WORLD TRADE ORGANIZATION

Dispute Settlement Reports

2006
Volume IX

Pages 3789–4408

CAMBRIDGE
UNIVERSITY PRESS

CAMBRIDGE UNIVERSITY PRESS
Cambridge, New York, Melbourne, Madrid, Cape Town, Singapore, São Paulo, Delhi

Cambridge University Press
The Edinburgh Building, Cambridge CB2 8RU, UK

Published in the United States of America by Cambridge University Press, New York

www.cambridge.org
Information on this title:www.cambridge.org/9780521896627

First published 2008

Printed in the United Kingdom at the University Press, Cambridge

A catalogue record for this publication is available from the British Library

ISBN 978-0-521-89662-7 hardback

THE WTO DISPUTE SETTLEMENT REPORTS

The *Dispute Settlement Reports* of the World Trade Organization (the "WTO") include panel and Appellate Body reports, as well as arbitration awards, in disputes concerning the rights and obligations of WTO Members under the provisions of the *Marrakesh Agreement Establishing the World Trade Organization*. The *Dispute Settlement Reports* are available in English. Volumes comprising one or more complete cases contain a cumulative list of published disputes. The cumulative list for cases that cover more than one volume is to be found in the first volume for that case.

This volume may be cited as DSR 2006:IX

TABLE OF CONTENTS

Page

European Communities – Selected Customs Matters (WT/DS315)

Report of the Appellate Body 3791
Report of the Panel 3915

Cumulative List of Published Disputes 4391

EUROPEAN COMMUNITIES – SELECTED CUSTOMS MATTERS

Report of the Appellate Body
WT/DS315/AB/R

Adopted by the Dispute Settlement Body on 11 December 2006

United States, *Appellant/Appellee*
European Communities, *Appellant/Appellee*
Argentina, *Third Participant*
Australia, *Third Participant*
Brazil, *Third Participant*
China, *Third Participant*
Hong Kong, China, *Third Participant*
India, *Third Participant*
Japan, *Third Participant*
Korea, *Third Participant*
Separate Customs Territory of Taiwan, Penghu, Kinmen, and Matsu, *Third Participant*

Present:
Ganesan, Presiding Member
Janow, Member
Taniguchi, Member

TABLE OF CONTENTS

Page

I. INTRODUCTION 3798
II. ARGUMENTS OF THE PARTICIPANTS AND THE THIRD PARTICIPANTS 3803
  A. Claims of Error by the United States – Appellant 3803
    1. The Panel's Terms of Reference 3803
    2. Claims regarding Article X:3(a) of the GATT 1994 3807
    3. The Panel's Interpretation of Article X:3(b) of the GATT 1994 3810
  B. Arguments of the European Communities – Appellee 3812
    1. The Panel's Terms of Reference 3812

2. Claims regarding Article X:3(a) of the GATT 1994 3814

3. The Panel's Interpretation of Article X:3(b) of the GATT 1994 3817

C. Claims of Error by the European Communities – Other Appellant 3820

1. The Panel's Terms of Reference 3820

2. Claims regarding Article X:3(a) of the GATT 1994 3821

3. Conditional Appeal of the European Communities 3826

D. Arguments of the United States – Appellee 3827

1. The Panel's Terms of Reference 3827

2. Claims regarding Article X:3(a) of the GATT 1994 3829

3. Conditional Appeal of the European Communities 3833

E. Arguments of the Third Participants 3835

1. Japan 3835

2. Korea 3836

III. ISSUES RAISED IN THIS APPEAL 3837

IV. THE PANEL'S TERMS OF REFERENCE 3839

A. Interpretation of the Term "Measures at Issue" under Article 6.2 of the DSU 3840

B. Confinement of the Measures at Issue to Areas of Customs Administration 3845

C. The United States' Claim Challenging the European Communities' System of Customs Administration "As a Whole" 3852

1. Challenging a Legal System "As a Whole" or "Overall" 3855

2. Whether the Panel Request Included a Challenge to the European Communities' System of Customs Administration "As a Whole" or "Overall" 3857

3. The Panel's Finding with respect to the "Design and Structure" of the European Communities' System of Customs Administration 3859

D. Temporal Limitations of the Panel's Terms of Reference 3860

V. CLAIMS REGARDING ARTICLE X:3(A) OF THE GATT 1994 3864

A. Administration of European Communities Customs Law through Penalty Provisions and Audit Procedures of Member States 3864

1. Whether the Substantive Content of a Legal Instrument May Be Challenged under Article X:3(a) of the GATT 1994 3864

2. Differences in Penalty Provisions and Audit Procedures 3867

B. The Administrative Process and the Requirement of Uniformity in Article X:3(a) of the GATT 1994 3872

C. The Administrative Process Leading to the Tariff Classification of Blackout Drapery Lining 3875

D. Tariff Classification of Liquid Crystal Display Flat Monitors with a Digital Video Interface 3880

E. Administration of the Successive Sales Provision 3886

F. Completing the Analysis with respect to the "As a Whole" Challenge of the United States under Article X:3(a) of the GATT 1994 3889

VI. THE PANEL'S INTERPRETATION OF ARTICLE X:3(B) OF THE GATT 1994 3895

VII. CONDITIONAL APPEAL OF THE EUROPEAN COMMUNITIES 3900

VIII. FINDINGS AND CONCLUSIONS 3901

ANNEX I Notification of an Appeal by the United States

ANNEX II Notification of an Other Appeal by the European Communities

ANNEX III Request for the Establishment of a Panel by the United States

TABLE OF CASES CITED IN THIS REPORT

Short Title	Full Case Title and Citation
Argentina – Hides and Leather	Panel Report, *Argentina – Measures Affecting the Export of Bovine Hides and Import of Finished Leather*, WT/DS155/R and Corr.1, adopted 16 February 2001, DSR 2001:V, 1779
Australia – Salmon	Appellate Body Report, *Australia – Measures Affecting Importation of Salmon*, WT/DS18/AB/R, adopted 6 November 1998, DSR 1998:VIII, 3327
Brazil – Desiccated Coconut	Appellate Body Report, *Brazil – Measures Affecting Desiccated Coconut*, WT/DS22/AB/R, adopted 20 March 1997, DSR 1997:I, 167
Canada – Dairy (Article 21.5 – New Zealand and US)	Appellate Body Report, *Canada – Measures Affecting the Importation of Milk and the Exportation of Dairy Products – Recourse to Article 21.5 of the DSU by New Zealand and the United States*, WT/DS103/AB/RW, WT/DS113/AB/RW, adopted 18 December 2001, DSR 2001:XIII, 6829

Short Title	Full Case Title and Citation
Canada – Gold Coins	GATT Panel Report, *Canada – Measures Affecting the Sale of Gold Coins*, L/5863, 17 September 1985, unadopted
Chile – Price Band System	Appellate Body Report, *Chile – Price Band System and Safeguard Measures Relating to Certain Agricultural Products*, WT/DS207/AB/R, adopted 23 October 2002, DSR 2002:VIII, 3045
Dominican Republic – Import and Sale of Cigarettes	Appellate Body Report, *Dominican Republic – Measures Affecting the Importation and Internal Sale of Cigarettes*, WT/DS302/AB/R, adopted 19 May 2005
EC – Bananas III	Appellate Body Report, *European Communities – Regime for the Importation, Sale and Distribution of Bananas*, WT/DS27/AB/R, adopted 25 September 1997, DSR 1997:II, 591
EC – Bed Linen (Article 21.5 – India)	Appellate Body Report, *European Communities – Anti-Dumping Duties on Imports of Cotton-Type Bed Linen from India – Recourse to Article 21.5 of the DSU by India*, WT/DS141/AB/RW, adopted 24 April 2003, DSR 2003:III, 965
EC – Chicken Cuts	Appellate Body Report, *European Communities – Customs Classification of Frozen Boneless Chicken Cuts*, WT/DS269/AB/R, WT/DS286/AB/R, and Corr.1, adopted 27 September 2005
EC – Computer Equipment	Appellate Body Report, *European Communities – Customs Classification of Certain Computer Equipment*, WT/DS62/AB/R, WT/DS67/AB/R, WT/DS68/AB/R, adopted 22 June 1998, DSR 1998:V, 1851
EC – Computer Equipment	Panel Report, *European Communities – Customs Classification of Certain Computer Equipment*, WT/DS62/R, WT/DS67/R, WT/DS68/R, adopted 22 June 1998, modified by Appellate Body Report, WT/DS62/AB/R, WT/DS67/AB/R, WT/DS68/AB/R, DSR 1998:V, 1891
EC – Hormones	Appellate Body Report, *EC Measures Concerning Meat and Meat Products (Hormones)*, WT/DS26/AB/R, WT/DS48/AB/R, adopted 13 February 1998, DSR 1998:I, 135
EC – Poultry	Appellate Body Report, *European Communities – Measures Affecting the Importation of Certain Poultry Products*, WT/DS69/AB/R, adopted 23 July 1998, DSR 1998:V, 2031

Short Title	Full Case Title and Citation
EC – Sardines	Appellate Body Report, *European Communities – Trade Description of Sardines*, WT/DS231/AB/R, adopted 23 October 2002, DSR 2002:VIII, 3359
EC – Selected Customs Matters	Panel Report, *European Communities – Selected Customs Matters*, WT/DS315/R, 16 June 2006
India – Patents (US)	Appellate Body Report, *India – Patent Protection for Pharmaceutical and Agricultural Chemical Products*, WT/DS50/AB/R, adopted 16 January 1998, DSR 1998:I, 9
Japan – Apples	Appellate Body Report, *Japan - Measures Affecting the Importation of Apples*, WT/DS245/AB/R, adopted 10 December 2003, DSR 2003:IX, 4391
Japan – Film	Panel Report, *Japan – Measures Affecting Consumer Photographic Film and Paper*, WT/DS44/R, adopted 22 April 1998, DSR 1998:IV, 1179
Korea – Dairy	Appellate Body Report, *Korea – Definitive Safeguard Measure on Imports of Certain Dairy Products*, WT/DS98/AB/R, adopted 12 January 2000, DSR 2000:I, 3
Mexico – Anti-Dumping Measures on Rice	Appellate Body Report, *Mexico – Definitive Anti-Dumping Measures on Beef and Rice, Complaint with Respect to Rice*, WT/DS295/AB/R, adopted 20 December 2005
Thailand – H-Beams	Appellate Body Report, *Thailand – Anti-Dumping Duties on Angles, Shapes and Sections of Iron or Non-Alloy Steel and H-Beams from Poland*, WT/DS122/AB/R, adopted 5 April 2001, DSR 2001:VII, 2701
US – Carbon Steel	Appellate Body Report, *United States – Countervailing Duties on Certain Corrosion-Resistant Carbon Steel Flat Products from Germany*, WT/DS213/AB/R and Corr.1, adopted 19 December 2002, DSR 2002:IX, 3779
US – Corrosion-Resistant Steel Sunset Review	Appellate Body Report, *United States – Sunset Review of Anti-Dumping Duties on Corrosion-Resistant Carbon Steel Flat Products from Japan*, WT/DS244/AB/R, adopted 9 January 2004, DSR 2004:I, 3
US – Cotton Yarn	Appellate Body Report, *United States – Transitional Safeguard Measure on Combed Cotton Yarn from Pakistan*, WT/DS192/AB/R, adopted 5 November 2001, DSR 2001:XII, 6027

Short Title	Full Case Title and Citation
US – FSC (Article 21.5 – EC II)	Appellate Body Report, *United States – Tax Treatment for "Foreign Sales Corporations" – Second Recourse to Article 21.5 of the DSU by the European Communities*, WT/DS108/AB/RW2, adopted 14 March 2006
US – Hot-Rolled Steel	Panel Report, *United States – Anti-Dumping Measures on Certain Hot-Rolled Steel Products from Japan*, WT/DS184/R, adopted 23 August 2001 modified by Appellate Body Report, WT/DS184/AB/R, DSR 2001:X, 4769
US – Oil Country Tubular Goods Sunset Reviews	Appellate Body Report, *United States – Sunset Reviews of Anti-Dumping Measures on Oil Country Tubular Goods from Argentina*, WT/DS268/AB/R, adopted 17 December 2004
US – Section 211 Appropriations Act	Appellate Body Report, *United States – Section 211 Omnibus Appropriations Act of 1998*, WT/DS176/AB/R, adopted 1 February 2002, DSR 2002:II, 589
US – Upland Cotton	Appellate Body Report, *United States – Subsidies on Upland Cotton*, WT/DS267/AB/R, adopted 21 March 2005
US – Upland Cotton	Panel Report, *United States – Subsidies on Upland Cotton*, WT/DS267/R, and Corr.1, adopted 21 March 2005, modified by Appellate Body Report, WT/DS267/AB/R
US – Wool Shirts and Blouses	Appellate Body Report, *United States – Measure Affecting Imports of Woven Wool Shirts and Blouses from India*, WT/DS33/AB/R and Corr.1, adopted 23 May 1997, DSR 1997:I, 323
US – Zeroing (EC)	Appellate Body Report, *United States – Laws, Regulations and Methodology for Calculating Dumping Margins ("Zeroing")*, WT/DS294/AB/R, adopted 9 May 2006

LIST OF ABBREVIATIONS USED IN THIS REPORT

Abbreviation	Description
BTI	Binding Tariff Information
CFI	Court of First Instance of the European Communities
Common Customs Tariff	Council Regulation (EEC) No. 2658/87 of 23 July 1987 on the tariff and statistical nomenclature and on the Common Customs Tariff
Community Customs Code	Council Regulation (EEC) No. 2913/92 of 12 October 1992 establishing the Community Customs Code
Court of Auditors Report	Court of Auditors, Special Report No. 23/2000 concerning valuation of imported goods for customs purposes (customs valuation), together with the Commission's replies, reproduced in *Official Journal of the European Communities*, C Series, No. 84, pp. 1-18 (14 March 2001)
DSB	Dispute Settlement Body
DSU	*Understanding on Rules and Procedures Governing the Settlement of Disputes*
DVI	digital video interface
EBTI	European Binding Tariff Information
EC Regulation 2171/2005	Commission Regulation (EC) No. 2171/2005 of 23 December 2005 concerning the classification of certain goods in the Combined Nomenclature
EC Treaty	Treaty Establishing the European Communities
ECJ	Court of Justice of the European Communities
GATT 1994	*General Agreement on Tariffs and Trade 1994*
Implementing Regulation	Commission Regulation (EEC) No. 2454/93 of 2 July 1993 laying down provisions for the implementation of Council Regulation (EEC) No. 2913/92 of 12 October 1992 establishing the Community Customs Code
LCD	liquid crystal display
Panel Report	Panel Report, *EC – Selected Customs Matters*
Panel request	*European Communities – Selected Customs Matters*, Request for the Establishment of a Panel by the United States, WT/DS315/8, 14 January 2005

Abbreviation	Description
TARIC	Integrated Tariff of the European Communities established by Council Regulation (EEC) No. 2658/87 of 23 July 1987 on the tariff and statistical nomenclature and on the Common Customs Tariff
Working Procedures	*Working Procedures for Appellate Review*, WT/AB/WP/5, 4 January 2005
WTO	World Trade Organization
WTO Agreement	*Marrakesh Agreement Establishing the World Trade Organization*

I. INTRODUCTION

1. The United States and the European Communities each appeal certain issues of law and legal interpretations developed in the Panel Report, *European Communities – Selected Customs Matters* (the "Panel Report").[1] The Panel was established to consider a complaint by the United States concerning the European Communities' system of customs administration under Articles X:3(a) and X:3(b) of the *General Agreement on Tariffs and Trade 1994* (the "GATT 1994").

2. Before the Panel, the United States claimed that the European Communities administers the following instruments of its customs law in a non-uniform manner, in violation of Article X:3(a) of the GATT 1994:

- Council Regulation (EEC) No. 2913/92 of 12 October 1992 establishing the Community Customs Code, including all annexes thereto, as amended (the "Community Customs Code");
- Commission Regulation (EEC) No. 2454/93 of 2 July 1993 laying down provisions for the implementation of Council Regulation (EEC) No. 2913/92 of 12 October 1992 establishing the Community Customs Code, including all annexes thereto, as amended (the "Implementing Regulation");
- Council Regulation (EEC) No. 2658/87 of 23 July 1987 on the tariff and statistical nomenclature and on the Common Customs Tariff, including all annexes thereto, as amended (the "Common Customs Tariff");
- the Integrated Tariff of the European Communities established by virtue of Article 2 of Council Regulation (EEC) No. 2658/87 of 23 July 1987 on the tariff and statistical nomenclature and on the Common Customs Tariff, including all annexes thereto, as amended (the "TARIC"); and

1 WT/DS315/R, 16 June 2006.

- for each of the above laws and regulations, all amendments, "implementing measures and other related measures".[2]

3. The United States submitted that various instances of alleged non-uniform administration of European Communities customs law illustrate that the European Communities' system of customs administration as a whole is inconsistent with the requirement of uniform administration contained in Article X:3(a) of the GATT 1994. In addition, the United States claimed that the European Communities does not provide for the prompt review and correction of administrative action relating to customs matters as required by Article X:3(b) of the GATT 1994.[3]

4. In the Panel Report, circulated to Members of the World Trade Organization (the "WTO") on 16 June 2006, the Panel concluded that its terms of reference authorized it to consider only "the manner of administration by the national customs authorities of the member States of the Community Customs Code, the Implementing Regulation, the Common Customs Tariff, the TARIC and related measures in the areas of customs administration specifically identified in the United States' request for establishment of a panel."[4] These areas of customs administration were "the classification and valuation of goods, procedures for the classification and valuation of goods, procedures for the entry and release of goods, procedures for auditing entry statements after goods are released into free circulation, penalties and procedures regarding the imposition of penalties for violation of customs rules and record-keeping requirements".[5] The Panel held that it was "authorized to examine particular cases or instances of administration of the Community Customs Code, the Implementing Regulation, the Common Customs Tariff and the TARIC and related measures in those areas of customs administration specifically identified in the United States' request".[6]

5. The Panel found that it was "precluded from considering 'as such' challenges of the design and structure of the [European Communities'] system of customs administration as a whole, and also the design and structure of the [European Communities'] system in the areas of customs administration ... specifically identified in the United States' request for the establishment of a panel."[7] However, at the conclusion of its analysis of the United States' claim under Article X:3(a) of the GATT 1994, the Panel observed that, even if it were authorized by its terms of reference to make findings on the design and structure of the European Communities' system of customs administration "as such", the United States had not demonstrated that the design and structure of the European Communities' system of customs administration, including components thereof, nec-

---

2 Request for the Establishment of a Panel by the United States, WT/DS315/8, 14 January 2005 (attached as Annex III to this Report), p. 1; Panel Report, para. 2.1. These laws and regulations are contained in Exhibits US-5, US-6, EC-16, and US-7, respectively, submitted by the United States and the European Communities to the Panel.

3 Panel Report, paras. 2.1 and 7.492.

4 *Ibid.*, para. 7.64.

5 *Ibid.*, para. 7.33.

6 Panel Report, para. 7.64.

7 *Ibid.*

essarily results in a violation of Article X:3(a). According to the Panel, the United States merely referred to "a number of apparently random instances of alleged violation of Article X:3(a) ..., without demonstrating ... that those examples are symptomatic and representative of underlying structural deficiencies in the [European Communities'] system of customs administration."[8]

6. The Panel examined individual instances of alleged non-uniform administration of European Communities' customs law in three different areas: *customs classification*, *customs valuation*, and *customs procedures*.[9] First, the Panel examined the United States' claims alleging non-uniform administration in the area of *customs classification*. The Panel found no violation of Article X:3(a) of the GATT 1994 with respect to the tariff classification of network cards for personal computers[10] and no violation regarding the tariff classification of drip irrigation products.[11] The Panel found, however, that the administrative process leading to decisions on tariff classification of blackout drapery lining by German customs authorities amounts to non-uniform administration and therefore constitutes a violation of Article X:3(a) of the GATT 1994.[12] The Panel also found a violation of the same provision with respect to the tariff classification of liquid crystal display ("LCD") monitors with digital video interface ("DVI").[13]

7. The Panel also found that the United States had not proved any violation of Article X:3(a) of the GATT 1994 with respect to: (i) the tariff classification of unisex articles or shorts[14]; (ii) the failure of customs authorities in one member State to treat Binding Tariff Information ("BTI") issued in other member States as binding[15]; (iii) the refusal to withdraw the revocation of BTI by the United Kingdom's customs authorities with respect to the tariff classification of the *Sony PlayStation2* in the context of the *Sony PlayStation2* case[16]; or (iv) the interpretation and application of the amended Explanatory Notes to the Common Customs Tariff concerning camcorders in the context of the *Camcorders* case.[17]

8. Secondly, the Panel examined individual instances of customs administration in the area of *customs valuation*. The Panel found that the administration of Article 147(1) of the Implementing Regulation (the "successive sales provision") amounts to a violation of Article X:3(a), because some member States impose a

[8] *Ibid.*, para. 7.490.

[9] The Panel found that Article 221 of the Community Customs Code, which is entitled "Recovery of the amount of the Customs Debt", was not covered by any of the areas of customs administration specifically identified in the United States' request for the establishment of a panel and therefore fell outside the Panel's terms of reference. (*Ibid.*, para. 7.487)

[10] *Ibid.*, para. 7.207.

[11] *Ibid.*, para. 7.218.

[12] *Ibid.*, para. 7.276.

[13] Panel Report, para. 7.305.

[14] *Ibid.*, para. 7.228.

[15] *Ibid.*, para. 7.329.

[16] *Ibid.*, para. 7.343 (referring to *Sony Computer Entertainment Europe Ltd. v. Commissioners of Customs and Excise*, Judgment of the High Court of Justice, Chancery Division (2005), EWHC 1644 (Ch) (Exhibit US-70 submitted by the United States to the Panel)).

[17] *Ibid.*, para. 7.354 (referring to Explanatory Notes to the Combined Nomenclature of the European Communities, *Official Journal of the European Communities* (13 July 2000), 316 (Exhibit US-62 submitted by the United States to the Panel)).

"form of prior approval" requirement while others do not.[18] The Panel found no violation with respect to the administration of Article 29(3)(a) of the Community Customs Code concerning vehicle repair costs covered under warranty.[19] The Panel found that the United States had not proved that differences among member States regarding the manner in which royalties are apportioned to the customs value of identical goods imported by the same company according to Article 32(1)(c) of the Community Customs Code amount to a violation of Article X:3(a) of the GATT 1994.[20] The Panel also found that the United States had not proved that the administration of Article 29 of the Community Customs Code and Article 143(1)(e) of the Implementing Regulation concerning the circumstances in which parties are to be treated as "related" for customs valuation purposes is non-uniform within the meaning of Article X:3(a) of the GATT 1994.[21]

9. Thirdly, the Panel examined individual instances of customs administration in the area of *customs procedure*. The Panel found no violation of Article X:3(a) with respect to the manner of administration of Article 78(2) of the Community Customs Code, which allows customs authorities to conduct audits following release of goods for free circulation within the European Communities.[22] The Panel also found no violation of Article X:3(a) with respect to "the substantive differences in penalty laws between member States" on the ground that "the substantive content of penalty laws ... cannot be viewed as acts of administration" under Article X:1.[23] The Panel further found that the United States had not proved that "the manner of administration of Article 133 of the Community Customs Code and Articles 502(3) and 552 of the Implementing Regulation regarding processing under customs control is non-uniform among member States in violation of Article X:3(a) of the GATT 1994."[24] Finally, the Panel found that "the United States ha[d] not proved that Articles 263-267 of the Implementing Regulation are administered in a non-uniform manner in violation of Article X:3(a) of the GATT 1994."[25]

10. Finally, with respect to the United States' claim of violation of Article X:3(b) of the GATT 1994, the Panel found that the European Communities does not violate the obligation to provide prompt review and correction of administrative action relating to customs matters "merely because the decisions regarding review of administrative action relating to customs matters ... do not apply to all agencies in the [European Communities] and do not have effect throughout the territory of the European Communities".[26]

11. The Panel therefore recommended:

---

[18] *Ibid.*, para. 7.385.
[19] *Ibid.*, para. 7.403.
[20] *Ibid.*, para. 7.371.
[21] *Ibid.*, para. 7.418.
[22] Panel Report, para. 7.434.
[23] *Ibid.*, para. 7.444.
[24] *Ibid.*, para. 7.465.
[25] *Ibid.*, para. 7.477.
[26] *Ibid.*, para. 7.556.

> ... that the Dispute Settlement Body request the European Communities to bring itself into conformity with respect to:
>
> (a) the administration of the Common Custom[s] Tariff regarding the administrative process leading to the tariff classification of blackout drapery lining;
>
> (b) the administration of the Common Customs Tariff regarding the tariff classification of liquid crystal display monitors with digital video interface;
>
> (c) the administration of Article 147(1) of the Implementing Regulation regarding the imposition by customs authorities in some member States of a form of prior approval with respect to the successive sales provision in the context of customs valuation.[27]

12. On 14 August 2006, the United States notified the Dispute Settlement Body (the "DSB") of its intention to appeal certain issues of law covered in the Panel Report and certain legal interpretations developed by the Panel, pursuant to Article 16.4 of the *Understanding on Rules and Procedures Governing the Settlement of Disputes* (the "DSU"), and filed a Notice of Appeal[28] pursuant to Rule 20 of the *Working Procedures for Appellate Review* (the "*Working Procedures*").[29] On 21 August 2006, the United States filed an appellant's submission.[30] On 28 August 2006, the European Communities notified the DSB of its intention to appeal certain issues of law covered in the Panel Report and certain legal interpretations developed by the Panel, pursuant to Article 16.4 of the DSU, and filed a Notice of Other Appeal [31] pursuant to Rule 23(1) and (2) of the *Working Procedures*. On 29 August 2006, the European Communities filed an other appellant's submission.[32] On 11 September 2006, the United States and the European Communities each filed an appellee's submission.[33] On the same day, Japan and Korea each filed a third participant's submission[34], and Argentina, Australia, Brazil, China, Hong Kong, China, India, and the Separate Customs Territory of Taiwan, Penghu, Kinmen, and Matsu each notified the Appellate Body Secretariat of its intention to appear at the oral hearing as a third participant.[35]

13. By letter dated 15 September 2006, Japan requested authorization from the Appellate Body Division hearing the appeal to correct a "clerical error" in its third participant's submission, pursuant to Rule 18(5) of the *Working Procedures*. On 18 September 2006, the Division invited all participants and third participants to comment on Japan's request. None of the participants or third participants objected to Japan's request. On 20 September 2006, the Division author-

---

27 Panel Report, para. 8.2.

28 WT/DS315/11 (attached as Annex I to this Report).

29 WT/AB/WP/5, 4 January 2005.

30 Pursuant to Rule 21(1) of the *Working Procedures*.

31 WT/DS315/12 (attached as Annex II to this Report).

32 Pursuant to Rule 23(3) of the *Working Procedures*.

33 Pursuant to Rules 22 and 23(4) of the *Working Procedures*.

34 Pursuant to Rule 24(1) of the *Working Procedures*.

35 Pursuant to Rule 24(2) of the *Working Procedures*.

ized Japan, pursuant to Rule 18(5), to correct the clerical error in its third participant's submission.

14. The oral hearing in this appeal was held on 28 and 29 September 2006. The participants and the third participants presented oral arguments (with the exception of Argentina, Brazil, Hong Kong, China, India, Korea, and the Separate Customs Territory of Taiwan, Penghu, Kinmen, and Matsu) and responded to questions posed by the Members of the Division hearing the appeal.

II. ARGUMENTS OF THE PARTICIPANTS AND THE THIRD PARTICIPANTS

A. Claims of Error by the United States – Appellant

1. The Panel's Terms of Reference

15. The United States requests the Appellate Body to reverse the findings of the Panel concerning its terms of reference. According to the United States, the Panel erred in three respects: first, in finding that, under Article 6.2 of the DSU, the measure at issue must be the "manner of administration" when a claim is made under Article X:3(a) of the GATT 1994; secondly, in finding that the specific measure at issue in this dispute was confined to the six areas of customs administration identified in the third paragraph of the request for the establishment of a panel by the United States (the "panel request")[36]; and finally, in concluding that, due to the wording and content of the panel request, the United States was precluded from challenging the European Communities' system of customs administration "as a whole".

(a) The "Measures at Issue" for Purposes of a Claim under Article X:3(a) of the GATT 1994

16. According to the United States, the Panel erroneously found that, when a violation of Article X:3(a) of the GATT 1994 is alleged, the measure to be identified in the panel request must be a "manner of administration".[37] For the United States, in making this finding, the Panel relied primarily on what it described as "an inter-linkage between the reference to the term 'measure' in Article 19.1 of the DSU and to the term 'measures at issue' in Article 6.2 of the DSU."[38] The Panel also reasoned that, under Article 19.1 of the DSU, a Member breaching Article X:3(a) of the GATT 1994 would be required "to alter the *manner* in which the relevant laws, regulations, decisions and/or rulings are being *administered* in order to abide by that recommendation."[39]

17. The United States contends that this reasoning of the Panel is flawed because a "manner of administration" is not a "measure" but, rather, a description

---

[36] Request for the Establishment of a Panel by the United States, WT/DS315/8 (attached as Annex III to this Report).

[37] Panel Report, para. 7.20.

[38] United States' appellant's submission, para. 45 (referring to Panel Report, para. 7.14).

[39] *Ibid.*, para. 46 (referring to Panel Report para. 7.21). (original emphasis)

of how a measure operates.[40] The United States adds that this approach blurs the distinction between measures and claims.[41] By finding the "manner of administration" to be the measure at issue, the Panel confused the measure at issue in an Article X:3(a) dispute with the obligation under that provision. The United States also argues that the Panel's reasoning leads to illogical consequences for complaints under other WTO provisions as well, because, under such an approach, the measure at issue is not "distinguishable" from the legal basis of the complaint for purposes of Article 6.2 of the DSU.[42] Regarding the "inter-linkage" between Articles 6.2 and 19.1 of the DSU identified by the Panel, the United States points out that the mere fact that a breach of Article X:3(a) may be removed by changing a law's administration cannot be a basis for concluding that the law is not the measure at issue.[43] The United States argues that, although Article 19.1 of the DSU contemplates a recommendation that a Member bring a measure into conformity with a covered agreement, it is silent as to how this is to be done.[44]

(b) Confinement of the Measures at Issue to Certain Areas of Customs Administration

18. The United States contends that the Panel erred in confining the specific measures at issue to the areas of customs administration indicated in the panel request, because the Panel failed to construe the panel request "as a whole". The United States also argues that the Panel confused arguments, on the one hand, with measures and claims, on the other hand.[45] For the United States, had the Panel construed the panel request "as a whole", it could not have avoided the conclusion that, first, the specific measures at issue were the Community Customs Code, the Implementing Regulation, the Common Customs Tariff, the TARIC, and, for each of these measures, all amendments, "implementing measures, and other related measures"; and, secondly, that the legal basis of the complaint was the administration of those measures in a manner inconsistent with Article X:3(a) of the GATT 1994.[46] The United States emphasizes that the list of areas of customs administration provided in the panel request was only illustrative, aimed to give an indication of the argument underlying the United States' claim, and did not constitute the claim itself or the specific measures at issue.[47] According to the United States, the Panel read individual phrases in the panel request in isolation, focusing on "particular text ... taken out of its context".[48] The United States maintains that the Panel's characterization of the illustrative list as a specification of the measures at issue "ignored the introduction to the list, which stated that '[l]ack of uniform, impartial and reasonable administration of

---

40 United States' appellant's submission, para. 47.
41 *Ibid.*
42 *Ibid.*, para. 49.
43 *Ibid.*, para. 48.
44 *Ibid.*
45 *Ibid.*, para. 52.
46 *Ibid.*, paras. 54-55.
47 United States' appellant's submission, para. 57.
48 *Ibid.*, para. 58.

the above-identified measures is manifest in differences among member States in a number of areas, including, but not limited to, the following.'"[49]

19. The United States also points out that the Panel gave no consideration to the fact that the request included a claim that the absence of mechanisms or institutions to secure uniform administration in the European Communities' system of customs administration "as a whole" results in a breach of Article X:3(a).[50] For the United States, the Panel missed the fundamental point that "nowhere in the system as a whole ... are there mechanisms or institutions which achieve the uniformity in administration which Article X:3(a) requires".[51] With respect to the analogy made by the Panel to the *EC – Computer Equipment* dispute, the United States considers that the Panel erred because, in *EC – Computer Equipment*, the scope of the measures at issue depended on the identity of the products subject to the measures; also, the claim put forward in that case was not "systemic" and did not relate to the system "as a whole".[52]

20. The United States considers that the Panel's approach led to a confusion of claims and measures, on the one hand, with arguments, on the other hand. The United States does not believe it was required to list the areas in which the manner of administration of the specific measure at issue was inconsistent with Article X:3(a); however, in the view of the United States, such a list made the panel request more transparent, in that it anticipated certain arguments the United States would make in its submissions and statements to substantiate its claims. For the United States, rather than understanding the discussion in the panel request as intended, the Panel mischaracterized it as "an elaboration of what it understood to be the measure at issue".[53]

(c) Challenging the European Communities' System of Customs Administration "As a Whole"

21. The United States contends that the Panel erred by construing the panel request to exclude a claim that the European Communities' system of customs administration "as a whole" results in non-uniform administration of European Communities customs law in breach of Article X:3(a) of the GATT 1994. For the United States, the Panel erred in considering that, in order to challenge the European Communities' system of customs administration "as a whole", the United States would have had to list separately "each and every area of customs administration".[54] This aspect of the Panel's reasoning, the United States argues, would make it "virtually impossible" to challenge a responding Member's system "as a whole" or overall.[55]

---

[49] *Ibid.*, para. 59.
[50] *Ibid.*, para. 61.
[51] *Ibid.*
[52] *Ibid.*, para. 62.
[53] *Ibid.*, para. 66.
[54] United States' appellant's submission, para. 70.
[55] *Ibid.*

22. The United States maintains that the panel request made it clear that its claim related to the European Communities' system of customs administration "as a whole", because it identified the measures that constitute the main instruments of European Communities customs legislation and addressed the manner of administration of these instruments collectively.[56] For the United States, the heart of the problem is that "the [European Communities] administers its customs law through 25 separate, independent customs authorities and does not provide any institution or mechanism to reconcile divergences automatically and as a matter of right when they occur."[57] The United States underlines that, throughout the panel request, the measures at issue were discussed collectively, and that this "is precisely what one would expect in a panel request challenging a system of customs administration as a whole."[58]

23. According to the United States, the Panel's interpretation of the panel request rested on its view that the word "manner", as used in the panel request, was not related to "the design and structure of something"[59], and the Panel assumed that a challenge to the design and structure of the European Communities' system of customs administration must refer to "actions taken and/or procedures and institutions existing at the [European Communities] level".[60] For the United States, these aspects of the Panel's reasoning are problematic; given that the very essence of the Article X:3(a) obligation is the "manner" of administration of certain types of measures, it would be "illogical to assume that [the] use of the word 'manner' in a claim involving Article X:3(a) of the GATT 1994 necessarily suggests that the claim does not relate to a Member's system of customs administration as a whole."[61] Furthermore, the United States is of the view that, because "the defining characteristic of the design and structure of the [European Communities'] system of customs administration ... is the *absence* of procedures and institutions" at the European Communities level, a challenge to the design and structure of this system must necessarily address administration undertaken by member State customs authorities.[62]

24. The United States considers that it clearly articulated a challenge to the European Communities' system of customs administration in the panel request.[63] The United States submits that the absence of an explicit reference to the terms "as such" or "*per se*" in the panel request does not preclude a claim with respect to the European Communities' system of customs administration "as a whole". What is important, the United States argues, is that the responding party be aware of the claim against it so that its ability to defend itself is not prejudiced.[64] For the United States, it is clear from statements by the European Communities

---

56 *Ibid.*, para. 72.
57 *Ibid.*, para. 69.
58 *Ibid.*, para. 74.
59 *Ibid.*, para. 76 (quoting Panel Report, para. 7.59).
60 *Ibid.*, para. 78 (quoting Panel Report, para. 7.60).
61 United States' appellant's submission, para. 77.
62 *Ibid.*, para. 78. (original emphasis)
63 *Ibid.*, para. 82.
64 *Ibid.*, paras. 83-84.

at meetings of the DSB, and from the European Communities' submissions and statements during the Panel proceedings, that the European Communities was aware that the United States had made a claim with respect to the European Communities' system of customs administration "as a whole".[65] For the United States, the "consistent articulation" by the United States throughout the Panel proceedings of a claim concerning the European Communities' system of customs administration "as a whole" is "a strong indication [that the European Communities] did not suffer any prejudice on account of any lack of clarity in the panel request".[66]

2. *Claims regarding Article X:3(a) of the GATT 1994*

(a) The Panel's Interpretation of the Term "Administer" in Article X:3(a) of the GATT 1994

25. The United States submits that the Panel erred in its interpretation and application of the term "administer" in Article X:3(a) of the GATT 1994, and its consequent treatment of differences in penalty provisions and audit procedures among the member States of the European Communities.[67] The Panel itself noted that the existence of substantive differences in penalty provisions and audit procedures among member States is not disputed between the parties.[68] In the United States' view, these divergences in laws among the member States, in and of themselves, lead to non-uniform administration of European Communities customs law in breach of Article X:3(a).[69] The United States asserts that the arguments it made with respect to the Panel's approach to divergences in penalty laws apply equally with respect to the Panel's approach to audit procedures.[70]

26. The United States agrees with the Panel that measures are administered when they are "put into practical effect".[71] The United States contends that penalty and audit regimes put the measures subject to those regimes into practical effect because they encourage compliance with, and deter breaches of, those measures.[72] The United States submits that the different penalty regimes put European Communities customs law into effect differently among the member States and that this amounts to a failure by the European Communities to administer its customs law in a uniform manner.[73]

27. Further, the United States refers to the Panel's finding that "the substantive content of penalty laws of the member States used to enforce [European Communities] customs law cannot be viewed as acts of administration".[74] The

[65] *Ibid.*, paras. 86-87, 88-91, and 93-97.
[66] *Ibid.*, para. 98 (quoting Appellate Body Report, *Thailand – H-Beams*, para. 95).
[67] *Ibid.*, para. 109. See also Panel Report, paras. 7.444, 8.1(d)(ii), 7.434, and 8.1(d)(i), respectively.
[68] United States' appellant's submission, para. 109 (referring to Panel Report, para. 7.444).
[69] *Ibid.*, para. 110.
[70] *Ibid.*, paras. 111 and 150.
[71] *Ibid.*, para. 118 (quoting Panel Report, para 7.104).
[72] *Ibid.*, para. 120.
[73] *Ibid.*, paras. 121 and 123.
[74] Panel Report, para. 7.444 (quoted in United States' appellant's submission, para. 113).

United States contends that a breach of Article X:3(a) can be substantiated not only by particular "acts of administration", but also by the laws themselves. According to the United States, if divergences between individual acts of administration (for example, individual impositions of penalties for identical breaches of European Communities customs law) constitute non-uniform administration, then, *a fortiori*, divergences in the penalty provisions that govern the individual acts of administration carried out by different customs authorities must also constitute non-uniform administration.

28. The United States alleges that the Panel's findings in the present case are inconsistent with the findings regarding Article X:3(a) of the GATT 1994 made by the panel in *Argentina – Hides and Leather*. In the view of the United States, the Panel should have recognized the distinction that the panel in *Argentina – Hides and Leather* recognized between measures of general application whose manner of administration is at issue under Article X:3(a), and measures of general application that put the measures at issue into practical effect.[75]

29. Furthermore, the United States submits that the Panel's reasoning concerning penalty laws is contradicted by other parts of the Panel Report. In the United States' view, the Panel recognized that a measure of general application may be put into practical effect through an instrument that happens also to be a measure of general application, and that it is appropriate to consider the substance of that instrument to determine how the measure at issue is being administered. In this respect, the United States mentions two aspects of the Panel Report: first, with respect to the tariff classification of blackout drapery lining, the Panel referred to the fact that one customs authority (in Germany) relied on an interpretative aid not relied on by customs authorities of other member States; and secondly, with respect to LCD monitors with DVI, the Panel referred to the substance of a Tariff Notice issued by the United Kingdom customs authority and a decree issued by the Dutch customs authority as showing a lack of uniform administration of the European Communities classification rules at issue. The United States submits that the Panel itself considered the substance of a measure of general application concerning blackout drapery lining and LCD monitors with DVI to determine how the Common Customs Tariff was being administered. In the United States' view, the same rationale should have been applied to the administration of penalty provisions.[76]

30. With respect to the Panel's finding concerning differences in audit procedures among the member States of the European Communities, the United States submits that the Panel erred in limiting the scope of the claim to the non-uniform administration of Article 78(2) of the Community Customs Code. The United States submits further that, even if the Panel had been correct in limiting its examination to Article 78(2) of the Community Customs Code, the Panel's reasoning was based on an incorrect interpretation of the term "administer" in Article X:3(a) of the GATT 1994. The United States contends that the error in the

[75] United States' appellant's submission, para. 132 (referring to Panel Report, *Argentina – Hides and Leather*, paras. 11.72, 11.94, and 11.101).

[76] *Ibid.*, paras. 134-139.

Panel's analysis is essentially the same as the error in its analysis of penalty provisions. Therefore, the United States considers the arguments it presented in the context of penalty provisions equally valid in the context of audit proceedings.[77]

31. In the event that the Appellate Body reverses the Panel's findings regarding penalty provisions and audit procedures, the United States requests the Appellate Body to complete the Panel's analysis and to find that divergences in penalty provisions and audit procedures in the European Communities amount to non-uniform administration of European Communities customs law in breach of Article X:3(a).[78]

(b) Completing the Analysis with respect to the "As a Whole" Challenge of the United States under Article X:3(a) of the GATT 1994

32. In the event the Appellate Body reverses the Panel's finding that its terms of reference regarding the United States' claim under Article X:3(a) of the GATT 1994 do not include a challenge to the European Communities' system of customs administration "as a whole", or an "as such" challenge with respect to the design and structure of this system, the United States requests the Appellate Body to complete the analysis and find that the design and structure of the European Communities' system of customs administration "as a whole" is inconsistent with Article X:3(a).[79] The United States submits that, in this dispute, "a reversal of the Panel's findings without a completion of the analysis would fail 'to secure a positive solution to [the] dispute'".[80]

33. The United States submits that the analysis can be completed on the basis of undisputed facts and the Panel's findings of fact regarding the European Communities' system of customs administration.[81] The United States recalls that "[t]he crux of the [United States'] claim ... was that the existence of a system of customs administration in which 25 separate, independent authorities exercise judgment in interpreting and applying [European Communities] customs law, without any procedures or institutions to ensure against divergences or to reconcile them promptly and as a matter of right when they occur necessarily constitutes a lack of uniform administration, in breach of Article X:3(a)."[82] The United States points to statements made by the Panel with respect to various mechanisms and institutions in the European Communities that, according to the European Communities, are supposed to ensure against divergences or to reconcile divergences when they occur.[83] The United States mentions as particular examples, the Customs Code Committee[84], Article 10 of the *Treaty Establishing the European Communities* (the "EC Treaty"), and the system of preliminary refer-

[77] *Ibid.*, para. 154.
[78] United States' appellant's submission, para. 159.
[79] *Ibid.*, para. 99.
[80] *Ibid.*, para. 101.
[81] *Ibid.*, para. 102.
[82] *Ibid.* (footnote omitted)
[83] *Ibid.*
[84] Committee established by Articles 247a(1) and 248a(1) of the Community Customs Code.

ence of questions of European Communities customs law to the Court of Justice of the European Communities (the "ECJ").[85] The United States also refers to the Panel's statement that the European Communities' system of customs administration "as a whole" is "complicated and, at times, opaque and confusing".[86] According to the United States, by these various statements, the Panel rejected the European Communities' argument that the institutions and procedures to which the European Communities referred ensure the uniform administration of European Communities customs law.[87] Thus, for the United States, in the light of the Panel's statements regarding "the institutions and mechanisms the [European Communities] held out as securing uniform administration of [European Communities] customs law, completion of the Panel's analysis should be straightforward"[88] and should lead to the conclusion that "the [European Communities'] system of customs administration as a whole is inconsistent with the [European Communities'] obligation of uniform administration under Article X:3(a) of the GATT 1994."[89]

3. *The Panel's Interpretation of Article X:3(b) of the GATT 1994*

34. The United States submits that the Panel erred in finding that the tribunals and procedures for review of customs administrative actions in the European Communities are consistent with Article X:3(b) of the GATT 1994, despite the fact that their decisions do not govern the practice of *all* the agencies entrusted with administrative enforcement *throughout the territory* of the European Communities.

35. The United States notes that review tribunals or procedures of the European Communities consist of the courts of various member States. Each court issues decisions that govern the practice of only the agency in the respective member State.[90] The United States claims that, in reaching its conclusion concerning interpretation and application of Article X:3(b), the Panel made a number of interpretive errors. In the United States' view, the Panel misconstrued the ordinary meaning of the terms "the agencies" and "such agencies"; confused the concepts of "implement" and "govern the practice of"; and failed to take into account the context provided by Article X:3(a) of the GATT 1994.[91] The United States submits that the Panel effectively disregarded the ordinary meaning of those terms when it stated that "it is difficult to know what significance should be attached, if any, to the reference to agencies in the plural."[92] The United States submits that the ordinary meaning of the plural form encompasses "the agencies"—without limitation—as opposed to only one such agency or just

85 United States' appellant's submission, paras. 103, 104, and 105.
86 United States' appellant's submission, para. 107 (quoting Panel Report, para. 7.191).
87 *Ibid.*, para. 108.
88 *Ibid.*
89 *Ibid.*
90 *Ibid.*, para. 31.
91 *Ibid.*, para. 163.
92 Panel Report, para. 7.528 (quoted in United States' appellant's submission, para. 164).

"some of" or a subset of "the agencies".[93] The United States argues that the use of the plural form contemplates multiple agencies and, given the absence of any basis in the text for distinguishing among multiple agencies, it must contemplate all the agencies entrusted with administrative enforcement.[94]

36. Furthermore, in the United States' view, Article X:3(b) must be read in the light of the obligation of uniform administration in Article X:3(a) of the GATT 1994. According to the United States, the review of decisions that are inconsistent with "established principles of law or the actual facts" contemplated by Article X:3(b) also embodies the principle of uniform administration.[95] The United States submits that procedures leading to decisions that have effect only in particular regions of a WTO Member's territory are therefore inconsistent with Article X:3(b). In addition, the United States alleges that the Panel did not give meaning to the two distinct requirements of "govern the practice" and "implement" in Article X:3(b).[96] In the United States' view, the Panel assumed incorrectly that, if a decision can be implemented by a single agency, then the decision need govern the practice of only that agency, even though, pursuant to Article X:3(b), it must be effectuated by "such agencies" entrusted with administrative enforcement.[97] The United States submits that Article X:3(b) does not contemplate such a geographical limitation of the "govern the practice" requirement.[98]

37. With respect to the Panel's assessment of what is "reasonable" in the light of "most legal systems", the United States submits that the Panel ignored the feature that distinguishes the system of the European Communities from most legal systems, namely, that most legal systems have only one central agency entrusted with enforcement of customs law. The United States points out that this is not the case in the European Communities because its legal system combines review tribunals with geographically limited jurisdiction with customs authorities whose practice is limited to particular geographical regions.[99] In the United States' view, this results in a geographically fragmented administration of the customs law in the European Communities.[100]

38. In the United States' view, should the Appellate Body reverse the Panel's finding on Article X:3(b) of the GATT 1994, it should also complete the Panel's analysis and find the European Communities to be in breach of its obligation under Article X:3(b) "by failing to provide review tribunals or procedures whose decisions govern the practice of all of the agencies that the [European Communities] entrusts with administrative enforcement of its customs laws."[101]

---

[93] United States' appellant's submission, para. 165.
[94] *Ibid.*, para. 166.
[95] *Ibid.*, para. 181.
[96] *Ibid.*, para. 174.
[97] *Ibid.*
[98] *Ibid.*, para. 191.
[99] *Ibid.*, para. 189.
[100] *Ibid.*
[101] United States' appellant's submission, para. 200.

B. *Arguments of the European Communities – Appellee*

1. The Panel's Terms of Reference

39. The European Communities submits that the Panel did not err in finding that the measure at issue was only the "manner of administration" of European Communities customs law in the specific areas identified by the United States in the panel request. Furthermore, the European Communities agrees with the Panel's conclusion that its terms of reference did not include a claim against the European Communities' system of customs administration "as a whole", or "as such".

(a) The "Measures at Issue" for Purposes of a Claim under Article X:3(a) of the GATT 1994

40. The European Communities agrees with the Panel that the measure at issue with respect to the United States' claim under Article X:3(a) of the GATT 1994 is the "manner of administration" of European Communities customs law.[102] The European Communities considers that, by referring to the "manner of administration", the Panel did not blur the distinction between the measure at issue and the claims under Article X:3(a). The Panel used the term "manner of administration" to distinguish "administration" (the measure at issue in this dispute) from the laws and regulations of general application under Article X:1 of the GATT 1994, which are the subject of administration. According to the European Communities, the Panel used the term "manner of administration" synonymously with "administration".[103] The European Communities is of the view that this "minor ambiguity"[104] is not enough to reverse the Panel's finding that when a violation of Article X:3(a) is claimed, the panel request must identify a "manner of administration".

41. The European Communities contends that the United States is trying to confuse the laws to be administered with their administration.[105] In this respect, the European Communities observes that, in *EC – Bananas III*, the Appellate Body distinguished, in the context of Article X:3(a), between the administration of the laws and the laws to be administered.[106] According to the European Communities, the panel request refers to the manner of administration[107], "clearly distinguishes the administration from the laws which are being administered", and, thus, "identifies the 'administration', rather than those laws, as the measure at issue in the dispute."[108]

---

102 European Communities' appellee's submission, para. 97.
103 *Ibid.*, para. 91.
104 *Ibid.*, para. 92.
105 *Ibid.*, para. 94 (referring to Appellate Body Report, *EC – Bananas III*, para. 200).
106 European Communities' appellee's submission, para. 94.
107 *Ibid.*, para. 95.
108 *Ibid.*, para. 96.

(b) Confinement of the Measures at Issue to Certain Areas of Customs Administration

42. For the European Communities, the Panel was fully justified in concluding that the measure at issue was only the administration of customs law in the areas identified in the third paragraph of the panel request. The European Communities reiterates that, in this case, the measure at issue is not the set of legal instruments listed in the first paragraph of the panel request but, rather, their administration.[109] The European Communities submits that the United States is trying to engage in a selective reading of the panel request by asking the Appellate Body to ignore the third paragraph of the panel request.[110] Furthermore, given the "vast body of law"[111] referred to by the United States in the first paragraph of the panel request, it would not have been possible for the European Communities to prepare adequately its defence purely on the basis of a challenge against the administration of European Communities customs law "as a whole" without specifying the relevant provisions or sectors. In the view of the European Communities, "an identification of the specific issue or provision with respect to which a claim of non-uniform administration is made was ... necessary ... to protect [its] due process rights".[112]

43. The European Communities contends that the Panel correctly referred to the general principle set out in *EC – Computer Equipment* that "what is necessary for identification of the 'specific measures at issue' depends on the circumstance of the case."[113] In the circumstances of the present case, given the vast body of law to which the United States referred, the Panel was justified in requiring specification of areas of customs administration.

44. Regarding the terms "including but not limited to" contained in the third paragraph of the panel request, the European Communities relies on the Appellate Body Report in *India – Patents (US)* in asserting that "these words cannot have the effect of including, contrary to the requirements of Article 6.2 [of the] DSU, the administration of the entire body of [European Communities] customs law into the Panel's terms of reference."[114] The European Communities adds that the United States' interpretation of this phrase would reduce the third paragraph of the panel request to inutility[115] and would "prejudice [the defendant's] due process rights by leaving the actual subject matter of the case unclear."[116]

(c) Challenging the European Communities' System of Customs Administration "As a Whole"

45. According to the European Communities, the Appellate Body should uphold the Panel's findings that the United States' claims regarding the European

---

[109] *Ibid.*, para. 99.
[110] *Ibid.*, para. 100.
[111] *Ibid.*, para. 103.
[112] *Ibid.* (footnote omitted)
[113] *Ibid.*, para. 105.
[114] European Communities' appellee's submission, para. 106.
[115] *Ibid.*, para. 108.
[116] *Ibid.*, para. 109.

Communities' system "as a whole" and "as such" are outside its terms of reference. The European Communities considers the "as a whole" claim to be outside the Panel's terms of reference because the measure at issue is "only the [European Communities'] manner of administration in the areas of customs law specifically identified in [the] Panel request".[117] The European Communities also maintains that "[i]t is thus incorrect to suggest that the [European Communities'] system of customs administration could be assessed 'as a whole', independently of the specific needs and requirements of the sector or area in question, and the tools and mechanisms existing in such area."[118]

46. The European Communities argues that the panel request did not indicate that the United States intended to challenge the European Communities' system of customs administration "as such". For the European Communities, the panel request identified as the measure at issue the "manner of administration", and these terms are "diametrically opposed to those which one could have expected to be used in the case of a challenge against a measure 'as such'."[119] Regarding the United States' argument that the measures at issue were the instruments listed in the first paragraph of the panel request, and that they constitute the main instruments of the European Communities customs legislation, the European Communities reiterates its view that the measures at issue are not these instruments but, rather, their administration in the areas listed in the third paragraph of the panel request. The European Communities adds that its system of customs administration is broader than the instruments listed in the first paragraph of the panel request, because it includes other instruments such as the EC Treaty itself and more specific instruments existing in the field of customs cooperation, or budgetary and financial control.[120]

47. With respect to the United States' reliance on a number of statements made by the parties during or outside the Panel proceedings[121], the European Communities recalls that "the compliance of a [p]anel request with Article 6.2 [of the] DSU must be assessed primarily on the face of the [p]anel request".[122] The European Communities reiterates that at no point did it recognize or acknowledge that its system of customs administration "as such" was the measure at issue in this dispute.[123]

2. *Claims regarding Article X:3(a) of the GATT 1994*

(a) The Panel's Interpretation of the Term "Administer" in Article X:3(a) of the GATT 1994

48. The European Communities submits that the Panel was correct to distinguish between the laws to be administered and the administration of those laws,

117 *Ibid.*, para. 113.
118 *Ibid.*, para. 117.
119 *Ibid.*, para. 125.
120 European Communities' appellee's submission, para. 128.
121 United States' appellant's submission, paras. 84-98.
122 European Communities' appellee's submission, para. 131. See also paras. 87 ff.
123 *Ibid.*, para. 133.

and disagrees with the United States that laws themselves can constitute administration. According to the European Communities, the administration of a law or a regulation of general application, by definition, implies its application in concrete cases.[124]

49. The European Communities argues that the Panel did not err in finding that substantive differences in the penalty laws of the member States of the European Communities, in and of themselves, do not constitute a violation of Article X:3(a) of the GATT 1994.

50. According to the European Communities, the United States did not demonstrate that differences in the penalty laws of the member States lead to nonconformity in the administration of European Communities customs law. The European Communities explains that, although administrative or penalty provisions applicable to violations of customs law are set out in the individual laws of the member States, the member States do not have complete freedom in the determination of the appropriate level of penalties. Rather, in accordance with the binding principles of European Communities customs law, sanctions for the violation of customs law that member States provide must be effective, proportionate, and dissuasive.[125] In the European Communities' view, these principles ensure uniform application of customs law throughout the European Communities.[126]

51. The European Communities emphasizes that the objective of ensuring uniform application of European Communities customs law does not require full harmonization of penalty provisions among the member States, and that differences in penalties do not necessarily lead to a lack of uniformity in the application of the provisions.[127] The European Communities submits that, if sanctions are dissuasive and effective, then it must be assumed that the related substantive provisions will be respected, regardless of differences in the level of sanctions applicable. The European Communities contends that the United States has not provided any evidence concerning the actual nature and level of sanctions imposed by the laws of member States for specific violations of customs provisions. Therefore, in the European Communities' view, the United States has not established that differences in penalty laws result in differences in the administration of European Communities customs law.[128]

52. With respect to the administration of audit procedures, the European Communities submits that the Panel was correct to find no violation of Article X:3(a).[129] The European Communities disagrees with the United States that the same arguments it submitted when challenging the Panel's findings with respect to penalty laws apply with equal force to the Panel's findings with respect to audit procedures. In the European Communities' view, these claims are sub-

[124] *Ibid.*, paras. 207-215.
[125] European Communities' appellee's submission, paras. 202 and 222.
[126] *Ibid.*, para. 222.
[127] *Ibid.*, para. 223.
[128] *Ibid.*, paras. 221-232.
[129] *Ibid.*, paras. 46 and 233.

stantially different, because audit procedures are not primarily set out in member States' laws.[130] The European Communities asserts that uniform practice in this respect is ensured by the Community Customs Audit Guide.[131]

53. The European Communities notes the discretionary character of Article 78(2) of the Community Customs Code but argues that, nevertheless, the mere exercise of discretion in one way or another does not constitute non-uniform administration.[132] The European Communities submits that "the [United States] has not provided any evidence to substantiate its allegation that there are significant differences in the audit procedures followed by the ... [m]ember States"[133], and "has also not been able to demonstrate what impact, if any, such differences would have on the uniform administration of [European Communities] customs law."[134]

54. Regarding the United States' request that the Appellate Body complete the analysis under Article X:3(a) with respect to penalty provisions and audit procedures, the European Communities maintains that the Panel did not make the necessary findings of fact and that there are no undisputed facts on the record that would enable the Appellate Body to complete the analysis.[135]

(b) Completing the Analysis with respect to the "As a Whole" Challenge of the United States under Article X:3(a) of the GATT 1994

55. In the event that the Appellate Body reverses the Panel's findings regarding its terms of reference, the European Communities submits that the Appellate Body is not in a position to complete the legal analysis and should decline to find that the European Communities' system of customs administration "as a whole" and "as such" is inconsistent with Article X:3(a) of the GATT 1994.[136]

56. The European Communities disagrees with the United States that there are enough factual findings made by the Panel, or enough undisputed facts on record, that would enable the Appellate Body to find that the European Communities' system of customs administration "as such" and "as a whole" is inconsistent with Article X:3(a). According to the European Communities, the Panel's statements to which the United States refers are isolated remarks in the Panel Report where the Panel commented on individual aspects of the European Communities' system of customs administration.[137] These statements, the European Communities argues, would not allow the Appellate Body to assess whether the European Communities' system of customs administration "as a whole" and "as such" is in conformity with Article X:3(a) of the GATT 1994, given that they do

---

[130] *Ibid.*, para. 234.

[131] *Ibid.*, para. 237 (referring to Community Customs Audit Guide, a framework for post-clearance and audit-based controls (Exhibit EC-90 submitted by the European Communities to the Panel)).

[132] *Ibid.*, para. 241.

[133] *Ibid.*, para. 249.

[134] European Communities' appellee's submission, para. 250.

[135] *Ibid.*, paras. 231 and 251.

[136] *Ibid.*, paras. 141-142.

[137] *Ibid.*, para. 159.

not contain findings of fact in this regard, and were not intended by the Panel to constitute such findings.[138] The European Communities notes that these statements are contained in a section where the Panel set out its understanding of the European Communities' system of customs administration as "context" for the evaluation of the United States' claims regarding individual instances of application.[139]

57. Furthermore, the European Communities emphasizes that the Panel observed, *inter alia*, that "the United States did not demonstrate that the design and structure of the [European Communities'] system of customs administration, including components thereof, necessarily result in a violation of Article X:3(a) of the GATT 1994".[140] Thus, in the European Communities' view, the Panel explicitly confirmed that the United States did "not even come close" to establishing that the European Communities' system of customs administration "as such" and "as a whole" entails a violation of Article X:3(a) of the GATT 1994.[141]

58. Finally, the European Communities submits that the United States' claim regarding the European Communities' system of customs administration "as a whole" is a claim that has not been explored by the Panel, and the Panel has therefore not made any legal findings and interpretations on this claim that the Appellate Body could reverse. For the European Communities, a claim of violation of the obligation of uniform administration directed against individual instances of application is fundamentally different from a claim directed against a system of customs administration "as such" and "as a whole".[142] Adjudging the claim regarding the European Communities' system of customs administration "as such" and "as a whole" would, therefore, violate the due process rights of the participants, and of the European Communities in particular. Appellate Body proceedings have to take place within a narrow time-frame, and are focused on issues of law and legal interpretations. For the European Communities, such proceedings are manifestly not suited for investigating a claim against a system of customs administration "as a whole" and "as such".[143]

3. *The Panel's Interpretation of Article X:3(b) of the GATT 1994*

59. The European Communities argues that the Panel was correct in finding that the European Communities has not violated Article X:3(b) of the GATT 1994, because this provision does not require that the review of administrative action relating to customs matters must have effect throughout the territory of the European Communities.[144]

---

[138] *Ibid.*, para. 160.

[139] *Ibid.*

[140] European Communities' appellee's submission, para. 29 (quoting Panel Report, para. 7.490).

[141] *Ibid.*, paras. 171-172.

[142] *Ibid.*, paras. 188-189.

[143] *Ibid.*, paras. 193-195.

[144] *Ibid.*, paras. 257 and 342.

60. As a general matter, the European Communities notes that all disputes concerning European Communities law that are not subject to the jurisdiction of the ECJ and the Court of First Instance of the European Communities (the "CFI") fall within the competence of the national courts of the member States. The European Communities explains that national courts have a dual function: when deciding a dispute governed by national law, they form part of the national legal order; when deciding a case governed by European Communities law, they belong, from the functional point of view, to the European Communities' legal order.[145]

61. The European Communities points out that, in the case of actions brought before a national court that relate to the interpretation of an issue of European Communities law, the national court may request the ECJ to interpret a question of European Communities law (referred to as "references for a preliminary ruling").[146] Member State courts, against whose decisions there is no judicial remedy under national law, are required to refer issues of interpretation of European Communities law to the ECJ.[147] Since European Communities customs law is implemented through the customs authorities of the member States, an appeal for judicial review is lodged before the court of the member State whose customs authorities have issued the decision.[148] According to the European Communities, the main objective of the preliminary reference procedure is to guarantee the proper and uniform interpretation and application of European Communities law throughout all the member States, while avoiding the establishment of a long and expensive appellate system before the ECJ.[149] The European Communities notes that a preliminary ruling by the ECJ is binding on the national court hearing the case in which the ruling is given, and that it has effect also on persons who are not parties to the case referred.[150] The European Communities points out that, in exceptional cases, a right of appeal against member State customs decisions may also be available directly to the CFI.[151]

62. The European Communities submits that the Panel gave the correct meaning to the terms "the agencies entrusted with administration enforcement" and "such agencies" in Article X:3(b) of the GATT 1994. In the European Communities' view, the Panel correctly explained that the use of the plural when referring to "agencies" in Article X:3(b) could flow from the fact that the review "tribunals and procedures" required under the same provision are also referred to in the plural.[152] The European Communities disagrees with the United States' argument that the use of the singular in the *proviso* indicates that only one entity within a WTO Member should be permitted "to pursue" the review. In the European

[145] European Communities' appellee's submission, paras. 260-261.

[146] *Ibid.*, para. 266.

[147] *Ibid.*, para. 267.

[148] *Ibid.*, para. 274.

[149] *Ibid.*, para. 270.

[150] *Ibid.*, para. 272.

[151] *Ibid.*, para. 279. This is the case when the European Commission takes decisions that are of direct and individual concern to individuals.

[152] *Ibid.*, para. 288 (referring to Panel Report, para. 7.527).

Communities' view, the *proviso* covers the "central administration of any of those agencies existing in the WTO [M]ember".[153]

63. In response to the United States' argument that the Panel failed to give meaning to the distinct requirements in Article X:3(b) that review decisions must be "implemented by" and "govern the practice of" such agencies[154], the European Communities submits that the differences between the terms "to implement" and "govern the practice of" are irrelevant for interpreting the term "the agencies". Furthermore, the European Communities notes that the absence of an express reference to Article X:3(a) in Article X:3(b) of the GATT 1994 contrasts with the explicit reference by Article X:3(c) to Article X:3(b) of the GATT 1994. The European Communities agrees with the Panel that this absence precludes an inference that the obligation to ensure review of administrative action under Article X:3(b) could be read as simultaneously requiring uniform administration in accordance with Article X:3(a) of the GATT 1994, because "such an interpretation would amount to merging different requirements that are currently contained in separate subparagraphs of Article X of the GATT 1994."[155] The European Communities argues that this interpretation is also supported by the negotiating history of Article X.[156] The European Communities concurs with the Panel that it would not be reasonable to infer that "first instance independent review tribunals and bodies, whose jurisdiction in most legal systems is normally limited in substantive and geographical terms, should have the authority to bind all agencies entrusted with administrative enforcement throughout the territory of a Member".[157]

64. Finally, the European Communities submits that the United States' interpretation would lead to a major conflict between the *Marrakesh Agreement Establishing the World Trade Organization* (the "*WTO Agreement*") and the EC Treaty, because the creation of a central European Communities customs court of first instance would require a profound constitutional amendment of the EC Treaty that would require ratification by its 25 member States. The European Communities recalls that, when the *WTO Agreement* was negotiated and concluded, the United States never raised any concern about the European Communities' system of judicial review, which had already existed for almost 40 years.[158]

[153] European Communities' appellee's submission, para. 291.
[154] *Ibid.*, para. 293 (referring to United States' appellant's submission, para. 174).
[155] *Ibid.*, para. 302 (quoting Panel Report, para. 7.534).
[156] See *ibid.*, paras. 313-322.
[157] *Ibid.*, para. 325 (referring to United States' appellant's submission, para. 188).
[158] *Ibid.*, para. 339.

C. *Claims of Error by the European Communities – Other Appellant*

1. *The Panel's Terms of Reference*

(a) Temporal Limitations of the Panel's Terms of Reference

65. The European Communities contends that the Panel took an excessively wide approach to the temporal reach of its terms of reference.[159] For the European Communities, a panel may, in principle, consider only measures that are in existence at the time of its establishment[160] and, therefore, the Panel erred in considering that it had "a general competence to also consider measures which 'pre-date' or 'post-date' its establishment."[161] The European Communities refers to past Appellate Body and panel reports in support of its arguments.[162] The European Communities argues that, furthermore, the manner of administration "cannot be regarded as a 'continuum' without [a] clear start or end point", contrary to what the Panel suggests.[163] According to the European Communities, the Panel's approach would produce absurd results: it would imply that "violations which occurred far in the past and which no longer have any current effect could be claimed to be continuing because 'administration has no end point'"[164]; similarly, "violations which had not yet occurred at the time the Panel was established might be regarded as indicative of violations pre-dating the Panel's establishment because administration 'has no starting point'."[165]

66. The European Communities considers that, on the basis of the panel request, it was entitled to assume that the complainant's case related to measures in existence at the time of the Panel's establishment. The European Communities contends that, by defining "administration" under Article X:3(a) of the GATT 1994 as a "phenomenon without any boundaries in time", the Panel violated the due process rights of the defendant protected by Article 6.2 of the DSU, because the preparation of the defence for past instances of administration is "unduly difficult", and including future instances of administration in the measure at issue would make the subject matter of the case a "moving target".[166]

67. The European Communities also argues that the Panel's reasoning would render establishing compliance almost impossible. If administration has no clear start or end point, it would be difficult for a WTO Member found to be in violation of Article X:3(a) to establish that it has altered its manner of administration

---

[159] European Communities' other appellant's submission, para. 40.

[160] *Ibid.*, para. 46 (referring to Appellate Body Report, *EC – Chicken Cuts*, para. 156).

[161] *Ibid.*, para. 47.

[162] The European Communities refers to Appellate Body Reports in *Chile – Price Band System*, para. 139; *EC – Chicken Cuts*, para. 56; *EC – Computer Equipment*, para. 81; and *US – Upland Cotton*, paras. 262-263 and 272; and to Panel Reports in *EC – Computer Equipment*, para. 8.14; *Japan – Film*, para. 10.58; and *US – Upland Cotton*, paras. 7.158-7.160. (*Ibid.*, paras. 46-59)

[163] *Ibid.*, para. 63; Panel Report, para. 7.37.

[164] European Communities' other appellant's submission, para. 65.

[165] *Ibid.*

[166] European Communities' other appellant's submission, para. 66.

so that compliance with Article X:3(a) is achieved.[167] The European Communities contends that "the Panel's approach to the temporal limitations to its terms of reference is incompatible with Article[s] 7.1 and 6.2 [of the] DSU"[168] and requests the Appellate Body to reverse the Panel's findings on the temporal limitations of its terms of reference.[169]

2. *Claims regarding Article X:3(a) of the GATT 1994*

(a) The Administrative Process and the Requirement of Uniformity

68. The European Communities submits that the Panel erred in finding that "Article X:3(a) of the GATT [1994] requires uniformity of administrative processes irrespective of their impact on the uniform administration of the laws."[170]

69. The European Communities agrees with the Panel that the term "to administer" relates to the application of laws, and that this may potentially include both the administrative processes as well as their results. However, for the European Communities, Article X:3(a) does not require that the administrative process "be fully uniform in all cases and respects".[171] The European Communities emphasizes that "[i]n most administrations, procedures are not fully regulated or harmonised."[172] The European Communities doubts that a total uniformity of administrative procedures is required in order to ensure that traders are treated fairly and consistently. In the view of the European Communities, whether the requirement of uniform administration in Article X:3(a) is met should be evaluated primarily on the basis of the administrative outcome. The European Communities argues that "[a]part from the case that the administrative process is regulated in laws or regulations of general application themselves, the obligation of uniform administration only extends to the administrative process to the extent that the administrative process has a direct and significant impact on the outcome of the process".[173] Accordingly, the European Communities requests the Appellate Body to reverse the Panel's finding that Article X:3(a) of the GATT 1994 requires uniformity of administrative processes irrespective of their impact on the uniform administration of the laws.[174]

(b) The Administrative Process Leading to the Tariff Classification of Blackout Drapery Lining

70. The European Communities submits that the Panel erred in finding that the European Communities has violated Article X:3(a) of the GATT 1994 with

[167] *Ibid.*, para. 68.
[168] *Ibid.*, para. 69.
[169] *Ibid.*, para. 70; Panel Report, paras. 7.36-7.37.
[170] European Communities' other appellant's submission, para. 82; Panel Report, paras. 7.102-7.113 and 7.119.
[171] European Communities' other appellant's submission, para. 76.
[172] *Ibid.*, para. 78.
[173] European Communities' other appellant's submission, para. 81.
[174] *Ibid.*, para. 82.

respect to the tariff classification of blackout drapery lining.[175] In particular, the European Communities challenges the Panel's findings relating to the administrative process governing the tariff classification of blackout drapery lining. The European Communities notes that the Panel reached these findings "even though it also found that there was no evidence of an actual divergence in the tariff classification of [blackout drapery lining]".[176] For the European Communities, the Panel erred because it overstepped its terms of reference by making findings with respect to expired measures, failed to make an objective assessment of the facts as required by Article 11 of the DSU, and misapplied the requirements of Article X:3(a) of the GATT 1994.

71. The European Communities contends that the findings of the Panel concerning blackout drapery lining are outside its terms of reference because they are exclusively based on the reasoning of the decisions and letters of the German customs authorities in two isolated past cases. The European Communities points out that the letter of the Main Customs Office Hamburg to Ornata GmbH dates from July 1998, the opinion of the ZPLA Hamburg in the Bautex-Stoffe GmbH case dates from February 2003, and the decision of the Main Customs Office Hamburg in the same case dates from September 2004.[177] For the European Communities, these decisions and letters are expired measures because they concern past transactions and they no longer have any effects for the future. The European Communities submits that the Panel's findings regarding the "administrative process" relating to the tariff classification of blackout drapery lining are outside its terms of reference and should be reversed.[178]

72. With respect to the Panel's findings that the German customs authorities relied on an interpretative aid that is particular to Germany, the European Communities argues that the description of the facts made by the Panel does not correspond to an objective assessment of the facts, as required by Article 11 of the DSU.[179] The European Communities argues that the decisions and letters to which the Panel referred did not rely on a German explanatory aid or on certain classification criteria in a way that would have been incompatible with the uniform application of European Communities customs law.[180] The European Communities also recalls that the interpretive aid referred to by the Panel "is purely a non-binding text which does not in any way derogate from the application of [European] Communit[ies] law".[181]

73. With respect to the alleged failure of the German customs authorities to take into account the decisions of customs authorities of other member States, the European Communities argues that the decisions and letters to which the Panel referred do not indicate that the German customs authorities wished to

[175] *Ibid.*, para. 148.
[176] *Ibid.*, para. 95 (referring to Panel Report, para. 7.265).
[177] *Ibid.*, para. 106.
[178] *Ibid.*, para. 110.
[179] European Communities' other appellant's submission, para. 111.
[180] *Ibid.*, paras. 114-115.
[181] *Ibid.*, para. 132 (referring to Panel Report, para. 7.239).

ignore the decisions of other customs authorities.[182] The European Communities adds that the factual basis for the Panel's findings is "extremely tenuous"[183], because the Panel based its findings on one single case and ignored a letter that clearly illustrates that the German customs authorities do take into account the practice of other customs authorities concerning the classification of similar goods when they are made aware of them.[184] The European Communities contends that the Panel's statement that "German customs authorities are not obliged to make reference to the decisions of other customs authorities when classifying blackout drapery lining, even in cases where there is a possibility that the products ... subject [to] those decisions are the same or similar"[185], contradicts Articles 6(3) and 2(1) of the Community Customs Code.

74. For the European Communities, even if the facts set out in the Panel Report were correct, they would not amount to an "act of non-uniform administration" within the meaning of Article X:3(a).[186] The European Communities considers that the Panel's findings are based on the "motivation" of decisions and letters issued by the German authorities, which can hardly be regarded as part of the "administration process".[187] Even if it were to be regarded as such, not every variation in the reasoning of the decisions of customs authorities could be regarded as amounting to non-uniform administration, because a violation of that obligation can only be assumed to exist where the divergence has a direct impact on administrative outcomes.[188] In the European Communities' view, Article X:3(a) does not require the reasoning of decisions of customs authorities to be uniform; this would be contrary to the very purpose of the "motivation", which is to set out the reasons that led to the decision in the circumstances of the particular case.[189] The European Communities points out that the Panel recognized that "there was no evidence that there had been a lack of uniformity as regards the actual tariff classification."[190]

(c) Tariff Classification of Liquid Crystal Display Monitors with Digital Video Interface

75. The European Communities submits that the Panel erred in finding that the European Communities has violated Article X:3(a) of the GATT 1994 with respect to the tariff classification of LCD monitors with DVI.[191] According to the European Communities, "[t]he Panel overstepped its terms of reference by basing its findings of violation primarily on instances of administration which post-

182 *Ibid.*, paras. 118-119 and 141.
183 *Ibid.*, para. 144.
184 *Ibid.*, paras. 120-121.
185 Panel Report, para. 7.276 (quoted in European Communities' other appellant's submission, para. 122).
186 European Communities' other appellant's submission, para. 124.
187 *Ibid.*, paras. 126-127 and 138.
188 European Communities' other appellant's submission, paras. 128 and 138.
189 *Ibid.*, para. 19.
190 *Ibid.*, para. 128.
191 *Ibid.*, para. 202.

date its establishment".[192] Specifically, the European Communities refers to the Dutch decree of 8 July 2005 and the German BTI of 19 July 2005.[193] The European Communities also argues that the Panel did not make an objective assessment of the facts, as required by Article 11 of the DSU, because "the Panel did not have any evidence before it to support a finding that at the time of its establishment, there was a lack of uniform administration with regard to the tariff classification of LCD monitors."[194]

76. The European Communities submits that, "even if ... the Panel was justified in considering instances of administration which post-dated the time of its establishment", it nevertheless erred in finding a violation of Article X:3(a).[195] The European Communities notes that uniformity under Article X:3(a) must be established "within a reasonable period of time"[196], and maintains that this has been achieved with the adoption of Commission Regulation (EC) No. 2171/2005 ("EC Regulation 2171/2005") on 23 December 2005, as well as with the withdrawal, in January 2006, of the Dutch decree and the German BTI.[197] In this respect, the European Communities submits that the Panel erred in failing to take into account draft EC Regulation 2171/2005, because it had not yet been formally adopted.[198] Also, the European Communities argues, the Panel erred in rejecting the evidence contained in exhibits provided by the European Communities at the interim review stage.[199] According to the European Communities, the Panel's decision was not in accordance with Article 15.2 of the DSU, because this evidence related to precise aspects of the Panel's Interim Report.[200] The European Communities considers that the strict approach taken by the Panel with respect to the evidence submitted by the European Communities during the interim review stage is "incompatible with its duty to make an objective assessment of the facts ... [g]iven the Panel's own liberal attitude towards its terms of reference, as well as the late admission of evidence provided by the United States".[201] The European Communities, therefore, requests the Appellate Body to

---

[192] *Ibid.*, para. 150.

[193] *Ibid.*, para. 166 (referring to Douanerechten. Indeling van bepaalde LCD monitoren in de gecombineerde nomenclatuur [Customs Law: Classification of certain LCD monitors in the Combined Nomenclature], No. CPP2005/1372 M, 8 July 2005; and BTI DEM/2975/05-1, 19 July 2005 (Exhibits US-77 and US-78, respectively, submitted by the United States to the Panel).

[194] *Ibid.*, para. 182.

[195] *Ibid.*, para. 183.

[196] *Ibid.*, para. 185.

[197] European Communities' other appellant's submission, para. 186 (referring to Commission Regulation (EC) No. 2171/2005 of 23 December 2005 concerning the classification of certain goods in the Combined Nomenclature; Dutch Ministry of Finance, Telefaxbericht, No. BCPP 2006/389 M, dated February 2006, on the withdrawal of decree No. CPP2005/1372 M; extract from the EBTI data base on the expired BTI DEM/2975/05-1 (Exhibits EC-167, EC-168, and EC-169, respectively, submitted by the European Communities to the Panel)). See also Panel Report, para. 6.3.

[198] European Communities' other appellant's submission, para. 190.

[199] The European Communities refers to Exhibits EC-167, EC-168, and EC-169, *supra*, footnote 197. See also Panel Report, paras. 6.3 and 6.6.

[200] European Communities' other appellant's submission, paras. 196-197.

[201] *Ibid.*, para. 199.

find that the Panel erred in rejecting exhibits submitted by the European Communities at the interim review stage.[202]

(d) Administration of the Successive Sales Provision

77. The European Communities appeals the Panel's finding that the administration of Article 147(1) of the Implementing Regulation (the "successive sales provision") amounts to a violation of Article X:3(a) of the GATT 1994 because some member States of the European Communities impose a "form of prior approval" requirement while others do not.[203]

78. The European Communities submits that, in reaching this finding, the Panel failed to make an objective assessment of the facts and misapplied Article X:3(a).[204] The European Communities claims that the Panel erred, in particular, in concluding that the United States had established a *prima facie* case that certain member States were imposing a requirement of prior approval.[205] In the European Communities' view, the Panel erred in shifting the burden of proof from the United States to the European Communities.[206]

79. The European Communities submits that the United States supported its claim exclusively with a statement in the European Communities Court of Auditors Special Report No. 23/2000 concerning the valuation of imported goods for customs purposes[207] (the "Court of Auditors Report"). The European Communities contends that the Court of Auditors' observation was not shared by other institutions of the European Communities and that, in particular, the European Commission confirmed that member States do not impose any requirement of prior approval.[208]

80. The European Communities contends that the Court of Auditors Report was not sufficient to establish a *prima facie* case of non-uniform administration of Article 147(1) of the Implementing Regulation, which does not contain a requirement of prior approval. The European Communities submits that: first, the statements relied upon by the Panel are excessively vague, because the Court of Auditors Report does not specify the precise nature of the "form of prior approval"; secondly, the Court of Auditors Report reflects the opinion of only one institution of the European Communities and does not take into account the opinions of other institutions, such as the European Commission; and thirdly, in the European Communities' view, the United States should have demonstrated non-

---

[202] *Ibid.*, para. 201 (referring to Panel Report, para. 6.6 and Exhibits EC-167, EC-168, and EC-169 submitted by the European Communities to the Panel).

[203] *Ibid.*, paras. 203-229.

[204] *Ibid.*, para. 204.

[205] European Communities' other appellant's submission, para. 204.

[206] See *ibid.*, paras. 214-222.

[207] Court of Auditors, Special Report No. 23/2000 concerning valuation of imported goods for customs purposes (customs valuation), together with the Commission's replies, reproduced in *Official Journal of the European Communities*, C Series, No. 84, pp. 1-18 (14 March 2001) (Exhibit US-14 submitted by the United States to the Panel).

[208] European Communities' other appellant's submission, para. 207 (referring to Court of Auditors Report, *supra*, footnote 207, p. 17).

uniform administration with evidence of actual administration rather than with the Court of Auditors Report.[209] Finally, the European Communities argues that the Court of Auditors detected only "minor variations" in administrative practices, which do not "automatically translate" into a violation of Article X:3(a).[210] In the European Communities' view, such variations will violate the obligation of uniform administration only if they are shown to have an impact on administrative outcomes.[211]

81. The European Communities submits that, even if the Panel was correct to assume that the burden of proof had shifted to the European Communities, it failed to give due weight to the information provided by the European Communities regarding the practice of its member States.[212] As a result, the Panel erred in rejecting as evidence the communication between the European Communities and its member States, which the European Communities provided in its comments on the Panel's Interim Report.[213]

3. *Conditional Appeal of the European Communities*

82. The European Communities conditionally appeals the Panel's finding that Article XXIV:12 of the GATT 1994 cannot be relied upon to attenuate or to derogate from the provisions of Article X:3 of the GATT 1994. The European Communities requests a review of this finding only in the event that the Appellate Body's conclusions imply that the European Communities should "create a centralised customs agency replacing its [m]ember States in the implementation of [European Communities] customs law", or that the European Communities should "create [a European Communities]-level tribunal for the first-instance review of customs decisions".[214]

83. The European Communities does not contest that it is obliged to ensure uniform administration of its customs law, even where this law is being administered by its member States.[215] However, the European Communities disagrees with the Panel's interpretation that Article XXIV:12 of the GATT 1994 "does not constitute an exception nor a derogation from the obligation of uniform administration in Article X:3(a) of the GATT 1994".[216] The European Communities submits that the question is not whether Article XXIV:12 is a "positive obligation" but, rather, what the content of this obligation is.[217] The European Communities refers to the general principle of international law that States are responsible for the acts of all their organs and emanations, including their sub-federal and

---

209 *Ibid.*, paras. 217-221.

210 *Ibid.*, para. 221.

211 *Ibid.*

212 European Communities' other appellant's submission, para. 223.

213 *Ibid.*, para. 227 (referring to Panel Report, paras. 6.6 and 7.427; and Exhibit EC-170 submitted by the European Communities to the Panel).

214 *Ibid.*, para. 235.

215 *Ibid.*, para. 233.

216 Panel Report, para. 7.145 (quoted in European Communities' other appellant's submission, para. 241).

217 European Communities' other appellant's submission, para. 242.

regional governments.[218] According to the European Communities, this general principle did not require a specific confirmation in the GATT.

84. The European Communities emphasizes the specific reference in Article XXIV:12 to "reasonable measures as may be available" and submits that this language not only confirms the responsibility of WTO Members for their local and regional governments, it also sets out a standard for the type of measures that must be taken by WTO Members with respect to their local and regional governments.[219] In the European Communities' view, the GATT panel in *Canada – Gold Coins* recognized this fact when it stated that "the consequences of ... non-observance [of GATT obligations] by the local government for trade relations with other [Members] are to be weighed against the domestic difficulties of securing observance".[220] Therefore, the European Communities submits that Article XXIV:12 of the GATT 1994 serves as a "useful and necessary safeguard" in cases where a WTO Member is faced with claims that could be addressed only through major changes in the federal system within that WTO Member, as would be the case for a requirement to create a European Communities customs agency or customs court.[221]

D. Arguments of the United States – Appellee

1. The Panel's Terms of Reference

(a) Temporal Limitations of the Panel's Terms of Reference

85. The United States is of the view that the Panel did not err in its approach to the temporal scope of its terms of reference.[222] The United States observes that the legal instruments it identified as the measures at issue in the panel request were in existence on the date when the Panel was established.[223] For the United States, the European Communities' argument "confuses *administration* of [European Communities] customs law in existence when the Panel was established with individual *acts of administration* that occurred prior to establishment and with *evidence* that came to light during the panel proceeding that confirm the existence of non-uniform administration at the time of panel establishment."[224] For the United States, the Panel correctly explained that "it would take account

[218] The European Communities refers, in paragraph 243 of its other appellant's submission, to Article 4 of the Articles on the Responsibility of States for Internationally Wrongful Acts 2001. (Text adopted by the International Law Commission at its fifty-third session, in August 2001, and submitted to the General Assembly as a part of the Commission's report covering the work of that session.) The report, which also contains commentaries on the draft articles, appears in the *Official Records of the General Assembly, Fifty-sixth Session, Supplement No. 10* (A/56/10). The text is reproduced in the annex to General Assembly Resolution 56/83 of 12 December 2001.

[219] European Communities' other appellant's submission, para. 243.

[220] GATT Panel Report, *Canada – Gold Coins*, para. 69 (quoted in European Communities' other appellant's submission, para. 244).

[221] European Communities' other appellant's submission, para. 247.

[222] United States' appellee's submission, para. 51.

[223] *Ibid.*, para. 17.

[224] *Ibid.*, para. 15. (original emphasis; footnote omitted)

of individual instances of administration pre-dating and post-dating panel establishment not to determine whether each established a WTO-inconsistency in its own right, but as a means of elucidating the manner of administration that may be in existence at the time of panel establishment."[225] The United States considers that the Panel referred to individual acts of administration that pre-dated its establishment "*not* as potential breaches of Article X:3(a) of the GATT 1994 in and of themselves, but as evidence of the manner of administration of the relevant provisions of [European Communities] customs law."[226]

86. The United States is also of the view that the European Communities misreads the logical distinction the Panel made between administration as an ongoing phenomenon and individual instances of administration.[227] For the United States, although the European Communities has referred to the general principle that a panel may consider only measures in existence at the time of panel establishment, it made "no distinction between acts of administration themselves being considered as potential breaches of Article X:3(a) and acts of administration being considered as evidence of an ongoing course of administration that potentially is a breach of Article X:3(a)."[228] The United States points out that nothing in the text of Article X:3(a) or its context suggests that a breach of Article X:3(a) "is demonstrated only when individual acts of administration in existence on the date a panel is established diverge."[229] According to the United States, the European Communities' view is that administration is not a continuum, and that only individual acts of administration in existence at the time of panel establishment can be challenged as breaching Article X:3(a). If this understanding were correct, the United States argues, the obligation of uniform administration under Article X:3(a) would be rendered "ineffective"[230] and would not meet the minimum standards of predictability for traders set out in Article X:3(a).[231]

87. Regarding the European Communities' argument concerning events that post-dated the Panel's establishment, the United States maintains that, contrary to the European Communities' assertions, the Panel's references to evidence post-dating its establishment do not show the Panel overstepping its terms of reference. According to the United States, "[t]hey show the Panel properly [took] account of evidence relevant to understanding the manner of administration of [European Communities] customs law existing at the time of panel establishment."[232]

---

[225] *Ibid.*, para. 18 (referring to Panel Report, paras. 7.36-7.37).
[226] United States' appellee's submission, para. 22. (original emphasis)
[227] *Ibid.*, para. 23.
[228] *Ibid.*, para. 27.
[229] *Ibid.*, para. 31.
[230] *Ibid.*, para. 35.
[231] *Ibid.*, paras. 32 and 41.
[232] *Ibid.*, para. 46.

2. *Claims regarding Article X:3(a) of the GATT 1994*

(a) The Administrative Process and the Requirement of Uniformity

88. The United States asks the Appellate Body to reject the European Communities' request for a reversal of the Panel's finding that Article X:3(a) of the GATT 1994 "requires uniformity of administrative processes irrespective of their impact on the uniform administration of the laws".[233]

89. The United States disagrees with the European Communities' view that "the obligation of uniform administration only extends to the administrative process to the extent that the administrative process has a direct and significant impact on the outcome of the process".[234] The United States points out that the European Communities failed to explain what it means by "administrative outcome" and how to distinguish administrative outcomes from administrative processes.[235] For the United States, the exclusion of administrative processes from the obligation of uniform administration has no basis in the text of Article X:3(a).[236] The United States considers that the European Communities' approach is too restrictive and would imply that significant areas of customs administration could be conducted in a non-uniform manner without breaching Article X:3(a).[237] For the United States, from the trader's view, there is no basis for assuming that the outcome of administrative processes consists only of the release of an imported good with a particular classification and valuation into the customs territory of the European Communities, and does not also include the burden associated with the administrative process.[238]

90. According to the United States, whether requiring uniformity of administrative processes under Article X:3(a) would exclude *de minimis* variations in the administration of customs law is not at issue in this dispute.[239] Indeed, the United States maintains that, where the Panel found divergences in administrative processes inconsistent with Article X:3(a), the divergences were material to traders' decisions to convey goods into the European Communities through one region rather than through another.[240]

(b) The Administrative Process Leading to the Tariff Classification of Blackout Drapery Lining

91. The United States submits that the Panel did not err in its findings regarding the tariff classification of blackout drapery lining. In the United States' view, the European Communities attempts to reargue certain factual issues, and in so

233 United States' appellee's submission, para. 63 (referring to European Communities' other appellant's submission, para. 82).
234 European Communities' other appellant's submission, para. 81.
235 United States' appellee's submission, paras. 53-54.
236 *Ibid.*, para. 55.
237 *Ibid.*, para. 58.
238 *Ibid.*, para. 59.
239 *Ibid.*, paras. 60-61.
240 *Ibid.*, para. 61.

doing misrepresents the relevant facts.[241] The United States disagrees with the European Communities' assertion that the product considered by the German customs authorities in the instances of administration the Panel reviewed was different from the product considered by other customs authorities in other member States of the European Communities.[242] Regarding the European Communities' allegation that the Panel was mistaken when it stated that all decisions or letters of the German customs authorities relied on an interpretative aid particular to Germany, the United States points out that there was an explicit reference to that aid in the documents issued by the German customs authorities.[243] The United States requests the Appellate Body not to disturb the Panel's factual findings or reweigh the evidence that was before it.[244]

92. The United States asserts that the case of tariff classification of blackout drapery lining is a specific example of the European Communities' mistake of confusing administration as an ongoing phenomenon with individual acts of administration. For the United States, divergence in how the German customs authorities and customs authorities in other member States administer the Common Customs Tariff constitutes a lack of uniform administration.[245]

93. The United States argues that the Panel correctly found that non-uniform administrative processes in classifying blackout drapery lining are inconsistent with Article X:3(a). The United States observes that the Panel did not find that differences between the blackout drapery lining presented to the German customs authorities and the blackout drapery lining presented to other customs authorities in the European Communities justified different tariff classifications; rather, the United States asserts that what the Panel found was an absence of evidence to support a finding of divergent tariff classifications between Germany and the other member States.[246] The United States contends that a finding of insufficient evidence of divergent classifications is not the same as a finding that different customs authorities correctly reached different tariff classifications. For the United States, the European Communities' argument regarding the classification of blackout drapery lining is a variation of its general argument that the obligation of uniform administration under Article X:3(a) covers administrative processes only to the extent that they have a direct and significant impact on administrative outcomes.[247] Finally, according to the United States, the distinction the European Communities seeks to draw between the "motivation" of a decision and "administrative processes" is without basis.[248]

94. The United States agrees with the Panel's finding that the German customs authorities failed to take into account the decisions of customs authorities

[241] United States' appellee's submission, para. 73.
[242] *Ibid.*, para. 77.
[243] *Ibid.*, para. 80.
[244] *Ibid.*, para. 85.
[245] *Ibid.*, para. 86.
[246] *Ibid.*, para. 90.
[247] United States' appellee's submission, para. 89.
[248] *Ibid.*, para. 94.

of other member States regarding the classification of blackout drapery lining.[249] For the United States, it is important to consider the context in which German customs authorities administer European Communities customs law, as it does not include any requirement of "reference by customs authorities to decisions taken by other customs authorities operating within the same system".[250] The United States considers it important that "the German [customs] authority by its own admission was aware of other authorities [in the European Communities] having classified 'comparable goods', yet gave scant consideration to such classification and apparently undertook no investigation of those other authorities' findings."[251]

(c) Tariff Classification of Liquid Crystal Display Monitors with Digital Video Interface

95. The United States requests the Appellate Body to uphold the Panel's finding that the European Communities has violated Article X:3(a) of the GATT 1994 with respect to the tariff classification of LCD monitors with DVI. For the United States, the European Communities' claim misrepresents key facts and ignores the distinction between administration and evidence of administration. The United States also disagrees with the European Communities' argument that the Panel erred by declining to consider new evidence introduced following the issuance of the Panel's Interim Report.[252]

96. The United States submits that the Panel's finding that the European Communities acknowledged tariff classification of LCD monitors with DVI to be non-uniform in 2004 was based on an objective assessment of the facts.[253] The United States emphasizes that it had established this fact before the Panel, and that various statements made by the European Communities in the course of the Panel proceedings suggested that the European Communities "was aware of the issue and was working to address it".[254]

97. The United States notes that the European Communities argued before the Panel that it had taken three steps to address the non-uniform administration with respect to the classification of LCD monitors with DVI: the June/July 2004 "conclusions" of the Customs Code Committee; Council Regulation (EC) No. 673/2005 of 25 April 2005 establishing additional customs duties on imports of certain products originating in the United States; and Commission Regulation (EC) No. 634/2005 of 26 April 2005 concerning the classification of certain goods in the Combined Nomenclature.[255] The United States maintains that the Panel made an objective assessment of the facts as it considered each of these

---

249 *Ibid.*, para. 107.
250 *Ibid.*, para. 100 (quoting Panel Report, para. 7.272).
251 *Ibid.*, para. 102 (quoting Panel Report, paras. 7.273-7.274).
252 *Ibid.*, para. 108.
253 *Ibid.*, para. 109.
254 United States' appellee's submission, para. 110.
255 *Ibid.*, para. 117 (referring to European Communities' first written submission to the Panel, paras. 351-353, 356, and 361).

measures and found that none of them resolved the problem of non-uniform administration.[256]

98. For the United States, the Panel did not overstep its terms of reference by referring to acts of administration that post-dated the Panel's establishment, because the Panel did not refer to these acts as breaches of Article X:3(a) in their own right, but as evidence of the manner of administration in breach of Article X:3(a) that was in existence at the time the Panel was established.[257] Thus, the United States argues, the European Communities again confuses administration with individual acts of administration. According to the United States, the Dutch decree of 8 July 2005 and the German BTI of 19 July 2005 are relevant evidence supporting the Panel's finding that "measures put into place since 2004 have not resolved the problem of non-uniform administration and may well have increased confusion."[258]

99. According to the United States, the Panel properly gave no weight to draft EC Regulation 2171/2005 concerning the tariff classification of LCD monitors and was correct to decline considering new evidence the European Communities introduced at the interim review stage.[259] Regarding draft EC Regulation 2171/2005, the United States argues that the European Communities' characterization of this piece of evidence as a new instance, rather than a continuation, of non-uniform administration in existence since 2004 is unfounded, and that the Panel could not have assumed that this draft Regulation would be adopted.[260] The United States adds that the European Communities' argument regarding the draft Regulation is "self-contradictory"[261] because, on the one hand, it argues that the relevant point in time for establishing a violation is the date of panel establishment while, on the other hand, it faults the Panel for not taking account of draft EC Regulation 2171/2005, which came into existence late in the Panel proceedings. Regarding the Panel's decision not to consider new evidence introduced at the interim review stage, the United States emphasizes that the interim review stage is not an appropriate time to introduce new evidence, and disagrees with the European Communities' assertion that there should be an exception for evidence introduced to correct errors of fact.[262]

(d) Administration of the Successive Sales Provision

100. The United States requests the Appellate Body to uphold the Panel's finding that the European Communities has violated Article X:3(a) of the GATT 1994 as a result of the imposition of a form of prior approval with respect to the

---

256 *Ibid.*, para. 123.

257 *Ibid.*, para. 125.

258 *Ibid.*, para. 126 (referring to Panel Report, para. 7.300).

259 *Ibid.*, paras. 128, 132, and 140 (referring, *inter alia*, to Exhibits EC-167, EC-168, and EC-169 submitted by the European Communities to the Panel).

260 *Ibid.*, paras. 129 and 131.

261 United States' appellee's submission, para. 130.

262 *Ibid.*, paras. 134-136. The United States makes reference to Appellate Body Report, *EC – Sardines*, para. 301, in support of its argument.

successive sales provision by customs authorities of some member States of the European Communities.[263]

101. The United States asserts that the statement of the European Communities' Court of Auditors Report that, "in practice, some customs authorities do impose a form of prior approval even though this has no basis in [European] Communit[ies] law"[264], amounts to an admission of non-uniform administration by the European Communities.[265] With respect to the European Commission's comment on this statement in the Court of Auditors Report[266], the United States submits that the European Communities has not accurately rendered the Commission's comment, because the words "in some member States" were omitted from the European Communities' quotation of the Commission's comment. In the United States' view, this reveals that the European Commission did not disagree with the Court of Auditors on the existence of divergent practices.[267] For the United States, the very fact that, in its replies to the Court of Auditors Report, the Commission disagreed with the Court of Auditors on a variety of issues but not on the Court's finding of divergent administration among customs authorities of member States, supports the Panel's view that the Court's finding was an admission of non-uniform administration in the European Communities.[268] The United States considers that it did not need to adduce additional evidence in order to establish its *prima facie* case, because it had provided the Panel with an admission of non-uniform administration by the European Communities.

102. The United States maintains that the Panel properly declined to consider evidence introduced by the European Communities at the interim review stage to rebut its admission of non-uniform administration, because this evidence could have been submitted at an earlier stage. Furthermore, according to the United States, even under the European Communities' own reasoning, it was proper for the Panel not to consider this new evidence concerning the administration of the successive sales provision, because the European Communities had not clarified that this evidence was intended merely to correct an error of fact.[269] Finally, the United States alleges that the e-mail correspondence the European Communities sought to introduce at the interim review stage consisted of statements made by persons with a vested interest in the outcome of the dispute.[270]

3. Conditional Appeal of the European Communities

103. The United States requests the Appellate Body to reject the European Communities' conditional appeal to reverse the Panel's finding that Arti-

---

[263] United States' appellee's submission, para. 141.
[264] Court of Auditors Report, *supra*, footnote 207, para. 64; Panel Report, para. 7.381.
[265] United States' appellee's submission, para. 143.
[266] See *supra*, para. 79.
[267] United States' appellee's submission, para. 145.
[268] *Ibid.*, para. 146.
[269] United States' appellee's submission, para. 157.
[270] *Ibid.*, para. 158.

cle XXIV:12 of the GATT 1994 cannot be relied upon to attenuate or to derogate from the provisions of the GATT 1994, including Article X:3.[271]

104. The United States asserts that the question of the possible relevance of Article XXIV:12 to the European Communities' obligations under Article X:3(b) is outside the scope of appellate review as circumscribed by Article 17.6 of the DSU.[272] According to the United States, the European Communities never raised the issue of the relevance of Article XXIV:12 to its obligations under Article X:3(b), but referred to it only in relation to the obligation of uniform administration under Article X:3(a) of the GATT 1994.[273]

105. The United States maintains that Article XXIV:12 of the GATT 1994 is not relevant to this dispute, because that provision applies to the "observance of the provisions of [the GATT 1994] by the regional and local governments and authorities within [each Member's] territories" whose measures "the federal government cannot control because they fall outside its jurisdiction under the constitutional distribution of competences."[274] In the United States' view, this dispute does not concern the observance of Article X:3(a) of the GATT 1994 by regional and local governments within the European Communities; but, rather, that the European Communities itself has failed to establish institutions or other mechanisms necessary to ensure uniform administration of its customs law. In this regard, the United States distinguishes the present dispute from the dispute in *Canada – Gold Coins*, which involved a measure adopted by a provincial government that put Canada in breach of its obligation under Article III of the GATT 1947.[275]

106. Finally, the United States argues that, even if Article XXIV:12 were applicable to this dispute, and even if it could potentially attenuate or derogate from the European Communities' obligations under Article X:3(a), it would not do so in this dispute, because the European Communities offered no evidence to show that the measures it is taking to ensure observance of Article X:3(a) by regional and local governments within its territories are "such reasonable measures as may be available to it", as required by Article XXIV:12.[276] With respect to the European Communities' argument that the "safeguards and mechanisms"[277] under its system of customs administration constitute such "reasonable measures", the United States submits that a mere assertion does not amount to proof, and that the question of whether the measures a Member is taking satisfy the requirements of Article XXIV:12 is not "self-judging".[278]

---

[271] *Ibid.*, para. 160; Panel Report, para. 7.145.

[272] United States' appellee's submission, para. 161.

[273] *Ibid.* (referring to European Communities' first written submission to the Panel, para. 220; and European Communities' response to Question 68 posed by the Panel, para. 113, Panel Report, pp. A-65 and A-66).

[274] United States' appellee's submission, paras. 164 and 163, respectively (referring to GATT Panel Report, *Canada – Gold Coins*, para. 56).

[275] *Ibid.*, para. 164 (referring to European Communities' other appellant's submission, paras. 234 and 244).

[276] *Ibid.*, para. 174.

[277] European Communities' other appellant's submission, para. 235.

[278] United States' appellee's submission, para. 174.

E. Arguments of the Third Participants

107. Pursuant to Rule 24(2) of the *Working Procedures*, Argentina, Australia, Brazil, China, Hong Kong, China, India, and the Separate Customs Territory of Taiwan, Penghu, Kinmen, and Matsu chose not to submit a third participant's submission but attended the oral hearing. In its statement at the oral hearing, Australia presented its views regarding the Panel's terms of reference, the interpretation of the scope of the term "administer" in Article X:3(a) of the GATT 1994, and the irrelevance of Article XXIV:12 of the GATT 1994 to the facts of this dispute. China, in its statement at the oral hearing, addressed issues relating to the Panel's terms of reference.

1. Japan

108. Japan agrees with the Panel that "the measure at issue", for purposes of Article X:3(a) of the GATT 1994, can be the "manner of administration" rather than certain laws, regulations, decisions, and rulings themselves.[279] According to Japan, previous WTO jurisprudence has indicated that "[i]n principle, *any act or omission* attributable to a WTO Member can be a *measure* of that Member for purposes of dispute settlement proceedings".[280] Japan submits that the United States' distinction between a "measure" and a "claim" is not convincing.[281] Japan considers that the manner of administration "can be described objectively" and that the "description of how a government administers laws, regulations and [other instruments] is nothing more than a description of an act or omission attributable to a WTO Member."[282]

109. Japan maintains that the Panel failed to provide sufficient reasoning for its finding that Article 6.2 of the DSU requires the complainant to identify specific areas of customs administration in the panel request, because the United States challenged before the Panel the administration of laws and regulations that cumulatively contain "thousands of different provisions".[283] Japan submits that the Panel's reasoning in this respect was insufficient, because "the Panel did not explain why the specification of the 'areas' of customs administration, each one of which still contains numerous different provisions to be administered, was sufficient to inform the defendant and the third parties of the legal basis of complaints."[284] In Japan's view, the Panel also failed to explain why it relied on the Appellate Body's finding in *EC – Computer Equipment*, despite the differences between that case and the present case. Japan is of the opinion that the Panel ought to have provided "sufficient reasoning for its finding, since fixing the

279 Japan's third participant's submission, paras. 8-17.

280 *Ibid.*, para. 11 (referring to Appellate Body Report, *US – Corrosion-Resistant Steel Sunset Review*, para. 81). (emphasis added by Japan)

281 *Ibid.*, para. 10.

282 *Ibid.*, para. 12.

283 *Ibid.*, para. 14; Panel Report, para. 7.30.

284 Japan's third participant's submission, para. 16.

scope of the terms of reference of a panel is quite important in that it will directly affect the rights and obligations of the parties to disputes."[285]

110. Japan also considers that the Panel failed to give due consideration to the European Communities' understanding of the claim against it in making findings on the scope and nature of the United States' challenge under Article X:3(a) of the European Communities' system of customs administration.[286] Japan asserts that the Panel must give full effect to the specificity requirements in Article 6.2 of the DSU, and that it must assess whether or not the defendant was sufficiently informed of the legal basis of the claim against it.

111. Japan is "sceptical" about the Panel's finding that expired measures may properly be the subject of recommendations by a panel, since "it is practically impossible for a defendant to bring a measure into conformity with its WTO obligations when the measure is no longer in existence."[287]

112. With regard to the relevance of Article XXIV:12 of the GATT 1994 for the interpretation of Article X:3(a), Japan asserts that the Panel properly concluded that "Article XXIV:12 ... is drafted as a positive obligation rather than a defence", and that Article XXIV:12 "imposes an obligation on Members to take all reasonable measures to ensure that local authorities comply with WTO obligations."[288]

2. *Korea*

113. Korea asserts that the Panel failed to take into account "the panel request of the United States, and the comments and arguments submitted during the underlying panel proceeding"[289], which unequivocally challenged the European Communities' system of customs administration "as a whole" rather than individual instances of non-uniform customs administration. As a result, Korea argues, the Panel erroneously narrowed its terms of reference by addressing only the individual instances of alleged non-uniformity. Korea submits that "a panel must construe a panel request as a whole and ... it must consider how the different parts of a panel request relate to one another."[290]

114. With respect to the United States' claim concerning Article X:3(b) of the GATT 1994, Korea contends that the European Communities has failed to provide a mechanism for the prompt review and correction of administrative actions related to customs matters. Korea submits that the terms "the agencies" and "such agencies" without any qualification unambiguously refer to the collective government entity in charge of customs matters within a Member's territory. In addition, Korea submits that Article X:3(a) of the GATT 1994, when read as

285 *Ibid.*, para. 17.

286 *Ibid.*, para. 18.

287 Japan's third participant's submission, paras. 24 and 26 (referring to Panel Report, para. 7.36).

288 *Ibid.*, para. 28 (quoting Panel Report, para. 7.144).

289 Korea's third participant's submission, para. 5.

290 *Ibid.*, para. 12. Korea makes reference to Appellate Body Report, *US – FSC (Article 21.5 – EC II)*, paras. 66-68, and Appellate Body Report, *US – Carbon Steel*, para. 127, in support of its argument.

context to Article X:3(b) of the GATT 1994, indicates that the obligation contained in Article X:3(b) relates to all, rather than only to some, of the agencies.[291]

115. Finally, Korea supports the United States' request that the Appellate Body complete the Panel's analysis and find that the European Communities' system of customs administration as a whole is inconsistent with the European Communities' obligation under Article X:3(a) of the GATT 1994.[292] Korea also supports the United States' request that the Appellate Body complete the analysis with regard to Article X:3(b) of the GATT 1994 and find that the European Communities fails to provide review tribunals or procedures whose decisions govern the practice of "all the agencies entrusted with administrative enforcement" within the territory of the European Communities.[293]

III. ISSUES RAISED IN THIS APPEAL

116. The following issues are raised in this appeal:

(a) with respect to the Panel's terms of reference:

(i) whether the Panel erred in finding that the "measure at issue" for the purposes of a claim under Article X:3(a) of the GATT 1994 must necessarily be "the manner of administration that is allegedly non-uniform, partial and/or unreasonable"[294];

(ii) whether the Panel erred in finding that the specific measure at issue in this dispute is "the manner of administration ... of the Community Customs Code, the Implementing Regulation, the Common Customs Tariff, the TARIC and related measures"[295], and, furthermore, that it was confined to "the areas of customs administration specifically identified in the United States' request for establishment of a panel"[296];

(iii) whether the Panel erred in finding that, due to the wording and content of the panel request, it was precluded from considering "as such" challenges of the design and structure of the European Communities' system of customs administration as a whole or overall[297]; and

(iv) whether the Panel erred in its interpretation of the temporal scope of its terms of reference in respect of "steps and acts

---

[291] Korea's third participant's submission, para. 18.

[292] Korea's third participant's submission, para. 14.

[293] *Ibid.*, para. 20.

[294] Panel Report, para. 7.20.

[295] *Ibid.*, para. 7.33. These laws and regulations are defined *supra*, para. 2 and footnote 2 thereto.

[296] *Ibid.*, para. 7.64.

[297] *Ibid.*, paras. 7.50, 7.63, and 7.64.

of administration that pre-date or post-date the establishment of a panel"[298];

(b) with respect to Article X:3(a) of the GATT 1994:

(i) whether the Panel erred in finding that the term "administer" in Article X:3(a) of the GATT 1994 "relates to the application of laws and regulations, including administrative processes and their results, but not to laws and regulations as such"[299], and whether, consequently, the Panel erred in finding that different penalty provisions and audit procedures found among the member States of the European Communities are not inconsistent with Article X:3(a) of the GATT 1994[300];

(ii) whether the Panel has made an interpretation to the effect that Article X:3(a) of the GATT 1994 requires uniformity of "administrative processes"; whether the Panel erred in finding, in paragraph 7.119 of the Panel Report, that the term "administer" relates to administrative processes; and whether the Panel erred in finding that the administrative process leading to the tariff classification of blackout drapery lining amounts to non-uniform administration within the meaning of Article X:3(a) of the GATT 1994, and that the European Communities has violated Article X:3(a) of the GATT 1994 with respect to the tariff classification of blackout drapery lining[301];

(iii) whether the Panel erred in finding that the European Communities has violated Article X:3(a) of the GATT 1994 with respect to the tariff classification of liquid crystal display flat monitors with a digital video interface[302];

(iv) whether the Panel erred in finding that the European Communities' administration of the "successive sales provision"[303] amounts to a violation of Article X:3(a) of the GATT 1994 because some member States of the European Communities impose a "form of prior approval" requirement while others do not[304]; and

(v) in the event that the Appellate Body concludes that the Panel erred in its identification of the specific measures at issue in this dispute, and in the event that the Appellate Body concludes that the United States was not precluded

298 Panel Report, paras. 7.36-7.37.

299 *Ibid.*, para. 7.119.

300 *Ibid.*, paras. 7.434 and 7.444.

301 *Ibid.*, para. 7.276.

302 *Ibid.*, para. 7.305.

303 Article 147(1) of the Implementing Regulation.

304 Panel Report, para. 7.385.

from challenging the European Communities' system of customs administration as a whole or overall, whether the Appellate Body is in a position to complete the analysis regarding this claim;

(c) with respect to Article X:3(b) of the GATT 1994:

whether the Panel erred in finding that "Article X:3(b) [of the GATT 1994] does not necessarily mean that the decisions of the judicial, arbitral or administrative tribunals or procedures for the review and correction of administrative action relating to customs matters must govern the practice of *all* the agencies entrusted with administrative enforcement *throughout the territory* of a particular [WTO] Member"[305]; and

(d) with respect to Article XXIV:12 of the GATT 1994:

in the event that the conditions posited by the European Communities' appeal are fulfilled, whether the Panel erred in its interpretation of Article XXIV:12 of the GATT 1994.[306]

117. We proceed to analyze these issues in the order set out above.

IV. THE PANEL'S TERMS OF REFERENCE

118. With respect to the Panel's terms of reference, the United States' appeal can be divided into three issues.

119. The first issue raised is whether the Panel erred in finding that, "when a violation of Article X:3(a) of the GATT 1994 is being claimed, the relevant request for establishment of a panel must identify the manner of administration that is allegedly non-uniform, partial and/or unreasonable."[307] (*infra*, Section IV.A) The second issue is whether the Panel erred in finding that the specific measure at issue in this dispute is "the manner of administration ... of the Community Customs Code, the Implementing Regulation, the Common Customs Tariff, the TARIC and related measures" and, furthermore, that it was confined to the six areas of customs administration specifically identified in the third paragraph of the request for the establishment of a panel by the United States (the "panel request").[308] (*infra*, Section IV.B) While these two issues relate to the identification of the specific *measure* at issue, the third issue raised by the United States relates to the Panel's construction of the nature and scope of the *claim* set out in the panel request. With respect to this third issue, the United States contends that the Panel erred in finding that, due to the wording and content of the panel request, the United States was precluded from challenging the European Communities' system of customs administration "as a whole" or "as such". (*infra*, Section IV.C)

---

305 *Ibid.*, paras. 7.539, 7.556, and 8.1(e). (original emphasis)

306 *Ibid.*, para. 7.145.

307 Panel Report, para. 7.20.

308 *Ibid.*, para. 7.33.

120. In its other appeal, the European Communities contends that the Panel erred in its interpretation of the temporal scope and limitations of its terms of reference in respect of "steps and acts of administration that pre-date or post-date the establishment of a panel".[309] (*infra*, Section IV.D)

121. We now examine these four issues in detail.

A. Interpretation of the Term "Measures at Issue" under Article 6.2 of the DSU

122. The first issue is whether the Panel erred in finding that the "measure at issue" for purposes of a claim under Article X:3(a) of the GATT 1994 must be the "manner of administration" that is allegedly non-uniform, partial, and/or unreasonable.[310]

123. The Panel was of the view that the term "measures at issue" in Article 6.2 of the DSU should be interpreted in the light of the specific WTO obligation that is allegedly being violated by that measure in a particular dispute. The Panel considered that this approach is necessary because the "measure at issue" identified in the panel request will be the subject of a recommendation, pursuant to Article 19.1 of the DSU, if that measure is found to be in violation of a WTO obligation.[311]

124. Based on this general proposition, the Panel turned to the interpretation of the nature of a "measure at issue" with respect to the obligation contained in Article X:3(a) of the GATT 1994. The Panel considered that the essence of the obligation under this Article is to "administer [the legal instruments of the kind described in Article X:1] in a uniform, impartial and reasonable manner".[312] For the Panel, "this essential aspect of the obligation contained in Article X:3(a) of the GATT 1994 [implies that] when a violation of Article X:3(a) of the GATT 1994 is being claimed, the ... request for establishment of a panel must identify the manner of administration that is allegedly non-uniform, partial and/or unreasonable."[313] The Panel further reasoned that, if a WTO Member were found to be in violation of Article X:3(a), this would mean that the manner in which the legal instruments are being administered by that Member is not uniform, impartial, or reasonable. In order to comply with a recommendation made under Article 19.1 of the DSU to bring the measure at issue into conformity with Article X:3(a) of the GATT 1994, "the Member would need to alter the *manner* in which the relevant laws, regulations, decisions and/or rulings are being *administered*".[314] Thus, for the Panel, the specific WTO obligation alleged to be violated and the means of compliance with a recommendation made under Article 19.1 of the DSU should govern the identification of the specific measure at issue under Article 6.2 of the DSU. The Panel therefore found that, for purposes of a claim

[309] *Ibid.*, para. 7.37.
[310] *Ibid.*, paras. 7.20 and 7.22.
[311] Panel Report, para. 7.17.
[312] *Ibid.*, para. 7.20.
[313] *Ibid.*
[314] *Ibid.*, para. 7.21. (original emphasis)

under Article X:3(a), the "measure at issue" to be identified in the panel request under Article 6.2 of the DSU must be the "manner of administration" of the legal instruments of the kind described in Article X:1 of the GATT 1994.[315]

125. On appeal, the United States challenges this interpretation of the Panel. For the United States, "manner of administration" is not a "measure"[316]; rather, it is, "[a]s the Panel uses the term, ... a *description* of how a measure operates so as to breach an Agreement provision."[317] The United States emphasizes that the Panel's reasoning blurs the distinction between "measures" and "claims".[318] The United States also finds fault with the Panel's recourse to Article 19.1 of the DSU in identifying the measure at issue. The United States point out that, "because DSU Article 19.1 requires that the breaching 'measure' be brought into conformity", it does not follow that "the measure in the case of Article X:3(a) must be the 'manner of administration' of 'laws, regulations, judicial decisions or administrative rulings,' rather than the laws, regulations, judicial decisions, or administrative rulings themselves."[319] For the United States, "[t]he mere fact that a breach of Article X:3(a) may be removed by changing a law's administration is not a basis for concluding that the law is not the measure at issue."[320] The United States also argues that the Panel's reasoning leads to illogical consequences for complaints not only under Article X:3(a) of the GATT 1994 but under other WTO provisions as well, because, under this approach, the measure at issue will not be "distinguishable" from the legal basis of the complaint, namely, the claim under Article 6.2 of the DSU.[321]

126. The European Communities agrees with the Panel that the measure at issue with respect to the United States' claim under Article X:3(a) in this dispute is the "manner of administration" of European Communities customs law.[322] The European Communities argues that, by referring to the "manner of administration", the Panel did not blur the distinction between the measure at issue and the claim under Article X:3(a). According to the European Communities, the Panel used the term "manner of administration" to distinguish "administration"—which is the measure at issue under Article X:3(a)—from the laws, regulations, judicial decisions, and administrative rulings of general application under Article X:1 of the GATT 1994, which are the subject of administration.[323] The European Communities is of the view that the Panel used the term "manner of administration" synonymously with "administration"[324], and submits that this "minor ambiguity"[325] is not enough to reverse the Panel's finding that, when a violation of Arti-

---

[315] *Ibid.*

[316] United States' appellant's submission, para. 47. See also United States' response to Question 1 posed by the Panel, Panel Report, p. A-2.

[317] United States' appellant's submission, para. 47. (original emphasis)

[318] *Ibid.*

[319] *Ibid.*, para. 48.

[320] *Ibid.*

[321] *Ibid.*, para. 49.

[322] European Communities' appellee's submission, para. 97.

[323] *Ibid.*, para. 91.

[324] *Ibid.*

[325] *Ibid.*, para. 92.

cle X:3(a) is claimed, the panel request must identify the "manner of administration". The European Communities contends that the United States is trying to confuse the laws to be administered with their administration.[326] The European Communities points out that the panel request itself refers specifically to the manner of administration[327], "clearly distinguishes the administration from the laws which are being administered"[328], and, thus, "identifies the 'administration', rather than [the] laws, as the measure at issue in the dispute".[329]

127. We are thus called upon to determine whether the Panel erred in finding that, when a violation of Article X:3(a) of the GATT 1994 is being claimed, the "measure at issue" must necessarily be the "manner of administration" of the legal instruments of the kind described in Article X:1, and that such legal instruments cannot themselves be identified as the "measures at issue".

128. We begin our analysis with the text of Article 6.2 of the DSU, which provides:

> The request for the establishment of a panel shall be made in writing. It shall indicate whether consultations were held, identify the specific measures at issue and provide a brief summary of the legal basis of the complaint sufficient to present the problem clearly. In case the applicant requests the establishment of a panel with other than standard terms of reference, the written request shall include the proposed text of special terms of reference.

129. Article 6.2 sets forth the requirements applicable to a request for the establishment of a panel. As the Appellate Body stated in *US – Carbon Steel*, there are two distinct requirements, namely:

> ... identification of *the specific measures at issue*, and the provision of a *brief summary of the legal basis of the complaint* (or the *claims*).[330] (original emphasis)

130. These two requirements relate to different aspects of the complainant's challenge to measures taken by another Member. The "specific measure" to be identified in a panel request is the object of the challenge, namely, the measure that is alleged to be causing the violation of an obligation contained in a covered agreement. In other words, the measure at issue is *what* is being challenged by the complaining Member. In contrast, the legal basis of the complaint, namely, the "claim" pertains to the specific provision of the covered agreement that contains the obligation alleged to be violated. A brief summary of the legal basis of the complaint required by Article 6.2 of the DSU aims to explain succinctly *how* or *why* the measure at issue is considered by the complaining Member to be violating the WTO obligation in question. This brief summary must be sufficient to present the problem clearly. Taken together, these different aspects of a panel

---

[326] *Ibid.*, para. 94.
[327] *Ibid.*, para. 95.
[328] European Communities' appellee's submission, para. 96.
[329] *Ibid.*
[330] Appellate Body Report, *US – Carbon Steel*, para. 125.

request serve not only to define the scope of a dispute, but also to meet the due process requirements.

131. Pursuant to Article 7.1 of the DSU, a panel's terms of reference are governed by the request for the establishment of a panel. In other words, the panel request identifies the measures and the claims that a panel will have the authority to examine and on which it will have the authority to make findings. The question of whether a measure falls within a panel's terms of reference is a threshold issue, distinct from the question of whether the measure is consistent or not with the legal provision(s) of the covered agreement(s) to which the panel request refers. Therefore, questions pertaining to the identification of the "measures at issue" and the "claims" relating to alleged violation of WTO obligations, set out in a panel request, should be analyzed separately.

132. At the heart of the Panel's reasoning stands the proposition that the term "measure at issue" in Article 6.2 of the DSU should be interpreted in the light of the specific WTO obligation that is raised in a particular claim. This reasoning appears to us to be flawed. The Panel's proposition would introduce uncertainty because the identification of the measure would vary depending on the substance of the legal provision invoked by a complainant and the interpretation that a panel might give to that provision. As we noted above, Article 6.2 of the DSU sets out "two distinct requirements" applicable to requests for the establishment of a panel: "identification of *the specific measures at issue*, and the provision of a *brief summary of the legal basis of the complaint* (or the *claims*)" sufficient to present the problem clearly.[331] These two requirements are conceptually different and they should not be confused. In finding that the term "measures at issue" in Article 6.2 should be interpreted in the light of the specific WTO obligation that is alleged to be violated, the Panel blurred the distinction between *measures* and *claims*.

133. In our view, a complainant is entitled to include in its panel request an allegation of inconsistency with a covered agreement of any measure that may be submitted to WTO dispute settlement. In *US – Corrosion-Resistant Steel Sunset Review*, the Appellate Body provided guidance on the types of measures that may be the subject of dispute settlement. Relying on, *inter alia*, Article 3.3 of the DSU, which refers to "situations in which a Member considers that any benefits accruing to it directly or indirectly under the covered agreements are being impaired by *measures taken by another Member*", the Appellate Body stated that "[i]n principle, any act or omission attributable to a WTO Member can be a measure of that Member for purposes of dispute settlement proceedings."[332] As long as the specificity requirements of Article 6.2 are met, we see no reason why a Member should be precluded from setting out in a panel request "any act or omission" attributable to another Member as the measure at issue.

134. The Panel considered that, when a violation of Article X:3(a) of the GATT 1994 is claimed, the measure at issue must necessarily be a "manner of

---

[331] *Ibid.*

[332] Appellate Body Report, *US – Corrosion-Resistant Steel Sunset Review*, para. 81. (emphasis added; footnote omitted)

administration" because, if such a violation is found, the WTO Member concerned would need to alter the manner of administration in order to comply with a recommendation made pursuant to Article 19.1 of the DSU. In our view, this reasoning of the Panel is flawed because it conflates the threshold question of whether a measure falls within a panel's terms of reference with the question of the means of implementation in the event that a violation is found. Through the recommendation under Article 19.1, the Member found to have violated a provision of a covered agreement is required to take corrective action to remove the violation. The recommendation envisaged in Article 19.1 concerns the stage of implementation and not the question of whether a measure falls within a panel's terms of reference. Moreover, the Member concerned has a degree of discretion with respect to the nature and type of action that it undertakes in order to achieve compliance. Therefore, we have difficulty in understanding how the means of compliance with a recommendation under Article 19.1 of the DSU should govern the identification of the specific measure at issue in a panel request. We agree, in this respect, with the United States that "[t]he mere fact that a breach of Article X:3(a) may be removed by changing a law's administration is not a basis for concluding that the law is not the measure at issue."[333]

135. In *US – Upland Cotton*, the Appellate Body emphasized that the nature of a recommendation a panel may make under Article 19.1 of the DSU with respect to a measure "is not ... dispositive of the preliminary question of whether a panel can address claims in respect of that measure".[334] In that case, the Appellate Body had to address the issue of whether an expired measure can be a "measure at issue" within the meaning of Article 6.2 of the DSU. The Appellate Body rejected the United States' argument that, because an expired measure is not susceptible to a recommendation under Article 19.1 of the DSU, it cannot be a "measure at issue" under Article 6.2. For the Appellate Body, the question of whether a panel can address claims in respect of an expired measure is to be distinguished from the question of whether that measure is susceptible to a recommendation under Article 19.1.[335] Although the issue addressed by the Appellate Body in *US – Upland Cotton* is not identical to that raised by the United States' appeal in this case, the Appellate Body's reasoning in *US – Upland Cotton* supports our position that Article 19.1 of the DSU does not place restrictions on the type of measure that can be identified in a panel request under Article 6.2 of the DSU.

136. Interpreting the term "measure at issue" in Article 6.2 of the DSU in the light of the substance of the specific WTO obligation that is allegedly being violated[336] would generate uncertainty and complexity in WTO dispute settlement proceedings. When drafting a request for the establishment of a panel, the complainant would have to foresee the possible restrictions that the substance of the legal provisions might impose on the type of measure that could be challenged.

---

[333] United States' appellant's submission, para. 48.
[334] Appellate Body Report, *US – Upland Cotton*, para. 272. (footnote omitted)
[335] *Ibid.*, para. 222.
[336] Panel Report, para. 7.17.

The identification of the measures at issue in the panel request might prove to be even more complex where the challenge concerns a plurality of provisions of the covered agreements. Moreover, the existence, nature, and scope of possible restrictions would depend on the panel's interpretation of the substance of those legal provisions. The respondent might also be placed in an uncertain situation in presenting its defence because it would have to guess what the panel would identify as the measure at issue on the basis of the panel's interpretation of the substance of the alleged violation. This could lead to unnecessary litigation on a panel's terms of reference, as the responding party may choose to contend at a preliminary stage that, in the light of the substance of the legal provision on which a specific claim is based, the measure identified in the panel request does not fall within the panel's terms of reference.

137. In the light of these considerations, we *reverse* the Panel's finding, in paragraph 7.20 of the Panel Report, that the "measure at issue" for purposes of a claim under Article X:3(a) of the GATT 1994 must necessarily be "the manner of administration that is allegedly non-uniform, partial and/or unreasonable."

B. Confinement of the Measures at Issue to Areas of Customs Administration

138. We next address the issue of whether the Panel erred in finding that the specific measure at issue in this dispute was "the manner of administration ... of the Community Customs Code, the Implementing Regulation, the Common Customs Tariff, the TARIC and related measures"[337], and furthermore, that it was confined to the areas of customs administration identified in the third paragraph of the panel request.

139. In the first paragraph of the panel request, the United States stated that it "considers that the manner in which the European Communities ... administers its laws, regulations, decisions and rulings of the kind described in Article X:1 of the ... GATT 1994 ... is not uniform, impartial and reasonable, and therefore is inconsistent with Article X:3(a) of the GATT 1994."[338] Also, in the third paragraph of the panel request, the United States asserted that the lack of uniform, impartial, and reasonable administration of measures relating to customs matters is manifest in differences among member States of the European Communities in a number of areas. The United States went on to state that these areas include, but are not limited to:

- classification and valuation of goods;
- procedures for the classification and valuation of goods, including the provision of binding classification and valuation information to importers;
- procedures for the entry and release of goods, including different certificate of origin requirements, different criteria

[337] *Ibid.*, para. 7.33.

[338] Request for the Establishment of a Panel by the United States (attached as Annex III to this Report), p. 1.

among member States for the physical inspection of goods, different licensing requirements for importation of food products, and different procedures for processing express delivery shipments;

- procedures for auditing entry statements after goods are released into the stream of commerce in the European Communities;
- penalties and procedures regarding the imposition of penalties for violation of customs rules; and
- record-keeping requirements.[339]

140. The Panel was of the view that "[t]he terms of the United States' request for establishment of a panel indicate that it challenges the manner of administration of certain aspects of [European Communities] customs law."[340] According to the Panel, "[t]he request clarifies that the administration challenged by the United States is that undertaken by the 'national customs authorities of [European Communities] member States'", and that "the specific forms of administration by national customs authorities challenged by the United States under Article X:3(a) of the GATT 1994 include, *inter alia*, laws, regulations, handbooks, manuals and administrative practices."[341]

141. The Panel stated that "the requirements in Article 6.2 of the DSU, including the obligation to *specifically* identify the 'measure at issue', serve the important due process objective of notifying the parties and third parties to a dispute of the nature of the complainant's case".[342] The Panel noted that the United States had challenged measures that "cumulatively contain, literally, thousands of different provisions [that] relate to a vast array of different customs areas, and may entail administration in a multitude of diverse ways."[343] In the light of this, the Panel considered that, "in the context of this dispute, the specificity requirement in Article 6.2 of the DSU additionally requires the identification of the customs areas in the context of which the obligation contained in Article X:3(a) of the GATT 1994 is alleged by the United States to be violated", because "without such additional specificity regarding the customs areas at issue, the European Communities would not have been accorded its due process right to be informed of the nature of the United States' claim under Article X:3(a) of the GATT 1994."[344]

142. Also, the Panel drew an analogy with the Appellate Body Report in *EC – Computer Equipment*, where the Appellate Body noted that, even though "Article 6.2 does *not* explicitly require that the products to which the 'specific measures' at issue apply be identified ... with respect to certain WTO obligations, in order to identify 'the specific measures at issue', it may ... be necessary to iden-

339 Request for the Establishment of a Panel by the United States, p. 2.
340 Panel Report, para. 7.25.
341 *Ibid.*
342 *Ibid.*, para. 7.27. (original emphasis)
343 Panel Report, para. 7.30.
344 *Ibid.*

tify the products subject to the measures in dispute".[345] According to the Panel, because, in the context of the present case, the "measure at issue" is the manner of administration of instruments relating to customs matters, the "identification of the areas of customs administration at issue is necessary to *specifically* identify the 'measures at issue' in the same way as suggested by the Appellate Body in *EC – Computer Equipment*" with respect to the products subject to the measure at issue in that case.[346]

143. The Panel noted:

> [T]he list of the areas of customs administration contained in the United States' request for establishment of a panel is preceded by the following text: "Lack of uniform, impartial and reasonable administration of the above-identified measures is manifest in differences among member States in a number of areas, *including, but not limited to, the following* ...".[347] (emphasis added by the Panel)

However, the Panel was of the view that the phrase "including, but not limited to" on its own does not have the legal effect of incorporating into the Panel's terms of reference all areas of customs administration in the European Communities' system of customs administration, in addition to those specifically identified in the panel request. For the Panel, interpreting that phrase as having the legal effect of including areas not specifically identified in the panel request "would undermine an important due process objective of the requirements of Article 6.2 of the DSU—namely, to provide sufficient notice and information to the responding party and third parties to a dispute of the nature of the complainant's case."[348]

144. On this basis, the Panel concluded:

> [T]he United States' request for establishment of a panel indicates that the "specific measure at issue" in this dispute for the purposes of Article 6.2 of the DSU is the manner of administration by the national customs authorities of the member States of the Community Customs Code, the Implementing Regulation, the Common Customs Tariff, the TARIC and related measures in the areas of customs administration specifically identified in the United States' request for establishment of a panel – namely, the classification and valuation of goods, procedures for the classification and valuation of goods, procedures for the entry and release of goods, procedures for auditing entry statements after goods are released into free circulation, penalties and procedures regarding the imposition of penalties for violation of customs rules and record-keeping requirements.[349]

345 Appellate Body Report, *EC – Computer Equipment*, para. 67. (original emphasis)
346 Panel Report, para. 7.31. (original emphasis)
347 *Ibid.*, para. 7.49.
348 Panel Report, para. 7.49
349 *Ibid.*, para. 7.33.

145. On appeal, the United States contends that the Panel erred in finding the specific measure at issue to be confined to areas of customs administration listed in the panel request, because the Panel failed to construe the panel request as a whole.[350] The United States also argues that the Panel confused arguments, on the one hand, with measures and claims, on the other hand.[351] For the United States, had the Panel construed the panel request as a whole, it could not have avoided the conclusion that, first, the specific measures at issue were the Community Customs Code, the Implementing Regulation, the Tariff Regulation, the TARIC, and, for each of these instruments, all amendments, "implementing measures, and other related measures"; and secondly, that the legal basis of the complaint was the administration of those measures in a manner inconsistent with Article X:3(a) of the GATT 1994.[352] The United States emphasizes that the list of areas provided in the third paragraph of the panel request was merely illustrative, aimed to give an indication of the argument underlying the United States' claim, and did not constitute the claim itself or the specific measure at issue.[353] According to the United States, the Panel made a selective reading of the panel request, focusing on particular text taken out of its context.[354] The Panel's characterization of the illustrative list as a specification of the measures at issue "ignored the introduction to the list, which stated that '[l]ack of uniform, impartial and reasonable administration of the above-identified measures is manifest in differences among member States in a number of areas, including, but not limited to, the following.'"[355] The United States argues that such a listing of the areas was not required; the list merely made the panel request more transparent, in that it anticipated certain arguments the United States would make in its submissions and statements to substantiate its claims.

146. The United States also argues that "the Panel gave no consideration to the fact that the request included a claim that the absence of mechanisms or institutions in the European Communities' system of customs administration as a whole results in the non-uniform administration of the measures at issue, in breach of Article X:3(a) of the GATT 1994."[356] The United States considers that the Panel erred in drawing an analogy between the *EC – Computer Equipment* dispute and the present case because, in *EC – Computer Equipment*, the scope of the measures at issue depended on the identity of the products subject to the measures; also, the claim put forward in that case was not "systemic" and did not relate to a system as a whole.[357] In these respects, *EC – Computer Equipment* is to be distinguished from this case.

147. For the European Communities, the Panel correctly concluded that the measure at issue was only the administration of European Communities customs

---

[350] These areas of customs administration are presented *supra*, para. 139.
[351] United States' appellant's submission, paras. 52 and 66.
[352] *Ibid.*, paras. 54-55.
[353] *Ibid.*, para. 57.
[354] *Ibid.*, para. 58.
[355] United States' appellant's submission, para. 59.
[356] *Ibid.*, para. 61.
[357] *Ibid.*, para. 62.

law in the areas identified in the third paragraph of the panel request. The European Communities asserts that, in this case, the measure at issue is not the set of legal instruments listed in the first paragraph of the panel request but, rather, their administration.[358] The European Communities submits that the United States attempts to engage a selective reading of the panel request by asking the Appellate Body to ignore the third paragraph of the panel request.[359] Furthermore, given the "vast body of law"[360] referred to by the United States in the first paragraph of the panel request, it would not have been possible for the European Communities to prepare adequately its defence purely on the basis of a challenge against the administration of European Communities customs law "as a whole" without an indication of the relevant provisions or sectors. In the view of the European Communities, "an identification of the specific issue or provision with respect to which a claim of non-uniform administration is made was ... necessary to protect ... [its] due process rights."[361]

148. The European Communities contends that the Panel correctly referred to the general principle set out in the Appellate Body Report in *EC – Computer Equipment* that "what is necessary for identification of the 'specific measures at issue' depends on the circumstances of the case."[362] In the circumstances of the present case, given the vast body of law to which the United States referred, the Panel was justified in requiring specification of areas of customs administration. Regarding the terms "including but not limited to" contained in the third paragraph of the panel request, the European Communities relies on the Appellate Body Report in *India – Patents (US)* in asserting that "these words cannot have the effect of including, contrary to the requirements of Article 6.2 of the DSU, the administration of the entire body of [European Communities] customs law into the Panel's terms of reference."[363] The European Communities adds that the United States' interpretation of this phrase would reduce the third paragraph of the panel request to inutility[364] and would "prejudice its due process rights by leaving the actual subject matter of the case unclear".[365]

149. We begin our analysis by recalling that, "[i]n principle, any act or omission attributable to a WTO Member can be a measure of that Member for purposes of dispute settlement proceedings."[366] Under Article 6.2 of the DSU, a complaining Member enjoys certain discretion in the identification of the specific measure at issue. Having said this, we must determine what is identified in the panel request as the specific measure at issue in this case.

---

358 European Communities' appellee's submission, para. 99.
359 *Ibid.*, para. 100.
360 *Ibid.*, para. 103.
361 *Ibid.*
362 European Communities' appellee's submission, para. 105.
363 *Ibid.*, para. 106.
364 *Ibid.*, para. 108.
365 *Ibid.*, para. 109.
366 Appellate Body Report, *US – Corrosion-Resistant Steel Sunset Review*, para. 81. (footnote omitted)

150. We note that the first paragraph of the panel request contains a list of instruments, introduced by the phrase "[t]he measures consist of:" The United States lists the following instruments:

- Council Regulation (EEC) No. 2913/92 of 12 October 1992 establishing the Community Customs Code, including all annexes thereto, as amended (the "Community Customs Code");
- Commission Regulation (EEC) No. 2454/93 of 2 July 1993 laying down provisions for the implementation of Council Regulation (EEC) No 2913/92 of 12 October 1992 establishing the Community Customs Code, including all annexes thereto, as amended (the "Implementing Regulation");
- Council Regulation (EEC) No. 2658/87 of 23 July 1987 on the tariff and statistical nomenclature and on the Common Customs Tariff, including all annexes thereto, as amended (the "Common Customs Tariff");
- the Integrated Tariff of the European Communities established by virtue of Article 2 of Council Regulation (EEC) No. 2658/87 of 23 July 1987 on the tariff and statistical nomenclature and on the Common Customs Tariff, including all annexes thereto, as amended (the "TARIC"); and
- for each of the above laws and regulations[367], all amendments, "implementing measures and other related measures".

Subsequently, in the panel request, the United States referred to the instruments listed in the first paragraph with the expressions "these measures" (in the second paragraph of the panel request) and "the above-identified measures" (in the third and fourth paragraphs).

151. We further note, as the Panel did, that the panel request refers repeatedly and consistently to the *administration* of the legal instruments listed in the first paragraph of the panel request. The panel request begins by stating that the United States "considers that the manner in which the European Communities ... *administers* its laws, regulations, decisions and rulings of the kind described in Article X:1 of the ... GATT 1994". (emphasis added) In the second sentence of the first paragraph, the United States submits that "the European Communities fails to *administer*", in a manner consistent with Article X:3(a), the legal instruments cited therein. (emphasis added) The second paragraph of the panel request, in each of its sentences, also refers to the "administration" of the legal instruments listed in the first paragraph; so does the introductory sentence of the third paragraph of the panel request. Thus, the panel request makes it clear that the United States does not challenge under Article X:3(a) the substantive content of the legal instruments listed in the first paragraph of the panel request, but their administration collectively. The United States confirmed at the oral hearing that

[367] These laws and regulations are defined *supra*, para. 2 and footnote 2 thereto.

it had challenged under Article X:3(a) these legal instruments *as administered* collectively.[368]

152. We recall that Article 6.2 of the DSU requires the identification of the "specific measures at issue" in the request for the establishment of a panel. The word "specific" in Article 6.2 establishes a specificity requirement regarding the identification of the measures that serves the due process objective of notifying the parties and the third parties of the measure(s) that constitute the object of the complaint. We therefore examine the question whether the presentation in the panel request meets the specificity requirement in Article 6.2 of the DSU. In our view, this specificity requirement is met with respect to the Community Customs Code, the Implementing Regulation, the Common Customs Tariff, and the TARIC. For each of these instruments, a specific citation is provided. Also, the panel request indicates clearly that the United States was challenging the manner in which these legal instruments are administered collectively. In our view, the first paragraph of the panel request is sufficiently specific to give notice to the parties and the third parties of the measures that constitute the object of the complaint.[369]

153. We turn next to the question whether the panel request confines the measure at issue to areas of customs administration. We read the third paragraph of the panel request as an illustrative list of areas where the United States considers European Communities customs law is not administered in a uniform way. Thus, the substance of the third paragraph of the panel request should be viewed as an anticipation of the United States' arguments. In this paragraph, the United States explains—briefly and in general terms—why it considers that the legal instruments listed in the first paragraph of the panel request are administered in a manner that is inconsistent with the uniformity requirement in Article X:3(a). Article 6.2 of the DSU requires that the *claims*—not the *arguments*—be set out in a panel request in a way that is sufficient to present the problem clearly.[370] Nothing in Article 6.2 prevents a complainant from making statements in the panel request that foreshadow its arguments in substantiating the claim. If the complainant chooses to do so, these arguments should not be interpreted to narrow the scope of the measures or the claims. Accordingly, we are of the opinion that the Panel erred when it found that the list of areas of customs administration

---

[368] See also United States' responses to Questions 1 and 4 posed by the Panel, Panel Report, pp. A-1 and A-4. In its response to Question 1, the United States stated that, "[i]n this dispute, the United States is challenging the manner in which [European Communities] customs law is *administered.*" (emphasis added) In its response to Question 4, the United States explained that it is, "indeed, challenging the absence of uniformity overall with respect to the *administration* of the [European Communities'] customs system." (emphasis added)

[369] We observe that the first paragraph of the panel request also lists among the measures at issue the "implementing measures and other related measures" for the Community Customs Code, the Implementing Regulation, the Common Customs Tariff, and the TARIC. This reference is vague and does not allow the identification of the specific instruments that the reference aims to cover. We are of the view that the phrase "implementing measures and other related measures" does not "identify the specific measures at issue", as required in Article 6.2 of the DSU.

[370] Appellate Body Report, *EC – Bananas III*, para. 143. See also Appellate Body Report, *India – Patents (US)*, para. 88; Appellate Body Report, *Korea – Dairy*, para. 139; and Appellate Body Report, *Dominican Republic – Import and Sale of Cigarettes*, para. 121.

in the third paragraph of the panel request limits the scope of the "specific measures at issue".[371]

154. In the light of these considerations, we *reverse* the Panel's finding, in paragraphs 7.33 and 8.1(a)(i) of the Panel Report, that "the specific measure at issue in this dispute ... is the manner of administration ... of the Community Customs Code, the Implementing Regulation, the Common Customs Tariff, the TARIC and related measures in the areas of customs administration specifically identified in the United States' request for establishment of a panel."[372] We *find*, instead, that the specific measures at issue identified in the panel request are the Community Customs Code, the Implementing Regulation, the Common Customs Tariff, and the TARIC, as administered collectively.

C. The United States' Claim Challenging the European Communities' System of Customs Administration "As a Whole"

155. We now turn to the question whether the Panel erred in finding that, due to the terms of the panel request, the United States was precluded from challenging the European Communities' system of customs administration *as a whole or overall.*

156. The Panel made separate findings regarding the scope and the nature of the United States' challenge under Article X:3(a) of the GATT 1994 of the European Communities' system of customs administration.[373] With respect to the scope of the United States' challenge, the Panel found that, due to the wording and content of the panel request, the United States was precluded from challenging the European Communities' system of customs administration as a whole or overall, and that its terms of reference regarding the scope of the United States' claim under Article X:3(a) were restricted to the specific areas of customs administration referred to in the panel request.[374] Although the Panel acknowledged the permissibility of challenging "a responding Member's system as a whole or overall"[375], it considered that, in this case, the reference in the panel request to a number of areas of customs administration indicated that the United States' claim under Article X:3(a) extends to some, but not all, areas of customs administration.[376] In reaching its conclusion, the Panel noted that the areas of customs administration listed in the panel request did not cover the totality of the European Communities' system of customs administration.[377]

157. With respect to the nature of the United States' challenge, the Panel concluded that, on the basis of the language and content of the panel request, the

---

371 Panel Report, para. 7.33.

372 Panel Report, para. 8.1(a)(i).

373 *Ibid.*, paras. 7.50 and 7.63.

374 *Ibid.*, para. 7.46.

375 *Ibid.*, para. 7.44.

376 *Ibid.*, para. 7.47.

377 *Ibid.*, para. 7.48. In this respect, the Panel noted that areas of customs administration, such as transit procedures, customs debt, inward processing, outward processing, exportation, and re-exportation, were absent from that list.

United States was precluded from making an "as such" challenge to the design and structure of the European Communities' system of customs administration as a whole, as well as in the areas of customs administration specifically identified in the panel request.[378] For the Panel, "there is nothing in the text of the United States' request for establishment of a panel that could be construed as clearly suggesting that the United States' challenge under Article X:3(a) of the GATT 1994 relates to the design and structure of the [European Communities'] system of customs administration."[379] The Panel further held that, in the panel request, the United States was concerned with the manner of administration by member State customs authorities, rather than with the design and structure of the customs administration system at the European Communities level "as such"[380]; in addition, such a challenge "is not obviously linked to the essence of the obligation contained in Article X:3(a) of the GATT 1994—namely, the obligation to administer in a uniform manner".[381] Finally, the Panel observed that the panel request makes no explicit reference to the terms "as such" or "*per se*".[382]

158. On appeal, the United States contends that the Panel erred by construing the panel request to exclude a claim that the European Communities' system of customs administration as a whole results in non-uniform administration of European Communities customs law, in breach of Article X:3(a) of the GATT 1994.[383] For the United States, the Panel erred in considering that, in order to challenge the European Communities' system of customs administration as a whole, the United States would have had to list separately each and every area of customs administration.[384] The United States maintains that the panel request made it clear that its claim related to the European Communities' system of customs administration as a whole, because it identified the measures that constitute the main instruments of European Communities customs legislation and addressed the manner of administration of these instruments collectively.[385] For the United States, the crux of its claim was that "the [European Communities] administers its customs law through 25 separate, independent customs authorities and does not provide any institution or mechanism to reconcile divergences automatically and as a matter of right when they occur."[386] In the United States' view, the Panel failed to consider the panel request "as a whole".[387] The United States emphasizes that the measures at issue were discussed collectively throughout the panel request, and that this is "precisely what one would expect in a panel request challenging a system of customs administration as a whole".[388]

378 Panel Report, para. 7.63.
379 *Ibid.*, para. 7.58.
380 *Ibid.*, paras. 7.59-7.60.
381 *Ibid.*, para. 7.61.
382 *Ibid.*, para. 7.62.
383 United States' appellant's submission, para. 67.
384 *Ibid.*, para. 70.
385 *Ibid.*, para. 72.
386 *Ibid.*, para. 69. See also paras. 2, 19, 21, and 102.
387 United States' appellant's submission, para. 73.
388 *Ibid.*, para. 74.

159. According to the United States, it clearly articulated a challenge of the European Communities' system of customs administration as a whole, as evident from the very first sentence of the panel request.[389] It would be "illogical to assume that [the] use of the word 'manner' in a claim involving Article X:3(a) of the GATT 1994 necessarily suggests that the claim does not relate to a Member's system of customs administration as a whole."[390] Furthermore, the United States is of the view that, because "the defining characteristic of the design and structure" of the European Communities' system of customs administration is the absence of procedures and institutions at the European Communities level, a challenge to the design and structure of this system necessarily must address administration undertaken by member State customs authorities.[391]

160. The United States also points out that the absence of an explicit reference to the terms "as such" or "*per se*" in the panel request does not preclude a claim with respect to the European Communities' system of customs administration as a whole: what is important, is that the responding party be aware of the claim against it so that its ability to defend itself is not prejudiced.[392] The United States maintains that the European Communities was aware that the United States had made a claim with respect to the European Communities' system of customs administration, as can be seen from the statements of the European Communities at meetings of the DSB[393] and the European Communities' submissions and statements during the Panel proceedings.[394]

161. According to the European Communities, the Appellate Body should uphold the Panel's finding that the United States' claims regarding the European Communities' system of customs administration "as a whole" and "as such" are outside its terms of reference. The European Communities considers the "as a whole" claim to be outside the Panel's terms of reference, because the measure at issue set out in the panel request is "only the [European Communities'] manner of administration in the areas of customs law specifically identified in [the] Panel Request".[395] The European Communities also maintains that "[i]t is incorrect to suggest that the [European Communities'] system of customs administration could be assessed 'as a whole', independently of the specific needs and requirements of the sector or area in question, and the tools and mechanisms existing in such area."[396]

162. The European Communities argues that the panel request did not indicate that the United States intended to challenge the European Communities' system of customs administration "as such". For the European Communities, the panel request identified, as the measure at issue, only the "manner of administration". In the European Communities' view, the term "manner of administration" is

---

[389] *Ibid.*, para. 82.
[390] *Ibid.*, para. 77.
[391] *Ibid.*, para. 78.
[392] *Ibid.*, para. 83.
[393] *Ibid.*, paras. 86-87.
[394] *Ibid.*, paras. 88-91.
[395] European Communities' appellee's submission, para. 113.
[396] European Communities' appellee's submission, para. 117.

"diametrically opposed to [what] one could have expected to be used in the case of a challenge against a measure 'as such'."[397] The European Communities adds that its system of customs administration is broader than the instruments listed in the first paragraph of the panel request, because it includes other instruments such as the *Treaty Establishing the European Communities* (the "EC Treaty") and more specific instruments existing in the field of customs cooperation or budgetary and financial control.[398]

163. With respect to the United States' reliance on a number of statements made by the parties during or before the Panel proceedings[399], the European Communities submits that "the compliance of a [p]anel request with Article 6.2 [of the] DSU must be assessed primarily on the face of the [p]anel request."[400] The European Communities also asserts that at no point did it recognize or acknowledge that the European Communities' system of customs administration "as such" was the measure at issue.[401]

164. The United States' appeal raises three questions that we address in turn. First, is a Member allowed to challenge within the WTO dispute settlement proceedings another Member's legal system *as a whole* or *overall*? Secondly, assuming that such a challenge could be made, did the Panel err in finding that, due to the wording and content of the panel request, the United States was "precluded from challenging the [European Communities'] system of customs administration as a whole or overall"?[402] Thirdly, did the Panel err in considering that the United States' contention on the "design and structure" of the European Communities' system of customs administration as a whole was outside its terms of reference?

1. Challenging a Legal System "As a Whole" or "Overall"

165. The United States contends that its claim relates to the European Communities' system of customs administration "as a whole or overall". As a preliminary observation, we do not think that, by challenging the European Communities' system of customs administration as a whole, the United States made an "as such" claim.[403] Indeed, before the Panel, the United States made it clear that it was "*not challenging the substance* of the measures mentioned in its request for establishment of a panel".[404] This was confirmed by the United States

[397] *Ibid.*, para. 125.

[398] *Ibid.*, para. 128.

[399] United States' appellant's submission, paras. 84-98.

[400] European Communities' appellee's submission, para. 131.

[401] *Ibid.*, para. 133.

[402] Panel Report, para. 7.46.

[403] See also our explanation *infra*, para. 174.

[404] Panel Report, para. 7.5. (emphasis added) We recall that an "as such" claim challenges an "act[] setting forth rules or norms that are intended to have general and prospective application". (Appellate Body Report, *US – Corrosion-Resistant Steel Sunset Review*, para. 82. See also Appellate Body Report, *US – Oil Country Tubular Goods Sunset Reviews*, para. 172) In other words, an "as such" claim in WTO parlance challenges the substantive content of the measure at issue regardless its application in individual instances.

in response to questioning at the oral hearing. Also at the oral hearing, the United States explained that, in this dispute, the claim made by the United States under Article X:3(a) is not readily classifiable in the categories of "as such" and "as applied" claims, that it would be inaccurate to characterize its claim as an "as such" claim, and that it did not wish to add a further category of claims.

166. We agree with the Panel that "there is nothing in the DSU nor in the other WTO agreements that would prevent a complaining Member from challenging a responding Member's system as a whole or overall."[405] We also agree with the Panel that a challenge that a system "as a whole or overall" is WTO-inconsistent must be presented in a manner that meets the two distinct requirements in Article 6.2 of the DSU.[406] A panel request must identify, with a sufficient degree of specificity, the measures that constitute or underlie the legal system challenged "as a whole or overall", and must also provide the legal basis of the complaint (or the claims) so as to present the problem clearly.[407] We already concluded in the previous section that, in the panel request, the United States has identified the measures at issue in this dispute in a manner that satisfies the specificity requirement in Article 6.2 of the DSU. We also disagreed with the Panel's view that, in the context of this dispute, the specificity requirement in Article 6.2 of the DSU "additionally requires the identification of ... customs areas".[408] We also recognize, as the Panel did, that, in this case, the legal instruments referred to by the United States in the panel request, "cumulatively, contain" a vast number of provisions that relate to a variety of customs areas and that "entail administration in ... diverse ways".[409] However, the essence of the United States' claim was not the administration or application of individual provisions of these legal instruments, but the absence of any mechanism or procedure at the European Communities level to reconcile divergences in the administration of these instruments by the member States of the European Communities.[410] Therefore, we do not think that the due process rights of the European Communities were infringed merely because the claim of the United States related to the manner of administration of the European Communities customs law as a whole or overall.

167. Under Article 6.2 of the DSU, a panel request must also provide a brief summary of the legal basis of the complaint sufficient to present the problem clearly. In other words, a panel request must summarize the claim made in a manner that will "serve the *due process* objective of notifying the parties and third parties to a dispute of the nature of the complainant's case".[411] As the Appellate Body stated in *Thailand – H-Beams*, the due process objective is "fundamental to ensuring a fair and orderly conduct of dispute settlement proceed-

---

405 Panel Report, para. 7.44.

406 *Ibid.*

407 See Appellate Body Report, *US – Carbon Steel*, para. 125.

408 Panel Report, para. 7.30.

409 *Ibid.*

410 United States' appellant's submission, paras. 2, 19, 21, 69, and 102.

411 Appellate Body Report, *US – Carbon Steel*, para. 126. (original emphasis) See also Appellate Body Report, *Brazil – Desiccated Coconut*, at 186; and Appellate Body Report, *EC – Bananas III*, para. 142.

ings".[412] In *Korea – Dairy*, the Appellate Body emphasized that, although Article 6.2 of the DSU demands only a summary of the legal basis of the complaint (or the claim), this summary must be "sufficient to present the problem clearly", and it is not enough only to "summarily identify" the legal basis of the complaint.[413] Compliance with the requirement of summarizing the claim in the panel request in a manner that "presents the problem clearly"[414] must be demonstrated, in principle, on the face of the panel request.[415] With these general considerations in mind, we address the question of whether the panel request included a challenge to the European Communities' system of customs administration as a whole or overall under Article X:3(a) of the GATT 1994.

2. *Whether the Panel Request Included a Challenge to the European Communities' System of Customs Administration "As a Whole" or "Overall"*

168. The United States' appeal requires us to examine the wording and content of the panel request. Determining the scope of the claims that are set out in a panel request requires that the panel request be construed as a whole.[416] We will be able to conclude that the panel request included a challenge to the European Communities' system of customs administration as a whole or overall only if we are convinced that the panel request, read as a whole, states this claim in a way that is "sufficient to present the problem clearly".

169. As we concluded earlier, the specific measures at issue identified in the panel request are the Community Customs Code, the Implementing Regulation, the Common Customs Tariff, and the TARIC, *as administered* collectively.[417] It is not in dispute that these are major instruments of European Communities customs legislation. Together, they delineate the legal architecture of the European Communities' customs regime. In other words, the administration of these legal instruments covers, if not the entirety, almost the whole of the European Communities' system of customs administration.[418]

170. The wording and content of the panel request shows that the United States' challenge under Article X:3(a) of the GATT 1994 concerns the manner of administration of these measures *collectively* or *as a whole*. The panel request begins by stating: "the manner in which the European Communities ... adminis-

[412] Appellate Body Report, *Thailand – H-Beams*, para. 88.
[413] Appellate Body Report, *Korea – Dairy*, para. 120.
[414] Article 6.2 of the DSU.
[415] Appellate Body Report, *US – Carbon Steel*, para. 127.
[416] See Appellate Body Report, *US – FSC (Article 21.5 – EC II)*, paras. 66-68; and Appellate Body Report, *US – Carbon Steel*, para. 127.
[417] See *supra*, para. 154.
[418] In this respect, we note the European Communities' contention that the European Communities' system of customs administration is somewhat broader than the administration of the four legal instruments to which the first paragraph of the panel request refers, and that the European Communities' system of customs administration rests as well on other measures such as "the EC Treaty itself" and "more specific instruments existing in the field of customs cooperation or budgetary and financial control". (European Communities' appellee's submission, para. 128)

ters its laws, regulations, decisions and rulings of the kind described in Article X:1 of [the GATT 1994] is not uniform." The second sentence of the first paragraph begins, "[f]or purposes of this request, the laws, regulations, decisions and ruling (collectively, 'measures')".

171. In turn, the second paragraph of the panel request states that "[a]dministration of these measures in the European Communities is carried out by the national customs authorities of [European Communities] member States" and that "[s]uch administration takes numerous different forms." In this paragraph, it is further stated that "the myriad forms of administration of these measures include, but are not limited to, laws, regulations, handbooks, manuals, and administrative practices of customs authorities of member States of the European Communities." The third paragraph of the panel request states that the "[l]ack of uniform, impartial and reasonable administration of the above-identified measures is manifest in differences among member States in a number of areas." In our view, these statements in the panel request present with sufficient clarity the complaint of the United States, namely, that the instruments identified in the first paragraph of the panel request are administered collectively, or as a whole, in breach of Article X:3(a). The fact that the panel request does not refer, explicitly or implicitly, to the manner of administration of particular provisions or instruments supports the view that the claim of the United States relates to the manner in which these instruments are administered collectively or as a whole.

172. In its appellant's submission as well as in response to questioning at the oral hearing, the United States has emphasized that the crux of its claim under Article X:3(a) is that "the existence of a system of customs administration in which 25 separate, independent authorities exercise judgment in interpreting and applying [European Communities] customs law, without any procedures or institutions to ensure against divergences or to reconcile them promptly and as a matter of right when they occur, necessarily constitutes a lack of uniform administration, in breach of Article X:3(a)."[419] Before the Panel, the United States also stressed the *absence* of such a reconciliation mechanism at the European Communities level. We observe that the panel request does not state in the same way this central element of the challenge the United States makes of the European Communities' system of customs administration. We think that the panel request could have been drafted with more precision. Had the United States explicitly stated in the panel request that the heart of the problem is the *absence* of any procedures or institutions or mechanisms to ensure against divergences or to reconcile them promptly and as a matter of right when they occur, there would have been little doubt as to whether the panel request set out a claim under Article X:3(a) against the European Communities' system of customs administration as a whole. Nevertheless, as we indicated above, by highlighting the nature and extent of the differences that exist in the administration of European Communities customs law by the member States, the panel request presents with sufficient clarity, as required by Article 6.2 of the DSU, that the claim made under Arti-

---

[419] United States' appellant's submission, para. 102. See also paras. 2, 19, 21, and 69.

cle X:3(a) concerned the European Communities' system of customs administration as a whole or overall.

3. *The Panel's Finding with respect to the "Design and Structure" of the European Communities' System of Customs Administration*

173. The Panel concluded that, on the basis of the language and content of the panel request, the United States was precluded from making an "as such" challenge with respect to the "design and structure" of the European Communities' system of customs administration.[420] This finding is challenged on appeal by the United States.

174. As we concluded earlier, the specific measures at issue are the four legal instruments identified in the first paragraph of the panel request, as administered collectively. The United States' claim is that the European Communities' system of customs administration as a whole results in non-uniform administration of European Communities customs law, in breach of Article X:3(a) of the GATT 1994. As we noted earlier, the claim of the United States in this dispute is not an "as such" claim, in the sense that it does not challenge the substantive content of the measures at issue.[421]

175. Before the Panel, and again in this appellate proceeding, the United States argues that the "design and structure" of the European Communities' system of customs administration *necessarily* result in non-uniform administration, because customs laws are administered by "25 separate, independent authorities ... without any procedures or institutions to ensure against divergences or to reconcile them promptly and as a matter of right when they occur."[422] By referring to the "design and structure" of the European Communities' system of customs administration, the United States sought to demonstrate how and why the instruments

---

[420] Panel Report, para. 7.63.

[421] On the distinction between challenging a set of measures or a legal system as a whole and an "as such" claim, see also *supra*, para. 165 and footnote 404 thereto.

[422] United States' response to Question 126 posed by the Panel concerning the European Communities' system of customs administration, Panel Report, p. B-4. We note that, in its response to Question 126, the United States stated that it understands the "design and structure" to mean the following:

- Customs law in the [European Communities] is prescribed by [European Communities] institutions: the Council and the Commission.
- [European Communities] customs law is administered by 25 different authorities, each responsible for a different part of the territory of the [European Communities].
- The [European Communities] has in place certain procedures and institutions which it contends secure uniform administration among the 25 different authorities. These include a general duty of cooperation among member States, guidelines on various matters (e.g., the conduct of customs audits), discretionary mechanisms (e.g., referral of questions to the Customs Code Committee), and the opportunity for traders to appeal customs administrative action to member State courts, with the possibility of such courts eventually referring questions of [European Communities] law to the ECJ.

The United States further noted: "[W]ithout any mechanism or other means even ostensibly present to ensure that the different authorities acted uniformly".

identified in the first paragraph of the panel request, as a whole, are administered in a manner leading to a lack of uniformity in their administration.[423] Thus, the United States' contention on the "design and structure" of the European Communities' system of customs administration was made as an argument to substantiate its "as a whole" challenge set out in the panel request. We therefore disagree with the Panel's characterization of the United States' contention on the "design and structure" of the European Communities' system of customs administration as a claim in itself. We noted earlier that the "as a whole" challenge of the United States is set out in the panel request consistently and according to the specificity requirements contained in Article 6.2 of the DSU. We therefore see no reason why the Panel was precluded from considering the United States' arguments on the "design and structure" of the European Communities' system of customs administration.

176. In the light of these considerations, we *reverse* the Panel's finding, in paragraphs 7.50, 7.64, and 8.1(a)(iii) of the Panel Report, that, due to the wording and content of the panel request, the United States was precluded from challenging the European Communities' system of customs administration as a whole or overall. We also *reverse* the Panel's finding, in paragraphs 7.63, 7.64, and 8.1(a)(iii) of the Panel Report, that the Panel was precluded from considering the United States' argument that the "design and structure" of the European Communities' system of customs administration necessarily result in a violation of Article X:3(a) of the GATT 1994.

D. *Temporal Limitations of the Panel's Terms of Reference*

177. The European Communities requests the Appellate Body to review whether the Panel erred in its interpretation of the temporal scope and limitations of its terms of reference in respect of "steps and acts of administration that predate or post-date the establishment of a panel".[424] The European Communities' other appeal focuses on the Panel's reasoning on the temporal scope of its terms of reference as set out in paragraphs 7.36 and 7.37 of the Panel Report.

178. The European Communities argues that the Panel took an excessively wide approach in interpreting the temporal limitations on its terms of reference.[425] For the European Communities, a panel may, in principle, consider only measures that are in existence at the time of its establishment[426] and, therefore, the Panel erred in considering that it had "a general competence to also consider measures which 'pre-date' or 'post-date' its establishment".[427] The European Communities also contends that the manner of administration "cannot be re-

---

[423] We note that, in response to questioning by the Panel, the United States stated that "the support for the [United States'] claim under Article X:3(a) includes evidence of *both* the design and structure of the [European Communities'] system of customs administration *and* specific instances of non-uniform administration." (United States' response to Question 173 posed by the Panel, Panel Report, p. B-29 (original emphasis))

[424] Panel Report, para. 7.37.

[425] European Communities' other appellant's submission, para. 40.

[426] *Ibid.*, para. 46.

[427] *Ibid.*, para. 47.

garded as a 'continuum' without [a] clear start or end point"[428], contrary to what the Panel suggests.[429] According to the European Communities, the Panel's approach would produce awkward results: it would imply that "violations which occurred far in the past and which no longer have any current effect could be claimed to be continuing because 'administration has no end point'."[430] Similarly, "violations which had not yet occurred at the time the Panel was established might be regarded as indicative of violations pre-dating the Panel's establishment because administration 'has no starting point'."[431]

179. The European Communities considers that, on the basis of the panel request, it was entitled to assume that the complainant's case related to measures in existence at the time of the Panel's establishment. By defining "administration" under Article X:3(a) of the GATT 1994 as "a phenomenon without any boundaries in time", the Panel violated the due process rights of the defendant protected by Article 6.2 of the DSU, because preparation of the defence for past instances of administration is "unduly difficult", and the inclusion of future instances of administration in the measure makes the subject matter of the case a "moving target".[432]

180. The European Communities also argues that the Panel's reasoning would make compliance almost impossible. If administration has no clear starting or ending point, it would be difficult for a WTO Member found to be in violation of Article X:3(a) to establish that it has altered its manner of administration so as to achieve compliance with Article X:3(a).[433] The European Communities submits that "the Panel's approach to the temporal limitations to its terms of reference is incompatible with Article[s] 7.1 and 6.2 [of the] DSU"[434] and therefore requests the Appellate Body to "reverse the Panel's findings in paragraphs 7.36 and 7.37".[435]

181. The United States is of the view that the Panel did not err in its approach to the temporal scope of its terms of reference.[436] The United States observes that the legal instruments identified in the panel request were in existence on the date when the Panel was established.[437] According to the United States, the European Communities' argument "confuses *administration* of [European Communities] customs law in existence when the Panel was established with individual *acts of administration* that occurred prior to establishment and with *evidence* that came to light during the panel proceeding that confirm the existence of non-uniform administration at the time of panel establishment."[438] For the United States, the Panel correctly explained that "it would take account of individual instances of

[428] *Ibid.*, para. 63.
[429] Panel Report, para. 7.37.
[430] European Communities' other appellant's submission, para. 65.
[431] *Ibid.*
[432] *Ibid.*, para. 66.
[433] *Ibid.*, para. 68.
[434] *Ibid.*, para. 69.
[435] *Ibid.*, para. 70.
[436] United States' appellee's submission, para. 51.
[437] *Ibid.*, para. 17.
[438] *Ibid.*, para. 15. (original emphasis)

administration pre-dating and post-dating panel establishment not to determine whether each established a WTO-inconsistency in its own right, but as a means of elucidating the manner of administration that was in existence at the time of panel establishment."[439]

182. The United States is also of the view that the European Communities misreads the distinction the Panel made between administration as an ongoing phenomenon and individual instances of administration.[440] For the United States, although the European Communities has referred to the principle that a panel may consider only measures in existence at the time of panel establishment, it made "no distinction between acts of administration themselves being considered as potential breaches of Article X:3(a) and acts of administration being considered as evidence of an ongoing course of administration that potentially is a breach of Article X:3(a)".[441] The United States underscores that nothing in the text of Article X:3(a) or its context suggests that a breach of that provision "is demonstrated only when individual acts of administration in existence on the date a panel is established diverge".[442]

183. With respect to the European Communities' argument concerning events that post-dated panel establishment, the United States maintains that, contrary to the European Communities' assertion, the Panel's references to evidence post-dating panel establishment do not show the Panel overstepped its terms of reference. According to the United States, these references "show the Panel properly [took] account of evidence relevant to understanding the manner of administration of [European Communities] customs law existing at the time of panel establishment."[443]

184. We begin our analysis by recalling the Appellate Body's statement in *EC – Chicken Cuts*:

> The term "specific measures at issue" in Article 6.2 suggests that, as a general rule, the measures included in a panel's terms of reference must be measures that are in existence at the time of the establishment of the panel.[444] (footnote omitted)

This general rule, however, is qualified by at least two exceptions. First, in *Chile – Price Band System*, the Appellate Body held that a panel has the authority to examine a legal instrument enacted after the establishment of the panel that amends a measure identified in the panel request, provided that the amendment does not change the essence of the identified measure.[445] Secondly, in *US – Upland Cotton*, the Appellate Body held that panels are allowed to examine a measure "whose legislative basis has expired, but whose effects are alleged to be impairing the benefits accruing to the requesting Member under a covered

---

[439] United States' appellee's submission, para. 18 (referring to Panel Report, paras. 7.36-7.37).
[440] *Ibid.*, para. 23.
[441] *Ibid.*, para. 27.
[442] *Ibid.*, para. 31.
[443] *Ibid.*, para. 46.
[444] Appellate Body Report, *EC – Chicken Cuts*, para. 156.
[445] Appellate Body Report, *Chile – Price Band System*, para. 139.

agreement" at the time of the establishment of the panel.[446] The summary presented by the Panel in paragraph 7.36 of the Panel Report is in line with what the Appellate Body said in *EC – Chicken Cuts*, *Chile – Price Band System*, and *US – Upland Cotton*.[447] Therefore, we see no error in the Panel's legal interpretation contained in paragraph 7.36 of the Panel Report.

185. Turning to paragraph 7.37 of the Panel Report, we note that the Panel sought to apply in the specific context of this dispute the legal interpretation it had set out in paragraph 7.36 of its Report. The Panel recalled first its view that, in this case, the specific measure at issue "comprises the *manner of administration* of the Community Customs Code, the Implementing Regulation, the Common Customs Tariff, the TARIC and related measures."[448] As the Panel identified the measure at issue as the *manner of administration*, it went on to discuss the temporal scope of the *manner of administration* for purposes of defining its terms of reference. In particular, the Panel said that "the manner of administration in a particular case may not have a clear starting point or end point", and that "administration may comprise a continuum of steps and acts, some of which may pre-date or post-date the step or act of administration that is considered by a panel at the time of establishment of that panel."[449] On this basis, the Panel concluded that "the steps and acts of administration that pre-date or post-date the establishment of a panel may be relevant to determining whether or not a violation of Article X:3(a) of the GATT 1994 exists at the time of establishment."

186. We agree with the conclusion of the Panel that "the steps and acts of administration that pre-date or post-date the establishment of a panel may be relevant to determining whether or not a violation of Article X:3(a) of the GATT 1994 exists at the time of establishment."[450] We are, however, of the view that the reasoning that led the Panel to this conclusion is incorrect.

187. In our opinion, the Panel's reasoning is incorrect to the extent that the Panel assumed that the measure at issue is the *manner of administration*.[451] As we concluded earlier, the measure at issue in this dispute is not the *manner of administration* but, rather, the legal instruments identified in the first paragraph of the panel request, as administered collectively or as a whole. In the light of the principles set out by the Panel in paragraph 7.36 of the Panel Report, the Panel's review should therefore have focused on these legal instruments as they existed and were administered at the time of establishment of the Panel.

188. In order to determine whether the measures at issue have been administered at the time of the Panel's establishment in a manner that is inconsistent with Article X:3(a) of the GATT 1994, the Panel was, however, entitled to rely on *evidence* of acts of administration. Thus, it is important to distinguish between,

---

[446] Appellate Body Report, *US – Upland Cotton*, para. 263.

[447] See Appellate Body Report, *Chile – Price Band System*, para. 139; Appellate Body Report, *EC – Chicken Cuts*, para. 156; and Appellate Body Report, *US – Upland Cotton*, para. 263.

[448] (original emphasis)

[449] (footnote omitted)

[450] Panel Report, para. 7.37.

[451] As we explained above, we disagree with the Panel's interpretations of Article 6.2 of the DSU and its reading of the panel request that led the Panel to this assumption.

on the one hand, the measures at issue and, on the other hand, acts of administration that have been presented as evidence to substantiate the claim that the measures at issue are administered in a manner inconsistent with Article X:3(a) of the GATT 1994. The Panel failed to make the distinction between *measures* and pieces of *evidence*. While there are temporal limitations on the measures that may be within a panel's terms of reference, such limitations do not apply in the same way to evidence. Evidence in support of a claim challenging measures that are within a panel's terms of reference may pre-date or post-date the establishment of the panel. A panel is not precluded from assessing a piece of evidence for the mere reason that it pre-dates or post-dates its establishment.[452] In this case, the United States was not precluded from presenting evidence relating to acts of administration before and after the date of Panel establishment. A panel enjoys a certain discretion to determine the relevance and probative value of a piece of evidence that pre-dates or post-dates its establishment.

189. We therefore *uphold*, albeit for different reasons, the Panel's interpretation, in paragraph 7.37 of the Panel Report, that "the steps and acts of administration that pre-date or post-date the establishment of a panel may be relevant to determining whether or not a violation of Article X:3(a) of the GATT 1994 exists at the time of [panel] establishment."

V. CLAIMS REGARDING ARTICLE X:3(A) OF THE GATT 1994

A. Administration of European Communities Customs Law through Penalty Provisions and Audit Procedures of Member States

1. Whether the Substantive Content of a Legal Instrument May Be Challenged under Article X:3(a) of the GATT 1994

190. We now turn to the question whether the Panel erred in finding that the term "administer" in Article X:3(a) of the GATT 1994 relates to the application of laws and regulations, but not to laws and regulations themselves, and whether, consequently, the Panel erred in finding that divergent penalty provisions and audit procedures found in member States of the European Communities are not inconsistent with Article X:3(a) of the GATT 1994. We first address the Panel's interpretation of the term "administer". Subsequently, we address the question of differences in penalty provisions and audit procedures among the member States.

[452] However, we recall that, in *US – Cotton Yarn*, the Appellate Body stated (when reviewing a textile safeguards determination) that a Member cannot be expected to examine "evidence that did not exist and that, therefore, could not possibly have been taken into account when the Member made its determination. ... Consequently, a panel must not consider evidence which did not exist *at that point in time*." (Appellate Body Report, *US – Cotton Yarn*, paras. 77 and 78 (original emphasis; footnote omitted)) We also note the Appellate Body's statement in *EC – Sardines* that "[t]he interim review stage is not an appropriate time to introduce new evidence." (Appellate Body Report, *EC – Sardines*, para. 301)

191. The Panel found that the text of Article X:3(a) does not contemplate the possibility that laws and regulations can *simultaneously* qualify as laws, regulations, judicial decisions, and administrative rulings of the kind described in Article X:1 of the GATT 1994 and as acts of administration within the meaning of Article X:3(a). The Panel concluded:

> [T]he term "administer" in Article X:3(a) of the GATT 1994 relates to the application of laws and regulations, including administrative processes and their results but not to laws and regulations as such.[453]

192. The Panel arrived at this interpretation after its analysis of the ordinary meaning of the term "administer":

> [T]here would appear to be nothing in the ordinary meaning of the term "administer" that would suggest that it covers *laws and regulations as such*. On the contrary, the relevant dictionary definitions indicate that the term "administer" refers to positive action or steps taken to put into effect measures such as laws and regulations, but not the laws and regulations themselves, which merely exist without effect until they are actually applied in practice.[454] (original emphasis)

193. The Panel found that this understanding of Article X:3(a) was confirmed by the context of the provision. In the Panel's view, Article X of the GATT 1994 contains a "due process theme", which suggests that the aim of Article X:3(a) is to ensure that traders are treated fairly and consistently when seeking to import from or export to a particular WTO Member. In this respect the Panel concluded:

> [T]he term "administer" in Article X:3(a) of the GATT 1994 relates to the *application* of laws in particular cases and, particularly, to *administrative processes and their results*, since the application of the obligation of uniformity (and, for that matter, the obligation of reasonableness and impartiality) to such processes and their result pursuant to Article X:3(a) of the GATT 1994, helps to ensure that traders are treated fairly and consistently. ... It is not clear that it should be inferred from this objective that Article X:3(a) of the GATT 1994 requires laws and regulations themselves to also be uniform, reasonable and impartial.[455] (original emphasis)

194. On appeal, the United States contends that the Panel erred in its interpretation of the term "administer". According to the United States, penalty provisions and audit procedures of the member States of the European Communities are themselves acts of administration in the sense of Article X:3(a) and, therefore, divergences in these provisions and procedures from member State to

[453] Panel Report, para. 7.119.
[454] *Ibid.*, para. 7.106.
[455] Panel Report, para. 7.108.

member State, by themselves, constitute non-uniform administration of customs laws in breach of Article X:3(a).[456]

195. The European Communities submits that the Panel was correct to distinguish between the laws to be administered and the administration of those laws, and disagrees with the United States that laws themselves can constitute administration within the meaning of Article X:3(a). The European Communities maintain that it would be "incompatible with the internal logic, wording, and purpose of Article X [of the] GATT" to assume that a law or regulation of general application could be "executed" or "put into effect" by another law or regulation of general application.[457]

196. We begin our analysis by recalling the text of Article X:3(a) of the GATT 1994:

> Each Member shall administer in a uniform, impartial and reasonable manner all its laws, regulations, decisions and rulings of the kind described in paragraph 1 of this Article.

197. With respect to the scope of Article X:3(a), the Appellate Body stated in *EC – Bananas III*:

> The text of Article X:3(a) clearly indicates that the requirements of "uniformity, impartiality and reasonableness" do not apply to the laws, regulations, decisions and rulings *themselves*, but rather to the *administration* of those laws, regulations, decisions and rulings. The context of Article X:3(a) within Article X, which is entitled "Publication and Administration of Trade Regulations", and a reading of the other paragraphs of Article X, make it clear that Article X applies to the *administration* of laws, regulations, decisions and rulings. To the extent that the laws, regulations, decisions and rulings themselves are discriminatory, they can be examined for their consistency with the relevant provisions of the GATT 1994.[458] (original emphasis)

198. In *EC – Poultry*, the Appellate Body made a reference to the above statement and concluded:

> [T]o the extent that Brazil's appeal relates to the *substantive content* of the [European Communities'] rules themselves and not to their *publication* or *administration*, that appeal falls outside the scope of Article X of the GATT 1994. The WTO-consistency of such substantive content must be determined by reference to provisions of the covered agreements other than Article X of the GATT 1994.[459] (original emphasis)

199. Thus, in *EC – Bananas III* and *EC – Poultry*, the Appellate Body distinguished between, on the one hand, the laws, regulations, judicial decisions, and

---

456 United States' appellant's submission, para. 110.

457 European Communities' appellee's submission, paras. 209-210.

458 Appellate Body Report, *EC – Bananas III*, para. 200.

459 Appellate Body Report, *EC – Poultry*, para. 115.

administrative rulings of general application set out in Article X:1 of the GATT 1994 and, on the other hand, the administration of these legal instruments. The Appellate Body reasoned that, as Article X:3(a) establishes disciplines on the *administration* of the legal instruments of the kind described in Article X:1, claims concerning the *substantive content* of these Article X:1 legal instruments fall outside the scope of Article X:3(a).

200. The statements of the Appellate Body in *EC – Bananas III* and *EC – Poultry* do not exclude, however, the possibility of challenging under Article X:3(a) the substantive content of a legal instrument that regulates the administration of a legal instrument of the kind described in Article X:1. Under Article X:3(a), a distinction must be made between the legal instrument being administered and the legal instrument that regulates the application or implementation of that instrument. While the substantive content of the legal instrument being administered is not challengeable under Article X:3(a), we see no reason why a legal instrument that regulates the application or implementation of that instrument cannot be examined under Article X:3(a) if it is alleged to lead to a lack of uniform, impartial, or reasonable administration of that legal instrument.

201. This distinction has implications for the type of evidence required to support a claim of a violation of Article X:3(a). If a WTO Member challenges under Article X:3(a) the substantive content of a legal instrument that regulates the administration of a legal instrument of the kind described in Article X:1, it will have to prove that this instrument necessarily leads to a lack of uniform, impartial, or reasonable administration. It is not sufficient for the complainant merely to cite the provisions of that legal instrument. The complainant must discharge the burden of substantiating how and why those provisions necessarily lead to impermissible administration of the legal instrument of the kind described in Article X:1.

2. *Differences in Penalty Provisions and Audit Procedures*

202. We now turn to the question whether divergences in penalty provisions and audit procedures among member States necessarily lead to non-uniform administration in breach of Article X:3(a) of the GATT 1994.

203. First, with respect to penalty provisions, the Panel observed that neither the Community Customs Code nor the Implementing Regulation defines offences at the European Communities level. It further noted the statement by the Court of Justice of the European Communities (the "ECJ") in the case *José Teodoro de Andrade v. Director da Alfândega de Leixões* that, "[as] regards customs offences, the [ECJ] has pointed out that in the absence of harmonization of the Community legislation in that field, the member States are empowered to choose the penalties which seem appropriate to them."[460] The Panel then made a

---

[460] Panel Report, para. 7.443 (quoting case C-213/99, *José Teodoro de Andrade v. Director da Alfândega de Leixões*, [2000] ECR I-11083 (7 December 2000) (Exhibit US-31 submitted by the United States to the Panel), para. 20).

reference to its own interpretation of the term "administer" (summarized above) and concluded:

> For the purposes of Article X:3(a) of the GATT 1994, the substantive content of penalty laws of the member States used to enforce [European Communities] customs law cannot be viewed as acts of administration with respect to laws, regulations, decisions and rulings covered by Article X:1 of the GATT. Therefore, substantive differences in penalty laws between member States cannot be considered to be in violation of Article X:3(a) of the GATT 1994.[461]

204. Secondly, with respect to the question whether substantive differences in audit procedures among member States lead to non-uniform administration of the Community Customs Code and the Implementing Regulation in violation of Article X:3(a) of the GATT 1994, the Panel found no such violation in audit procedure requirements of Article 78(2) of the Community Customs Code[462], based on the following reasoning:

> [D]ivergences resulting from the exercise of discretion in the law being administered do not necessarily fall foul of Article X:3(a) of the GATT 1994 provided that the existence and exercise of discretion do not unduly compromise the underlying due process objective of Article X:3(a) of the GATT 1994 and do not render the trading environment insecure and unpredictable without just cause.[463]

205. The United States challenges the Panel's finding that penalty provisions and audit procedures are not themselves acts of administration and, therefore, divergences in those provisions or procedures cannot constitute a lack of uniform administration of European Communities customs law.[464] With respect to penalty provisions, the United States submits that, if divergences between individual acts of administration (for example, the imposition of different penalties for the same breaches of European Communities customs law) constitute non-uniform administration, then, *a fortiori*, divergences between the penalty provisions that govern the individual acts of administration carried out by different customs authorities must also constitute non-uniform administration.[465]

---

[461] *Ibid.*, para. 7.444.

[462] Article 78(2) of the Community Customs Code provides:

> The customs authorities may, after releasing the goods and in order to satisfy themselves as to the accuracy of the particulars contained in the declaration, inspect the commercial documents and data relating to the import or export operations in respect of the goods concerned or to subsequent commercial operations involving those goods. Such inspections may be carried out at the premises of the declarant, of any other person directly or indirectly involved in the said operations in a business capacity or of any other person in possession of the said document and data for business purposes. Those authorities may also examine the goods where it is still possible for them to be produced.

[463] Panel Report, para. 7.434.

[464] United States' appellant's submission, para. 109.

[465] *Ibid.*, para. 125.

206. With respect to audit procedures, the United States submits that the Panel erred in limiting the scope of the United States' claim to the non-uniform administration of Article 78(2) of the Community Customs Code. The United States further submits that, even if the Panel had been correct in limiting its examination to Article 78(2) of the Community Customs Code, the Panel's reasoning is based on an incorrect interpretation and application of the term "administer" contained in Article X:3(a) of the GATT 1994. The United States submits that the error in the Panel's analysis is essentially the same as the error in its analysis of penalty provisions. Therefore, the arguments presented by the United States in that context are equally valid in the context of audit procedures.[466]

207. In reply, the European Communities refers to the binding principles of European Communities law, according to which penalties must be effective, proportionate, and dissuasive[467], and submits that these principles ensure uniform application of customs laws throughout the European Communities. The European Communities also points out that the United States has not provided concrete evidence concerning the nature and level of sanctions set out in member States' laws for specific violations of customs provisions and thus has not established that, in practice, differences in penalty laws result in differences in the administration of European Communities customs law.[468]

208. With respect to the administration of audit procedures, the European Communities submits that these claims are substantially different from the claims relating to differences in penalty provisions, because audit procedures "are not set out in [m]ember States' law".[469] The European Communities asserts that uniform practice in this respect is ensured by the Community Customs Audit Guide.[470] The European Communities also notes the discretionary character of Article 78(2) of the Community Customs Code and argues that the mere exercise of discretion in one way or another does not constitute non-uniform administration.[471]

209. In our analysis, we first note the Panel's observation that the existence of differences among penalty provisions for violations of European Communities customs law is not disputed between the parties.[472] The parties confirmed this understanding at the oral hearing. We also recall the European Communities' assertion that, under European Communities customs law, sanctions for the violation of customs laws which member States provide must be effective, proportionate, and dissuasive.[473]

---

[466] United States' appellant's submission, para. 154.

[467] European Communities' appellee's submission, paras. 202 and 222.

[468] *Ibid.*, paras. 221-232.

[469] *Ibid.*, para. 234.

[470] *Ibid.*, para. 237 (referring to the Community Customs Audit Guide, a framework for post-clearance and audit-based controls (Exhibit EC-90 submitted by the European Communities to the Panel)).

[471] *Ibid.*, para. 241.

[472] Panel Report, para. 7.444.

[473] European Communities' appellee's submission, para. 202 (referring to Case C-68/88, *Commission/Greece*, [1989] ECR 2965, paras. 23-25 (Exhibit EC-38 submitted by the European Communities to the Panel); similarly, Case C-326/88, *Hansen*, [1990] ECR I-2911, para. 17 (Exhibit EC-39

210. We already found that the substantive content of legal instruments that regulate the application or implementation of laws, regulations, decisions, and administrative rulings of the kind described in Article X:1 can be challenged under Article X:3(a).[474] We therefore consider that the penalty laws of member States, as instruments of implementation of European Communities customs law, can be examined under Article X:3(a). However, the United States must substantiate how and why divergences in penalty laws among member States necessarily lead to non-uniform administration of European Communities customs law.

211. In our view, differences in penalty provisions, in and of themselves, do not necessarily lead to a violation of Article X:3(a). Whether differences would lead to non-uniform administration depends on both the nature of the penalty provisions and the nature of the customs law provisions that they seek to enforce. No evidence was adduced by the United States before the Panel on either the degree of differences in the penalty provisions of the member States or the impact of such differences in the enforcement of the provisions of European Communities customs law.

212. Furthermore, the effects of the differences in penalty provisions would need to be evaluated against the degree of uniformity in administration of European Communities customs law that is envisaged by Article X:3(a). The effects of the differences among member States' laws on uniformity in the administration of European Communities customs law has not been established. Therefore, we do not need to address the question of what degree of uniformity in the administration of laws of the kind described in Article X:1 is required by Article X:3(a).[475]

213. The United States' case rests essentially on the plea that, if divergences in the individual acts of administration can constitute non-uniform administration, then, *a fortiori*, divergences in the penalty provisions that govern the individual acts of administration carried out by different customs authorities must also constitute non-uniform administration. This argument presupposes that differences between individual acts of administration are a reflection of differences between the penalty provisions. However, in our view, this need not always be the case. The differences may stem as well from the exercise of discretion in the application of the law and the specific circumstances of the case.

214. The United States has not provided concrete examples of the application of penalty provisions in member States that demonstrate non-uniform admini-

---

submitted by the European Communities to the Panel); Case C-36/94, *Siesse*, [1995] ECR I-3573, para. 20 (Exhibit EC-40 submitted by the European Communities to the Panel); Case C-213/99, *Andrade*, [2000] ECR I-11083, paras. 19-20 (Exhibit US-31 submitted by the United States to the Panel); as well as to a Council Resolution of 29 June 1995 on the effective uniform application of Community law and on the penalties applicable for breaches of Community law in the internal market, *Official Journal of the European Communities*, C Series, No. 188, pp. 1-3 (22 July 1995) (Exhibit EC-41 submitted by the European Communities to the Panel)).

[474] *Supra*, para. 200.

[475] We note that this question is not before us, as neither the United States nor the European Communities has appealed the Panel's findings relating to the interpretation of the term "uniform" in Article X:3(a) of the GATT 1994.

stration of European Communities customs law. The United States referred only to a single sentence in the European Commission document "An Explanatory Introduction to the modernized Customs Code", which reads:

> Specific offences may be considered in one Member State as a serious criminal act possibly leading to imprisonment, whilst in another Member State the same act may only lead to a small—or even no—fine.[476]

Clearly, this single sentence is not sufficient. Thus, the United States has not established that the mere existence of differences in penalty provisions among member States, in and of themselves, has led to non-uniform administration of European Communities customs law.

215. With respect to differences in audit procedures among member States of the European Communities, we note at the outset that Article 78(2) of the Community Customs Code empowers customs authorities to conduct audits following the release of goods for free circulation, but it does not oblige them to do so.[477] We are also aware that a certain degree of uncertainty as to when and under what conditions an audit will be carried out is in the interest of sound customs administration and must be accepted by traders as part of a normal customs regime.[478]

216. As we indicated in relation to penalty laws, the mere existence of differences in the laws themselves is not sufficient to show a breach of the uniformity requirement in Article X:3(a) with respect to the administration of European Communities customs law. In order to establish its claim, the United States would have had to show that differences in audit procedures necessarily lead to non-uniform administration of European Communities customs law in particular cases. In our view, the United States did not make such a demonstration before the Panel. Different results in the application of a law or provision do not necessarily reflect non-uniform administration of the law itself, but may stem as well from the exercise of discretion in the application of the law or circumstances of the case. The United States did not submit to the Panel any concrete example of the application of audit procedures that led to non-uniform administration of European Communities customs law.

217. In the light of the above, we *reverse* the Panel's finding, in paragraph 7.119 of the Panel Report, that, without exception, Article X:3(a) of the GATT 1994 always relates to the application of laws and regulations, but not to laws and regulations as such.[479] In our view, the possibility of challenging under Article X:3(a) the substantive content of a legal instrument that regulates the administration of a legal instrument of the kind described in Article X:1 cannot be excluded. Yet, we consider that the Panel did not err when it found that differences

---

[476] United States' appellant's submission, para. 123 (quoting European Commission document Directorate-General for Taxation and Customs Union, TAXUD/447/2004 Rev 2, An Explanatory Introduction to the modernized Customs Code (24 February 2005) (Exhibit US-32 submitted by the United States to the Panel), p. 13).

[477] Panel Report, para. 7.429.

[478] *Ibid.*, para. 7.432.

[479] Panel Report, para. 7.119.

in penalty provisions and audit procedures, themselves, do not establish a breach of the uniformity requirement in Article X:3(a) of the GATT 1994. We therefore *uphold* the Panel's conclusions, in paragraphs 7.434, 7.444, 8.1(d)(i), and 8.1(d)(ii) of the Panel Report, that substantive differences in penalty laws and audit procedures among the member States of the European Communities alone do not constitute a violation of Article X:3(a) of the GATT 1994.

B. The Administrative Process and the Requirement of Uniformity in Article X:3(a) of the GATT 1994

218. We now turn to the question whether Article X:3(a) of the GATT 1994 requires uniformity of administrative processes.

219. The Panel found that the term "administer" in Article X:3(a) of the GATT 1994 relates to the application of laws and regulations, including administrative processes and their results.[480] The Panel reasoned that the ordinary meaning of this term implies that it "covers the *application* of laws, regulations, decisions and rulings in particular cases"[481] and that "the application of a law in a particular case encompasses the *administrative process* entailed in that application, because the administrative process represents the series of steps, actions or events that are taken or occur in pursuance of what is required by the law in question."[482] The Panel added that "the application of a law in a particular case encompasses the *results of administrative processes* ... because [they] are the final manifestation of the application of a law in a particular case."[483]

220. Moving to contextual interpretation, the Panel noted that "[t]he title as well as the content of the various provisions of Article X of the GATT 1994 indicate that that Article, at least in part, is aimed at ensuring that due process is accorded to traders when they import or export."[484] For the Panel, "[t]he due process theme underlying Article X of the GATT 1994" ultimately suggests that "the term 'administer' in Article X:3(a) of the GATT 1994 relates to the *application* of laws in particular cases and, particularly, to *administrative processes and their results*, since the application of the obligation of uniformity (and, for that matter, the obligations of reasonableness and impartiality) to such processes and their results pursuant to Article X:3(a) of the GATT 1994, helps to ensure that traders are treated fairly and consistently."[485]

221. In its other appeal, the European Communities considers that the Panel's reasoning is incorrect because it implies that "the obligation of uniform administration in Article X:3(a) [of the] GATT does not only apply to the outcomes of administration, but also to 'administrative processes'."[486] For the European Communities, Article X:3(a) does not require that the administrative process

---

480 *Ibid.*, para. 7.113.
481 *Ibid.*, para. 7.104. (original emphasis)
482 *Ibid.*, para. 7.105. (original emphasis; footnote omitted)
483 *Ibid.* (original emphasis)
484 Panel Report, para. 7.107.
485 *Ibid.*, para. 7.108. (original emphasis)
486 European Communities' other appellant's submission, para. 73.

"must be fully uniform in all cases and respects".[487] The European Communities also emphasizes that, "[i]n most administrations, procedures are not fully regulated or harmonised."[488] The European Communities doubts that total uniformity of administrative procedures is required in order to ensure that traders are treated fairly and consistently.[489] In the view of the European Communities, whether the requirement of uniformity in Article X:3(a) is fulfilled should be evaluated primarily on the basis of the administrative outcome.[490] The European Communities argues that "[a]part from the case that the administrative process is regulated in laws or regulations of general application themselves, the obligation of uniform administration only extends to the administrative process to the extent that the administrative process has a direct and significant impact on the outcome of the process."[491] Accordingly, the European Communities requests the Appellate Body to reverse the Panel's finding that Article X:3(a) of the GATT 1994 requires uniformity of administrative processes irrespective of their impact on the uniform administration of the laws covered by Article X:1 of the GATT 1994.[492]

222. The United States disagrees with the European Communities' view that "the obligation of uniform administration only extends to the administrative process to the extent that the administrative process has a direct and significant impact on the outcome of the process."[493] The United States points out that the European Communities failed to explain what it means by "administrative outcome" and how to distinguish administrative outcomes from administrative processes.[494] For the United States, the exclusion of administrative processes from the obligation of uniform administration has no basis in the text of Article X:3(a).[495] The United States considers that the European Communities' approach is too restrictive and would imply that significant areas of customs administration could be carried out in a non-uniform manner without breaching Article X:3(a).[496] According to the United States, whether requiring uniformity of administrative processes under Article X:3(a) would exclude *de minimis* variations in the administration of customs law is not an issue that arises in this dispute.[497] Indeed, the United States maintains that, where the Panel found divergences in administrative processes inconsistent with Article X:3(a), the divergences were material to traders' decisions to convey goods into the European Communities through one region rather than through another.[498]

223. We first address the European Communities' contention that the Panel found that Article X:3(a) of the GATT 1994 *requires* uniformity of the adminis-

---

[487] *Ibid.*, para. 76.
[488] *Ibid.*, para. 78.
[489] *Ibid.*
[490] *Ibid.*, para. 81.
[491] *Ibid.*
[492] *Ibid.*, para. 82.
[493] European Communities' other appellant's submission, para. 81.
[494] United States' appellee's submission, paras. 53-54.
[495] *Ibid.*, para. 55.
[496] *Ibid.*, para. 58.
[497] *Ibid.*, paras. 60-61.
[498] *Ibid.*, para. 61.

trative processes.[499] We do not see such a finding in the Panel Report. The Panel found that the term "administer" in Article X:3(a) *relates* to administrative processes[500], but it did not find that Article X.3(a) *requires* uniformity as regards administrative processes.

224. We turn to the question of whether the term "administer" in Article X:3(a) may include administrative processes and whether it requires uniformity of administrative processes. We agree with the Panel that the term "administer" may include administrative processes. In its broadest sense, an administrative process may be understood as a series of steps, actions, or events that are taken or occur in relation to the making of an administrative decision. Given this broad definition of administrative process, it appears to us that Article X:3(a) of the GATT 1994 does not contemplate uniformity of administrative processes. In other words, non-uniformity or differences in administrative processes do not, by themselves, constitute a violation of Article X:3(a). This Article contains an obligation to administer in a uniform manner legal instruments of the kind described in Article X:1—laws, regulations, judicial decisions, and administrative rulings of general application pertaining to the subject matters set out in that provision. We agree with the Panel that the term "administer" in Article X:3(a) refers to *putting into practical effect*, or *applying*, a legal instrument of the kind described in Article X:1.[501] Thus, under Article X:3(a), it is the *application* of a legal instrument of the kind described in Article X:1 that is required to be uniform, but not the processes leading to administrative decisions, or the tools that might be used in the exercise of administration.

225. This does not mean that the characteristics of an administrative process are irrelevant for purposes of assessing whether a legal instrument of the kind described in Article X:1 is uniformly applied or put into practical effect in particular cases. The features of an administrative process that govern the application of a legal instrument of the kind described in Article X:1 may constitute relevant evidence for establishing uniform or non-uniform administration of that legal instrument. The probative value of such evidence will, however, depend on the circumstances of each case and will necessarily vary from case to case. Thus, we may conceive of cases where a panel might attach much weight to differences that exist at the level of the administrative processes, because it considers these differences to be so significant that they have caused, or are likely to cause, the non-uniform application of the legal instrument at issue. On the other hand, a panel might conclude, after an overall assessment of the evidence, that the consistent nature of the results of the application of the legal instrument shows that the measure at issue is administered in a uniform manner, even though differences may exist at the level of the administrative process.

226. As the term "administer" in Article X:3(a) may include the administrative processes, evidence relating to the features of an administrative process can be adduced in support of a claim of a violation of Article X:3(a). However, in order

---

[499] European Communities' other appellant's submission, heading IV.B.

[500] Panel Report, para. 7.119.

[501] Panel Report, para. 7.104.

to substantiate a claim of violation based on an administrative process, it is not sufficient that the complainant merely recites the features of the administrative processes; it will also have to show how and why those features necessarily lead to a lack of uniform, impartial, or reasonable administration of a legal instrument of the kind described in Article X:1.

227. In the light of the foregoing consideration, we *uphold* the Panel's finding, in paragraph 7.119 of the Panel Report, that the term "administer" in Article X:3(a) of the GATT 1994 may include administrative processes that put into effect the legal instruments of the kind described in Article X:1 of the GATT 1994. We also find that Article X:3(a) of the GATT 1994 does not require uniformity of administrative processes.

C. *The Administrative Process Leading to the Tariff Classification of Blackout Drapery Lining*

228. We address next the question whether the Panel erred in finding that the European Communities has violated Article X:3(a) of the GATT 1994 with respect to "the administrative process leading to the tariff classification of blackout drapery lining".[502]

229. Regarding the tariff classification of blackout drapery lining, the Panel did not find that the divergent classification decisions by, on the one hand, the German customs authorities and, on the other hand, the customs authorities in the United Kingdom, Ireland, the Netherlands, and Belgium amounted to non-uniform administration in violation of Article X:3(a) of the GATT 1994.[503] However, the Panel noted that the "United States has also implicitly challenged the *administrative process* that led to divergent classification decisions regarding blackout drapery lining"[504], and went on to assess the consistency with Article X:3(a) of the administrative process followed by the German customs authorities. Relying on decisions and letters in two cases, the Bautex-Stoffe GmbH case ("Bautex") and the Ornata GmbH case [505], the Panel found that, with respect to the tariff classification of blackout drapery lining, the German customs authorities relied on an interpretative aid that is particular to Germany[506] and that is not contained in the relevant chapters of the Common Customs Tariff.[507] The Panel also noted that it "has not been provided with any evidence to indicate that any other member States are relying upon an aid akin to that used by the German customs authorities with respect to the tariff classification of blackout drapery lining."[508] For the Panel:

> ... a system of customs administration which allows or, at least, does not prevent customs authorities from unilaterally relying

---

[502] Panel Report, para. 7.276.
[503] *Ibid.*, para. 7.265.
[504] *Ibid.* (original emphasis)
[505] *Ibid.*, paras. 7.268-7.270.
[506] *Ibid.*, para. 7.268.
[507] *Ibid.*, para. 7.271.
[508] *Ibid.*

> upon interpretative aids in carrying out their functions, which are not provided for in the binding rules applicable to all customs authorities, such as in the European Communities, could lead to non-uniform administration in violation of Article X:3(a) of the GATT 1994 in certain circumstances.[509]

On this basis, the Panel concluded that "the German customs authorities' reliance upon the interpretative aid in question amounts to non-uniform administration in violation of Article X:3(a) of the GATT 1994."[510]

230. The Panel also observed:

> [A] customs administration system which does not *require* reference by customs authorities to decisions taken by other customs authorities operating within the same system and/or cooperation between customs authorities before customs decisions are taken, such as in the European Communities, could lead to non-uniform administration in violation of Article X:3(a) of the GATT 1994 in certain circumstances.[511] (original emphasis)

Relying on decisions and letters in the Bautex case, the Panel found that German customs authorities failed to consider seriously classification decisions for blackout drapery lining by other customs authorities. On this basis, the Panel concluded that "the treatment by the German customs authorities of classification decisions for blackout drapery lining issued by other customs authorities amounts to non-uniform administration in violation of Article X:3(a) of the GATT 1994."[512]

231. The European Communities challenges in its other appeal the Panel's findings on the administrative process leading to the tariff classification of blackout drapery lining by the German customs authorities. The European Communities notes first that the Panel reached these findings "even though it also found that there was no evidence of an actual divergence in the tariff classification of [blackout drapery lining]."[513] For the European Communities, the Panel erred because it overstepped its terms of reference by making findings with respect to expired measures, failed to make an objective assessment of the facts as required by Article 11 of the DSU, and misapplied the requirements in Article X:3(a) of the GATT 1994.

232. The European Communities argues that the findings of the Panel regarding blackout drapery lining are outside its terms of reference because they are based exclusively on the reasoning of the decisions and letters of the German customs authorities in two isolated cases. The European Communities point out that the letter of the Main Customs Office Hamburg to Ornata GmbH dates from July 1998, the opinion of the ZPLA Hamburg in the Bautex case dates from February 2003, and the decision of the Main Customs Office Hamburg in the same

[509] *Ibid.*, para. 7.267.
[510] Panel Report, para. 7.271.
[511] *Ibid.*, para. 7.272. (footnote omitted)
[512] *Ibid.*, para. 7.275.
[513] European Communities' other appellant's submission, para. 95.

case dates from September 2004.[514] For the European Communities, these decisions and letters are expired measures, relate to past cases, and do not produce any effects for the future.[515]

233. The European Communities contends that the description of the facts made by the Panel with respect to the reliance by the German customs authorities on an interpretative aid that is particular to Germany does not correspond to an objective assessment of the facts, as required by Article 11 of the DSU.[516] According to the European Communities, the decision of the Main Customs Office Hamburg in the Bautex case and the letter of the Bremen Main Customs Office to Ornata GmbH do not contain any explicit reference to the interpretative aid allegedly relied on by the German customs authorities, contrary to what the Panel suggested.[517] With respect to the alleged failure of the German customs authorities to take into account the decisions of other customs authorities, the European Communities also contends that the assessment of the facts by the Panel is flawed. With respect to the statements made by the Bremen Main Customs Office and the Hamburg ZPLA regarding the classification decisions of other customs authorities, the European Communities explains that these statements give no indication that these customs authorities wished to dismiss the relevance of the classification decisions of customs authorities of other member States.[518] According to the European Communities, the Panel ignored a letter from the Main Customs Office Hamburg to Ornata GmbH[519], which clearly illustrates that the German customs authorities do take into account the practice of other customs authorities concerning the classification of similar goods when they are made aware of them.[520]

234. The European Communities considers that the Panel's findings are based on an assessment of the "motivation" of the decisions and letters that were issued by the German customs authorities[521], and that such reasoning cannot properly be regarded as part of the "administrative process".[522] In any event, not every divergence in the reasoning between the decisions of customs authorities could be regarded as amounting to non-uniform administration, because a violation of that obligation caused by differences in administrative process can only be assumed to exist where a divergence has a direct impact on administrative outcomes.[523] In the European Communities' view, Article X:3(a) does not require that the reasoning of decisions by customs authorities be uniform, since this would be contrary to the very purpose of the "motivation", which is to set out the reasons for the decision in the circumstances of the particular case.[524]

---

514 *Ibid.*, para. 106.
515 European Communities' other appellant's submission, para. 107.
516 *Ibid.*, para. 111.
517 *Ibid.*, para. 112.
518 *Ibid.*, para. 141.
519 Exhibit US-50 submitted by the United States to the Panel.
520 European Communities' other appellant's submission, paras. 120-121.
521 *Ibid.*, paras. 126 and 138.
522 *Ibid.*, paras. 127 and 138.
523 *Ibid.*, paras. 128 and 138.
524 European Communities' other appellant's submission, para. 19.

235. The United States submits that the Panel did not err in its findings regarding the tariff classification of blackout drapery lining. In the United States' view, the European Communities attempts to reargue certain factual issues and, in so doing, misrepresents the relevant facts.[525] Regarding the European Communities' allegation that the Panel was wrong to state that all the decisions or letters of the German customs authorities regarding the classification of blackout drapery lining relied on the German interpretative aid, the United States points out that there was an explicit reference to that aid in the documents issued by the German customs authorities.[526] The United States requests the Appellate Body not to disturb the Panel's factual findings or reweigh the evidence that was before it.[527]

236. The United States contends that the Panel correctly found that differences in the administrative processes leading to the classification of blackout drapery lining were inconsistent with Article X:3(a). The United States observes that the Panel did not find that differences between the blackout drapery lining presented to the German customs authorities and the blackout drapery lining presented to other customs authorities justified different tariff classifications; but, rather, that there was an absence of evidence to support a finding of divergent tariff classifications in Germany, on the one hand, and in other member States, on the other hand.[528] The United States argues that a finding of insufficient evidence of divergent classification decisions is not the same as a finding that different customs authorities correctly reached different tariff classification decisions. According to the United States, the distinction the European Communities seeks to draw between the "motivation" of a decision and "administrative processes" is unfounded.[529]

237. The United States agrees with the Panel's finding that the German customs authorities failed to take into account the decisions of other customs authorities in the European Communities regarding the classification of blackout drapery lining.[530] According to the United States, the German customs authorities are not required to refer to decisions taken by other customs authorities operating within the same system of European Communities customs administration.[531] The United States considers it important that "the German customs authority by its own admission was aware of other authorities having classified 'comparable goods', yet gave scant consideration to such classification and apparently undertook no investigation of those other authorities' findings."[532]

238. At the outset of our analysis, we observe that the Panel reached what seem to be two opposite conclusions on the tariff classification of blackout drapery lining by the German customs authorities. On the one hand, the Panel found that the decisions of the German customs authorities regarding the tariff classifi-

---

[525] United States' appellee's submission, para. 73.
[526] *Ibid.*, para. 80.
[527] *Ibid.*, para. 85.
[528] *Ibid.*, para. 90.
[529] *Ibid.*, para. 94.
[530] *Ibid.*, para. 107.
[531] United States' appellee's submission, para. 100 (quoting Panel Report, para. 7.272).
[532] *Ibid.*, para. 102.

cation of blackout drapery lining did not amount to non-uniform administration in violation of Article X:3(a) of the GATT 1994. Indeed, the Panel considered that, on the basis of the evidence before it, there was an objective factual basis that justified the German customs authorities to classify the product in a manner different from that of customs authorities in other member States.[533] On the other hand, for the reasons we set out above, the Panel found that "the administrative process leading to the tariff classification of blackout drapery lining amounts to non-uniform administration within the meaning of Article X:3(a) of the GATT 1994."[534] As a result of this finding, the Panel ultimately concluded that there was "a violation of Article X:3(a) of the GATT 1994 with respect to the tariff classification of blackout drapery lining".[535]

239. As we explained in Section V.B of this Report, the term "administer" may include administrative processes, but this does not mean that Article X:3(a) of the GATT 1994 *requires* uniformity of administrative processes. In order to find that an administrative process has led to non-uniform administration of a measure under Article X:3(a), a panel cannot merely rely on identifying the features of an administrative process that it may view as non-uniform; a panel must go further and undertake an analysis to determine whether those features of the administrative process necessarily lead to non-uniform administration of a legal instrument of the kind described in Article X:1.[536]

240. In this case, the Panel highlighted and criticized the use by the German customs authorities of an interpretative aid that is particular to Germany[537], as well as the absence of any formal requirement for the customs authorities in Germany to refer to the decisions of customs authorities of other member States when classifying blackout drapery lining.[538] In this respect, we observe that the Panel viewed the resort to an interpretative aid that is particular to Germany and the absence of any requirement to refer to tariff classification decisions issued in other member States as features of the administrative process that German customs authorities follow in making tariff classification decisions regarding blackout drapery lining. Irrespective of whether this characterization is correct, we note that the Panel did not explain how and why these two features of the administrative process would necessarily lead to non-uniform classification of blackout drapery lining.

241. Indeed, as we noted earlier, the Panel found that the divergent decisions regarding the tariff classification of blackout drapery lining by, on the one hand, the German customs authorities and, on the other hand, customs authorities in other member States were justified by an "objective factual basis" and, therefore, did not amount to non-uniform administration, in violation of Article X:3(a) of the GATT 1994.[539] Given this opposite conclusion on the tariff classification

---

533 Panel Report, para. 7.265.

534 *Ibid.*, para. 7.276.

535 *Ibid.*

536 See our development on this issue in Section V.B of this Report.

537 Panel Report, paras. 7.267-7.271.

538 Panel Report, paras. 7.272-7.275.

539 *Ibid.*, para. 7.265.

decisions of the German customs authorities on blackout drapery lining, we fail to see how, on the basis of the aforesaid two features of the administrative process, the Panel could have come to the conclusion of a violation of Article X:3(a) of the GATT 1994.[540]

242. Accordingly, we *reverse* the Panel's finding, in paragraphs 7.276 and 8.1(b)(iv) of the Panel Report, that the administrative process leading to the tariff classification of blackout drapery lining amounts to non-uniform administration within the meaning of Article X:3(a) of the GATT 1994, and that the European Communities has violated Article X:3(a) of the GATT 1994 with respect to the tariff classification of blackout drapery lining.

243. The European Communities also claims that the Panel's findings regarding the administrative process leading to the tariff classification of blackout drapery lining were not based on an objective assessment of the facts as required by Article 11 of the DSU. As we concluded that the Panel erred in finding a violation of Article X:3(a) of the GATT 1994 with respect to the tariff classification of blackout drapery lining, we do not consider it necessary, for purposes of resolving this dispute, to rule on whether the Panel's findings regarding the administrative process in question were based on an objective assessment of the facts, as required by Article 11 of the DSU.

D. *Tariff Classification of Liquid Crystal Display Flat Monitors with a Digital Video Interface*

244. We now turn to the question whether the Panel erred in finding that the European Communities has violated Article X:3(a) of the GATT 1994 with respect to the tariff classification of liquid crystal display ("LCD") flat monitors with digital video interface ("DVI").

245. This issue concerns the tariff classification of LCD monitors with DVI that are shipped separately from computers. For these monitors, the question is whether they are to be classified as computer monitors or as video monitors. Video monitors fall under heading 8528 of the European Communities' Common Customs Tariff and are subject to a duty rate of 14 per cent. Computer monitors fall under heading 8471 of the Common Customs Tariff and are imported duty-free (as they are subject to the Information Technology Agreement). The classification of these monitors has acquired significance as a result of the increasing technological developments and the convergence of information technology and consumer electronics. Before the Panel, the United States challenged the divergence in the tariff classification of LCD monitors with DVI among the customs authorities of the member States of the European Communities.

246. The Panel found that "the tariff classification of LCD monitors with DVI amounts to non-uniform administration within the meaning of Article X:3(a) of the GATT 1994."[541] The Panel relied on a divergence in the tariff classification of this product between, on the one hand, the customs authorities in the Nether-

---

[540] *Ibid.*, para. 7.276.
[541] Panel Report, para. 7.305.

lands, which classified LCD monitors with DVI as video monitors under heading 8528, and, on the other hand, customs authorities in other member States, which classified this product as computer monitors under heading 8471. The Panel also noted that the European Communities did not "appear to dispute" the existence of this divergence.[542] The European Communities argued before the Panel that certain actions had been taken by the European Communities since 2004 to resolve the divergence in the tariff classification of LCD monitors with DVI among customs authorities of the member States. After analyzing the evidence placed before it[543], the Panel concluded that "the action taken by the European Communities has not had the effect of rectifying the divergence in the tariff classification of LCD monitors with DVI among customs authorities of the member States."[544]

247. The Panel further noted "the existence of a draft Regulation [2171/2005] concerning the classification of LCD monitors contained in Exhibit EC-163".[545] The Panel took the view that, "at the time the Panel issued its Interim Report to the parties, the Panel had not been provided with evidence to indicate that that draft regulation had the effect of removing [the] divergence in tariff classification of such monitors which became evident in 2004."[546]

248. In its comments on the Interim Report, the European Communities indicated to the Panel that the draft Regulation contained in Exhibit EC-163 had been adopted as Commission Regulation (EC) No. 2171/2005 ("EC Regulation 2171/2005") on 23 December 2005. It also informed the Panel that, following the adoption of that Regulation, the decree of 8 July 2005 issued by the Dutch customs authorities had been withdrawn and the German Binding Tariff Information ("BTI") dated 19 July 2005 had ceased to be valid.[547] These comments of the European Communities at the interim review stage were supported by three new exhibits.[548] The Panel declined to consider these exhibits on the ground that "the

---

[542] *Ibid.*, para. 7.294.

[543] This evidence included:

- Council Regulation (EC) No. 483/2005 of 16 March 2005 (Exhibit US-62 submitted by the United States to the Panel);
- Commission Regulation (EC) No. 634/2005 of 26 April 2005 (Exhibit EC-85 submitted by the European Communities to the Panel);
- an opinion of the Customs Code Committee taken at its 346th Meeting of 30 June–2 July 2004 (European Communities' first written submission to the Panel, para. 353); and
- Tariff Notice 13/04 issued by the customs authority of the United Kingdom (according to the Panel, apparently published following the issuance of the opinion of the Customs Code Committee); the decree of 8 July 2005 issued by the Dutch customs authority; and a BTI dated 19 July 2005 issued by the German customs authority; Letters respectively dated 2 September 2005 and 6 December 2005 from the Director-General of the European Information, Communications and Consumer Electronics Technology Industry Associations (EICTA) to a high-ranking official of the European Commission (Exhibits US-76, US-77, US-78, US-75, and US-81, respectively, submitted by the United States to the Panel).

[544] Panel Report, para. 7.304.

[545] *Ibid.*, footnote 580 to para. 7.305.

[546] *Ibid.*

[547] European Communities' comments on the Interim Panel Report, paras. 67 and 69.

[548] Exhibits EC-167, EC-168, and EC-169 submitted by the European Communities to the Panel.

terms of Article 15.2 preclude[d] [it] from taking into consideration evidence which is not reflected in the Interim Report."[549]

249. In its other appeal, the European Communities challenges the Panel's finding that "the tariff classification of LCD monitors with DVI amounts to non-uniform administration within the meaning of Article X:3(a) of the GATT 1994."[550] For the European Communities, the Panel "overstepped its terms of reference by basing its findings of violation primarily on instances of administration which post-date its establishment".[551] Specifically, the European Communities refers to the Dutch decree of 8 July 2005 and the German BTI of 19 July 2005.[552] The European Communities also argues that the Panel did not make an objective assessment of the facts, as required by Article 11 of the DSU, because "the Panel did not have any evidence before it to support a finding that at the time of its establishment, there was a lack of uniform administration with regard to the tariff classification of LCD monitors."[553] The European Communities contends that, "apart from one inconclusive press release by a law firm, the United States did not provide any evidence as to the [European Communities'] classification practice prior to the Panel's establishment."[554]

250. The European Communities considers that the Panel erred in finding a violation of Article X:3(a), even assuming that it was justified to consider "instances of administration which post-dated ... its establishment".[555] For the European Communities, uniformity under Article X:3(a) must be "established within a reasonable period of time"[556], and maintains that this has been achieved with the adoption of EC Regulation 2171/2005 on 23 December 2005, as well as with the withdrawal, in January 2006, of the Dutch decree and the German BTI.[557] In this respect, the European Communities asserts that the Panel erred in failing to take into account draft EC Regulation 2171/2005. In the European Communities' view, a regulation should not be ignored simply because it has not yet been adopted.[558] The European Communities also argues that the Panel erred in rejecting the evidence contained in exhibits provided by the European Communities at the interim review stage.[559] Rejecting this evidence was not in accordance with Article 15.2 of the DSU because the evidence related to precise aspects of the Interim Report.[560] The European Communities, therefore, requests the Appellate

---

549 Panel Report, para. 6.6.
550 Panel Report, para. 7.305.
551 European Communities' other appellant's submission, para. 150.
552 *Ibid.*, para. 166 (referring to Exhibits US-77 and US-78 submitted by the United States to the Panel).
553 *Ibid.*, para. 182.
554 *Ibid.*, para. 21.
555 *Ibid.*, para. 183.
556 *Ibid.*, para. 185.
557 *Ibid.*, para. 186.
558 *Ibid.*, para. 190.
559 The European Communities refers to Exhibits EC-167, EC-168, and EC-169 submitted to the Panel.
560 European Communities' other appellant's submission, para. 197.

Body to "reverse the Panel's decision in paragraph 6.6 of the [Panel Report] not to admit the evidence contained in Exhibits EC-167, EC-168 and EC-169."[561]

251. The United States contends that the European Communities' other appeal misrepresents key facts and ignores the distinction between administration and evidence of administration. The United States also disagrees with the European Communities' argument that the Panel erred by declining to consider new evidence introduced only at the interim review stage.[562]

252. In the United States' view, the Panel made an objective assessment of the facts when it found that, in 2004, the European Communities acknowledged that tariff classification of LCD monitors with DVI was not uniform.[563] The United States emphasizes that it had established this fact before the Panel and that various statements made by the European Communities in the course of the Panel proceedings suggested that "the [European Communities] was aware of the issue and was working to address it."[564] The United States observes that the European Communities argued before the Panel that three steps were taken by European Communities institutions in order to address the non-uniform classification of LCD monitors with DVI (namely, "the June/July 2004 Customs Code Committee 'conclusions', the EU Council duty suspension regulation and EU Commission Regulation 634/2005").[565] The Panel analyzed each of these measures and found that none of them resolved the problem of non-uniform administration.[566]

253. For the United States, the Panel did not overstep its terms of reference by referring to acts of administration that post-dated the Panel's establishment, because the Panel referred to these acts as evidence of the manner of administration at the time of Panel establishment that is alleged to be inconsistent with Article X:3(a). According to the United States, the Dutch decree of 8 July 2005 and the German BTI of 19 July 2005 are relevant evidence supporting the Panel's finding that "measures put into place since 2004 have not resolved the problem of non-uniform administration and may well have increased confusion."[567] The United States contends that the Panel was correct to attribute no weight to draft EC Regulation 2171/2005 on LCD monitors and declined to consider new evidence introduced by the European Communities at the interim review stage.[568] Regarding the Panel's decision not to consider new evidence introduced at the interim review stage, the United States underlines that the interim review stage is not an appropriate time to introduce new evidence, and disagrees with the Euro-

---

[561] European Communities' other appellant's submission, para. 201.

[562] United States' appellee's submission, para. 108.

[563] *Ibid.*, para. 109.

[564] *Ibid.*, para. 110.

[565] *Ibid.*, para. 117.

[566] *Ibid.*, para. 123 (referring to European Communities' first written submission to the Panel, paras. 351-353, 356, and 361).

[567] *Ibid.*, para. 126 (referring to Panel Report, para. 7.300).

[568] United States' appellee's submission, paras. 128, 132, and 140 (referring, *inter alia*, to Exhibits EC-167, EC-168, and EC-169 submitted by the European Communities to the Panel).

pean Communities' assertion that there should be an exception for evidence introduced to correct errors of fact.[569]

254. As we explained above, had the Panel properly identified the measures at issue, its task would have been to determine whether the measures at issue had been administered collectively in a uniform manner *at the time the Panel was established*[570], that is to say, in March 2005. In order to make this determination, the Panel could rely on *evidence* that pre-dated or post-dated the time of the Panel's establishment to the extent that it was evidence relevant for the assessment of whether the European Communities acted consistently with Article X:3(a) at the time of the Panel's establishment.[571] In our view, the Panel did not err in referring, in its analysis, to "evidence related to instances of administration which occurred after its establishment"[572], because this evidence was relevant to the task of determining whether there was a violation of Article X:3(a) at the time of the establishment of the Panel. The Dutch decree of 8 July 2005 and the German BTI of 19 July 2005 had come into existence within a short time after the establishment of the Panel. In our view, it was not unreasonable for the Panel to consider that this evidence was relevant for assessing how the measures at issue were administered at the time the Panel was established. Accordingly, we reject the European Communities' argument that the Panel "overstepped its terms of reference by basing its findings of violation primarily on instances of administration which post-date its establishment."[573]

255. Another point raised by the European Communities' other appeal is whether the Panel failed to make an objective assessment of the facts, as required by Article 11 of the DSU, because it did not have any evidence before it to support a finding that, at the time of the establishment of the Panel, there was a lack of uniform administration with regard to the tariff classification of LCD monitors with DVI. However, the Panel Report shows that the Panel did analyze various pieces of evidence and came to the conclusion that the divergence in tariff classification of LCD monitors with DVI, found to have existed in 2004, had not been subsequently rectified.[574] The Panel's analysis of the evidence also shows that some confusion did indeed exist in 2004 and 2005 among customs authorities of the member States on the tariff classification of LCD monitors with DVI, and that this confusion might also have caused divergences in tariff classification.[575]

256. Thus, it seems to us not correct to state, as the European Communities does, that "the Panel *did not have any evidence before it* to support a finding that at the time of its establishment, there was a lack of uniform administration with

---

569 *Ibid.*, paras. 134-136 (referring to Appellate Body Report, *EC – Sardines*, para. 301).

570 See Section IV.D of this Report. As we concluded in Section IV.B, the measures at issue in this dispute are the Community Customs Code, the Implementing Regulation, the Common Customs Tariff, and the TARIC, *as administered* collectively.

571 See Section IV.D of this Report.

572 European Communities' other appellant's submission, para. 166.

573 *Ibid.*, para. 150.

574 This evidence is presented *supra*, footnote 543.

575 Panel Report, paras. 7.300-7.303.

regard to the tariff classification of LCD monitors."[576] The Panel did analyze various pieces of evidence, and we see nothing in the Panel's examination, weighing, and analysis of the evidence relating to the tariff classification of LCD monitors with DVI that would amount to a violation of its duty to make "an objective assessment of the facts" within the meaning of Article 11 of the DSU.

257. Finally, we turn to the last question raised by the European Communities' other appeal, namely, whether the Panel erred in failing to take into account draft EC Regulation 2171/2005, and in declining to consider Exhibits EC-167, EC-168, and EC-169 submitted by the European Communities at the interim review stage.

258. With respect to draft EC Regulation 2171/2005, we disagree with the European Communities that the Panel did not consider this draft Regulation. Draft EC Regulation 2171/2005 was discussed by the Panel in footnote 580 to paragraph 7.305 of the Panel Report. The European Communities might have wished the Panel had attached more weight than it did to this piece of evidence. It is, however, well-established that the weighing of the evidence is, in principle, within the discretion of the panel as the trier of facts.[577] Thus, the Panel was "not required to accord to factual evidence of the parties the same meaning and weight as do the parties".[578] We also recall that "a mere divergence of views between a party and a panel on the inferences to be drawn from pieces of evidence is not a sufficient ground to conclude that the Panel failed to 'make ... an objective assessment of the facts of the case'."[579]

259. With respect to Exhibits EC-167, EC-168, and EC-169 (which relate to the adoption of EC Regulation 2171/2005 and its consequences), we are of the view that the Panel did not err in declining to consider these pieces of evidence.[580] As the Appellate Body stated in *EC – Sardines*, "[t]he interim review stage is not an appropriate time to introduce new evidence."[581] The Panel's decision to decline to consider Exhibits EC-167, EC-168, and EC-169 appears to us to be in line with the Appellate Body's statement in *EC – Sardines* that "only ... 'precise aspects' of the [interim] report ... must be verified during the interim review ... [a]nd this ... cannot properly include an assessment of new and unanswered evidence."[582] In any event, although Exhibits EC-167, EC-168, and EC-169 might have arguably supported the view that uniform administration had been achieved by the time the Panel Report was issued, we fail to see how these exhibits showed uniform administration at the time of the establishment of the Panel.

260. In the light of the above considerations, we *uphold* the Panel's finding, in paragraphs 7.305 and 8.1(b)(v) of the Panel Report, that "[t]he tariff classifica-

---

[576] European Communities' other appellant's submission, para. 182. (emphasis added)

[577] See Appellate Body Report, *EC – Bed Linen (Article 21.5 – India)*, para. 181.

[578] Appellate Body Report, *Japan – Apples*, para. 221; Appellate Body Report, *Australia – Salmon*, para. 267.

[579] Appellate Body Report, *Dominican Republic – Import and Sale of Cigarettes*, para. 84.

[580] See Panel Report, para. 6.6.

[581] Appellate Body Report, *EC – Sardines*, para. 301.

[582] *Ibid.*

tion of liquid crystal display monitors with digital video interface amounts to non-uniform administration within the meaning of Article X:3(a) of the GATT 1994."

E. *Administration of the Successive Sales Provision*

261. We now turn to the question whether the European Communities' administration of the successive sales provision (Article 147(1) of the Implementing Regulation)[583] leads to a violation of Article X:3(a) of the GATT 1994 because some member States of the European Communities impose a "form of prior approval" requirement while others do not.

262. The Panel concluded:

> The imposition by customs authorities in some member States of a form of prior approval with respect to the successive sales provision, which is inconsistent with [European Communities] customs law and which is not imposed by customs authorities in other member States means that the European Communities does not administer its customs law concerning successive sales—in particular, Article 147(1) of the Implementing Regulation—in a uniform manner in violation of Article X:3(a) of the GATT 1994.[584]

263. In reaching its conclusion, the Panel relied on the European Communities' Court of Auditors Special Report No. 23/2000 concerning valuation of imported goods for customs purposes[585] (the "Court of Auditors Report") submitted by the United States to the Panel as Exhibit US-14. The Court of Auditors Report suggests that, "in practice, some customs authorities do impose a form of prior approval even though this has no basis in [European Communities] law." At the same time, however, the European Commission, it its replies to the Court of Auditors Report, contests the Court of Auditors' assertion that, "in practice, some customs authorities do impose a form of prior approval".[586] The Panel Report reflects that the Panel took into account the Court of Auditor's statement that

---

[583] Article 147 of the Implementing Regulation sets out the conditions under which a sale other than the last sale that led to the introduction of the goods into the European Communities may be used as the basis for the valuation of the goods. It provides, in relevant part:

> For the purposes of Article 29 of the Code, the fact that the goods which are the subject of a sale are declared for free circulation shall be regarded as adequate indication that they were sold for export to the customs territory of the Community. In the case of successive sales before valuation, only the last sale, which led to the introduction of the goods into the customs territory of the Community, or a sale taking place in the customs territory of the Community before entry for free circulation of the goods shall constitute such indication.
>
> Where a price is declared which relates to a sale taking place before the last sale on the basis of which the goods were introduced into the customs territory of the Community, it must be demonstrated to the satisfaction of the customs authorities that this sale of goods took place for export to the customs territory in question.

[584] Panel Report, para. 7.385.

[585] Court of Auditors Report, *supra*, footnote 207.

[586] The Commission's replies are published together with the Court of Auditors Report pursuant to Article 248(4) second subparagraph of the EC Treaty.

only some customs authorities impose a "form of prior approval". However, it is not clear from the Panel Report that the Panel also took into account the European Commission's replies to the Court of Auditors Report, which are an integral part of Exhibit US-14. The Panel considered that, since the United States had presented a section of the Court of Auditors Report to sustain its claim, it was incumbent on the European Communities to submit evidence to rebut the Court of Auditors' assertion. The Panel stated:

> ... at the time the Panel issued its Interim Report to the parties, the European Communities had not submitted any evidence to substantiate its assertion in this regard.* [587]
>
> ---
>
> *The Panel considers that it was incumbent upon the European Communities to submit such evidence in the light of aspects of the [European Communities'] Court of Auditor's report referred to in paragraph 7.383 above, which tend to call the European Communities assertion in this regard into question.

264. On appeal, the European Communities claims that the Panel "unduly shifted the burden of proof from the United States to the European Communities" to establish whether or not there was a lack of uniformity in the application of Article 147(1) of the Implementing Regulation. In the European Communities' view, the United States had not established a *prima facie* case of violation of Article X:3(a) of the GATT 1994 with respect to the administration of the successive sales provision. The European Communities also submits that, by shifting the burden of proof, the Panel failed to make an objective assessment of the matter before it as required by Article 11 of the DSU.[588]

265. In the view of the United States, the statement in the Court of Auditors Report that, "in practice, some customs authorities do impose a form of prior approval even though this has no basis in Community law"[589], amounts to an admission of non-uniform administration by the European Communities.[590] The United States considers that it did not need to adduce additional evidence in order to establish its *prima facie* case, given that it had provided the Panel with an admission by the European Communities.[591]

266. We begin our analysis by recalling that the Appellate Body addressed the question of allocation of the burden of proof in *US – Wool Shirts and Blouses*. In that case, the Appellate Body held:

> The burden of proof rests upon the party, whether complaining or defending, who asserts the affirmative of a particular claim or defence. If that party adduces evidence sufficient to raise a presumption that what is claimed is true, the burden then shifts to the other

---

587 Panel Report, para. 7.382 and original footnote 671 thereto.

588 European Communities' other appellant's submission, para. 214.

589 Court of Auditors Report, *supra*, footnote 207, para. 64; Panel Report, para. 7.381.

590 United States' appellee's submission, para. 143.

591 *Ibid.*, para. 147.

> party, who will fail unless it adduces sufficient evidence to rebut the presumption. (footnote omitted)
>
> In the context of the GATT 1994 and the *WTO Agreement*, precisely how much and precisely what kind of evidence will be required to establish such a presumption will necessarily vary from measure to measure, provision to provision, and case to case.[592]

267. The Appellate Body defined the nature of a *prima facie* case in *EC – Hormones*. It stated:

> [A] *prima facie* case is one which, in the absence of effective refutation by the defending party, requires a panel, as a matter of law, to rule in favour of the complaining party presenting the *prima facie* case.[593] (footnote omitted)

268. Bearing this in mind, we examine whether the United States had established a *prima facie* case in assessing non-uniform administration of the successive sales provision. The United States submitted to the Panel one document to substantiate its claim, that is, Exhibit US-14.[594] Exhibit US-14 contains two opposing statements: first, the Court of Auditors Report suggests that, in practice, some customs authorities do impose a form of prior approval even though this has no basis in European Communities law; and second, the European Commission's replies to the Court of Auditors Report, in which the Commission contests the Court of Auditor's assertion by saying that "customs authorities in some member States do not 'impose' such a notification".[595] The Court of Auditors Report and the Commission's replies are contained in the same document submitted to the Panel as Exhibit US-14. Given this rebuttal, we cannot agree with the United States that Exhibit US-14 amounts to an admission by the European

---

[592] Appellate Body Report, *US – Wool Shirts and Blouses*, p. 14, DSR 1997:I, 323, at 335.

[593] Appellate Body Report, *EC – Hormones*, para. 104. See also Appellate Body Report, *US – Wool Shirts and Blouses*, p. 14, DSR 1997:I, 323, at 335.

The Appellate Body has subsequently relied on this statement in various instances. (See, for example, Appellate Body Report, *US – Zeroing (EC)*, para. 217; and Appellate Body Report, *Mexico – Anti-Dumping Measures on Rice*, para. 167 and footnote 160 thereto)

[594] The Court of Auditors Report states, in relevant part:

> The Court was unable to identify the full extent to which importers use or seek to use the successive sales provision. One reason for this is that, in order to apply the successive sales provision, unlike some other customs provisions, there is no legal requirement for an importer to obtain prior permission or authorisation. However, the Court found that, in practice, some customs authorities do impose a form of prior approval even though this has no basis in Community law. As in other aspects of customs valuation the Court found variations in the extent to which customs authorities allow the use of the provision or consult with each other. The Court has established that certain importers use the successive sales provision in one or more Member States but not in others and has drawn some significant examples of inconsistency to the attention of the Commission.
>
> ...
>
> The Commission's view is that customs authorities in some Member States do not 'impose' such a notification.

(Court of Auditors Report, *supra*, footnote 207, para. 64, and Commission's replies thereto, p. 17)

[595] European Commission's comments on paragraphs 62-64 of the Court of Auditors Report, *supra*, footnote 207, p. 16.

Communities of the fact that some member States impose a prior approval requirement in the administration of the successive sales provision.

269. Furthermore, we observe that the United States has not provided sufficient evidence for its assertion. It has not specified, for example, which member States impose "a form of prior approval"; what "forms of prior approval" the customs authorities of those member States impose; or how frequently such a requirement has been imposed. In addition, the United States has made no specific reference to instances of administration of the successive sale provision, or given examples where prior approval was imposed by, or would have been required by, a member State in practice.

270. In the light of these considerations, we disagree with the Panel that the United States has established a *prima facie* case with respect to its claim alleging lack of uniform administration of the successive sales provision. We therefore *reverse* the Panel's finding, in paragraphs 7.385 and 8.1(c)(ii) of the Panel Report, that "the European Communities does not administer its customs law concerning successive sales—in particular, Article 147(1) of the Implementing Regulation—in a uniform manner, in violation of Article X:3(a) of the GATT 1994." In the light of this finding, we do not consider it necessary, for purposes of resolving this dispute, to rule on whether the Panel's finding with respect to the administration of the successive sales provision was based on an objective assessment of the matter as required by Article 11 of the DSU.

F. Completing the Analysis with respect to the "As a Whole" Challenge of the United States under Article X:3(a) of the GATT 1994

271. We now examine whether the Appellate Body is in a position to complete the analysis and to determine whether the measures at issue (that is, the Community Customs Code, the Implementing Regulation, the Common Customs Tariff, and the TARIC), collectively or "as a whole", are administered by the European Communities in a manner inconsistent with its obligation under Article X:3(a) of the GATT 1994.

272. The Panel concluded that, "based on the language and content of the Panel's terms of reference, the Panel is precluded from considering 'as such' challenges of the design and structure of the [European Communities'] system of customs administration as a whole and also the design and structure of the [European Communities'] system in the areas of customs administration that have been specifically identified in the [panel request]."[596] For the reasons we set out in Section IV.C of this Report, we reversed this finding of the Panel. In our view, the terms of the panel request indicate that the United States properly made a claim that the Community Customs Code, the Implementing Regulation, the Common Customs Tariff, and the TARIC, collectively, are administered in a non-uniform manner, in violation of Article X:3(a) of the GATT 1994. The Panel should have examined this claim, but it did not. Consequently, we have

[596] Panel Report, para. 7.64.

now to determine whether we are in a position to complete the analysis with respect to the United States' claim under Article X:3(a) of the GATT 1994.

273. The United States is of the view that the Appellate Body should complete the analysis, and find that the European Communities' system of customs administration "as a whole" is inconsistent with Article X:3(a).[597] For the United States, in this dispute, "a reversal of the Panel's findings without a completion of the Panel's analysis would fail 'to secure a positive solution to [the] dispute.'"[598] The United States submits that the analysis can be completed on the basis of undisputed facts and the Panel's findings of fact regarding the European Communities' system of customs administration.[599] The United States recalls that "[t]he crux of the [United States'] claim ... was that the existence of a system of customs administration in which 25 separate, independent authorities exercise judgment in interpreting and applying [European Communities] customs law, without any procedures or institutions to ensure against divergences or to reconcile them promptly and as a matter of right when they occur necessarily constitutes a lack of uniform administration, in breach of Article X:3(a)."[600] The United States points to statements made by the Panel with respect to various mechanisms and institutions in the European Communities that, according to the European Communities, ensure against divergences or reconcile them when they occur.[601] The United States also refers to the Panel's "overall assessment" that the European Communities system of customs administration "as a whole" is "complicated and, at times, opaque and confusing".[602] According to the United States, by these statements, the Panel rejected the European Communities' argument that the institutions and procedures to which the European Communities referred ensure the uniform administration of European Communities customs law.[603] For the United States, in the light of the Panel's statements regarding "the institutions and mechanisms the [European Communities] held out as securing uniform administration of [European Communities] customs law, completion of the Panel's analysis should be straightforward"[604], and should lead to the conclusion that "the [European Communities'] system of customs administration as a whole is inconsistent with the [European Communities'] obligation of uniform administration under Article X:3(a) of the GATT 1994."[605]

274. The European Communities disagrees with the United States that there are enough factual findings made by the Panel, or undisputed facts on record, that would enable the Appellate Body to make the finding requested by the United States regarding the European Communities' system of customs administration "as such" and "as a whole". According to the European Communities,

[597] United States' appellant's submission, paras. 29, 99, and 204(a).
[598] *Ibid.*, para. 101.
[599] *Ibid.*, para. 102.
[600] *Ibid.* (footnote omitted)
[601] *Ibid.*, paras. 103-106 (referring to Panel Report, paras. 7.156-7.192).
[602] *Ibid.*, para. 107 (referring to Panel Report, para. 7.191).
[603] *Ibid.*, para. 108.
[604] *Ibid.*
[605] *Ibid.*

the Panel's statements to which the United States refers are isolated remarks in the Panel Report where the Panel comments on individual aspects of the European Communities' system of customs administration.[606] These comments, the European Communities argues, do not allow the Appellate Body to assess whether the European Communities' system of customs administration "as a whole" and "as such" is in conformity with Article X:3(a) of the GATT 1994, because they do not contain findings of fact with respect to the European Communities' system of customs administration, and were not intended by the Panel to constitute such findings.[607] The European Communities observes that these comments are contained in a section of the Panel Report where the Panel set out its understanding of the European Communities' system of customs administration as "context" for the evaluation of the United States' claims regarding individual instances of application.[608] The European Communities also emphasizes that, if the United States' challenge concerns the European Communities' system of customs administration as a whole, then the "system must be evaluated with all its constituent interlocking elements and mechanisms, and not individual elements in isolation."[609]

275. Furthermore, the European Communities emphasizes that, in paragraph 7.490 of the Panel Report, the Panel observed, *inter alia*, that "the United States did not demonstrate that the design and structure of the [European Communities'] system of customs administration, including components thereof, necessarily result in a violation of Article X:3(a) of the GATT 1994." Thus, according to the European Communities, the Panel found that "the [United States] has not even come close to establishing that the [European Communities'] system 'as such' and 'as a whole' entails a violation of Article X:3(a) [of the] GATT."[610]

276. Finally, the European Communities submits that the United States' claim regarding the European Communities' system of customs administration "as a whole" is a claim that has not been explored by the Panel, and on which the Panel has therefore not made any legal findings and interpretations that the Appellate Body could reverse. For the European Communities, a claim of violation of the obligation of uniform administration directed against individual instances of application is fundamentally different from a claim directed against a system of customs administration "as such" and "as a whole".[611] Adjudging the claim regarding the European Communities' system of customs administration "as such" and "as a whole" would, therefore, violate the due process rights of the participants, and of the European Communities in particular.[612]

277. In response to questioning at the oral hearing, the United States confirmed that it does not consider that Article X:3(a) requires a centralized system of customs administration at the European Communities level. Therefore, for the

---

606 European Communities' appellee's submission, para. 159.
607 *Ibid.*, para. 160.
608 *Ibid.* (referring to Panel Report, paras. 7.156-7.191).
609 *Ibid.*, para. 163. (footnote omitted)
610 *Ibid.*, para. 172. See also para. 171.
611 European Communities' appellee's submission, paras. 188-189.
612 *Ibid.*, paras. 193-195.

United States, the administration of European Communities customs law by 25 national customs authorities does not, in itself, constitute a breach of Article X:3(a). According to the United States, the structural shortcoming that undermines the European Communities' system of customs administration is, rather, the absence of "any procedures or institutions to ensure against divergences or to reconcile them promptly and as a matter of right when they occur."[613] The United States contends that the absence of any procedures, institutions, or mechanisms to ensure uniform administration necessarily results in a breach of Article X:3(a) of the GATT 1994 by the European Communities.[614]

278. It is well settled that the Appellate Body will be in a position to complete the legal analysis if it has before it sufficient factual findings of the panel or undisputed facts on the panel record.[615] In this case, the Panel did not examine the United States' claim that the measures at issue, collectively, are administered in a non-uniform manner. Therefore, we have to consider whether the factual findings or general observations made by the Panel with respect to the claims it did examine, can be utilized in the context of completing the analysis. In considering this question, we also have to take into account the nature and breadth of the United States' challenge, that is, whether the Community Customs Code, the Implementing Regulation, the Common Customs Tariff, and the TARIC, collectively, are administered in a non-uniform manner, in violation of Article X:3(a) of the GATT 1994.

279. We begin our analysis by noting that, before the Panel, the European Communities referred to certain institutions and mechanisms existing in the European Communities to secure uniformity of administration of European Communities customs law. According to the European Communities, these institutions and mechanisms play "an instrumental role in achieving uniform administration of [European Communities] customs law by the customs authorities of the member States."[616] The Panel took the view that it was not authorized to make any findings in relation to these institutions and mechanisms given that it had found that its terms of reference precluded it from considering challenges to the design and structure of the European Communities' system of customs administration, including components thereof.[617] Nevertheless, the Panel chose to discuss these institutional mechanisms in a section of the Panel Report entitled "Relevant Aspects of the EC System of Customs Administration". It did so because it was of the view that "its understanding of certain aspects of the manner in which the [European Communities'] system of customs administration functions ... is important *context* for the examination of the particular instances of

---

613 United States' appellant's submission, para. 102.

614 *Ibid.* See also paras. 2, 19, 21, and 69; United States' opening statement at the oral hearing; and United States' response to Question 126 posed by the Panel, Panel Report, pp. B-4 and B-5.

615 See Appellate Body Report, *US – Hot-Rolled Steel*, para. 235; Appellate Body Report, *Canada – Dairy (Article 21.5 – New Zealand and US)*, para. 98; and Appellate Body Report, *US – Section 211 Appropriations Act*, para. 343.

616 Panel Report, para. 7.489.

617 *Ibid.*, para. 7.490.

alleged violations of Article X:3(a) of the GATT 1994 in respect of which such aspects have been raised."[618]

280. The institutions and mechanisms of the European Communities' system of customs administration that the Panel addressed include the following: (i) the Customs Code Committee; (ii) Article 10 of the EC Treaty; (iii) the preliminary reference system (Article 234 of the EC Treaty); (iv) infringement proceedings; (v) the European Ombudsman; (vi) complaints to the European Commission; (vii) restrictions on the adoption of national measures by customs authorities of the member States; (viii) consultations and mutual assistance between member State customs authorities; and (ix) best practice guidelines, such as the European Binding Tariff Information (the "EBTI") guidelines, which refer to the EBTI database, and the Compendium of Customs Valuation texts.

281. The European Communities identified the Customs Code Committee as "an important institution that helps to ensure uniform administration of [European Communities] customs law among the customs authorities of the member States."[619] The Panel noted that "the opinions of the Customs Code Committee are not legally binding on the customs authorities of the member States."[620] After considering certain other features of the Community Customs Code, the Panel concluded that "it would appear that the Customs Code Committee has limited power to impose uniform administration of [European Communities] customs law on customs authorities of the member States."[621]

282. With respect to the "duty of cooperation" contained in Article 10 of the EC Treaty, the Panel observed that "the extent to which Article 10 of the EC Treaty contributes to the uniform administration of [European Communities] customs law is unclear."[622] The European Communities also cited Article 234 of the EC Treaty, according to which national courts of the member States may refer any question regarding the interpretation of European Communities law to the ECJ (the preliminary reference system). The European Communities submitted that "it is through preliminary rulings issued by the ECJ, which are binding on all courts of the member States, that divergences ... can be avoided and the effective application of European Communities law be assured."[623] The Panel noted, however, that "a trader is not authorized under [European Communities] law to proceed directly to the ECJ for a preliminary ruling"[624], and that "the use of the preliminary reference system to secure uniform administration ... in the area of customs administration during the period of 1995–2005 appears low."[625]

283. With respect to the infringement proceedings that may be instituted before the ECJ against member States for failure to fulfil an obligation under European Communities law, and the role played by the European Ombudsman, the

[618] *Ibid.*, para. 7.155. (emphasis added)
[619] *Ibid.*, para. 7.157. (footnote omitted)
[620] *Ibid.*, para. 7.160.
[621] *Ibid.* (footnote omitted)
[622] Panel Report, para. 7.164.
[623] *Ibid.*, para. 7.166.
[624] *Ibid.*, para. 7.167.
[625] *Ibid.*, para. 7.168.

Panel noted that the use of both mechanisms appeared to be "low"[626], and opined that "the extent to which the European Ombudsman is effective in ensuring uniform administration ... is unclear."[627] The Panel made observations that were largely descriptive in nature with respect to: the possibility of bringing a complaint to the European Commission; the existence of restrictions on the adoption of national measures by customs authorities of the member States; the mechanisms of consultation and mutual assistance between member State customs authorities; and best practice guidelines. In particular, the Panel noted that the customs authorities of the member States are not obliged to consult with one another before making customs decisions[628], that there is no obligation on the part of customs authorities of the member States to consult the EBTI database when they classify a good[629], and that "the commentaries contained in the Compendium of Customs Valuation texts have no legal status and, therefore, do not have binding effect."[630]

284. Finally, under a section of the Panel Report entitled "General observations regarding the institutions and mechanisms involved in the administration of the EC customs laws", the Panel noted that, "in its consideration of the [European Communities'] system of customs administration as a whole, the Panel found the system complicated and, at times, opaque and confusing."[631] Later, in a section entitled, "Overall observations regarding the United States' allegations of non-uniform administration under Article X:3(a) of the GATT 1994", the Panel observed that "certain features associated with a number of those institutions and mechanisms would not necessarily enhance uniform administration of [European Communities] customs law by the customs authorities of the member States and, at worst, might even cause non-uniform administration."[632]

285. From the description of the institutions and mechanisms involved in the administration of the European Communities customs law provided in paragraphs 7.157 to 7.191 of the Panel Report, it appears that there are institutions and mechanisms in the European Communities that seek to ensure that divergences in administration among the customs authorities of the member States do not occur or are reconciled in the event that they do occur. What is less clear from these general observations is whether the Panel made factual findings or reached definitive conclusions with respect to these institutions and mechanisms. Certainly, the Panel raised doubts about the effectiveness of these institutions and mechanisms in bringing about uniformity of administration of European Communities customs law. However, the Panel did not find that these institutions and mechanisms are structurally flawed in such a way that the European Communities' system of customs administration would necessarily lead to non-uniform administration, in a violation of Article X:3(a) of the GATT 1994. On

---

626 *Ibid.*, paras. 7.170 and 7.172.
627 *Ibid.*, para. 7.172.
628 *Ibid.*, paras. 7.177, 7.180, 7.187, and 7.190.
629 *Ibid.*, para. 7.181.
630 *Ibid.*, para. 7.186. (footnote omitted)
631 Panel Report, para. 7.191.
632 *Ibid.*, para. 7.489.

the contrary, the Panel stated that, "even if the Panel were authorized to make such findings, ... the United States did not demonstrate that the design and structure of the [European Communities] system of customs administration, including components thereof necessarily result in a violation of Article X:3(a) of the GATT 1994."[633] Accordingly, it appears to us that these general observations of the Panel do not constitute a sufficient foundation of factual findings or undisputed facts upon which we can rely for completing the analysis.

286. Further, as we said above, these general observations by the Panel with respect to the institutions and mechanisms involved in the administration of European Communities customs law were made in the context of an analysis based on the Panel's narrow interpretation of the measure at issue and the claim set out in the panel request.[634] We have reversed this interpretation of the Panel. Therefore, the general observations made by the Panel in paragraphs 7.157 to 7.191 of the Panel Report do not provide a sufficient foundation for us to complete the analysis. Moreover, the Panel examined the operation of these institutions and mechanisms in isolation and did not discuss how these institutions and mechanisms interact in the administration of European Communities customs law. Finally, given the breadth and the nature of the claim set out by the United States in the panel request, we are of the view that paragraphs 7.157 to 7.191 of the Panel Report do not constitute a sufficient basis to enable us to complete the analysis.

287. In the light of all these considerations, we are unable to complete the analysis.

VI. THE PANEL'S INTERPRETATION OF ARTICLE X:3(B) OF THE GATT 1994

288. We now turn to the question whether Article X:3(b) of the GATT 1994 requires that decisions of the judicial, arbitral, or administrative tribunals, or procedures for the review and correction of administrative action relating to customs matters, must govern the practice of *all* the agencies entrusted with administrative enforcement *throughout the territory* of a particular WTO Member.

289. The Panel found:

> [N]either the ordinary meaning of the various terms of Article X:3(b) of the GATT 1994 nor the legal context for the interpretation of Article X:3(b) of the GATT 1994 provide a clear answer to the specific question the Panel has been called upon to address—namely, whether Article X:3(b) of the GATT 1994 requires the decisions of the judicial, arbitral or administrative tribunals or procedures for the review and correction of administrative action relating to customs matters to govern the practice of *all* the agen-

---

[633] *Ibid.*, para. 7.490.
[634] *Ibid.*, para. 7.33.

> cies entrusted with administrative enforcement *throughout the territory* of a particular [WTO] Member.[635] (original emphasis)

290. The Panel considered, however, that it would not be "reasonable" to infer that first instance independent review tribunals and bodies, whose jurisdiction in most legal systems is normally limited in substantive and geographical terms, should have the authority to bind all agencies entrusted with administrative enforcement throughout the territory of a WTO Member, such as the European Communities.[636]

291. On appeal, the United States claims that the Panel failed to give meaning to the terms "the agencies entrusted with administrative enforcement" and "such agencies" in Article X:3(b).[637] In the United States' view, the Panel effectively disregarded the ordinary meaning of these terms when it stated that "it is difficult to know what significance should be attached, if any, to the reference to agencies in the plural."[638] The United States submits that the ordinary meaning of the plural form encompasses "the agencies"—without limitation—as opposed to only one such agency, or just "some of" or "a subset of" the agencies. The use of the plural form contemplates multiple agencies and, given the absence of any basis in the text for distinguishing among multiple agencies, it must contemplate *all* the agencies entrusted with administrative enforcement.[639] Furthermore, the United States maintains that Article X:3(b) must be read in the light of the requirement of uniform administration in Article X:3(a) of the GATT 1994, and that it follows from this context that procedures leading to decisions that have effect only in particular regions of a Member's territory are inconsistent with Article X:3(b) of the GATT 1994.

292. In the European Communities' view, the Panel correctly explained that the use of the plural form when referring to "agencies" in Article X:3(b) could flow from the fact that the review "tribunals and procedures" required under the same provision are also referred to in the plural.[640] The European Communities concurs with the Panel that it would not be reasonable to infer "that first instance independent review tribunals and bodies, whose jurisdiction in most legal systems is normally limited in substantive and geographical terms, should have the authority to bind all agencies entrusted with administrative enforcement throughout the territory of a [WTO] Member."[641] Furthermore, the European Communities submits that the absence of an express reference to Article X:3(a) in Article X:3(b) of the GATT 1994 contrasts with the explicit reference in Article X:3(c) to Article X:3(b) of the GATT 1994, and argues that this absence precludes an inference that the obligation to ensure review of administrative action

---

[635] Panel Report, para. 7.537.

[636] *Ibid.*, para. 7.538. We note that the European Communities and its member States are WTO Members in their own rights.

[637] United States' appellant's submission, paras. 164-172.

[638] Panel Report, para. 7.528.

[639] United States' appellant's submission, para. 166.

[640] European Communities' appellee's submission, para. 288 (referring to Panel Report, para. 7.527).

[641] *Ibid.*, para. 325 (referring to United States' appellant's submission, para. 188).

under Article X:3(b) could be read as simultaneously requiring uniform administration within the meaning of Article X:3(a) of the GATT 1994.

293. Our analysis begins with the text of Article X:3(b) of the GATT 1994, which stipulates:

> Each Member shall maintain, or institute as soon as practicable, judicial, arbitral or administrative tribunals or procedures for the purpose, *inter alia*, of the prompt review and correction of administrative action relating to customs matters. Such tribunals or procedures shall be independent of the agencies entrusted with administrative enforcement and their decisions shall be implemented by, and shall govern the practice of, such agencies unless an appeal is lodged with a court or tribunal of superior jurisdiction within the time prescribed for appeals to be lodged by importers; *Provided* that the central administration of such agency may take steps to obtain a review of the matter in another proceeding if there is good cause to believe that the decision is inconsistent with established principles of law or the actual facts. (original emphasis)

294. At the outset, we note that both parties agree that Article X:3(b) relates to *first* instance review. The Panel agreed with this interpretation. It found support for this interpretation in the separate reference in Article X:3(b) to the possibility of filing an appeal with "a court or tribunal of superior jurisdiction within the time prescribed for appeals to be lodged by importers". We agree that the phrase "unless an appeal is lodged with a court or tribunal of superior jurisdiction" contemplates the possibility that there may be an appeal to bodies of "superior jurisdiction" and confirms the view that Article X:3(b) relates to first instance review. We note that the Panel also relied on the proviso of Article X:3(b), which provides that the "central administration of such agency may take steps to obtain a review of the matter in another proceeding if there is good cause to believe that the decision is inconsistent with established principles of law or the actual facts."[642]

295. Article X:3(b) requires that first instance review decisions "shall be implemented by, and shall govern the practice of, such agencies" (that is, agencies entrusted with the administration of customs matters). The question before us is whether, as argued by the United States, Article X:3(b) requires that first instance review decisions must govern the practice of *all* the agencies entrusted with administrative enforcement *throughout the territory* of a WTO Member.

296. The United States emphasizes that Article X:3(b) contains two separate references to "agencies" in the plural: the first reference is to "the agencies entrusted with administrative enforcement"; and the second reference is to "such agencies".[643] From that, the United States infers that review decisions should govern the practice of "*all* of the agencies entrusted with administrative enforcement". We address each of these references in turn.

---

[642] Panel Report, para. 7.521.

[643] United States' appellant's submission, para. 166.

297. The use in Article X:3(b) of the term "the agencies entrusted with administrative enforcement" in the plural form suggests that reference is made to more than a single agency. However, it does not follow from the use of the plural that first instance review decisions concerning administrative action taken by an agency must necessarily be binding on all other agencies throughout a WTO Member's territory. In our view, the interpretation proposed by the United States would mean reading words into the treaty text that are not there. We can conceive of several explanations for the use of the plural when referring to "agencies" in Article X:3(b) of the GATT 1994: there could be several agencies in a WTO Member having different areas of substantive competence; various agencies could also have competence for different geographical areas. The use of the plural for "agencies" might also be a consequence of the reference to "tribunals" and "procedures" in the plural.[644] The reference to "tribunals" and "procedures" in the plural suggests to us that WTO Members are free to establish several first instance review tribunals and procedures that have different substantive or geographic areas of competence. Article X:3(b) does not, in our view, preclude a WTO Member from establishing first instance review tribunals and procedures governing the practice of all administrative agencies in their entire territory; however, it also does not require WTO Members to do so. Therefore, we are not convinced that the reference to "agencies" in the plural implies that first instance review decisions must govern the practice of "*all* agencies" of a WTO Member.

298. The United States also argues that the absence of criteria for distinguishing among multiple "agencies" implies that the reference to "such agencies" means all agencies. A plain reading of Article X:3(b) suggests that "such agencies" are not all agencies, but only those agencies whose action has been subject to review by a tribunal or procedure and that are bound by the decisions of that tribunal or procedure "with respect to identical factual situations that may arise in the future concerning identical legal issues".[645] We agree with the Panel that what is required by Article X:3(b) is that "the decisions of judicial, arbitral or administrative tribunals and procedures for the prompt review and correction of administrative action must govern the practice of the agency whose action was the subject of review by a tribunal or procedure in a particular case."[646] Article X:3(b) leaves the specific structure of the review mechanism to the discretion of the Member concerned. Therefore, "such agencies" may encompass more or fewer agencies depending on the structure of the review mechanism. However, we do not see why the jurisdiction of a review tribunal or procedure and the binding effect of a review decision of that tribunal would always or necessarily have to extend to all agencies of a Member.

299. In addition, we recall that Article X:3(b) relates to first instance review and contemplates the possibility of appeals to bodies of "superior jurisdiction" as well as the seeking of "a review of the matter" by a centralized agency. This

---

644 European Communities' appellee's submission, para. 288.

645 Panel Report, para. 7.531.

646 *Ibid.*, para. 7.528.

would also suggest that the first instance review required by that provision need not necessarily cover the entire territory of a WTO Member.

300. Accordingly, we are of the view that it does not follow from the ordinary meaning of Article X:3(b) that decisions of judicial, arbitral, or administrative tribunals or procedures for first instance review and correction of administrative action relating to customs matters must govern the practice of *all* the agencies entrusted with administrative enforcement *throughout the territory* of a WTO Member.

301. We address next the question whether *context* suggests otherwise. We consider that Article X:3(a) of the GATT 1994 is relevant as context. The Panel, however, noted that Article X:3(b) of the GATT 1994 does not contain an express textual link to the obligation of uniform administration of customs laws in Article X:3(a). The Panel contrasted this with Article X:3(c) of the GATT 1994, which explicitly cross-references Article X:3(b).[647] Against this background, the Panel considered that it was not possible to infer that the drafters of the GATT 1994 intended the obligation of Article X:3(b) to be read as simultaneously requiring uniform administration in accordance with Article X:3(a). In the Panel's view, this would amount to "merging different requirements that are currently contained in separate sub-paragraphs of Article X".[648] We see no reason to disagree with the Panel's interpretation. We are also of the view that the requirement of "uniformity" contained in Article X:3(a) does not imply that under Article X:3(b) decisions of review tribunals must govern the practice of all agencies entrusted with customs enforcement throughout the territory of a WTO Member. Article X:3(a) requires, *inter alia*, uniformity of administration. In contrast, Article X:3(b) relates to the review and correction of administrative action by independent mechanisms.

302. Finally, turning briefly to the treaty's object and purpose, we note the Panel's view that the due process objective underlying Article X:3(b) is that "a trader who has been adversely affected by a decision of an administrative agency has the ability to have that adverse decision reviewed."[649] We believe this due process objective is not undermined even if first instance review decisions do not govern the practice of all the agencies entrusted with customs enforcement throughout the territory of a WTO Member, so long as there is a possibility of an independent review and correction of the administrative action of every agency.

303. For these reasons, we are of the view that Article X:3(b) of the GATT 1994 requires a WTO Member to establish and maintain independent mechanisms for prompt review and correction of administrative action in the area of customs administration. However, neither text nor context nor the object and purpose of this Article require that the decisions emanating from such first instance review must govern the practice of *all* agencies entrusted with administrative enforcement *throughout the territory* of a particular WTO Member.

---

[647] Likewise, this is in contrast with Article X:3(a), which contains a cross-reference to Article X:1.

[648] Panel Report, paras. 7.534.

[649] *Ibid.*, para. 7.538.

304. We therefore *uphold* the conclusion of the Panel, in paragraphs 7.539, 7.556, and 8.1(e) of the Panel Report, that "Article X:3(b) of the GATT 1994 does not necessarily mean that the decisions of the judicial, arbitral or administrative tribunals or procedures for the review and correction of administrative action relating to customs matters must govern the practice of *all* agencies entrusted with administrative enforcement *throughout the territory* of a particular [WTO] Member."[650] We *conclude* that the Panel did not err in finding the tribunals and procedures for review of customs administrative action provided by the European Communities to be consistent with Article X:3(b) of the GATT 1994.

VII. CONDITIONAL APPEAL OF THE EUROPEAN COMMUNITIES

305. The Panel found that Article XXIV:12 of the GATT 1994 cannot be relied upon to attenuate or to derogate from the provisions of the GATT 1994 (including Article X:3(a)), to which Article XXIV:12 refers.[651] In the light of this reasoning, the Panel concluded:

> Article XXIV:12 of the GATT does not constitute an exception nor a derogation from the obligation of uniform administration in Article X:3(a) of the GATT 1994. Therefore, Article XXIV:12 of the GATT 1994 has no impact upon our examination of the United States' claims under Article X:3(a) of the GATT 1994.[652] (footnote omitted)

306. The European Communities conditionally appeals this finding in the event that the Appellate Body's conclusions on the United States' appeal imply that the European Communities should "create a centralised customs agency replacing its [m]ember States in the implementation of [European Communities] customs law"[653], or that the European Communities should "create an [European Communities]-level tribunal for the first-instance review of customs decisions".[654]

307. The United States requests the Appellate Body to reject the European Communities' conditional appeal because the question of the possible relevance of Article XXIV:12 of the GATT 1994 is outside the scope of these appellate proceedings and because this provision applies to the observance of GATT 1994 laws by regional and local governments and authorities, which is not at issue in this appeal.

308. We already found that we were unable to complete the analysis with respect to whether the measures at issue, taken as a whole, have been administered in a manner inconsistent with the requirements in Article X:3(a) of the GATT 1994. In addition, we upheld the Panel's conclusion that the European Communities did not breach Article X:3(b) of the GATT 1994. It thus follows that the

---

[650] (original emphasis)

[651] Panel Report, para. 7.144. (footnote omitted)

[652] *Ibid.*, para. 7.145.

[653] European Communities' other appellant's submission, para. 235.

[654] *Ibid.*

conditions on which this aspect of the European Communities' appeal is predicated are not satisfied. Therefore we do not consider it further.

VIII. FINDINGS AND CONCLUSIONS

309. For the reasons set out in this Report, the Appellate Body:

(a) with respect to the Panel's terms of reference:

(i) *reverses* the Panel's finding, in paragraph 7.20 of the Panel Report, that the "measure at issue" for purposes of a claim under Article X:3(a) of the GATT 1994 must necessarily be "the manner of administration that is allegedly non-uniform, partial and/or unreasonable";

(ii) *reverses* the Panel's finding, in paragraphs 7.33 and 8.1(a)(i) of the Panel Report, that the specific measure at issue in this dispute is "the manner of administration ... of the Community Customs Code, the Implementing Regulation, the Common Customs Tariff, the TARIC and related measures in the areas of customs administration specifically identified in the United States' request for establishment of a panel"[655]; and *finds*, instead, that the specific measures at issue identified in the panel request are the Community Customs Code, the Implementing Regulation, the Common Customs Tariff, and the TARIC, as administered collectively;

(iii) *reverses* the Panel's finding, in paragraphs 7.50, 7.64, and 8.1(a)(iii) of the Panel Report, that, due to the wording and content of the panel request, the United States was precluded from challenging the European Communities' system of customs administration as a whole or overall; and *reverses* also the Panel's finding, in paragraphs 7.63, 7.64, and 8.1(a)(iii) of the Panel Report, that the Panel was precluded from considering the United States' argument that the "design and structure" of the European Communities' system of customs administration necessarily result in a violation of Article X:3(a) of the GATT 1994; and

(iv) *upholds*, albeit for different reasons, the Panel's interpretation, in paragraph 7.37 of the Panel Report, that "the steps and acts of administration that pre-date or post-date the establishment of a panel may be relevant to determining whether or not a violation of Article X:3(a) of the GATT 1994 exists at the time of [panel] establishment";

(b) with respect to claims under Article X:3(a) of the GATT 1994:

---

655 Panel Report, para. 8.1(a)(i).

(i) *reverses* the Panel's finding, in paragraph 7.119 of the Panel Report, that, without exception, Article X:3(a) of the GATT 1994 always relates to the application of laws and regulations, but not to laws and regulations as such; but *upholds* the Panel's conclusions, in paragraphs 7.434, 7.444, 8.1(d)(i), and 8.1(d)(ii) of the Panel Report, that substantive differences in penalty laws and audit procedures among the member States of the European Communities alone do not constitute a violation of Article X:3(a) of the GATT 1994;

(ii) *concludes* that the Panel did not find that Article X:3(a) of the GATT 1994 requires uniformity of "administrative processes"; *upholds* the Panel's finding, in paragraph 7.119 of the Panel Report, that the term "administer" in Article X:3(a) of the GATT 1994 may include administrative processes that put into effect the legal instruments of the kind described in Article X:1 of the GATT 1994; but *reverses* the Panel's finding, in paragraphs 7.276 and 8.1(b)(iv) of the Panel Report, that the administrative process leading to the tariff classification of blackout drapery lining amounts to non-uniform administration within the meaning of Article X:3(a) of the GATT 1994, and that the European Communities has violated Article X:3(a) of the GATT 1994 with respect to the tariff classification of blackout drapery lining;

(iii) *upholds* the Panel's finding, in paragraphs 7.305 and 8.1(b)(v) of the Panel Report, that "[t]he tariff classification of liquid crystal display monitors with digital video interface amounts to non-uniform administration within the meaning of Article X:3(a) of the GATT 1994";

(iv) *reverses* the Panel's finding, in paragraphs 7.385 and 8.1(c)(ii) of the Panel Report, that "the European Communities does not administer its customs law concerning successive sales—in particular, Article 147(1) of the Implementing Regulation—in a uniform manner, in violation of Article X:3(a) of the GATT 1994"; and

(v) *is unable to complete* the analysis with respect to the United States' claim that the European Communities' system of customs administration as a whole or overall is not administered in a uniform manner, as required by Article X:3(a) of the GATT 1994;

(c) with respect to Article X:3(b) of the GATT 1994:

upholds the conclusion of the Panel, in paragraphs 7.539, 7.556, and 8.1(e) of the Panel Report, that "Article X:3(b) of the GATT 1994 does not necessarily mean that the decisions of the judicial, arbitral or administrative tribunals or procedures for the review and correction of administrative action relating to customs matters must govern the practice of *all* the agencies entrusted with administrative enforcement *throughout the territory* of a particular [WTO] Member"[656]; and

(d) with respect to Article XXIV:12 of the GATT 1994:

finds that the conditions on which the European Communities' appeal is predicated are not satisfied, and therefore *does not consider* it.

310. The Appellate Body *recommends* that the DSB request the European Communities to bring its measures, which have been found in this Report, and in the Panel Report as modified by this Report, to be inconsistent with the GATT 1994, into conformity with its obligations under that Agreement.

[656] (original emphasis)

ANNEX I

WORLD TRADE ORGANIZATION

WT/DS315/11
17 August 2006

(06-3905)

Original: English

EUROPEAN COMMUNITIES – SELECTED CUSTOMS MATTERS

Notification of an Appeal by the United States under Article 16.4 and Article 17 of the Understanding on Rules and Procedures Governing the Settlement of Disputes (DSU), and under Rule 20(1) of the Working Procedures for Appellate Review

The following notification, dated 14 August 2006, from the Delegation of the United States, is being circulated to Members.

Pursuant to Article 16 of the *Understanding on Rules and Procedures Governing the Settlement of Disputes* ("DSU") and Rule 20 of the *Working Procedures for Appellate Review*, the United States hereby notifies its decision to appeal to the Appellate Body certain issues of law covered in the Report of the Panel on *European Communities – Selected Customs Matters* (WT/DS315/R) and certain legal interpretations developed by the Panel.

The United States seeks review by the Appellate Body of the following aspects of the Report of the Panel.

I. *Terms of Reference*

The United States seeks review of three sets of errors committed by the Panel with respect to its analysis of its terms of reference.

(A) As the first step in its analysis the Panel found, in paragraph 7.20 of the Report, that "when a violation of Article X:3(a) of the [*General Agreement on Tariffs and Trade 1994*] is being claimed," the "measure at issue" that Article 6.2 requires to be identified in the request for establishment of a panel is "the manner of administration that is allegedly non-uniform, partial and/or unreasonable." This finding is in error and is based on erroneous findings on issues of law and related legal interpretations contained in paragraphs 7.8 through 7.22 of the Panel Report. In making this finding, the Panel misinterpreted or misapplied Article 6.2 of the DSU.

While the Panel's finding that "manner of administration" is the measure at issue in a dispute involving Article X:3(a) of the *General Agreement on Tariffs and Trade 1994* ("GATT 1994") was in error and should not be allowed to stand, the U.S. panel request did in fact identify the manner of administration of European Communities ("EC") laws, regulations, decisions, and rulings of the kind described in Article X:1 of the GATT 1994 at issue (referred to hereafter collectively as "EC customs law"), and the Panel did not find against the United States on this ground.

(B) Having incorrectly found "manner of administration" to be the measure at issue in a dispute involving Article X:3(a) of the GATT 1994, the Panel also misconstrued the specific measures at issue identified in the U.S. panel request as confined to the manner of administration of EC customs law in certain specific areas, as opposed to the manner of administration of such measures irrespective of area. Thus, the Panel found in paragraph 7.33 of the Report that the "specific measure at issue" in this dispute, within the meaning of Article 6.2 of the DSU, was:

> [T]he manner of administration by the national customs authorities of the member States of the Community Customs Code, the Implementing Regulation, the Common Customs Tariff, the TARIC and related measures in the areas of customs administration specifically identified in the United States' request for establishment of a panel – namely, the classification and valuation of goods, procedures for the classification and valuation of goods, procedures for the entry and release of goods, procedures for auditing entry statements after goods are released into free circulation, penalties and procedures regarding the imposition of penalties for violation of customs rules and record-keeping requirements.

This finding is in error and is based on erroneous findings on issues of law and related legal interpretations contained in paragraphs 7.23 through 7.32 and 8.1(a)(i) of the Panel Report. In making this finding, the Panel misinterpreted or misapplied Articles 6.2 and 7.1 of the DSU.

(C) The Panel then made the erroneous legal conclusion that its terms of reference excluded the U.S. claim that the design and structure of the EC system of customs administration as a whole results in the administration of EC customs law in a non-uniform manner, contrary to Article X:3(a) of the GATT 1994. For example, paragraph 7.50 of its Report, the Panel made the erroneous finding that "its terms of reference regarding the U.S. claim under Article X:3(a) of the GATT 1994 do not include a challenge to the EC system of customs administration overall or as a whole under Article X:3(a) of the GATT 1994." The Panel made a similarly erroneous finding in paragraph 7.63, stating that "the United States is precluded from making an 'as such' challenge with respect to the design and structure of the EC system of customs administration as a whole and also with respect to the design and structure of the EC system in the areas of customs administration that have been specifically identified in the United States' request." This finding is repeated at paragraph 8.1(a)(iii) of the Panel's Report.

These findings are in error and are based on erroneous findings on issues of law and related legal interpretations contained in paragraphs 7.11 through 7.20, 7.23 through 7.32, 7.40 through 7.50, 7.53 through 7.63, and 8.1(a)(iii) of the Panel Report. In making these findings, the Panel misinterpreted or misapplied Articles 6.2 and 7.1 of the DSU.

The Panel's error in excluding from its terms of reference the U.S. challenge with respect to the EC system of customs administration as a whole did not depend on its first two errors with respect to its terms of reference. Even if the first two findings in the Panel's analysis of its terms of reference were correct (which we contend they were not), the Panel still should not have excluded the U.S. challenge with respect to the EC's system of customs administration as a whole. The U.S. claim was about features that are absent from the EC system of customs administration, which result in the EC administering its customs laws in a non-uniform manner, contrary to Article X:3(a) of the GATT 1994. That central aspect of the U.S. complaint – which was evident from the panel request, elaborated in U.S. submissions and statements, and well understood by the EC as evidenced by its submissions and statements – was part of the U.S. panel request whether that request is understood as encompassing the administration of EC customs law in all areas or only in certain areas (as the Panel found).

Accordingly, the United States asks the Appellate Body to reverse the Panel's finding that this claim was outside the Panel's terms of reference. Additionally, the United States asks the Appellate Body to complete the Panel's analysis based on the undisputed facts and the Panel's factual findings regarding the EC system of customs administration. In light of the Panel's factual findings that the various institutions and mechanisms that the EC held out as securing the uniform administration of its customs laws – in an environment where administration is the responsibility of 25 separate, independent customs authorities – do not actually do so, the Appellate Body should find that the EC system of customs administration as a whole results in the non-uniform administration of EC customs law, in breach of Article X:3(a) of the GATT 1994.

II. *Interpretation of the term "administer" in Article X:3(a) of the GATT 1994 as it relates to the existence of divergent penalty laws and audit procedures*

The United States seeks review of the Panel's legal conclusions that the existence of divergent penalty laws and audit procedures are not inconsistent with Article X:3(a) of the GATT 1994, and the related issues of law and legal interpretation. At paragraph 7.444, for example, the Panel found "no violation of Article X:3(a) of the GATT 1994 with respect to the substantive differences in penalty laws between member States." At paragraph 7.434, for example, the Panel found "no violation of Article X:3(a) of the GATT 1994 with respect to the manner of administration of the audit procedure requirements in the European Communities by the member States applicable to goods following their release for free circulation."

In finding that the EC does not breach its Article X:3(a) obligation of uniform administration to the extent that it puts EC customs law into practical effect through divergent penalty laws and audit procedures, the Panel erred in its interpretation of the term "administer" as used in that provision. The Panel's error regarding its approach to differences in customs penalty laws is based on erroneous findings on issues of law and related legal interpretations contained in paragraphs 7.113 through 7.119, 7.442 through 7.444, and 8.1(d)(ii) of the Panel Report. Its error regarding its approach to differences in audit procedures is based on erroneous findings on issues of law and related legal interpretations contained in paragraphs 7.113 through 7.119, 7.425 through 7.434, and 8.1(d)(i) of the Panel Report.

The United States asks the Appellate Body to reverse the Panel's legal conclusions that the existence of divergent penalty laws and audit procedures are not inconsistent with Article X:3(a) of the GATT 1994. The United States further asks the Appellate Body to complete the Panel's analysis. In light of the Panel's findings and undisputed facts regarding the existence of divergent penalty laws and audit procedures, the Appellate Body should find that the EC fails to administer EC customs law in a uniform manner, in breach of Article X:3(a) of the

GATT 1994, to the extent it gives effect to EC customs law through the maintenance of divergent penalty laws and audit procedures.

III. *Interpretation of Article X:3(b) of the GATT 1994*

The United States seeks review of the Panel's legal conclusion that "the European Communities does not violate Article X:3(b) of the GATT 1994 merely because the decisions regarding review of administration action relating to customs matters, which are taken by authorities in the member States acting as organs of the European Communities, do not apply and have effect throughout the territory of the European Communities." Panel Report, para. 7.554; *id.,* paras. 7.539, 7.556, and 8.1(e). That conclusion represents an erroneous interpretation of Article X:3(b) of the GATT 1994, which was based on erroneous findings on issues of law and related legal interpretations contained in paragraphs 7.526 through 7.538.

The United States asks the Appellate Body to reverse the Panel's erroneous interpretation of and conclusion under Article X:3(b). Further, the United States asks the Appellate Body to complete the Panel's analysis. It is undisputed that each of the tribunals and procedures the EC provides is limited to reviewing the administrative actions of the customs authority within a particular EC member State. It also is undisputed that none of these tribunals or procedures issues decisions that govern the practice of all of the agencies entrusted with administrative enforcement of the EC's customs law (that is, the customs authorities of the 25 EC member States). In light of these undisputed facts, the Appellate Body should find that the EC is in breach of its obligation under Article X:3(b) of the GATT 1994.

ANNEX II

WORLD TRADE ORGANIZATION

WT/DS315/12
28 August 2006

(06-4123)

Original: English

EUROPEAN COMMUNITIES – SELECTED CUSTOMS MATTERS

Notification of an Other Appeal by the European Communities under Article 16.4 and Article 17 of the Understanding on Rules and Procedures Governing the Settlement of Disputes (DSU), and under Rule 23(1) of the Working Procedures for Appellate Review

The following notification, dated 28 August 2006, from the Delegation of the European Commission, is being circulated to Members.

---

1. Pursuant to Article 16.4 and Article 17 of the DSU and to Rule 23.1 of the Working Procedures for Appellate Review, the European Communities submits its Notice of Other Appeal on certain issues of law in the Report of the Panel on *European Communities – Selected Customs Matters*[657] and certain legal interpretations developed by the Panel.

2. The European Communities seeks review by the Appellate Body of the following:

    (a) the Panel's decision not to admit certain evidence submitted by the European Communities during the interim review stage, and in particular Exhibits EC-167 to EC-170 (paragraphs 6.5 and 6.6 of the Panel report). This decision is incompatible with Article 15.2

[657] WT/DS315/R, circulated on 16 June 2005.

of the DSU and with the Panel's duty to make an objective assessment of the facts as required by Article 11 of the DSU;

(b) the Panel's finding regarding the temporal limitations of its terms of reference, according to which it may consider measures, including acts of administration, which were no longer in existence, or not yet in existence, at the time of its establishment (paragraph 7.36 to 7.37 of the Panel Report). These findings are inconsistent with Articles 6.2 and 7.1 of the DSU;

(c) the Panel's finding that Article X:3(a) GATT requires uniformity of administrative processes irrespective of their impact on the uniform administration of the laws (paragraphs 7.102 to 7.113 and 7.119 of the Report). This finding is based on an incorrect interpretation of Article X:3(a) GATT;

(d) the Panel's finding that Article XXIV:12 GATT cannot be relied upon to attenuate or to derogate from the provisions of the GATT 1994, including Article X:3 GATT, and does not constitute an exception from such provisions (paragraphs 7.140 to 7.145 of the Panel Report). This finding is based on an incorrect interpretation Article XXIV:12 GATT;

(e) the Panel's finding that the EC has violated Article X:3(a) GATT with respect to the process leading to the tariff classification of blackout drapery lining (paragraphs 7.266 to 7.276, 8.1(b)(iv) and 8.2(a) of the Panel Report). In reaching this finding, the Panel has erred in its interpretation of Article X:3(a) GATT, and failed to make an objective assessment of the facts as required by Article 11 of the DSU;

(f) the Panel's finding that the EC has violated Article X:3(a) GATT with respect to the tariff classification of LCD Monitors with DVI (paragraphs 7.291 to 7.305, 8.1(b)(v) and 8.2(b) of the Panel Report). In reaching this finding, the Panel has erred in its interpretation of Article X:3(a) GATT, and failed to make an objective assessment of the facts as required by Article 11 of the DSU;

(g) the Panel's finding that the EC has violated Article X:3(a) GATT with respect to the imposition by the customs authorities of certain Member States of a form of prior approval with respect to the successive sales provision (paragraphs 7.376 to 7.385, 8.1(c)(ii) and 8.2(c) of the Panel Report). In reaching this finding, the Panel has erred in its interpretation of Article X:3(a) GATT, and failed to make an objective assessment of the facts as required by Article 11 of the DSU.

ANNEX III

WORLD TRADE ORGANIZATION

WT/DS315/8
14 January 2005

(05-0192)

Original: English

EUROPEAN COMMUNITIES – SELECTED CUSTOMS MATTERS

Request for the Establishment of a Panel by the United States

The following communication, dated 13 January 2005, from the delegation of the United States to the Chairperson of the Dispute Settlement Body, is circulated pursuant to Article 6.2 of the DSU.

The United States considers that the manner in which the European Communities ("EC") administers its laws, regulations, decisions and rulings of the kind described in Article X:1 of the *General Agreement on Tariffs and Trade 1994* ("GATT 1994") is not uniform, impartial and reasonable, and therefore is inconsistent with Article X:3(a) of the GATT 1994. For purposes of this request, the laws, regulations, decisions and rulings (collectively, "measures") that the European Communities fails to administer in such a manner pertain to the classification and valuation of products for customs purposes and to requirements, restrictions or prohibitions on imports. The measures consist of:

- Council Regulation (EEC) No 2913/92 of 12 October 1992 establishing the Community Customs Code, including all annexes thereto, as amended (the "Code");
- Commission Regulation (EEC) No 2454/93 of 2 July 1993 laying down provisions for the implementation of Council Regulation (EEC) No 2913/92 of 12 October 1992 establishing the Community Customs Code, including all annexes thereto, as amended (the "Commission Regulation");

- Council Regulation (EEC) No 2658/87 of 23 July 1987 on the tariff and statistical nomenclature and on the Common Customs Tariff, including all annexes thereto, as amended (the "Tariff Regulation");
- the Integrated Tariff of the European Communities established by virtue of Article 2 of Council Regulation (EEC) No 2658/87 of 23 July 1987 on the tariff and statistical nomenclature and on the Common Customs Tariff, including all annexes thereto, as amended (the "TARIC"); and
- for each of the above laws and regulations, all amendments, implementing measures and other related measures.

Administration of these measures in the European Communities is carried out by the national customs authorities of EC member States. Such administration takes numerous different forms. The United States understands that the myriad forms of administration of these measures include, but are not limited to, laws, regulations, handbooks, manuals, and administrative practices of customs authorities of member States of the European Communities.

Lack of uniform, impartial and reasonable administration of the above-identified measures is manifest in differences among member States in a number of areas, including, but not limited to, the following:

- classification and valuation of goods;
- procedures for the classification and valuation of goods, including the provision of binding classification and valuation information to importers;
- procedures for the entry and release of goods, including different certificate of origin requirements, different criteria among member States for the physical inspection of goods, different licensing requirements for importation of food products, and different procedures for processing express delivery shipments;
- procedures for auditing entry statements after goods are released into the stream of commerce in the European Communities;
- penalties and procedures regarding the imposition of penalties for violation of customs rules; and
- record-keeping requirements.

In addition, the European Communities has failed to maintain, or institute as soon as practicable, judicial, arbitral or administrative tribunals or procedures for the purpose, *inter alia*, of the prompt review and correction of administrative action relating to customs matters. The above-identified measures, including in particular Articles 243 through 246 of the Code, expressly provide that EC member States are responsible for the implementation of procedures for appeals from decisions by member State customs authorities. Accordingly, the ability to obtain review of a customs decision by a tribunal of the European Communities does not arise until after an importer or other interested party has pursued review through national administrative and/or judicial tribunals. For this reason, the European Communities is in breach of Article X:3(b) of the GATT 1994.

The EC measures are also inconsistent with Article X:1 of the GATT 1994.

On 21 September 2004, the United States requested consultations with the European Communities pursuant to Articles 1 and 4 of the *Understanding on Rules and Procedures Governing the Settlement of Disputes* ("DSU") and Article XXII:1 of the GATT 1994 (WT/DS315/1). The United States held consultations with the European Communities in Geneva on 16 November 2004. Unfortunately, these consultations did not resolve the dispute.

Accordingly, the United States respectfully requests the Dispute Settlement Body to establish a panel pursuant to Article 6 of the DSU to examine this matter with standard terms of reference as set out in Article 7.1 of the DSU.

EUROPEAN COMMUNITIES – SELECTED CUSTOMS MATTERS

Report of the Panel

WT/DS315/R

Adopted by the Dispute Settlement Body on 11 December 2006 as Modified by the Appellate Body Report

TABLE OF CONTENTS

Page

TABLE OF ANNEXES 3932

TABLE OF CASES CITED IN THIS REPORT 3935

LIST OF ABBREVIATIONS 3939

I. INTRODUCTION 3941

II. FACTUAL ASPECTS 3942

A. The Legislative Framework for Administration of EC Customs Law 3943

1. The Community Customs Tariff 3943

2. The Community Customs Code 3944

3. The Implementing Regulation 3944

B. Institutions and Mechanisms Involved in the Administration of the EC Customs Laws 3944

1. The Commission 3944

2. The member States 3945

(a) Legal effect of EC customs law on member States 3945

(b) Administration of EC customs law 3946

3. The Customs Code Committee 3946

4. EC courts 3948

(a) Role and function of the courts of member States 3948

(b) Role and function of the ECJ 3949

5. Cooperation between the member States and between the member States and the Commission 3949

(a) Council Regulation (EC) No. 515/97 3949
(b) Action programmes 3950
6. Training 3950
7. Budgetary and financial control 3951
C. Specific Areas of Customs Administration Referred to by the United States in its Submissions 3951
1. Tariff Classification 3951
(a) Classification Regulations 3952
(b) HS Explanatory Notes and WCO Opinions 3952
(c) Explanatory Notes of the Combined Nomenclature 3952
(d) Opinions of the Customs Code Committee 3953
(e) Binding tariff information 3953
2. Customs valuation 3955
3. Audit following release for free circulation 3957
4. Penalties for infringements of EC customs law 3958
5. Processing under customs control 3958
6. Local clearance procedures 3959
7. Recovery of customs debt 3960
D. Review of Customs Decisions 3960
1. Decisions the subject of judicial review 3960
2. Review by member States' customs authorities and courts 3960
3. Direct appeals to the ECJ 3961
III. PARTIES' REQUESTS FOR FINDINGS AND RECOMMENDATIONS 3961
A. United States 3961
B. European Communities 3962
IV. ARGUMENTS OF THE PARTIES 3962
A. First Written Submission of the United States 3962
1. Introduction 3962
2. The EC fails to administer its customs law in a uniform manner 3963
(a) Customs classification 3963
(b) Customs valuation 3965
(c) Customs procedures 3967
(d) The Commission, acting through the Customs Code Committee, does not provide

uniformity to the administration of EC customs law 3969

3. The EC does not provide tribunals or procedures for the prompt review and correction of administrative action relating to customs matters 3970

4. Conclusion 3973

B. first written submission of the european communities 3973

1. Introduction 3973

2. Factual background 3974

(a) General principles of the EC legal system 3974

(i) The EC institutions and the EC legislative process 3974

(ii) The implementing powers of the European Commission 3975

(iii) The legal effect of Community law 3976

(iv) The Commission, the member States, and the execution of Community law 3977

(b) The administration of EC customs law 3978

(i) The basic principles of the EC Customs Union 3978

(ii) The EC's international commitments in the field of customs administration and cooperation 3979

(iii) The legislative framework of the EC Customs Union 3979

(iv) The Commission, the member States, and the Customs Code Committee 3981

(v) Tariff classification 3982

(vi) Customs valuation 3986

(vii) Processing under customs control 3987

(viii) Local clearance procedure 3988

(ix) Penalties for violations of customs law 3989

(x) EC customs cooperation 3989

(xi) Budgetary and financial aspects 3991

(xii) The continuous evolution of EC customs law 3991

(c) Judicial control in EC law 3992

(i) The EC court system 3992

(ii) Judicial protection in the EC legal system 3993

(iii) Preliminary rulings: the Court of Justice and the uniform interpretation and application of Community law 3994

(iv) Judicial review of customs decisions 3995

(d) The US system in comparison 3996

(i) The administration of US customs law ... 3996

(ii) Review of customs decisions in US law 3997

3. The US claims under Article X:3(a) GATT 3998

(a) The requirements of Article X:3(a) GATT 3998

(i) Article X:3(a) GATT concerns the administration of customs laws, not the customs laws themselves 3998

(ii) Article X:3(a) GATT does not prescribe the ways in which WTO Members must administer their customs laws 3998

(iii) Article X:3(a) GATT lays down minimum standards 4000

(iv) The meaning of "uniform administration" 4000

(b) The burden of proof 4001

(c) General issues underlying the US claims under Article X:3(a) GATT 4002

(i) The fact that EC customs law is administered by the customs authorities of EC member States is compatible with Article X:3(a) GATT... 4002

(ii) The EC has measures in place to ensure the uniform administration of EC customs laws throughout the EC 4003

(iii) Some necessary corrections regarding the role and functioning of the Customs Code Committee 4004

(iv) The role of the Court of Justice in ensuring uniformity in the administration of EC customs law 4005

(d) The US claims under Article X:3(a) GATT 4006

(i) Tariff classification 4006

(ii) Customs valuation 4012

(iii) Processing under customs control 4015

(iv) Local clearance procedure 4015

(v) Penalties for violations of customs law... 4016

4. The US claim under Article X:3(b) GATT 4017

(a) The requirements of Article X:3(b) GATT 4017

(b) The EC provides for prompt review of customs decisions.. 4018

(i) The claim regarding the absence of an EC customs court.................................. 4018

(ii) Promptness in the review....................... 4019

C. First Oral Statement of the United States 4020

D. First Oral Statement of the European Communities................ 4030

1. The significance of the case 4030

(a) The constitutional significance of the case for the EC 4030

(b) The systemic importance of the case for the WTO 4031

2. The uniform administration of EC customs law........... 4032

(a) The requirements of Article X:3(a) GATT 4032

(b) The burden of proof 4033

(c) The claims raised by the United States 4034

(i) Tariff classification................................ 4034

(ii) Customs valuation 4035

(iii) Processing under customs control and local clearance procedure....................... 4036

(iv) Penalties for violations of customs law... 4036

3. The prompt review of customs decisions in the EC 4037

(a) The requirements of Article X:3(b) GATT 4037

(b) The burden of proof 4038

(c) The claims raised by the United States 4038

(i) The absence of an EC customs court 4038

(ii) The lack of promptness in the review..... 4039

E. Second Written Submission of the United States 4040

1. Introduction... 4040

2. GATT 1994 Article X:3 does not contain a relative, Member-specific standard 4041

(a) The obligations in GATT 1994 Article X:3 do not vary according to the particular features of a Member's customs administration system 4041

(b) The United States does not seek the harmonization of WTO Members' customs administration systems 4042

3. GATT 1994 Article X:3(a) is not a "subsidiary," "minimum standards provision" that is breached only when the non-uniform administration of a Member's customs laws exhibits a discernible pattern........ 4043

(a) There is no basis for the EC's characterization of GATT 1994 Article X:3(a) as a "subsidiary," "minimum standards provision" ... 4043

(b) The United States is not required to demonstrate a "pattern" of non-uniform administration to establish that the EC is in breach of its GATT 1994 Article X:3(a) obligation 4044

(i) The "pattern" requirement asserted by the EC has no basis in GATT 1994 Article X:3(a)........ 4044

(ii) The EC fails to even explain what it believes the United States must establish to meet the so-called "pattern" requirement........ 4044

(iii) The reference to a "pattern" in the panel report in US – Hot-Rolled Steel is not relevant to the present dispute....... 4045

(c) The EC acknowledges the existence of divergences among member State authorities in the administration of EC customs law 4046

4. The instruments that the EC holds out as ensuring uniform administration do not do so 4046

(a) Most of the instruments that the EC holds out as securing uniform administration are non-binding, discretionary, or extremely general in nature 4047

(b) Binding tariff information does not secure uniform administration........ 4047

(i) The EC system permits "shopping" for favorable BTI from among the 25 member State customs authorities 4047

(ii) The power of a member State customs authority to revoke BTI based on nothing more than its own reconsideration of the applicable classification rules, as affirmed in the Timmermans decision, detracts from uniform administration 4048

(c) The availability of review by member State courts as the "normal" means of reconciling divergences in member State administration of EC customs laws does not fulfill the EC's GATT 1994 Article X:3(a) obligation to administer its customs laws in a uniform manner 4050

5. In arguing that matters such as penalties and audit procedures are outside the scope of its obligation under GATT 1994 Article X:3(a), the EC relies on an erroneous understanding of what it means to "administer" customs laws 4051

(a) The EC relies on an erroneous understanding of what it means to "administer" customs laws 4052

(b) Penalties and audit procedures play a critical role in carrying out EC customs laws................ 4053

(c) Member States' penalties and audit procedures are properly characterized as tools for the administration of EC customs laws 4054

(i) A law may be a tool for administering other laws... 4054

(ii) Basing a claim of non-uniform administration on differences among member State laws that are tools for administering the EC's customs laws is not inconsistent with the Appellate Body's finding that a GATT 1994 Article X:3(a) claim must concern the administration of customs laws rather than their substance................................. 4054

(iii) The findings of the panel in Argentina – Hides and Leather are directly relevant to the present dispute................ 4055

(d) Reference to "penalties" for "minor breaches" in GATT 1994 Article VIII:3 does not put penalties outside the scope of Article X:3(a) 4056

(e) The US argument does not imply a requirement of harmonization of all sub-federal laws of WTO Members that have any similarity in subject matter to federal laws 4056

6. The decisions of review tribunals in the EC do not govern the practice of "the agencies" entrusted with administrative enforcement of EC customs laws, contrary to GATT 1994 Article X:3(b) 4057

(a) The decisions of the tribunals or procedures a WTO Member provides pursuant to GATT 1994 Article X:3(b) must govern the practice of "the agencies" entrusted with administrative enforcement of the Member's customs laws 4057

(b) The US argument does not imply a requirement for every WTO Member to establish a single, centralized customs court...... 4058

F. Second Written Submission of the European Communities..... 4060

1. The measures at issue in the present dispute 4060

2. The US claims under Article X:3(a) GATT 4061

(a) The requirements of Article X:3(a) GATT 4061

(i) Article X:3(a) GATT concerns the administration of customs laws, not the customs laws themselves 4061

(ii) Article X:3(a) GATT does not prescribe the ways in which WTO Members must administer their customs laws... 4063

(iii) Article X:3(a) GATT lays down minimum standards................................ 4064

(iv) The meaning of "uniform administration"....................................... 4064

(b) The burden of proof.. 4065

(c) General issues underlying the US claims under Article X:3(a) GATT 4067

(i) The US case is aimed at compelling the EC to create an EC customs agency.. 4068

(ii) The United States misrepresents the EC legal system 4069

(d) The US claims under Article X:3(a) GATT....... 4070

(i) Tariff classification................................ 4070

(ii) Customs valuation 4079

(iii) Processing under customs control........... 4082

(iv) Local clearance procedure 4083

(v) Penalties for violations of customs law... 4084

3. The US claim under Article X:3(b) GATT 4087

(a) Nature of the review: independent tribunals or procedures... 4087

(b) Time requirement: promptness in the review..... 4090

G. Second Oral Statement of the European Communities............ 4091

1. The EC is not obliged to create an EC customs agency and a customs court... 4091

2. The US claims under Article X:3(a) GATT 4094

(a) The United States misrepresents the requirements of Article X:3(a) GATT 4094

(i) Article X:3(a) GATT is a non-prescriptive, minimum standards provision 4094

(ii) Article X:3(a) GATT requires the United States to demonstrate the existence of a pattern of non-uniform administration 4095

(b) The US has not provided any evidence of a lack of uniformity in the EC's administration of its customs laws 4096

(c) The US criticisms of the EC's system of customs administration are unjustified, and do not demonstrate any incompatibility with Article X:3(a) GATT 4098

(i) Administrative guidance and the duty of cooperation 4098

(ii) The EBTI system 4099

(iii) Judicial review by member States' Courts... 4100

(d) Article X:3(a) GATT does not require the EC to harmonize member States' penalty provisions... 4102

(i) Penalty provisions are not covered by Article X:3(a) GATT 4102

(ii) Article X:3(a) GATT does not require the harmonization of laws which exist in a WTO Member at sub-federal level .. 4103

(iii) Community law ensures a sufficient degree of uniformity of penalty provisions.. 4104

3. The US claim under Article X:3(b) GATT 4105

(a) The ECJ and the requirement of prompt review.. 4105

(b) The requirement that the decisions of the tribunals must govern the practices of the agencies.. 4106

(c) The US interpretation of Article X:3(b) GATT requires the establishment, in every WTO Member, of a single and centralized customs court or a single and centralized customs agency. 4108

4. Closing statement... 4109

H. Second Oral Statement of the United States............................ 4116

1. Introduction.. 4116

2. The EC fails to rebut evidence supporting US Claims 4117

(a) EC admissions of non-uniform administration .. 4117

(b) There is no requirement to show a "pattern" of non-uniform administration 4118

(c) Difficulty of certain customs administration questions does not counter evidence of non-uniform administration and, in fact, highlights the problem 4118

(d) Resolution of divergences among member States after months or years does not counter evidence of non-uniform administration. 4118

3. Recent cases confirm that processes EC holds out as securing uniform administration fail to do so............... 4119

4. It is appropriate for the Panel to exercise its authority under DSU Article 13 4121

5. The EC fails to rebut evidence that classification rules are administered in a non-uniform manner........... 4122

(a) BTI does not secure uniform administration...... 4122

(b) LCD monitors 4123

(c) Blackout drapery lining..................................... 4124

6. The EC fails to rebut evidence that valuation rules are administered in a non-uniform manner 4125

7. The EC fails to rebut evidence that customs procedures are administered in a non-uniform manner 4126
 (a) Processing under customs control 4126
 (b) Penalties 4127
8. Member State courts, whose decisions govern only the customs authorities in their respective territories, do not fulfil the EC's obligation under Article X:3(b) of the GATT 1994 4128
9. Closing statement 4130

V. ARGUMENTS OF THE THIRD PARTIES 4133
A. Third Party Written Submission of China 4133
1. Issues relating to interpretation and application of Article X:3(a) 4133
 (a) The scope of application of Article X:3(a) of the GATT 1994 4133
 (b) The meaning of "uniform" as used in Article X:3(a) of the GATT 1994 4134
 (c) The standard of uniformity required by Article X:3(a) of the GATT 1994 4135
2. Conclusion 4135
B. Third Party Written Submission of Japan 4136
1. Introduction 4136
2. Consistency of the challenged measures with Article X:3(a) of the GATT 4136
 (a) The meaning of the term "uniform" administration in Article X:3(a) of the GATT 1994 4136
 (b) Article X:3(a) of the GATT does not prescribe the specific means a Member must employ in order to ensure a uniform administration of customs laws; such uniformity should be determined in respect of the particular customs system as a whole 4137
3. Consistency of the challenged measures with Article X:3(b) of the GATT 4138
 (a) The measure in question 4138
 (b) The consistency of the challenged measure with Article X:3(b) of the GATT 4139
4. Conclusion 4139
C. Third Party Written Submission of the Republic of Korea 4140

1. Introduction 4140
2. Legal arguments 4140
(a) The EC's non-uniform administration of laws and regulations concerning customs classification, valuation and other procedures violate Article X:3(a) of GATT 1994 4140
(b) EC judicial system's failure to provide a viable mechanism to promptly review customs related administrative actions violate Article X:3(b) of GATT 1994 4142
3. Conclusion 4143

D. Third Party Written Submission of the Separate Customs Territory of Taiwan, Penghu, Kinmen and Matsu 4143
1. Introduction 4143
2. Arguments 4143
3. Conclusion 4146

E. Third Party Oral Statement of Argentina 4146
1. Introduction 4146
2. The link between subparagraph (b) and subparagraph (a) of Article X:3 of the GATT 1994 4147
3. "Promptness" as an obligation in Article X:3(b) 4147

F. Third Party Oral Statement of Australia 4148

G. Third Party Oral Statement of China 4149
1. The scope of application of Article X:3(a) of the GATT 1994 4149
2. The meaning of "uniform" as used in Article X:3(a) of the GATT 1994 4150
3. The standard of uniformity required by Article X:3(a) of the GATT 1994 4151

H. Third Party Oral Statement of Japan 4151
1. Arguments relating to the consistency of the challenged measures with Article X:3(a) of the GATT 4151

I. Third Party Oral Statement of the Republic of Korea 4153
1. The EC's non-uniform administration of laws and regulations concerning customs classification, valuation and other procedures violate Article X:3(a) of GATT 1994 4153
2. The EC judicial system's failure to provide a viable mechanism to promptly review customs related

administrative actions violates Article X:3(b) of GATT 1994 4154

VI. INTERIM REVIEW 4155

A. New Evidence Referred to in Comments During the Interim Review Stage 4155

B. Panel's Terms of Reference 4156

1. Manner of administration 4156

2. Challenge of the EC system as a whole/overall 4156

3. Administration by "national customs authorities of EC member States" of "laws, regulations, handbooks, manuals and administrative practices" 4157

4. Temporal issues 4158

(a) Expired measures or measures not yet in existence at the time of panel establishment 4158

(b) The temporal scope of "administration" 4159

(c) "Currently" 4160

5. Retroactive recovery of customs duties 4161

C. Interpretation of Article x:3(a) of the GATT 1994 4161

1. "Object and purpose" 4161

2. "Supplementary means of interpretation" 4162

3. "Minimum standards" 4163

4. "Uniform" 4163

(a) Nature of the challenge 4163

(b) "Reasonable period of time" 4164

D. Panel's Observations Regarding the EC System of Customs Administration 4165

E. Specific Instances of Alleged Violation of Article X:3(A) of the GATT 1994 4166

1. Tariff classification of blackout drapery lining 4166

2. Tariff classification of liquid crystal display flat monitors with digital video interface 4168

3. Revocation of BTI concerning candlesticks and preserved fruits and nuts in the context of the Timmermans case 4168

4. Penalties against infringements of EC customs legislation 4169

F. EC and Member State Obligations 4169

G. Other Requests for Review 4170

VII. FINDINGS 4171

A. Article x of the GATT 1994 4171
B. The Panel's Terms of Reference 4172
1. The measure(s) at issue 4172
(a) Summary of the parties' arguments 4172
(b) Analysis by the Panel 4174
(i) Interpretation of the term "measures at issue" under Article 6.2 of the DSU........ 4174
(ii) The "measure(s) at issue" for the purposes of a claim under Article X:3(a) of the GATT 1994 4177
(iii) The "measure at issue" for the purposes of the United States' claim under Article X:3(a) of the GATT 1994 in this dispute 4178
(iv) Summary 4182
2. Temporal matters concerning the Panel's terms of reference 4182
(a) Summary of the parties' arguments 4182
(b) Analysis by the Panel 4183
3. The scope of the United States' challenge of the EC system of customs administration under Article X:3(a) of the GATT 1994 4184
(a) Summary of the parties' arguments 4184
(b) Analysis by the Panel 4185
4. The nature of the United States' challenge of the EC system of customs administration under Article X:3(a) of the GATT 1994 4188
(a) Summary of the parties' arguments 4188
(b) Analysis by the Panel 4190
5. Overall conclusions regarding the Panel's terms of reference 4194
C. Procedural Issues 4194
1. Admissibility of certain evidence 4194
(a) Evidence contained in section III of the United States' oral statement at the second substantive meeting 4194
(b) Evidence relied upon by the United States in sections of its oral statement at the second substantive meeting other than that contained in section III 4198

(c) Summary and conclusions 4200
2. Requests by the United States that the Panel exercise its discretion under Article 13 of the DSU 4200
D. Claims under Article x:3(a) of the GATT 1994 4203
1. Article X:3(a) of the GATT 1994 4203
2. Findings requested by the United States under Article X:3(a) of the GATT 1994 4203
(a) Summary of the parties' arguments 4203
(b) Analysis by the Panel 4205
3. Interpretation of Article X:3(a) of the GATT 1994 4207
(a) Interpretation of "administer" 4207
(i) Summary of the parties' arguments 4207
(ii) Analysis by the Panel 4209
(b) Interpretation of "uniform" 4215
(i) Summary of the parties' arguments 4215
(ii) Analysis by the Panel 4215
4. Relevance of Article XXIV:12 of the GATT 1994 for the interpretation of Article X:3(a) of the GATT 1994 in the context of this dispute 4220
(a) Summary of the parties' arguments 4220
(b) Analysis by the Panel 4222
5. Burden of proof 4225
(a) Summary of parties' arguments 4225
(b) Analysis by the Panel 4227
6. Specific alleged violations of Article X:3(a) of the GATT 1994 4229
(a) Relevant aspects of the EC system of customs administration 4229
(i) Administration by customs authorities in the EC member States 4229
(ii) Institutions and mechanisms involved in the administration of the EC customs laws 4229
(b) Allegations of non-uniform administration of the Common Customs Tariff in the area of tariff classification 4244
(i) Tariff classification of network cards for personal computers 4244
(ii) Tariff classification of drip irrigation products 4249

(iii) Tariff classification of unisex articles or shorts ... 4252

(iv) Tariff classification of blackout drapery lining ... 4255

(v) Tariff classification of liquid crystal display flat monitors with digital video interface ... 4276

(vi) Treatment of BTI in member States other than the issuing member State ... 4290

(vii) Refusal to withdraw revocation of BTI concerning Sony PlayStations2 in the context of the Sony PlayStation2 case ... 4297

(viii) Interpretation and application of an amendment to an explanatory note concerning camcorders in the Camcorders case ... 4302

(ix) Summary and conclusions ... 4307

(c) Allegations of non-uniform administration of the Community Customs Code and the Implementing Regulation in the area of customs valuation ... 4308

(i) Royalty payments ... 4308

(ii) Valuation on a basis other than the transaction of the last sale (or "successive sale") ... 4313

(iii) Vehicle repair costs covered under warranty ... 4317

(iv) Relationship between EC importer and non-EC manufacturers ... 4323

(v) Summary and conclusions ... 4330

(d) Allegations of non-uniform administration of the Community Customs Code and the Implementing Regulation in the area of customs procedures ... 4330

(i) Audit following release for free circulation ... 4330

(ii) Penalties against infringements of EC customs legislation ... 4338

(iii) Processing under customs control ... 4344

(iv) Local clearance procedures ... 4352

(v) Summary and conclusions ... 4356

(e) Allegations of non-uniform administration regarding Article 221(3) of the Community Customs Code 4357

(i) Summary of the parties' arguments 4357

(ii) Analysis by the Panel 4359

(f) Overall observations regarding the United States' allegations of non-uniform administration under Article X:3(a) of the GATT 1994 4362

E. Claims Under Article X:3(b) of the GATT 1994 4363

1. Article X:3(b) of the GATT 1994 4363

2. Findings requested by the United States under Article X:3(b) of the GATT 1994 4363

(a) Summary of the parties' arguments 4363

(b) Analysis by the Panel 4364

3. Interpretation of Article X:3(b) of the GATT 1994 4365

(a) Summary of the parties' arguments 4365

(i) Relevant features of review bodies 4365

(ii) Geographical coverage and substantive effect of decisions of review bodies 4366

(b) Analysis by the Panel 4373

4. Specific alleged violations of Article X:3(b) of the GATT 1994 4380

(a) Summary of the parties' arguments 4380

(b) Analysis by the Panel 4382

(i) Discharge of the European Communities' obligation under Article X:3(b) of the GATT 1994 4383

(ii) Review of administrative action relating to customs matters by authorities in the member States 4385

(iii) Summary and conclusions 4386

VIII. CONCLUSIONS AND RECOMMENDATIONS 4386

TABLE OF ANNEXES

ANNEX A

RESPONSES TO QUESTIONS POSED BY THE PANEL AND OTHER PARTIES AFTER THE FIRST SUBSTANTIVE MEETING OF THE PANEL

Contents	
Annex A-1	Responses of the United States to Questions posed by the Panel after the First Substantive Meeting
Annex A-2	Responses of the United States to Questions posed by the European Communities after the First Substantive Meeting
Annex A-3	Responses of the European Communities to Questions posed by the Panel after the First Substantive Meeting
Annex A-4	Responses of the European Communities to Questions posed by the United States after the First Substantive Meeting
Annex A-5	Responses of Argentina to Questions posed by the Panel after the First Substantive Meeting
Annex A-6	Responses of China to Questions posed by the Panel after the First Substantive Meeting
Annex A-7	Responses of Japan to Questions posed by the Panel after the First Substantive Meeting
Annex A-8	Responses of Korea to Questions posed by the Panel after the First Substantive Meeting
Annex A-9	Responses of the Separate Customs Territory of Taiwan, Penghu, Kinmen and Matsu after the First Substantive Meeting

ANNEX B

RESPONSES TO QUESTIONS POSED BY THE PANEL AND OTHER PARTIES AFTER THE SECOND SUBSTANTIVE MEETING OF THE PANEL

Contents	
Annex B-1	Responses of the United States to Questions posed by the Panel after the Second Substantive Meeting
Annex B-2	Responses of the European Communities to Questions posed by the Panel after the Second Substantive Meeting
Annex B-3	Comments of the United States on the European Communities' Responses to Questions posed by the Panel after the Second Substantive Meeting
Annex B-4	Comments of the European Communities on the United States' Responses to Questions posed by the Panel after the Second Substantive Meeting

ANNEX C

RESPONSES TO SUPPLEMENTARY QUESTIONS POSED BY THE PANEL REGARDING SECTION III OF THE UNITED STATES SECOND ORAL STATEMENT

Contents	
Annex C-1	Response of the European Communities to the Panel's Question No. 172 regarding section III of the US Second Oral Statement
Annex C-2	Responses of the United States to Supplementary Questions posed by the Panel regarding section III of the US Second Oral Statement
Annex C-3	Responses of the European Communities to Supplementary Questions posed by the Panel regarding section III of the US Second Oral Statement

ANNEX D

REQUEST FOR THE ESTABLISHMENT OF A PANEL

Contents	
Annex D-1	Request for the Establishment of a Panel by the United States (WT/DS315/8)

ANNEX E

PANEL'S WORKING PROCEDURES

Contents	
Annex E-1	Panel's Working Procedures

ANNEX F

LISTS OF EXHIBITS SUBMITTED BY THE PARTIES

Contents	
Annex F-1	List of Exhibits submitted by the United States
Annex F-2	List of Exhibits submitted by the European Communities

TABLE OF CASES CITED IN THIS REPORT

Short Title	Full Case Title and Citation of Case
Argentina – Footwear (EC)	Appellate Body Report, *Argentina – Safeguard Measures on Imports of Footwear*, WT/DS121/AB/R, adopted 12 January 2000
Argentina – Hides and Leather	Panel Report, *Argentina – Measures Affecting the Export of Bovine Hides and the Import of Finished Leather*, WT/DS155/R and Corr.1, adopted 16 February 2001
Argentina – Textiles and Apparel	Appellate Body Report, *Argentina – Measures Affecting Imports of Footwear, Textiles, Apparel and Other Items*, WT/DS56/AB/R and Corr.1, adopted 22 April 1998
Brazil – Desiccated Coconut	Appellate Body Report, *Brazil – Measures Affecting Desiccated Coconut*, WT/DS22/AB/R, adopted 20 March 1997
Canada – Gold Coins	GATT Panel Report, *Canada – Measures Affecting the Sale of Gold Coins*, L/5863, 17 September 1985
Canada – Wheat Exports and Grain Imports	Appellate Body Report, *Canada - Measures Relating to Exports of Wheat and Treatment of Imported Grain*, WT/DS276/AB/R, adopted 27 September 2004
Canada – Wheat Exports and Grain Imports	Panel Report, *Canada - Measures Relating to Exports of Wheat and Treatment of Imported Grain*, WT/DS276/R, adopted 27 September 2004 as upheld by the Appellate Body Report, WT/DS276/AB/R
Chile – Price Band System	Appellate Body Report, *Chile – Price Band System and Safeguard Measures Relating to Certain Agricultural Products*, WT/DS207/AB/R, adopted 23 October 2002
EC – Bananas III	Appellate Body Report, *European Communities – Regime for the Importation, Sale and Distribution of Bananas*, WT/DS27/AB/R, adopted 25 September 1997
EC – Chicken Cuts	Appellate Body Report, *European Communities – Customs Classification of Frozen Boneless Chicken Cuts*, WT/DS/269/AB/R, WT/DS286/AB/R

Short Title	Full Case Title and Citation of Case
EC – Chicken Cuts	Panel Report, *European Communities – Customs Classification of Frozen Boneless Chicken Cuts*, Complaint by Thailand, WT/DS286/R
EC – Computer Equipment	Appellate Body Report, *European Communities – Customs Classification of Certain Computer Equipment*, WT/DS62/AB/R, WT/DS67/AB/R; WT/DS68/AB/R, adopted 5 February 1998
EC – Hormones	Appellate Body Report, *EC Measures Concerning Meat and Meat Products (Hormones),* WT/DS26/AB/R, WT/DS48/AB/R, adopted 13 February 1998
EC – Poultry	Appellate Body Report, *European Communities – Measures Affecting the Importation of Certain Poultry Products*, WT/DS69/AB/R, adopted 23 July 1998
EC – Sardines	Appellate Body Report, *European Communities – Trade Description of Sardines*, WT/DS231/AB/R, adopted 23 October 2002
EC – Tariff Preferences	Appellate Body Report, *European Communities – Conditions for the Granting of Tariff Preferences to Developing Countries*, WT/DS246/AB/R, adopted 20 April 2004
EC – Trademarks and Geographical Indications (US)	Panel Report, *European Communities – Protection of Trademarks and Geographical Indications for Agricultural Products and Foodstuffs, Complaint by the United States*, WT/DS174/R, adopted 20 April 2005
EEC – Dessert Apples	GATT Panel Report, *European Economic Community – Restrictions on Imports of Dessert Apples – Complaint by Chile*, L/6491, adopted 22 June 1989, BISD 36S/93
Guatemala – Cement I	Appellate Body Report, *Guatemala – Anti-Dumping Investigation Regarding Portland Cement from Mexico*, WT/DS60/AB/R, adopted 25 November 1998
India – Patents (US)	Appellate Body Report, *India – Patent Protection for Pharmaceutical and Agricultural Chemical Products,* WT/DS50/AB/R, adopted 16 January 1998
Japan – Agricultural Products II	Appellate Body Report, *Japan – Measures Affecting Agricultural Products*, WT/DS76/AB/R, adopted 19 March 1999

Short Title	Full Case Title and Citation of Case
Japan – Alcoholic Beverages II	Appellate Body Report, *Japan – Taxes on Alcoholic Beverages*, WT/DS8/AB/R, WT/DS10/AB/R, WT/DS11/AB/R, adopted 1 November 1996
Japan – Film	Panel Report, *Japan – Measures Affecting Consumer Photographic Film and Paper*, WT/DS44/R, adopted 22 April 1998
Korea – Dairy	Appellate Body Report, *Korea – Definitive Safeguard Measure on Imports of Certain Dairy Products*, WT/DS98/AB/R, adopted 12 January 2000
Thailand – H-Beams	Appellate Body Report, *Thailand – Anti-Dumping Duties on Angles, Shapes and Sections of Iron or Non-Alloy Steel and H-Beams from Poland*, WT/DS1222/AB/R, adopted 5 April 2001
US – Carbon Steel	Appellate Body Report, *United States – Countervailing Duties on Certain Corrosion-Resistant Carbon Steel Flat Products from Germany*, WT/DS213/AB/R and Corr.1, adopted 19 December 2002
US – Corrosion-Resistant Steel Sunset Review	Appellate Body Report, *United States – Sunset Review of Anti-Dumping Duties on Corrosion-Resistant Carbon Steel Flat Products from Japan*, WT/DS244/AB/R, adopted 9 January 2004
US – Corrosion-Resistant Steel Sunset Review	Panel Report, *United States – Sunset Review of Anti-Dumping Duties on Corrosion-Resistant Carbon Steel Flat Products from Japan*, WT/DS244/R, adopted 9 January 2004, as modified by the Appellate Body Report, WT/DS244/AB/R
US – Gambling	Panel Report,*United States – Measures Affecting the Cross-Border Supply of Gambling and Betting Services*, WT/DS285/R, adopted 20 April 2005, as modified by the Appellate Body Report, WT/DS285/AB/R
US – Gasoline	Appellate Body Report, *United Sttates – Standards for Reformulated and Conventional Gasoline*, WT/DS2/AB/R, adopted 20 May 1996
US – Gasoline	Panel Report, *United States – Standards for Reformulated and Conventional Gasoline*, WT/DS2/R, adopted 20 May 1996, as modified by the Appellate Body Report, WT/DS2/AB/R

Short Title	Full Case Title and Citation of Case
US – Hot-Rolled Steel	Panel Report, *United States – Anti-Dumping Measures on Certain Hot-Rolled Steel Products from Japan*, WT/DS184/R, adopted 23 August 2001 as modified by the Appellate Body Report, WT/DS184/AB/R
US – Malt Beverages	GATT Panel Report, *United States – Measures Affecting Alcoholic and Malt Beverages*, adopted 19 June 1992, BISD 39S/206
US – Offset Act (Byrd Amendment)	Appellate Body Report, *United States – Continued Dumping and Subsidy Offset Act of 2000*, WT/DS217/AB/R, WT/DS234/AB/R, adopted 27 January 2003
US – Oil Country Tubular Goods from Mexico	Appellate Body Report, *Anti-Dumping Measures on Oil Country Tubular Goods (OCTG) from Mexico,* WT/DS282/AB/R, adopted 28 November 2005
US – Oil Country Tubular Goods Sunset Reviews	Appellate Body Report, *United States – Sunset Reviews of Anti-Dumping Measures on Oil Country Tubular Goods from Argentina*, WT/DS268/AB/R, adopted 17 December 2004
US – Section 301 Trade Act	Panel Report, *United States – Sections 301-310 of the Trade Act 1974*, WT/DS152/R, adopted 27 January 2000
US – Shrimp	Appellate Body Report, *United States – Import Prohibition of Certain Shrimp and Shrimp Products*, WT/DS58/AB/R, adopted 6 November 1998
US – Stainless Steel	Panel Report, *United States – Anti-Dumping Measures on Stainless Steel Plate in Coils and Stainless Steel Sheet and Strip from Korea*, WT/DS179/R, adopted 1 February 2001
US – Underwear	Appellate Body Report, *United States – Restrictions on Imports of Cotton and Man-made Fibre Underwear,* WT/DS24/AB/R, adopted 25 February 1997
US – Upland Cotton	Panel Report, *United States – Subsidies on Upland Cotton*, WT/DS267/R, adopted 21 March 2005 as modified by the Appellate Body Report, WT/DS267/AB/R
US – Wool Shirts and Blouses	Apellate Body Report, *United States – Measures Affecting Imports of Woven Wool Shirts and Blouses from India*, WT/DS33/AB/R and Corr.1, adopted 23 May 1997

LIST OF ABBREVIATIONS

BDL	Blackout drapery lining
BTI	Binding Tariff Information
CCC, the Code	Community Customs Code, Council Regulation (EEC) 2913/92
CFI	European Court of First Instance
CIS	Customs Information System
CN	European Communities Combined Nomenclature
Comitology Decision	Council Decision 1999/468/EC of 28 June 1999 laying down the procedures for the exercise of implementing powers conferred on the Commission
Commission, EC Commission	Commission of the European Communities
Council, EC Council	Council of the European Union
Court of Justice, European Court of Justice	Court of Justice of the European Communities
Customs Code Committee, the Committee	Committee established by Articles 247a (1) and 248a (1) of the CCC
Customs Valuation Agreement	Agreement on Implementation of Article VII of the General Agreement on Tariffs and Trade 1994
DSB	Dispute Settlement Body
DSU	Understanding on Rules and Procedures Governing the Settlement of Disputes
EBTI	European Binding Tariff Information
EC	European Communities
ECJ	European Court of Justice
ECR	European Court of Justice, Reports of Cases before the Court
EC Treaty	Treaty establishing the European Community
EU Treaty	Treaty on European Union

GATT	General Agreement on Tariffs and Trade 1994
HS	Harmonized Commodity and Coding System
HS Convention	International Convention on the Harmonized Commodity and Coding Sysdtem
Implementing Regulation,	Commission Regulation (EEC) 2454 of 2 July 1993 laying down provisions for the Implementation of the CCC
Kyoto Convention	International Convention on the Simplification and Harmonization of Customs Procedures
LCD monitors with DVI	Liquid crystal display flat monitors with digital video interface
LCP	Local clearance procedures
Member States, EC member States	Member States of the European Union
Official Journal	Official Journal of the European Union
PCC	Processing under customs control procedure
RIL	Reebok International Limited
Taric	Integrated Tariff of the European Communities
Tariff, the	Community Customs Tariff, Council Regulation (EEC) 2658/87
US	United States
USCIT	United States Court of International Trade
USTR	United States Trade Representative
WCO	World Customs Organization
WTO	World Trade Organization
WTO Agreement	Marrakesh Agreement Establishing the World Trade Organization

I. INTRODUCTION

1.1 On 21 September 2004, the United States requested consultations with the European Communities (EC) pursuant to Articles 1 and 4 of the Understanding on the Rules and Procedures Governing the Settlement of Disputes (DSU) and Article XXII:1 of the General Agreement on Tariffs and Trade 1994 (GATT 1994) (WT/DS315/1).

1.2 The request referred to the alleged non-uniform manner in which the European Communities administers its laws, regulations, decisions and rulings of the kind described in Article X:1 of GATT 1994 pertaining to the classification and valuation of products for customs purposes and to requirements, restrictions or prohibitions on imports.

1.3 The request identified the following measures: Council Regulation (EEC) No. 2913/92 of 12 October 1992 establishing the Community Customs Code, including all annexes thereto, as amended (the "Code"); Commission Regulation (EEC) No. 2454/93 of 2 July 1993 laying down provisions for the implementation of Council Regulation (EEC) No. 2913/92 of 12 October 1992 establishing the Community Customs Code, including all annexes thereto, as amended (the "Commission Regulation"); Council Regulation (EEC) No. 2658/87 of 23 July 1987 on the tariff and statistical nomenclature and on the Common Customs Tariff, including all annexes thereto, as amended (the "Tariff Regulation"); the Integrated Tariff of the European Communities established by virtue of Article 2 of Council Regulation (EEC) No. 2658/87 of 23 July 1987 on the tariff and statistical nomenclature and on the Common Customs Tariff, including all annexes thereto, as amended (the "TARIC"); and for each of the above laws and regulations, all amendments, implementing measures and other related measures.

1.4 The request also referred to the alleged failure of the European Communities to institute judicial, arbitral or administrative tribunals or procedures for the purpose, *inter alia*, of the prompt review and correction of administrative action relating to customs matters.

1.5 The United States and the European Communities held consultations on 16 November 2004 but failed to reach a mutually satisfactory resolution of the matter. Consequently, in a communication dated 13 January 2005[658], the United States requested the Dispute Settlement Body (DSB) to establish a panel. Accordingly, at its meeting of 21 March 2005, the DSB established the Panel with standard terms of reference. The terms of reference for the Panel are, therefore, the following:

> "To examine, in the light of the relevant provisions of the covered agreements cited by the United States in document WT/DS315/8, the matter referred to the DSB by the United States in that document and to make such findings as will assist the DSB in making the recommendations or in giving the rulings provided for in those agreements."

[658] WT/DS315/8 contained in Annex C.

1.6 On 17 May 2005, the United States requested the Director-General to determine the composition of the Panel, pursuant to paragraph 7 of Article 8 of the DSU. That paragraph provides:

> If there is no agreement on the panelists within 20 days after the date of the establishment of a panel, at the request of either party, the Director-General, in consultation with the Chairman of the DSB and the Chairman of the relevant Council or Committee, shall determine the composition of the panel by appointing the panelists whom the Director-General considers most appropriate in accordance with any relevant special or additional rules or procedures of the covered agreement or covered agreements which are at issue in the dispute, after consulting with the parties to the dispute. The Chairman of the DSB shall inform the Members of the composition of the panel thus formed no later than 10 days after the date the Chairman receives such a request.

1.7 On 27 May 2005, the Director-General accordingly composed the Panel as follows:

Chairman:	Mr. Nacer Benjelloun-Touimi
Members:	Mr. Mateo Diego-Fernández
	Mr. Hanspeter Tschäni

1.8 Argentina; Australia; Brazil; China; Hong Kong, China; India; Japan; Korea; and Chinese Taipei reserved their third party rights to participate in the Panel's proceedings.

1.9 The Panel held the first substantive meeting with the parties on 14-16 September 2005. The session with the third parties took place on 15 September 2005. The Panel's second substantive meeting with the parties was held on 22-23 November 2005.

1.10 On 10 January 2005, the Panel issued the Descriptive Part of its Panel Report. The Interim Report was issued to the parties on 10 February 2006 and the Final Report was issued to the parties on 31 March 2006.

II. FACTUAL ASPECTS

2.1 This dispute concerns, *inter alia*, the question of whether the manner in which the European Communities administers its laws, regulations, decisions and rulings of the kind described in Article X:1 of GATT 1994, pertaining to the classification and valuation of products for customs purposes and to requirements, restrictions or prohibitions on imports, complies with the obligation of uniform administration contained in Article X:3(a) of the GATT 1994. In particular, the United States argues that the following measures are not being administered in a uniform way by the European Communities in violation of Article X:3(a): (a) the "Community Customs Code" contained in Council Regulation (EEC) No. 2913/92 of 12 October 1992; (b) the "Implementing Regulation" implementing the Community Customs Code contained in Commission Regulation

(EEC) No. 2454/93 of 2 July 1993; (c) the "Common Customs Tariff", which was originally promulgated in Council Regulation (EEC) No. 2658/87 but which is updated annually in the EC Official Journal; (d) the "Taric", which is the Integrated Tariff of the European Communities established by virtue of Article 2 of the Council Regulation (EEC) No. 2658/87 of 23 July 1987 and (d) "related measures". The United States also challenges the alleged failure of the European Communities to provide for the review and correction of administrative action relating to customs matters in the manner prescribed by Article X:3(b) of the GATT 1994.

A. *The Legislative Framework for Administration of EC Customs Law*

2.2 The EC Treaty establishes a common commercial policy. According to Article 133(1) of the EC Treaty, the common commercial policy is based on uniform principles, particularly with regard to changes in tariff rates, the conclusion of tariff and trade agreements, the achievement of uniformity in measures of liberalisation, export policy, and measures to protect trade such as those to be taken in the event of dumping or subsidies. The ECJ has confirmed that the customs union and the common commercial policy, which includes administration of customs matters, fall within the exclusive competence of the European Communities.[659]

2.3 The three main instruments comprising the legislative framework for customs administration in the European Communities are: the Community Customs Tariff; the Community Customs Code; and the Implementing Regulation. Each of these instruments are EC regulations. Pursuant to Article 249(2) of the EC Treaty, they are binding in their entirety and directly applicable in all member States.

1. *The Community Customs Tariff*

2.4 The Community Customs Tariff was established by Council Regulation (EC) No. 2658/87 on 23 July 1987, which covers customs tariffs and the collection of international trade statistics. In turn, the Community Customs Tariff establishes the Combined Nomenclature (CN). Being a signatory to the HS Convention, the European Communities based the CN on the Harmonized System (HS). In particular, Article 1(2) of Regulation No. 2658/87 states that the CN is comprised of: (a) the harmonized system nomenclature; (b) EC subdivisions/headings to that nomenclature (where a corresponding duty rate is specified); and (c) preliminary provisions, additional sections or chapter notes and footnotes relating to subheadings. The preliminary provisions contain, *inter alia*, general rules for the interpretation of the CN.

2.5 The actual tariff nomenclature is contained in the Annex to Regulation No. 2658/87, which is updated on a periodic basis pursuant to Article 12 of the

[659] Opinion 1/75, *Local Cost Standard*, [1975] ECR 1355 (Exhibit EC-13).

Regulation. The current version of the Annex was published on 7 September 2004 and came into force on 1 January 2005 as Commission Regulation (EC) No. 1810/2004.

2.6 The CN has eight-digit codes, with the first six digits representing the HS codes (as required by the HS Convention) and the last two digits identifying CN subheadings. Additionally, there may be a 9th digit reserved for the use of national statistical subdivisions and a 10th and 11th digit for the Integrated Tariff of the European Communities, known as the "Taric".[660] Similar to the HS, the CN consists of 21 sections, covering 99 chapters. Some sections and chapters of the CN are preceded by notes.

2. *The Community Customs Code*

2.7 Council Regulation (EEC) No. 2913/92 establishes the Community Customs Code.[661] The Community Customs Code comprises 253 articles and is divided into nine Titles, dealing with the following topics – Title I: Scope and basic definitions; Title II: Factors on the basis of which import duties or export duties and the other measures prescribed in respect of trade in goods are applied; Title III: Provisions applicable to goods brought into the customs territory of the Community until they are assigned a customs-approved treatment or use; Title IV: Customs-approved treatment or use; Title V: Goods leaving the customs territory of the Community; Title VI: Privileged operations; Title VII: Customs debt; Title VIII: Appeals; Title IX: Final provisions.

3. *The Implementing Regulation*

2.8 According to Article 247 of the Community Customs Code, the measures necessary for the implementation of the Community Customs Code are to be adopted by the Commission. On the basis of Article 247, the Commission adopted Regulation (EEC) No. 2454 of 2 July 1993 laying down provisions for the Implementation of the Community Customs Code (the "Implementing Regulation").[662] The Implementing Regulation sets out in detail the provisions necessary for the implementation of the Community Customs Code. Its structure broadly follows that of the Community Customs Code.

B. *Institutions and Mechanisms Involved in the Administration of the EC Customs Laws*

1. *The Commission*

2.9 The Commission is not normally directly involved in the administration of EC customs law. Rather, Article 211 of the EC Treaty provides that the

---

[660] Article 2 of Regulation No. 2658/87 provides that the Taric shall be based on the CN. Section I of the TARIC explicitly states that it incorporates, *inter alia,* (a) the provisions of the HS; and (b) the provisions of the CN. The current version of the Taric is contained in Exhibit US-7.

[661] The current version of the Community Customs Code is contained in Exhibit US-5.

[662] The current version of the Implementing Regulation is contained in Exhibit US-6.

Commission shall "ensure that the provisions of this Treaty and the measures taken by the institutions pursuant thereto are applied". Generally, in the area of customs administration, the function of the European Commission as the guardian of the Treaty pursuant to Article 211 is to monitor the correct and uniform application of EC customs laws by the member States. Where the Commission considers that a member State has failed to fulfil an obligation under the Treaty, the Commission has the possibility, in accordance with the procedures of Article 226 of the EC Treaty, to bring the matter before the ECJ. Such "infringement proceedings" can be brought in response to any violation of Community law by a member State and can also concern the incorrect application of Community law by the administrations of the member States. In addition, there is a standardised procedure for complaints by individuals to be addressed to the European Commission regarding alleged infringements of Community law. Such complaints, which may also concern the application of Community law by national administrations, may lead to the institution of infringement proceedings by the Commission. In accordance with Article 228(1) of the EC Treaty, if the ECJ finds that a member State has failed to fulfil an obligation under the EC Treaty, the member State concerned is required to take the necessary measures to comply with the judgment of the ECJ. Where the member State concerned fails to comply with the judgment, the ECJ may impose a penalty payment on the member State pursuant to Article 228 (1) of the EC Treaty.

2.10 In the exercise of its duties under the EC Treaty, the public service of the European Commission is guided by a Code of Conduct which is part of the Commission's rules of procedure, and which sets out the principles of good administrative behaviour to be observed by all Commission staff.[663] In particular, Part 4 of the Code of Conduct provides that all enquiries must be dealt with as quickly as possible, and sets out time limits within which correspondence should be answered. Complaints regarding non-compliance with the Code of Conduct may be addressed to the Secretariat-General of the Commission. In addition, the Commission is politically responsible to the European Parliament. Moreover, in accordance with Article 194 of the EC Treaty, any citizen may direct a petition to the European Parliament on any matter which comes within the Community's fields of activity. Finally, in accordance with Article 195 of the EC Treaty, the European Parliament has appointed an Ombudsman empowered to receive complaints from individuals concerning instances of maladministration in the activities of the Community institutions or bodies.

2. *The member States*

(a) Legal effect of EC customs law on member States

2.11 Jurisprudence of the ECJ has established that the law of the European Community, including EC customs law, has primacy over the national law of the

[663] Exhibit EC-12.

member States.[664] The principle of primacy applies to all provisions contained in the EC Treaty (primary Community law) and in acts of the EC institutions (secondary Community law). It also applies in respect of any provision of national law at any level, including member States' constitutions.[665] In practical terms, the principle means that, whenever a court of a member State encounters a conflict between a provision of Community law and a provision of its national law, it must set aside the provision of national law and only apply Community law.

2.12 Jurisprudence of the ECJ has also established that Community law is directly effective in member States. This means that Community law may create rights for individuals, which can be directly invoked by those individuals in proceedings before national courts and authorities.[666] The principle of "direct effect" may apply both to primary Community law as well as to secondary Community law.

(b) Administration of EC customs law

2.13 Community customs law is executed by the national authorities of the member States. This arrangement is referred to as "executive federalism".[667] The principle of executive federalism within the European Communities reflects the principle of subsidiarity, which is enshrined in Article 5(2) of the EC Treaty, according to which the Community should take action only if and in so far as the objectives of the proposed action cannot be sufficiently achieved by the member States.

2.14 Article 10 of the EC Treaty imposes the following obligation on the member States regarding their administration, *inter alia* of EC customs law :

> Member States shall take all appropriate measures, whether general or particular, to ensure fulfilment of the obligations arising out of this Treaty or resulting from action taken by the institutions of the Community. They shall facilitate the achievement of the Community's tasks.
>
> They shall abstain from any measure which could jeopardise the attainment of the objectives of this Treaty.

3. The Customs Code Committee

2.15 The Customs Code Committee is established by Articles 247a(1) and 248a(1) of the Community Customs Code. The Customs Code Committee has

[664] Case 6/64, *Costa/E.N.E.L.*, [1964] ECR 1251, 1270 (Exhibit EC-4); Case 106/77, *Simmenthal II*, [1978] ECR 629, para. 17-18 (Exhibit EC-5).

[665] Case 11/70, *Internationale Handelsgesellschaft*, [1970] ECR 1125, para. 3 (Exhibit EC-6).

[666] Case 26/62, *Van Gend en Loos*, [1963] ECR 1, 25 (Exhibit EC-7).

[667] Koen Lenaerts/Piet van Nuffel, *Constitutional Law of the European Union*, 2nd ed, para. 14-047 (2005) (Exhibit EC-10).

adopted its own Rules of Procedure[668], which are based – with some minor modifications – on the standard rules of procedure for comitology committees.[669]

2.16 In accordance with Article 1(1) of its Rules of Procedure, the Customs Code Committee comprises the following sections: Section for General Customs Rules; Origin Section; Duty-Free Arrangements Section; Customs Valuation Section; Section for Customs Warehouses and Free Zones; Section for Customs Procedures with Economic Impact; Transit Section; Single Administrative Document Section; Repayment Section; Tariff and Statistical Nomenclature Section; Section on the Movement of Air or Sea Passengers' Baggage; Economic Tariff Questions Section; Counterfeit Goods Section; Section for favourable treatment (end-use of goods). The Customs Code Committee is composed of representatives from each member State and chaired by a representative of the Commission.

2.17 Article 249 of the Community Customs Code states that the Customs Code Committee has the authority to examine any question concerning customs legislation which is raised by its chairman, either on his own initiative or at the request of a member State's representative. A similar provision is found in Article 8 of Regulation No. 2658/87 establishing the Common Customs Tariff, according to which the Committee may examine any matter referred to it by its chairman, either on his own initiative or at the request of a representative of a member State, concerning the CN or the Taric.

2.18 In practice, the Customs Code Committee undertakes the following tasks: gives opinions on amendments to the Community Customs Code or implementing measures proposed by the Commission; examines questions concerning the interpretation of customs provisions or definitions of terms used in customs legislation; exercises powers granted by virtue of specific customs legislation e.g., Article 9(1) of Regulation No. 2658/87 regarding: (a) amendment of the CN (including the creation of statistical Taric sub-headings); (b) consideration of classification regulations; (c) determination of the position of the European Communities in the Harmonized System Committee. The opinions of the Customs Code Committee are not legally binding.[670]

2.19 Articles 247a and 248a of the Community Customs Code provide that the Customs Code Committee shall act as a regulatory or management committee. Article 247 of the Community Customs Code foresees that the measures necessary for the implementation of the Community Customs Code are normally adopted according to the regulatory procedure. In certain cases, including those mentioned in Article 248 of the Community Customs Code, the management procedure applies instead.

[668] Exhibit US-9. The Rules of Procedure of the Committee are also available on the public website of the European Commission:
http://europa.eu.int/comm/taxation_customs/customs/procedural_aspects/general/community_code/index_en.htm

[669] These standard rules of procedure have been published in the Official Journal (Exhibit EC-2).

[670] Joined Cases 69 and 70/76, *Dittmeyer*, [1977] ECR 231 (Exhibit EC-31).

2.20 According to Article 2 of the "Comitology Decision" contained in Decision 1999/468/EC,[671] the regulatory procedure should be applied for the adoption of "measures of general scope designed to apply essential provisions of basic instruments". Article 5 of the Comitology Decision provides that the Commission can adopt a proposed measure only if the Committee has agreed by qualified majority.[672] If no such majority has been reached or a qualified majority is against the proposal, the draft is submitted to the European Council. The European Council must then decide by qualified majority within 3 months, including to reject the measure in question. If no decision is taken within this time limit, the Commission adopts the proposed measure.

2.21 The "management procedure", which applies to "management measures",[673] is prescribed in Article 4 of Decision 1999/468/EC. That Article provides that, under this procedure, the Commission can adopt a proposed measure even when the Committee does not agree. However, if a negative opinion is rendered with a qualified majority by the Committee, the Commission must involve the European Council who can take a different decision with qualified majority within 3 months. The Commission can defer the application of the measure in such cases. In the event that the European Council takes no decision within three months, the suspended measure becomes applicable.

2.22 Community legal acts other than the Community Customs Code may also include references to the Customs Code Committee. In such cases, the applicable decision-making procedure is laid down in the provision attributing decision-making power to the Commission. One example is Article 10 of Regulation No. 2658/87 establishing the Common Customs Tariff, which provides that the Commission will be assisted by the Customs Code Committee in accordance with the management procedure.

4. *EC courts*

(a) Role and function of the courts of member States

2.23 The courts of the member States perform a dual role. When determining a dispute governed by national law, they form part of the national legal order. However, these national courts assume the status of Community courts when determining a case governed by Community law. The courts of the member States are competent to determine any dispute in cases where jurisdiction is not expressly conferred on the ECJ nor on the EC Court of First Instance. Pursuant to Article 234 of the EC Treaty, courts of member States may refer questions to the ECJ.

---

671 Exhibit US-10.

672 A "qualified majority" decision involves a weighing of the votes of the member States pursuant to Article 205(2) of the Treaty Establishing the European Community, as amended by Article 3 of the Protocol on the Enlargement of the European Union.

673 Article 2 of the Comitology Decision explains that "management measures" include measures relating to the application of the common agricultural and common fisheries policies, or to the implementation of programmes with substantial budgetary implications.

(b) Role and function of the ECJ

2.24 The ECJ and the Court of First Instance of the European Communities are constituted under the EC Treaty and the Protocol on the Statute of the ECJ annexed to it.[674] Both Courts are composed of one judge per member State and they normally decide in chambers of three or five judges. The ECJ is assisted by eight Advocates General, who provide opinions on cases.

2.25 According to Article 220 of the EC Treaty, the central task of the ECJ and the Court of First Instance is to ensure that, in the interpretation and application of the Treaty, the law is observed. Actions may be taken directly to the ECJ such as actions against member States for failure to fulfil an obligation under Community law (Articles 226-228 of the EC Treaty), actions for the annulment of a Community measure (Articles 230-231 of the EC Treaty), actions for failure by a Community institution to act (Article 232 of the EC Treaty), and actions for damages relating to the Community's non-contractual liability (Article 235 of the EC Treaty).

2.26 Proceedings before the ECJ may also originate from a national court under Article 234 of the EC Treaty. According to Article 234 EC, national courts may refer any question regarding the interpretation of Community law to the ECJ. With certain exceptions, member States' courts against whose decision there is no judicial remedy under national law are obliged to refer such questions to the ECJ.

2.27 Article 225(1) of the EC Treaty provides that the Court of First Instance shall have jurisdiction at the first instance in respect of actions for annulment, actions for failure to act, actions founded on non-contractual liability, staff cases and cases under arbitration clauses in Community contracts, with the exception of those reserved to the ECJ. According to Article 51 of the Statue of the Court of Justice, the ECJ shall hear actions brought by the Member States, the institutions of the Communities and by the European Central Bank. The ECJ may hear appeals on points of law from decisions of the Court of First Instance, where that Court has jurisdiction at first instance.

5. *Cooperation between the member States and between the member States and the Commission*

(a) Council Regulation (EC) No. 515/97

2.28 Council Regulation (EC) No. 515/97 on mutual assistance between the administrative authorities of the member States and cooperation between the latter and the Commission seeks to ensure the correct application of, *inter alia*, the law on customs matters.[675]

2.29 Title I of Regulation No. 515/97 deals with the provision of assistance on request between member States customs authorities. Title II deals with spontaneous assistance between customs authorities. Title III deals with relations between

[674] Exhibit US-42.
[675] Exhibit EC-42.

member States' customs authorities and the Commission. Title V establishes the Customs Information System, which is an automated information system for the use of the administrative authorities of the member States and the Commission to assist EC customs authorities in preventing, investigating, and prosecuting operations that are in breach of customs law.

(b) Action programmes

2.30 The Community has adopted and implemented successive action programmes aimed at strengthening the effective implementation of the EC customs union. The current action program, "Customs 2007", applies for the period of 1 January 2003 to 31 December 2007. It is established by Decision 253/2003/EC of the European Parliament and the Council.[676] The objectives of Customs 2007 are set out in Article 3 (1) of Decision 253/2003. According to this Article, the objectives of the program are to ensure that the member States' customs administrations:

(a) carry out coordinated action to ensure that customs activity matches the needs of the Community's internal market through implementing the strategy set out in the aforementioned Commission communication and Council resolution on a strategy for the customs union;

(b) interact and perform their duties as efficiently as though they were one administration and achieve equivalent results at every point of the Community customs territory;

(c) meet the demands placed on them by globalisation and increasing volumes of trade and contribute towards strengthening the competitive environment of the European Union;

(d) provide the necessary protection of the financial interests of the European Union and provide a secure and safe environment for its citizens;

(e) take the necessary steps to prepare for enlargement and to support the integration of new member States.

2.31 Customs 2007 foresees a number of programme actions, which include actions in the field of communication and information exchange systems, benchmarking, exchanges of officials, seminars, workshops and project groups, training activities, monitoring actions, and external actions in the form of technical assistance and training.

6. Training

2.32 The training of customs officials of the member States takes place primarily at the national level. In addition, a "Common Customs Training Programme" was developed in the context of Customs 2007.

---

[676] Exhibit EC-43.

7. Budgetary and financial control

2.33 According to Article 2(1)(b) of the Council Decision 2000/597/EC, Euratom on the system of the European Communities' own resources[677], common customs tariff duties and other duties established in respect of trade with non-member countries shall constitute an "own resource" entered into the budget of the European Communities. Article 17(1) of Council Regulation (EC/Euratom) No. 1150/2000[678] provides that member States must take all requisite measures to ensure that the amounts corresponding to the Community's entitlement are made available to the Community as specified in that Regulation. In accordance with Article 18(2)(a) of Regulation No. 1150/2000, the member States must, at the request of the EC Commission, carry out additional inspections, with which the Commission shall be associated at its request. According to Article 18(3) of Regulation No. 1150/2000, the Commission may also itself carry out inspection measures on the spot.

C. Specific Areas of Customs Administration Referred to by the United States in its Submissions

1. Tariff Classification

2.34 The term "tariff classification" is defined in Article 20(6) of the Community Customs Code as the relevant subheading of: (a) the CN or any other nomenclature based on it, with or without further subdivisions, which is used for the application of Community tariff measures relating to trade in goods (e.g., tariff suspensions, tariff preferences, anti-dumping duties); or (b) any other Community nomenclature based on the CN, with or without further subdivisions, which is used for the application of non-tariff measures relating to trade in goods (e.g., import quotas for textile products, export refunds for agricultural goods).

2.35 The obligation to classify products under the Community Customs Code is borne by "customs authorities", which are defined in Article 4(3) of the Community Customs Code as the authorities responsible *inter alia* for applying customs rules. In the context of the European Communities, which is a customs union and which has a common customs tariff between EC member States and third countries, the member State administrations are responsible for all operations relating to the implementation on a day-to-day basis of the CN, including the making of classification decisions.

2.36 Jurisprudence of the ECJ establishes that tariff classification is carried out on the basis "of the objective characteristics and properties of products which can be ascertained when customs clearance is obtained".[679] Classification instruments that may be applicable throughout the European Communities include classification regulations, HS explanatory notes and opinions, EC explanatory

---

[677] Exhibit EC-44.

[678] Exhibit EC-45.

[679] Case 38/76, *Luma*, [1976] ECR 2027, para. 7 (Exhibit EC-18); Case C-233/88, *van de Kolk*, [1990] ECR I-265, para. 12 (Exhibit EC-19).

notes, and opinions of the Customs Code Committee and binding tariff information.

(a) Classification Regulations

2.37 Pursuant to Article 9(1)(a) of Regulation No. 2658/87, the Commission may adopt regulations on the classification of goods. Such classification regulations are adopted by the Commission in accordance with the management procedure referred to in Article 10 of Regulation No. 2658/87. Classification regulations determine the tariff subheading to be applied to the specific good described in the Regulation but may also become relevant by analogy to products similar to those described in the regulation.[680] A classification regulation is binding throughout the Community in accordance with Article 249(2) of the EC Treaty but cannot amend the CN.[681]

(b) HS Explanatory Notes and WCO Opinions

2.38 According to Article 7(1)(b) of the HS Convention, the HS Committee can prepare Explanatory Notes, classification opinions and other advice as guidance to the interpretation of the HS. The ECJ has stated in its case law that, even though they are not normally binding in Community law, HS Explanatory Notes and classification opinions of the World Customs Organization (WCO) are important aids in the interpretation of the Common Customs Tariff.[682] Nevertheless, the ECJ has also judged that an interpretation of the HS approved by the WCO Council is binding on the Community when it reflects general practice followed by the member States, unless it is incompatible with the wording of the heading concerned or goes manifestly beyond the discretion conferred on the WCO.[683]

(c) Explanatory Notes of the Combined Nomenclature

2.39 According to Article 9(1)(a) of Regulation No. 2658/87, the Commission may issue explanatory notes to the CN. Such explanatory notes are adopted by the Commission in accordance with the management procedure foreseen in Article 10 of that Regulation. Explanatory notes may clarify particular issues of tariff classification arising under the CN but are distinct from the notes which introduce the chapters of the CN.[684] Explanatory notes to the CN are not legally bind-

---

[680] Case C-130/02, *Krings*, judgment of 4 March 2004 (not yet in the official reports), para. 35 (Exhibit EC-20).

[681] Case C-401/93, *GoldStar*, [1994] ECR I-5587, para. 19 (Exhibit EC-21); Case C-265/89, *Vismans*, [1990] ECR I-3411, para. 13 (Exhibit EC-22).

[682] Case C-396/02, *DFDS*, judgment of 16 September 2004 (not yet published), para. 28 (Exhibit EC-25); Case 14/70, *Deutsche Bakels,* [1970] ECR 1001, paras 9-10 (Exhibit EC-26).

[683] Cf. Case C-233/88, *van de Kolk*, [1990] ECR I-265, para. 9 (Exhibit EC-19).

[684] Case 183/73, *Osram,* [1974] ECR 477, para. 12 (Exhibit EC-27); Case 149/73, *Witt,* [1973] ECR 1587, para. 3 (Exhibit EC-28).

ing, and cannot amend the CN. However, the ECJ has repeatedly acknowledged that explanatory notes are an important aid in the interpretation of the CN.[685]

(d) Opinions of the Customs Code Committee

2.40 On the basis of Article 8 of Regulation No. 2658/87, the Customs Code Committee may adopt opinions on questions relating to the application and interpretation of the CN. Such opinions are distinct from opinions which the Committee adopts in the context of a comitology procedure on measures proposed by the Commission. Opinions adopted by the Committee are not legally binding. However, the ECJ has held that that such opinions constitute an important means of ensuring the uniform application of the common customs tariff by the authorities of the member States and, as such, can be considered as a valid aid to the interpretation of the Common Customs Tariff.[686]

(e) Binding tariff information

2.41 The basic provisions on binding tariff information ("BTI") are set out in Article 12 of the Community Customs Code. Further rules concerning binding information are contained in Title II of Part I of the Implementing Regulation (Articles 5-14). These additional provisions address, in particular, the procedures for obtaining binding information, measures to be taken in the event of binding information, the legal effect of binding information, and the expiry of binding information. In addition, the Commission has issued administrative guidelines on the European Binding Tariff Information (EBTI) System and its operation.[687]

2.42 The aim of binding information is to enable the trader to proceed with certainty where there are doubts as to the classification or origin of goods, thereby protecting the trader against any subsequent change in the position adopted by the customs authorities.

2.43 According to Article 6(1) of the Implementing Regulation, applications for binding information are to be made in writing, either to the customs authorities in the member State or member States in which the information is to be used, or to the competent customs authorities in the member State in which the applicant is established. In accordance with Article 6(5) of the Implementing Regulation, a list of the member States' authorities competent to issue BTI is regularly published in the Official Journal.[688]

2.44 The application must be made on a standard application form conforming to the specimen contained in Annex 1B to the Implementing Regulation. The details that an application for BTI must contain are set out in Article 6(3)(A) of the Implementing Regulation. According to Article 6(3)(A)(j), the application must contain the indication by the applicant whether, to his knowledge, BTI for

---

685 Case C-396/02, *DFDS*, judgment of 16 September 2004 (not yet published), para. 28 (Exhibit EC-25); Case C-259/97, *Clees*, [1998] ECR I-8127, para. 12 (Exhibit EC-29).

686 Joined Cases 69 and 70/76, Dittmeyer, [1977] ECR 231, para. 4 (Exhibit EC-31).

687 Exhibit EC-32.

688 Exhibit EC-33.

identical or similar goods has already been applied for, or issued in the Community.

2.45 Article 8(1) of the Implementing Regulation provides that a copy of the application for BTI, a copy of BTI notified to the applicant, and the information contained in copy 4 of the BTI form shall be transmitted to the Commission. This transmission is done by electronic means. In accordance with Article 8(3) of the Implementing Regulation, this data is stored in a database of the Commission, called the EBTI data base. There are two versions of this database. One is available to the public for consultation; the other is exclusively available to the Commission and issuing customs authorities of the member States. The version available to the public allows searches of valid BTI by issuing country, start and end date of validity, BTI reference, CN code, keyword, or product description. The public version of the EBTI database is accessible on the website of the European Commission.[689] The version available to the Commission and customs authorities of the member States contains additional information of a confidential nature, which is not made available to the public (i.e. the name and address of the applicant, holder and agent, if one has been appointed, confidential commercial details concerning the goods for which the BTI has been issued, including trade names). The version available to the Commission and issuing customs authorities also contains all applications for BTI that have been submitted to member State customs administrations and BTI that has ceased to be valid.[690] According to the administrative guidelines issued by the Commission on the EBTI system, the EBTI database should be consulted by customs authorities prior to the issuance of BTI in cases where there is a doubt regarding the correct classification, or where different headings merit consideration.[691]

2.46 As for who is responsible for issuing BTI, this is the task of member State customs authorities. In particular, Article 12 of the Community Customs Code provides that member State customs authorities must, upon written request, issue BTI. When the customs authorities have possession of all the elements necessary for them to determine the classification of the goods, BTI shall be notified to the applicant as soon as possible in accordance with Article 7(1) of the Implementing Regulation.

2.47 Article 10 of Implementing Regulation provides that BTI may only be invoked by the holder of the information or the holder's representative.[692] Articles 5 and 11 of the Implementing Regulation provide that BTI is binding on the administration of all member States. Further, according to Article 12(2) of the Community Customs Code, BTI will be binding on the customs authorities as against the holder of the BTI. Article 12(3) of the Community Customs Code clarifies that BTI will be binding only in respect of the tariff classification of

[689] http://europa.eu.int/comm/taxation_customs/dds/en/ebticau.htm.

[690] A copy of the search interface of the database available to the Commission and issuing authorities of the member States are contained in Exhibit EC-34.

[691] Exhibit EC-32, p. 7.

[692] Article 5(3) of the Implementing Regulation defines the "holder" of BTI to mean "the person in whose name the binding information is issued." The "holder" of BTI need not be the same as the "applicant" for BTI.

goods that correspond in every respect to those described in the information. Article 12(4) of the Community Customs Code indicates that BTI will be valid for a period of six years but may be annulled where the customs authorities determine that the information is based on inaccurate or incomplete information from the applicant. Article 12(5) of the Community Customs Code identifies the circumstances in which BTI shall cease to be valid, including where BTI is revoked or amended in accordance with Article 9. Article 9 of the Community Customs Code, in turn, provides for revocation or amendment of BTI where "one or more of the conditions laid down for its issue were not or are no longer fulfilled." The ECJ has held that a member State customs authority is entitled to consider that one of the provisions laid down for the issuance of BTI is no longer fulfilled and to revoke that BTI where, on more detailed examination, it appears to that authority that its initial interpretation of the legal provisions applicable to the tariff classification of the goods concerned "is wrong, following an error of assessment or evolution in the thinking in relation to tariff classification"[693].

2.48 The procedure that will apply in the event of inconsistencies arising in BTI is set out in Article 9 of the Implementing Regulation. In particular, such inconsistencies may be considered by the Customs Code Committee if it has been placed on the agenda of the next meeting of the Committee by the Commission or at the request of a representative of a member State. Article 9 further provides that, in light of such inconsistencies, the Commission must adopt a measure to ensure the uniform application of the CN rules, as applicable, as soon as possible and within six months following the meeting at which the inconsistency is placed on the agenda of the Customs Code Committee. The measures foreseen in Article 9(1) of the Implementing Regulation may take the form of a classification regulation adopted by the Commission on the basis of Article 9(1)(a) of Regulation No. 2658/87. In accordance with Article 12(5)(a)(i) of the Community Customs Code, where such a regulation is adopted, BTI which is not in accordance with it will cease to be valid. Alternatively, the Commission may also, on the basis of Article 12(5)(a)(iii) of the Community Customs Code and Article 9(1) of the Implementing Regulation, adopt a decision obliging the member State who issued BTI to revoke it.

2. *Customs valuation*

2.49 Where customs duties are calculated on an *ad valorem* basis – that is, they are expressed as a percentage of the value of the good – the assessment of duties owed must include the valuation of the good.

2.50 The basic provisions on customs valuation are contained in Chapter 3 of Title II of the Community Customs Code (Articles 28-36). More detailed provisions are contained in Title V of the Implementing Regulation (Articles 141-181a). Title V is subdivided into seven chapters, concerning general provisions;

---

[693] *Timmermans Transport & Logistics BV v. Inspecteur der Belastingdienst – Douanendistrict Rososendaal and Hoogenboom Production Lts. v. Inspecteur der Belastingdienst – Douanendistrict Rotterdam*, Joined Cases C-133/02 and C-134/02, 2004 ECR I-01125, 22 January 2004, para. 25 (Exhibit US-2).

royalties and licensing fees; the place of introduction into the Community; transport costs; rates of exchange; simplified procedures for perishable goods; and declarations of particulars and documents to be furnished. In addition, Annex 23 of the Implementing Regulation contains interpretative notes on customs valuation. Article 141(1) of the Implementing Regulation requires that, when applying the provisions of the Community Customs Code and the Implementing Regulation, member States shall comply with the interpretative notes.

2.51 Pursuant to Article 29 of the Community Customs Code, the primary basis for determination of customs value in the European Communities is the "transaction value" – that is, the price actually paid or payable for the imported goods. The transaction value may be used for imported goods provided that none of the restrictions or conditions leading to the rejection of the transaction value applies.

2.52 According to Article 32 of the Community Customs Code, the transaction value must be adjusted by *additions* to the price for: (a) commissions and brokerage; (b) the cost of containers and packing; (c) goods and services supplied by the buyer; (d) any royalties or licence fees related to the goods; (e) the proceeds to the seller of any subsequent resale, disposal or use of the imported merchandise; and (f) the costs of transport, insurance, loading and handling charges in the exporting country. Articles 157 - 159 of the Implementing Regulation provide further guidance concerning the meaning of "royalties" and the circumstances when they should be included in the transaction value. Article 33 of the Community Customs Code provides that the transaction cost must also be adjusted by *deductions* to the price for, for example: (a) costs for transportation within the European Communities; and (b) EC customs duties, antidumping duties and other charges payable in the European Communities by reason of the importation or sale of the goods.

2.53 The transaction value is the preferred and primary method of valuation and is used in most instances. However, pursuant to Article 29(1)(b) of the Community Customs Code, the transaction value may be rejected if, *inter alia*, the buyer and seller are "related" parties. Article 143 of the Implementing Regulation defines "related" parties to include cases such as: (a) where the parties are legally recognized partners in business; and (b) one of them directly or indirectly controls the other. Article 29(2) of the Community Customs Code makes it clear that the existence of a legal relationship between the buyer and seller does not necessarily mean that the transaction value will be rejected. This will only occur if the relationship influences the price. Annex 23 of the Implementing Regulation, which contains interpretative notes on custom value, explains in more detail when the transaction value should be disregarded in light of the relationship between buyer and seller.

2.54 Article 30 of the Community Customs Code provides that, if the transaction value cannot be used, alternative bases for valuation are to be used in the following sequential order: (a) the transaction value of identical goods; (b) the transaction value of similar goods; (c) the unit price at which the imported or identical or similar goods are sold in the greatest aggregate quantity to persons not related to the sellers; and (d) the computed value, which is the production cost including general expenses and the usual amount of profit. Annex 23 of the Implementing Regulations provides additional guidance regarding when these alternative methods can be used.

2.55 Article 147(1) of the Implementing Regulation provides that, for the purposes of Article 29 of the Community Customs Code, the fact that the goods which are the subject of a sale are declared for free circulation shall be regarded as adequate indication that they were sold for export to the customs territory of the Community. Article 147(1) of the Implementing Regulation further provides that, in the case of successive sales before valuation, only the last sale, which led to the introduction of the goods into the customs territory of the Community, or a sale taking place in the customs territory of the Community before entry for free circulation of the goods, shall constitute such indication.

2.56 Where a need for further detailed rules on valuation occurs, the Commission may, in accordance with the procedure referred to in Article 247 of the Community Customs Code, amend the valuation rules contained in the Implementing Regulation, which will be legally binding in all member States. In addition, in accordance with Article 249 of the Community Customs Code, the Customs Code Committee (through its Customs Valuation Section) may examine questions concerning the application of EC customs legislation in the field of valuation. The Commission has also issued a Compendium of Customs Valuation texts which contains commentaries prepared and conclusions reached by the Customs Code Committee on specific issues of customs valuation on the basis of Article 249 of the Community Customs Code. In addition, it contains excerpts from relevant judgments of the ECJ on valuation issues, as well as indices of other relevant texts.[694]

3. *Audit following release for free circulation*

2.57 Article 78 of the Community Customs Code authorizes customs authorities to inspect the commercial documents and data relating to any imports or exports or to subsequent commercial operations involving them. Such inspections help customs authorities to be in a position to satisfy themselves as to the accuracy of the particulars contained in the relevant customs declaration. Such inspections may be carried out at the premises of the declarant or of any person directly or indirectly involved in these operations. Customs authorities may also examine goods where it is still possible for them to be produced.

2.58 No provisions in the Community Customs Code nor in the Implementing Regulation oblige customs authorities to conduct audits following the release of goods for free circulation or impose any obligations on the manner in which such audits are to be conducted. However, the EC Commission in conjunction with the member States has prepared a Community Customs Audit Guide[695], which sets out a framework for post-clearance and audit-based controls.

---

[694] Exhibit EC-37.

[695] Exhibit EC-90.

4. *Penalties for infringements of EC customs law*

2.59 There are no provisions in the Community Customs Code nor in the Implementing Regulation that define the penalties applicable for violations of EC customs law. Therefore, as a general rule, the nature and level of such penalties, whether administrative or criminal in nature, are determined by the national laws of the member States. Nevertheless, in furtherance of Article 10 of the EC Treaty, member States must take all measures necessary for the proper implementation and application of EC law, including the provision of penalties for violations of EC law. In particular, they must ensure that particular infringements of Community law are penalized under conditions, both procedural and substantive, which are analogous to those applicable to infringements of national law of a similar nature and importance and which, in any event, make the penalty effective, proportionate and dissuasive.[696] This has been confirmed by Council resolution of 29 June 1995 on the effective uniform application of Community law and on the penalties applicable for breaches of Community law in the internal market, which recalls the relevant case law of the ECJ and calls upon member States to ensure that "Community law is duly applied with the same effectiveness and thoroughness as national law and that, in any event, the penalty provisions adopted are effective, proportionate and dissuasive".[697] Where a member State fails to provide such effective, proportionate and dissuasive penalities, it fails to fulfil its obligations under the EC Treaty.[698]

5. *Processing under customs control*

2.60 Article 130 of the Community Customs Code states that the procedure for processing under customs control allows non-Community goods to be used in the customs territory of the Community in operations which alter their nature or state, without being subject to import duties or commercial policy measures, and thereafter allows the processed products to be released for free circulation at the rate of import duty applicable to the processed products.

2.61 Article 85 of the Community Customs Code provides that the use of the procedure for processing under customs control (which is defined as a customs procedure with economic impact) is conditional upon authorization being issued by the customs authorities at the request of the person who carries out the processing or arranges for it to be carried out. Authorization will only be granted if certain conditions are fulfilled. One such condition is contained in Article 133(e) of the Community Customs Code.

2.62 Article 133(e) of the Community Customs Code provides that, before granting authorization under Article 85, the customs authorities must examine

---

[696] Case C-68/88, *Commission/Greece*, [1989] ECR 2965, para. 23-25 (Exhibit EC-38); similarly, Case C-326/88, *Hansen*, [1990] ECR I-2911, para. 17 (Exhibit EC-39); Case C-36/94, *Siesse*, [1995] ECR I-3573, para. 20 (Exhibit EC-40); Case C-213/99, *Andrade*, [2000] ECR I-11083, para. 19, 20 (Exhibit US-31).

[697] Exhibit EC-41.

[698] Case C-68/88, *Commission/Greece*, [1989] ECR 2965, para. 23-25 (Exhibit EC-38), where Greece was found to have violated its obligations under Article 10 of the EC Treaty.

the economic consequences of the use of the processing under customs control procedures to determine whether or not the procedure helps to create or maintain a processing activity in the European Communities without adversely affecting the essential interests of EC producers of similar goods. Article 502(3) of the Implementing Regulation provides that, in respect of processing under customs control arrangements, the examination shall establish whether the use of non-Community sources enables processing activities to be created or maintained in the Community.

2.63 Article 552 and Part A of Annex 76 of the Implementing Regulation set out the cases in which the economic conditions are deemed to be fulfilled so that, in those cases, an examination of the economic conditions is not necessary. For the types of goods and operations mentioned in Part B of Annex 76 of the Implementing Regulation and those not covered by Part A of that Annex, the examination of the economic conditions must take place at Community level, through the relevant Committee procedure. For the types of goods and operations not mentioned in Annex 76 of the Implementing Regulation, pursuant to Articles 502(1) and 552(1) of the Implementing Regulation, the examination of the economic conditions shall take place at national level. When examinations take place at the national level, member States must communicate to the Commission relevant information in accordance with Article 522 of the Implementing Regulation. Furthermore, pursuant to Articles 503 and 504 of the Implementing Regulation, if a member State objects to an authorization issued or if the customs authorities concerned wish to consult before or after issuing an authorization, an examination of the economic condition may take place at Community level.

6. *Local clearance procedures*

2.64 Pursuant to Article 263 of the Implementing Regulation, customs authorities of EC member States may allow, upon request, the use of the "local clearance procedure" to any applicant wishing to have goods released for free circulation at the applicant's premises or at other designated places. In other words, an importer may have goods released for free circulation at its own premises or certain other designated locations without having to present the goods to customs.

2.65 The basic provision for the local clearance procedure is Article 76(1)(c) of the Community Customs Code. Additionally, where a data-processing technique is used, Article 77 of the Community Customs Code shall apply. More detailed provisions are laid down in Articles 263 – 267 of the Implementing Regulation.

2.66 Under Article 263 of the Implementing Regulation, authorisation to use the local clearance procedure shall be granted to any person wishing to have goods released for free circulation at his premises or at the other places designated or approved by the customs authorities in respect of goods subject to certain procedures (transit or customs procedures with economic impact) or which are brought into the customs territory of the Community with an exemption from the requirement that they be presented to customs. Article 264(1) of the Implementing Regulation provides that authorisation for local clearance will be granted provided that the applicant's records enable the customs authorities to carry out effective checks.

7. *Recovery of customs debt*

2.67 Revenue from import and export duties based on the Common Customs Tariff constitutes "own resources" pursuant to Article 2(1)(b) of the Council Decision 2000/597/EC, Euratom. Articles 217 – 220 of the Community Customs Code govern the entry into the accounts of the member States and, therefore, constitute the link between, on the one hand, the obligations of the debtor to pay import or export duty to the national customs administration and, on the other hand, the member States' obligation to make the "own resources" available to the European Communities. Pursuant to Article 221 of the Community Customs Code, as soon as the amount has been entered into the accounts, it must be communicated to the debtor in accordance with the appropriate procedures. Article 221(3) of the Community Customs Code stipulates the period of time within which the debt must be communicated to the debtor.

D. *Review of Customs Decisions*

1. *Decisions the subject of judicial review*

2.68 A "decision" is defined in Article 4(5) of the Community Customs Code as any "official act by the customs authorities pertaining to customs rules giving a ruling on a particular case, such act having legal effects on one or more specific or identifiable persons; this term covers, *inter alia*, binding information within the meaning of Article 12 [of the Community Customs Code]". In addition, Article 6(3) of Community Customs Code provides that "[d]ecisions adopted by the customs authorities in writing which either reject requests or are detrimental to the persons to whom they are addressed shall set out the grounds on which they are based. They shall refer to the right of appeal provided for in Article 243".

2.69 Article 243(1) of the Community Customs Code provides that any person directly and individually concerned by a *decision* of the customs authorities regarding the application of customs legislation has the right to lodge an appeal. An appeal is also possible where a requested decision has not been taken within the time period stipulated in Article 6(2) of the Community Customs Code.

2. *Review by member States' customs authorities and courts*

2.70 Article 243(1) of the Community Customs Code states that an appeal must be lodged in the member State where the relevant decision has been taken or applied for. In addition, Article 245 of the Community Customs Code states that "provisions for the implementation of the appeals procedure shall be determined by the member States", meaning that appeals procedures are laid down in the national laws of the member States.

2.71 Article 243(2) indicates that the right of appeal may be exercised: (a) initially before the customs authorities designated for that purpose by the member States; and (b) subsequently, before an independent body, which may be a judicial authority or an equivalent specialised body, according to the provisions in force in the member States.

2.72 With respect to review by customs authorities designated in member States, this is required in most member States. However, in Belgium, Estonia, Greece, Cyprus, France, Malta and Portugal, administrative reviews are voluntary. Further, in Sweden, there is no administrative review and the administrative decision has to be appealed directly to the courts. Administrative authorities in the member States can repeal, revoke, alter or replace a disputed administrative decision.

2.73 Regarding appeals to member States' courts, most such courts are only entitled to annul the administrative decision should they consider it unlawful. However, in some cases, the courts may substitute their own decisions in cases involving the payment of duties. A few national courts have the power to substitute or amend the administrative decision challenged: Denmark, Latvia, the Netherlands, Sweden and Slovenia.

3. Direct appeals to the ECJ

2.74 Article 230 of the EC Treaty vests individuals with the right to approach the Court of First Instance directly in certain cases. Article 230, which concerns actions for annulment, deals with the jurisdiction of the ECJ to review the legality of acts jointly adopted by the European Parliament and the Council, the European Commission and the ECB, or by the Council itself or the Parliament where the act is intended to produce legal effects vis-à-vis third parties. An action for annulment under Article 230 does not cover acts adopted by a national authority. Nor does it extend to the EC Treaty and its amendments.

III. PARTIES' REQUESTS FOR FINDINGS AND RECOMMENDATIONS

A. United States[699]

3.1 The United States requests the Panel to:

(a) find that the European Communities is not in conformity with Article X:3(a) and Article X:3(b) of the GATT 1994;

(b) recommend that the European Communities bring itself into compliance with Article X:3(a) and Article X:3(b) of the GATT 1994 promptly.

[699] US First Written Submission, para. 155, and Second Written Submission, para. 117.

B. European Communities[700]

3.2 The European Communities requests the Panel to reject the claims raised by the United States.

IV. ARGUMENTS OF THE PARTIES

4.1 The arguments of the parties' are set out in their written and oral submissions to the Panel, and in their answers to questions. The parties' arguments as presented in their submissions are summarized in this section. The summaries are based on the executive summaries submitted by the parties. The parties' written answers to questions from the Panel and from each other are set out in the Annexes to this Report (see list of Annexes at page xvi).

A. First Written Submission of the United States

1. Introduction

4.2 This dispute raises two questions: First, does the European Communities ("EC") administer its customs laws, regulations, judicial decisions and administrative rulings of general application in a uniform, impartial and reasonable manner, as required by Article X:3(a) of the *General Agreement on Tariffs and Trade 1994* ("GATT 1994")? Second, does the EC have in place judicial, arbitral or administrative tribunals or procedures for the purpose, *inter alia*, of the prompt review and correction of administrative action relating to customs matters, as required by Article X:3(b) of the GATT 1994? The answer to both questions is, no.

4.3 Instead of administering its basic customs law in a uniform way, the EC administers it in 25 different ways. As administration is the responsibility of each member State, questions of classification and valuation may be subject to as many as 25 different interpretations, and traders are subject to 25 different procedural regimes for bringing goods into free circulation in the EC. The net result is an administration that distorts rather than facilitates trade and that imposes transaction costs that should not exist where administration is uniform.

4.4 This problem is magnified by the absence of EC tribunals or procedures for the prompt review and correction of administrative action relating to customs matters. Like the administration of EC customs measures, appeals from customs decisions are a matter for each member State. As a result, there are 25 different appellate regimes in the EC, none of which can yield a decision with EC-wide effect, unless and until a question is referred to the Court of Justice of the European Communities ("the ECJ").

4.5 In the EC, the basic elements of the customs system are laid out in three pieces of legislation: the Community Customs Code ("CCC"), the CCC Implementing Regulation ("Implementing Regulation" or "CCCIR"), and the Common Customs Tariff ("the Tariff"). These measures (as well as related measures) are

[700] EC First Written Submission, para. 477, and Second Written Submission, para. 246.

administered separately by the customs authorities in each of the 25 member States of the EC. There is a Customs Code Committee ("the Committee"), consisting of representatives of each of the member States and chaired by a representative of the Commission. Ostensibly, one of its functions is to reconcile divergences that emerge in member State administration of EC customs law. However, serious institutional constraints prevent it from fulfilling that function on a systematic basis.

4.6 Where a trader disputes a decision by a member State's customs authorities, its only recourse is to appeal that decision through the courts or other review tribunals of the member State. There is no EC forum to which a trader can promptly appeal a decision by a member State's customs authorities, including a decision that diverges from decisions of other member State authorities.

4.7 As a Member of the WTO in its own right, that is, separately from its constituent member States, the EC has an obligation to provide for administration of its customs laws and to provide for the prompt review and correction of administrative action relating to customs matters in the manner prescribed by GATT Articles X:3(a) and (b), respectively. The first question raised by this dispute is whether the EC administers its customs law in a uniform manner, as required by Article X:3(a). Considering the ordinary meaning to be given to the terms of that article, the question is whether the EC manages, carries on, or executes its customs law in a manner that is the same in different places or circumstances, or at different times. Of particular relevance here is uniformity with respect to different places.

4.8 One of the few panels to probe Article X:3(a) in any detail was the panel in *Argentina – Measures Affecting the Export of Bovine Hides and the Import of Finished Leather* ("*Argentina – Hides and Leather*"). The panel report in that dispute supports the proposition that the requirement of uniform administration in Article X:3(a) includes administration that is uniform across the territory of a WTO Member. The EC does not administer its customs law in a manner that is uniform across different places in the EC, as Article X:3(a) requires. It administers its customs law in a manner that varies from member State to member State and fails to provide an EC mechanism for the systematic reconciliation of such variations.

2. *The EC fails to administer its customs law in a uniform manner*

(a) Customs classification

4.9 One area in which divergent administration of EC customs law is especially troubling is customs classification. Not surprisingly, when 25 different authorities are tasked with interpreting a complex nomenclature system, the possibilities for divergent interpretations are substantial. Indeed, the EC evidently was quite candid about this in its dispute with Thailand and Brazil over the classification of frozen boneless chicken cuts (*European Communities – Customs Classification of Frozen Boneless Chicken Cuts*). Neither the Code, nor any other provision of EC law of which the United States is aware, requires one member State to follow another member State's interpretation of the Tariff. If one member State classifies a product under a particular tariff subheading, there is no requirement that other member States classify it under the same subheading. *A fortiori*, there is no requirement that other member States follow the rationale of the first member State in classifying *similar* goods.

4.10 It is instructive to consider administration of the EC's provision for advance classification rulings, known as binding tariff information ("BTI"). Under the BTI system, an importer or other interested party applies to a member State's customs authorities for issuance of BTI confirming the classification that will be assigned to particular goods on importation into the territory of that member State. The application may be made by the "holder" of the BTI (i.e. the person in whose name it is issued), or by another "applicant" (defined as any person who applies for BTI). The holder or other applicant chooses the member State to which it will make the application.

4.11 Once issued, BTI is "binding on the customs authorities as against the holder of the information." Article 11 of the Implementing Regulation states that BTI issued by the authorities of one member State is "binding on the competent authorities of all the Member States under the same conditions." However, in reality member States do not always treat BTI issued by other member States as binding, and the BTI system does not ensure uniform administration of customs classifications. Moreover, pre-existing BTI issued by one member State does not prevent an applicant from trying to persuade a second member State that the classification in the original BTI was mistaken. In issuing the new BTI, nothing in the Code or Implementing Regulation requires the authorities to adhere to the findings contained in the previously issued BTI.

4.12 There are several ways in which the BTI system fails to achieve uniform administration with respect to classification. The first way is that it results in BTI shopping. In theory, the Commission should be able to control BTI shopping by exercising its authority to reconcile inconsistent BTI. However, there are several impediments to the Commission performing this function. First, it may be difficult to detect whether, in fact, "different binding information exists." BTI is particular to the holder. Thus, it is possible for two different holders to possess conflicting BTI for identical merchandise. That "different binding information exists" would not be readily apparent in that case. Even where the same holder possesses conflicting BTI, the existence of the conflict may not be readily apparent to the Commission or the representative of a member State. The holder of the BTI may choose not to bring the conflict to the attention of the Committee. Other persons interested in having the difference reconciled (e.g., competitors) would not necessarily be aware of the conflict. Conversely, where a holder or other interested person is aware of conflicting BTI and wants to see the conflict resolved, it has no right to have the matter put before the Committee for resolution within a prescribed period of time.

4.13 Moreover, differences in classification of identical goods from member State to member State need not necessarily manifest themselves through conflicting BTI. It is possible for an applicant to receive unfavorable BTI from one member State and simply import the goods at issue through another member State (possibly incurring additional shipping, distribution, or other costs) without necessarily seeking BTI from that State. In that case, the existence of a difference would not necessarily be apparent to the Commission.

4.14 The EC does have in place an electronic database available to the public for searching BTI. In theory, one might be able to use the database to determine whether different member States had issued conflicting BTI for identical products. However, as a practical matter, such a search is extremely difficult, if not impossible.

4.15 Moreover, the inability to achieve uniform application of the Tariff through the BTI system is further demonstrated by the relative autonomy that each member State has with respect to revocation or amendment of BTI. In a recent decision, in a case known as *Timmermans*, the ECJ held that a member State customs authority can revoke BTI based on its own reconsideration of the Tariff (as opposed to the revelation of facts not before it when the BTI was issued). The Court reached this conclusion, even though the Advocate General had recommended the opposite conclusion, observing that "the possibility of revoking BTI in this way is not readily compatible either with the objective of the uniform application of the customs nomenclature or with the objective of legal certainty pursued by the introduction of BTI." Indeed, this is precisely the problem from the point of view of GATT Article X:3(a). Whatever limited potential the BTI system might have to provide for some degree of uniformity across the EC with respect to the particular goods and holder that are the subject of the BTI is further undermined by the fact that revisions to BTI are not even ostensibly "binding."

4.16 Finally, the problem of non-uniform administration of EC law on customs classification is illustrated by two recent (but by no means isolated) cases. In one case, German customs authorities have diverged from other member State authorities in the classification of a specialized textile product (blackout drapery lining) for five years, and EC institutions have not reconciled the divergence. In the second case, involving liquid crystal display flat monitors with digital video interface, the question of divergent classification (between the Netherlands, on the one hand, and other member States, on the other) was brought before the Committee in 2004 and, with respect to a major subset of the product concerned, remains unresolved today (and is subject to a temporary solution only with respect to the rest).

(b) Customs valuation

4.17 In some respects, the problems of non-uniform administration of customs law are even more pronounced in the area of valuation than they are in the area of classification. Unlike classification, EC customs law on valuation does not even provide a system comparable to BTI – that is, an information system that is ostensibly binding (albeit in a very limited way) and that (depending on how designed and administered) could at least be a step towards achieving uniform administration. In general, the ability of EC institutions to step into the breach to impose uniformity is limited. The valuation section of the Committee does not have the authority to examine individual cases with a view to reconciling differences in administration from member State to member State.

4.18 The ways in which the valuation provisions of the Code and Implementing Regulation have been applied differently in different member States were catalogued in great detail in a December 2000 report by the EC Court of Auditors. One highlight of the Court's report is differential treatment of royalty payments. Under Article 32(1)(c) of the Code, royalties and license fees related to the goods being valued are supposed to be added to the price actually paid or payable, to the extent not already included. The Court found that in a number of cases, different member States apportioned royalties differently to the customs value of identical goods imported by the same company. Significantly, it found that in the cases identified, the member States involved either did not bring the disparate treatment to the attention of the Committee, or the matter was not examined by the Committee.

4.19 Another issue the Court examined was application of the rule that allows imported goods, in certain cases, to be valued on a basis other than the transaction of the last sale which led to the introduction of the goods into the customs territory of the EC. The Court found that authorities in some member States but not others required importers to obtain prior approval for valuation on a basis other than the transaction value of the last sale.

4.20 A third issue identified by the Court was differential treatment of vehicle repair costs covered under warranty. In at least one member State – Germany – the Court found that customs authorities reduced the customs value of imported vehicles by the value of repairs undertaken in the territory of the EC and reimbursed by the foreign seller. Other member States – in particular, Italy, the Netherlands, and the United Kingdom – declined requests for similar customs value reductions. Of particular note, the Court observed that the Commission had been aware of differential treatment among member States for at least ten years and had not taken any steps to reconcile the difference. In response, the Commission noted that since 1997 it had "attempted to align by means of implementing legislation diverging practices in the Community" but was unable to attain the necessary majorities in the Committee.

4.21 A recent case involving non-uniform administration of EC customs valuation law concerns divergent approaches to the determination of whether an importer has a control relationship with its off-shore suppliers. In that case, Spanish customs authorities found Reebok International Limited (RIL) to have a control relationship with suppliers outside the EC based on its contracts with those suppliers, while other member States (in particular, the Netherlands) found no such relationship. The different interpretation has significant consequences. Member State authorities that agreed with RIL that it did not have a control relationship with its suppliers allowed it to declare the customs value of its goods on the basis of the "sale for export" transaction value rule set out in Article 29 of the Code. On the other hand, the Spanish authorities required RIL to apply a different methodology. The net impact on RIL was an additional customs liability of 350,000 Euros per year (390,000 Euros when value-added tax and interest are included).

4.22 In sum, valuation, like classification, is an area in which the EC does not provide for uniform administration of its customs law. Each member State's authorities make their own interpretations of the Code and Implementing Regulation, and even where differences between member States are identified, the EC lacks the capacity systematically to reconcile them.

(c) Customs procedures

4.23 With respect to customs procedures, non-uniform administration is evident in various phases of the customs process. It comes up, for example, in the audits that different member State authorities perform after goods have been released for free circulation. It is not uncommon for a member State's authorities to perform an audit to verify the value that an importer declared for goods that were released for free circulation. The December 2000 Court of Auditors Report found that different member State authorities take different approaches to such valuation audits, with important consequences for importers.

4.24 In the case of at least one member State, the Court found that the customs authorities lack the right to perform post-importation audits at all, except in cases of fraud. Even among States in which authorities are permitted to perform post-importation audits, the Court found differences among working practices, including the balance between reliance on examinations of goods at time of importation and post-release audits. Significantly, the Court found that differences in working procedures mean that "individual customs authorities are reluctant to accept each other's decisions." One audit procedure that the Court highlighted was the issuance of written valuation decisions. While some member States regularly issue written valuation decisions with binding effect going forward, others rarely issue such decisions.

4.25 Another area in which administration varies from member State to member State concerns penalties for violation of customs law. This area of divergence is one that has been noted by the ECJ on a number of occasions. The Commission itself has recognized (in its explanatory note accompanying a recent proposed revision to the Code) that "[e]conomic operators have complained for a long time about the lack of harmonization with regard to penalties against infringements of the customs rules. Specific offences may be considered in one Member State as a serious criminal act possibly leading to imprisonment, whilst in another Member State the same act may only lead to a small – or even no – fine."

4.26 Yet another area in which the administration of EC customs law differs among member States is the decision to permit what is known as "processing under customs control." Where this procedure is permitted, goods may be brought into the EC without being subject to duty and processed into downstream products in the EC, with those products then being released for free circulation at the applicable duty rate. Permission to engage in processing under customs control is subject to an economic conditions assessment, which different member States administer differently. Guidance issued by the United Kingdom customs authorities states that there are "*two aspects* to the economic test" and requires an applicant to provide evidence of the impact on its business of processing under customs control as well as evidence of "the impact upon any other community producers of the imported goods." In contrast, French regulations, for example, do not impose the additional test of demonstrating the absence of harm to competitors in the EC.

4.27 Another area in which non-uniform administration is evident is local clearance procedures ("LCP"). Under LCP, an importer may have goods released for free circulation at its own premises or certain other designated locations (as opposed to customs premises). While the general concept of how LCP is supposed to operate is set forth in the Implementing Regulation, the particular requirements vary from member State to member State. This is evident in the information that member States require LCP importers to transmit to customs authorities before goods are released. Some require only the electronic transmittal of manifest data. Others require that manifest data be translated or supplemented. Variations also are evident in the involvement of customs authorities prior to goods being released. Some member States rely on post-release audits, while others reserve the right to inspect goods prior to release. Member States typically require that supplementary information be transmitted to customs authorities following release under LCP, though here, too, the requirements vary. For example, some member States require transmittal of the EC's DV1 valuation form, whereas others do not. Some require the transmittal of invoices, certificates, and other supporting documentation, whereas others do not. Finally, requirements for retaining documents supporting LCP imports vary widely, ranging from four years in the United Kingdom to ten years in the Netherlands.

4.28 As the panel correctly observed in *Argentina – Hides and Leather*, "Article X:3(a) requires an examination of the real effect that a measure might have on traders operating in the commercial world" (para. 11.77). To that end, "[e]very exporter and importer should be able to expect treatment of the same kind, in the same manner both over time *and in different places*..." (para. 11.83; emphasis added). Article X:3(a) thus acts as a check against certain distortions to trade that may come about through administration that varies depending on factors such as point of entry within the territory of a Member.

4.29 A system that subjects traders to different procedures and different interpretations of classification and valuation law depending on the member State through which goods are imported into the territory of the EC is contrary to this basic principle. At a minimum, it makes it difficult for a trader to have a reasonable expectation of the treatment goods will receive when they are imported into the EC. It may also cause traders to make decisions about how to bring goods into the EC based on known differences among member States.

(d) The Commission, acting through the Customs Code Committee, does not provide uniformity to the administration of EC customs law

4.30 The mechanism provided in the Code for the Commission to address questions of administration of EC customs law is the Customs Code Committee. The Committee consists of representatives of each of the member States and is chaired by a representative of the Commission. Individual traders have no right to raise matters with the Committee. That right is reserved to the chairman of the Committee and member State representatives. A trader may petition a member State to bring a question before the Committee (though the Code does not require member States to have a petition process). However, the member State is under no obligation to respond favorably to such a petition.

4.31 For the most part, the Committee operates under the "regulatory procedure" laid down in the EC's so-called "comitology" decision. In matters relating to binding advance rulings that member States may issue on the classification or origin of goods, and in certain matters relating to preferential tariff treatment, the Committee operates under the comitology decision's "management procedure." Under both the regulatory procedure and the management procedure, a decision by the Committee requires the support of a majority of the member State representatives and at least 231 votes out of a total of 321 (based on weighting by member State as set out in the EC Treaty), and failure to reach a decision can lead to referral of the matter to the Council of the European Union, with different consequences depending on the applicable procedure. However, in practice, with respect to matters of customs administration, the Commission turns to the Council only on extremely rare occasions. Given institutional disincentives to refer matters to the Council, they may linger before the Committee indefinitely, as the Commission attempts to achieve the necessary majorities. This may mean that in controversial cases, no decision at all is taken.

4.32 The Code provides for adoption by the Committee of its own rules of procedure. Those rules are notable for purposes of the present dispute primarily for what they do *not* say. First, the rules do not contain any process for a trader affected by a member State's application of the Code to petition the Committee. Second, the rules contain no requirement that the Committee publish its agenda in advance of its meetings. Thus, a trader that may be affected by a question put before the Committee has no assurance that it will be made aware of the pendency of the matter. Third, while the rules contain an Article entitled "Admission of third parties," that Article does not establish a right for potentially affected parties to submit evidence and arguments to the Committee or even to be present at Committee meetings. It merely authorizes the Committee Chairman to invite experts to address the Committee and allows observers of certain third countries or organizations as specified in other EC instruments to be present at Committee meetings. Finally, there is no requirement that records of the Committee's proceedings be made public. In fact, Article 15 of the rules expressly provides that decisions on public access to the Committee's documents are subject to the discretion of the Commission and that, in any event, "[t]he Committee's discussions shall be kept confidential."

4.33 Traders as well as EC institutions have acknowledged the limits of the Committee procedure's ability to reconcile differences in administration among member State customs authorities. For example, in the Court of Auditors Valuation Report, it was observed that in using the valuation section of the Committee, the Commission "has to rely on discussion, persuasion and encouragement as the means of achieving common treatment of identical problems in Member States." In reply, the Commission itself acknowledged that the Committee "can ...only deal with a limited number of important cases that are brought before it."

4.34 In sum, the Committee process through which the Commission operates in matters of customs administration is not designed to systematically achieve uniform administration where divergences are shown to exist. From the point of view of "traders operating in the commercial world" (the relevant perspective for examining the Article X:3(a) obligation, as noted by the panel in *Argentina – Hides and Leather*), a WTO Member does not provide for uniform administration where there is doubt as to whether the mechanism ostensibly available for bringing about uniformity will or will not operate in the case of any given divergence. The mechanism theoretically available for bringing uniformity to the administration of customs law in the EC lacks a process for doing so on a systematic basis, and this absence of a process leads back to the conclusion that the EC simply does not provide for the uniform administration required by Article X:3(a).

3. *The EC does not provide tribunals or procedures for the prompt review and correction of administrative action relating to customs matters*

4.35 The second aspect of the US claim concerns the EC's failure to provide for an EC court or other forum to which a member State customs decision can be promptly appealed. Under the EC system, review of a member State customs decision is available in the courts of that member State. The only court with jurisdiction to issue decisions with EC-wide effect on matters of customs administration is the ECJ. However, the referral of questions to that court is not automatic, and even when a question does get referred to the ECJ, the time and steps necessary from the initial rendering of a customs decision by a member State's authorities to issuance of a decision by the ECJ makes review in that forum far from prompt.

4.36 The issue of reviewability of customs decisions is linked to the issue of uniform administration of customs law. To the extent that the administration of customs law is fragmented, the provision for review in the courts of each of 25 member States does not alleviate the fragmentation and may well compound it. In contrast, a single system of review could alleviate the different initial results that may occur in different ports from time to time.

4.37 The GATT 1994 provision pertinent to appellate review of customs decisions is Article X:3(b), which requires *each* WTO Member to "maintain, or institute as soon as practicable, judicial, arbitral or administrative tribunals or procedures for the purpose, *inter alia*, of the prompt review and correction of administrative action relating to customs matters." The EC is a WTO Member in its own right and is subject to Article X:3(b). Accordingly, the EC must have such tribunals or procedures.

4.38 Relevant context for interpreting Article X:3(b) includes the immediately preceding subparagraph in the paragraph in which the obligation at issue appears. That subparagraph calls for the "uniform, impartial, and reasonable" administration of customs laws. Thus, the decisions of the tribunals or procedures must provide for the review and correction of customs matters for the EC as a whole, not just within limited geographical regions within the EC. It is inconsistent with Article X:3(b) to require a trader who had received adverse customs decisions in three different member States, each at odds with the prevailing interpretation of EC customs law in other member States, to pursue separate appeals in each of those States.

4.39 The Community Customs Code says little on the question of appeals. It merely establishes that there shall be a right to appeal from customs decisions; provides that, in the first instance, appeals may be exercised before a member State's customs authorities and subsequently before a court or other independent body; and provides that, except in certain specified circumstances, "the lodging of an appeal shall not cause implementation of the disputed decision to be suspended." Beyond that, the Code simply states that "[t]he provisions for the implementation of the appeals procedure shall be determined by the Member States."

4.40 Thus, the Code leaves wide discretion to the individual member States in establishing procedures for appeals from customs decisions, and that discretion is evidenced in the diversity of procedures in fact available in the different member States. Indeed, even if it could be argued (contrary to what the United States argues here) that the EC might fulfill its obligation under Article X:3(b) merely by requiring member States to have appellate procedures in place, it is notable that nothing in the Code requires that review by member State tribunals be prompt. The Code is silent on the question of timing.

4.41 In fact, appellate procedures vary from member State to member State with respect to factors such as the availability of first-level review by the customs authorities themselves, time-periods for first-level review by the customs authorities (where such review is mandatory before proceeding to court), requirements to post security in order to avoid immediate enforcement of the decision on appeal, and availability of review by courts of superior jurisdiction. For example, the time periods for first instance reviews conducted by member State customs authorities can vary widely (from 30 days in Ireland, to one year in the Netherlands). Moreover, differences among procedures are even more pronounced after the first stage of review.

4.42 At the top of the review structure is the ECJ. Unlike the decisions of the courts in individual member States, the decisions of the ECJ do have effect throughout the territory of the EC. It is only at this stage, after a trader has pursued its appeal through a member State's court system, that the trader reaches a forum for review and correction provided by the EC itself. However, given the time it necessarily takes to reach this forum, it can hardly be considered to meet the EC's Article X:3(b) obligation to provide "tribunals or procedures for the purpose ...of the *prompt* review and correction of administrative action relating to customs matters."

4.43 In commenting on the request for the establishment of a panel in this dispute, the EC referred to the ECJ as the second institution (alongside the Commission) that enforces "harmonized customs rules and institutional and administrative measures ...to prevent divergent practices." That the EC views the ECJ as serving this function is instructive and cause for examining the role actually filled by the ECJ. What that examination reveals is significant institutional limitations on the ability of the ECJ "to prevent divergent practices" and a failure of the ECJ to constitute a tribunal or procedure for prompt review and correction of administrative action relating to customs matters, as required by Article X:3(b). The principal manner in which a question of a member State's administration of EC customs law is likely to come before the ECJ is through a referral by the court of a member State, pursuant to Article 234 of the EC Treaty. However, with the exception of courts of last resort, referral of questions by member State courts is discretionary. Moreover, even when a question does get referred to the ECJ, the answer of the ECJ does not finally decide the matter. Rather the answer is sent back to the requesting court, which then decides the case before it in light of the ECJ's guidance.

4.44 In his opinion in the 1997 *Weiner* case before the ECJ, the EC's Advocate General urged member State courts to exercise self-restraint in referring questions of customs classification law to the ECJ. The Advocate General found it "clear that the Court's contribution to uniform application of the Common Customs Tariff by deciding on the classification of particular products will always be minimal." The Advocate General's reasoning is easily transferrable to valuation and other areas in which member States' administration of EC law may diverge. A key lesson to be drawn from *Weiner* is that the ECJ is not suited to be the EC's tribunal or procedure for prompt review and correction of administrative action relating to customs matters required by Article X:3(b). Its place within the EC system – as the highest level adjudicator of questions of EC law – and the manner in which questions are put to it – typically, through discretionary referral by member State courts – make it incapable of serving that role.

4.45 As the ECJ is not set up to be an EC customs court – and, in any event, as the time it takes for a question raised in a member State's customs decision ultimately to get to ECJ review hardly qualifies such review as prompt – what is left is a patchwork of member State customs authorities whose work is reviewed by member State courts, with no EC tribunal or procedure providing prompt review and correction of customs decisions in a way that would bring about uniformity in the administration of EC customs law. In sum, the EC provides no tribunal or procedure for the prompt review and correction of administrative action relating to customs matters, as required by Article X:3(b) of the GATT 1994.

4. *Conclusion*

4.46 For the reasons set forth in the First Written Submission of the United States, the EC fails to comply with the obligations in Articles X:3(a) and X:3(b) of the GATT 1994. It does not administer its customs laws, regulations, decisions and rulings in a uniform, impartial, and reasonable manner. Nor does it maintain judicial, arbitral, or administrative tribunals or procedures for the purpose of the prompt review and correction of administrative action relating to customs matters. The United States asks that the Panel find the EC is not in conformity with Articles X:3(a) and X:3(b) of the GATT 1994 and recommend that it come into compliance promptly.

B. *First Written Submission of the European Communities*

1. *Introduction*

4.47 The United States alleges that the EC does not fulfil its obligations under Article X:3(a) of the GATT by failing to administer its customs laws in a uniform manner. Moreover, the United States alleges that the EC does not comply with its obligations under Article X:3(b) GATT by not providing judicial, arbitral or administrative tribunals or procedures for the prompt review and correction of administrative action relating to customs matters.

4.48 These claims of the United States are unfounded. The United States does not provide evidence that the EC fails to administer its customs laws in a manner contrary to Article X:3(a) GATT. Apart from a small number of isolated and misleading examples, the United States provides very little information about the actual administration of EC customs law. Since it does not provide any evidence to the effect that the EC administers its customs laws in a non-uniform manner, the United States fails to establish a *prima facie* case in support of its claims.

4.49 The focus of the United States case is not on the actual administration of EC customs laws, but on the EC system of customs administration. Put simply, the United States objects to the fact that the EC administers EC customs laws not through an EC customs agency, but through the national administrations of its member States. Similarly, the United States objects to the fact that judicial review of customs decisions in the EC is provided not through "EC-level tribunals", but through tribunals of the EC member States. With these claims, the United States is putting into question fundamental structural elements of the EC legal order, without providing a shred of proof that these structural elements are indeed incompatible with the requirements of Article X:3(a) and (b) GATT.

4.50 The US interpretation of Article X:3(a) and (b) GATT is without basis in the text of these provisions. According to the United States, Article X:3(a) and (b) GATT seems to prescribe in detail the way in which a WTO Member must implement its customs laws. The EC does not believe that this is the objective underlying Article X:3 GATT. Article X:3 GATT is a provision laying down minimum standards for the administration of customs law, not a legal basis for the harmonization of the systems of customs administration of WTO Members.

4.51 The weakness of the US case is also illustrated by the lukewarm reaction of traders to the US case. In response to a request for input by the United States Trade Representative following the consultation request, USTR received a mere three submissions. Only one of these submissions is referred to in the US First Written Submission. Of the other two submissions, one was unsubstantiated, one unhelpful to the US case since it provided an example of the uniform application of EC classification rules.

2. *Factual background*

(a) General principles of the EC legal system

4.52 The progress of European integration has largely been built on legislation. Over the decades, the EC has built a large body of Community law covering an increasing range of policy areas on the basis of the powers attributed to it in its founding treaties.

4.53 The success of European integration is based on the direct and uniform application of Community law in the legal order of the member States of the Community. The European Community is therefore very much a Community based on the rule of law. This fact is explicitly recognized in Article 6(1) EU Treaty.

4.54 However, with the exception of some limited policy fields, the EC does not itself administer Community law through an EC-level administration. Rather, the execution of EC law takes place through the national administrations of the member States, and similarly through the Courts of the member States. This principle of administration through the member States can be described as "executive federalism".

4.55 The US attack on the EC system of customs administration directly puts into question fundamental principles of EC law. In order to place these issues in their proper context, a deeper explanation of the basic principles of EC constitutional law is required.

(i) The EC institutions and the EC legislative process

4.56 According to Article 5 of the EC Treaty, the Community shall act within the limits of the powers conferred upon it by the Treaty. Furthermore, Article 5 EC Treaty requires the EC to act in accordance with the principles of subsidiarity and proportionality. The EC Treaty sets up a number of institutions which shall carry out the tasks entrusted to the European Community. The main institutions involved with the EC legislative process are the European Parliament, the Council of Ministers, and the European Commission.

4.57 The legislative procedure applicable to the adoption of a particular legal act is laid down in the specific legal basis conferring the powers on the Community to adopt such an act. In the large majority of cases, the adoption of a legislative act of the Community will require a proposal from the European Commission. In most cases, the EC Treaty foresees that legislative acts shall be adopted jointly by the European Parliament and the Council in accordance with the co-decision procedure set out in Article 251 EC Treaty. To this extent, the European Parliament and the Council can be regarded as the primary legislative organs of the EC. In certain cases, the Treaty also provides that the Council may adopt legislative acts alone, usually after consultation of the European Parliament.

(ii) The implementing powers of the European Commission

4.58 Article 202, third indent, of the EC Treaty provides that the Council may confer on the Commission powers for the implementation of Community law. Article 202, third indent, further provides that the Council may impose certain requirements in respect of the exercise of those powers. Finally, the last sentence of Article 202, third indent, EC Treaty provides that these procedures must be "consonant with principles and rules to be laid down in advance by the Council, acting unanimously on a proposal from the Commission and after obtaining the opinion of the European Parliament".

4.59 On the basis of Article 202, third indent, of the EC Treaty, the Council has adopted Decision 1999/468. This decision, also known as the "Comitology Decision", lays down, at a general level, the procedures for the exercise of implementing powers which the Council may delegate to the Commission.

4.60 The Comitology Decision distinguishes three types of procedure: the advisory procedure, the management procedure, and the regulatory procedure. In accordance with Article 2 of the Decision, the regulatory procedure should be applied for the adoption of "measures of general scope designed to apply essential provisions of basic instruments". The management procedure is applicable to the adoption of "management measures", such as those relating to the application of the common agricultural and common fisheries policies, or to the implementation of programmes with substantial budgetary implications. The advisory procedure is applicable in all other appropriate cases.

4.61 The specific procedures to be followed are respectively set out in Articles 3, 4 and 5 of the Comitology decision. Under each of the procedures, the Commission is assisted by a committee composed of representatives of the member States, and chaired by a representative of the Commission. The Commission shall submit a draft of the measures to be adopted to the Committee.

4.62 Where the advisory procedure is applicable, the Committee shall deliver its opinion by simple majority. In contrast, where the management and the regulatory procedure are applicable, the Committee shall deliver its opinion by qualified majority, which involves a weighing of the votes of the member States as foreseen in Article 205(2) EC Treaty.

4.63 The main difference between the three procedures lies in the consequences of a negative opinion of the Committee. In the case of the advisory procedure as described in Article 3 of the Comitology Decision, the Commission shall take "utmost account" of the opinion delivered by the Committee. However, it may adopt the measure even if it is not in accordance with the opinion of the Committee.

4.64 In the case of the management procedure described in Article 4 of the Comitology Decision, the Commission adopts measures which shall apply immediately. However, if these measures are not in accordance with the opinion of the committee, they shall be communicated by the Commission to the Council. In that event, the Commission may defer application of the measures on which it has decided for a period to be laid down in each basic instrument but which shall in no case exceed three months from the date of such communication. The Council, acting by qualified majority, may take a different decision within the period provided for by paragraph 3 of Article 4 of the Decision.

4.65 In the case of the regulatory procedure as described in Article 5 of the Comitology Decision, if the measure is not in accordance with the opinion of the Committee, the Commission shall submit to the Council a proposal relating to the measures to be taken. In this case, the applicable procedure is set out in Article 5(6) of the Decision.

4.66 Accordingly, the committees established pursuant to the Comitology Decision fulfil an important role in the Community's internal decision-making process. In particular, in the context of the management and the regulatory procedure, the opinion of the Committee may determine whether a measure can be adopted by the Commission, or must be referred to the Council.

4.67 In accordance with Article 7(1) of the Comitology decision, each Committee shall establish its own rules of procedure on the proposal of its chairman on the basis of standard rules of procedure.

(iii) The legal effect of Community law

4.68 On the basis of the powers attributed to the European Community in the EC Treaty, the institutions may adopt a number of legislative and other acts. Article 249(1) EC Treaty states that the competent institutions may adopt regulations, directives, decision, recommendations, and opinions. The legal effect of these acts is described in Article 249(2) EC Treaty.

4.69 According to the constant case law of the Court of Justice, the law of the European Community has primacy over the national law of the member States. This primacy of Community law is a fundamental principle of the Community legal order. It applies to all provisions contained in the EC Treaty and in acts of the EC institutions. It also applies against any provision of national law at any level, including member States' constitutions. This means that whenever a Court of a Member State encounters a conflict between a provision of Community law and a provision of its national law, it must set aside the provision of national law, and apply Community law only.

4.70 A second fundamental principle of Community law is that of direct effect. As the Court has held in its constant case law, Community law may create rights for individuals which can be directly invoked by those individuals in proceedings before national courts and authorities. This direct effect may apply both to provisions of the founding treaties and to acts of secondary Community law.

4.71 Taken together, the principles of supremacy and of direct effect are essential for the effective and uniform application of Community law. They enable individuals to invoke provisions of Community law in proceedings before national courts. They thereby enable national judges – acting in constant dialogue with the European Court of Justice through the preliminary reference procedure – to safeguard the respect of Community law.

4.72 Moreover, the Court of Justice held that when the conditions under which individuals may rely on the provisions of Community law before the national courts are met, all organs of the administration, including decentralized authorities, are obliged to apply those provisions and if necessary must directly set aside national provisions that are in contradiction with EC law.

(iv) The Commission, the member States, and the execution of Community law

4.73 Community law is typically implemented through the national administrations of the member States. Only in a limited number of policy fields is the execution of Community law directly carried out by European Commission.

4.74 The system of the execution of EC law has frequently been referred to as "executive federalism". The principle of executive federalism within the EC also reflects the principle of subsidiarity enshrined in Article 5(2) EC Treaty, according to which the Community should take action only if and in so far as the objectives of the proposed action cannot be sufficiently achieved by the member States.

4.75 The executive federalism of the EC is fully compatible with the requirements of uniformity in the interpretation and application of Community law. In this regard, the principles of primacy and direct effect once again have an important role. Through those principles, Community law becomes directly binding on national administrations, and may be invoked against them. This enables the European Court of Justice to ensure, through the preliminary reference procedure, the uniform interpretation and application of Community law.

4.76 Moreover, Article 10 EC Treaty imposes on the member States a duty of cooperation, which applies also to the execution of Community law by the member States.

4.77 In addition, Article 211, first indent, of the EC Treaty provides that the Commission shall "ensure that the provisions of this Treaty and the measures taken by the institutions pursuant thereto are applied". In reflection of this role, the Commission is frequently referred to as the "guardian of the Treaty".

4.78 Where the Commission considers that a Member State has failed to fulfil an obligation under the Treaty, the Commission has the possibility, in accordance with the procedures of Article 226 EC Treaty, to bring this matter before the Court of Justice. Such "infringement proceedings" can be brought in response to any violation of Community law by a Member State, and can also concern the incorrect application of Community law by the administrations of the member States.

4.79 In accordance with Article 228(1) EC Treaty, if the Court of Justice finds that a Member State has failed to fulfil an obligation under the EC Treaty, the State concerned shall be required to take the necessary measures to comply with the judgment of the Court of Justice. Where the Member State concerned fails to comply with the judgment, the possibility exists under Article 228(1) of the EC Treaty for the Court of Justice to impose a penalty payment on the Member State.

4.80 Individuals have a vital role in detecting infringements of Community law. There is a standardized procedure for complaints to be addressed to the European Commission regarding infringements of Community law. Such complaints, which may also concern the application of Community law by national administrations, can lead to the institution of infringement proceedings by the Commission.

4.81 The public service of the European Commission is guided by a code of conduct which is part of the Commission's rules of procedure, and which sets out the principles of good administrative behaviour to be observed by all Commission staff. The Code of Conduct provides in particular that all enquiries must be dealt with as quickly as possible, and sets out time limits within which correspondence should be answered. Complaints regarding non-compliance with the Code of Conduct may be addressed to the Secretariat-General of the Commission.

4.82 The Commission in the exercise of its duties is also subject to certain other controls. In particular, the Commission is politically responsible to the European Parliament. Moreover, in accordance with Article 194 EC Treaty, any citizen may direct a petition to the European Parliament on any matter which comes within the Community's fields of activity. Finally, in accordance with Article 195 EC Treaty, the European Parliament has appointed an Ombudsman empowered to receive complaints from individuals concerning instances of maladministration in the activities of the Community institutions or bodies.

(b) The administration of EC customs law

(i) The basic principles of the EC Customs Union

4.83 According to Article 23(1) EC Treaty, the Community shall be based upon a customs union which shall cover all trade in goods and which shall involve the prohibition between member States of customs duties on imports and exports and of all charges having equivalent effect, and the adoption of a common customs tariff in relation to third countries.

4.84 Accordingly, the EC customs union has an internal and an external dimension. As regards the internal dimension, Article 25 EC Treaty provides for the prohibition of all customs duties and charges having equivalent effect in trade between the member States. Articles 28 and 29 EC Treaty contain a prohibition of quantitative restrictions and measures having equivalent effect on imports and exports between the EC member States.

4.85 As for the external dimension, the EC Treaty establishes a common commercial policy. According to Article 133(1) EC Treaty, the common commercial policy is based on uniform principles, particularly in regard to changes in tariff rates, the conclusion of tariff and trade agreements, the achievement of uniformity in measures of liberalization, export policy, and measures to protect trade such as those to be taken in the event of dumping or subsidies. As the Court of Justice has confirmed on numerous occasions, the customs union and the common commercial policy fall within the exclusive competence of the EC.

4.86 The internal dimension of the EC customs union also benefits products originating in third countries. According to Article 23(2) EC Treaty, the prohibitions contained in Articles 25, 28 and 29 EC Treaty shall also apply to products from third countries which are in free circulation in member States. Article 24 EC Treaty defines products from third countries as being in free circulation when the import formalities have been complied with and any customs duties or charges having equivalent effect which are payable have been levied in that Member State, and if they have not benefited from total or partial drawback of such duties or charges. In other words, once goods from a third country are in free circulation in the EC, they are treated in every respect like Community goods, and benefit from the free movement of goods in the internal market in the same way as goods originating in the Community.

(ii) The EC's international commitments in the field of customs administration and cooperation

4.87 The EC is a founding Member of the WTO. As such, the EC respects and implements its commitments under the covered agreements. In particular, EC customs law implements, and fully respects, relevant WTO agreements such as the GATT, the Customs Valuation Agreement, or the Agreement on Rules of Origin.

4.88 While the EC is not yet a Member of the World Customs Organization (WCO), the EC is a party to numerous Conventions negotiated under the auspices of the WCO. Notably, the EC is a party to the International Convention on the Harmonized Commodity and Coding System (HS Convention), and the International Convention on the Simplification and Harmonization of Customs Procedures (Kyoto Convention).

4.89 The EC also has concluded a number of bilateral agreements with third countries on customs cooperation. In particular, the EC has concluded such an agreement with the United States.

(iii) The legislative framework of the EC Customs Union

4.90 On the basis of the powers attributed to them in the EC Treaty, the EC institutions have adopted a number of legislative acts which establish the legal framework of the EC customs union. The three main instruments of EC customs legislation are the Community Customs Tariff, the Community Customs Code

(CCC), and the Implementing Regulation. It is noteworthy that all these instruments are regulations, which, according to Article 249(2) EC Treaty, are binding in their entirety and directly applicable in all member States.

4.91 The Community Customs Tariff is established by Council Regulation (EEC) 2658/87. The Community Customs Tariff establishes a combined nomenclature (CN) with a description of goods up to an eight-digit code. The CN is based on the six-digit HS nomenclature, to which it adds Community subdivisions, referred to as "CN subheadings".

4.92 In addition, the CN contains preliminary provisions. These preliminary provisions notably contain general rules for the interpretation of the CN, other general provisions, as well as special provisions for certain types of goods. In addition, the CN also contains section and chapter notes, as well as footnotes relating to the application of duty rates.

4.93 The CN is contained in Annex I to Council Regulation 2658/87. In accordance with Article 12 of this Regulation, the Commission adopts each year a regulation containing the complete version of the CN. The CN contains the conventional rate of duties applicable on importation to the Community and, where applicable, lower autonomous rates.

4.94 In accordance with Article 2 of Regulation 2658/87, an integrated tariff of the European Communities (Taric) is established by the Commission. The Taric is based on the CN, and contains all measures contained in the CN, additional Community subdivisions, referred to as Taric subheadings, which are needed for the implementation of specific policies, any other information necessary for the implementation or management of the Taric, as well as the rates of customs duty applicable and other import and export charges, including duty suspensions and preferential tariff rates. Taric codes include the 8-digit CN codes plus a 9th and 10th digit. The Taric is established and continuously updated by the Commission, and available online through the internet.

4.95 Article 9(1)(b), (d), (e) and (f) of Regulation 2658/87 also give the Commission the possibility to amend the combined nomenclature in certain respects. Such amendments must be adopted in accordance with the management procedure referred to in Article 10 of the Regulation.

4.96 Council Regulation (EEC) 2913/92 establishes the Community Customs Code (CCC). The CCC comprises 253 articles and is divided into nine Titles. The CCC together with its implementing provisions constitutes a comprehensive codification of the rules for the administration of customs throughout the Community.

4.97 According to Article 247 CCC, the measures necessary for the implementation of the CCC are to be adopted by the Commission in accordance with the Regulatory Procedure referred to in Article 247a CCC. Article 247a refers to Article 5 of the Comitology Decision.

4.98 On the basis of Article 247 CCC, the Commission has adopted Regulation (EEC) No. 2454 of 2 July 1993 laying down provisions for the Implementation of the CCC. The Implementing Regulation is a voluminous text comprising ca.

800 articles and over 100 annexes. It sets out in detail the provisions necessary for the implementation of the CCC. Its structure follows broadly that of the CCC.

(iv) The Commission, the member States, and the Customs Code Committee

4.99 As is generally the case for Community law, Community customs law is executed by the national authorities of the EU member States. Member States' customs authorities are bound by Community customs law, which applies directly and uniformly through the Community legal order.

4.100 As in other fields of Community law, the Commission is not normally directly involved with the administration of EC customs law. There are only a limited number of cases in which the Commission may itself take decisions regarding the application of EC customs law. Generally, the function of the European Commission as the guardian of the Treaties is to monitor the correct and uniform application of EC customs laws by the member States.

4.101 A specific forum for cooperation between the member States and the Commission is the Customs Code Committee. This Committee is established by Articles 247a(1) and 248a(1) of the CCC. It is composed of representatives of all member States and chaired by a representative of the Commission. It has adopted its own Rules of Procedure, which are based on the standard rules of procedure for comitology committees.

4.102 In accordance with Article 1(1) of its Rules of Procedure, the Customs Code Committee comprises a number of sections covering specific areas of customs law and administration. The Customs Code Committee has a number of functions which are attributed to it in Community legislation. Articles 247a and 248a CCC provide that the Customs Code Committee shall act as a regulatory or management committee within the meaning of the Comitology Decision. Article 247 CCC foresees that the measures necessary for the implementation of the CCC are normally adopted according to the regulatory procedure. In certain cases, including those mentioned in Article 248 CCC, it is the management procedure which shall apply.

4.103 Legal acts other than the CCC may also include references to the Customs Code Committee. In this case, the specific procedure applicable is laid down in the respective provision attributing the decision-making power to the Commission. One example is Article 10 of Regulation 2658/87 establishing the Common Customs Tariff, which provides that the Commission will be assisted by the Customs Code Committee in accordance with the management procedure.

4.104 In addition, Article 249 CCC provides that the Committee may examine any question concerning customs legislation which is raised by its chairman, either on his own initiative or at the request of a Member State's representative. A similar provision is also found in Article 8 of Regulation 2658/87 establishing the Common Customs Tariff, according to which the Committee may examine any matter referred to it by its chairman, either on his own initiative or at the request of a representative of a Member State, concerning the combined nomenclature or the Taric nomenclature.

4.105 The Customs Code Committee is not a mechanism for the administrative or judicial review of customs decisions. Rather, it is an integral part of the Community's regulatory process, through which the member States' expertise is integrated into this process. The US complaints are accordingly based on an erroneous understanding of the nature and functions of the Committee.

4.106 However, any individual with a concern regarding the administration of customs matters can bring this issue to the attention of the Commission, which will consider the matter and respond in accordance with the Commission's Code of Conduct. If the Commission considers that the matter requires consideration by the Committee, it will put this matter on the Committee's agenda. In a similar fashion, a concerned individual may also address the administration of a Member State, which may equally decide to raise the matter in the Committee.

4.107 Moreover, Article 9(1) of the Committee's Rules of Procedure allows the Chairman, on his initiative or at the request of a Member, to invite experts to talk on particular matters. Thus, where this is justified by the complexity of a particular issue, the Committee may also hear representatives of the concerned industry or traders, and has done so in the past.

(v) Tariff classification

4.108 According to Article 20(1) of the CCC, duties legally owed where a customs debt is incurred shall be based on the Common Customs Tariff. In accordance with the constant case law of the Court of Justice, tariff classification is carried out on the basis "of the objective characteristics and properties of products which can be ascertained when customs clearance is obtained".

4.109 In principle, the classification of goods is the responsibility of the customs authorities of the member States which carry out the customs clearance of the goods concerned. In addition, there exists a variety of tools which ensure a uniform classification practice throughout the Community. These tools include classification regulations, HS explanatory notes and opinions, EC explanatory notes, and opinions of the Customs Code Committee. Moreover, the CCC provides for binding information on questions of tariff classification. In this way, Community law provides for a graduated set of tools adaptable to the circumstances of the specific case in order to ensure a uniform classification practice. Finally, judgments of the Court of Justice also are an important tool for ensuring a uniform classification practice.

4.110 According to the first indent of Article 9(1)(a) of Regulation 2658/87, the Commission may adopt Regulations on the classification of goods. Such classification regulations are adopted by the Commission in accordance with the management procedure referred to in Article 10 of Regulation 2658/87.

4.111 Classification regulations will determine the tariff subheading to be applied to the specific good described in the Regulation. The Court of Justice has confirmed that under certain circumstances, classification regulations may also become relevant by analogy to products similar to those described in the regulation. A classification regulation is binding throughout the Community in accordance with Article 249(2) EC Treaty. However, classification regulations cannot amend the CN, and must therefore respect the Common Customs Tariff.

4.112 Where a national Court has doubts about the validity of a classification regulation, it may refer this question to the Court of Justice in accordance with Article 234(1)(b) of the EC Treaty. If the question arises before a national court against the decision of which there is no further remedy, the Court must refer this question to the Court of Justice. In determining whether or not the Commission has exceeded its powers, the Court of Justice has sought to establish whether the Commission has committed "a manifest error of assessment".

4.113 In contrast, since classification regulations are acts of general applicability, they would normally not be of direct and individual concern to individuals as required by Article 230(4) EC Treaty. Accordingly, classification regulations cannot normally be challenged through a direct annulment action before the Tribunal of First Instance. Only under exceptional circumstances, where a classification regulation is so specific that it affects only the applicant by virtue of certain attributes which are peculiar to it, can a classification regulation also be challenged directly through an annulment action.

4.114 The Community is a party to the HS Convention, and the common customs tariff is based on the HS nomenclature. According to Article 7(1)(b) of the HS Convention, the HS Committee can prepare Explanatory Notes, Classification Opinions and other advice as guidance to the interpretation of the HS. The EC considers that WCO explanatory notes and classification opinions constitute an important tool for uniform tariff classification not only within the Community, but also beyond. The EC participates actively in the drafting of the explanatory notes and classification opinions, and has up to now adopted all of the HS measures.

4.115 The Court of Justice has stated in its case law that even though they are not normally binding in Community law, HS Explanatory Notes and Classification Opinions of the WCO are an important aid in the interpretation of the Community customs tariff. In other cases, the Court of Justice has also judged that an interpretation of the HS approved by the WCO Council is binding on the Community when it reflects the general practice followed by the member States, unless it is incompatible with the wording of the heading concerned or goes manifestly beyond the discretion conferred on the Customs Cooperation Council.

4.116 According to Article 9(1)(a), second indent, of Regulation 2658/87, the Commission may issue explanatory notes. Such explanatory notes are adopted by the Commission in accordance with the management procedure foreseen in Article 10 of the Regulation.

4.117 Explanatory notes may equally clarify particular issues of tariff classification arising under the CN. They must, of course, be distinguished from the notes which introduce the chapters of the CN, and which are an integral part of the tariff and cannot be modified by explanatory notes. EC explanatory notes are not legally binding, and cannot amend the CN. However, the Court of Justice has repeatedly acknowledged that explanatory notes are an important aid in the interpretation of the CN.

4.118 On the basis of Article 8 of Regulation 2658/87, the Customs Code Committee may adopt opinions on questions relative to the application and interpretation of the combined nomenclature. Such opinions must be distinguished from opinions which the Committee adopts in the context of a comitology procedure on measures proposed by the Commission.

4.119 Opinions adopted by Committee are not legally binding. However, the Court of Justice has held that that such opinions constitute an important means of ensuring the uniform application of the common customs tariff by the authorities of the member States and as such can be considered as a valid aid to the interpretation of the tariff.

4.120 According to Article 12(1) of the CCC, the customs authorities shall, upon written request, issue binding tariff information (BTI). The basic provisions on binding tariff information are set out in Article 12 CCC. Further rules concerning binding information are contained in Title II of Part I of the Implementing Regulation (Articles 5-14). These additional provisions address in particular the procedures for obtaining binding information, measures to be taken in the event of binding information, the legal effect of binding information, and the expiry of binding information. In addition, in order to ensure a harmonious and uniform application of the rules on binding tariff information, the Commission has issued administrative guidelines on the European Binding Tariff Information (EBTI) System and its operation.

4.121 According to Article 6(1) of the Implementing Regulation, applications for binding information are to be made in writing, either to the customs authorities in the Member State or member States in which the information is to be used, or to the competent customs authorities in the Member State in which the applicant is established.

4.122 The application shall be made on a standard application form conforming to the specimen contained in Annex 1 B to the Implementing Regulation. The details which an application for BTI must contain are set out in Article 6(3)(A) of the Implementing Regulation. According to Article 6(3)(A)(j), the application must in particular contain the indication by the applicant whether, to his knowledge, binding tariff information for identical or similar goods has already been applied for, or issued in the Community. When customs have possession of all the elements necessary for them to determine the classification of the goods, binding information shall be notified to the applicant as soon as possible in accordance with Article 7(1) of the Implementing Regulation.

4.123 Article 8(1) of the Implementing Regulation provides that a copy of the application for BTI, a copy of BTI notified to the applicant, and the information contained in copy 4 of the BTI form shall be transmitted to the Commission. This transmission is done by electronic means. In accordance with Article 8(3) of the Implementing Regulation, this data is stored in a database of the Commission, which is called the EBTI data base.

4.124 There are two versions of this database. One is available to the public for consultation, the other is exclusively available to the Commission and issuing authorities of the member States. The version available to the public allows searches of valid BTI by issuing country, start and end date of validity, BTI reference, CN code, keyword, or product description. The public version of the EBTI database is accessible on the website of the European Commission.

4.125 The version available to the Commission and national customs authorities contains additional information of a confidential nature which is not made available to the public (i.e. the name and address of the applicant, holder and agent, if one has been appointed, confidential commercial details concerning the goods for which the BTI has been issued, including trade names). The version available to the Commission and issuing customs authorities also contains all applications for BTI which have been submitted to customs administrations and BTI that has ceased to be valid.

4.126 The EBTI database is an important tool for securing a uniform BTI practice. In particular, according to the administrative guidelines issued by the Commission on the EBTI system, the EBTI data base must be consulted by customs authorities prior to the issuance of BTI in all cases where there is a doubt regarding the correct classification, or where different headings merit consideration.

4.127 According to Article 12(2) CCC, BTI will be binding on the customs authorities as against the holder of the BTI. It follows furthermore from Article 12(2) CCC and Article 5 No. 1 of the Implementing Regulation that BTI is binding not only on the administration which has issued it, but on the administrations of all member States.

4.128 According to Article 12(3) CCC, BTI will be binding only in respect of the tariff classification of goods which correspond in every respect to those described in the information. In accordance with Article 12(4) CCC, BTI will be valid for a period of six years. Further details regarding the legal effect of binding information are set out in Articles 10 to 12 of the Implementing Regulation.

4.129 Article 12(5) CCC sets out the cases in which BTI shall cease to be valid. According to Article 12(6) of the CCC, the holder of binding information which ceases to be valid may still use that information for a period of six months, provided that he concluded binding contracts for the purchase or sale of the goods in question, on the basis of the BTI, before the measure was adopted. Further details are set out in Articles 13 and 14 of the Implementing Regulation.

4.130 In the event that despite the procedural safeguards described above, different BTI exists, Article 9(1) gives the Commission the power to adopt the necessary measures to ensure the uniform application of the CN. The measures foreseen in the second indent of Article 9(1) of the Implementing Regulation may take the form of a classification regulation adopted by the Commission on the basis of Article 9(1)(a) of Regulation 2658/87. In accordance with Article 12(5)(a)(i) of the CCC, where such a regulation is adopted, BTI which is not in accordance with it will cease to be valid. Alternatively, the Commission may also, on the basis of Article 12(5)(a)(iii) CCC and the second indent of Article 9(1) of the Implementing Regulation, adopt a decision obliging the Member State who issued the BTI to revoke it.

4.131 A decision requiring the revocation of BTI is of direct and individual concern to the holder of the BTI. Therefore, the holder may bring a direct action for the annulment of such a decision by the Commission before the Court of First Instance in accordance with Article 230(4) EC. In contrast, a direct action for annulment is normally not possible against a classification regulation. However, the validity of such classification could be raised in the context of proceedings before a national tribunal, and could then be referred to the Court of Justice in accordance with the preliminary reference procedure.

(vi) Customs valuation

4.132 Community customs law contains a complete set of rules for customs valuation in the EC. The basic provisions are contained in Chapter 3 of Title II of the CCC (Articles 28 through 36). More detailed provisions are contained in Title V of the Implementing Regulation (Articles 141 to 181a). Title V is subdivided into seven chapters, concerning general provisions, royalties and licensing fees, the place of introduction into the Community, transport costs, rates of exchange, simplified procedures for perishable goods, and declarations of particulars and documents to be furnished.

4.133 In addition, Annex 23 to the Implementing Regulation contains interpretative notes on customs value, which reflect the interpretative notes contained in Annex I to the WTO Valuation Agreement. Article 141(1) of the Implementing Regulation requires that when applying the provisions the provisions of the CCC and the Implementing Regulation, member States shall comply with the interpretative notes. In addition, Article 141(2) of the Implementing Regulation refers to Annex 24 to the Regulation, which sets out the generally accepted accounting principles to be applied for the determination of customs value. Finally, Annex 25 to the Implementing Regulation contains details on the calculation of air transport costs to be included in the customs value.

4.134 In accordance with the WTO Valuation Agreement, Article 29(1) of the CCC provides that the customs value of imported goods shall normally be the transaction value, i.e. the price actually paid or payable for the goods when sold for export to the customs territory of the Community. The details and exceptions to this rule are contained in the Community legislation referred to above, in accordance with the WTO Valuation Agreement.

4.135 EC customs law also provides for a number of mechanisms to ensure the uniform application of EC valuation rules. These tools are not as numerous as those available in the case of tariff classification. However, this is due to the substantial differences between tariff classification and valuation which must be kept in mind.

4.136 First, it should be noted that the EC valuation rules are extremely detailed. For this reason, the room for specific additional interpretations is relatively small. Second, since the valuation of goods is normally based on the transaction value, customs valuation very much depends on evaluations to be carried out on a case-by-case basis. This means that valuation rules typically must be of a general and abstract character, rather than product specific. In other words, whereas it may be possible to decide in the abstract on the classification of a defined type of good, it is not possible to lay down once and for all in the abstract the value of a particular good.

4.137 Where a need for further detailed rules on valuation occurs, the Commission may, in accordance with the procedure of Article 247 CCC, amend the valuation rules contained in the Implementing Regulation. Such amendments will be legally binding in all member States. From this perspective, amendments to the Implementing Regulation and its annexes may, in relation to specific issues, be regarded as functionally similar to classification regulations.

4.138 Moreover, in accordance with Article 249 CCC, the Customs Code Committee (through its Customs Valuation Section) may examine any questions concerning the application of EC customs legislation in the field of valuation. On this basis, the CCC may issue opinions on specific issues of application of EC valuation rules. Whereas such opinions are not legally binding, they may constitute useful guidance for the interpretation of the applicable EC law.

4.139 The Commission has also issued a Compendium of Customs Valuation texts. This Compendium contains commentaries prepared and conclusions reached by the Customs Code Committee on specific issues of customs valuation on the basis of Article 249 CCC. In addition, it contains excerpts from relevant judgments of the Court of Justice on valuation issues, as well as indices of other relevant texts.

4.140 As in other areas of EC customs law, the ECJ plays an important role in ensuring the uniform interpretation of EC valuation rules. Wherever a dispute occurs between an importer and EC customs authorities on the interpretation and application of EC valuation rules, the national court may – and sometimes must – refer the question to the Court of Justice in accordance with Article 234 EC Treaty.

(vii) Processing under customs control

4.141 The processing under customs control procedure (PCC) allows the nature or state of non-Community goods to be altered without subjecting them to import duties or commercial policy measures. The resulting products are released for free circulation at the rate of import duty applicable to the processed products in order to benefit from a lower import duty amount or to fulfil technical requirements for placing the goods on the market.

4.142 The detailed provisions governing PCC are laid down in Articles 84 to 90 and 130 to 136 of the CCC and Articles 496 to 523 and 551 to 552 of the Implementing Regulation. The use of the procedure requires an authorization, which is granted only if certain conditions are fulfilled. The US First Written Submission deals only with one type of condition, the so-called "economic conditions" which are described in Article 133(e) CCC. EC law ensures the uniform application of the assessment of the economic conditions by several means.

4.143 For the types of goods and operations mentioned in Annex 76, Part A, of the Implementing Regulation, which represent the majority of the cases, the economic conditions shall be deemed to be fulfilled in accordance with Article 552(1) first subparagraph of the Implementing Regulation. This means that, in these cases, customs authorities do not examine the economic conditions.

4.144 For the types of goods and operations mentioned in Annex 76, Part B, of the Implementing Regulation and not covered by Part A of that Annex, the examination of the economic conditions shall take place at Community level, through the relevant Committee procedure. This means that a uniform assessment of the economic conditions is ensured for so-called sensitive goods because the examination has to take place at Community level.

4.145 Third, for the types of goods and operations not mentioned in Annex 76 of the Implementing Regulation, the examination of the economic conditions shall take place at national level. An examination at national level is required only in rare cases because, as mentioned before, either the economic conditions are deemed to be fulfilled or the examination takes place at Community level. Nevertheless, transparency and uniform application of the assessment of the economic condition is also ensured in these rare cases because member States have to communicate to the Commission relevant information in accordance with Article 522 of the Implementing Regulation. The Commission makes these particulars available to the customs administrations. Furthermore, if a Member State objects to an authorization issued or if the customs authorities concerned wish to consult before or after issuing an authorization, an examination of the economic condition may take place at Community level.

(viii) Local clearance procedure

4.146 Community customs legislation contains simplified procedures in order to facilitate completion of formalities for placing goods under a custom procedure as far as possible while ensuring that operations are conducted in a proper manner. The local clearance procedure is one of those simplified procedures, where an importer may have goods released for free circulation at its own premises or certain other designated locations without having to present the goods to customs.

4.147 The basic provision for the local clearance procedure is Article 76(1)(c) CCC. Where a data-processing technique is used, Article 77 CCC applies in addition. More detailed provisions are laid down in Articles 263 to 267 of the Implementing Regulation.

4.148 According to Article 263 of the Implementing Regulation, authorization to use the local clearance procedure shall be granted to any person wishing to have goods released for free circulation at his premises or at the other places designated or approved by the customs authorities in respect of goods subject to certain procedures (transit or customs procedures with economic impact) or which are brought into the customs territory of the Community with an exemption from the requirement that they be presented to customs.

4.149 Under Article 267 of the Implementing Regulation, the authorization shall lay down the specific rules for the operation of the procedure. Article 266 of the Implementing Regulation imposes some obligations on the holder of the authorization in order to enable the customs authorities to satisfy themselves as to the proper conduct of the operations. Generally speaking, these obligations consist in the notification to the customs authorities of some events (like the arrival of the goods to the place designated for release or the holder's desire to have the goods released for free circulation) and the obligation to enter the goods in the holder's records.

(ix) Penalties for violations of customs law

4.150 EC customs law does not explicitly set out the sanctions which apply in case of a violation by individuals of provisions of EC customs law. Accordingly, the nature and level of such penalties, whether administrative or criminal in nature, is determined by the national laws of the member States.

4.151 However, this does not mean that the member States have complete freedom in the determination of the appropriate level of penalties. In its constant case law, the European Court of Justice has repeatedly stated that Article 10 EC Treaty requires the member States to take all measures necessary for the proper implementation and application of Community law, including the provision of penalties for violations of EC law.

4.152 According to the case law of the Court, member States are obliged to provide for effective, proportionate and dissuasive penalities for any violation of EC law. Where a member States fails to provide such effective, proportionate and dissuasive penalities, it fails to fulfil its obligations under the EC Treaty. This has been confirmed by the ECJ specifically also in respect of the application of EC customs law.

4.153 The principles set out in the case law of the ECJ regarding the imposition of penalties for the violation of EC law can be regarded as generally accepted principles of EC law. This is illustrated by the Council resolution of 29 June 1995 on the effective uniform application of Community law and on the penalties applicable for breaches of Community law in the internal market. This resolution recalls the relevant case law of the Court of Justice, and calls upon member States to ensure that "Community law is duly applied with the same effectiveness and thoroughness as national law and that, in any event, the penalty provisions adopted are effective, proportionate and dissuasive".

(x) EC customs cooperation

4.154 An important instrument in the field of EC customs cooperation is Regulation (EC) 515/97 on mutual assistance between the administrative authorities of the member States and cooperation between the latter and the Commission to ensure the correct application of the law on customs and agricultural matters.

4.155 Title I of Regulation 515/97 deals with assistance on request between member States customs authorities. According to Article 4(1) of the Regulation, EC customs authorities must transmit to one another, upon request, any information necessary to ensure compliance with the provisions of EC customs legislation. The modalities of such assistance are set out in the following articles of Regulation 515/97. Article 7 provides that at the request of a customs authority, the requested authority shall keep a special watch for certain persons, places, movements of goods, or means of transport. Article 9 provides that customs authorities shall, at the request of another customs authority, carry out investigations concerning operations which appear to constitute a breach of customs legislation.

4.156 Title II deals with spontaneous assistance between customs authorities. Article 15 provides in particular that EC customs authorities must provide each other spontaneously any information concerning operations which appear to constitute violations of EC customs legislation.

4.157 Title III deals with relations between member States' customs authorities and the Commission, and obliges member States in particular to provide information to the Commission on all operations which appear to constitute breaches of EC customs law. According to Article 18(3) of the Regulation, in response to a reasoned request from the Commission, the member States' authorities shall take the actions foreseen in Articles 4 to 8 of the Regulation. According to Article 18(4) of the Regulation, where the Commission considers that irregularities have taken place, it may prompt a Member State to carry out an inquiry, at which Commission officials may be present under the conditions set out in Articles 9(2) and 11 of the Regulation. The Member State authorities shall, as soon as possible, communicate to the Commission the findings of the enquiry.

4.158 Title V establishes the Customs Information System (CIS). The CIS is an automated information system for the use of the administrative authorities of the member States and the Commission. In accordance with Article 23(2) of the Regulation, its aim is to assist the EC customs authorities in preventing, investigating, and prosecuting operations which are in breach of customs law by allowing the rapid dissemination of relevant information among all EC customs authorities. The conditions for the operation and use of the CIS are set out in detail in the following chapters of Title V of the Regulation.

4.159 Finally, customs cooperation is obviously an area which is subject to constant evolution, reflecting changing circumstances and technological and practical needs. For this reason, the Community has adopted and implemented successive action programmes aimed at strengthening the effective implementation of the EC customs union. The current action program is Customs 2007, which applies for the period of 1 January 2003 to 31 December 2007. It is established by Decision No. 253/2003/EC of the European Parliament and the Council.

4.160 The objectives of Customs 2007 are set out in Article 3(1) of Decision 253/2003. For the attainment of its objectives, Customs 2007 foresees a number of programme actions, which include actions in the field of communication and information exchange systems, benchmarking, exchanges of officials, seminars, workshops and project groups, training activities, monitoring actions, and external actions in the form of technical assistance and training. According to Article 14 of the Decision, the financial framework for the operations to be undertaken is set at €133 million.

(xi) Budgetary and financial aspects

4.161 The uniform implementation of the EC customs union is also important for the EC for budgetary and financial reasons. According to Article 2(1)(b) of the Council Decision 2000/597/EC, Euratom on the system of the European Communities' own resources, common customs tariff duties and other duties established in respect of trade with non-member countries shall constitute an own resource entered into the budget of the European Communities. According to Article 2(3) of the Decision, of the amount collected, Members shall retain an amount of 25% by way of collection cost. Accordingly, the correct implementation of Community customs law has direct implications for the EC budget, and is also for this reason closely monitored by the EC institutions, and in particular the European Commission.

4.162 Council Regulation (EC/Euratom) No. 1150/2000 sets out further procedures for the implementation of the own resources decision. This Regulation provides further tools for the uniform implementation of Community customs law, and therefore deserves to be considered here. According to Article 17(1) of the Regulation, member States must take all requisite measures to ensure that the amounts corresponding to the Community's entitlement are made available to the Community as specified in the Regulation. In accordance with Article 18(2)(a) of the Regulation, the member States must, at the request of the Commission, carry out additional inspections, with which the Commission shall be associated at its request. According to Article 18(3) of the Regulation, the Commission may also itself carry out inspection measures on the spot.

4.163 A failure to make available the Community's own resources is an infringement of the treaty, which can give rise to infringement proceedings against the Member State concerned. Where such a failure results from an incorrect application of EC customs law, the infringement procedures may at the same time also result in a finding that the member States has incorrectly applied EC customs law.

(xii) The continuous evolution of EC customs law

4.164 The EC institutions keep EC customs law under constant review in order to ensure that EC customs authorities can operate under the best possible conditions possible.

4.165 As the most recent example in this respect, the European Commission has launched a process of public consultations with a view to the preparation of a modernized customs code. The draft versions of the customs code have been submitted to several rounds of public consultations, in which traders, national administrations and third countries were provided with an opportunity to comment on the envisaged amendments. The United States did not provide any comments in the context of these consultations, even though it would have been perfectly possible for it to do so.

4.166 The Unites States has stated that "the most vocal critics of the EC frequently have been the EC's own officials". However, the statements to which the

United States refers simply reflect the ongoing process of reform and review of EC customs law. Indeed, the EC is not complacent about its own system, and is committed to continue developing it in accordance with changing needs and circumstances. However, this does not prove that the EC is in any way failing to comply with its obligations under Article X:3(a) and (b) GATT.

(c) Judicial control in EC law

(i) The EC court system

4.167 In the EC, all disputes concerning matters governed by Community law which are not subject to the jurisdiction of the Court of Justice of the EC (and the EC Court of First Instance) fall within the competence of the national courts. The national courts thus assume the status of Community courts of general competence, in the sense that they are competent to determine any dispute that is not expressly conferred on the EC Court of Justice and on the EC Court of First Instance. The situation of the national courts is such that they perform a dual functional role. When determining a dispute governed by national law, they continue to form part of the national legal order. When determining a case governed by Community law, they belong from the functional point of view to the Community legal order. Since the very foundation of the EC, the use of national courts to implement Community law has been considered as the best way of ensuring justice in a swift manner close to the citizens.

4.168 The EC Treaty itself established the role of the national courts in the application of the Community legal order, as well as the scope and consequences thereof, by virtue of its Article 234 concerning references to the Court of Justice by national Courts. Such role cannot be negated by Community legislation. Therefore, any modification in the boundaries between the competences of the Court of Justice and the national Courts would require the amendment of the EC Treaty.

4.169 The Court of Justice and the Court of First Instance of the European Communities are constituted under the EC Treaty and the Protocol on the Statute of the Court of Justice annexed to it. Both Courts are composed of one judge per Member State and they normally decide in chambers of three or five judges. The Court of Justice is assisted by eight Advocates General, who act with complete impartiality and independence in delivering an individual reasoned opinion on cases which require his or her involvement.

4.170 According to Article 220 of the EC Treaty, the central task of the Court of Justice and the Court of First Instance is to ensure that in the interpretation and application of the Treaty, the law is observed. This is done through different procedures, which delimitate the jurisdiction of both European Courts between themselves and with the national courts. The Court of Justice and the Court of First Instance are to act within the limits of the powers conferred upon them by the founding treaties.

4.171 The main division between the different kinds of proceedings before the Court of Justice is between those originating and terminating before the Court itself and those originating and terminating before national courts. In addition, the Court of Justice is competent to hear appeals on points of law from decisions of the Court of First Instance, where that Court has jurisdiction at first instance.

4.172 The main kinds of proceedings originating and terminating before the Court of Justice are, amongst others, actions against member States for failure to fulfil an obligation under Community law, actions for the annulment of a Community measure, actions for failure by a Community institution to act, and action for damages relating to the Community's non-contractual liability. The second category of proceedings before the Court of Justice is actions which originate before a national court but are referred to the Court of Justice for a ruling on the interpretation or validity of a point of Community law.

4.173 Article 225(1) of the EC Treaty provides that the Court of First Instance shall have jurisdiction at first instance in actions for annulment, actions for failure to act, actions founded on non-contractual liability, staff cases and cases under arbitration clauses in Community contracts, with the exception of those reserved in the Statute to the Court of Justice. As the Statute reserves to the Court actions for annulment and actions for failure to act brought by institutions and member States in some sectors, the jurisdiction conferred on the Court of First Instance covers virtually all direct actions brought by natural or legal persons as well as direct actions by member States challenging executive action by the Community institutions. In the fields thus defined, the Court of First Instance has exclusive jurisdiction at first instance, its decisions being subject to a right of appeal on points of law only to the Court of Justice.

(ii) Judicial protection in the EC legal system

4.174 As a Community based on the rule of law, the Community recognizes the right of individuals to judicial protection. This right to an effective remedy before a tribunal is, first of all, recognized in Article 47 of the Charter of Fundamental Rights of the European Union, which reflects, in accordance with Article 6(2) EU Treaty, the constitutional traditions of the member States. It should be also stressed that all EC members States are parties to the Council of Europe Convention for the Protection of Human Rights and Fundamental Freedoms of 14 November 1950, where Article 6(1) lays down the right to a fair trial by an independent and impartial tribunal established by law.

4.175 In the EC legal system, national courts guarantee this right when a decision taken by national authorities is challenged. This also applies to acts of the member States through which they implement Community law. While the judicial organization and procedures in the member States result from their various political, constitutional and legal traditions, they all provide complete legal protection in relation to administrative decisions.

4.176 As regards the decisions of the EC institutions, the main action to exercise this right is the action for annulment. Under Article 230 of the EC Treaty, the Court is to review the legality of acts, amongst others, adopted jointly by the European Parliament and the Council, of the acts of the Council, and of the Commission, other than recommendations or opinions. Generally speaking, an action for annulment is available in the case of all measures adopted by the institutions, whatever their nature or form, which are intended to have legal effects. However, this jurisdiction does not cover acts adopted by a national authority. Neither does it extend to the Treaty and its amendments.

4.177 Under Article 230(4) of the EC Treaty, natural or legal persons may institute proceedings against a decision addressed to that person or against a decision which, although in the form of a regulation or a decision addressed to another person, is of direct and individual concern to the former person. The Court of Justice has interpreted "of direct concern" to mean that the effect of the measure on the person's interests must not depend on the discretion of another person, including the relevant Member State. The requirement of "individual concern" is fulfilled where the measure in question affects specific natural or legal persons by reason of certain attributes peculiar to them, or by reason of a factual situation which differentiates them from all other persons and distinguishes them individually in the same way as the addressee.

(iii) Preliminary rulings: the Court of Justice and the uniform interpretation and application of Community law

4.178 The Court of Justice plays a central role in the uniform interpretation and application of Community law throughout the Community by means of the preliminary reference procedure set out in Article 234 EC Treaty.

4.179 Where a question as to any of these matters arises before any court or tribunal of a Member State, that court or tribunal may, if it considers that a decision on the question is necessary to enable it to give Judgment, request the Court of Justice to give a ruling on it. Where any such question is raised in a case pending before a court or tribunal of a Member State, against whose decisions there is no judicial remedy under national law, that court or tribunal must bring the matter before the Court of Justice.

4.180 However, where the validity of a Community act is challenged before a national court, the Court of Justice has declared that the power to declare the act invalid must be reserved to the latter. Therefore, if a national court considers that an act of an EC institution is invalid, it is obliged to make a reference to the Court of Justice. The latter has justified this case law with the need to secure the uniform application of all acts of the Community.

4.181 In a recent case, the Court of Justice confirmed that the principle of Member State liability for breaches of Community law also applies when a breach is attributable to a Member State court, because it fails to refer a case to the Court of Justice. In such cases, the affected claimant is entitled to bring another suit, affording the national judge hearing that case the opportunity to refer the issue to the Court of Justice at the second attempt.

4.182 When entertaining a preliminary reference, the Court of Justice does not exercise an appellate power to approve or overrule determinations of the referring courts. Rather, it assists the national court in coming to a decision which has not been made at the time of the reference. The relationship between national courts and the Court of Justice is co-operative and not hierarchical, based on the recognition that each court has a different function, and on mutual goodwill and respect.

4.183 The main objective of this preliminary reference system is to guarantee the proper and uniform interpretation and application of Community law throughout all the member States, avoiding the establishment of a long and expensive appellate system before the Court of Justice. This is extremely important because the administration of the Community is, to a large extent, carried out by the member States rather than by the Community institutions and because Community legislation may require implementing measures to be adopted by national legislatures or executives. It is through preliminary references that divergences within and between the member States can be avoided and the effective application of Community law be assured. At the same time, the reference procedure constitutes the principal method by which the compatibility of national law and administrative decisions with Community law is tested.

4.184 Apart from providing a means of ensuring uniformity throughout the Community, individual litigants find that their national cases are referred to the Court of Justice as to the validity or interpretation of an act of a Community institution. All parties to the main action are entitled to participate in the preliminary reference proceedings, as well as Members States and Community institutions. It is the practice of the Commission to participate in every case before the Court of Justice, as a consequence of its role as guardian of the Community interest. A preliminary ruling given by the Court of Justice is binding on the national court hearing the case in which the ruling is given. Besides, national courts and tribunals implement faithfully the preliminary rulings of the Court of Justice. If a referring court does not follow the ruling of the Court of Justice, this would constitute a breach of the obligations of the Member State under the Treaty, which could be brought before the Court of Justice under Articles 226 to 228 of the EC Treaty.

4.185 A preliminary ruling has also an effect on persons who are not parties to the case referred. In *Simitzi v. Municipality of Kos*, the Court held that Greece could no longer reasonably have believed that a duty was compatible with Community law after the date of the Judgment in which a comparable French charge was held not to be. In a recent case, the Court of Justice has expanded the effects of preliminary rulings to certain *res judicata* situations. The Court declared that, in view of the obligation on all the authorities of the member States to ensure observance of Community law and because of the principle of cooperation arising from Article 10 EC, an administrative body may be under an obligation to review a final administrative decision in order to take account of the interpretation of the relevant provision given by the Court in a subsequent preliminary ruling.

(iv) Judicial review of customs decisions

4.186 Article 243(1) CCC provides that any person shall have the right to appeal against decisions taken by the customs authorities which relate to the application of customs legislation and which concern him or her directly and individually. Article 243(1) CCC also provides that any person who has applied to the customs authorities for a decision relating to the application of customs legislation and has not obtained a ruling on that request within the period referred to in Article 6(2) CCC shall also be entitled to exercise the right of appeal. Article 243(1) finally provides that the appeal must be lodged in the member State where the decision has been taken or applied for.

4.187 Since Community customs law is implemented through the customs authorities of the member States, the appeal is lodged before a tribunal of the member State whose customs authorities have issued the decision. In accordance with Article 245 CCC, the provisions governing the appeals procedure are laid down in the national laws of the member States. The CCC abstains from harmonising the national law on administrative and judicial appeals against customs decisions. This reflects the fact that such procedural laws often apply uniformly to the whole field of national administration. Harmonization might therefore have led to the fragmentation of hitherto uniform national appeals procedures.

4.188 As it has already been explained above, the role of the member States' courts in the judicial review of customs decision is fully compatible with the uniform application of EC customs law. member States' courts are obliged to apply EC law according to the interpretation given by the Court of Justice and set aside any national provision or measure that is inconsistent with EC law. Wherever a question of interpretation of Community law arises, such a question may be referred to the Court of Justice in accordance with Article 234 EC. Where the national court is a court of last instance or any national court considers that the Community measure is invalid, such court is obliged to refer the question to the ECJ.

4.189 Finally, it should be noted that in exceptional cases, a right of appeal against customs decisions may also be available directly to the EC Court of First Instance. This is the case when the European Commission takes decisions applying EC customs law which are of direct and individual concern to individuals within the meaning of Article 230(4) EC Treaty. Examples for such decisions are Commission decisions revoking BTI. Another example would be Commission decisions on the repayment or remission of import duties on equitable grounds on the basis of Article 907 of the Implementing Regulation.

(d) The US system in comparison

(i) The administration of US customs law

4.190 In the United States, customs laws, which are federal laws, are essentially administered by US Customs and Border Protection. US Customs and Border Protection is an agency of the US Federal Government part of the US Department of Homeland Security. US Customs and Border Control has 20 Field Operations Offices which oversee 317 US ports of entry and 14 preclearance offices.

4.191 However, it is noteworthy that the fact that US customs law is implemented by a federal agency is not specific to customs matters. On the contrary, it reflects a fundamental interpretation of US constitutional law according to which Congress may not require US states to implement federal law. This has been confirmed by the US Supreme Court in the case *Printz vs. United States.*

4.192 The US dual federalism is diametrically opposed to the basic principles of the EC legal order. The US system is characterized by a principle of "dual sovereignty", in which the individual States may not be "conscripted" or "commandeered" to administer federal law. EC law is characterized by the principle of executive federalism, where all EC law must be executed by the national authorities of the member States, acting under the guidance and supervision of the EC institutions.

4.193 The EC does not intend to question the constitutional choices which the United States has made. However, in response to the US claims under Article X:3(a) GATT, it is important to stress that the EC's executive federalism is just as fundamental and legitimate a constitutional choice as the US system of dual sovereignty. The EC considers that its constitutional choices should be afforded the same respect as those of the United States.

(ii) Review of customs decisions in US law

4.194 Judicial review in the US concerning customs and trade issues is in the first step attributed to the United States Court of International Trade (the "USCIT"), which is a federal court established under Article III of the US Constitution. The USCIT is equal in rank to a federal district court.

4.195 Appeals against the USCIT's decisions may in all cases be taken as of right to the US Court of Appeals for the Federal Circuit (the "CAFC"). It is a specialized appellate court with the rank of a federal circuit court, which has exclusive jurisdiction over appeals from the USCIT as well as a disparate group on non-USCIT issues, patents appeals being the most common. Ultimately, an appeal to the US Supreme Court, via petition for writ of certiorari, can be lodged.

4.196 It is worth noting that this centralized first instance judicial review at federal level through the USCIT is a political choice that the United States has made. Under US law, State courts have also a role in enforcing federal law, as was clearly explained by the US Supreme Court in the case *Claflin v. Houseman.*

4.197 The EC does not intend to question the political choices which the United States has made to organize its judiciary in relation to customs matters. However, in response to the US claims under Article X:3(b) GATT, it is important to stress that the EC's judiciary system is just as fundamental and legitimate a constitutional choice as the US centralized system. The EC considers that its constitutional choices should be afforded the same respect as those of the United States.

3. *The US claims under Article X:3(a) GATT*

(a) The requirements of Article X:3(a) GATT

(i) Article X:3(a) GATT concerns the administration of customs laws, not the customs laws themselves

4.198 The requirements of Article X:3(a) GATT do not concern the customs laws themselves, but only their *administration*. This was clearly spelt out by the Appellate Body in *EC – Bananas III*.

4.199 This distinction is highly important for the present case. It means that Article X:3(a) GATT does not require a harmonization of laws within a Member where, for instance, different legal regimes are applicable within different parts of the territory of a WTO Member.

4.200 This is particularly relevant for all WTO Members which have a federal structure. In a federal State or entity, different laws may apply in the different parts of the territory of the Member concerned, depending on whether it is the federal or the sub-federal level which has legislated on a particular issue.

4.201 Article X:3(a) GATT does not interfere with the question of whether a particular issue should be dealt with at the federal or the sub-federal level. It guarantees merely that whatever laws exist must be administered in uniform manner. However, where laws apply only in part of the territory of a Member, this requirement is met provided that those laws are applied uniformly within the part of the territory in which they are applicable.

4.202 Further confirmation for this interpretation is found in Article XXIV:12 GATT. The Panel in *Canada – Gold Coins* found that this provision has the "function of allowing federal States to accede to the General Agreement without having to change the federal distribution of competence". Accordingly, any interpretation of Article X:3(a) GATT which would affect the internal distribution of competence is incompatible with Article XXIV:12 GATT.

4.203 In other words, Article X:3(a) GATT does not require that customs laws be regulated at the central level of each WTO Member. The WTO Agreements respect the internal structure and divisions of competences in each WTO Member. Where sub-federal laws exist in a particular WTO Member, it is therefore to the administration of those laws that Article X:3(a) GATT refers.

(ii) Article X:3(a) GATT does not prescribe the ways in which WTO Members must administer their customs laws

4.204 Article X:3(a) GATT does not prescribe the specific way in which WTO Members should administer their customs laws. It merely sets out an obligation to administer customs laws in a uniform manner.

4.205 Article X:3(a) GATT is not the only provision of the covered agreements dealing with the administration of customs laws. Indeed, a number of Agreements contained in Annex 1A to the WTO Agreement deal with specific matters of customs administration, notably the Valuation Agreement, the Agreement on Rules of Origin, and the Agreement on Import Licensing Procedures.

4.206 Wherever it was felt necessary to lay down specific disciplines on how WTO Members should administer their customs laws, appropriate provisions were included in the respective agreements. For example, Articles 2(h) and 3(f) of the Agreement on Rules of Origin require WTO Members to issue advance rulings on the origin of goods. If it had been felt necessary to include similar obligations for the issuance of advance rulings on other issues, such as tariff classification or customs valuation, such provisions could have been included in the covered agreements. If they were not, it must be concluded that WTO Members did not consider such obligations appropriate.

4.207 Article X:3(a) GATT must therefore not be interpreted in such a way as to create WTO obligations where WTO Members consciously abstained from laying them down. In other words, Article X:3(a) GATT is not a legal basis for engaging in a harmonization of the customs law and administrations of WTO Members through the DSU.

4.208 Respect of these principles is particularly necessary since the revision of Article X GATT is currently the subject of the ongoing Doha negotiations on trade facilitation. In the context of these negotiations, WTO Members have made a large number of proposals to supplement and improve Article X GATT, including on issues which are the subject of the US claims. This also applies to the United States itself, which has made a number of proposals in relation to Article X GATT, including a proposal to create an obligation to "make available, upon request of a trader, binding rulings in certain specific subject areas (e.g., tariff classification, customs valuation, duty deferral)". Proposals on advance rulings, the majority of which however is limited to issues of tariff classification, have also been made by a number of other countries.

4.209 These ongoing negotiations underline that on those matters in which it is currently silent, Article X GATT in fact does not contain any obligations. It is unclear to the EC how the United States can simultaneously make proposals for the creation of new obligations going beyond Article X GATT, and then argue that very similar obligations are already owed under Article X GATT as it currently stands.

4.210 The US case is motivated less by legal than by political considerations. In fact, this has been explicitly admitted by the United States in a press release that was issued by USTR to announce the US request, which indicated that "pressing a major player in world trade to administer its customs laws and regulations in a uniform manner will help to advance" the Doha Round trade facilitation negotiations. The EC is highly concerned by this attempt by the United States to instrumentalize the DSU for the purposes of influencing the ongoing Doha Round negotiations.

(iii) Article X:3(a) GATT lays down minimum standards

4.211 In line with the foregoing, it must be considered that Article X:3(a) GATT only lays down minimum standards. It does not oblige WTO Members to meet the highest possible standard achievable at a given point in time. This character of Article X:3(a) as a minimum standard has been emphasized by the Appellate Body in *US – Shrimp*. The Panel in *Argentina – Hides and Leather* has also cautioned against reading too much into Article X:3(a) GATT.

4.212 Moreover, minor administrative differences in treatment cannot be regarded as implying a violation of Article X:3(a) GATT. This was clearly stated by the GATT Panel in *EC – Dessert Apples*, which confirmed that certain variations between EC member States in the administration of import licensing, e.g., as regards the form in which licence applications could be made and the requirement of pro-forma invoices, did not constitute a breach of Article X:3(a) GATT.

4.213 Overall, Article X:3(a) GATT is therefore a minimum standards provision which guarantees only a certain minimum level of uniformity in administration. Moreover, Article X:3(a) GATT does not prohibit administrative variations where such variations are minor or do not significantly affect the interests of traders.

(iv) The meaning of "uniform administration"

4.214 The meaning of the requirement of "uniform administration" must be established in the light of the foregoing observations. Moreover, account must be taken of the practical realities in which customs administrations must work.

4.215 The administration of customs laws in the real world involves a number of difficulties and challenges. First of all, the administration of customs frequently involves complex questions of law and fact. Second, the circumstances under which customs authorities operate are in continuous evolution due to changes in goods traded or commercial behaviour. This requires customs authorities to continuously adapt to new realities. Third, customs administration is a mass business.

4.216 Therefore, a measure of realism is required in the application of Article X:3(a) GATT. If customs authorities struggle with a complex new question of law and fact, this does not already mean that authorities in the member concerned administer customs law in a non-uniform manner. Similarly, if it takes a certain amount of time to come to an established practice on a new and complex issue of customs law, this does not yet mean that customs laws are being administered in a non-uniform way.

4.217 A complete uniformity in the application of customs laws could never be achieved by any Member, even those with the most efficient systems of customs administration. In a large country with a large bureaucracy, a minimum degree of non-uniformity is *de facto* unavoidable. This may occur, for instance, because a trader in a particular case does not challenge a particular decision even though it was illegal. In such a case, non-uniformity may be the result, but this does not mean that the Member in question fails to meet its obligations under Article X:3(a) GATT. The EC notes that the United States appears to agree with this, since it states that "the fact that divergences occur is not problematic in and of itself".

4.218 The proposition that individual instances of administration are not probative for a violation of Article X:3(a) GATT also finds support in the case law under the DSU. In *EC – Poultry*, the Appellate Body already confirmed that individual measures of application do not fall within the scope of Article X GATT. In *US – Hot Rolled Steel*, the Panel stated that rather than relying on individual instances of administration, it was necessary for the complaining party to establish a pattern of decision making contrary to Article X:3(a) GATT.

4.219 Accordingly, whether a particular member meets the requirement of "uniformity" cannot be established merely by looking at an individual example of practice. Rather, uniformity can be assessed only on the basis of an overall pattern of customs administration. Only if, on the basis of such general patterns, a WTO Member's administration of its customs laws can be shown to be non-uniform, is the standard of Article X:3(a) GATT violated.

(b) The burden of proof

4.220 It is established case law under the DSU that the party which asserts a particular claim bears the burden of proof. In the present case, it is the United States which claims that the EC does not administer its customs laws in a uniform manner. It is accordingly the United States which must adduce evidence to establish a *prima facie* case that its claim is true. Only if the United States discharges this burden of proof will the burden shift to the EC to rebut the US case.

4.221 The United States does not even come close to discharging this burden of proof. In fact, the United States adduces only very sparse evidence regarding the actual administration of EC customs law. The examples given by the United States are partially irrelevant, partially inconclusive, and in any event do not show a general pattern of non-uniform administration of EC customs law.

4.222 Instead of adducing concrete evidence regarding the administration of EC customs law, the United States tries to build its case on systemic criticisms of the EC system of customs administration, arguing for instance that because EC law is administered by the authorities of the 25 EC member States, "divergences will inevitably occur". However, the assertion that such "divergences are inevitable", which the EC strongly contests, does not replace the proof that divergences actually occur.

4.223 The entirely speculative nature of the US case is also illustrated by the US references to the expected effects of the enlargement of the EU by 10 new member States on 1 May 2004. In the press release of USTR announcing the US Panel Request, the anticipated effects of EU enlargement were cited as the primary reason for requesting a Panel.

4.224 At the time the United States made its request for a Panel, EU enlargement had been in effect for less than eight months. The United States has not referred to any lack of uniformity in the implementation of EC customs law by the administrations of the 10 new member States. Pure speculation about possible future developments cannot replace facts and evidence as a basis for claims made under the DSU.

4.225 In its efforts to avoid its own burden of proof, the United States prefers to refer to pronouncements of EC officials or institutions, which it claims are the "most vocal critics" of the EC system. However, these references are taken out of context, and do not support the conclusions the Unites States would draw from them. In any event, the desire to make further progress is natural in the context of a healthy system of customs administration. Such statements have nothing to do with the question of whether the EC is in compliance with its obligations under Article X:3(a) GATT, and do not exempt the United States from the necessity of discharging its burden of proof.

4.226 Finally, that the US case is not really based on any pattern of non-uniformity in the administration of customs in the EC is strikingly confirmed by the almost complete lack of reaction to the call for input by the United States Trade Representative following the consultation request. If really there was a pattern of non-uniformity, as the United States alleges, one could have expected that the United States would receive more than three contributions, two of which were not even pertinent to the US case.

(c) General issues underlying the US claims under Article X:3(a) GATT

(i) The fact that EC customs law is administered by the customs authorities of EC member States is compatible with Article X:3(a) GATT

4.227 Article X:3(a) GATT does not prescribe the ways in which a WTO Member must implement its customs laws. This also includes the question through what authorities or administration customs laws are administered. Article X:3(a) GATT in no ways excludes that in a federal or quasi-federal state or entity, customs laws could be administered by authorities at the sub-federal level. Contrary to the United States, it does not prescribe the creation of a customs agency similar to US Customs and Border Protection.

4.228 Moreover, when they administer EC customs law, the EC member States act as the organs of the EC. This has been confirmed with by the recent Panel report in *EC – Trademarks and Geographical Indications (US)*, where the Panel noted that when EC member States execute a particular EC regulation, they do so as organs of the EC, for which the EC is responsible under public international law.

4.229 For this reason, the United States is wrong to assert that there "is no EC customs authority to speak of". The customs authorities of the EC member

States, acting together with and under the supervision of the competent institutions of the EC, are the EC customs authority. That this system of customs administration is different from that of the United States is of no relevance under Article X:3(a) GATT. It should also be recalled that the United States itself has accepted, in the EC-US Agreement on customs cooperation, the fact that the EC member States together with the European Commission constitute the EC customs authority.

4.230 The United States is also wrong to assert that due to the involvement of EC member States in the administration of EC customs law, "divergences inevitably occur". As the EC has already shown, and will recall again in the following section, the EC has numerous mechanisms in place to ensure that the administration of EC customs law takes place in a uniform manner. In addition, the US statement that in the EC system, a lack of uniformity would be "inevitable" is unsupported by evidence.

(ii) The EC has measures in place to ensure the uniform administration of EC customs laws throughout the EC

4.231 The US claim that the EC does not provide for the systematic reconciliation of divergences in the application of EC customs law is false. It reflects a biased and incomplete presentation of the EC system, in which the United States focuses on a small number of instruments while ignoring a wide range of other instruments which equally contribute to the uniform interpretation and application of EC customs law. Moreover, the United States fails to take into account the overall context of the EC legal system and the ways in which uniformity is ensured within the EC system.

4.232 The EC finds it remarkable that the United States would make sweeping statements about the uniformity of EC law without ever once mentioning such fundamental principles of EC law as the supremacy and direct effect of EC law, the duty of cooperation, infringement proceedings, the various instruments of EC customs cooperation, or the budgetary control aspects.

4.233 A particularly striking example of the highly selective US approach is customs classification, where the United States concentrates mainly on the EC BTI system, without giving any consideration to the other tools for ensuring a uniform classification practice within the EC, such as classification regulations, HS instruments, EC explanatory notes, or opinions of the Customs Code Committee. Even where the US considers parts of the EC system, it presents these in a highly distorted way.

4.234 The question of whether the EC, at a systematic level, administers EC customs law in a uniform manner cannot be evaluated by simply considering one single instrument in isolation. Rather, the EC system has to be evaluated as a whole, taking into account all of the relevant instruments in their proper context.

4.235 This evaluation should be made taking into account the structural elements of the EC legal system and the overall record and experience of European integration. The structural elements which the United States criticises are not specific to the administration of customs laws, but are general structural elements of the EC constitutional order. More than fifty years of successful integration in Europe based on the EC's model of executive federalism should not lightly be dismissed.

(iii) Some necessary corrections regarding the role and functioning of the Customs Code Committee

4.236 The United States argues that the Customs Code Committee does not function efficiently enough and that individual traders are not given enough rights in the context of the proceedings of the Committee. These US criticisms are unfounded.

4.237 As regards the alleged inefficiency in the Committee's operation, the United States relies essentially on general statements about "institutional disincentives" which would keep the Commission from putting matters to a vote. These allegations regarding "institutional disincentives" are unfounded and are not supported by any evidence. Moreover, the United States neglects that the conditions under which the Chairman puts a matter to the vote or may postpone a vote are laid down in Article 6 of the Rules of Procedure of the Committee.

4.238 The fact that in some cases, the Committee may have to be seized more than one time of the same or of related matters has nothing to do with "institutional disincentives". Rather, this may reflect the complexity of the issue in question and the need to gather a full understanding of the factual situation before a decision can be taken.

4.239 The entirely speculative nature of the US claims is also illustrated by the references it makes to the supposed negative effects of EU enlargement on the efficiency of the Committee. The United Sates makes these statements without being able to support them with any concrete evidence.

4.240 As regards the rights of individual traders in respect of the proceedings of the Committee, the United States makes these arguments in the context of a discussion of whether the EC administers its customs laws uniformly in accordance with Article X:3(a) GATT. The EC does not understand the relevance of these arguments regarding the rights of private traders before the Committee for the question of whether EC customs law is uniformly applied throughout the EC.

4.241 The US complaints seem to be based on a fundamental misunderstanding of the role of the Customs Code Committee. The Committee is not a mechanism for the administrative or judicial review of customs decisions. Rather, it is an integral part of the Community's regulatory process, through which member States expertise is integrated into this process. There is accordingly no basis for the extensive rights of private traders requested by the United States.

4.242 Any individual with a concern regarding the administration of customs matters can bring this issue to the attention of the Commission, which will consider the matter and respond in accordance with the Commission's Code of Conduct. If the Commission considers that the matter requires consideration by the

Committee, it will put this matter on the Committee's agenda. In a similar fashion, a concerned individual may also address the administration of a Member State, which may equally decide to raise the matter in the Committee.

4.243 As regards the publication of agendas or reports of the Committee, there is no obligation of publication in this respect. The United States also has not raised any claim under Article X:1 GATT. In any event, the US claims are factually wrong. Documents relating to the Customs Code Committee, including agendas and summary records of meetings, are available on the public register of comitology of the European Commission. Moreover, access to the agendas and records of the Committee is governed by the EC rules on access to documents laid down in Regulation EC/1049/2001.

(iv) The role of the Court of Justice in ensuring uniformity in the administration of EC customs law

4.244 The United States contests that uniform administration can be guaranteed by the Court of Justice through preliminary references made by national courts. To sustain its arguments, the United States relies on the opinion of AG Jacobs in *Wiener*. However, AG Jacobs′ position departs from the case-law of the Court of Justice and, what is even more fundamental, his position as to the exercise of a greater measure of self-restraint either on the part of the Court or by national courts was not followed by the Court.

4.245 AG Jacobs proposed to the Court that the question referred by the Bundesfinanzhof should be answered by reminding the principles enshrined in the case-law of the Court of Justice in relation to customs classification. Contrary to the conclusions of the AG, the Court of Justice provided a specific answer to the question of how the goods in question were to be classified.

4.246 As to AG Jacobs' advice for self-restraint addressed to national courts, the ruling of the Court of Justice is completely silent on this issue. Therefore, AG Jacobs' non-binding opinion constitutes a doctrinal position with no influence on the case law of the Court of Justice.

4.247 Concerning AG Jacob's statement about the supposedly minimal contribution of the Court to the uniform application of the Common Customs Tariff, the United States has clearly taken it out of context. What AG Jacobs underlined in its opinion is that, considering the detailed character of the Common Customs Tariff, there were also other ways of ensuring uniformity in the field of customs classification and gave the Commission's classification regulations as an example.

4.248 To confirm that AG Jacobs' advice for self-restraint is being followed by national courts, the United States refers to two Judgments given by two different UK courts. Thus the support found by the United States to its arguments is limited to two cases in one of the 25 EC member States. No evidence is provided on the position taken by the other 24 national judiciary branches in relation to the AG's advice (should such a position exist). The EC considers that these two UK cases are not sufficient to support the US claim.

4.249 Moreover, in *Anchor Foods Limited*, the UK Queen's Bench Division did not rely on AG Jacobs´ opinion to decide that there was no need to refer to Court of Justice. Indeed, the Queen´s Bench Division decided not to refer because of the limited importance of the case. It should also be pointed out that the Queen's Bench Division did not act in this case as a court of last instance and that, therefore, it was not under an obligation to refer the case to the Court of Justice.

(d) The US claims under Article X:3(a) GATT

(i) Tariff classification

The ECJ and tariff classification

4.250 The United States argues that the ECJ as an institution is ill-equipped to bring uniformity to the administration of the Tariff. This statement, which is solely based on the Opinion of AG Jacobs, in Wiener, is wrong.

4.251 Concerning specifically the role of the ECJ in classification disputes, the EC disagrees with the US opinion that because of this fact-intensive nature of classification questions, the ECJ cannot play a useful role in securing a uniform administration of EC classification rules. Even if classification questions may typically be fact-intensive, this does not make them fundamentally different from other questions of law, which also involve the application of abstract rules to factual situations.

4.252 Moreover, it is in the nature of classification issues that they concern the classification of specific goods. To which extent a classification of particular goods may be transposable by analogy to different, but similar goods is a complex question which can be evaluated only on a case-by-case basis. Once again, however, this is a general issue of classification, and is not in any way specific to the role of the Court.

4.253 Finally, the US attempts to belittle the role of the Court are strikingly at odds with its allegations that the EC acts in a non-uniform manner. The US comments would actually seem to cast doubt on whether classification questions can be regulated effectively at all. The concerns expressed by the United States concerning the fact-intensive nature of classification questions arise regardless of whether the final decision-maker is a Court or an administrative agency.

4.254 Overall, the US line of argument leaves the EC perplexed. The United States seems to practically claim that a uniform classification cannot be achieved, and then fault the EC for not doing enough to achieve it.

Binding tariff information

4.255 Article X:3(a) GATT is a provision which sets out minimum standards, and does not prescribe the specific means a Member must employ in order to ensure a uniform administration of customs laws. For this reason, there is no obligation under WTO law for a Member to have a system of binding tariff information in place. This is clearly illustrated also by the US proposals in the context of the Doha Round trade facilitation negotiations, which aim at supplementing Article X GATT by introducing an obligation to provide for advance rulings on classification matters.

4.256 The United States alleges that the EBTI system encourages "BTI shopping" and thus leads to an increased risk of divergent BTIs. These US allegations are based on numerous misconceptions about the EBTI system. The United States claims that the "holder or other applicant chooses the member States to which it will make the application". This is misleading. EC customs law does not allow applicants to "pick and choose" the member State which will issue the BTI. According to Article 6(1) of the Implementing Regulation, applications for BTI must be made either to the competent authorities in the Member State or member States in which the information is to be used, or to the competent authorities in the Member State were the applicant is established.

4.257 The United States also complains that a BTI "is not binding on the holder, in the sense that it does not need to be invoked by the holder". First, this is not entirely true. According to Article 10(2)(a) of the Implementing Regulation, the customs authorities may require the holder, when fulfilling customs formalities, to inform the customs authorities that he is in possession of BTI in respect of the goods being cleared through customs.

4.258 Second, the EC fails to see the practical relevance of this issue from the point of view of a uniform BTI practice. The United States states that a person that has received unfavourable BTI in one Member State "may ignore it, not apply for BTI in another State, and simply attempt to import merchandise through another member State asserting the more favourable classification without relying on BTI at all". This may be so, but the situation would be no different if no BTI had been granted at all. BTI is granted for the benefit of the holder. In the situation described by the United States, it would therefore be more natural for the person which has received the unfavourable BTI to challenge it, if it believes it to be wrong. Moreover, there is no reason to assume that other EU customs authorities will apply a different tariff classification than the one foreseen in the BTI, just because the BTI is not invoked.

4.259 The US claim that an applicant may apply in one Member State and, if it is not favourable, decline to invoke it and apply for BTI in another member State is wrong. According to Article 6(3)(A)(j) of the Implementing Regulation, when applying for BTI, the applicant must indicate whether, to his knowledge, binding tariff information for identical or similar goods has already been applied for, or issued in the Community. Moreover, Box 11 of the Standard BTI Application form requires the applicant to declare whether he has applied or been issued with BTI for similar or identical goods. The United States cannot here try to show deficiencies in the EC system by constructing scenarios which are based on flagrant violations of EC rules. In addition, Article 12(4) CCC provides that BTI based on inaccurate or incomplete information from the applicant shall be annulled.

4.260 The United States argues that where divergent BTIs exist, the EC system does not provide for sufficient mechanisms to correct these divergences. The scenarios and supposed difficulties which the United States describes in detecting divergent BTIs are largely theoretical. Classification differences typically occur in cases where several headings potentially merit consideration, and the choice between them is not entirely obvious. Such cases do not remain secret for long. It is the customs authorities themselves which will first notice the difficulty, and if they do not, traders will make them aware of it by challenging decisions which they perceive as unfavourable to them. If a challenge occurs, the question may be referred to the Court of Justice, which will ultimately lead to its being clarified.

4.261 However, even before the Courts have been seized or have given judgment, frequently the national customs authorities themselves will raise the issue in the Customs Code Committee. Alternatively, they may first seize the Commission of the matter, which may decide to bring it before the Customs Code Committee.

4.262 Individual traders also frequently approach the Commission or member States authorities with particular problems of customs classification, who can then decide to take the necessary action, including raising the issue before the Customs Code Committee. In brief, difficulties in detecting "hidden" divergent BTI are greatly exaggerated by the United States; experience in fact shows that such divergences, if they have economic implications, do not remain hidden for long.

4.263 The EC also has the EBTI data base, which allows searches of all BTIs both by the public and by the customs authorities. This data base is an important instrument of transparency in the EBTI system. The EBTI database is very well received by traders and used frequently; in the first six months of 2005, for instance, the average number of consultations per month was about 324.000.

4.264 The United States is wrong to argue that the search might be difficult because product descriptions might vary. First, that product descriptions might vary is true, but this is hardly a barrier to conducting a search. Searches of the public EBTI data base can be conducted using a variety of parameters, and a careful targeting of criteria will yield results. Keywords are available in all official languages of the EC. There is also a translation facility available to translate keywords into any of the 19 languages. Accordingly, language should not be a major difficulty in making searches.

4.265 Moreover, as the EC has also explained, there exists a version of the EBTI data base accessible to the member States' customs authorities and the Commission. This data base allows searches of BTI using additional parameters, including notably the name and address of holder and applicant. Moreover, this data base also allows searches of pending applications for BTI. Detailed instructions for the EC customs authorities as to how to conduct searches have also been included in the Administrative Guidelines on the EBTI system issued by the European Commission.

4.266 It is untrue that the EC has no means of detecting divergent BTIs. It is interesting to note that the United States, in order to illustrate its claim of a divergent classification practice regarding blackout drapery lining has provided as an exhibit excerpts from the public EBTI data base. Thus, the United States has itself disproved its claim that use of the EBTI data base is impossible.

4.267 The US criticisms of the judgment in decision of the Court of Justice in Case C-133/02, *Timmermans*, are without merit. There is no reason to assume, as the United States does, that a revocation of a BTI as allowed by the Court in *Timmermans* would lead to less uniformity. On the contrary, a revocation may precisely be necessary in order to take into account that other customs authorities have adopted a different classification practice, which is confirmed to be the correct one. This in fact is precisely what happened in *Timmermans*, where the withdrawal of the BTI occurred because "on a closer examination and in consultation with the customs authorities of a neighbouring district concerning the interpretation of the applicable nomenclature, it had become apparent the goods in question should be classified under" a different subheading. The same reasoning could also have been applied if the divergence had arisen in relation to the practice of the authorities of another Member State.

4.268 In any event, the Timmermans judgment does not primarily concern a question of uniform application, but a question of legal security for the trader. The Court of Justice held that the legitimate interests of the trader were sufficiently protected by the provisions of Article 12(6) CCC, which under certain conditions allow continued use of the BTI for a limited period of time. This is not problematic under Article X:3(a) GATT.

Alleged divergences in EC classification practice

4.269 In order to support its claim, the United States has referred to two cases in which the EC allegedly has administered its laws in the field of tariff classification in a non-uniform manner. However, both cases do not show any lack of uniformity in the EC's administration.

4.270 The first case of alleged divergences concerns the classification of Blackout Drapery Lining (BDL). However, in this case, the goods examined by the German customs authorities were not identical to those described in the BTI, since they were not flocked with a layer of textile flock. Whether the product was flocked or not is an important difference, which justifies the different classification of the product. Accordingly, since the United States has not shown that the products were identical in the relevant respect, the United States fails to show that there is in fact any inconsistency.

4.271 Moreover, the EC would like to recall that according to Article 12(3) CCC, the holder of BTI must be able to prove that the good declared correspond in every respect to those described in the information. Goods as described in the decision of the German customs authorities would not appear to fall under the description contained in the BTIs.

4.272 In addition, it should be noted that according to Article 6(3)(A)(d) of the Implementing Regulation, it is the applicant which must provide a detailed description of the goods permitting their identification and the determination of their classification in the customs nomenclature. In contrast, the United States has not provided information as to whether samples were submitted to the authorities issuing the BTI, and whether these samples were indeed identical with the ones that were analysed by the German authorities.

4.273 Even if a mistake had occurred in the factual appraisal of the products, this does not mean that there is a lack of uniformity in the application of EC customs law. In particular, if the importer in question felt that the German authorities had erred in their appraisal of the good in question, he could have appealed the decision of the Main Customs Office of Bremen before the Bremen Tax Court. The United States has not provided information whether the importer in question has made an appeal. If the importer has chosen not to appeal, then this cannot be used to claim a lack of uniformity in the EC's system of customs classification. The EC would also note that neither the importer nor the producer have ever brought the issue of classification of BDL to the attention of the European Commission.

4.274 The administrative aids referred to by the lower German customs office contain nothing contrary to Community law, and in any event is purely an interpretative aid prepared for administrative purposes which does not in any way have force of law, and does not derogate from Community law. That handbooks, guidance or other compilations prepared by member States have no legally binding character in Community law has been clarified by the European Court of Justice in *Binder*.

4.275 Finally, it is not without interest to note that the United States has had its own difficulties in classifying BDL, and has had to revoke previous classification rulings regarding BDL.

4.276 As regards the case of LCD monitors, the essential question is whether they are to be classified as computer monitors or as video monitors. The correct classification of these monitors is a relatively recent question which has arisen due to the increasing convergence of information technology and consumer electronics. Many LCD monitors, by virtue of their design and technical characteristics, can serve both as a computer monitor and as a video monitor. It is therefore difficult for customs authorities to establish on an objective basis the precise purpose for which a particular monitor is intended.

4.277 In addition, there are a high number of different types of LCD monitors on the market. These monitors differ in various aspects, including their size, the interfaces they possess and the signals they can process, and their general design. To the extent that such features may have an impact on their use, such differences between different types of monitors may also need to be taken into account.

4.278 The US claims that the EC does not ensure a uniform classification practice in respect of LCD monitors must be regarded as unfounded. In fact, the EC institutions have kept this particular classification issue under very close review from the outset, and have taken the necessary measures to ensure a correct and uniform classification practice in this respect.

4.279 The Customs Code Committee was seized of the issue for the first time in April 2004 and has reviewed the situation at regular intervals since. Since the classification issue also requires technical input from industry, the Committee also has, in accordance with Article 9 of its Rules of Procedure, heard representatives of the industry. At its meeting of 30 June to 2 July 2004, the Customs Code Committee concluded that unless an importer can demonstrate that a monitor is only to be used with an ADP machine (heading 8471) or to be used as an indicator panel (heading 8531), it has to be classified under heading 8528.

4.280 The allegation that the Netherlands wrongly classifies LCD Monitors as Video Monitors is therefore misplaced. In principle, such a classification is in line with the CN, as confirmed by the Customs Code Committee. It must of course also be taken into account that the actual classification of LCD monitors depends on the concrete monitor.

4.281 The EC institutions have taken further measures to ensure a uniform practice. The first such measure is Council Regulation (EC) 493/2005 of 16 March 2005. The purpose of this measure is to provide certainty about tariff treatment to the concerned importers through a suspension of duties for a transitional period of time. From a practical purpose, the suspension of the duties fulfils exactly the same purpose as that of a classification regulation, since it assures traders that, regardless of whether the goods fall under heading 8471 or 8528, their goods will receive the same tariff treatment.

4.282 The US claim that the example of LCD Video Monitors shows that the Customs Code Committee is inadequate to reconcile differences in member States interpretations is misplaced. The Customs Code Committee has shown itself perfectly able to adopt the necessary conclusions, and it continues to be involved in the continuous monitoring of the situation.

4.283 The EC has adopted another relevant measure, namely Regulation 634/2005, which classifies LCD monitors of a particular type under heading 8528. Currently, the Commission keeps monitoring the situation, and may adopt further classification regulations for LCD Monitors or other appropriate measures as and when the need arises.

4.284 The US customs authorities have also found it difficult to properly classify LCD monitors. For instance, in a ruling of June 3, 2003, US Customs found that it was not possible to determine the principal function of a particular type of LCD monitor, and therefore decided to classify it under heading 8528 in application of General Interpretative note 3(c), which foresees classification under the heading which occurs last in numerical order.

4.285 Of the two cases which the United States has raised, neither shows any lack of uniformity in the EC's administration of tariff classification. Both cases involve classification questions of a high technical complexity, with which the United States has had its own difficulties. Accordingly, the United States is far from having established any significant pattern of non-uniformity in EC tariff classification practice. On the contrary, the preceding discussion has shown that the EC customs administration has the necessary mechanisms in place to ensure uniformity in tariff classification.

(ii) Customs valuation

The uniform administration of valuation rules in the EC

4.286 Valuation questions are regulated in Articles 28 through 36 of the CCC and in Articles 141 to 181 a of the Implementing Regulation, with further details being contained in Annexes 23 to 29 to the Implementing Regulation. These provisions constitute an exhaustive regulation of customs valuation, which overall does not leave room for discretion to member States' administration.

4.287 The EC rules are based on, and fully integrate, all the rules contained in the WTO Valuation Agreement. According to the third preambular paragraph of the WTO Valuation Agreement, the central objective of the WTO Valuation Agreement was to "provide greater uniformity and certainty" in the implementation of valuation rules. The EC wonders how the WTO Valuation Agreement can achieve this objective if, as the US argues, it leaves "significant discretion" to WTO Members in the valuation of goods for customs purposes.

4.288 There is no obligation under WTO law to institute a system of binding information for valuation matters. Article X:3(a) GATT does not prescribe the specific ways in which WTO Member must implement their customs laws. This is particularly obvious in the area of customs valuation, which is governed by the WTO Valuation Agreement. If WTO Members had wished to provide for a specific obligation to introduce or maintain systems of binding information on valuation matters, it would have been natural to include such a an obligation in the Valuation Agreement. Further support for this view comes from the fact that the US itself has, in the context of the Doha Negotiations on trade facilitation, proposed to supplement Article X GATT by creating an obligation to provide for advance rulings on customs issues including customs valuation.

4.289 The case for binding valuation information as a tool for ensuring uniformity is far less clear than it is for binding tariff information. Specific goods do not change much over time, and are certainly identical regardless of the place of import. On the other hand, customs valuation is based on sets of data which can change from transaction to transaction, and from importer to importer. This makes the matter of direct comparability between transactions, and importers, rather difficult. Moreover, valuation data is of a relatively temporal nature, since sales contracts, prices and other factors such as relationships between parties, and the details of royalty and licence fee agreements, can change very frequently.

4.290 For these reasons, the content of binding valuation information would have to differ considerably from the content of binding tariff information. In particular, unlike for tariff information, where it is possible to provide in the abstract for the classification of a good corresponding to a particular description, it is not possible to lay down in the abstract the value of a good. Rather, binding information on valuation would have to take on a much more nuanced and specific character, focussing for instance on the characterization of specific elements inherent in certain recurrent transactions between the same parties.

4.291 Classification and valuation have inherent differences which must be taken into account. Therefore, elements such as classification regulations and binding tariff information are not easily transposable to the area of valuation. Instead, the Commission can carry out necessary clarifications through amendments to the Implementing Regulation. Such amendments can be seen as fulfilling a function which is rather similar to that of classification regulations or EC explanatory notes. Moreover, the Customs Code Committee, and in particular its valuation section, has a very important role in the area of valuation, and has contributed to uniformity in particular by elaborating commentaries and conclusions on numerous topical issues relating to the administration of valuation rules.

4.292 The general mechanisms for providing for a uniform application of EC law also apply in the area of customs valuation. First, if an individual trader feels incorrectly treated by a decision of a member States' customs authority, he can bring an action against such decision before the member States' court. If there is an issue of Community law to be clarified, such question can, and in certain circumstances must be, referred to the European Court of Justice. In this way, the Court of Justice has clarified numerous issues of Community law in the area of customs valuation.

4.293 Second, if the Commission finds that a member State applies Community provisions in the field of customs valuation incorrectly, the European Commission can bring infringement proceedings against such member State in accordance with Article 226 EC Treaty. There is no evidence whatsoever that this system of administration does not suffice to ensure a uniform administration of EC valuation rules.

4.294 It is remarkable that the United States has never raised any problem regarding the administration of EC valuation law in the WTO Committee on Customs Valuation, nor in the Technical Committee. Moreover, not a single case has ever been brought under the DSU against the EC for a violation of the WTO Valuation Agreement.

Report 23/2000 of the EC Court of Auditors

4.295 The Court of Auditors is an institution which, through its examination and reporting activity, equally contributes to the uniform application of Community customs law. Therefore, Report 23/2000 is evidence for the ability of the EC system to detect difficulties wherever they occur.

4.296 Report 23/2000 is only the expression of the views of one EC institution, which are not necessarily shared by other institutions, or by the EC as a whole. Moreover, it is clear that the Report of the Court of Auditors also contains certain political and technical judgments, which cannot necessarily be assumed to be correct.

4.297 The objective of the Court of Auditors is to ensure the optimal collection and utilization of the Community's own resources. This is entirely unrelated to the question of whether the EC is compliant with Article X:3(a) of the GATT. Therefore, it cannot simply be assumed, as the United States seems to do, that a criticism made by the Court of Auditors in its Report translates into a violation of Article X:3(a) GATT.

4.298 Report 23/2000 relates to a set of facts as examined by the Court in 1999-2000. It is striking that the United States in its First Written Submission never asks the question as to what the EC might have done in order to address the criticisms or suggestions raised by the Court of Auditors. As the EC will show, the EC has in fact systematically worked through the issues raised by the Court of Auditors, and wherever necessary taken the measures to ensure uniformity. A clear example for this is the adoption of Commission Regulation 444/2002, which now clarifies the issue of warranties. Even to the extent that any lack of uniformity actually existed, it cannot therefore be assumed that such situation continues to exist today.

4.299 The Report of the Court of Auditors is a highly synthetic document, which reflect the results of a number of audits carried out by the Court at the time. Consequently, the conclusions in the Court's report are of a certain level of generality. For this reason also, they are not adequate for addressing the question of the EC's compliance with its obligations under Article X:3(a) GATT.

4.300 Accordingly, the United States should not be allowed to rely on the Report of the Court of Auditors, but rather be required to establish its *prima facie* case. In any event, Report 23/2000 of the EC Court of Auditors does not show that the EC is in any way non-compliant with its obligations under Article X:3(a) GATT.

The Reebok case

4.301 The only concrete example that the United States provides in support of its allegation of non-uniform administration of EC valuation rules is a case concerning Reebok International Limited (RIL). However, this case does not support the US claim that the EC fails to administer its valuation laws in a uniform manner.

4.302 The case, which is relatively complex, is currently being examined by the Commission. Moreover, the Commission submitted the issue to the Customs Code Committee (Valuation Section), where it was discussed at two instances in October and December 2004. On the basis of the information which had been submitted by RIL, the Committee did not establish any incompatibility with EC law, or lack of uniformity between EC member States.

4.303 In any event, the EC notes that if the Spanish customs authorities had erred in assessing the conditions of Article 143(1)(e) of the Implementing Regulation, RIL can appeal this decision before the competent Spanish courts, and such an appeal is currently pending. If there are questions of Community law arising, such questions can then be referred to the Court of Justice via a request for a preliminary ruling.

4.304 Overall, the Reebok case provides any support for the US allegation that the EC fails to administer is customs valuation rules in a uniform manner. The EC institutions have taken the necessary action in response to the concerns of Reebok. Moreover, and appeal is currently pending. The Customs Code Committee is not a substitute for the normal appeals mechanisms before the national courts.

(iii) Processing under customs control

4.305 The US claim that the UK authorities apply tests that go beyond the requirements of Community law in respect of processing under customs control is wrong. The UK requirements are exactly the same two laid down by Article 133(e) CCC.

4.306 Article 502(3) of the Implementing Regulation repeats the first part of the sentence and this has to be considered as an abbreviated reference to the requirements laid down in Article 133(e) CCC. It cannot be otherwise considering that this Regulation, which has been adopted by the Commission, is implementing legislation and cannot modify the requirements laid down by the CCC.

4.307 Indeed, both documents, the CCC and the UK guidance, require the same two conditions (amongst others) for the granting of an authorization for processing under customs control, which are named as "economic conditions. Furthermore, it is worth noting that, contrary to what the US states, the French "Bulletin officiel des douanes" also refers to the test relating to the absence of harm to competitors in the EC. The US claim on Article X:3(a) is not founded in relation to processing under customs control.

(iv) Local clearance procedure

4.308 The US presentation is flawed in that it does not differentiate between the three steps of the summary declaration, the local clearance notification and the supplementary declaration. All goods brought into the EC customs territory have to be presented to customs and the summary declaration is the act by which this presentation is formalized. The lodging of the summary declaration is, therefore, not a formality which is part of the local clearance procedure. Moreover, contrary to the US claims, all these declarations may be lodged either under a paper-based or an electronic procedure.

4.309 Due to this confusion between the general obligations stemming from border crossing and those attached to LCP, the description of the situation in the UK in the US First Written Submission is inaccurate and does not correspond to the actual situation in this Member State.

4.310 In relation to the customs involvement prior to release, the fact that, at the frontier, anti-smuggling and admissibility checks are made electronically does not mean that there is no involvement of customs. Moreover, if the goods do not fulfil these checks, there will be a customs action (physical check, seizure...). It is therefore wrong to state that there is no customs involvement prior to release in the UK.

4.311 Concerning the requirements after release, the United States makes a misleading description of the use of electronic clearance systems versus paper-based systems. Both systems can be used in all member States. As far as LCP is concerned, detailed Community rules for paper-based clearance can be found in Articles 263 to 267 of the Implementing Regulation. Where the clearance system used is electronic, additional rules are applicable and can be found in Articles 4(a) to (c) and Articles 222-224 of the same Regulation.

4.312 As regards supporting document requirements, all EC member States apply identical rules. The issue raised by the United States concerning the valuation form "DV1" again stems from a confusion, since all member States allow operators having regular trade flows with the same suppliers to submit only once the relevant DV1 together with the initial application to benefit from LCP.

4.313 In relation to the document retention requirements, the information on the Netherlands provided by the United States is wrong. Moreover, Article 16(1) CCC provides that the requisite documents shall be retained for a minimum period of three years, but leaves member States the possibility to stipulate longer periods taking into account their general administrative and fiscal needs and practices. The resulting time-frame differences between the EC member States for which the United States submits evidence are not fundamental. Besides, the EC has already explained above that Article X:3(a) GATT concerns the administration of customs laws, not the customs laws themselves and this provision does not impose an obligation to harmonize legislation within a WTO member.

4.314 In addition, in the light of the GATT Panel in *EEC – Dessert Apples*, the EC considers that any such differences are not substantial in nature and do not entail a lack of uniformity in the application of customs laws contrary to Article X:3(a) GATT.

(v) Penalties for violations of customs law

4.315 The US claim that the EC violates is obligations under Article X:3(a) GATT by not providing for a uniform administration of penalties for violations of customs laws must fail for three reasons. First, penalty provisions are not covered by Article X:3(a) GATT. Second, Article X:3(a) does not require the harmonization of member States' penalty provisions. Third, EC law does ensure a sufficient degree of uniformity of member States' penalty provisions.

4.316 The obligation of uniform administration in Article X:3(a) GATT applies only to the administration of the laws referred to in Article X:1 GATT. In this respect, it is necessary to distinguish between the customs laws themselves, and the provisions which set out the nature and level of the penalty applicable for a violation of such laws. This is regardless of whether the penalty is criminal or administrative in character, or whether it involves a fine, a prison term, or another sanction. Therefore, penalty provisions, which provide for a sanction in the case of a violation of a provision of customs laws, are not themselves customs laws. It must also be noted that the imposition of sanctions concerns illegal behaviour, i.e. it concerns illegitimate actions rather than legitimate trade, which is the focus of Article X:3(a) GATT.

4.317 Moreover, Article X:3(a) GATT concerns only the *administration* of customs laws, not the substance of the customs laws themselves. This means in particular that Article X:3(a) GATT does not create an obligation to harmonize laws which may exist within a WTO Member at the sub-federal level. It merely requires that such laws be administered uniformly within the territory in which they apply.

4.318 The penalties applicable for violations of customs laws are set out in the national laws of the member States, which of course must respect the principles set out by Community law. Accordingly, it is not the administration of penalty provisions which varies within the EC; it is the laws themselves which are different, albeit within the limits set by Community law.

4.319 The United States has not shown that the administration of those penalty provisions varies within the member States which have adopted them. Rather, the United States is effectively requiring a harmonization of penalty provisions within the EC. Article X:3(a) provides no legal basis for such a claim.

4.320 The European Court of Justice has developed clear guidelines for penalty provisions for violations of EC customs law, which must be effective, proportionate, and dissuasive. These principles have also been confirmed by the Council of the European Union.

4.321 Contrary to the US submission, in *Andrade*, the Court confirmed that member States cannot act freely when laying down penalty provisions, but must ensure that the penalty is effective, proportionate and dissuasive. In other words, member States are limited in two directions. They cannot lay down penalties which are excessively severe and therefore violate the principle of proportionality. On the other hand, they cannot lay down penalties which are so lenient that they have no dissuasive effect and therefore do not ensure the effective application of Community law.

4.322 These fundamental principles are sufficient to ensure uniformity in the application of customs laws. This is also confirmed by Article VIII:3 GATT, which specifically addresses the issue of sanctions for violations of customs regulations, by merely laying down minimum standards of proportionality.

4. *The US claim under Article X:3(b) GATT*

(a) The requirements of Article X:3(b) GATT

4.323 Article X:3(b) GATT requires the WTO members to have tribunals or procedures of a judicial, arbitral or administrative nature with the main purpose of reviewing and correcting promptly administrative decisions in customs matters. There are, therefore, four conditions laid down in the provision: the material scope of the control (administrative decisions in customs matters), its nature (tribunals or procedures of a judicial, arbitral or administrative nature), its purpose (review and correction), and a time requirement principle (promptness).

4.324 In relation to the nature of the control, the provision allows a certain margin of discretion to the WTO members. The control may consist not only in tribunals but also in procedures, which implies that there is no obligation to create a separate body to ensure the control. Furthermore, the nature of the control may be not judicial but also arbitral or administrative. But what is particularly important in our case is that Article X:3(b) refers to each of these controls in plural: WTO members are obliged to have "tribunals or procedures" not "a tribunal" or "a procedure". The Spanish and French versions of the provision also use the equivalent terms in plural. This clearly allows the WTO members to have several tribunals, each of them covering a part of its geography and being competent for the review of the administrative decisions taken by their different customs offices.

4.325 Finally, the Appellate Body's interpretation of Article X GATT in *EC – Poultry* and *EC – Bananas III* further supports that this provision does not impose any specific structure for the review system (specific type of courts or procedures, number of instances, degree of centralization of the review system…).

4.326 The EC may also comply with its obligation under X:3(b) through the courts of its member States, as it has already been recognized by the Panel in *EC – Trademarks and Geographical Indications (US).* The reasoning of this Panel does not only apply to the executive authorities, but also to the judicial authorities of the member States when they apply and interpret Community law.

4.327 As to the time requirement, Article X:3(b) GATT requires a "*prompt* review and correction" (emphasis added). Though the three linguistic versions of Article X:3(b) do not have exactly the same meaning, all of them have a common denominator: the period of time to review a customs decision has to be reasonably short. To be more precise on this question will certainly require making an analysis on a case by case basis.

4.328 The EC does not agree with the US argument that the relevant context for the interpretation of Article X:3(b) GATT includes the immediately preceding subparagraph in the paragraph in which the obligation at issue appears, and that therefore the decisions of the tribunals or procedures must provide for the review and correction of customs matters for the EC as a whole, not just within limited geographical regions within the EC. Subparagraphs (a) and (b) lay down different obligations: one of uniform administration, the other on remedies. From a legal point of view, Article X:3 GATT does not make any link between both subparagraphs, which should, therefore be considered as separate obligations.

(b) The EC provides for prompt review of customs decisions

(i) The claim regarding the absence of an EC customs court

4.329 The United States affirms that the EC fails "to provide for an EC court […] to which a member State customs decision can be promptly appealed". This is clearly wrong. Article X:3(b) GATT does not require a central court or procedure to appeal administrative decisions in customs matters. There is no obligation under the GATT for the WTO members to establish a court similar to the US Court of International Trade. Decisions of the member States' customs authorities, which are based on EC law, are reviewed by the national courts and tribunals acting as the ordinary judges for EC law. Customs decisions adopted by the EC institutions are reviewed by the Court of Justice (and, in some cases, by the Court of First Instance) through direct actions or preliminary rulings on validity. There is, therefore, a complete system of judicial protection in place.

4.330 Furthermore, the US analysis of the review system established by the EC and its member States relies on an erroneous interpretation of Article X:3(b), which is based on the existence of a link between this provision and Article X:3(a). However, there is no such link. Assuming, *ad arguendo*, that there were a link between those two provisions, the US analysis would be partial and biased because it does not take into account the EC mechanisms to ensure uniform administration in the customs sector.

4.331 The *Bantex* decision mentioned by the United States shows the artificial analysis made by the United States. In the absence of a real problem in the EC remedies system, the United States relies on an individual case and tries to transform it into a systemic problem by relying on two hypotheses ("if another member State's authorities had correctly classified Bantex's products" and "if a trader in Bantex's position invokes the United Kingdom BTI in the territory of another member State"). None of these two situations have occurred in Bantex and, therefore, the US arguments have to be rejected as not based on real facts.

4.332 On the contrary, the final outcome of the Bantex case shows that EC legal remedies ensure uniform administration in customs matters. Following the UK High Court judgment, the HM Customs and Excise decided on 23 March 2004 to revoke the BTIs on the basis of Articles 12(5)(a)(iii) and 9 CCC and in the light of the Judgment of the Court of Justice in *Timmermans*. This case proves that preliminary rulings given by the Court of Justice are taken into consideration by national authorities other than those directly involved in the specific case. It also shows that the *Timmermans* Judgment in fact contributes to the uniform administration of EC law.

4.333 The United States misunderstands the EC system when it claims that "at the top of the structure for reviewing customs authorities' administration of EC customs law is the ECJ". This is not correct. The European Court of Justice does not review national customs administrations decisions. On the contrary, as we have already explained several times, it helps the national courts in such a review through the preliminary ruling procedure. This procedure is based on a cooperation relationship between the Court of Justice and national courts, not on a hierarchical one.

(ii) Promptness in the review

4.334 The US First Written Submission provides no arguments for why customs decisions are appealed before the national courts of the EC member States in a manner that cannot be qualified as "prompt". The only argument of the United States is that "the time periods for first instance reviews conducted by member State customs authorities can vary widely", for which purpose it compares the time period for administrative reviews in three member States. Three other eventual divergences between member States are mentioned in the US First Written Submission but the United States neither develops these allegations in its argumentation nor provides representative specific examples in the member States mentioned.

4.335 The EC recalls, first, that the burden is on the United States, as complainant, to make a *prima facie* case in support of its position, and that, therefore, this burden cannot be shifted on the EC, as respondent, by using the tactics of making general and unsubstantiated assertions.

4.336 In relation to the time periods for first instance administrative reviews conducted by member State customs authorities, the only US claim is that they vary widely in the three member States mentioned above. Again, the United States does not give the reasons to conclude that the three time periods do not comply with the Article X:3(b) GATT requirement for a "prompt" review. Differences as to time periods are not contrary to that provision, which does not impose the obligation on the WTO to harmonize time periods in administrative, judicial or arbitral reviews of customs administrative decisions. A different interpretation would be contrary to the intrinsic nature of Article X GATT, which is a provision, as it is spelled in its heading, on publication and administration of trade rules, not on their contents.

C. *First Oral Statement of the United States*

4.337 In its First Written Submission, the United States demonstrated that the European Communities fails to administer its customs laws in the uniform manner required by Article X:3(a) of the GATT. The United States also demonstrated that the EC fails to provide the tribunals or procedures for the prompt review and correction of administrative action relating to customs matters that Article X:3(b) of the GATT requires.

4.338 The EC responded to the US claims in part by re-casting them, incorrectly, as either broad-based attacks on European federalism or narrow complaints about the particular outcomes of specific cases. To the extent that the EC confronted the US arguments directly, its responses appeared to fall into five categories: (1) that Article X:3(a) is a narrow provision setting out "minimum" obligations; (2) that material divergences in member State administration of customs laws do not occur or are systematically reconciled when they do occur; (3) that various principles, instruments, and institutions in the EC ensure the uniform administration that Article X:3(a) requires; (4) that where certain material differences admittedly exist among member State practices, these differences do not concern administration of customs law at all but, rather, matters of general member State administrative law; and (5) that, with respect to Article X:3(b), the EC fulfills its obligation by virtue of the fact that each member State provides a separate forum for review of customs administrative decisions.

4.339 The claims of the United States are straightforward. Both claims stem from the fact that the EC, as a Member of the WTO in its own right – as distinct from its constituent member States – is bound by the obligations set forth in Articles X:3(a) and X:3(b). With respect to Article X:3(a), the EC provides for the administration of its customs law by each of its 25 member States while failing to ensure that the member States administer that law uniformly. That divergences among the member States occur is undeniable. This fact is admitted by the EC even in its own Written Submission. Outside the context of this dispute, it has been acknowledged by EC officials and has been a constant complaint of traders. The claim of the United States is that no EC institution systematically provides for the reconciliation of such divergences, so as to achieve the uniformity of administration required by Article X:3(a).

4.340 The US Article X:3(b) claim is that the EC fails to provide any forum for the prompt review and correction of administrative action by member State customs authorities. While review is provided for under the laws of individual member States, that review does not meet the EC's obligation under Article X:3(b). Fragmentation of review, on a member State-by-member State basis, is not consistent with Article X:3(b). That obligation must be interpreted in light of its context, which includes Article X:3(a).

4.341 The issues raised by these claims are not new. Contrary to the EC's suggestion, this dispute is not the first time the United States has raised these issues with the EC. In fact, the United States has raised these issues routinely in the context of EC trade policy reviews since 1997. The United States also has raised these issues in other WTO and bilateral settings. The United States has decided to pursue its claims through dispute settlement precisely because the underlying problems persist despite its efforts to address them in other fora.

4.342 It is important to make clear what this dispute is *not* about. The United States complaint is not that the very decision to retain competence over customs administration in the hands of member State authorities is per se inconsistent with the obligation of uniform administration under Article X:3(a). The US complaint is that because the retaining of competence over customs administration in the hands of member State authorities is not coupled with the systematic reconciling of divergences among member State authorities, it is inconsistent with the obligation of uniform administration under Article X:3(a). The EC is not subject to a lower requirement of uniform administration than every other WTO Member simply by virtue of its "executive federalist" structure.

4.343 Just as this dispute is not about the EC's right to adopt an executive federalist form of government, it also is not about the particular decisions of individual member State authorities in particular cases. In its First Submission, the United States set forth a number of illustrations to demonstrate the lack of uniform administration of customs law in the EC. In its First Submission, the EC treats these cases not as illustrations but as actual matters in dispute. The US argument is not that any particular good should be classified or valued one way or another. Rather, the argument is that the system for administering customs law in the EC does not ensure the uniformity that Article X:3(a) requires.

4.344 In its First Submission, the United States identified the obligation of uniform administration in Article X:3(a) and explained the scope of that obligation applying customary rules of treaty interpretation of public international law. In particular, the United States considered the ordinary meaning of the operative terms in Article X:3(a) in their context and in light of the object and purpose of the GATT 1994. Applying this rule, the United States identified the relevant question as whether the EC manages, carries on, or executes its customs law in a manner that is the same in different places or circumstances, or at different times. The United States also discussed the report of the panel in *Argentina – Hides and Leather*, which confirmed this understanding of the concept of uniform administration.

4.345 In its First Submission, the EC entirely avoids the ordinary meaning of the operative terms of Article X:3(a). Tellingly, its discussion under the heading "The meaning of 'uniform administration'" does not actually discuss the meaning of "uniform administration." Instead, it discusses supposed limitations on the obligation of uniform administration. Thus, the EC asserts that the obligation of uniform administration must be qualified by "practical realities," that "a minimum degree of non-uniformity is *de facto* unavoidable," and that "uniformity can be assessed only on the basis of an overall pattern of customs administration."

4.346 Not only does the EC's explanation of "uniform administration" fail to come to grips with the ordinary meaning of those words, but the limitations that it posits would effectively render the obligation of uniform administration meaningless. For example, the EC suggests a limitation of "practical realities," but identifies no standard by which that limitation might be assessed. Similarly, while it asserts that "a minimum degree of non-uniformity is *de facto* unavoidable," it offers no standard for judging the degree of non-uniformity that may exist without running afoul of Article X:3(a).

4.347 Moreover, the EC's contention that non-uniformity is impermissible only when it amounts to a *pattern* of non-uniformity is entirely misplaced. The EC draws this proposition from two reports that are not at all on point. First, it purports to rely on the Appellate Body's report in *EC – Poultry*. However, the relevant issue there was not the meaning of "uniform administration," but rather, the applicability of Article X at all to a particular import license issued with respect to a particular shipment.

4.348 Similarly, in the panel report in *US - Hot-Rolled Steel* on which the EC relies, the panel did not reach the question of what "uniform administration" means. As is clear from the sentence immediately preceding the extract on which the EC relies, the relevant issue was "whether the final anti-dumping measure before [the panel] in [that] dispute can be considered a measure of 'general application.'"

4.349 More importantly, neither of the reports from which the EC seeks support concerned the issue presented by this dispute, which is lack of *geographical* uniformity in administration of a Member's customs laws. Whatever the relevance of showing a pattern of non-uniformity may be in other contexts, the EC has failed to demonstrate its relevance to establishing a breach of Article X:3(a) based on geographical non-uniformity.

4.350 The EC's other arguments attempting to narrow the obligation of uniform administration are similarly flawed. For example, the EC characterizes as "highly important for the present case" the distinction between the substance of customs laws and their administration. The significance the EC apparently attaches to this distinction is that differences among member States' laws – as, for example, in the area of penalties – are beyond the purview of Article X:3(a), as they are differences of substance rather than differences of administration.

4.351 The problem with this argument is that it ignores the different forms that administration can take. It assumes that laws cannot be instruments that administer other measures. That assumption, however, is plainly incorrect. Customs laws may be administered through instruments which are themselves laws. This is the case with respect to penalty laws, which are instruments for administering customs laws by enforcing compliance with those laws. To the extent different EC member States use different penalty measures to enforce compliance with EC customs laws, they administer EC customs laws non-uniformly.

4.352 This latter observation is supported by the panel report in *Argentina – Hides and Leather*. In that dispute, the EC had challenged as inconsistent with Article X:3(a) an Argentinian measure that provided for private persons to be present during the customs clearance for export of certain goods. Argentina defended in part on the ground that the EC really was complaining about the substance of a measure rather than its administration. In rejecting Argentina's argument, the panel stated: "Of course, a WTO Member may challenge the substance of a measure under Article X. The relevant question is whether the substance of such a measure is administrative in nature or, instead, involves substantive issues more properly dealt with under other provisions of the GATT 1994.... If the substance of a rule could not be challenged, even if the rule was administrative in nature, it is unclear what could ever be challenged under Article X...."

4.353 Likewise, in the present dispute, the line the EC draws between substance and administration would render Article X:3(a) meaningless. By characterizing all laws, regulations, and rules pertaining to customs matters as substantive measures, the EC would put all laws, regulations, and rules that are instruments of customs administration beyond the reach of the disciplines Members have agreed to in Article X:3. It defies logic to suggest that a GATT obligation can be eliminated simply by virtue of such characterization.

4.354 In its second line of argument, the EC challenges the proposition that in the administration of customs law, divergences among member State authorities occur and are not systematically reconciled by the EC. In our First Submission, we demonstrated this point through evidence of the EC's own admissions, statements by traders, and illustrations of particular cases in which divergences have occurred. The EC's response does not rebut this evidence.

4.355 When it comes to admissions by the EC or EC officials, the EC does not deny the truth of the statements asserted. At most, it belittles them. For example, a statement by the EC's Commissioner for Taxation and Customs Union recognizing that the Community Customs Code "may result in divergent application of the common rules" is summarily dismissed by the EC as "reflect[ing] the ongoing process of reform and review of EC customs law." Statements by the EC's Court of Auditors identifying systemic problems in reconciling divergent administration of customs valuation laws are similarly tossed aside as "the expression of the views of one EC institution." Admissions by the EC in the context of another recent dispute – *European Communities – Customs Classification of*

Frozen Boneless Chicken Cuts – regarding institutional difficulties in monitoring divergences in binding tariff information issued by different member States are not acknowledged at all.

4.356 Unlike the EC, the United States finds statements by EC institutions and officials highly relevant to the matter at hand. These statements are blunt acknowledgments of how the system of customs law administration operates by persons who are in positions to have the information and experience to know. The cumulative message that there is a problem of divergent administration and no mechanism to systematically reconcile divergences is undeniable.

4.357 Nor is the EC's treatment of the illustrative cases cited by the United States any more effective at rebutting this point. For example, in its First Submission the United States laid out an illustrative case concerning divergent classification of LCD monitors. The United States noted that a regulation by the Council of the European Union suspended duties on a subset of such monitors, but that member States continued to apply different classifications to other monitors. In particular, the United States noted that the Netherlands continues to classify monitors with a diagonal measurement of greater than 19 inches as video monitors, whereas other member State classify them as computer monitors. The EC's terse response is that the classification by the Dutch authorities "is in line with the CN, as confirmed by the Customs Code Committee."

4.358 That response is quite revealing for at least three reasons. First, it does not deny the divergence among member State authorities on this matter. Second and relatedly, by characterizing the Dutch classification as "in line" with the CN, the EC suggests that more than one classification may be "in line" with the CN. But this is precisely the point of the illustration: Where more than one classification is "in line" with the CN, the EC does not provide a mechanism for systematically reconciling different classifications adopted by different member State authorities. Third, the Customs Code Committee conclusion with which the Dutch classification supposedly is "in line" is not itself in line with the relevant Chapter Note from the Common Customs Tariff. Specifically, the Committee conclusion would prohibit a monitor from being classified as a computer monitor (under Tariff heading 8471) unless an importer can demonstrate that it is "*only* to be used with an ADP machine" – a computer machine. However, under the relevant Tariff chapter notes, a monitor may be classified as a computer monitor if "it is of a kind solely *or principally* used in an automatic data-processing system." It hardly is conducive to uniform administration for member State authorities to have to reconcile notes to the Common Customs Tariff that say one thing and a Customs Code Committee conclusion that says something entirely different.

4.359 To take another example, in its First Submission the United States described the illustrative case of differential administration of EC valuation rules with respect to Reebok International Limited. The United States described a situation in which different member State authorities have reached different conclusions as to whether RIL's contracts with non-EC suppliers establish a control relationship for customs valuation purposes, and EC institutions have not reconciled the divergence. The EC dismisses this case as "relatively complex" and states without explanation that, upon its consideration of the matter, the Customs Code Committee "did not establish any incompatibility with EC law, or lack of uniformity between EC Member States." Then, the EC goes on to state that "the Customs Code Committee is not a substitute for the normal appeals mechanisms before the national courts."

4.360 This response is notable for at least two reasons. First, the EC does not deny the essential facts as described in the US First Submission. It merely calls them "complex" and states that the Customs Code Committee found no lack of uniformity. Second, in stressing that "the Customs Code Committee is not a substitute for the normal appeals mechanisms before the national courts" the EC in effect reinforces the crux of the US argument: There is no EC mechanism for ensuring uniform administration. In any case, in numerous other parts of its First Submission, the EC readily acknowledges that divergences among member States exist.

4.361 In its third line of argument, the EC challenges the proposition that there is no EC mechanism to ensure uniform administration of EC customs law. In its First Submission, the United States demonstrated that customs law in the EC is administered by 25 different member State authorities, that this results in divergences of administration, and that no EC institution exists to systematically reconcile those divergences. To demonstrate this last point, the United States focused on the role of the Commission and the Court of Justice in matters of customs administration. The United States focused on these two institutions, because the EC had asserted to the DSB that it was through the operation of these two institutions that uniform administration is enforced. The United States showed that neither institution functions in a way that results in uniform administration. Its discussion of the role of the Commission logically led the United States to focus on the Customs Code Committee which, as the EC acknowledges, "is an integral part of the Community's regulatory process."

4.362 Because of the integral part played by the Committee, it is important to understand how the Committee functions. The United States demonstrated that various aspects of the Committee's operation make it ineffective as a mechanism to systematically bring uniformity to the administration of customs law. These include the absence of any right for a trader affected by a member State's administration of the law to petition the Committee and the difficulty of obtaining answers to technical questions of divergence in member State customs administration where those answers require the support of qualified majorities of 25 member State representatives.

4.363 With respect to the ECJ, the United States demonstrated that limitations on the ability to get questions reviewed by the ECJ, procedural hurdles that must be passed before doing so, and the time it takes to get questions answered by the ECJ make this institution, too, an ineffective mechanism to systematically bring uniformity to the administration of customs law.

4.364 The EC challenges the US understanding of the operation of EC law and institutions, contending that in seeking to identify EC mechanisms that ensure uniformity of administration the United States has focused inappropriately on the

Customs Code Committee and given inadequate attention to principles of EC law as well as EC institutions and instruments of administration. The main problem with this argument is that, on closer inspection, the individual elements that the EC describes as contributing to uniform administration do not add up to a mechanism that systematically leads to uniform administration where administration in the first instance is the responsibility of 25 different member State authorities.

4.365 For example, the EC refers to the existence of detailed substantive laws. But, detailed substantive laws surely do not themselves ensure uniform administration. Indeed, the EC itself stresses the distinction between substance and administration. Moreover, the cataloging of divergent administration in the EC Court of Auditors report on customs valuation (Exhibit US-14) demonstrates that detailed laws are not themselves a substitute for uniform administration.

4.366 In other instances, the mechanisms the EC identifies represent an ideal of uniform administration to which the EC aspires. For instance, the EC refers to the "duty of cooperation" in Article 10 of the EC Treaty. It also attaches importance to the principles of supremacy and direct effect as doctrines that are "essential for the effective and uniform application of Community law." However, it cannot be assumed that by virtue of the duty of cooperation or the doctrines of supremacy and direct effect uniformity of administration necessarily is achieved. Indeed, these principles do not answer the question of what happens when EC law itself permits more than one manner of administration.

4.367 Another instrument for achieving uniform administration that the EC describes is the ability of traders to address matters of concern to the Commission or to member State representatives, which may or may not, in turn, address them to the Customs Code Committee. As the EC itself acknowledges, the Commission and member State representatives are under no obligation to bring any given matter before the Committee.

4.368 The EC also emphasizes the role of appeals to national courts, with the possibility of preliminary references to the ECJ, as a means of ensuring uniform administration. Where a trader encounters a lack of uniform administration, its recourse is to appeal one or more of the divergent actions to a national court which (unless it is a court from which there is no recourse) may or may not make a preliminary reference to the ECJ. Even if the court does make a preliminary reference to the ECJ, the matter still may take years to decide.

4.369 In short, where a trader detects a lack of uniform administration it has no right to appeal to an EC institution to correct the lack of uniformity. Instead, it must proceed through "the normal appeals mechanisms before the national courts" in the hope that this may lead eventually to an elimination of the non-uniformity. The proposition that the normal appeals mechanism is a key instrument of uniform administration is notable for at least three reasons. First, litigation is a particularly cumbersome tool to achieve the day-to-day operational uniformity of administration that Article X:3(a) contemplates. Second, the EC's contention in this regard is at odds with its separate contention – in discussing the US Article X:3(b) claim – that the obligation of uniform administration and the obligation to provide remedies from administrative action are discrete obligations without any inherent link to one another. Here, the EC suggests that they are inherently intertwined. Third, the EC's emphasis on the normal appeals mechanisms leaves open the critical question of what happens if a national court or, eventually, the ECJ finds that both the administrative action appealed and the divergent administrative action to which it is compared are consistent with the applicable provision of EC customs law. In other words, the EC does not, and cannot, contend that lack of uniformity itself is grounds for appeal from and correction of administrative action. Thus, the emphasis the EC places on a trader's right to pursue the "normal appeals mechanisms" does not really answer the question of how non-uniformity is eliminated when EC law permits two or more non-uniform measures to co-exist.

4.370 In a similar vein, the EC's reference to the Commission's power to bring infringement proceedings against member States that violate EC law is of little relevance. It may be that there are instances in which a divergence in administration of EC law is so extreme as to give rise to an infringement proceeding. But, this extraordinary tool hardly serves to achieve uniformity of administration where divergent practices do not give rise to breaches of EC law.

4.371 In short, a large part of the EC's argument is devoted to painting a picture of customs law administration in the EC in which various instruments combine to ensure uniformity. But, when looked at closely, the elements of that picture do not add up to a mechanism that provides for the systematic reconciliation of divergences among member State customs authorities. What is glaringly absent from this picture is any EC mechanism to systematically reconcile divergences in member State administrative actions.

4.372 The EC's fourth line of argument is that certain divergences in member State practice – in particular, penalty provisions and audit procedures – are not really matters of administration of EC customs law at all. It characterizes such matters as part of the general administrative law of individual member States. It follows, according to the EC's reasoning, that the EC has no Article X:3(a) obligation with respect to these matters. The only Article X:3(a) obligation applies to the particular member States in which the laws at issue apply, according to the EC.

4.373 By the EC's logic, one could define away almost any obligation under Article X:3(a). Where a divergence in administration takes the form of different measures applicable in different regions within a Member's territory, the Member could label the measures as substantive law rather than instruments of administration of customs law and thus avoid the obligation of Article X:3(a) entirely. The panel in *Argentina – Hides and Leather* saw through and rejected a similar argument.

4.374 The EC's argument in this dispute is even more troubling than the argument that the panel rejected in *Argentina – Hides and Leather*, because the EC is suggesting that the obligation of uniform administration does not necessarily extend to the limits of each WTO Member's territory. The obligation is mutable, according to the EC. For any given law being administered, it applies only to the limits of the territory covered by that law. By this logic, there is no obligation of uniform administration from region to region or even from locality to locality.

4.375 This argument has no basis in Article X:3(a). That Article applies to "each Member." Like other GATT obligations, the obligation of uniform administration is an obligation on the Member. It is not a separate obligation on each individual region or locality within the Member's territory. Were it otherwise, any instance of geographical non-uniform administration could be argued away simply by sub-dividing the Member's territory and treating each sub-division separately for purposes of Article X:3(a).

4.376 It is especially puzzling that the EC characterizes penalty provisions and audit procedures as outside the scope of Article X:3(a). Those instruments go to the heart of the way substantive customs rules are administered. Indeed, that penalties are a critical tool for administering other laws is expressly acknowledged in the Council Resolution on penalties set forth in Exhibit EC-41.

4.377 The EC also asserts that penalties fall outside the scope of Article X:3(a) because they pertain to "illegitimate actions rather than legitimate trade." That argument mischaracterizes both Article X and the concept of penalties. Article X does not make the distinction between legitimate and illegitimate trade that the EC posits. Even if it did make such a distinction, it is not the case that penalties apply only to illegitimate trade. The *de Andrade* case cited in the US First Submission is a perfect example of the application of a penalty in the context of legitimate trade. The only offense at issue there was a failure to clear goods through customs within the time period specified in the Community Customs Code.

4.378 The EC argues in the alternative that even if Article X:3(a) does apply to penalties, fundamental principles of EC law ensure that penalties meet the requirements of uniform administration. The fundamental principles to which the EC refers are requirements that penalties be "effective, proportionate, and dissuasive." But, these very general principles permit a wide range of member State practices. As the EC itself acknowledges, "Specific offences may be considered in one Member State as a serious criminal act possibly leading to imprisonment, whilst in another Member State the same act may only lead to a small – or even no – fine."

4.379 The same flaws attach to the EC's discussion of customs audits. The US First Submission called attention to significant divergences in auditing practices identified in the EC Court of Auditors report. As with penalties, the EC summarily asserts that "questions of auditing are not part of customs procedures, and therefore do not concern the administration of customs law as such." Nowhere does the EC state the basis for its assertion, which is entirely incorrect. Like penalties, audits are essential tools in administering substantive customs laws.

4.380 The US First Submission explained that, in connection with audits, some member State authorities provide traders with binding valuation guidance that may be relied upon in future transactions, while others do not. The EC dismisses this observation by stating that "[w]hether such advise might be legally binding is a question of general administrative law of the Member States." By a simple act of characterization, the EC again purports to remove a matter from review under Article X:3(a). The United States sees no basis for this assertion that different member State approaches to valuation guidance are not "significant from the point of view of Article X:3(a)."

4.381 The United States turns, finally, to the EC's argument regarding Article X:3(b). In its First Submission, the United States demonstrated that the EC does not provide tribunals or procedures for the prompt review and correction of administrative action relating to customs matters. The individual member States provide fora for review of customs decisions, but the existence of these fora does not fulfill the obligation of the EC, as a WTO Member in its own right. The United States argued that the Article X:3(b) obligation must be interpreted in light of its context, which includes Article X:3(a), and that a fragmentation of review of customs decisions across the territory of a Member runs contrary to that provision's obligation of uniform administration.

4.382 The EC's assertion that there is no link between subparagraphs (a) and (b) of Article X:3 and no obligation to interpret the latter in light of the former is especially surprising, given the EC's explanation of how uniformity of customs law administration is achieved in the EC. A theme repeated throughout the EC's First Submission is that appeals of customs decisions to national courts, coupled with the possibility of national courts making preliminary references to the ECJ, constitutes a critical instrument of ensuring uniform administration of customs law. In other words, in its Article X:3(a) argument, the EC effectively contends that reviews of customs decisions and administration of customs laws are closely intertwined. That position supports interpreting the obligation to provide reviews of customs decisions in light of the obligation to administer customs laws uniformly.

4.383 Moreover, the EC simply is wrong to assert that Article X:3 "does not make any link" between subparagraphs (a) and (b). The second sentence of subparagraph (b) expressly states that the decisions of the tribunals or procedures maintained or instituted in accordance with that subparagraph "shall govern the practice of" "the agencies entrusted with administrative enforcement." Administrative enforcement, in turn, is the subject of subparagraph (a).

4.384 The EC's contention that use of the plural form in Article X:3(b) "clearly allows" the provision of separate review tribunals covering different parts of a Member's territory is equally flawed. Use of the plural form in Article X:3(b) might allow for the possibility that a Member may provide different fora for different types of review. For example, a Member might provide an administrative tribunal for reviews of classification and valuation decisions and a separate judicial tribunal for reviews of penalty decisions. This interpretation gives effect to use of the plural form in Article X:3(b) without running afoul of the obligation to interpret that provision in light of the context of Article X:3(a).

4.385 Finally, the EC asserts that it fulfills its Article X:3(b) obligation, because member State courts are EC courts when it comes to the application and interpretation of EC law. To support this assertion, the EC refers to the panel report in *EC – Trademarks and Geographical Indications (US)*. There, the panel found that in the exercise of certain executive functions, member State authorities "'act *de facto* as organs of the Community.'" Without any explanation at all, the EC asserts that the panel's reasoning in that dispute applies with equal force to member State judicial authorities exercising adjudicatory functions.

4.386 The EC's assertion does not, in fact, flow from the statement it quotes from that panel report. First, the issue presented there was substantially different from the one presented here. The issue there had absolutely nothing to do with obligations of the EC; it had to do with obligations of particular member States. The question was whether an individual member State executing an EC regulation in a manner that discriminated between persons of other EC member States, on the one hand, and persons of non-EC member States, on the other, violated a most-favored-nation obligation. This very different context makes it impossible to extrapolate from the finding in that dispute to the issue presented in this dispute.

4.387 Second, the nature of the Article X:3(b) obligation is such that it cannot be carried out in a geographically fragmented way in a single Member, such as the EC. It cannot be assumed that one panel's recognition of member State *executive* authorities as *de facto* EC authorities for one particular purpose in the context of one particular WTO obligation means that another panel must recognize member State *judicial* authorities as *de facto* EC authorities for a different purpose in the context of an entirely different WTO obligation.

4.388 In short, the fact that the EC may consider member State courts to be acting as *de facto* EC courts when they interpret and apply EC law does not mean that the EC itself provides the tribunals or procedures required by Article X:3(b). It remains the fact that member State tribunals interpret and apply the law within the territory of their respective member States. They can bind administrative agencies only within their respective member States. This arrangement does not meet the EC's obligation under Article X:3(b).

D. *First Oral Statement of the European Communities*

1. *The significance of the case*

(a) The constitutional significance of the case for the EC

4.389 The US case constitutes an unprecedented attack on fundamental principles of the EC legal order. By challenging the involvement of the customs authorities of the EC member States in the administration of EC customs law, the United States is essentially requesting the EC to establish an EC customs agency. This runs counter to the principle of executive federalism in the EC legal order, according to which EC law is generally implemented through the authorities of the member States.

4.390 Similarly, the US claim that the EC is obliged to provide judicial review through "EC-level tribunals" is diametrically opposed to a fundamental structural principle of the EC judicial system, in which judicial review of decisions of the member States authorities is provided by the tribunals of the member States.

Thus, on the sole basis of Article X:3(b) GATT, the United States is effectively requiring the EC to engage in a complete overhaul of its judicial system, a task which could not be carried out without a modification of the founding treaties of the EC.

4.391 The EC would like to emphasize that it recognizes and fully respects its obligations under Article X GATT. The EC does not claim that it is in any way subject to different or lesser obligations under Article X GATT than other WTO Members. However, the EC also believes that its constitutional arrangements for the administration of customs laws, and review of customs decisions, are fully compatible with the WTO Agreements. Indeed, the WTO Agreements respect and uphold the constitutional autonomy of the WTO members. It is therefore a matter of great concern that, in the present case, fundamental constitutional arrangements are as such made the subject of WTO dispute settlement.

4.392 In fact, with its present challenge, the United States seems to expect the EC to establish a customs agency and a customs court similar to those existing in the United States. The EC believes that Article X:3 GATT provides no legal basis for such a claim. Moreover, whereas the EC fully respects the right of the United States to opt for a centralized system of customs administration and judicial review, it believes its own constitutional choice of a system based on federal principles deserves an equal measure of respect.

(b) The systemic importance of the case for the WTO

4.393 The present case is highly important for the WTO Membership at large. Indeed, in its criticisms of specific instruments of EC customs administration, the United States adopts a maximalist approach that should be of genuine concern to WTO members.

4.394 With this approach, the United States overstretches the legal requirements of Article X:3 GATT beyond all recognition. Indeed, what is a stake in the present dispute is essentially whether Article X:3 GATT should become a legal basis for the harmonization of the systems of customs administration of WTO Members through the DSU.

4.395 The EC emphatically believes that it should not. The DSU is not a peer review process through which the optimal design of customs administrations can be sought. Rather, the purpose of the DSU is, in accordance with Article 3.2 DSU, to preserve the rights and obligations of the Members under the covered agreements, and thus prevent the nullification and impairment of benefits accruing to Members under such agreements.

4.396 A rigorous focus on legal obligations is also made necessary by the overlap between the present dispute and the ongoing negotiations on trade facilitation of the Doha Round. According to a public statement by the United States Trade Representative, one of the essential objectives of the United States in the present dispute is to enhance the Doha Trade Facilitation Negotiations "by pressing a major player in world trade". This political motivation behind the US case is also illustrated by the overlap between some of the criticisms made by the United

States in the present case and its own proposals in the context of the Doha Round.

4.397 The EC is fully committed to the success of the Doha Round Negotiations, including the negotiations on trade facilitation. However, as Japan has correctly pointed out in its Written Submission, specific initiatives to ensure a uniform administration of customs laws should be addressed through the Doha Negotiations, and not through the dispute settlement process.

2. *The uniform administration of EC customs law*

(a) The requirements of Article X:3(a) GATT

4.398 Article X:3(a) GATT requires WTO Members to administer the laws and regulations referred to in Article X:1 GATT in a uniform manner. In its First Submission, the United States significantly overstates the requirements imposed by Article X:3(a) GATT. Moreover, the United States ignores almost completely the existing case law on this provision.

4.399 First, it is consistent case law since the Appellate Body Report in *EC – Bananas* that Article X:3(a) GATT concerns only the *administration* of laws and regulations, and not those laws and regulations themselves. This is a highly important point for Members which have a federal structure, and where certain matters are regulated at a sub-federal level. Where laws and regulations exist at a sub-federal level, all that Article X:3(a) GATT requires is that such laws are administered in a uniform manner in the area where they apply. Article X:3(a) GATT does not impose any requirement to harmonize sub-federal laws within a WTO Member.

4.400 Second, Article X:3(a) GATT merely requires WTO Members to administer their laws and regulations in a uniform manner, but is neutral as to the means which WTO Members employ for this purpose. In other words, Article X:3(a) GATT does not prescribe the specific instruments and structures which WTO Members should use in the administration of their customs laws. Accordingly, Article X:3(a) GATT does not have the purpose of harmonising the customs laws and practices of WTO Members, and is not a legal basis for achieving such a result through the DSU.

4.401 Third, as the Appellate Body has stressed in *US – Shrimp*, and as Japan has equally confirmed, Article X:3(a) GATT is a minimum standards provision. It is a subsidiary provision which provides WTO Members with certain minimum guarantees of uniformity in the administration of customs laws and regulations. Wherever more precise and ambitious disciplines were necessary, the corresponding obligations have been laid down in other provisions of the covered agreements.

4.402 Fourth, given the character of Article X:3(a) GATT as a minimum standards provision, not every minor variation in administrative law and practice constitutes a lack of uniformity contrary to Article X:3(a) GATT. This follows clearly from the GATT Panel Report in *EEC – Dessert Apples*, where the Panel held that certain variations between EC member States in the implementation of import licensing arrangements were minor and therefore did not amount to a violation of Article X:3(a) GATT. In other words, there is a certain minimal threshold in Article X:3(a) GATT, which implies that a variation in administrative practice must have a significant impact on the administration of customs laws in order to constitute a breach of Article X:3(a) GATT.

4.403 Fifth, it is very important to recall the findings of the Panel in *US – Hot Rolled Steel*, according to which it is not possible to establish a lack of uniformity solely on the basis of an individual instance of administration. Rather, as Japan has convincingly explained, it is necessary to establish that there is a *pattern* of non-uniform administration with a significant impact on how customs laws are administered. Such an interpretation of Article X:3(a) GATT is particularly necessary given that customs authorities have to operate in complex and rapidly changing circumstances, to which they constantly need to adapt. Moreover, systems of customs administration are complex, and their outcomes are determined by many factors, not all of which can be controlled by the WTO Member in question. For instance, where an individual trader does not exhaust all the remedies and procedural possibilities afforded to him by the system of a WTO Member, a resulting lack of uniformity cannot be attributed to a failure in that Member's system. Similarly, if a trader in an individual case abuses procedural possibilities, or violates provisions of the law of the Member in question, this cannot be regarded as proof of a lack of uniformity contrary to Article X:3(a) GATT.

(b) The burden of proof

4.404 The burden of proof for establishing that there is a pattern of non-uniformity in the administration of the EC's customs laws is on the United States. The United States does not even come close to discharging this burden of proof.

4.405 The United States has not primarily focussed on the actual administration of customs laws in the EC, but rather on systemic aspects of the EC's system of customs administration. At the most general level, the United States challenges the involvement of the EC's member States authorities in the administration of EC customs law. At a second level, the United States criticizes the role or capacity of various EC institutions and arrangements, such as the European Commission, the Court of Justice, or the Customs Code Committee. Finally, at the management level, the United States also criticizes various aspects of the EC's system of customs administration, such as the design of the EC's EBTI system.

4.406 None of these arguments are relevant for the application of Article X:3(a) GATT, and none of them amount to proof that there is a pattern of non-uniformity in the EC's customs administration. To take the most fundamental point, the United States submits to the Panel that the involvement of the authorities of EC member States in the administration of EC customs law is incompatible with Article X:3(a) GATT because "divergences inevitably occur". The EC strongly contests this statement. The EC would also express its amazement that the United States would assert that a fundamental element of the EC legal order is incompatible with the GATT without offering any proof for such a statement.

4.407 As regards the more specific instruments and institutions of the EC system, and as the EC has already shown in its First Written Submission, the US criticisms are based on misunderstandings or misrepresentations of the EC system. In addition, Article X:3(a) GATT leaves WTO Members a large measure of freedom as to how they administer their customs law, provided they do so in a uniform manner. Therefore, the US criticisms are irrelevant for the purposes of assessing the EC's compliance with Article X:3(a) GATT.

4.408 Moreover, in its First Written Submission, the United States presents an incomplete and distorted picture of the EC's system of customs administration. On the basis of this inadequate presentation of the facts, the United States chooses to address only those specific issues where it perceives the EC system exhibits a weakness. However, in order to assess whether there is a deficiency in the EC system, it is not sufficient to look at a particular issue or instrument in isolation. Rather, as Japan has aptly explained, it is necessary to look at the EC's system as a whole.

4.409 As regards the actual administration of EC customs law, the US Submission remains almost silent. In essence, the United States presents the Panel with two examples of alleged non-uniformity in the area of tariff classification, and with one example in the area of customs valuation. Even if these cases actually demonstrated a lack of non-uniformity, one or two cases in a particular area hardly amount to a statistically significant sample on which to assess whether there is a pattern of non-uniformity. Moreover, as the EC has shown in its First Written Submission, none of the examples adduced by the United States, all of which involve questions of customs administration of a high technical complexity, in fact shows a lack of uniformity in the EC's administration.

4.410 No single fact could illustrate the weakness of the US case more clearly than the tepid reaction which the USTR received when it launched a call for comments following its consultation request in the present dispute. In response to this call, USTR received a mere three submissions, two of which the United States itself does not seem to have judged helpful for its case. The EC would submit that if there indeed was a significant pattern of non-uniformity in the EC's practice, a stronger reaction from interested industry and traders could have been expected.

4.411 Overall, the United States fails to establish that there is a pattern of non-uniformity in the EC's system of customs administration.

(c) The claims raised by the United States

(i) Tariff classification

4.412 The first area in which the United States alleges that there exists a lack of uniformity is tariff classification. The United States bases this claim essentially on a criticism of the role of the Court of Justice, and of the EC system of binding tariff information. In addition, the US sets out two examples of classification of specific products, which it alleges demonstrate a lack of uniformity in the EC's practice.

4.413 As regards the two systemic issues, the US criticisms are unwarranted. The ECJ, acting in particular through the preliminary reference procedure, plays an important role in ensuring a uniform interpretation and application of EC classification rules, and will continue to do so in the future.

4.414 Similarly, the EC's BTI system is an important tool for providing uniformity in tariff classification throughout the EC, and security to traders. However, the EC is under no obligation under Article X:3(a) GATT to establish a BTI system, let alone to design this system in a particular way.

4.415 Moreover, as Japan as pertinently remarked, both the ECJ and the EBTI system are only part of the EC's classification system. As the EC has already noted, in order to assess whether the EC administers classification rules in a uniform manner, it is not sufficient to only consider two elements in isolation. Rather, the EC system should be considered as a whole, including also instruments such as classification regulations, HS explanatory notes and opinions, and EC explanatory notes.

4.416 The two specific examples given by the United States concern the classification of blackout drapery lining and of LCD monitors. However, neither case demonstrates a lack of uniformity in the EC's classification practice. In fact, both cases involve classification issues of a high complexity, with which the United States itself has experienced certain difficulties. Accordingly, rather than demonstrate a lack of uniformity in the EC's practice, these cases simply serve as an illustration of the technical complexities of tariff classification in the rapidly evolving world of today.

(ii) Customs valuation

4.417 The second field where the United States alleges a lack of uniformity is customs valuation. However, the US case here is as unsubstantiated as its claim in the field of tariff classification.

4.418 At a systemic level, the United States complains that the EC does not even provide for binding valuation rulings. However, these complaints are unjustified. The EC is not obliged under Article X:3(a) GATT to provide for binding rulings on valuation questions or any other issues.

4.419 Moreover, there are considerable structural differences between tariff classification and customs valuation which explain why the EC provides for binding information in the area of tariff classification, but not in the area of valuation. In particular, customs valuation is normally based on the transaction value, and therefore involves data which can change from transaction to transaction, and from importer to importer.

4.420 At the same time, EC valuation rules are quite detailed, and guide the EC customs authorities in all relevant circumstances. Wherever clarification is necessary, this can be achieved through amendments to the valuation rules contained in the Implementing Regulation or the Customs Code. Moreover, the European Commission, the Customs Code Committee, and the European Court of Justice all play an important role in securing a uniform valuation practice.

4.421 In order to substantiate its allegations, the United States mainly relies on a report of 2000 by the EC Court of Auditors. However, this report does not support the US case. In fact, as much as anything else, it is evidence of the EC's ability to itself ensure uniformity in its customs administration. Where necessary, the report has given rise to the appropriate action by the EC institutions, and therefore does not constitute relevant evidence today. In addition, the EC would also point out that the Court of Auditors did not in any way make judgments as to whether the EC was in compliance with Article X:3(a) GATT, and it cannot be assumed that the issues raised in the report of the Court of Auditors translate into a violation of the GATT.

4.422 At the level of actual practice, the United States presents only one example, concerning a valuation dispute between Reebok International Limited (RIL) and the Spanish customs authorities. However, this is a complex valuation dispute concerning the assessment of whether RIL has a control relationship with certain of its suppliers. The European Commission has kept this case, which is currently pending before a Spanish court, under close review, and has also discussed it in the Customs Code Committee. However, it must also be recalled that neither the European Commission nor the Customs Code Committee are a substitute for the normal appeals mechanisms before the national courts.

(iii) Processing under customs control and local clearance procedure

4.423 The United States alleges that there is a lack of uniformity as regards two customs procedures, namely processing under customs control and the local clearance procedure. These US arguments are based on wrong interpretations and factual errors.

4.424 In relation to processing under customs control, the reality is that Community customs legislation and the UK and French guidances require the same two "economic conditions" for the granting of an authorization for processing under customs control. Therefore, there is no evidence showing that the EC customs authorities administer this procedure in a non-uniform manner.

4.425 As to the local clearance procedure, the US First Written Submission is deficient in four aspects. First, the United States does not provide a single exhibit to illustrate and support its claim. Second, from the description provided in the US First Written Submission, it is clear that the United States has misunderstood the different steps in the process followed when goods are imported through this procedure. Third, the US description of the procedure and of the documents retention requirements contains fundamental errors. Finally, any variations which might remain are not substantial in nature and therefore do not exceed the minimal threshold of Article X:3(a) GATT.

(iv) Penalties for violations of customs law

4.426 Finally, the United States also claims that the EC fails to comply with its obligations by not administering penalties for violations of customs laws in a uniform manner. This US claim must be rejected for three reasons.

4.427 First, the EC submits that provisions which establish the penalty for a violation of customs laws are not themselves related to the administration of customs laws and therefore do not fall within the scope of Article X:3(a) GATT.

4.428 Second, it is important to note that the penalties applicable to violations of customs laws are set out in laws and regulations of the EC member States. Accordingly, it is not the administration of the laws which varies, but rather it is the laws themselves which are different. However, as the EC has already explained, there is no requirement in Article X:3(a) GATT to harmonize laws which apply in a WTO Member at a sub-federal level.

4.429 Finally, EC law does provide for a sufficient degree of harmonization of sanctions for violations of customs law. As the European Court of Justice has clarified in its case law, member States penalty provisions must be effective, proportionate and dissuasive. Through these principles, a uniform application of customs law throughout the EC is sufficiently safeguarded.

3. *The prompt review of customs decisions in the EC*

(a) The requirements of Article X:3(b) GATT

4.430 Article X:3(b) GATT merely requires WTO Members to ensure that administrative decisions in customs matters are reviewed promptly by an independent tribunal or through an independent procedure. The United States misrepresents the requirements imposed by Article X:3(b) GATT.

4.431 The EC would like to recall once more that it is consistent case law since the Appellate Body Reports in *EC – Bananas* and *EC – Poultry* that Article X GATT, and, therefore, its subparagraph 3(b), does not impose any requirement of harmonization of laws within a WTO Member. This means that where, within a WTO Member, separate systems of judicial review exist at a sub-federal level, Article X:3(b) GATT does not require that such separate systems be harmonized. It merely requires that in each of these separate systems of judicial review, a prompt review of customs decisions is ensured.

4.432 In addition, it should also be recalled that Article X:3(a) and (b) GATT are separate obligations. Accordingly, Article X:3(b) GATT, unlike Article X:3(a) GATT, is not concerned with questions of uniformity, but exclusively with the prompt review of customs decisions.

4.433 It should also be noted that in the EC, the review of customs decisions currently takes place as part of the general systems for review of administrative decisions in the field of administrative law or tax law. Creating a separate jurisdiction for customs matters at EC level would, therefore, lead to more, rather than less fragmentation of procedures for judicial review. This would not be in the interest of traders, who in this case, rather than being able to have recourse to lawyers qualified in general administrative or tax litigation in a particular Member State, would have to have recourse to specialized lawyers experienced in specific EC-level procedures.

4.434 Moreover, Article X:3(b) GATT is neutral as to the means which WTO Members employ for ensuring prompt review. In other words, this provision does not prescribe the specific bodies or instruments, structures and time periods which WTO Members should use to ensure prompt review of customs decisions. Accordingly, Article X:3(b) GATT does not have the purpose of harmonising the laws of WTO Members, and is not a legal basis for achieving such a result through the DSU.

(b) The burden of proof

4.435 The burden of proof for establishing that the EC does not guarantee a prompt review of customs decisions is on the United States. Again, as in the field of uniform administration, the United States does not come close to discharging this burden of proof.

4.436 The United States has not primarily focussed on the actual review of customs decisions in the EC, but rather on a systemic question of the EC's court system. At the most general level, the United States considers insufficient the involvement of the EC's member States' courts and tribunals in the review of customs decisions. The United States submits to the Panel that the involvement of the courts and tribunals of EC member States in the application of EC customs law is incompatible with Article X:3(b) GATT because "the burden to traders of non-uniform administration is not alleviated through the appeals process". The EC strongly contests this statement.

4.437 As regards the actual functioning of EC court system, the US Submission remains almost silent. In essence, the United States refers only to the maximum time-limits for the administrative reviews in three EC member States and one of these references is not even accurate.

(c) The claims raised by the United States

(i) The absence of an EC customs court

4.438 The first US criticism is about the nature of the judicial review system established in the EC. According to the United States, the absence of an EC-level review reinforces the divergences in interpretation between the authorities in two different member States.

4.439 This interpretation is wrong in that it makes an unwarranted link between the two subparagraphs in Article X:3 GATT and because Article X:3(b) GATT does not require a central procedure or court, like the US Court of International Trade (USCIT), to appeal administrative decisions in customs matters. In its Third Party Submission, Japan has supported the EC´s interpretation.

4.440 Moreover, as the EC has explained in its Written Submission, where the tribunals of the member States provide judicial review of decisions taken by the member States' customs authorities, they act as organs of the EC, through which the EC discharges its obligations under Article X:3(b) GATT. This view also finds support in the recent Panel Report in *EC – Geographical Indications and Trademarks (US)*.

(ii) The lack of promptness in the review

4.441 The second criticism made by the United States of the EC system is that it does not guarantee a prompt review of customs decisions.

4.442 First of all, this US allegation is based on the divergence of the maximum time periods for administrative reviews between three EC member States. However, the information given by the United States in relation to the Netherlands is not fully correct. Point 6.2.7 of the Regulation to the General Tax Act of the Netherlands provides that the tax authorities, which include the customs authorities, will in principle decide on all objections within six weeks. According to the same provision, the legal time limit of one year, which is laid down in a separate act, is only to be applied in exceptional cases, e.g., in the case of mass complaints, or where the complainant does not provide the necessary cooperation.

4.443 Second, the US First Written Submission alleges that the time periods for administrative reviews in the EC member States can vary widely. However, the United States provides no actual evidence for this statement. In particular, it should be kept in mind that the periods referred to by the United States are purely maximum time limits, and do therefore not necessarily provide information on the actual length of administrative reviews.

4.444 The EC has already explained that Article X:3(b) GATT does not impose an obligation of harmonization. Besides, the fact that an EC Member provides a one-year period instead of the three-months period of another Member State does not mean that the former does not guarantee a prompt review.

4.445 Even in the United States, the statutory maximum time-limit for deciding on protests is two years. The United States does not explain why this maximum time limit would be compatible with Article X:3(b) GATT, whereas the shorter periods provided for in certain EC member States would not be. As a further illustration, it is also instructive to consider the practice of the US Court of International Trade. In three recent classification cases, the USCIT invested nearly four years as an average to take a decision.

4.446 These examples illustrate that establishing what is "prompt" and what is no longer "prompt" may not be quite as straightforward as the United States would seem to suggest. Indeed, the actual length for the administrative and judicial review of a customs decisions may depend on a number of factors, not all of which are always fully under the control of the WTO Member concerned. Such factors may include the caseload, the factual and legal complexity of the case, the behaviour of the complainant, the involvement of other parties, as well as questions of administrative and judicial procedure and organization. It is therefore highly difficult to provide abstract rules on the length of administrative and, even more so, judicial procedures, since there may always be exceptional cases where a longer duration is justified by special circumstances of the case.

4.447 For this reason, the EC also submits that whether a WTO Member complies with its obligation under Article X:3(b) GATT cannot be established on the basis of isolated individual cases. Rather, it would have to be established that there is a general pattern of a lack of prompt review in order to consider that the obligation of Article X:3(b) GATT is violated.

E. *Second Written Submission of the United States*

1. *Introduction*

4.448 The 25 member States of the European Communities do not act as one when it comes to the administration of EC customs law or the review and correction of customs administrative decisions. Even though the EC in this proceeding disputes the US claims, the EC and EC officials have readily acknowledged the underlying problem in statements outside the dispute settlement context.

4.449 Not surprisingly, uniformity is a goal to which the EC aspires. For example, in the Decision adopting the EC's "Customs 2007" program (Exhibit EC-43), the European Parliament and the Council of the European Union called for the continuous adaptation of customs policy "to ensure that national customs administrations operate as efficiently and effectively as would one single administration." However, the system of customs administration and review currently in place not only falls far short of that goal, it also falls far short of the requirements of GATT 1994 Article X:3, and therefore is in breach of that article.

4.450 Before countering the key themes that have emerged in the EC's response to US claims, it is necessary to discuss two general points that cut across the EC's various arguments. First, the EC repeatedly strikes an alarmist tone in responding to the US arguments. The Panel should regard the EC's prediction of widespread upheaval with a healthy dose of skepticism. Nowhere does the United States argue that Article X:3 compels WTO Members to have identical systems for customs administration and review, nor is that the implication of US arguments.

4.451 Similarly flawed is the proposition that accepting the US arguments will lead to a requirement of harmonization of non-customs-related provisions typically regulated at the regional or local level of government. The EC draws that inference from the fact that the United States calls attention to certain tools of administration of EC customs law – in particular, penalty provisions and audit procedures – which vary dramatically from member State to member State. However, the EC disregards that the US argument is directed at laws and regulations at the sub-federal (i.e. member State) level that are used to verify and enforce compliance with laws and regulations prescribed at the federal (i.e. EC) level. The US argument is not directed at the vast body of laws and regulations at the sub-federal level that have nothing at all to do with verification and enforcement of compliance with other laws and regulations or that concern only verification and enforcement of compliance with other sub-federal laws and regulations.

4.452 Moreover, in suggesting that the logic of the US argument on Article X:3(b) would force every WTO Member to have a single, centralized customs court, the EC again distorts the US position. It is not the US view that Article X:3(b) requires every WTO Member to have a single, centralized customs court. It is the US view that Article X:3(b) requires every WTO Member to have review tribunals or procedures whose "decisions ...govern the practice of" "the agencies entrusted with administrative enforcement" of its customs laws. A Member may be able to accomplish that where courts with regional jurisdiction review actions of a single customs authority. But, this does not occur where, as in the EC, fragmentation of review is coupled with fragmentation of administration.

4.453 Just as the Panel should not be swayed by the EC's prediction of a parade of horribles should it accept the US arguments, it also should not be swayed by the EC's contention that coming into compliance with its obligations would be difficult. Difficulty of coming into compliance has no bearing on whether the EC is or is not currently in compliance with its obligations under GATT 1994 Article X:3. Relative difficulty of compliance sheds no light on the ordinary meaning of the treaty's terms. Nor is it an element of context or the treaty's object and purpose.

2. *GATT 1994 Article X:3 does not contain a relative, Member-specific standard*

(a) The obligations in GATT 1994 Article X:3 do not vary according to the particular features of a Member's customs administration system

4.454 The EC incorrectly urges on the Panel a relative view of Article X:3(a). The EC suggests that the obligation of uniform administration may mean different things for different WTO Members, depending on the design of each Member's customs administration system. A relative standard is suggested by, among other statements, the EC's allusion to GATT 1994 Article XXIV:12. That Article simply provides that each WTO Member "shall take such reasonable measures as may be available to it to ensure observance of the provisions of [the GATT 1994] by the regional and local governments and authorities within its territories." It is not applicable here, because the present dispute does not concern "observance of the provisions of [the GATT 1994] by the regional and local governments and authorities" in the EC. Rather, it concerns observance of the provisions of Article X:3 of the GATT 1994 by the EC itself.

4.455 Moreover, the EC does not formally invoke Article XXIV:12, but it does argue that "any interpretation of Article X:3(a) which would affect the internal distribution of competence is incompatible with Article XXIV:12 GATT." The EC appears to be trying to turn Article XXIV:12 on its head. Paragraph 13 of the *Understanding on the Interpretation of Article XXIV of the General Agreement on Tariffs and Trade 1994* makes it clear that Article XXIV:12 does not excuse or alter a Member's obligations. That paragraph explicitly states that "[e]ach Member is fully responsible under GATT 1994 for the observance of all provisions of GATT 1994." The EC instead seems to be saying that read in light of Article XXIV:12, Article X:3(a) will mean different things for different Members depending on whether, as a matter of "the internal distribution of competence," a Member has decided that certain tools for the administration of its customs law (such as penalties and audits) are to be prescribed and applied by regional governments.

4.456 This construction of Article X:3(a) as applying differently to different Members has no basis in Article X:3(a) or in Article XXIV:12. Article XXIV:12 does not limit or otherwise qualify the obligation of uniform administration. Indeed, Article XXIV:12 does not qualify the *applicability* of GATT obligations at all. Rather, it is a narrow provision concerning the *implementation* of certain obligations, which must be construed to avoid "imbalances in rights and obligations between unitary and federal States." (GATT Panel Report, *Canada – Gold Coins*, paras. 63-64)

4.457 That GATT 1994 Article XXIV:12 does not support a construction of Article X:3(a) that varies from Member to Member is further demonstrated by contrasting that provision to a provision in another WTO agreement – the *General Agreement on Trade in Services* ("GATS") – that does, in fact, qualify Members' obligations. GATS Article VI:2(a), like GATT 1994 Article X:3(b), requires Members to provide tribunals or procedures for the prompt review of certain administrative decisions. However, that obligation is expressly qualified in the next subparagraph, which states that "subparagraph (a) shall not be construed to require a Member to institute such tribunals or procedures where this would be inconsistent with its constitutional structure or the nature of its legal system." No similar exception appears in GATT 1994 Article X:3.

4.458 Moreover, it should not pass without notice that despite its oblique assertion of "constitutional implications" and its reference to "fundamental principles of the EC legal order," the EC does not formally invoke Article XXIV:12. Had it done so, it would have had the burden to demonstrate that lapses in the uniform administration of EC customs law concern matters "which the central government cannot control under the constitutional distribution of powers." (GATT Panel Report, *US – Beverages*, para. 5.79) Evidently this is a burden that the EC is not prepared to assume.

(b) The United States does not seek the harmonization of WTO Members' customs administration systems

4.459 Finally, an essential aspect of the EC's urging a relative standard for application of Article X:3 is its mischaracterization of US claims as seeking "the harmonization of the systems of customs administration of WTO Members through the DSU." Contrary to the EC's assertion, the United States does not argue that Article X:3 requires each Member to have a single customs agency and customs court. The United States recognizes the diversity of systems of customs administration among WTO Members, which is evidenced in part by the responses to the Panel's Questions No. 10 and 11 to third parties. It is notable, however, that each of these third parties prominently identified the existence of a single, centralized customs agency in explaining how it ensures uniform administration of customs laws across its territory. Just as it would be improper for the United States to argue that Article X:3(a) requires harmonization of Members' systems of customs administrations, it is improper for the EC to argue that its unique status within the WTO as perhaps the only Member without a single, centralized customs agency makes it subject to a different standard with respect to the obligation of uniform administration.

3. *GATT 1994 Article X:3(a) is not a "subsidiary," "minimum standards provision" that is breached only when the non-uniform administration of a Member's customs laws exhibits a discernible pattern*

(a) There is no basis for the EC's characterization of GATT 1994 Article X:3(a) as a "subsidiary," "minimum standards provision"

4.460 The EC persists in characterizing Article X:3(a) as "a minimum standards provision" or "a subsidiary provision." This characterization is based entirely on a passing reference by the Appellate Body in its report in *US – Shrimp*. That statement, however, does not support the diminished significance the EC attaches to Article X:3(a).

4.461 The EC misreads the phrase "minimum standards" as used in the *US – Shrimp* report to mean, in effect, "low standards" or "minor standards." In context, however, it is clear that this was not the sense in which the Appellate Body used the term. At issue was a law for which the United States had invoked an exception under Article XX of the GATT. The Appellate Body looked to Article X:3 as a provision establishing requirements analogous to "due process" that would be relevant to analyzing whether the requirements in the chapeau of Article XX had been met. (para. 182) However, the Appellate Body was not probing how strict or lenient the Article X:3 standard is. In fact, it found it to be clear that various aspects of the measure at issue were "contrary to the spirit, if not the letter, of Article X:3 of the GATT 1994." (para. 183)

4.462 Thus, in context, it is evident that in using the phrase "minimum standards," the Appellate Body in *US – Shrimp* was not making a judgment about how high or low the Article X:3 threshold is, only that there is a threshold that must be met.

4.463 In any event, it is not clear how the EC's characterization of Article X:3(a) as a "minimum standards provision" translates into a legal standard that may be applied by the Panel. The EC suggests that in using "minimum standards" and similar phrases, what it really meant was that a breach of the obligation of uniform administration can be established only if non-uniform administration is shown on the basis of "an overall pattern" or "general patterns" of customs administration.

(b) The United States is not required to demonstrate a "pattern" of non-uniform administration to establish that the EC is in breach of its GATT 1994 Article X:3(a) obligation

(i) The "pattern" requirement asserted by the EC has no basis in GATT 1994 Article X:3(a)

4.464 The Appellate Body report in *US – Shrimp* on which the EC relies for its characterization of Article X:3 as a "minimum standards provision" makes no reference at all to a pattern requirement. Indeed, the Appellate Body's finding that transparency and procedural fairness were lacking in administration of the measure at issue there was based on a finding that certain formal safeguards were absent from the system for administration of that measure, rather than a finding of any "pattern" of non-transparency or lack of procedural fairness as a matter of practice. (para. 181) Likewise, the EC provides no mechanism to safeguard against the non-uniform administration of EC customs laws by 25 different member State authorities.

4.465 More fundamentally, there is no basis in the text of Article X:3(a) (or any other WTO provision) for the proposition that a breach is established only when a pattern of non-uniform administration is shown. The one panel to have examined in any depth the obligation of uniform administration in Article X:3(a) – the *Argentina – Hides and Leather* panel – made no reference to a "pattern" requirement for establishing a breach of that obligation. (paras. 11.80-11.83) That panel found it "obvious ...that it is meant that Customs laws should not vary, that every exporter and importer should be able to expect treatment of the same kind, in the same manner both over time and in different places and with respect to other persons." (para. 11.83) As the obligation of uniform administration was explained there, it plainly is capable of being breached even if various instances of non-uniform administration do not exhibit a discernible pattern.

(ii) The EC fails to even explain what it believes the United States must establish to meet the so-called "pattern" requirement

4.466 The simple fact that "pattern" would be an element of a breach in addition to "non-uniform" administration demonstrates the fatal flaw in the EC's proposed approach. The text of Article X:3(a) does refer to administering in a "uniform manner." It does not refer to a "pattern of non-uniform" administration.

4.467 Furthermore, the EC's proposed approach does not make sense even divorced from the agreed text of the GATT 1994. The ordinary meaning of the word "pattern" as relevant here is "[a]n arrangement or order discernible in objects, actions, ideas, situations, etc." Central to the concept of a pattern is discernability of arrangement or order. Central to the concept of non-uniformity is the absence of these very qualities. Thus, a pattern of non-uniform administration would appear to refer, paradoxically, to a discernability of arrangement or order in something that lacks a discernability of arrangement or order (i.e. that is non-uniform). Despite this apparent anomaly, the EC does not elaborate on the asserted "pattern" requirement.

4.468 The EC does make oblique references to a "statistically significant sample" of non-uniformity, occurrences of non-uniformity that are "so widespread and frequent as to constitute an overall pattern of non-uniformity," and occurrences of non-uniformity "on a large scale," as if to imply that it equates the existence of a pattern of non-uniform administration with the frequency and scope of non-uniform administration. However, these references shed little light on what the EC believes must be shown in order to satisfy the so-called pattern requirement.

4.469 More importantly, the suggestion that there is some quantitative criterion for assessing uniformity of administration is at odds with the EC's own acknowledgment that "Article X:3(a) GATT does not require uniformity for its own sake, but rather intends to protect the interests of traders." The interests of traders in uniform administration of the customs laws do not depend on the statistical significance of occurrences of non-uniform administration, just as they do not depend on whether instances of non-uniform administration manifest a pattern, in the ordinary sense of that term, or occur in a haphazard way.

(iii) The reference to a "pattern" in the panel report in US – Hot-Rolled Steel is not relevant to the present dispute

4.470 Moreover, the EC's assertion of a pattern requirement relies on a single sentence from the panel report in *US – Hot-Rolled Steel*. The concept of a pattern was relevant to the question at issue in that dispute in a way that it is not relevant in the present dispute.

4.471 In any dispute involving a claim of *non-uniform* administration, it must be asked what *uniform* administration would look like. In the present dispute, which concerns a claim of overall geographical non-uniformity of administration, the actual system in the EC is contrasted to a system in which traders can reasonably expect treatment of the same kind, in the same manner when entering their goods through different EC member States. To the extent that traders do not receive treatment of the same kind, in the same manner when entering goods through different EC member States, that state of affairs is recognizable as non-uniform administration, whether or not such non-uniform administration constitutes a pattern.

4.472 Conversely, in *US – Hot-Rolled Steel* the relevant claim was that a particular application of US antidumping law to particular producers in a particular investigation amounted to non-uniform administration of US antidumping law. That proposition could be tested only if the panel had an understanding of what uniform administration of US antidumping law looked like.

4.473 The claim at issue in the present dispute is far different. The United States is arguing that the EC's system of customs law administration as a whole does not result in the uniform administration that Article X:3(a) requires. Evidence of a pattern is not necessary to distinguish the EC system of customs law administration as one that does not meet that obligation.

4.474 Curiously, in arguing for a generic "pattern" requirement, the EC cites the panel's summary of the US argument in *US – Hot-Rolled Steel*. But, in that dispute, the United States was not arguing for a generic "pattern" requirement. Quite to the contrary, the United States was arguing for a distinction to be made between the way the panel analyzed Japan's Article X:3 claims and the way panels had analyzed Article X:3 claims in disputes challenging the overall administration of particular measures of general application. The present dispute is one in which the United States challenges the overall administration of EC customs law. In that sense, the US claim is more like the claim at issue in *US – Shrimp* than the claim at issue in *US – Hot-Rolled Steel*.

(c) The EC acknowledges the existence of divergences among member State authorities in the administration of EC customs law

4.475 Finally, it is important to recall that the EC itself acknowledges that divergences in administration of its customs law among the 25 different member State authorities do in fact occur. It submits that when they occur they either are reconciled through various EC instruments and institutions, or they simply are immaterial or not relevant to the EC's Article X:3(a) obligation. But, it acknowledges that divergences occur, and this point should not be lost.

4.476 In addition to general acknowledgments by the EC of divergences in the administration of EC customs law, it has made particular acknowledgments of such divergences in the context of this dispute. Specifically, it has acknowledged divergences in the areas of penalties and audit procedures, approaches to permitting certain customs valuation methods, and administration of the economic conditions test for use of the procedure known as processing under customs control.

4.477 In calling attention to the EC's various acknowledgments of non-uniform administration of EC customs law, the US purpose is to show that the EC's argument concerning the US burden of proof is not written on a blank slate. While the EC charges that the United States has not met its burden, its own statements preclude it from asserting that the 25 separate member State customs authorities administer EC customs law as would a single EC-wide authority.

4. The instruments that the EC holds out as ensuring uniform administration do not do so

4.478 Central to the EC's argument that it complies with its obligation of uniform administration under GATT 1994 Article X:3(a) is its assertion that certain EC instruments prevent divergences among member States from occurring or correct them when they do occur.

(a) Most of the instruments that the EC holds out as securing uniform administration are non-binding, discretionary, or extremely general in nature

4.479 First, the EC's replies to the Panel's questions underscore the non-binding, discretionary, or extremely general nature of the instruments that supposedly secure uniform administration. For example: (a) The EC acknowledges that the Administrative Guidelines on the European Binding Tariff Information (EBTI) System and its Operation "are not legally binding;" (b) When asked about "practical mechanisms" to deal with the situation in which member States disagree on the classification for a particular good, the EC replies that the member States "*should* consult with one another," that if the disagreement persists the Customs Code Committee "*may* examine the question," and that "[i]n practice, the responsible official in the Member State concerned *will* submit the issue to the Commission" (though the EC does not say what rule will compel this submission); (c) When asked how, "in practical terms," the Customs Code Committee reconciles differences in the application of EC rules on customs valuation, the EC explains that "[t]he Committee may issue opinions" which, it later explains, are not legally binding on member States' customs authorities; and (d) When asked to explain "in practical terms" a finding by the ECJ that EC law must be applied uniformly in all member States, the EC states that "this means that they [the authorities of the member States] should interpret and apply Community law in accordance with all available guidance as to its proper meaning."

4.480 Frequently, in referring to instruments that secure uniform administration, the EC falls back on member States' general duty of cooperation under Article 10 of the EC Treaty. That provision sets forth a general obligation of member States under EC law. Tellingly, when the EC refers to it as an instrument to secure uniform administration, it does not refer to any measures making that general obligation operational in the specific area of customs administration.

(b) Binding tariff information does not secure uniform administration

4.481 A more concrete instrument for securing uniform administration that the EC identifies is binding tariff information. The EC's replies to questions confirm that BTI does not secure uniform administration.

(i) The EC system permits "shopping" for favorable BTI from among the 25 member State customs authorities

4.482 One reason that BTI does not secure uniform administration is that traders may engage in BTI shopping. That is, in a system where each of 25 different member State customs authorities is separately responsible for issuing BTI, traders may manipulate the system to obtain the optimal classification for their goods, regardless of whether such classification is uniformly agreed to among all member States. The opportunity for manipulation is facilitated by the fact that under Article 12(2) of the Community Customs Code (Exhibit US-5), BTI is "binding on the customs authorities as against the holder of the information," but it is not binding on the holder.

4.483 In fact, in its explanatory introduction accompanying the draft Modernized Community Customs Code (Exhibit US-32), the EC acknowledges the problem of BTI shopping as a factor detracting from uniform administration. Thus it states that "it is proposed to extend the binding effect of the decision [i.e. the BTI] also to the holder(s) of the decision in order to avoid the system only being used where the applicant is satisfied with the result." (p. 12) Similarly, in its arguments in the *EC – Chicken Cuts* dispute, the EC explained that "it is possible under EC law to withdraw an application for a BTI where the outcome is considered unfavourable by the importer." (Panel Report, para. 7.261)

4.484 At the first Panel meeting, the United States had understood the EC to assert that the situation in which BTI is used only where the applicant is satisfied with the result is a rather rare circumstance. In a question following the first Panel meeting, the United States asked the EC to substantiate that assertion. The EC's terse response was that it "does not have any evidence that would indicate that such situations are frequent," while also in effect conceding that it does not have evidence that such situations are "rare." This response is not surprising. A problem of BTI shopping from the point of view of uniform administration is precisely the fact that it is done in a way that does *not* generate evidence and thus is difficult to identify. Traders hardly can be expected to come forward and openly admit that they are taking advantage of the opportunity to seek optimal classification of their goods from among 25 different customs authorities.

(ii) The power of a member State customs authority to revoke BTI based on nothing more than its own reconsideration of the applicable classification rules, as affirmed in the Timmermans decision, detracts from uniform administration

4.485 The EC's discussion of the *Timmermans* case and the possibility for member State authorities to amend or revoke BTI on their own initiative also reinforces the point that BTI does not secure uniform administration of EC customs law. *Timmermans* was the case in which the Court held that a member State's customs authorities may amend or revoke BTI even where the only basis for amendment or revocation is the authorities' own reconsideration of the applicable classification rules. The Court reached that conclusion despite the Advocate General's observation (Exhibit US-21) that "the possibility of revoking BTI in this way is not readily compatible either with the objective of the uniform application of the customs nomenclature or with the objective of legal certainty pursued by the introduction of BTI." (para. 59)

4.486 In explaining its disagreement with the Advocate General's observation, the EC stated that "[t]he correct classification in the combined nomenclature is not a matter of discretion, and neither is the revocation of BTI which has been found to be incompatible with the combined nomenclature." The EC went on to point out that "the Court made clear that the Customs authorities may revoke the BTI only if it is wrong."

4.487 There is a serious flaw in the EC's logic. It assumes, without any basis, that the correct classification of any given good will always be objectively known to all member State authorities and, therefore, "is not a matter of discretion." Under this assumption, the application of classification rules is always a straightforward, mechanical exercise, and if a member State authority revokes BTI, it must be due to an obvious error in the performance of that exercise, the correction of which necessarily will advance uniformity.

4.488 The EC ignores the fact that applying classification rules to a particular good may require a customs authority to make certain judgments and that, especially in complex cases, these judgments may evolve upon further reflection. It is not the case that the correct classification is a matter of discretion, but the findings leading to determination of the correct classification may entail exercises of discretion, in the sense of judgment. It is incorrect for the EC to assume that the classification of a particular good will always be objectively known and obvious to all 25 customs authorities. In relying on the Court's finding that "the Customs authorities may revoke the BTI only if it is wrong," and asserting that discretion has no part in such action, the EC misunderstands the sense in which discretion is referred to and begs the question of who determines that BTI is wrong. Of course, absent a Commission regulation, it is *the member State authority itself* that determines that the original BTI is wrong. Accordingly, it cannot be assumed that, where a customs authority revokes BTI based on its revised assessment of the good's correct classification, such action will necessarily yield the objectively correct classification and thereby align it with the other member State customs authorities, resulting in uniform administration.

4.489 Where a member State authority initially issues BTI – presumably believing it has applied the classification rules correctly – that BTI is supposed to be binding on other member State authorities with respect to the particular holder of the BTI and the goods concerned. If that authority reconsiders its application of the classification rules – again, presumably believing that its revised application of the classification rules is correct – there is no mechanism to impose its reconsideration on a uniform basis. It is in this sense that the member State autonomy recognized in *Timmermans* detracts from uniform administration.

4.490 A final point that bears recalling with respect to BTI is the very limited sense in which BTI is ostensibly binding at all. As Korea underscores in its Third Party Submission, "The BTI from one member state does not necessarily bind another member state to classify similar or identical goods imported by a person other than the holder of the BTI in the same way, resulting in different classifications and treatment for the same or similar product." The EC itself called attention to this limited applicability of BTI in the *EC – Chicken* dispute.

(c) The availability of review by member State courts as the "normal" means of reconciling divergences in member State administration of EC customs laws does not fulfill the EC's GATT 1994 Article X:3(a) obligation to administer its customs laws in a uniform manner

4.491 The one instrument the EC holds out as securing uniform administration that is binding in character is review of customs administrative decisions by member State courts. The emphasis that the EC puts on this instrument is problematic for at least three reasons. First, as the decision of a member State court is binding only within that member State, an appeal to a member State court will not necessarily engender uniform administration. It is notable that the EC confirms that it has in place no mechanism to notify the courts of other member States of the outcome of review of a customs decision in one member State court. Absent such a mechanism, it is difficult to see how one member State court would be able to take account of relevant decisions of other member State courts, let alone take the step of seeking to bring about uniform administration by affirmatively aligning itself with other member State courts.

4.492 Second, while the pursuit of an appeal before one member State court might or might not lead to uniform administration in the case of a simple divergence between two member States, it does not address the situation of a divergence involving several member States. In that case, the EC evidently would require a trader to pursue an appeal through each of several member State courts in order to achieve uniform administration. This is a particularly onerous burden to impose on traders to achieve a result – uniform administration – that they are entitled to as a matter of procedural fairness in the first instance, pursuant to GATT 1994 Article X:3(a).

4.493 Third, the EC's emphasis on appeals to member State courts in effect stands GATT 1994 Article X:3(a) on its head. It takes a GATT obligation under which traders are *entitled* to certain elements of procedural fairness in customs administration and submits that it is fulfilled largely though a system that imposes a requirement on traders to overcome legal hurdles in order to attain those elements of procedural fairness. This can be seen, for example, in the EC's assertion in its statement at the first Panel meeting that "where an individual trader does not exhaust all the remedies and procedural possibilities afforded to him by the system of a WTO Member, a resulting lack of uniformity cannot be attributed to a failure in that Member's system."

4.494 Article X:3 contains a pair of complementary obligations that afford procedural fairness to traders. Pursuant to Article X:3(a), a trader may expect that, consistent with a Member's WTO obligations, its customs laws will be administered in a uniform, impartial and reasonable manner across the Member's territory. Pursuant to Article X:3(b), the trader may expect, consistent with the Member's WTO obligations, access to an independent forum for the prompt review and correction of particular instances of the uniform administration of the Member's customs laws. Pursuant to that same provision, the trader may expect not only that the decisions of such independent fora will be implemented by the authorities responsible for customs administration, but also that they will govern the practice of all such authorities, such that the customs laws will continue to be administered in a uniform manner in light of those decisions.

4.495 Yet the EC appears to say that compliance with Article X:3(b) would in and of itself necessarily equate to compliance with Article X:3(a). In other words, the EC's approach would mean that Article X:3(b) would render Article X:3(a) redundant. As the EC describes it, the trader is not necessarily entitled to expect that the EC's customs laws will be uniformly administered in the first instance. Rather, it is through exercise of the right to review that the trader eventually *may* attain uniform administration.

4.496 Moreover, according to the EC's explanation, a trader must be willing not only to pursue a first level of review in order to attain uniform administration, but to "exhaust all the remedies and procedural possibilities afforded to him by the system." Unless a trader is prepared to pursue multiple layers of appeals, possibly in more than one member State, including opportunities for preliminary reference of questions to the ECJ – a process which itself takes an average of 19 to 20 months to complete – then any resulting lack of uniformity in the administration of EC customs law "cannot be attributed to a failure in [the EC's] system."

4.497 The United States submits that in emphasizing appeals to member State courts as a key instrument in securing uniform administration, the EC has taken an obligation of the EC to provide an important element of procedural fairness to traders and shifted the obligation to traders to seek out that element of procedural fairness themselves. This is contrary to the text of GATT 1994 Article X:3 and the widely recognized focus of that Article on the interests of traders.

5. In arguing that matters such as penalties and audit procedures are outside the scope of its obligation under GATT 1994 Article X:3(a), the EC relies on an erroneous understanding of what it means to "administer" customs laws

4.498 There are no EC rules prescribing penalties for violations of EC customs laws. As the EC Commission itself has acknowledged, "Specific offences may be considered in one Member State as a serious criminal act possibly leading to imprisonment, whilst in another Member State the same act may only lead to a small – or even no – fine." (Exhibit US-32, p. 13)

4.499 With respect to audit procedures, there are differences among working practices, including the balance between reliance on examinations of goods at time of importation and post-release audits. As the EC Court of Auditors observed, due to such differences, "'individual customs authorities are reluctant to accept each other's decisions.'" (Exhibit US-14, para. 37) At the conclusion of audits, some member State authorities provide traders what amounts to binding valuation information, which they may invoke in future transactions, while others do not.

4.500 In dismissing the foregoing instances of non-uniform administration, the EC argued that they are outside the scope of its obligation under GATT 1994 Article X:3(a) because penalties and audit procedures are not measures of the type described in Article X:1, and because penalties and audit procedures do not constitute administration of measures that are described in Article X:1. Alternatively, the EC argued that certain EC guidelines cause penalties and audit procedures to be uniform within the meaning of Article X:3(a). Of these arguments, the main emphasis to have emerged is the proposition that differences among member States in penalties and audit procedures do not constitute non-uniform administration of EC measures that indisputably *are* within the scope of Article X:1.

(a) The EC relies on an erroneous understanding of what it means to "administer" customs laws

4.501 In its reply to the Panel's Question No. 93, the EC refers to the definition of the term "administer" and states that, in light of that definition, "Article X:3(a) GATT refers to the execution in concrete cases of the laws, regulations, decisions and rulings of general application referred to in Article X:1 GATT." It then reasons that since a law of a member State, such as a penalty law, "itself needs to be executed or applied," "it cannot be said that such a law 'executes' or 'applies' another." This reasoning is flawed for several reasons.

4.502 First and fundamentally, the EC relies on an exceedingly narrow, erroneous definition of the term "administer." It begins correctly by referring to the dictionary definition of "administer" as "execute." But, it then purports to paraphrase the definition and in so doing introduces a concept from outside the dictionary definition and relies heavily on that concept in its argument. Specifically, it asserts that "in Article X:3(a) GATT, to 'administer' means to execute the general laws and regulations, i.e. to apply them *in concrete cases*." Thus the EC argues that only when a member State authority applies EC customs laws "in concrete cases" is it administering those laws, and only divergences in the application of EC customs laws "in concrete cases" may constitute non-uniform administration. Conversely, according to the EC's reasoning, the mere employment of dramatically different tools by different member State customs authorities for giving effect to EC customs laws does *not* constitute non-uniform administration.

4.503 Of course, the concept of "concrete cases" appears nowhere in the definition of "administer" as quoted by the EC itself. The United States does not dispute that the application of laws and regulations in concrete cases is an action encompassed by the term "administer." However, the United States disputes the EC's suggestion that the term "administer" is *limited* to application in concrete cases.

4.504 In fact, the absence of any such limiting concept is evident from a closer examination of the term "administer." The EC correctly quotes the dictionary definition of "administer" as "execute." But, it does not probe further to define "execute." In fact, the ordinary meaning of "execute" as relevant here is "[c]arry out, put into effect." The question, then, is whether audit procedures and penalty provisions of different member States put EC customs laws into effect, or whether it is only the application of those laws by customs authorities in concrete cases that puts them into effect. The answer is that audit procedures and penalty provisions put EC customs laws into effect by verifying and enforcing compliance with those laws.

(b) Penalties and audit procedures play a critical role in carrying out EC customs laws

4.505 The administration of EC customs laws depends in large part on the actions of traders themselves. It is traders who make who make declarations and provide the customs authorities information concerning classification and valuation of goods. It would be impossible for the authorities to thoroughly inspect every shipment or verify the contents of every declaration before clearance. It is for this reason that tools for verifying and enforcing compliance with the customs laws are critical to "carrying out" or "putting into effect" those laws.

4.506 Given the critical role that audits and penalties play in giving effect to EC customs laws, it is somewhat surprising that the EC asserts, for example, that "provisions which establish the penalty for a violation of customs laws are not themselves related to the administration of customs laws." Indeed, in other contexts (e.g., Exhibit EC-41, p. 1) the EC has acknowledged the critical relationship between penalties and the administration of customs laws.

4.507 The EC's position with respect to audits is equally puzzling. In its First Written Submission, the EC asserted that audits, like penalties, "are not part of customs procedures, and therefore do not concern the administration of customs laws as such." In its response to the Panel's Question No. 64(e), the EC explained that it does not consider audits to be customs procedures "[b]ecause they are not one of the procedures referred to in Article 3(16) CCC." However, the specific sense in which the EC uses the term "customs procedure" for purposes of the CCC has absolutely no bearing on whether audits are customs procedures for administering the CCC. Indeed, the EC so acknowledged in response to the Panel's Question No. 64(c).

4.508 In other contexts, the EC has acknowledged that audits are tools for administering EC customs laws. For example, the Customs Audit Guide contained in Exhibit EC-90 refers to CCC Articles 13 to 16 as "a legal basis for the undertaking of audits." (A framework for post clearance and audit based controls, p. 4) CCC Article 13, in turn, states that member State customs authorities may "carry out all the controls they deem necessary to ensure that customs legislation is correctly applied."

(c) Member States' penalties and audit procedures are properly characterized as tools for the administration of EC customs laws

4.509 The EC contends that, in describing member States' disparate penalty and audit provisions as tools of the administration of EC customs law which constitute the non-uniform administration of those laws, "the US is undermining the clear distinction between the administration of laws and the laws themselves." In the EC's view, penalty and audit provisions are themselves laws that are administered and therefore cannot be described as tools for administering other laws (in this case, EC customs laws).

(i) A law may be a tool for administering other laws

4.510 The flaw in the EC's reasoning is its assumption that a law can be viewed only one way, as the thing that is administered and not also as a tool for administering something else. The United States does not disagree with the proposition that a law providing for penalties or audit procedures may be considered as something to be administered. But that does not exclude the possibility of considering the same law as a tool for administering other laws, for example, by putting those laws into effect through verification and enforcement. The EC itself recognized this precise point in *Argentina – Hides and Leather*, where it challenged the same Argentinian measure from the perspective of its substance *and* from the perspective of its character as a tool for administering other laws. (Panel Report, para. 4.203)

(ii) Basing a claim of non-uniform administration on differences among member State laws that are tools for administering the EC's customs laws is not inconsistent with the Appellate Body's finding that a GATT 1994 Article X:3(a) claim must concern the administration of customs laws rather than their substance

4.511 The distinction between administration and substance that the Appellate Body referred to in *EC – Bananas III* is not to the contrary. The Appellate Body there did not have occasion to consider whether the different licensing procedures at issue represented a non-uniformity in the administration of some other law. That question simply was not at issue there, as it is here.

4.512 By contrast, the panel in *Argentina – Hides and Leather* did have occasion to consider whether a regulation could be challenged under Article X:3(a) as a tool for administering Argentina's customs laws in a manner inconsistent with that provision. The EC in that dispute challenged a measure of Argentina (Resolution 2235) as a tool for administering Argentina's customs laws (set forth in other statutes and resolutions) in a manner inconsistent with Article X:3(a). Argentina defended, just as the EC does here, by arguing that the complaint was about the substance of a measure rather than its administration, and therefore was outside the scope of Article X:3(a) under the Appellate Body's reasoning in *EC – Bananas III*. The panel rejected that argument, noting that "[t]he relevant question is whether the substance of such a measure is administrative in nature or, instead, involves substantive issues more properly dealt with under other provisions of the GATT 1994." (para. 11.70) In finding that the measure in question was administrative in nature the panel observed, "Resolution 2235 does not create the classification requirements; it does not provide for export refunds; it does not impose export duties. It merely provides for a certain manner of applying those substantive rules." (para. 11.72)

4.513 Following the panel's reasoning in *Argentina – Hides and Leather*, the fact that tools for administration of EC customs laws themselves take the form of laws does not mean that the United States has ignored the difference between substance and administration highlighted in *EC – Bananas III*. Like Resolution 2235 in *Argentina – Hides and Leather*, member States' penalty and audit provisions do not prescribe rules on classification and valuation, but they do provide means of "putting into effect" laws that do prescribe rules on classification and valuation.

(iii) The findings of the panel in Argentina – Hides and Leather are directly relevant to the present dispute

4.514 The EC disputes the relevance of the panel report in *Argentina – Hides and Leather*. First, it asserts that a distinguishing feature of the measure challenged in *Argentina – Hides and Leather* was that it mandated administration in a manner inconsistent with Article X:3(a). Second, it suggests that unlike the measure challenged in *Argentina – Hides and Leather*, penalty provisions are not recognizable as being administrative in nature. Neither of these arguments is well founded.

4.515 The question of whether the measure at issue in *Argentina – Hides and Leather* mandated administrative behavior inconsistent with GATT 1994 Article X:3(a) or merely permitted it was entirely irrelevant to the panel's findings in that dispute. The EC's suggestion that the panel report in *Argentina – Hides and Leather* is irrelevant because unlike the measure at issue there penalty provisions are not readily distinguishable as "administrative" or "substantive" is addressed in the US response to the Panel's Question No. 90.

4.516 Of course, the relevant question for Article X:3(a) purposes is not whether a measure is *either* "administrative" *or* "substantive" in character. A measure may have both qualities depending on the perspective from which it is examined, as the EC argued in *Argentina – Hides and Leather*. Distinguishing a measure as "administrative" in character, as the panel in that dispute explained, is a matter of determining whether it prescribes the means for "executing" or "putting into effect" substantive rules on classification and valuation, for example, which themselves are set forth in other measures. Like the measure at issue in *Argentina – Hides and Leather*, EC member State penalty and audit provisions do not prescribe substantive rules on classification and valuation, but they do put such substantive rules as prescribed in EC regulations into effect.

4.517 Since, in the EC's view, a Member administers its customs laws only when it applies those laws "in concrete cases," the EC cannot conceive of the possibility that non-uniform administration of customs laws may take the form of different audit procedures and penalty provisions in different regions of the Member's territory. The EC's understanding ignores the ordinary meaning of "administer" as "execute," which in turn means "put into effect."

4.518 The EC recognizes that the focus of Article X:3 is on protecting the interests of traders. From traders' point of view, however, the liability they may face for misclassification of goods or technical errors in clearing goods through customs, the likelihood of being audited, and the possibility that at the conclusion of an audit the customs authorities may issue binding guidance that the traders may rely upon in the future all are considerations that can be as important as the consideration of how the customs authorities will classify and value their goods.

(d) Reference to "penalties" for "minor breaches" in GATT 1994 Article VIII:3 does not put penalties outside the scope of Article X:3(a)

4.519 The EC makes the additional argument that the mention of "penalties for minor breaches of customs regulations or procedural requirements" in GATT 1994 Article VIII:3 is evidence that penalties are not addressed by GATT 1994 Article X. But this argument is a non-sequitur. The fact that Article VIII:3 sets substantive parameters for penalties for certain types of breaches of customs regulations or procedural requirements – i.e. "minor breaches" – has nothing to do with whether penalties may be considered to be tools for administering a Member's customs laws.

4.520 Carried to its logical extension, the EC's reasoning would lead to manifestly absurd results. For example, it would mean that a Member could discriminate among other Members by applying penalties to customs breaches involving products of some Members but not applying penalties to customs breaches involving like products of other Members. This would not be a breach of GATT 1994 Article I, according to the EC's logic, because that article, like Article X:1, refers only to "charges" and not expressly to "penalties."

(e) The US argument does not imply a requirement of harmonization of all sub-federal laws of WTO Members that have any similarity in subject matter to federal laws

4.521 Equally unavailing is the EC's argument that a finding that differences in member States' penalty and audit provisions constitutes non-uniform administration of EC customs laws would have dire implications for all WTO Members in a variety of regulatory areas. This argument is based on the erroneous premise that under the US argument any sub-federal law that had any similarity in subject matter with a federal law (i.e. a "link") "could be said to constitute 'administration' of the law." However, it is not the mere existence of a "link" between member States' penalty and audit provisions and EC customs laws that makes the former administrative in nature. Rather, it is the fact that the very purpose of member States' penalty and audit provisions is to "execute" or "put into effect" EC customs laws that gives them that quality.

6. *The decisions of review tribunals in the EC do not govern the practice of "the agencies" entrusted with administrative enforcement of EC customs laws, contrary to GATT 1994 Article X:3(b)*

4.522 The EC fails to comply with Article X:3(b) because the one review tribunal that it provides whose decisions have EC-wide effect is the ECJ, and review by the ECJ does not meet the requirement of promptness. Review by member State courts does not fulfill the EC's obligation, as the decisions of each such court apply only within its respective member State. The decisions of any given member State's courts do not "govern the practice of" "the agencies entrusted with administrative enforcement" of customs laws in the EC as a whole. Further, Article X:3(b) must be read in light of the obligation of uniform administration in Article X:3(a); accordingly, where review leads to decisions whose effect is limited to particular regions within a Member's territory such review is not consistent with Article X:3(b).

(a) The decisions of the tribunals or procedures a WTO Member provides pursuant to GATT 1994 Article X:3(b) must govern the practice of "the agencies" entrusted with administrative enforcement of the Member's customs laws

4.523 The first sentence of Article X:3(b) requires Members to provide tribunals or procedures for the prompt review and correction of administrative action relating to customs matters. The second sentence requires that such tribunals or procedures "be independent of the agencies entrusted with administrative enforcement" *and* that their decisions "be implemented by, and ...govern the practice of, such agencies." It is the requirement that the decisions of review tribunals or procedures govern the practice of the agencies entrusted with administrative enforcement that makes clear that the EC does not fulfill its obligation under Article X:3(b), since each of the multiple review tribunals it provides renders decisions that govern the practice only of a subset of agencies entrusted with administrative enforcement within a particular region in the EC.

4.524 The EC states that "Article X:3(b) GATT, unlike Article X:3(a) GATT, is not concerned with questions of uniformity, but exclusively with the prompt review of customs decisions." But if this were so, there would be no need for Article X:3(b) to specify that the decisions of review tribunals must "govern the practice of" the agencies entrusted with administrative enforcement. It would suffice simply to require the provision of tribunals or procedures whose decisions are "implemented by" the agencies entrusted with administrative enforcement.

4.525 The ordinary meaning of the term "govern" as relevant here is "[c]ontrol, influence, regulate, or determine" or "[c]onstitute a law, rule, standard, or principle for." Accordingly, the distinct "govern the practice" requirement in Article X:3(b) looks beyond the simple implementation of a decision in the case at hand and requires that the decision "control, influence, regulate or determine" the practice of or "constitute a law, rule, standard, or principle for" "the agencies entrusted with administrative enforcement" of the customs laws.

4.526 Moreover, it is "*the* agencies entrusted with administrative enforcement" whose practice is required to be governed by the decisions of review tribunals or procedures. That requirement is not fulfilled where the decisions of review tribunals or procedures govern the practice of only *some of* the agencies entrusted with administrative enforcement.

4.527 This understanding is reinforced by the context provided by Article X:3(a). The EC concedes that Articles X:3(a) and X:3(b) must be interpreted "in a harmonious way." Where the decisions of review tribunals govern the practice of the agencies entrusted with administrative enforcement, they become part of the agencies' administration of the Member's customs laws in future cases. Since the Member's customs laws must be administered in a uniform manner, the decisions of review tribunals must govern the practice of "the agencies" throughout its territory.

4.528 Australia put the point succinctly in its statement at the first Panel meeting when it observed that "the decisions and rulings of the review bodies should be applied consistently and be available equally throughout the territory of the WTO member." That is not the case in the EC. Not only are the decisions of individual member State courts applicable only within their respective member States, and therefore not applied consistently throughout the EC's territory, but such decisions are not "available equally throughout the territory" of the EC. As the EC explained in response to the Panel's Question No. 72, there is no mechanism to ensure that member State courts are kept apprised of the customs review decisions of other member State courts.

4.529 The only review tribunal decisions that govern the practice of "the agencies" entrusted with administrative enforcement of EC customs laws throughout the EC's territory are decisions of the ECJ. However, review by the ECJ can hardly be considered to satisfy the Article X:3(b) requirement of prompt review. The ordinary way for questions to be put before the ECJ is through the preliminary reference procedure, in which it may take 19 to 20 months for the ECJ to render a decision (and that is only an average).

(b) The US argument does not imply a requirement for every WTO Member to establish a single, centralized customs court

4.530 The EC has indicated that the EC is not the only WTO Member to provide for review of customs administrative actions on a regional basis and suggested that the US argument would imply an obligation for each WTO Member to establish a single review tribunal with jurisdiction throughout its territory. However, whether or not there are other Members that provide for review of customs administrative action on a regional basis, the EC is the only WTO Member of which the United States is aware that has a combination of geographically fragmented customs administration *and* geographically fragmented review.

4.531 The United States does not argue that Article X:3(b) requires every WTO Member to have a single, centralized tribunal for the prompt review and correction of customs administrative actions. What the United States does argue is that Article X:3(b) requires that the decisions of the tribunals that a Member provides for the prompt review and correction of customs administrative actions govern the practice of the agencies entrusted with administrative enforcement of the customs laws *throughout the Member's territory.*

4.532 Where a Member has a single, centralized agency entrusted with the enforcement of its customs laws, it is conceivable that it may fulfill its obligation under Article X:3(b) even where it provides for review and correction through multiple tribunals each of whose jurisdiction is regionally limited. In that case, where the court for a given region renders a decision, the agency should be able both to implement that decision in the region and conform its practice throughout its territory. In this way, the Member's administration of its customs laws would be governed by that decision, and its customs law administration would be uniform. If the decision of a court in one region conflicts with a decision of a court in another region, the agency should be able to resolve the conflict by appealing one or the other decision to a court or tribunal of superior jurisdiction, a possibility contemplated by the second sentence of Article X:3(b).

4.533 Further evidence for the proposition that the review and correction provided for pursuant to Article X:3(b) must result in decisions that govern the administration of a Member's customs laws throughout its territory is the *proviso* in the second sentence, which states that "*the central administration of such agency* may take steps to obtain a review of the matter in another proceeding if there is good cause to believe that the decision is inconsistent with established principles of law or the actual facts." (Emphasis added.) The *proviso* contemplates "the central administration" challenging a tribunal's decision collaterally – i.e. "in another proceeding" – when the central administration determines that "the decision is inconsistent with established principles of law or the actual facts." But, that possibility makes sense only if the decision in the original proceeding would otherwise have effect outside of that proceeding. If the decision's effects were confined to the proceeding in which it was rendered, there would be no need or basis for a collateral challenge.

4.534 As the possibility of collateral challenge to tribunals' decisions implies that the effects of such decisions are not confined to the particular proceedings in which they are rendered, there is no basis for suggesting that Article X:3(b) contemplates these effects having a scope that is narrower than the Member's entire territory. Not only is there no basis for such a suggestion, but the reference to "the central administration" of the agency entrusted with administrative enforcement itself supports the proposition that the effects of tribunals' decisions are contemplated as having a scope that covers the Member's entire territory.

4.535 In sum, the combination of 25 separate EC member State customs authorities and review tribunals that are distinct to each member State results in review tribunal decisions that do not govern the practice of "*the* agencies entrusted with administrative enforcement" of the EC's customs laws. For this reason, the provision of review and correction of member State customs administrative decisions by member State tribunals fails to meet the EC's obligation under Article X:3(b).

F. Second Written Submission of the European Communities

1. The measures at issue in the present dispute

4.536 The US claim under Article X:3(a) GATT relates to "the manner in which the EC administers" its customs laws. As regards the US claim under Article X:3(b) GATT, the EC understands that the measure at issue is the alleged failure of the EC to provide for tribunals or procedures for the prompt review and correction of customs decisions.

4.537 However, in relation to the claim under Article X:3(a) GATT, the United States goes on to add that "the specific measure at issue" within the meaning of Article 6.2 DSU "are the laws regulations, decisions and rulings that make up EC customs law", i.e. the measures listed in the first paragraph of the US Panel request.

4.538 The EC does not agree that the measure listed in the first paragraph of the US panel request, which include notably the Community Customs Code, the Implementing Regulation, and the Community Customs Tariff, are the "measures at issue" in the present dispute within the meaning of Article 6.2 DSU. It follows clearly from the first sentence of the first paragraph of the US Panel request that the US claim relates to the manner in which the EC *administers* the measures listed, not to the measures themselves. The enumeration at the end of the first paragraph of the US request serves merely the purpose of identifying the laws which the EC allegedly fails to administer in a non-uniform manner. However, this does not mean that these laws themselves become measures at issue in the present dispute.

4.539 The EC also does not share the view of the United States that administration of laws "may not itself be a measure". As the Appellate Body has confirmed in *US – Corrosion-Resistant Steel Sunset Review*, any act or omission attributable to a WTO Member can be a measure of that Member for purposes of WTO dispute settlement. This also applies to the administration of laws as referred to in Article X:3(a) GATT.

4.540 Close attention to what is the measure at issue in the present dispute is particularly necessary given the specific features of Article X:3(a) GATT as the legal basis of the US claim. As the Appellate Body has confirmed in *EC – Bananas III*, Article X:3(a) GATT relates only to the administration of the laws and regulations referred to in Article X:1 GATT, not to those laws and regulations themselves.

4.541 The US suggestion that administration may not be a measure would lead to the absurd result that non-compliance with Article X:3(a) GATT could never be challenged under the DSU.

4.542 At the same time, the EC is concerned that the United States is trying to blur the distinction between the administration of measures, and the measures themselves, and thereby effectively attempts to enlarge the scope of the present dispute. For these reasons, the Panel should hold that the acts of general application listed in the US panel request are not measures at issue in the present dispute.

4.543 On a further point, the United States has refused to identify the specific aspects of EC customs administration that it was challenging. It has merely stated that it challenged the administration of the listed measures, which it described as "capturing the universe of measures that constitute EC customs law".

4.544 This does not constitute a sufficiently precise description of the measure at issue in the present dispute. EC customs legislation is a large and complex body of law. It would therefore not be sufficient to describe the measure at issue in the present as the "administration of EC customs law". Rather, the measure at issue in the present dispute is the administration of EC customs law in those respects referred to in the US Panel request, as further refined in the US First Written Submission, notably tariff classification, customs valuation, processing under customs control, local clearance procedure, and penalties. This is also confirmed by the title of the present dispute, which is "*Selected* Customs Matters", and thus cannot include simply all customs matters.

4.545 The United States attempts to keep the scope of the present panel proceedings vague are also illustrated by the US's refusal to provide an exhaustive list of the customs procedures in respect of which it alleges a lack of uniform administration, and instead claims that this lack is "not confined to any particular customs rule or group of rules". In this respect, the EC would remark that it cannot be expected to defend itself against nebulous charges of non-uniform administration in areas that the United States has not identified in its Panel request and its First Written Submission. Accordingly, the US attempt to keep the scope of the present proceedings vague should be rejected.

2. *The US claims under Article X:3(a) GATT*

(a) The requirements of Article X:3(a) GATT

(i) Article X:3(a) GATT concerns the administration of customs laws, not the customs laws themselves

4.546 The EC has explained, with reference to the relevant case law of the Appellate Body, that Article X:3(a) GATT does not concern the laws and regulations themselves, but only their *administration*. This means that Article X:3(a)

GATT does not require a harmonization of laws within a Member where, for instance, different legal regimes are applicable within different parts of the territory of a WTO Member. This is relevant in all areas where matters at issue in the present dispute are governed by laws of the EC member States, which is the case in particular with respect to penalties for vi c olations of customs law.

4.547 The United States contests this interpretation by arguing that "customs laws may be administered through instruments which are themselves laws".

4.548 The EC considers this interpretation to be manifestly incompatible with the wording of Article X:3(a) GATT, which refers only to the *administration* of the laws, regulations, decisions and rulings of the kind referred to in Article X:1(a) GATT. Article X:1 GATT specifies that these measures are all measures of *general application*. The administration of such measures is thus their application in concrete cases. Laws, which are of general application, can therefore not at the same time be regarded as measures of administration. The US argument would also be incompatible with the clear distinction made by the Appellate Body in *EC – Bananas III* between the administration of laws and the laws themselves.

4.549 The United States tries to escape from this conclusion by drawing a distinction between "substantive" and "administrative" laws, for which it claims as support the Panel Report in *Argentina – Hides and Leather*. According to the United States, only laws which are of an administrative nature must be administered in a uniform manner, whereas no such obligation would exist with respect to laws which are of a "substantive" character.

4.550 Apart from the fact that the United States furnishes no explanation of what it understands by "substantive" and what by "administrative" laws, the EC does not believe this interpretation to be correct. The Panel Report in *Argentina – Hides and Leather* does not provide any support for the US interpretation. The obligation of uniform application applies to all the measures of the kind referred to in Article X:1 GATT, regardless of whether they are "substantive" or "administrative" in nature. The real distinction for Article X:3(a) GATT is thus not between substantive and administrative measures, but between administration and the measures to be administered.

4.551 This matter is of great importance for all WTO Members where certain matters covered by Article X:3(a) GATT may be regulated at the sub-federal level. This is even more important since Article X:3(a) GATT does not only apply to the administration of customs laws, but also to laws regarding the internal taxation and internal sale of products. In many WTO Members, including the United States, such matters are frequently governed by sub-federal laws, which may result in the existence of divergent rules across the territory of such WTO Members. If the US arguments were accepted, differences in sub-federal legislation would have to be regarded as incompatible with Article X:3(a) GATT. This would upset the federal balance in numerous WTO Members, and can therefore not be a reasonable interpretation of Article X:3(a) GATT. This would be incompatible also with the findings of the GATT Panel in *Canada – Gold Coins*, which held that the GATT respects the internal distribution of competences within each WTO Member.

4.552 The United States has wrongly argued that the EC interpretation would put "all laws and regulations that are instruments of customs administration beyond the reach of the disciplines of Articles X:3(a) GATT".

4.553 First of all, the EC argument applies only to those matters which are the subject matter of sub-federal legislation, which is in the EC the case notably for penalties. In the EC, as in other WTO members, most areas of customs law are governed by laws at the federal level.

4.554 Moreover, even where a law exists at the sub-federal level, this does not mean it is "beyond the reach" of Article X:3(a) GATT. On the contrary, Article X:3(a) GATT requires the uniform administration of all laws, including those which might exist in a WTO Member at the sub-federal level, within the area in which they apply.

4.555 Finally, the United States looses sight of the actual object and purpose of Article X:3(a) GATT. The purpose of this provision to ensure a certain minimum level of predictability and security as regards the administration of the covered laws and regulation to WTO Members and traders. This objective is entirely respected if laws which apply at a sub-federal level within a WTO Member are applied in a uniform manner within the territory in which they apply. It is not compatible with this objective and purpose to transform Article X:3(a) GATT into a provision which requires legislative changes, and notably a harmonization of sub-federal within a WTO Member.

(ii) Article X:3(a) GATT does not prescribe the ways in which WTO Members must administer their customs laws

4.556 Article X:3(a) GATT contains an obligation to administer customs laws in a uniform manner, but does not prescribe the specific way in which WTO Members should administer their customs laws.

4.557 At the level of principle, the United States does not appear to contest this point. In fact, it states on a number of occasions that "prescribing the method for the EC to come into compliance with Article X:3(a) GATT is not necessary to resolve this dispute".

4.558 However, the reality of the US claims is rather different. In particular, the United States is effectively requiring the EC to establish a customs agency, which in addition should have competences to issue advance rulings for a number of matters. A more prescriptive application of Article X:3(a) GATT is hardly imaginable.

4.559 It is also interesting to note that the United States has so far not provided any explanation of how its claims relate to its own proposal made in the context of the Doha Round Trade Facilitation Negotiations, which in particular foresee the creation of an obligation to provide for advance rulings on tariff classification and valuation matters. The United States has also not contested that one of its essential motives behind the present case is to influence the Doha Trade Facilitation Negotiations.

4.560 The EC therefore maintains its view that the United States is seeking an application of Article X:3(a) GATT which would be highly prescriptive in character, and effectively transform Article X:3(a) GATT into a basis for the harmonization of customs laws and practices along the US model. The EC submits that such an interpretation should be rejected.

(iii) Article X:3(a) GATT lays down minimum standards

4.561 The United States has attempted to deny the importance of the statement of the Appellate Body in *US – Shrimp*, and criticized in particular that the Appellate Body "did not elaborate on what it meant by minimum standards". However, this does not change the fact that the Appellate Body qualified Article X:3 GATT as a provision which lays down certain minimum standards of transparency and procedural fairness. While this does not replace the need to interpret the actual terms of Article X:3(a) GATT, it does shed some light on the limited objective underlying this provision, which is directly opposed to the highly ambitious interpretation advocated by the United States.

4.562 In its First Written Submission, the EC has also explained, with reference to the GATT Panel Report in *EEC – Dessert Apples*, that minor administrative differences in treatment cannot be regarded as implying a violation of Article X:3(a) GATT. This view has also been shared by Japan. In its response to a question by the Panel, the EC has explained that this means that it is for the United States, as the complaining party, to show that variations of administrative practice, even where they existed, have a significant impact on traders.

4.563 The United States has tried to sweep this case law aside by claiming that it has "provided evidence of a system that engenders and fails to cure myriad divergences of administration in matters that go to the core of customs administration and affect traders liability for customs duty, as well as other aspects of their operations". The EC does not contest, for instance, that where the liability for customs duty is affected, this is significant for the competitive situation of a trader. However, as the EC has already remarked, for some of the other alleged differences, for instance as regards the local clearance procedure or valuation audits, the United States has so far provided no explanation as to why such differences, even if they existed, would be significant for traders.

(iv) The meaning of "uniform administration"

4.564 As the Panel in *US – Hot Rolled Steel* has held, uniformity can be assessed only on the basis of an overall pattern of customs administration. Only if, on the basis of such general patterns, a WTO Member's administration of its customs laws can be shown to be non-uniform, is the standard of Article X:3(a) GATT violated. Very similar views have also been expressed by certain of the third parties in the present case, namely Australia and Japan.

4.565 The United States has tried to distinguish the present case from *US – Hot Rolled Steel* and *EC – Poultry* by arguing that these cases were not concerned with "geographical uniformity". However, the US fails to explain why "geographical uniformity" should be treated any differently from other kinds of uniformity, e.g., uniformity across time. Nor is it clear why a different standard would apply to the requirement of uniform administration on the one hand, and the requirement of impartial and reasonable administration, on the other. The EC would also like to recall that it has been the United States itself, which – in cases such as *US – Hot Rolled Steel* – has argued against judging compliance with Article X:3(a) GATT only on the basis of individual cases.

4.566 In response to a question from the Panel, the United States has further elaborated that in the present case, "the question is not whether a particular administrative authority is applying a particular law in a uniform manner", but "whether different authorities across the territory of a WTO Member [...] are applying various laws uniformly". Apparently, the United States is thus suggesting that a stricter standard should apply to WTO Members with a decentralized system of customs administration compared to WTO Members with a centralized customs administration. The EC sees no basis for such double standards, which should therefore be rejected.

4.567 Finally, contrary to what the US claims, the EC has never suggested that the pattern of non-uniformity needed to be "neat". If instances of non-uniformity in the system of a WTO Member are so widespread and frequent as to have a significant impact on the administration of that Member's system, then this will amount to a pattern of non-uniform administration. There is no need for them to be arranged in a particular pattern. Therefore, the US argument that the standard set out by the Panel in *US – Hot Rolled Steel* would make it impossible to challenge an overall absence of uniformity is simply incorrect.

(b) The burden of proof

4.568 The burden of proof rests on the United States as the complainant in the present case. It is for the United States to bring forward sufficient evidence to establish that there is a pattern of non-uniform administration in respect of the aspects of EC customs law raised by the United States.

4.569 In its First Written Submission, the United States failed to bring forward any evidence to this effect. It limited itself to raising a small number of cases on issues of tariff classification and customs valuation. A limited number of cases in a particular area are insufficient for assessing the overall administration of the EC's system. Moreover, the cases raised by the United States in fact do not constitute examples of lack of uniformity in the EC's system.

4.570 The Panel asked the United States a number of questions aimed at obtaining from the United States evidence concerning the actual incidence of non-uniform administration in the areas of EC customs law raised by the United States.

4.571 In its responses, the United States does not furnish a single new piece of evidence of non-uniformity in the EC's system. Instead, it responds that its claim "does not turn on the statistical frequency of non-uniform administration". Moreover, it claims "that it is the EC, rather than the United States, that is likely to have the information sought in the question", and requests the Panel to exercise its authority under Article 13 of the DSU to seek relevant information from the EC. For instance, the United States suggests that the EC should be requested to provide "a statistically significant sample of BTI and other classification decisions from various member States (including explanations of the bases for those decisions) in order to determine the frequency of divergent administration". As another example, the United States suggests that the "Panel might seek from the EC information of the type that enabled the EC's Court of Auditors to make the findings contained in its report on customs valuation".

4.572 These responses must be regarded as transparent attempts of the United States to rid itself of the burden of proof, and should be rejected as such. It is not credible for the United States to claim, on the one hand, that there is a widespread pattern of non-uniform administration in the EC, and then to claim that it does not have any evidence to support this claim.

4.573 Instead, the United States wishes to pass the burden of proof to the EC by requesting that it should be the EC which provides the information requested. With this request, the United States is essentially suggesting that the EC should proof its own innocence. This request is not only completely without basis in WTO law, it also amounts to a logical impossibility. Whereas it should be possible for the United States to provide evidence of instances of non-uniform administration, if such instances in fact existed, it is logically impossible for the EC to proof that such instances never occur.

4.574 For this reason, it would be entirely impractical for the Panel to request the EC, as suggested by the United States, to provide "a statistically significant sample of BTI and other classification decisions from various member States (including explanations of the bases for those decisions) in order to determine the frequency of divergent administration". Similarly, it is impractical for the United States to suggest that the "Panel might seek from the EC information of the type that enabled the EC's Court of Auditors to make the findings contained in its report on customs valuation". The Report of the Court of Auditors was based on audit visits that took place on the premises of the Commission and the customs administrations of 12 EC member States in 1999-2000. The US suggestion therefore amounts in essence to requesting the EC to conduct a new audit of customs valuation. This is not a reasonable request to make of a defending party in the context of proceedings under the DSU.

4.575 Moreover, the request made by the United States goes considerably beyond the functions of a Panel under Articles 13 of the DSU. Whereas the Appellate Body has confirmed that Panel's have a certain investigative authority, this authority also has its limits, which were clearly spelt out by the Appellate Body in *Japan – Agricultural Products II*. In the present case, the United States is asking the Panel to do precisely what the Appellate Body said it should not. Having failed to make its own *prima facie* case, the United States is asking the Panel to seek the relevant information from the EC. In this way, the Panel would relieve the United States of its original burden of proof, and make the case for the complainant.

4.576 The United States seems to believe that it can establish a lack of uniformity by making broad allegations of absence of uniformity in particular areas. However, the administration of customs law in areas such as tariff classification or customs valuation depends on the particular circumstances of each case. Accordingly, whether administration is uniform or not cannot be established without knowledge of the "particular details of each case", and it is the responsibility of the United States as the complainant to provide these details.

4.577 Finally, while the EC can certainly not be expected to prove that it administers its laws in a uniform manner, it would like to point out that certain elements of the context of the present case provide an indication that the factual allegations made by the United States are incorrect. The EC has already, in its First Written Submission, pointed out the almost complete lack of reaction by US industry and traders to the request by USTR for input to the present case.

4.578 A similarly interesting indication is provided by the reactions of other WTO Members, and notably the third parties, to the present dispute. Of the nine WTO Members which have chosen to become a party to the present dispute, not one has pointed to the existence of any examples of lack of uniformity. The only third party which claimed that a lack of uniformity in the EC's practice existed is Korea. However, Korea refused to do so, invoking "the business confidential nature of the underlying business transactions". The EC considers that if Korea had indeed information which might be helpful for the EC to ensure a uniform administration of its customs laws, Korea should have shared this information in the first place with the EC. This would also be in accordance with the customs cooperation agreement between the EC and Korea, which provides for obligations of mutual information and assistance.

4.579 Finally, the United States keeps on referring to what it calls "blunt acknowledgements of how the EC system operates" by certain EC officials of institutions, and claims that the "cumulative message is that there is a problem of divergent administration". The United States is referring here to a handful of dispersed statements by EC officials and institutions, which are taken out of context, and are of no relevance for the present case. Most of these statements should be seen as a normal reflection of the process of self-monitoring and improvement which is necessary for any system of customs administration in the context of a rapidly evolving world. If every critical comment made in the context of WTO Member's administrative and regulatory processes were immediately interpreted as evidence of WTO-incompatibility, this would create a serious chilling effect on the internal policy debates of WTO Members.

(c) General issues underlying the US claims under Article X:3(a) GATT

4.580 In its First Written Submission, the EC has already addressed a number of general issues underlying the US claims under Article X:3(a) GATT, including the role of the member States, the Commission, the Court of Justice, and the

Customs Code Committee. The United States has so far not responded in detail to these explanations of the EC. Instead, its subsequent interventions have highlighted two central tendencies underlying the US case: first, the US attempt to force the EC to create an EC customs agency; and second, its tendency to belittle and ignore the functioning of the EC institutions and procedures designed to ensure a uniform application of Community law throughout the EC.

(i) The US case is aimed at compelling the EC to create an EC customs agency

4.581 The US submissions confirm that the US case is essentially aimed at compelling the EC to establish an EC customs agency. While the United States has formally claimed that prescribing the method for the EC to come into compliance with its obligations under Article X:3(a) GATT is "not necessary to resolve this dispute", its claims and submissions in the present dispute tell a very different story. Indeed, the alleged need for an EC customs agency is a recurrent theme in the submissions of the United States. Consequently, the United States has referred to the creation of such an agency as an "obvious option" for addressing its claims.

4.582 That the US case is exclusively aimed at the creation of an EC customs agency is also illustrated by the US response to a Panel's question on the specific measures the United States would expect the EC to adopt to address its claims. The United States referred only to creation of a customs agency. While the United States indicated that it did not "rule out" that other options might exist for addressing its claims, it failed to identify any other concrete measures which the EC could take.

4.583 The exclusive focus of the United States on the establishment of an EC customs agency is also revealed by the US response to a Question by the Panel, where it asked the United States to comment on the EC's observation that the US criticisms of the ECJ judgment in *Timmermans* was inconsistent with its criticism of the decision of the UK Court in *Bantex*. In response, the United States explained that in the absence of a centralized customs authority, any scenario would lead to non-uniform administration.

4.584 In the view of the United States, in the absence of such an agency, no modification to the EC's rules and procedures in the areas of tariff classification, customs valuation and customs procedures would be sufficient to address the US claims.

4.585 Another confirmation of the nature of the US claims is the "wish list" which the United States addressed to the EC following the consultations in the present dispute. This wish list included as its first point the "establishment of a single, centralized EC authority for issuing advance rulings, within a brief, specified period following request, to traders regarding matters including classification, valuation, and origin (both preferential and non-preferential)".

4.586 The United States has attempted to present this request as a sort of concession, since the agency in question would be responsible only for issuing advance rulings. In response, the EC would recall that there is – with the exception of origin matters – currently no obligation to provide for advance rulings on customs matters. Accordingly, the suggestion that the EC should create an agency with a competence to issue such rulings goes beyond current WTO commitments.

4.587 Overall, it becomes clear that the US case is not concerned with the actual administration of EC customs law, but is an extremely ambitious case aimed at a complete overhaul of the EC's system of customs administration. It would leave the EC with almost no other choice but to establish an agency with operational tasks which are unprecedented in the history of the EC. Such an enterprise would entail profound changes in the way EC law is administered, and have legal, financial and personnel implications which are very difficult to project at the current stage. The EC also doubts that this could be regarded as a "reasonable measure" within the meaning of Article XXIV:12 GATT.

4.588 More importantly still, executive federalism is a feature not just of EC customs law, but of EC law in general. Since Article X:3(a) GATT applies not only to customs matters, but to all the matters referred to in Article X:1 GATT, the issues raised in the present case do not seem necessarily limited to the field of customs, but concern almost areas of EC law. Accordingly, it is a frontal attack on the executive federalism of the EC legal order, with implications that would go far beyond the area of customs.

4.589 This claim cannot have a legal basis in Article X:3(a) GATT. This provision provides for certain minimum standards of procedural fairness and transparency. Like the WTO Agreements overall, it does not prejudge the internal autonomy of WTO Members on fundamental questions of internal organization and administration.

(ii) The United States misrepresents the EC legal system

4.590 In its First Written Submission, the EC has set out in detail how the EC legal system ensures the uniform interpretation and application of EC law through the EC. The EC has also set out how the various institutions and actors involved contribute to the uniform application of EC customs law.

4.591 In its subsequent submissions, the United States has provided almost no reaction to these explanations of the EC. Instead, the United States chooses to persist in its highly selective reading of the EC legal system, and ignores everything that does not fit into the negative picture it wishes to draw. The dismissive approach of the United States towards the EC legal system is reflected in a repeated statement, where the US claims that the EC system consists in "a loose web of principles, instruments, and institutions, including non-binding guidance, plus general obligations of cooperation between member States, plus discretionary referrals of matters to the Customs Code Committee".

4.592 The EC considers such statements to be derogatory towards the EC as a whole. The mechanisms which the EC has described are typical not only for the area of customs law, but for the way in which the uniform interpretation and application of EC law is ensured throughout the EC. Accordingly, if the United

States considers the EC customs union to constitute a "loose web", then presumably this must apply to the EC as a whole.

4.593 Such statements betray a lack of understanding and appreciation of the history and success of European integration over the last 50 years. It may also reflect the fact that there are considerable difference between the constitutional structures and processes of the United States on the one hand, and the EC on the other. However, such differences must be tolerated within the WTO, and cannot simply be presumed to amount to violations of Article X:3(a) GATT.

4.594 As regards the role of the Commission, the Court of Justice, and the Customs Code Committee, the United States has so far not further substantiated its criticisms. As regards the Customs Code Committee the United States, when asked whether it had any evidence to proof its allegation that decision-making in the Committee has become more difficult since the most recent enlargement on 1 May 2005, the United States failed to produce the requested evidence, and instead stated that this was "evident". In addition, it again referred to a statement from an EC official. However, this statement was made in a personal capacity and right after the entry into force of enlargement, and therefore can hardly be regarded as "evidence" of what has happened since enlargement.

(d) The US claims under Article X:3(a) GATT

(i) Tariff classification

Binding tariff information

The alleged risk of BTI shopping

4.595 The Panel asked the United States to provide evidence that "picking and choosing" actually occurs in the EC's BTI system. In response, the United States failed to provide such evidence. Instead, it attempts to circumvent the question by referring to observations which are of no relevance to the question.

4.596 First, the United States refers to a passage from Panel Report in *EC – Chicken Cuts*, in which the EC is reported to have stated that it is possible under EC law to withdraw an application for a BTI where the outcome is considered unfavourable by the importer. However, this statement does not contain anything that would indicate that BTI shopping occurs in the EC. Since BTI is granted upon application, and in the interest of the applicant, it is normal that the application can be withdrawn until the BTI has been issued. Before the issuance of BTI, the applicant will in most cases not know the tariff classification envisaged by the customs authorities. In contrast, once the BTI has been issued, the application can no longer be withdrawn. In addition, it should be noted that all applications, including those which have been withdrawn, are entered into the version of the EBTI data base to which the customs authorities have access.

4.597 Second, the United States claims that the issuance of BTI is "heavily skewed in favor of certain member States", and claims that this "skewing suggest strategic selection of the member States in which importers apply for BTI". The

EC considers that the fact that the authorities of certain member States issue more BTIs than others simply reflects differences between member States in terms of market size, geographical location, trading patterns, other practical considerations.

4.598 Finally, the US states that "importers regularly approach the US embassies in EC Member States to enquire as to the optimal authorities from which to apply for BTI". The EC would remark that even if such questions were asked, this is no proof that divergent practices in fact occur. Indeed, there is no "optimal authority", and the application should be submitted to the competent Member State authorities as determined by Article 6(1) of the Implementing Regulation.

The alleged difficulties of detecting and correcting divergent BTIs

4.599 The United States has also argued that the EC system does not provide for sufficient mechanisms to detect and correct divergences between BTIs, should they occur.

4.600 In its responses to the Panel's question, the United States has criticized that the EBTI data base "does not reveal in any detail the rationale applied by different authorities in classifying a particular good in a particular way". The EC is astonished by this statement. For each BTI issued, the EBTI data base (in both its versions) includes a detailed description of the product sufficient to permit their identification and classification, the CNN code under which the product was classified, and the justification of this classification. The justification will typically identify the interpretative rules and principles applied, and where appropriate other relevant authority, such as case law of the Court of Justice. The EC considers this information entirely sufficient to ensure full information about the BTI practice of EC customs authorities.

4.601 The EC has also explained that the EBTI data base is very well received and intensively used by traders and by customs authorities, as evidenced by the fact that the average number of consultations per month in the first half of 2005 was about 324.000. The United States has argued that this number might "indicate anything from academic curiosity to collection of statistical information". The EC finds the explanation that 324.000 consultations per months would be generated by "academic curiosity" or "collection of statistical information" remarkably far-fetched. It is clear that the EC EBTI data base is a useful tool for securing a uniform classification practice, which is widely used by traders and customs authorities alike.

The US claim that member States do not treat BTI issued by other member States as binding

4.602 In its First Written Submission, the United States has claimed that "Member States do not always treat BTI issued by other Member States as binding". Once again, the United States has failed to provide specific examples to prove its allegation. Instead, it points to a survey of a trade association to which it has already referred to in its First Written Submission. According to this survey, one company reported that "binding tariff information from Germany is still not accepted by other EU countries, especially Greece and Portugal".

4.603 The EC contests the existence of any problem regarding the recognition of BTI from Germany in other EC member States. The "survey" referred to by the United States is no "evidence" to the contrary. It merely reflects a comment made by one unidentified company which is not supported by any further explanation or evidence. Accordingly, it is impossible to verify the accuracy of the statement. The EC would remark that even if an importer claims that BTI was not accepted, this might in fact reflect a range of problems of an entirely different kind, for instance a lack of identity of the products imported with those described in the BTI. Moreover, if indeed a customs authority fails to recognize BTI issued by another Member State, the importer can obtain judicial review. The importer can also inform the European Commission, but the EC is not aware of this having occurred.

4.604 Second, the United States refers to a statement by the EC in the context of the dispute *EC – Chicken Cuts*, where the EC is quoted as asserting that a particular "interpretation" was not followed in other EC customs offices. As the EC will explain further below, there was no difference of interpretation or application of EC classification rules in this case. However, for the purposes of the present discussion, it suffices to point out that the EC's statement related only to "interpretation". Nowhere in the Panel Report in *EC – Chicken Cuts* has the EC said that BTI was not recognized when presented by the holder. Accordingly, the statement quoted by the United States is not a pertinent answer to the Panel's question.

4.605 Finally, the United States refers the Panel to the decision of the Main Customs Office Bremen in the *Bantex* case, in which the Customs Office noted that "numerous binding customs tariff decisions have been handed down regarding comparable goods". This remark once again betrays a misunderstanding of how the EC's BTI system works. BTI is binding on the customs authorities only as against the holder of the BTI and it does not appear that *Bantex* GmbH was the holder of BTI for the products at issue. Accordingly, once again, the United States responds to the Panel's question with an example that is of no relevance to the question. In addition, it is noted that in the *Bantex* case, the question was not whether there existed BTI for comparable goods, but whether the goods were identical to those described in the BTIs. As this was not the case, the example is even less apt to support the US claim.

The legal effect of BTI

4.606 In its First Written Submission, the United States has also made numerous criticisms of the legal effects of BTI, which relate notably to the *Timmermans* case law of the European Court of Justice. These criticisms are unfounded: the *Timmermans* case in fact can contribute to the uniform application of EC customs law. The EC has also pointed out that the US' arguments were inconsistent with its criticisms of the decision by the UK Court in the *Bantex* case.

4.607 When questioned by the Panel about this obvious inconsistency, the United States responded that "in the absence of a centralized customs administration", both situations, i.e. either allowing the revocation of BTI or not allowing it, could lead to a lack of uniformity. As the EC has already explained above, this US response demonstrates irrefutably that the specific features of the EC's BTI system are not in any way problematic from the point of view of the uniform application of EC classification rules. Rather, the US case is uniquely aimed at compelling the EC to create an EC customs agency.

4.608 That there is nothing wrong with the EC's BTI system, and notably the effect of BTI in the EC legal order, is also borne out by a comparison with the US rules on advance rulings. For instance, the United States has criticized in its First Written Submission that BTI in the EC is "specific to the holder". Interestingly, exactly the same appears to be true for advance rulings in the United States, where US law explicitly cautions that "no other person [than the one to whom the ruling is addressed] should rely on the ruling letter or assume that the principles of that ruling will be applied in connection with any transaction other than the one described in the letter".

4.609 Similarly, US law also provides that a ruling letter may only be invoked "in the absence of a change of practice or other modification or revocation which affects the principle of the ruling set forth in the ruling letter". The EC fails to see how this is fundamentally different from the *Timmermans* case law.

4.610 The rather limited effect of rulings issued by US Customs has also been confirmed by the US Supreme Court in *United States v. Mead Corp*, in which the Court held that ruling letters of US Customs have no legal force and that Customs has regarded a classification as conclusive only as between itself and the importer to whom it was issued.

Alleged divergences in EC classification practice

Blackout Drapery Lining

4.611 In its First Written Submission, the EC has already demonstrated that the products at issue were not identical to the products described in the BTI referred to by the United States, and that accordingly, this case does not demonstrate a lack of uniformity in the EC's classification practice.

4.612 When required by the Panel to comment on the EC's explanations, the United States starts its observations by contesting the EC's statement that the product "before the German authorities was not flocked". In support, the United States refers to a "decision" of the Main Customs Office Hamburg on which the Main Customs Office Bremen is supposed to have relied. These statements are incorrect as the letter of the Main Customs Office Hamburg related to an administrative appeal introduced by a company called Ornata GmbH. This appeal is in any way related to the administrative appeal introduced by Bautex-Stoffe GmbH which was the subject of the decision of the Main Customs Office Bremen, let alone that the Main Customs Office Bremen relied on the letter of the Main Customs Office Hamburg.

4.613 It is also noted that contrary to the US claims, that letter does not contain a decision, but rather requested the observations of the importer on the envisaged classification. In response to this letter, the Ornata GmbH withdrew its protest by letter of 16.9.1998.

4.614 As regards the substance, the United States accuses the decision of the Main Customs Office Bremen of being incompatible with an HS explanatory note to heading 59.07. This statement is manifestly wrong. HS explanatory note (G)(1) to heading 59.07 provides that the fabrics covered include "fabric, the surface of which is coated with glue (rubber glue or other), plastics, rubber or other materials and sprinkled with a fine layer of other materials such as (1) textile flock or dust to produce imitation suèdes". Therefore, the presence of textile flock or dust was a relevant criterion for the classification under heading 59.07. The decision of the Main Customs Office Bremen took account of this factor and, since the product was not flocked, it could accordingly not be classified under heading 59.07.

4.615 The United States also unwarrantedly criticises the decision of the Main Customs Office Bremen for having considered the density of the web of the product. According to Note (2)(a)(5) to Chapter 59 of the CN, heading 5903 does not apply to plates, sheets, or strips of cellular plastics, combined with textile fabric, where the textile fabric is present merely for reinforcing purposes. The question whether the web was fine is a relevant criterion for establishing whether it is present for reinforcement purposes or not.

4.616 The United States has also criticized the EC for having referred to a classification regulation concerning a type of ski trousers. This criticism is unwarranted. Commission Regulation 1458/97 concerned the classification of garments under heading 6210, which covers "garments made up of fabrics of heading 5602, 5603, 5903, 5906 or 5907". Accordingly, the classification regulation in question concerned implicitly the classification of the fabric out of which the trouser was made. In doing so, it had to apply Note 2(a)(5) to Chapter 59 of the combined nomenclature, i.e. determine whether the fabric serves merely for reinforcing purposes, and in this context took into account a.o. the "tight weave" of the fabric. Accordingly, Commission Regulation 1458/97 was certainly a relevant precedent for the interpretation of note 2(a)(5) to Chapter 59.

4.617 For the same reason, the EC can also not find anything contrary to Community law in the "interpretative aid" referred to by the lower German customs office: the criteria of the density of the web mentioned in that text was fully compatible with Community law and the German text was purely an interpretative aid without any legally binding character.

4.618 Finally, the United States also alleges that by relying on the tightness of the fabric, the Main Customs Office Bremen violated the chapeau of Note 2(a) to Chapter 59, which states that heading 5903 applies to "textile fabrics impregnated, coated, covered or laminated with plastics, whatever the weight per square meter". This criticism is equally unjustified because the weight referred to is the weight of the entire product, i.e. the fabric as impregnated, coated, covered or laminated. The Main Customs Office Bremen did not consider the weight of the product, but rather the density of the web of the polyester fabric, which is only a part of the product. Accordingly, the decision of the Office is entirely compatible with the Chapeau of Note 2(a) to Chapter 59.

4.619 Furthermore, the United States attempts to find fault with individual aspects of the reasoning of the German customs authorities are also irrelevant for the present case, which does not concern the question under which heading a particular product should properly have been classified, but the question of uniformity of administration of EC classification rules. Moreover, to the extent that the United States considers EC practice to be incompatible with an HS explanatory note, it could raise this matter in the context of the WCO in accordance with Article 10 of the HS Convention.

4.620 It is clear that the products as described in the decision of the Main Customs Office Bremen were not identical to the products described in the BTIs referred to by the United States, since the former were not flocked with textile flock, while the products in the BTIs are described as having been flocked. On the basis of these product descriptions, the products had to be classified differently. Accordingly, this difference in tariff classification is not a lack of uniformity, but on the contrary the result a correct application of the Combined Nomenclature.

4.621 Moreover, if an error had occurred in respect of the description of the goods by the German customs authorities, the importers in question could have challenged the decision before the German courts. However, no such action has been taken.

LCD Monitors

4.622 The EC has notably pointed to the fact that Council Regulation 493/2005, by suspending the tariff duties under heading 8528 for monitors up to a certain size, ensures a uniform tariff treatment for all the monitors covered by the Regulation. The United States continues to criticize this regulation as being "provisional" and a "stop-gap measure" and it argues that a duty suspension is "far different from a classification regulation".

4.623 The EC considers these objections to be unfounded. That the regulation is valid only until 31 December 2006 reduces in nothing its value for ensuring a uniform tariff treatment throughout the EC today. Moreover, before the expiration of the measure, the EC will examine the situation and will adopt the measures which are necessary. The United States cannot build an allegation of non-uniform administration on the mere speculation that the EC might fail to take certain measures in the future.

4.624 The United States is also wrong to claim that Regulation 493/2005 fails to ensure uniform administration because the measure concerns the suspension of a duty rate, rather than the classification of a product. The United States fails to appreciate that Article X:3(a) GATT does not require uniform administration for its own sake, but rather in order to ensure uniform conditions of treatment for traders. Accordingly, Article X:3(a) GATT can be held to be violated only where a variation of practice in fact has a significant impact on traders. In the case of LCD monitors, due to Regulation 493/2005, for the monitors covered by the regulation, there is no difference in tariff duties between monitors classified under heading 8471 and those classified under heading 8528, since the tariff rate for both will be 0%. Nor are there any other relevant differences in treatment. Accordingly, even if there were differences in tariff classification for the monitors at issue, this would have absolutely no impact on traders. This is why the trading community was in fact strongly supportive of the measure.

4.625 In addition, the EC considers that even if the Panel were to hold that there was an incompatibility with Article X:3(a) GATT, this incompatibility could not be held to constitute nullification or impairment of any benefit accruing to the United States under Article X:3(a) GATT. Since the United States has not contested that the tariff treatment for the monitors covered by Regulation 493/2005 is uniform, and the duty rate is 0%, the presumption of nullification and impairment established by Article 3.8 DSU would therefore have to be considered as rebutted in the present case.

4.626 The United States also criticizes the conclusions reached by the Customs Code Committee at its 346th meeting of 30 June to 2 July 2004, according to which "unless an importer can demonstrate that a monitor is only to be used with an ADP machine (heading 8471) or to be used as an indicator panel (heading 8531), its has to be classified in heading 8528". The US argues in particular that this conclusion is incompatible with Note 5 to Chapter 84 of the Common Customs Tariff, according to which a unit is to be regarded as part of a complete system if "it is of a kind solely or principally used in an automatic data-processing system".

4.627 The EC recalls that the present case does not concern the correctness of individual classifications, but rather the question of uniform administration. The United States does not show that there is any lack of uniformity; rather, it questions the substantive classification practice of the EC. Such arguments are not admissible under Article X:3(a) GATT. This has also been confirmed by *US – Hot Rolled Steel*, in which the Panel held that it was not "properly a Panel's task to consider whether a Member has acted consistently with its own domestic legislation".

4.628 Moreover, the US allegations that the conclusions of the Customs Code Committee are incompatible with note 5(a) to Chapter 84 are false. On the basis of several presentations by the industry concerned, the Committee concluded that industry had not succeeded in presenting any criteria on which principal use could be established.

4.629 The EC would add that it does not understand what purpose conclusions of the Customs Code Committee could have if, as the United States seems to suggest, they should be limited to restating the language of the Combined Nomenclature. In order to provide for a uniform application of the CN, it must be possible for the Committee to reach, on the basis of the facts available, and acting in conformity with the Combined Nomenclature, specific conclusions concerning the classification of particular goods. It is in this way that the Committee can and does contribute to the uniform classification of goods throughout the EC. The US suggestion that the Committee's conclusions "actually detracts rather than promotes uniformity" is thus manifestly unfounded.

4.630 The US' own practice does not seem to differ greatly from that of the EC on this point. In its First Written Submission, the EC had already pointed to a ruling in which US Customs had found it impossible to establish the "principal use" of a monitor. In another recent ruling on LCD monitors, US Customs found that "the dual purpose of the monitors is indicative of a lack of principal use for this good", and accordingly classified the good under heading 8528. Similarly, in a recent guidance to traders on flat panel display modules, US Customs stated the following: "The issue of principal/sole use has been difficult to ascertain in the past. As a result of this review by US Customs, it has been determined that only specific size flat panel display modules are principally used in ADP system [...]".

Further examples of alleged non-uniformity in classification practice

4.631 The Panel has asked the United States to provide evidence for its allegation that there are other instances of non-uniform administration in the classification practice of the EC. In response, the United States refers to a limited number of largely unsubstantiated statements which it had already made in its First Written Submission.

4.632 First, the United States refers to a questionnaire of a trade association of March 2005, in which a respondent company is reported to have stated that "[u]nisex articles or shorts have different classifications in Italy and Spain to those in Germany". This "survey" is based on a comment from a single unidentified company, and is not supported by further evidence or explanations. On this basis, it is impossible to ascertain the precise nature of the products concerned, or to identify the questions of tariff classification which might be involved. Accordingly, the EC considers that this statement does not provide any evidence of a lack of uniformity in EC classification practice.

4.633 Second, the United States refers once again to Case C-339/98, *Peacock*, in which Germany had classified certain network cards differently from the classification envisaged in BTIs issued by certain other member States. The EC fails to see how this case illustrates an absence of uniform administration. First, the EC would recall that this case relates to importations carried out before 1995. In 1995, however, the European Commission had, in order to ensure a uniform application of Community law, adopted Regulation 1165/95 foreseeing the classification of the adapter cards in question under heading 8517 (electrical apparatus for line telegraphy).

4.634 The classification by the German customs authorities was appealed in the competent courts, which referred the question to the European Court of Justice. By judgment of 19 October 2000 in case C-339/98, the Court of Justice decided that the products in question had to be classified under heading 8471 (automatic data-processing machines and parts thereof). In a further ruling, in case C-463/95, *Cabletron*, the Court of Justice confirmed this interpretation and decided that Regulation 1165/95 was invalid.

4.635 Overall, the case of network cards is a case in which the Commission had already in 1995 taken the necessary measures to ensure a uniform classification practice. As the United States itself has recognized, what is significant is not that a divergence may occur, but rather that it is addressed and removed once it occurs. This is precisely what happened in *Peacock*.

4.636 In addition, the EC would remark that the correct classification of network equipment is a complex technical question with which many customs authorities have had to come to terms. The United States itself experienced difficulties in classifying networked equipment, and has revoked or modified numerous rulings concerning the classification of such equipment. Finally, the classification of network equipment has also led to a WTO dispute between the EC and the United States concerning the correct classification of LAN equipment, in which the United States unsuccessfully alleged that due to its classification practice, the EC was not respecting its tariff concessions in respect of LAN equipment. The EC does not find it appropriate that the United States raises what is essentially a substantive classification question in the context of the present case, which is concerned with uniformity of administration under Article X:3(a) GATT.

4.637 Third, the United States refers to the dispute *EC – Chicken Cuts*. However, it must be recalled that *EC – Chicken Cuts* concerned the interpretation of the EC's tariff concessions, and incidentally the question of the correct classification of the products in question. In contrast, in *EC – Chicken Cuts*, the complainants did not make any claims under Article X:3(a) GATT, and it was never alleged that the EC's classification practice had not been uniform. On the contrary, the facts of the case show that for the entire period in question, the EC had measures in place which ensured the uniform tariff classification of the products. On this basis, the Panel and the Appellate Body came to the conclusion that the EC's classification practice had been entirely uniform.

4.638 Finally, the United States refers again to an alleged lack of uniformity regarding the classification of drip irrigation products. This is a case of temporarily diverging BTI which was promptly addressed through the adoption of a classification regulation, and which is today resolved.

4.639 Binding tariff information was issued by France on 6 July 1999 for a Roberts Irrigation Product (Ro-Drip) under CN code 8424 81 10. On 9 February 2001, Spain issued BTI in which it classified the product under CN code 3917 32 99. This issue of divergent BTI was discussed by the Tariff and Statistical Nomenclature Section of the Customs Code Committee. During the process, Roberts Irrigation Systems made a submission to the Committee. Furthermore, the US government also made several submissions to the Commission. The issue was resolved by the adoption of Commission Regulation (EC) No. 763/2002 of 3 May 2002, which classified the product under heading 3917 32 99. Consequently, France revoked and replaced the previously issued binding tariff information.

4.640 The United States has alleged that this case supports its claims because one or more member States did not treat as binding BTI issued by other member States. This remark appears beside the point, since the BTI were not issued for the same holders. In any event, as the United States has itself argued, what matters is not whether divergences occurred, but whether they are addressed and removed when they occur. In the case of drip irrigation products, this is precisely what happened. Once the divergent BTIs had been detected, the case was promptly addressed and solved within 15 months, which is a period of time that is reasonable for for definitely resolving a complex classification issue.

(ii) Customs valuation

Report 23/2000 of the EC Court of Auditors

4.641 The Panel asked the United States to provide evidence as regards the incidence of non-uniform administration with respect to the issues of customs valuation discussed in Report 23/2000 and referred to by the United States. In response, the United States declined to provide such evidence, arguing that its claim "does not turn on the statistical frequency of non-uniform administration".

4.642 The EC disagrees with this response. First of all, a violation of Article X:3(a) GATT requires the existence of a pattern of non-uniform administration. Accordingly, the statistical incidence of instances of non-uniform administration in the areas in question is a highly relevant question. Since the United States has failed to provide such evidence, it has failed to establish a *prima facie* case of violation of Article X:3(a) GATT.

4.643 More importantly still, with its references to Report 23/2000, the United States has not proved the existence of a lack of uniformity in the EC's system. The Report of the Court of Auditors did not have the purpose of assessing compliance with Article X:3(a) GATT. Moreover, for all the issues raised in the report, the report has been followed up by the EC institutions, and wherever necessary, the appropriate measures have been taken.

4.644 The US response to these remarks is to ask the Panel "to exercise its authority under Article of the 13 DSU [...] to seek information of the type that was made available to the Court of Auditors in preparing its report on valuation". As the EC has already remarked, this request amounts to shifting the burden of proof to the EC, and should therefore be rejected.

4.645 Moreover, the US request is also impracticable. Report 23/2000 was based on audit visits that took place on the premises of the Commission and the customs administrations of 12 EC member States in 1999-2000. Whatever information the Court of Auditors, which is an independent EC institution, may have collected at that time is in the possession of the Court of Auditors only. In addition, such information would reflect the situation in 1999-2000, but not the situation today. Accordingly, the US suggestion therefore amounts in essence to requesting the EC to conduct a new audit of customs valuation. In this way, the United States seems to want to transform an EC institution which is devoted to ensuring the proper collection and administration of the EC's own resources into a mechanism intended to provide it with the necessary evidence for conducting a WTO challenge. The US request must be regarded inadmissible.

4.646 As regards the issue of repair costs covered by a warranty, the United States now seems to accept that this issue has been resolved by Commission Regulation 44/2002, of 11 March 2002. However, the United States faults the EC for allegedly having taken more than 12 years to resolve the matter. First of all, it is not accurate that the EC tolerated a lack of uniformity for 12 years. More importantly still, what matters is that, on a complex issue of customs valuation, the EC itself detected the problem and took the necessary measures to correct it. Accordingly, rather than showing any failure in the EC's system, this case shows that the EC system functions properly.

4.647 The United States also refers again to the specific issue of valuation audits. In particular, the United States refers to a statement in the report of the Court of Auditors according to which one member States lacked the authority to perform post-importation audits.

4.648 In this respect, the EC would like to clarify that under Article 76(2) CCC, every Member State may proceed to all necessary verifications in order to satisfy themselves of the accuracy of the particulars contained in the declaration. This also includes all questions regarding the value of the goods. The Member State referred to by the Court of Auditors was Greece, which, in 2000, has established a service with powers to conduct post-clearance audits. In addition, the EC has also referred to the EC Customs Audit Guide, which ensures a uniform audit practice across the EC.

The Reebok case

4.649 The Panel has requested the United States to provide concrete evidence to support its submission that there is a lack of uniform application as regards the treatment of related parties under Article 143(e) of the Implementing Regulation. In its response, the United States informs that its description of the case is based on a "narrative account by the importer at issue". Moreover, the US states that "due to concerns relating to the pendency of litigation over the matter at issue and the commercial sensitivity of the information that supporting documentation would contain, the importer declined to provide documentation at this time".

4.650 The United States does therefore not provide any evidence for its claim that there is a lack of uniformity in the application of Article 143(1)(e) of the Implementing Regulation. The United States cannot justify this failure to discharge its burden of proof on the basis of the refusal of the importer in question to provide the necessary evidence. It is for the United States itself, as the complaining party, to provide the evidence for the claims it makes.

4.651 The United States has repeatedly stated that the "EC does not deny the essential facts". The EC has certainly not contested that it has been contacted by Reebok with a problem regarding the application of Article 143(1)(e) of the Implementing Regulation by the Spanish customs authorities. However, the EC contests that there is a problem of non-uniform application of this provision.

4.652 The United States also faults the EC for having stated that the Commission and the Customs Code Committee cannot serve as substitutes for the normal appeal procedures applicable in individual cases, and has claimed that there is "no EC institution before which the trader has a right to obtain uniform treatment". This is in stark contrast to the fact that according to the US' own statements, the case is currently pending before the Spanish courts, and the importer concerned refuses to share information on account of this pendency. Moreover, as the EC has explained repeatedly, where a court of a Member State applies Community law, it acts as an organ of the EC. Finally, if there is a question of interpretation of Community law, this question can – and in certain cases must – be referred to the European Court of Justice by way of a request for a preliminary ruling, which ensures a uniform interpretation of EC law throughout the Community.

4.653 In addition, the United States has referred to a decision by the European Ombudsman on a complaint by an individual importer. The EC can confirm that the complaint was made on behalf of Reebok, which claimed that the European Commission was not properly discharging its responsibilities in respect of the administration of customs valuation law.

4.654 At the outset, the EC would like to point out that the Ombudsman did not take a decision on the substance of the complaint. Rather, the complainant withdrew the complaint indicating that the he "was satisfied with the position the Commission had adopted on the matter and with its proposal to look into pending problematic issues".

4.655 Second, the EC would like to recall that the European Ombudsman is another mechanism which contributes to the proper administration of EC law by the EC institutions. The fact that there is a decision of the European Ombudsman is therefore not as such problematic, but rather shows the working of the various mechanisms of the EC's system.

4.656 Finally, the EC would remark that the facts as set out in the decision are not presented entirely correctly. Notably, the United States quotes from a letter of the European Commission of 20 December 2000, in which the Commission is supposed to have stated "that the interpretation issues raised by the complainant were a matter for the national customs authorities". This quotation is not correct. In its letter of 20.12.2000, the Commission stated that "[t]he application of this criterion [of Article 143(1)(e) Implementing Regulation] in individual cases is of course a matter for national administrations and the Commission Services could only express an opinion if a detailed file on all aspects of the case was to be forwarded by the customs services in question. However, our services do not, in general, have a responsibility to undertake a detailed examination of very specific cases, this being the task of the national administrations".

4.657 The EC considers that this statement reflects correctly the division of competences between the European Commission and the customs authorities of the member States, which are competent for the application of customs law in individual cases. It is neither possible nor appropriate for the Commission to substitute itself for the competent authority simply because in an individual case of application a trader is not satisfied with an approach taken by the customs authority. On the contrary, the European Commission is responsible for monitoring and ensuring the correct and uniform interpretation and application of EC customs law.

4.658 In the case in question, Reebok had simply not, at the time in question, submitted to the European Commission any evidence that showed an incorrect application of EC law, or a divergence in the application of EC law. Accordingly, the Commission did not see any need to intervene in the specific pending case.

4.659 Where the Commission is informed of a wrong interpretation of Community law, including Community customs law, the Commission will take the appropriate action. A pertinent example is furnished by a complaint submitted by Reebok regarding the imposition of compensatory interest by the Spanish customs authorities. Since this complaint showed an incompatibility with Community law, this complaint led the Commission to initiate infringement proceedings against Spain. The EC would underline that Reebok did not lodge a similar complaint as regards the application of Article 143(1)(e) CCC.

(iii) Processing under customs control

4.660 In relation to this customs procedure, the United States has progressively limited its claims. In its First Written Submission, the United States identified an eventual contradiction between Article 133 CCC and Article 502(3) of the Implementing Regulation, in that the former requires an applicant to provide information both on the creation or maintenance of processing activities in the EC and an absence of harm to essential interests of Community producers of similar goods, while, in contrast, the Implementing Regulation requires the former but not the latter. At the same time, the United States highlighted that, according to its interpretation, a guidance adopted by United Kingdom required both types of information, while the French guidance simply sets out the first condition.

4.661 The EC explained in its First Written Submission that there is no contradiction between the CCC and the Implementing Regulation, because the latter is subsidiary legislation and cannot modify the conditions laid down in the CCC. The EC also explained that both the United Kingdom and the French guidance required the importer to provide the two sets of information.

4.662 The United States insists that the French guidance makes no reference to information on harm to Community producers, which is, on the contrary, required by the United Kingdom's guidance.

4.663 The EC considers that the US criticism is based on an isolated and incorrect interpretation of the French guidance, which has to be interpreted in the context of the EC legislation. The guidance refers to the economic conditions required to obtain an authorization to process under customs control in the same way as Article 502(3) of the Implementing Regulation: by using an abbreviation of the requirements laid down in Article 133(e) CCC. The French authorities require the same kind of information as the United Kingdom: the information needed to assess whether "the necessary conditions for the procedure to help create or maintain a processing activity in the Community without adversely affecting the essential interests of Community producers of similar goods (economic conditions) are fulfilled".

4.664 This interpretation is also supported by paragraph 78 of the French guidance, which, within Chapter III "Examination of economic conditions", plays the role of a chapeau to Section I, where paragraph 83 is located. Contrary to what the United States affirms, this paragraph 78 is more than simply an introductory paraphrase of certain provisions from the CCC. This paragraph reminds, for Section I as a whole, that the absence of adverse effects on the essential interests of Community producers is a general economic condition that is common to the three customs procedures therein covered (inward processing, outward processing and processing under customs control), as it is clearly laid down in Articles 117(c), 148(c) and 133(e) CCC, respectively.

4.665 In the present case, the United States has not submitted any evidence on the application of the guidance issued by the French authorities. The EC would like to recall that according to the case law of the Appellate Body, it is the party which asserts that a measure of another Member is inconsistent with WTO obligations which has the burden of proving that the measure in question has the alleged content or meaning. Relevant evidence for establishing the meaning may also include evidence regarding the application of the measure. This was explained by the Appellate Body in *US – Carbon Steel* and in *US - Oil Country Tubular Goods Sunset Reviews*.

(iv) Local clearance procedure

4.666 In response to two questions from the Panel, the United States has explained its understanding of the procedures applicable in the EC for clearance of goods for free circulation and it has claimed that the lack of uniform administration described in its First Written Submission exists independently of the particular stages in which the clearance process is articulated.

4.667 The description made by the United States is still not correct. The US states that simplified procedures are separated into three groups (local clearance, warehousing and simplified declaration), but the correct classification in relation to declarations for release for free circulation should be "incomplete declarations" (Articles 254-259 of the Implementing Regulation), "simplified declaration procedure" (Articles 260-262) and "local clearance procedure" (Articles 263-267). The US description mixes local clearance procedure for release for free circulation and other simplifications for customs procedures with economic impact, like warehousing. In any case, the EC considers the United States has not explained the alleged divergences between the practices of the customs authorities and whether the differences occur between EC member States at equivalent steps in the same procedure.

4.668 Besides, the EC would like to insist that paragraphs 110 to 115 and the table in paragraph 116 of the US First Written Submission describe inexistent divergences. Thus, taking the United Kingdom and France as representative examples in relation to inspection of goods by the customs authorities prior to release, there is no contradiction between the practices in these two EC member States. In both cases, customs officials may (or may not) inspect goods prior to release. The EC already explained this question in its First Written Submission, without receiving an answer from the United States either in its First Oral Statement or in its response to the questions from the Panel. The same problems occur with the other divergences alleged by the United States.

4.669 It is clear that, contrary to what the United States claims, the EC disputes the existence of divergences in the administration of local clearance procedures and that the United States has not provided a single exhibit to illustrate and support its claim.

(v) Penalties for violations of customs law

Penalty provisions are not covered by Article X:3(a) GATT

4.670 The United States argues that penalty provisions are "tools" for the administration of customs laws. Interestingly, the United States itself appears to concede that penalty provisions are not as such laws pertaining the matters referred to in Article X:1 GATT. Indeed, the United States itself explains that "it is important to distinguish between the administration of penal laws and the application of penal laws to administer customs laws of the type described in Article X:1".

4.671 The EC does not contest that penalty provisions are relevant tools for ensuring a uniform administration of customs law. This is precisely why EC law provides that penalty provisions must be effective and dissuasive. However, the fact that penalty provisions are "tools" for the uniform administration of customs laws does not mean that they are themselves laws or regulations pertaining to the matters enumerated in Article X:1 GATT, in particular tariff classification, customs valuation, or rates of duty. If, as the United States correctly argues, penalty provisions are merely "tools" to ensure a uniform administration of those laws, then penalty provisions as such do not fall within the scope of Article X:3(a) GATT.

4.672 The United States has tried to counter this argument by arguing that standards for penalty provision also are addressed in the Kyoto Convention. However, the fact that the Kyoto Convention, which is a Convention negotiated in the context of the WCO, may contain certain provisions or standards on penalty provisions has nothing to do with the scope of Article X:3(a) GATT. On the contrary, the fact that the Kyoto Convention contains a harmonization of certain specific matters may rather provide an indication that the WCO Members considered that such matters were not yet sufficiently addressed in the GATT.

4.673 The United States has also contested the EC's argument that penalties are concerned with illegitimate actions rather than with legal trade. In support, it has referred to the example of the judgment of the ECJ in *de Andrade*, where, according to the US, "the only offense at issue was a failure to clear goods through customs within the period specified in the Community Customs Code".

4.674 The EC fails to see the basis for the US objection. Penalties for violations of customs law by definition are responses to contraventions of customs law. Penalties are sanctions for acts or omissions which are illegal. Penalty provisions therefore have a fundamentally different character from provisions which establish the conditions for legal trade, e.g., by setting tariff rates or establishing rules for customs valuation.

4.675 The *de Andrade* case referred to by the United States confirms precisely this point. In *de Andrade*, the importer had infringed Article 49 CCC, according to which, where goods are covered by a summary declaration, the formalities necessary for them to be assigned a customs-approved treatment of use must be carried out within certain specified time-limits. The measures taken by the customs authorities in *de Andrade* were a sanction for the failure of the importer to comply with these time-limits. The *de Andrade* case demonstrates simply that sanctions are a tool for ensuring compliance with EC law, and that EC member States apply the necessary sanctions. In contrast, *de Andrade* does nothing to support the view that penalty provisions as such fall within the scope of Article X:1 GATT.

Article X:3(a) GATT does not require the harmonization of member States' penalty provisions

4.676 Article X:3(a) GATT concerns only the administration of customs laws, not the substance of the laws themselves. This means in particular that Article X:3(a) GATT does not create an obligation to harmonize laws which may exist within a WTO Member at the sub-federal level. It merely requires that such laws be administered uniformly within the territory in which they apply.

4.677 The United States continues to claim that because penalty provisions are contained in laws of the EC member States, the EC administers its laws in a non-uniform manner. This is manifestly wrong. As the EC has already stressed, it is not the administration of penalty provisions which varies within the EC; it is the laws themselves which are different, albeit within the limits set by Community law.

4.678 In its submissions, the United States has not claimed that EC member States fail to administer their penalty provisions in a uniform manner. Indeed the United States has stated that "whether each individual member State administers its own penal law uniformly within its own territory is not relevant to our claim". This is a striking admission, because it shows that the US claim in fact has nothing to do with the administration of penalty provisions. Rather, the US claim is about the harmonization of legislation within the EC, which is a claim which has no basis in Article X:3(a) GATT.

4.679 The United States also reiterates its argument that the EC's reasoning would "dramatically diminish the effectiveness of Article X:3(a) GATT. However, this statement is incorrect. Article X:3(a) GATT applies to the administration of all of the laws referred to in Article X:1 GATT, regardless of whether they apply in all or part of the territory of a WTO Member. If Article X:3(a) GATT were held to apply penalty provisions, then it should apply to the administration of the penalty provisions of each Member State. Accordingly, the clear distinction drawn by the EC between the administration of measures and their content does not in any way diminish the effectiveness of Article X:3(a) GATT, but simply reflects the proper scope and content of this provision.

Community law ensures a sufficient degree of uniformity of penalty provisions

4.680 Finally, to the extent that penalty provisions can be regarded as relevant for ensuring a uniform administration of the laws referred to in Article X:1 GATT, the EC considers that EC law provides for a sufficient level of harmonization in this respect.

4.681 As the EC has already explained, the European Court of Justice has developed clear guidelines for penalty provisions for violations of EC customs law, which must in particular be effective, proportionate, and dissuasive. These principles have also been confirmed by the Council of the European Union.

4.682 The United States has not shown that the fact that penalty provisions are contained in laws of the member States leads in any way to a non-uniformity in the administration of the laws covered by Article X:1 GATT, in particular laws regarding tariff classification, customs valuation, and rates of duty.

4.683 Instead, the United States has simply stated that "[t]o the extent that different member States have different penalty provisions that apply to the violation of EC customs law [...] they administer EC customs law differently." This argumentation is logically flawed, since the US fails to distinguish between the application of the penalty provisions, and the application of the relevant substantive laws.

4.684 Indeed, it is not correct to assume that differences in penalties would necessarily lead to a lack of uniformity in the application of the provisions the violation of which is sanctioned. Such a consequence would result only if sanctions were not dissuasive or effective. If, on the contrary, sanctions are dissuasive and effective, then it must be assumed that the related substantive provisions will be respected, regardless of differences in the level of sanctions applicable.

4.685 Is is true that differences in the level of penalties may also be important from the point of view of proportionality. However, proportionality has nothing to do with the question of uniform administration under Article X:3(a) GATT. Rather, the proportionality of penalties is addressed in Article VIII:3 GATT, and the United States has not made any claim that the EC does not comply with this provision.

4.686 As the EC has explained, EC law requires that sanctions be effective, proportionate, and dissuasive. The United States has not shown that sanctions in the EC do not comply with these principles. Moreover, the United States has not shown that divergences in penalty provisions of the member States in any way lead to a non-uniformity in the application of the laws of the member States. The US case remains therefore purely theoretical, and unsupported by any facts.

4.687 The United States has also again referred to the EC's work on the modernized customs code, which includes proposals for a harmonization of administrative penalties for violations of customs law. In this respect, it must be stressed that the purpose of these proposals is to further develop and advance the EC the single market also in the field of penalties. This has nothing to do with the EC's obligations under Article X:3(a) GATT.

3. *The US claim under Article X:3(b) GATT*

(a) Nature of the review: independent tribunals or procedures

4.688 The United States agrees with the EC that a WTO Member complies with this obligation under Article X:3(b) GATT only when the review system is independent of the agencies entrusted with administrative enforcement in customs matters.

4.689 In this respect, the United States has raised no criticism about the independence of the remedies instituted by the EC, either at Community level or at Member State level. It should, however, be noticed that the United States applies a less strict standard of independence than the EC. The latter has considered that a body ensuring administrative review is independent of the agencies entrusted with administrative enforcement only when it is not integrated into the organization of the agencies. On the contrary, for the United States independence is already ensured when the office responsible for administrative review is functionally independent of the ports whose decisions it reviews, even if both offices form part of the same agency. The EC considers that the US interpretation is not in conformity with Article X:3(b), which requires that the reviewing tribunals or procedures must be independent of the agencies entrusted with administrative enforcement. This provision imposes an external separation between the tribunals or procedures and the agencies and an internal separation within an agency between the controller and the controlled is not sufficient to comply with Article X:3(b).

4.690 The thrust of the US claim concentrates on the fact that the review decisions taken by the EC member States "have effect only within their respective member States and not on EC agencies generally" and that "the provision of tribunals or procedures by individual member States within the EC does not satisfy the EC's obligations under Article X:3(b)".

4.691 The United States relies on several arguments to support that assertion. First, the United States has constantly argued that the Article X:3(b) GATT obligation must be interpreted in the light of Article X:3(a) GATT, which the United States considers to be its context.

4.692 The EC has explained several times that each of those two subparagraphs in Article X:3 GATT lay down separate obligations and that it cannot be considered that there is a legal relationship between these two provisions (i.e: the obligations from one provision cannot be imported into the other).

4.693 The structure of Article X:3 GATT itself already justifies that interpretation. First, subparagraph (b) does not make any reference to subparagraph (a), unlike subparagraph (c), which contains an explicit link to subparagraph (b). Second, Article X:3 GATT is not introduced by a chapeau allowing to affirm that the two separate subparagraphs are linked and that the obligations therein instituted have to be interpreted in light of the each other.

4.694 Moreover, contrary to what the United States claims, review of customs decisions by the courts of the EC member States does not run counter to the obligation of uniform administration. That type of review is perfectly compatible with the obligation of uniform administration, provided that the latter is ensured by other means that are appropriate to this aim.

4.695 Finally, there is a substantial reason to reject the US interpretation. If we consider that, as the United States has accepted, the review established by Article X:3(b) is only a review of first instance, to require uniformity at first instance would necessarily imply the establishment of a central court of first instance with jurisdiction over the whole territory of any WTO Member. This conclusion finds no support in the wording of Article X:3(b) GATT, which makes no reference to the obligation to establish such central court of first instance. Article X:3(b) GATT does not even require appeals to be decided by a central court or tribunal of superior jurisdiction. The conclusion is that Article X:3(b) does not deal with uniform administration/application of customs law, which is covered exclusively by subparagraph (a), but only with first instance remedies.

4.696 The United States is interpreting Article X:3(b) through the glass of its own legal system and requiring all WTO Members to establish the equivalent to its Court of International Trade. Japan has aligned with the EC in the rejection of this unilateral interpretation. It is worth noting that Australia has also argued that "Article X:3(b) is not a prescriptive Article and includes no obligation to have a central court".

4.697 Furthermore, the EC would like to recall that the establishment of a central customs court within the EC institutional framework runs contrary to one of its fundamental constitutional principles: that the EC Court of Justice and the Court of First Instance are to act within the limits of the powers conferred upon them by the founding treaties and that the courts of the EC member States act as "ordinary" EC courts when applying Community law. In the absence of a provision in the Treaties attributing a competence to any or both of those Courts to review decisions taken by the EC member States and in the presence of the preliminary reference system laid down by Article 234 of the EC Treaty, any modification in the boundaries between the competences of the Court of Justice or the Court of First Instance and the nationals courts would require the amendment of the EC Treaty.

4.698 The EC believes that similar problems, at least at legislative level, may arise in those WTO Members where a central tribunal or court of first instance in customs matters does not exist.

4.699 The United States claims to have found an argument to justify a relationship between subparagraphs (a) and (b) of Article X:3 in the second sentence of subparagraph (b), which states that the decisions of the tribunals or procedures shall govern the practice of the agencies entrusted with administrative enforcement.

4.700 The EC considers that sentence as a provision aimed at securing a fair implementation of tribunal decisions in administrative law matters. To ensure respect by an administrative authority of the decisions taken by a tribunal, most of the legal systems have developed different methods to enforce the *res iudicata* principle. That is the sense that the EC gives to the "shall govern the practice" sentence. It cannot mean, as it is sustained by the United States, that a first instance review decision on a specific case constitutes the source of a general obligation upon the relevant agency. Article X:3(b) only sets up an obligation to implement in fair terms the decision given by an independent tribunal or through an independent procedure.

4.701 Second, the United States has contested the EC's argument that the use of the plural form in Article X:3(b) GATT means that a WTO Member is allowed to have several different review tribunals, each of them covering a part of its geography. According to the United States, "the use of the plural form [...] might allow for the possibility that a Member State may provide for different types of review".

4.702 The EC contests this argument, because it does not take into account that the United States and the EC interpretations are not mutually exclusive: the use of the plural form may indicate that a WTO Member is entitled to maintain geographically limited tribunals and it may also indicate that a WTO Member is allowed to maintain multiple fora for review of customs decisions.

4.703 Third, in its First Written Submission, the EC has explained that when the courts of the member States apply Community law, they act as organs of the Community. This is one of the cornerstone principles in the EC constitutional framework. In support, the EC has also referred to the findings of the Panel in *EC – Trademarks and Geographical Indications (US)*.

4.704 In its First Oral Statement, the United States has argued that the Panel Report in *EC – Trademarks and Geographical Indications (US)* is not relevant, because "the issue presented there was substantially different from the one presented here". The EC disagrees. The issue in *EC – Trademarks and Geographical Indications* was a US claim that, by applying an EC regulation, EC member States were granting each other advantages not available to other third countries, and thus violating most-favoured nation obligations. In response to this claim, the Panel held that member States authorities, when implementing Community law, were acting as organs of the EC; for this reason, the Panel found that such application could not be regarded as the granting of advantages to "other countries". The finding of the Panel in *EC – Trademarks and Geographical Indications* that member States' authorities, when implementing EC law, act as organs of the EC, is highly relevant to the present case. The fact that in the present case, the United States has made a claim under Article X:3(a) GATT, and not regarding most-favoured national obligations, is no reason why the Panel should ignore this case law.

4.705 In addition, the United States argues "that it cannot be assumed that one Panel's recognition of member States *executive* authorities as *de facto* EC authorities [...] means that another panel must recognize member States *judicial* authorities as *de facto* EC authorities". The EC fails to see the basis of this distinction. Both executive and judicial authorities are relevant public authorities in each WTO Member. Both the actions of the executive and of the judicial branches may be relevant for compliance with WTO obligations. Accordingly, the EC sees no reason why only executive authorities, but not judicial authorities of the member States, should be recognized as authorities of the EC when implementing EC law.

4.706 The US arguments are also incompatible with principles of general international law regarding responsibility for wrongful acts. In this regard, the EC would refer to Article 4(1) of the Articles on responsibility of States for internationally wrongful acts elaborated by the International Law Commission (ILC).

4.707 It follows clearly from this provision that, when it comes to the acts of a State under international law, there is no distinction between acts of the legislative, executive and judicial organs. For this very same reason, it would seem unjustifiable to consider that only the executive authorities of the member States, but not the judicial authorities of the member States, can act as EC organs.

4.708 Similarly, it follows from the ILC's articles on state responsibility that the responsibility for internationally wrongful acts extends not only to organs of the central government, but also to organs of territorial units. Accordingly, the EC has never contested that it is responsible in international law for the compliance by EC member States with the obligations of the EC under the WTO Agreements.

4.709 With its argument that member States courts cannot be regarded as EC courts, the United States seems to suggest that whereas the EC is responsible for the actions of EC member States, it cannot have recourse to organs of the EC member States for discharging its obligations, such as the one under Article X:3(b) GATT. Such a result would be highly contradictory. Under the general principles of state responsibility, attribution of conduct relates to all acts and omission, regardless of their legality. Accordingly, not only must conduct be attributed for the purposes of establishing a violation of international obligations, but also in order to assess whether obligations have been complied with. In other words, it is perfectly possible for the EC to have recourse to its member States for the purposes of discharging international obligations, including the obligation to provide for prompt review under Article X:3(b) GATT.

(b) Time requirement: promptness in the review

4.710 Along these proceedings, the claim has been progressively reduced by the United States. Indeed, the United States has lately explained that it is not arguing the lack of promptness of review and correction provided by the EC member States tribunals.

4.711 As to the European Court of Justice and the Court of First Instance, the United States has never claimed that the proceedings before these two Courts, when reviewing decisions taken by the EC institutions, do not ensure prompt review. The only criticism sustained by the United States refers to "preliminary rulings" (i.e.: references to the Court of Justice by national courts). The United States argues that "the time it takes for questions to get presented to and decided by the ECJ and the fact that, in general, referral of questions to the ECJ is discretionary [...] means that the ECJ is not a tribunal or procedure for the prompt review and correction of customs administrative decisions".

4.712 The EC has already explained that this criticism underlay the US misunderstanding of the EC system: the ECJ does not review national customs administrations decisions, but it helps the national courts in such a review through the preliminary ruling procedure with the aim of ensuring the uniform application of Community law throughout the Community. Therefore, preliminary rulings by the ECJ are one of the EC mechanisms to ensure uniform administration of the EC trade laws, regulations, judicial decisions and administrative rulings of general application, as required by Article X:3(a) GATT, and cannot be considered as such a mechanism of "review" of national customs decisions.

G. Second Oral Statement of the European Communities

1. The EC is not obliged to create an EC customs agency and a customs court

4.713 The EC has already explained the significant constitutional implications of the present case for the EC as well as for the WTO Membership in general. It has also explained that the US claims under Article X:3 GATT are essentially directed at forcing the EC to create a centralized customs agency and a customs court.

4.714 The subsequent submissions of the United States have entirely confirmed this assessment. The US has offered no evidence of non-uniform administration of EC customs law, or of judicial review which would be less than prompt. Instead, it has focussed entirely on the involvement of the customs authorities of the EC member States in the administration of EC customs law, which it claims "as such" leads to a lack of uniformity contrary to Article X:3(a) GATT. Similarly, in its claims under Article X:3(b) GATT, the US has focussed entirely on the absence of an EC customs court.

4.715 The US has protested this as a "caricature" of its claims. However, as so often, caricature reveals the true nature of things. Immediately after assuring the Panel that it does not argue that Article X:3(a) GATT requires WTO Members to have a single customs agency, the US retreats from this assurance by stating that "establishing such an agency is the principal manner by which the United States understands the vast majority of WTO Members (if not all WTO Members) to have undertaken to discharge their obligation" under Article X:3(a) GATT. The US also claims that because the EC does not have a single customs agency, it is obliged to have a single customs court.

4.716 The US fixation on the creation of a centralized customs agency and a customs court has been a constant feature of the present proceedings. The creation of such an agency, which should be equipped also with a competence to issue advance rulings on a number of issues, was the first demand made by the United States of the EC during the consultation phase of the present dispute. The second demand was the creation of an EC customs court. Moreover, when questioned by the Panel as to which measures, short of establishing a customs agency and a customs court, the EC should take if the US were to prevail with its claims, the US failed to identify a single concrete measure.

4.717 The US is therefore wrong to complain about the EC's misrepresenting its claims. The US claim under Article X:3(a) GATT is clearly directed against the involvement of the customs authorities of the EC member States in the administration of EC customs law. It is thus a direct challenge to the EC's system of executive federalism, which is a general structural element of the EC legal order, and not only in the field of customs administration. The same is true for the US claim under Article X:3(b) GATT, which is aimed at replacing the courts of the member States by an EC customs court. The EC cannot be faulted for clearly spelling out the US claim.

4.718 The United States has accused the EC of advocating a relative view of Article X:3(a) GATT. This argument is unfounded. The obligation of uniform, impartial and reasonable administration in Article X:3(a) GATT is the same for all WTO Members, including the EC. The EC has never argued that it is subject to standards which are different from those applicable to other Members.

4.719 In support of its view, the US has referred to the fact that the EC, supported by Japan, has argued that whether there exists a lack of uniformity must be established taking into account the features of the system of customs administration in question. This is equally unfounded. It goes without saying that whether a lack of uniformity exists in a particular system of customs administration can only be determined on the basis of all relevant facts, which necessarily include the features of the customs system in question. This has nothing to do with advocating a relative standard, but is simply a requirement inherent in an objective assessment of the facts.

4.720 The US has claimed that "it is improper for the EC to argue that its unique status within the WTO as perhaps the only Member without a single centralized customs agency makes it subject to a different standard with respect to the obligation of uniform administration". The US has also stated that "the EC is the only WTO Member [...] that has a combination of geographically fragmented customs administration and geographically fragmented review". As the EC has already remarked, it is not arguing that it is subject to a different standard than other WTO Members. However, even if it were indeed the only WTO Member with a decentralized system of customs administration and judicial review, this does not mean that its system is in any way incompatible with Article X:3 GATT.

4.721 The EC is an original Member of the WTO. When the EC became a party to the WTO Agreements, including the GATT 1994, its system of customs administration and judicial review was perfectly well known to all Contracting Parties. With this knowledge, the Contracting Parties, including the United States, agreed that the EC should become an original Member of the WTO. It cannot seriously be argued that a fundamental characteristic of the EC such as the involvement of the EC member States in the administration of EC law, including customs law, and in the provision of judicial review, is nonetheless to be regarded as incompatible with Article X:3(a) GATT.

4.722 This point deserves particular emphasis because it is not limited to the area of customs laws. Article X:3(a) GATT applies to all the laws referred to in Article X:1 GATT. Accordingly, the interpretations of the US would not just apply to the area of customs law. Rather, they would make the involvement of sub-federal entities in the execution of federal laws generally impossible in large areas of economic regulation.

4.723 This is of considerable concern to the entire WTO Membership. While the US has a constitutional system in which the spheres of competence of the federal government and of the 50 states are clearly separated, other WTO Members have systems which are marked by a system of executive federalism, in which federal laws are implemented through sub-federal units. As has been recognized even by Judges of the US Supreme Court, executive federalism is a perfectly legitimate constitutional choice, and there is no reason why it could not also apply in the area of customs. Accordingly, the Panel should not accept an interpretation of Article X:3 GATT which would impose a particular US view as to how federal laws should be implemented on other WTO Members.

4.724 The United States has also faulted the EC for having referred to Article XXIV:12 GATT. These criticisms are unwarranted. The EC has invoked this provision as support for its view that GATT commitments, including Article X:3(a), were undertaken by the Contracting Parties in full respect of their respective constitutional systems. As the Panel in *Canada – Gold Coins* has explained, Article XXIV:12 GATT is a provision which has the "function of allowing federal states to accede to the General Agreement without having to change the federal distribution of competences". As a counterpart, Article XXIV:12 GATT requires every WTO Member to take such reasonable measures available to it to ensure observance of the provisions of the GATT at the sub-federal level.

4.725 The EC is fully committed to ensuring compliance by its member States with the requirements of Article X GATT, in accordance with Article XXIV:12 GATT. However, this is not what the US is asking of the EC. The US is arguing that the EC should create a centralized customs agency, a customs court, and should replace all relevant legislation of the member States, notably on the matter of penalties, by EC legislation. This would result in a radical shift in the federal balance within the EC. Such an interpretation is therefore not compatible with the purpose of Article XXIV:12 GATT.

4.726 As regards specifically the issue of a customs court, the US has also referred to Article VI:2(b) GATS, and argued that the EC is trying to transpose this provision to Article X:3 GATT. This argument is manifestly unfounded. Article VI:2(b) GATS contains a general exception which renders the obligation to institute the tribunals or procedures required by Article VI:2(a) GATS essentially facultative for certain members. To this extent, the provision can be regarded as a more far-reaching equivalent to Article X:3(c) GATT, which gives the possibility to provide review also through procedures which are administered by bodies which are not independent. However, this has nothing to do with the EC's arguments in the present case. The EC is not contesting that it is obliged to institute tribunals or procedures for the provision of judicial review which are independent of the agencies which they control. The EC merely points out that the question how the EC organizes its court system through which it provides judicial review is not prejudged by Article X:3 GATT.

4.727 The US has also argued that difficulties of coming into compliance should have no bearing on assessing whether the EC is in compliance with Article X:3 GATT. At a general level, the EC agrees that difficulties of compliance are not as such decisive for the interpretation of an international obligation. However, the US cannot expect that its claim should be accepted without any consideration of its practical implications. Whereas the Panel is not required to decide on which measures would be necessary for securing compliance, it should also not decide on this particular dispute without giving due consideration to the real-world implications of the US claims.

2. *The US claims under Article X:3(a) GATT*

(a) The United States misrepresents the requirements of Article X:3(a) GATT

(i) Article X:3(a) GATT is a non-prescriptive, minimum standards provision

4.728 The US has disputed the EC's characterization of Article X:3(a) GATT as a minimum standards provision. It also disputes the relevance of the Appellate Body Report in *US – Shrimp*, where the Appellate Body refers to the requirements of Article X:3(a) GATT as "minimum standards". In the view of the US, "minimum standards" does not mean that these standards are "low standards".

4.729 These US arguments amount to a mischaracterization of the EC's arguments. The EC has not argued that Article X:3(a) GATT contains a "relative" standard, nor has it taken a position on whether it is a "low" or a "high" standard. However, given the highly ambitious application of Article X:3(a) GATT sought by the US, it is necessary to reflect on the nature and purpose of the obligations contained in this provision.

4.730 Article X:3(a) GATT is not a provision which prescribes in detail how WTO Members should administer their customs laws. There are other provisions in the GATT, and in other covered agreements, which contain the detailed substantive disciplines with which Members must comply. Article X:3(a) GATT complements these disciplines of the GATT and its annexes in order to ensure that the enjoyment of the benefits of the GATT by other Members is not frustrated through measures of administration which are unreasonable, partial, or non-uniform. It cannot be lightly assumed that the administration of a WTO Member falls below these minimum standards.

4.731 This is confirmed by the Appellate Body in *US – Oil Country Tubular Goods Sunset Reviews*, in which it held as follows: "A claim under Article X:3(a) of the GATT 1994 must be supported by solid evidence; the nature and the scope of the claim, and the evidence adduced by the complainant in support of it, should reflect the gravity of the accusations inherent in claims under Article X:3(a) GATT". This clearly confirms that the Appellate Body considers that Article X:3(a) GATT sets out basic minimum standards, a violation of which cannot be assumed lightly. Moreover, in a very recent case, the United States itself argued that the evidence offered to support an Article X:3(a) GATT claim must reflect the gravity of such a claim.

(ii) Article X:3(a) GATT requires the United States to demonstrate the existence of a pattern of non-uniform administration

4.732 In its Second Written Submission, the United States contests that it is required to demonstrate the existence of a pattern of non-uniform administration in order to establish a violation of Article X:3(a) GATT. The United States has also contested that the Panel Report in *US – Hot-Rolled Steel* provides authority for such a requirement, and has claimed that the EC has based itself on "one single sentence" of this report. This is manifestly untrue. The reference by the Panel in *US – Hot Rolled Steel* to the requirement of a pattern was not a mere *dictum*, but based on a considered reflection of the requirements of Article X:3(a) GATT. It reflected the Panel's view that in order to amount to a violation of Article X:3(a) GATT, the actions in question must "have a significant impact on the overall administration of the law, and not simply on the outcome in the single case in question". This, incidentally, was also the submission of the United States in *US – Hot Rolled Steel*.

4.733 The US tries to distinguish *US – Hot Rolled Steel* by submitting that in the present case, it is not arguing that "a particular application" of EC customs law represents non-uniform administration, but rather that the "EC's system of customs law administration as a whole" does not comply with Article X:3(a) GATT. The EC is baffled by this argument. The US seems to believe that because it makes more sweeping claims, it needs to present less evidence. The EC submits that the opposite should be true. It is not comprehensible to the EC how the US can challenge the "overall administration" of the EC's system without actually showing how customs law is administered in that system. It seems to the EC that in order to condemn the EC's system of customs administration as a whole as incompatible with Article X:3(a) GATT, a very clear pattern of non-uniform administration would have to be demonstrated.

4.734 The US has also referred to the Panel Report in *Argentina – Hides and Leather*, and has stated that this Panel did not refer to the requirement of a pattern. However, the Panel *Argentina – Hides and Leather* provides no support for the US arguments. The measure challenged in *Argentina – Hides and Leather* was a resolution which authorized representatives of Argentinean industry to participate in certain parts of the administrative procedure. It thereby made it impossible for Argentina to ensure the protection of business confidential information, and administer its customs laws in an impartial and reasonable manner. It was not contested that in the practical application of the resolution, industry representatives did indeed participate in the process. Accordingly, since there was no doubt that the administration by Argentina was uniformly unreasonable and partial, there was no reason for the Panel to examine whether there was a pattern. This is entirely different from the present case, where no EC measure mandates non-uniform administration; quite on the contrary, EC measures ensure uniform administration, and the EC strongly contests that there is a lack of uniformity in the EC's administration of its customs laws.

4.735 Finally, the US takes to misrepresenting the EC's argument by claiming that the EC had requested it to show the existence of a "neat pattern" of non-uniform administration. The EC does not understand the Panel in *US – Hot Rolled Steel* to have required the pattern of instances of administration to be arranged in any particular order, or to be "neat". A pattern can also be constituted by a repetition of similar acts or omissions. Where such instances of administration become sufficiently widespread and frequent as to have an impact on the overall administration of the law, this constitutes a lack of uniformity contrary to Article X:3(a) GATT. This is the standard which the US must meet, no more, but also no less.

4.736 The US has also argued that a pattern cannot be required because "the interests of traders in [....] uniform administration of the customs laws do not depend on the statistical significance of occurrences of non-uniform administration". The EC disagrees. Article X:3(a) GATT protects traders against an administration of customs law in which they cannot reasonably predict the treatment they will receive. It does not protect them against individual instances of administrative error, which can and should be corrected through mechanisms of administrative and judicial review. Accordingly, how widespread and frequent instances of non-uniform administration are is a relevant consideration under Article X:3(a) GATT.

(b) The US has not provided any evidence of a lack of uniformity in the EC's administration of its customs laws

4.737 As the EC has already mentioned, the Appellate Body in *US – Oil Country Tubular Goods Sunset Reviews* has required that any claim under Article X:3(a) GATT must be supported by "solid evidence". The United States, which has the burden of proof as the complainant, has singularly failed to discharge this burden. Far from producing solid evidence, it has not produced any evidence to support its claim of non-uniform administration in the EC's system of customs administration.

4.738 When required by the Panel to provide evidence to support its claim, the United States has monotonously responded that such evidence was not relevant to its claim, and that if it were relevant, it should be the EC which should provide it. As the EC has already remarked, this is a transparent attempt to shift the burden of proof to the EC, which should be rejected by the Panel.

4.739 The US claims that the EC has "acknowledged" instances of non-uniform administration in the areas of penalties and audit procedures are unfounded. As regards the issue of penalties, there is no non-uniform administration, rather, as the EC will show further below, it is the laws of the member States containing sanctions provisions which are different. As regards the issue of audits, the EC has already contested, and continues to contest, that there is a lack of non-uniform administration. As explained, all member States have the necessary audit capacity, and the audit practices of the member States are sufficiently harmonized, with guidance provided by the EC Customs Audit Guide. This Guide also addresses the selection of audit targets, and the question of risk assessment. It therefore addresses the issue of the balance between inspections at import and post-clearance audits which has been raised by the US. The US therefore has not substantiated its allegation that there is a lack of uniformity in the EC's customs auditing practice.

4.740 The US also claims to have demonstrated that there is a lack of uniformity in the area of processing under customs control. The EC does not see the basis for this statement. The US has merely referred to guidance on this procedure, which it claims to contain certain divergences as regards the application of the economic conditions. The EC has contested this interpretation made by the US, which is not supported by the text of guidance. In contrast, the US has not provided any evidence of actual administration which would support its claim that there are differences in administration.

4.741 The US alleges that the EC has recognized that such differences exist by explaining that in certain cases, the examination of the economic conditions takes place at EC level. This statement is unfounded. The EC has merely correctly explained the various ways in which the economic conditions for processing under customs control are applied in the EC. That in certain cases, the conditions are examined at EC level, whereas in other cases, they are examined at member States level, does not mean that in the second case, there is a lack of uniform application. It is also noted that in accordance with Article 522 of the Implementing Regulation, member States are obliged to communicate to the Commission the information about authorizations issued and applications refused on the grounds that the economic conditions are not fulfilled. This allows the Commission to verify that the economic conditions are applied correctly.

4.742 Overall, the US has therefore not shown the existence of any lack of uniformity in the administration of EC customs law, let alone the existence of a pattern of non-uniform administration.

(c) The US criticisms of the EC's system of customs administration are unjustified, and do not demonstrate any incompatibility with Article X:3(a) GATT

4.743 Since the United States has been unable to demonstrate any actual lack of uniformity in the EC's practice, it has instead tried to build its case on criticism of the various elements of the EC's system of customs administration. Before addressing the specific arguments made by the United States, the EC would like to make three general remarks.

4.744 First, systemic criticism cannot replace proof of actual lack of uniform administration. As the EC has said time and time again, Article X:3(a) GATT does not prescribe how WTO Members should administer their laws. The specific design of the EC's system could therefore become relevant under Article X:3(a) GATT only if it necessarily led to a lack of uniformity. However, the US has provided no evidence for such a proposition. In this regard, it is also necessary to recall the findings of the Appellate Body in *US – Carbon Steel*, according to which it is the responsibility of the complainant who alleges that the municipal law of another member has a particular meaning or effect to provide evidence for such statement.

4.745 Second, in order to assess whether the EC's system ensures uniform administration of customs laws, it is not sufficient to look at one particular instrument or feature in isolation. Rather, the question is whether the EC's system as a whole, including all its relevant instruments, ensures uniform administration. The approach followed by the United States in its Second Written Submission is precisely the opposite. The US selects a particular instrument, mischaracterises it, and then triumphantly declares that such instrument is not sufficient to ensure uniform administration. It is obvious that such a way of proceeding does not constitute a fair and objective way of appraising the EC's system.

4.746 Third, the US shows a marked tendency to ignore all elements that do not suit it for the purposes of its claims. For instance, in its discussions of EC classification practice, the US focuses almost exclusively on the EBTI system, but does not acknowledge the existence of other binding instruments of Community law, such as classification regulations or explanatory notes. Similarly, the US has not acknowledged with one word the EC instruments existing in the field of customs cooperation, or the budgetary and financial instruments. To put it differently, whereas the US is happy to rely on a report of the Court of Auditors as alleged proof for a lack of uniformity in the EC's system, the US does not wish to acknowledge that such EC institutions might also contribute to uniformity, and therefore have to be taken into account in the evaluation of the overall system.

(i) Administrative guidance and the duty of cooperation

4.747 As the first of its systemic criticisms, the United States claims that "most of the instruments that the EC holds out as securing uniform administration are non-binding, discretionary, or extremely general in nature".

4.748 This statement turns the EC's system upside down. The EC's system of customs administration is based on a very comprehensive body of law, which is entirely binding. In all areas of customs law, the EC institutions dispose of the necessary powers to adopt legally binding measures as and wherever the need arises. This is complemented by a complete system of judicial protection and review, which includes rights of appeal of traders, but also the possibility to bring infringement proceedings. To claim, therefore, that the EC's system is primarily based on non-binding means is simply self-refuting.

4.749 The US also criticizes the reliance of the EC, in certain cases, on administrative guidance and other instruments which are not legally binding, such as the EBTI guidelines, or the conclusions of the Customs Code Committee. This criticism is unwarranted. The EC has recourse to non-binding guidance as a complement to binding measures whenever this is warranted by the specific issue at hand, given for instance its technical character. To take but one example, the EC does not see what would be gained by transforming the EBTI guidelines, which, for instance, contain instructions as to how and when to consult the EBTI data base, into a legally binding instrument. Moreover, more important is whether the guidelines are actually followed, and the US has produced no evidence to the contrary.

4.750 As regards the duty of cooperation, the US has criticized that this obligation is too general in nature. The EC does not agree. What matters is not that the duty of cooperation is a general obligation, but that it exists. Moreover, it is legally binding, and can be sanctioned by the Court of Justice. That cases before the Court may not be very frequent does not mean that the duty of cooperation does not have practical effect. Quite on the contrary, it shows that it is generally respected.

(ii) The EBTI system

4.751 The second systemic aspect criticized by the US is the EC's BTI system. The EC has already intensively responded to the US arguments in this respect, and will therefore highlight only a number of new aspects in the US arguments.

4.752 In its Second Written Submission, the US repeats its claim that the EC's system facilitates BTI shopping. However, as the EC has already noted, the US does not provide any evidence for this statement. In an apparent attempt to explain this failure, the US now states that BTI shopping "is done in such a way that it is does not generate evidence and thus is difficult to identify". Moreover, the US remarks that "traders can hardly be expected to come forward and openly admit that they are taking advantage of the opportunity to seek optimal classification of their goods". The EC would submit that alleged difficulties of providing evidence are not a reason for exempting the United States from discharging its burden of proof. The United States cannot expect the Panel to accept its claim on faith just because it states that providing evidence is too difficult.

4.753 Second, assuming for a moment that the United States presentation of the situation was right, the EC also wonders wherein precisely would lie the nullification or impairment of benefits to the US. It seems to the EC that if there is nullification and impairment, then the US should be able to support this with some evidence. Inversely, if its traders have no interest in the case, because they achieve optimal classification of their goods, then the US has itself rebutted the presumption of nullification and impairment in Article 3.8 DSU.

4.754 In its Second Written Submission, the US also continues its criticisms of the *Timmermans* case law of the Court of Justice, which it claims is contrary to the uniform application of EC customs law. In this respect, the EC can largely refer to its earlier submissions. However, a new element in the US arguments is that the US now appears to view classification a matter of discretion. In fact, the US argues that tariff classification requires a customs authority to make certain judgments, which may evolve over time. In this way, the US seems to take a highly dynamic approach to tariff classification, which for the US seems to be at least partially a policy issue.

4.755 This approach may explain the frequent reconsiderations of classification issues in US practice. It may also explain why the US seems to be much more concerned with geographical uniformity than with uniformity over time. However, the EC does not agree with the US's point of departure. Tariff classification, albeit complex, is a legal issue which is fully subject to judicial review. At any given moment, there is only one correct classification for a particular product, and this classification does not rapidly change on the basis of policy considerations.

4.756 Accordingly, the *Timmermans* case law does not in any way detract from the uniformity of EC law. On the contrary, it allows member States to correct errors, where such errors have been made. Contrary to the US view, this has nothing to do with applying the member States' "own interpretation", but rather with applying the correct interpretation. A perfect illustration for this is the *Bantex* case, where the *Timmermans* case law allowed the UK authorities to bring their classification practice into line with an EC classification regulation they had overlooked. Moreover, as the EC has already shown, US rules for the revocation of advance rulings in the event of error or change of practice do not seem to fundamentally differ from those in the EC.

(iii) Judicial review by member States' Courts

4.757 As the third and last issue, the US criticizes the EC for having referred to the judicial review of customs decisions as another mechanism for securing the uniform application of EC customs law.

4.758 The US' first objection is that because decisions of member States' courts are "binding only within that Member State", a decision in a particular case might be inconsistent with the decisions of the courts of other member States. This objection is spurious. Apart from the fact that there is no requirement, as the EC will show later, for first instance judgments to be "binding throughout the Community", the US is forgetting that the EC member States courts are not operating in a vacuum. Precisely in order to avoid the danger to which the United States refers, the EC Treaty has established has the preliminary reference procedure. This procedure allows the Court of Justice, acting in constant dialogue with the member States' courts, to ensure a uniform interpretation and application of Community law. It is important to note that in deciding whether a question of Community law should be referred to the ECJ, or whether it can be regarded as obvious, member States' courts must also consider whether the matter will be equally obvious to the courts of other member States. Accordingly, where courts of different member States have decided, or might decide, a question of Community law differently, this is a reason for referring the question to the European Court of Justice.

4.759 Furthermore, the US has criticized the fact that the EC has no system of notification of judgements between the courts of member States. In order to counter the EC's argument that such a system would be burdensome and ineffective, the US has referred to the existence, in the United States, of data bases such as Lexis and Westlaw. These remarks are beside the point. The EC understands the Panel's Question No. 72 to have referred to mechanisms of formal "notification" of judgments of one court to another. The EC does not understand the question to have aimed at privately-run data bases such as Lexis and Westlaw. As for such mechanism, similar data bases, as well as legal and technical journals, obviously also exist in the EC. Moreover, typically traders and brokers interested in the classification of a particular good are well aware of relevant judicial decisions throughout the EC, and will bring them to the attention of the courts, if these are not already aware of them.

4.760 Second, the US argues that it is excessively burdensome for a trader which operates in several member States to pursue his appeal in several courts. The EC does not agree. The situation described by the US is due to the fact that the competence of EC tribunals is territorially limited, and, as the EC will show, there is nothing wrong with that. Moreover, no trader is obliged to import the same good through various different ports in different member States, but if he does so, the result may be that different courts will be competent. Finally, this still does not mean that the trader would normally have to conduct several appeals in parallel. If a question is referred to the Court of Justice, the normal situation will be that other procedures in which the same question is relevant can be suspended until the Court has given judgment. Once the Court has given judgment, this interpretation will guide all member States courts. Moreover, each referral to the European Court of Justice, as well as judgments rendered, is published in the Official Journal of the European Union, which allows traders and judges of other EC member States to be fully informed about cases which arose in another member State.

4.761 Finally, the US complains that the EC should not be allowed to refer to judicial review as an instrument for securing uniform application since this is an "entitlement" of traders under Article X:3(b) GATT. Moreover, the US claims that the EC is arguing that compliance with Article X:3(b) would be sufficient for compliance with Article X:3(a) GATT.

4.762 These allegations are entirely unfounded. The EC has never claimed that the provision of judicial review is sufficient for complying with Article X:3(a) GATT. On the contrary, the EC has acknowledged that a system which purely relies on private rights of appeal would not normally appear to be compliant with Article X:3(a) GATT. This is however not the case in the EC, where judicial review is only one out of many mechanisms which contribute to the uniform application of EC law. That judicial review is also at the same time an entitlement under Article X:3(b) GATT is irrelevant. First of all, this provision concentrates solely on first-instance review. Secondly, there is nothing to prevent that it may also at the same time be a tool for securing uniform administration.

4.763 Overall, the United States has failed to show that there are any features in the EC system which necessarily would lead to a lack of uniformity in the EC's system of customs administration. Quite on the contrary, the EC's system contains numerous, interlocking mechanisms which together provide a high degree of assurance for a uniform interpretation and application of EC customs law. The US claims should therefore be dismissed.

(d) Article X:3(a) GATT does not require the EC to harmonize member States' penalty provisions

4.764 A final claim under Article X:3(a) GATT concerns the issue of penalties for customs violations. This US claim has nothing to do with the administration of laws, but rather is aimed at forcing the EC to harmonize the member States laws which contain penalty provisions and replace them with EC laws. This claim has no basis in Article X:3(a) GATT.

(i) Penalty provisions are not covered by Article X:3(a) GATT

4.765 First, the EC has explained that penalty provisions are not among the laws which are referred to in Article X:1 GATT, and therefore are not covered by Article X:3(a) GATT. So far, the United States has not provided any explanation as to why penalty provisions should be regarded as laws within the meaning of Article X:1 GATT, i.e. laws "pertaining to the classification or valuation of products for customs purposes, or to rates of duty, taxes, or other charges".

4.766 In fact, the United States does not even seem to argue that penalty provisions are laws within the meaning of Article X:1 GATT. Instead, it merely states that penalty laws are "tools" for the administration of the laws referred to in Article X:1 GATT. However, if penalty provisions are merely tools for the administration of the laws in Article X:1 GATT, they are not themselves such laws.

4.767 In its Second Written Submission, the US has also made an oblique reference to the term "charges" in Article X:1 GATT. However, the EC does not believe that this term covers penalties. "Charges" are contributions of a pecuniary nature, which are frequently "charged" in exchange for services rendered or goods provided. Penalties respond to illegal behaviour by imposing a sanction. Such sanctions may be financial in character, but can also take other forms. For instance, criminal sanctions may include not just fines, but also imprisonment or social work. Administrative sanctions may also include measures such as the destruction or forfeiture of the goods. It does not appear that all these different types of sanctions can be included under the term "charges". This is also illustrated by Article VIII GATT, which clearly distinguishes between fees and charges on the one hand, and penalties, on the other.

(ii) Article X:3(a) GATT does not require the harmonization of laws which exist in a WTO Member at sub-federal level

4.768 The second problem with the US claim is that member States' laws which contain penalty provisions are themselves laws of general application. Accordingly, even if these laws fell under Article X:1 GATT, it would be the administration of those laws to which Article X:3(a) GATT applies. The alleged differences between member States' penalty provisions to which the US has referred are not differences in administration, but differences between different legislative measures applicable in different territories. That a particular topic may be regulated differently in different parts of the territory of a WTO Member has nothing to do with non-uniform administration. Accordingly, Article X:3(a) GATT cannot be used to create a duty to harmonize sub-federal laws existing within a WTO Member.

4.769 The United States has tried to escape this conclusion by repeating its mantra that "laws can also be administered through laws", and that therefore, member States' penalty provisions are to be regarded as "administration" for the purpose of Article X:3(a) GATT. This interpretation is fundamentally at odds with the ordinary meaning of the wording of Article X:3(a) GATT.

4.770 The United States has defined the term to "administer" as "to execute", which in term it defines as "to carry out, put into effect". The EC can agree with these definitions. However, the EC does not agree that a penalty provision "puts into effect" or "carries out" the substantive rule the violation of which it is intended to sanction. For instance, a provision which provides for the imposition of a sanction for the failure to declare a good does not "carry out" or "put into effect" the provision which imposes the obligation to declare the good. The penalty provision itself needs to be carried out through an administrative or judicial act imposing the sanction. It is this latter act which can be regarded as executing the prohibition, and thus to constitute "administration". In contrast, the penalty provision complements the substantive provision, but does not itself put it into effect.

4.771 Indeed, the United States itself has explicitly recognized that a penalty provision "may be considered as something to be administered". This exposes the logical fallacy of the United States. A law that itself needs to be "put into effect" cannot be said to "put into effect" another law. Rather, penalty provisions and substantive provisions are both measures of general application which complement one another. That the former exists at the member States level and the latter at the EC level does not mean that the former administers the latter.

4.772 The US has criticized the EC for having defined "administration" as the execution of laws "in concrete cases". This criticism is unjustified. The administration of a law, which is defined as an act of general application, by definition implies its application in concrete cases. This follows clearly from the structure of Article X GATT. Article X:1 GATT defines the laws of general application which must be published by WTO Members. Article X:3(a) GATT then refers to these laws of general application as the acts to be administered in a uniform, impartial and reasonable manner. It defies the internal logic of Article X GATT to argue that laws to be administered can at the same time themselves constitute administration. This would undermine the clear distinction between "administration" and the laws to be administered recognized by the Appellate Body in *EC – Bananas III*.

4.773 The US has sought support for its interpretation in the Panel Report in *Argentina – Hides and Leather*, in which the Panel found that a particular Argentinean resolution constituted a violation of the requirement of impartial and reasonable administration. However, as the EC has already explained, this was because the Argentinean measure made it impossible for Argentina to administer its customs laws in a manner that was reasonable and impartial. Nowhere does the Panel Report in *Argentina – Hides and Leather* indicate that the Argentinean measure administered some other measure. Accordingly, *Argentina – Hides and Leather* provides not support to the US interpretation in the present case.

4.774 Overall, the US interpretation that "laws may implement other laws" is highly contrived and self-serving. It is designed to achieve a condemnation of the EC in the present case while safeguarding those areas of economic activity which in the United States itself are regulated in state law.

4.775 In the United States, a wine exporter may have to deal with 50 different sets of state requirement for the sale of alcoholic beverages. This is probably far more burdensome than the fact that an importer in the EC may have to reckon with the penalty provisions of one out of 25 member States, depending on where the offence is committed. It is therefore not clear why the EC should be obliged to harmonize its penalty provisions while the US is entitled to maintain sub-federal laws in numerous areas covered by Article X:3(a) GATT.

4.776 Of course, the United States has a system of dual federalism where State law may never implement federal law. However, this cannot mean that all WTO Members in which the borderlines between federal and state competence are less strict, and federal and state laws may therefore be complementing one another, are somehow in violation of Article X:3(a) GATT.

(iii) Community law ensures a sufficient degree of uniformity of penalty provisions

4.777 Finally, the EC would clarify that whereas it does not accept that penalty laws can be regarded as "administration", it does not contest that penalty laws may also be relevant for securing a uniform application of the laws referred to in Article X:1 GATT. This is precisely why Community law, as clarified by the Court of Justice, lays down certain basic rules for penalty provisions, which must be effective, proportionate, and dissuasive.

4.778 These general requirements are sufficient for securing a uniform application of EC customs laws, in accordance with Article X:3(a) GATT. The United States does not provide any evidence which would show that the absence of a full harmonization of penalty provisions in the EC leads to any lack of uniformity in the application of EC laws in areas referred to by Article X:1 GATT.

4.779 The US has repeatedly referred to the fact that the EC, in the context of the discussions on the modernized customs code, has considered including a provision which would provide for a further harmonization of administrative sanctions in the customs area. However, these discussions have nothing to do with the question of whether the EC is in compliance with the requirements of Article X:3(a) GATT. Where this is beneficial for the functioning of the internal market, the EC has adopted harmonising measures in numerous areas, without this necessarily being a reaction to a WTO obligation.

3. *The US claim under Article X:3(b) GATT*

(a) The ECJ and the requirement of prompt review

4.780 The US criticism on prompt review is limited to the role played by the ECJ through the preliminary reference procedure. The US has not presented any allegation concerning the actions for annulment of a Community measure, and, therefore, the US seems to admit that, in this type of procedure, the ECJ and the Court of First Instance comply with the requirement of prompt review.

4.781 It should be pointed out that preliminary references serve the purpose of ensuring the uniform application and interpretation of Community law by the tribunals of the member States. In this sense, the Court of Justice, when acting through the preliminary reference procedure, exercises a function, which is not dissimilar to that of a supreme court. As the EC has repeatedly explained, preliminary reference procedures at the same time also serve as one of the various instruments to ensure uniform administration in accordance with Article X:3(a) GATT. The EC has already affirmed that, in its view, "administer" means to execute the general laws and regulations, to apply them in concrete cases. Therefore, uniformity is ensured through a panoply of administrative and legal mechanisms, including some judicial ones, like preliminary references or appeals to a second instance court. In no respect, however, does the ECJ, through the preliminary reference procedure, provide "review" within the meaning of Article X:3(b) GATT, nor is this in any way required for the EC's compliance with this provision. In this context, it should be recalled that, as the US has already admitted, prompt review in Article X:3(b) GATT refers only to first instance.

4.782 In any case, even if the requirement of promptness is applied to cases where preliminary references are requested, the accumulated time span it takes for a case to go through the ECJ and the relevant national court rarely arrives to the nearly four years average of the USCIT cases mentioned by the EC in its First Oral Statement. In response to a question by the Panel, the US justifies these delays on "the fact that in the US courts the scheduling of proceedings is, to a significant extent, conducted by mutual consent of the parties". The EC finds it difficult to justify an exception to the "prompt review" obligation on the basis a procedural mechanism that relies on the discretionary will of the defending agency.

4.783 Moreover, the EC would like to recall that the average periods for review by the USCIT to which it has referred do not include the periods necessary for appeals to the US Court of Appeals for the Federal District or subsequently to the US Supreme Court. It would thus seem to the EC that if the activity of the US Supreme Court were to be regarded as "review", it would certainly be no more prompt than that provided by the ECJ.

(b) The requirement that the decisions of the tribunals must govern the practices of the agencies

4.784 The second US argument constitutes the core of its Second Written Submission in relation to Article X:3(b) GATT. This argument refers to the requirement that the decisions of the review tribunals govern the practice of the agencies entrusted with administrative enforcement of the WTO Member's customs law.

4.785 This argument has only appeared in these proceedings at a very last stage. The US used it for the first time in some of its replies to the first Panel questions, notably Question No. 35, where the Panel asked the US to identify what the US is challenging or alleging under Article X:3(b) GATT. This appears to replace the more general argument in the US First Written Submission, according to which "the opportunity for review and correction on a member-by-member State basis does not fulfil the EC's obligation under Article X:3(b)". This chapter included some arguments, mainly on timing and variations in review procedures, all of which seem to have been discarded in the course of the proceedings. Therefore, the US argument built on the second sentence of Article X:3(b) seems to be a last-minute fall-back position.

4.786 Although the late appearance of the argument has impeded a discussion between the parties, the EC will duly explain why the US position on the "govern the practice" requirement is a misrepresentation of Article X:3(b) GATT.

4.787 The US interpretation that any decision of a first instance tribunal binds the whole organization of the customs agencies throughout a WTO Member's territory is based on four grounds: three are related to the literal interpretation of the provision, namely the reference to two different obligations in the provision ("implement" and "govern"), " the ordinary meaning of the term "govern" and the use of the Article "the" before the term "agencies", while the fourth ground is based on the context provided by Article X:3(a) GATT.

4.788 The EC cannot agree with these arguments advanced by the US. In the first place, the EC has already explained in its Second Written Submission the meaning of "govern" compared to the expression "implement", and how the former refers first of all to an obligation of fairness when taking a second administrative decision following the issuance of an independent review decision.

4.789 Second, to interpret the term "govern", the different definitions of this term must be differentiated. Should we admit that "govern" means "control, regulate, determine, constitute a law, rule, standard or principle for", the decisions of first instance tribunals would be considered as having binding effects, contrary to a common element that is shared by most of the "civil law" and "common law" legal systems: that only high level or last instance tribunals take decisions that are considered as binding and, therefore, a general source of law.

4.790 The EC can admit that a decision of a first instance regional tribunal plays the role of guidance to other first instance regional tribunals. Thus, the ordinary meaning of "govern", among those provided by the US, would be "influence". The decisions of a first instance tribunal are only binding for the specific cases decided by the same tribunal and, therefore, contrary to an argument constantly repeated by the US, they are not an instrument ensuring uniform administration.

4.791 This interpretation reflects the situation in those third parties to the dispute having regional courts of first instance in customs matters, like Brazil, China, Japan and, partially, India. On the contrary, as their submissions have shown, those third parties having centralized courts for first instance review of administrative decisions in customs (Argentina, Australia and Korea) can easily share the far-reaching interpretation of Article X:3(b) that the US follows in this case.

4.792 Third, the use of the term "*the* agencies" in Article X:3(b) does not mean that those agencies are *all* the agencies throughout the WTO Member's territory, in our case the EC. "The agencies" must be read in context with the term to which it relates, "tribunals", which are tribunals of first instance. Therefore, "the agencies" must be understood as "the agencies" whose decisions are reviewed by these tribunals of first instance. In the EC, "the agencies" are those established in each of its member States, not the agencies established in the other member States.

4.793 Moreover, the US fails to give a proper meaning to the term "decision" in Article X:3(b) GATT. The "decision" of a tribunal in a particular case must be distinguished from the reasoning which led it to this decision. For instance, if a tribunal decides on an action for the annulment of a decision of the customs authorities, then the decision will be to annul the decision or not. If the decision is to annul, then this decision will govern the practice of the agency. In contrast, there is no basis in Article X:3(a) GATT for assuming that all questions of interpretation which the tribunal may have considered in the course of its reasoning equally become binding on the agency. This would give a role to judicial precedent which would go far beyond the practice of numerous WTO Members which do not have a legal system based on case law.

4.794 This does not imply that the decisions of a tribunal of first instance, including the reasoning contained in the judgement, do not produce any effects in the EC system. Such reasoning will constitute relevant judicial practice which will be taken into account by the customs agencies. Moreover, if a customs agency or a court in a EC member State does not share the interpretation of the EC legislation given by a court of another member State, it will take the initiatives that are proper to its respective position in the system: the customs agency shall consult and discuss the issue with the Commission and the other member States, the court in another member State will or shall refer to the EC Court of Justice.

4.795 Fourth, the US considers that its understanding of X:3(b) is reinforced by the context provided by Article X:3(a). The EC has already challenged any linkage between these to set of obligations in the course of these proceedings. The EC considers that the US interpretation finds no support in the language, structure or objectives of Article X:3 GATT. The fact that, as the US underlines, the EC has conceded that Articles X:3(a) and X:3(b) must be interpreted "in an harmonious way" does not mean that we agree to an interpretation that transforms Article X:3 GATT in a "totum revolutum" provision, where the different obligations are melted, with the unwarranted consequence that the obligation to grant independent review and correction of customs administrative decisions at first instance level is absorbed by the obligation to ensure uniform administration of the legislation.

4.796 Finally, it is not true, contrary to what the US declares, that "if they [i.e. the decisions of review tribunals] govern the practice of only some of the agencies then, by definition, the administration of the Member's laws will not be uniform". This categorical conclusion does not take into account that, as the EC has explained, there are other means of ensuring uniform administration and that the EC counts with a wide range of instruments which contribute to the uniform interpretation and application of EC customs law.

(c) The US interpretation of Article X:3(b) GATT requires the establishment, in every WTO Member, of a single and centralized customs court or a single and centralized customs agency.

4.797 The US claims that it does not argue that Article X:3(b) requires every WTO Member to have a single, centralized tribunal for the prompt review and correction of customs administrative actions. The US accepts the existence of first instance regional courts provided that the WTO Member has a single, centralized agency entrusted with the enforcement of customs law or that the various regional customs authorities take other steps to ensure that the decisions of review tribunals govern the practice of the agencies and that the Member continues to administer its customs laws in a uniform manner.

4.798 It is unclear to the EC why the existence of a centralized customs agency, which at best is a question under Article X:3(a) GATT, should be linked to the design of the court system under Article X:3(b) GATT. The United States explains that "if the decision of a court in one region conflicts with a decision of a court in another region, the agency should be able to resolve the conflict by appealing one or the other decision to a court or a tribunal of superior jurisdiction". This explanation is revealing, because it shows that even according to the United States, judgments of courts of first instance are not binding on other courts, since otherwise, the conflict should not have occurred at all. More importantly still, the US seems to forget that it is the courts which should control the agency, not the agency which controls the courts. In the view of the US, it would be the agency which would be charged with ensuring the uniformity of the practice of the first instance tribunals, and which would select the judgment it wishes to appeal. This is an interpretation which totally blurs the borderlines between the role of the customs authorities and of the courts, and which should not be accepted.

4.799 The only additional reason given by the US to sustain that a central agency would cure the lack of a central court is a proviso that constitutes the fourth phrase in the second sentence of Article X:3(b). This proviso provides the possibility, for the central administration of a customs agency, to request the review of a first instance court decision when there is good cause to believe that the decision is inconsistent with established principles of law or the actual facts. The US considers that "that possibility makes sense only if the decision in the original proceeding would otherwise have effect outside of that proceeding".

4.800 The US interpretation of this proviso is wrong in that it misunderstands the role played by the review mechanism laid down in that proviso. That mechanism is not established to rectify the effects of the original decision in the practice of the agencies but to provide a remedy, based on limited grounds, against a decision that is no more challengeable through ordinary means because it is time barred.

4.801 That is clear, first, from the structure of paragraph (b). The exception provided by the proviso refers to the time limits for appeals contained in the previous phrase in subparagraph (b) (the third phrase in the second sentence of the subparagraph), not to the "govern the practice" requirement, which is placed in the second phrase of the second sentence of Article X:3(b) GATT.

4.802 Second, that the proviso is not intended to rectify the effects of the original decision in the practice of the agencies also derives from the nature of this type of exceptional review. When the review is based on the lack of consistency with established principles of law, its purpose is to protect the cornerstones of a legal system, with the view to eliminate conflicts with the case-law of the highest courts, which are responsible for refining those principles of law. When the review is based on the lack of consistency with the actual facts, its purpose is to annul a judicial decision on discovery of facts that were unknown to the court and to the party claiming the revision when the decision was given. Neither of these two grounds of review is linked to the eventual effects of a first instance judicial decision on the practice of the customs agencies. The review based on the respect of principles has as its objective to ensure respect of the legal system and of the highest courts, the review based on the discovery of new facts produces its effects only on the original decision.

4. *Closing statement*

4.803 The EC will begin its closing remarks by first presenting a number of general comments on the present case. It will then present its closing arguments on the US claims under Article X:3(a) GATT. The EC will subsequently present its closing arguments on the US claims under Article X:3(b) GATT.

4.804 A first general remark the EC would like to make is that the present case is not like any other which has been litigated under the DSU. It constitutes a fundamental challenge against the entire system of customs administration and judicial review of a WTO Member, namely the EC. Contrary to what the US has alleged, this has nothing to do with "scare tactics", but simply describes the reality. From the discussions it can be seen that the case is not limited to issues of customs law and administration. Rather, it touches upon fundamental differences between legal traditions and cultures, between Members which have a federal structure and those who do not, between Members who have a system of executive federalism and others who do not, and between common law and continental law systems on the value of judicial precedent. The EC believes that such issues are not properly litigated under the DSU, but should be left to the constitutional autonomy of each WTO Member. The EC is confident that the Panel will also be mindful of these considerations in its interpretation of Article X GATT, which is not a provision which should be used to interfere with fundamental questions regarding a Member's domestic legal system.

4.805 A second general remark the EC would like to make is that the Panel should not lose sight of the real implications of the US claims. The US case is, as the EC has repeatedly emphasized, aimed at the creation of an EC customs agency and an EC Court, plus the harmonization of member States' laws in a number of areas. Despite all US professions to the contrary, this is the clear conclusion from numerous US statements where the US declared that "in the absence" of an EC customs agency or a customs court, such and such issue necessarily leads to a lack of uniformity. This all-or-nothing nature of the US arguments is troubling, since it represents a highly prescriptive application of Article X:3(a) GATT on structural elements of the EC legal order which were well known at the time the EC became a WTO Member.

4.806 As a third issue, the EC was planning to raise the issue of the US's late submission of evidence. Given the Panel's decision to modify the timetable, for which the EC would like to thank the Panel, the EC will not further enter into this question at this stage. Nonetheless, the EC regrets that the US has not presented its evidence earlier, and that the EC does not feel to be in the same position as it would have been had the US presented its evidence as early as it should have. The EC would also like to add that at the end of these proceedings, the feeling is still one of a lack of conclusion. In fact, the EC feels as if it had been in a sort of trade policy review mechanism exercise, and it seems discussions could still have continued on the EC's system of customs administration forever. It does not seem that this is really how the WTO dispute settlement mechanism should be used.

4.807 The following are the EC's closing remarks on Article X:3(a) GATT.

4.808 The present proceedings have shown that the parties have strongly different views of the requirements of Article X:3(a) GATT. The US views this provision as a highly demanding legal standard, which can be used to prescribe in detail how a WTO Member administers its customs law. Moreover, the US also appears to believe, despite its professions that divergences as such are not problematic, that a violation of Article X:3(a) can already be demonstrated through reference to individual instances of administration.

4.809 The EC does not agree with these views of the US. In the view of the EC, Article X:3(a) is purely a non-prescriptive, minimum standards provision which complements the substantive disciplines of other provisions of the covered agreements. Moreover, given the high number of administrative instances in the day-to-day management of customs, it cannot be assumed that a violation can already be accepted because of individual instances of non-uniform administration. Rather, as the Panel in *US – Hot-Rolled Steel* has stated, demonstration of a pattern of non-uniform administration is required. Moreover, as the Appellate Body has clarified in *US – Oil Country Tubular Goods Sunset Reviews*, "solid evidence" is needed corresponding to the gravity of the allegation.

4.810 In the bulk of its submissions, the United States has tried to base its case not on evidence of actual administration, but on systemic criticisms of EC's system of customs administration. In its submissions, the EC has already responded in detail to these allegations. It has also provided a comprehensive description of the EC's system of customs administration, which it hopes will assist the Panel in its task of proceeding to an objective assessment of the facts.

4.811 The EC would therefore limit itself to addressing some systemic claims raised in the US Second Oral Statement. First, there is the continued insistence of the US on its arguments that the EC system encourages "BTI shopping". In support, it refers to what it calls "skewing" of the issuing of BTI, and in particular the fact that some member States, notably Germany, issue a higher percentage of BTIs than other member States. As the EC has already remarked, this fact does not in any way prove that BTI shopping occurs. Rather, it reflects different commercial patterns and the general importance of Germany as the largest economy in the EC internal market. It may also reflect different habits of traders due to the fact that Germany was the first member State to introduce BTI in the EC before its Community-wide introduction through the EC Customs Code.

4.812 The US has also complained against a lack of obligations on the part of one member State authority to take into account the BTI issued by other member States. This statement distorts the legal situation in the EC. As the EC has explained, where a member State, for instance through consultation of the EBTI data base, learns of BTI divergent from the classification intended by it, the Member State may not simply go ahead issuing conflicting BTI, but rather must refer this matter to the Commission and/or the customs code committee.

4.813 Finally, the US also has continued its criticism of the preliminary reference procedure as a means for ensuring uniform administration. In support, it has, in its Second Oral Statement, referred to a recent judgment of the ECJ in *Intermodal Transport*, from which it has quoted very selectively. The EC had planed to comment on this issue in its closing remarks, but given the additional time granted by the Panel for comments on Part III of the US Second Oral Statement, the EC will reserve this for its written remarks.

4.814 Leaving the systemic issues, the EC turns now to what should be the focus of the US case: namely the actual administration of EC customs law. In other words, when one takes stock of the US submissions, has the US shown that there is a pattern of non-uniform administration of EC customs law? The answer is a resounding "no".

4.815 As regards the area of tariff classification, the US has essentially referred to only two single cases of application, namely LCD monitors and blackout drapery lining (BDL).

4.816 As regards LCD monitors, the US position was first that the duty suspension regulation did not ensure uniform application. More recently, and notably in its Second Oral Statement, the US has shifted focus to the monitors not covered by this regulation. In this context, it has referred to some extremely recent developments which occurred during the Panel proceedings, for instance BTI issued by the German authorities in July 2005, and industry comments addressed to the European Commission in September 2005. In the EC's view, these recent developments do not show that there is a problem of non-uniform application contrary to Article X:3(a) GATT, but rather that there is an issue in the process of resolution. In fact, the classification of the relevant monitors is an issue which is currently under review, and relevant measures will be submitted to the Customs Code Committee in the very near future.

4.817 As regards BDL, the US has not shown any lack of uniformity, either. As the EC has said before, there is no evidence that the products before the German authorities were covered with textile flock, and thus identical to those described in the BTI issued by the Dutch, Irish and UK authorities. In a last-minute attempt to paper over this difficulty, the US has submitted an affidavit by the Chairman of Rockland, the producer of BDL. The EC has already explained that this statement by a person with a clear interest in the classification of BDL has no probative value whatsoever. Moreover, the affidavit does not concern the question whether the products before the EC authorities were in fact identical. Rather, it contains merely an assurance that Rockland has never produced any product that is not flocked. This, however, is not the issue, since it is not clear that the products were all produced by Rockland, nor that all of Rockland's products are indeed identical. Overall, the question of whether the products were flocked is purely a question of the examination of the physical goods by the competent customs authorities. Moreover, the EC notes that both importers concerned by the German decisions, the Bautex GmbH and the Ornata GmbH, have not appealed the decisions. For this reason, the United States cannot now claim there to be a lack of uniformity attributable to the EC system.

4.818 In the area of customs valuation, the US has been even less forthcoming with evidence. It has mainly referred to the report of the Court of Auditors, which is however in itself a tool for ensuring uniform administration, has been implemented, and no longer represents an accurate description of the situation today. As regards actual cases, the US referred only to one single case, involving Reebok. However, it has entirely failed to substantiate this case with evidence of non-uniform administration, and has thus not fulfilled its burden of proof.

4.819 Finally, in the area of customs administration, the US seems to have entirely dropped its arguments regarding the local clearance procedure. As regards processing under customs control, the US simply repeats its erroneous interpretations of the French guidance, which it misinterprets so as to create the impression of a conflict with EC law. However, if fails to support its doubtful interpretation with any evidence as regards the actual application of the guidance.

4.820 When one passes in review the factual basis of the US claims, one must conclude that it is extremely thin. From the beginning, the United States has struggled to come forward with evidence of non-uniform application. It has started by bringing two examples in the area of classification and one in the area of valuation. When it saw these examples evaporate, it tried to add, in a last-ditch effort, two more cases, one of which even concerns a matter outside the Panel's terms of reference.

4.821 The EC submits that there is a stark mismatch between this lack of factual evidence, and the extremely broad allegations of the US. Millions of customs issues are dealt with by the EC customs authorities every year. If the EC's system of customs administration were truly as deficient as the United States alleges, then evidence of non-uniform administration should be abundant, and the US should have been able to provide numerous examples. But the opposite has been the case. Significantly also, of the numerous third parties in the present proceedings, none, not even those which in principle supported the US case, have pointed towards any examples of lack of uniformity in the EC's system. This difficulty of the US to provide evidence is essentially due to one fact: the EC's system is not anywhere near as bad as the US would want to make it appear, but on the contrary as a whole ensures a high degree of uniformity throughout the EC. For this reason, the US claims should be rejected.

4.822 Before concluding on Article X:3(a) GATT, the EC would like to make some last remarks on the issue of penalties. It has by now become clear that this US claim is rather different from the other claims in that it concerns not actual administration, but different legislation which exists at Member States level. As the EC has explained, this claim must fail for several reasons.

4.823 First, penalty provisions are not among the laws referred to in Article X:1 GATT. The US explanations in its Second Oral Statement that penalties somehow "pertain to classification", or would be "charges" or "requirements on imports" simply have no basis in the text of Article X:1 GATT.

4.824 Second, provisions which set out penalties do not constitute "administration", but rather are themselves laws of general application. That at the same time, they may be related to the substantive law which they sanction is neither here nor there. Laws may very well complement one another without for that reason becoming "administration".

4.825 Finally, to the extent that penalty laws have an impact on the uniform application of customs laws, the EC has taken the necessary measures to ensure that member States' legislation on sanctions does not undermine uniformity. In particular, the requirement that sanctions be dissuasive and deterrent means that traders will normally respect the substantive provisions of customs law; uniform application of these laws is thus ensured.

4.826 The US has, in its Second Oral Statement, argued that the uniform application of US customs laws "is not the point", because penalty laws still remain part of the "legal backdrop" against which traders decide into which member State of the Community they import. This is wrong for two reasons. First, because penalty provisions do not fall under Article X:1 GATT. And second, because Article X:3(a) GATT only concerns the administration of laws, but does not give traders the right to expect that in all parts of the territory of a WTO Member, the same laws will apply. In other words, the "legal backdrop" in a WTO Member with a federal structure may perfectly well include sub-federal laws, provided of course that these laws are administered in accordance with Article X:3(a) GATT.

4.827 Accordingly, the Panel should reject the US claim that the EC is obliged to harmonize the penalty laws of its member States.

4.828 Concerning Article X:3(b) GATT, the EC will mainly concentrate on some arguments put forward by the US recently.

4.829 First, the EC would like to insist that the US arguments concerning Article X:3(b) have been recently shifted to the requirement "govern the practice".

4.830 The EC will not repeat its arguments on this issue, tough it is worth insisting on the fact that the US carries out an interpretation that does not take into account that the obligations in Article X:3(b) apply to first instance courts.

4.831 The US claims that the "govern the practice" requirement means "that the review court decisions must control the way agencies administer the customs law". This interpretation imposes very far-reaching obligations for all WTO Members, which do not correspond to the legal traditions of most of the WTO Members of both "civil law or roman-germanic law" and the "common law" families. In the US interpretation, first instance courts will deliver judgments that will be binding outside the relevant proceedings and will participate in the elaboration of a case-law or precedents that will constitute a general source of law.

4.832 This surprising outcome is aggravated by the fact, as the EC has heard from the present discussions, that the US understands the term "decision" to cover not only the operative part of a judgment but also its reasoning. The US interpretation would imply a radical change in the nature of those courts.

4.833 The EC would insist on the need to reject the far-reaching interpretation of Article X:3(b) made by the US. The EC has provided the Panel with its own interpretation, which clearly confirms that the EC court system complies with the requirements of Article X:3(b).

4.834 Second, the EC would like to note that, contrary to US claims, its position on the interpretation of the "govern the practice" requirement is not in conflict with its interpretation of Article X:3(b) GATT.

4.835 In paragraph 89 of its Second Oral Statement, the US distorts the EC's arguments in this respect. The EC has never referred to the review of decisions of customs agencies by member States' courts of first instance as a key means to achieve the aim of uniform administration. What the EC has sustained is something which has nothing to do with the misleading summary presented by the US. The EC has explained that preliminary rulings by the European Court of Justice constitute an important instrument of ensuring uniform administration of customs law. This role is played not because preliminary references are made by courts of first instance, but because of the effects that the resulting rulings by the ECJ have on all courts in the different member States.

4.836 Third, the EC would like to refer to the US rebuttal of the EC's argument that the creation of an EC Customs Court would breach fundamental EC constitutional principles. The US has alleged in its Second Oral Statement that Article 225a of the EC Treaty lays ground-work for the establishment of new EC courts like the new Civil Service Tribunal.

4.837 This interpretation shows a total lack of understanding of the EC judicial system by the US.

4.838 Article 225a of the EC Treaty is just an organizational provision allowing the creation of judicial organs to decide at first instance certain classes of action or proceedings in specific areas. In other words, the creation of a new court would only imply the redistribution of the work of the European Court of First Instance (CFI) and in no way entails the attribution of new competences to EC Courts.

4.839 Therefore, no new court established according to Article 225a of the EC Treaty would be entitled to examine actions other than the actions for annulment of some acts of EC institutions for which the CFI has jurisdiction according to Articles 225 and 230 of the EC Treaty. No such court would be entitled to review decisions taken by the member States' authorities. This remains the task of the EC member States' courts under the system of attribution of competences laid down in the EC Treaty, and will remain so unless an amendment to the EC Treaty is ratified by all member States.

4.840 The creation of a centralized customs court in the EC, therefore, would require a reform of the EC Treaty.

4.841 The US kindly offers the EC another option to comply with its ambitious reading of the obligation under Article X:3(b): instead of creating a central customs court, the EC can always establish a centralized customs agency which, among other duties, will be in charge of ensuring that review decisions of courts of first instance "control" how agencies administer EC customs laws.

4.842 The EC has been repeatedly accused by the US of calling for a special standard in the application of Article X:3 GATT, accusation from which we have duly defended ourselves. It seems to the EC that it is rather the US who is trying to impose its own standard on the whole WTO membership, since their interpretation of the obligations under Article X:3(b) leads always to the imposition of one or the other body or institution found in the US system (a central customs agency and/or a central customs court). By contrast, the EC's interpretation of Article X:3(b) allows the US and other WTO Members to maintain their systems as long as they fulfill the important but distinct obligations of uniform administration and prompt review of administrative decisions.

H. Second Oral Statement of the United States

1. Introduction

4.843 This dispute is about two things: *first*, the fact that the EC, through its 25 different customs authorities, does not administer EC customs law in a uniform manner; and, *second*, the fact that the EC fails to provide tribunals and procedures for the prompt review and correction of customs administrative actions as required by Article X:3(b) of the GATT 1994.

4.844 With respect to Article X:3(a), the United States has shown that EC customs law is administered by 25 separate, independent customs authorities. Absent some process or institution to prevent divergences among these authorities or reconcile them when they occur, such a system plainly would not satisfy the EC's obligation of uniform administration. And, indeed, such a process or institution does not exist.

4.845 The EC asserts that such processes and institutions do exist. However, the processes and institutions that the EC holds out as securing uniform administration do nothing of the sort. They are either extremely general (e.g., the overarching duty of cooperation in EC Treaty Article 10), non-binding (e.g., explanatory notes, guidance, and other "soft law" instruments to which the EC has referred), or discretionary in nature (e.g., the possibility that a question may or may not be referred to the Customs Code Committee). The one process of a binding nature that the EC holds out as securing uniform administration – appeals to member State courts with the possibility of referral to the ECJ – in effect puts a heavy burden on the trader to seek out uniform administration, rather than providing for uniform administration in the first instance, as GATT Article X:3(a) requires. And, even this process does not actually secure uniform administration.

4.846 The EC and individual EC officials acknowledge that the instruments purported to secure uniform administration do not in fact do so. Traders share this view. In some areas (e.g., penalties and audit procedures) the tools of administration differ from member State to member State such that administration of EC customs law is undeniably non-uniform. The US has supported its arguments with illustrations of particular instances in which member States have administered EC customs law in a non-uniform way and the EC has failed to effectively and timely reconcile the divergences.

4.847 Moreover, the only tribunals or procedures available for the prompt review and correction of customs administrative action in the EC are member State courts. The decisions of these courts govern only the actions of the customs authorities in the member States concerned. As there is no tribunal for the prompt review and correction of customs administrative actions whose decisions govern the practice of customs authorities throughout the EC, the EC fails to meet its obligation under Article X:3(b) of the GATT 1994.

4.848 It is important to keep in mind that this dispute stems from the fact that the EC is a Member of the WTO in its own right. This dispute could not have been brought under the GATT 1947, as the EC itself (as distinct from individual member States) was not a Contracting Party to the GATT 1947. EC arguments ranging from the timing of the US claim to the intentions of the drafters of Article X:3 need to be understood with this fact in mind.

2. *The EC fails to rebut evidence supporting US Claims*

4.849 The EC mistakenly asserts that there is a lack of evidence to support the US claims. In fact, the US claims are amply supported by un-rebutted evidence of: the manner of operation of the very "procedures and institutions of the EC legal system" that the EC claims "provide for a uniform application and interpretation of EC law"; admissions by the EC and EC officials; statements of traders; and illustrations of particular cases of non-uniform administration.

(a) EC admissions of non-uniform administration

4.850 Somewhat awkwardly, the EC attempts to distance itself from its own past admissions or admissions by senior EC officials. In some cases, the EC dismisses such statements as irrelevant on the theory that the speaker was not addressing the consistency of EC actions with Article X:3 *per se*. In the EC's view, it seems that an admission is relevant evidence only if the speaker actually draws the legal conclusion that the action or inaction in question breaches Article X:3.

4.851 Thus, even though the EC Court of Auditors made a number of critical findings demonstrating lack of uniform administration of EC customs valuation rules, the EC dismisses those findings because "the Court of Auditors did not in any way make judgments as to whether the EC was in compliance with Article X:3(a) GATT." Likewise, even though the explanatory note accompanying the EC's draft Modernized Customs Code observed that "[s]pecific offences may be considered in one member State as a serious criminal act possibly leading to imprisonment, whilst in another member State the same act may only lead to a small – or even no – fine" (Exhibit US-32, p. 13) the EC asserts that acknowledgment to be irrelevant because it did not draw a legal conclusion with respect to GATT Article X:3(a).

4.852 An admission by the EC or an EC official need not state a legal conclusion in order to constitute relevant evidence. What matters is that the representations concerning factual matters tend to support a legal conclusion relevant to the dispute.

4.853 Similarly, the Panel should decline the EC's suggestion that it pay no heed to the statements of individual officials simply because they were not speaking officially on behalf of the EC. The point that the EC consistently misses is that in each of these cases, a senior official with extensive knowledge of the administration of EC customs law – whether the Commission's Head of Customs Legislation Unit or an Advocate General of the Court of Justice, for example – was speaking authoritatively on that subject.

4.854 Yet another instance of the EC distancing itself from its own admissions is its discussion of the *EC – Chicken Cuts* dispute. In that dispute, where it was convenient to its immediate interests, the EC asserted an absence of uniform administration (i.e. lack of consistent classification of the product at issue under one Tariff heading). And now, where a lack of uniform administration does *not* serve the EC's immediate purpose, it latches onto the Panel's finding of consistent classification and disavows its earlier statements.

(b) There is no requirement to show a "pattern" of non-uniform administration

4.855 In addition to distancing itself from its own admissions, the EC responds to US evidence in support of its Article X:3(a) claim by arguing that the evidence does not exhibit a "pattern." However, such a "pattern" requirement has no basis in Article X:3(a). Nor is it supported by the Panel report in *US – Hot-Rolled Steel*, on which the EC heavily relies.

(c) Difficulty of certain customs administration questions does not counter evidence of non-uniform administration and, in fact, highlights the problem

4.856 A further line of EC argument asserts that the cases identified by the United States as illustrating non-uniform administration concerned "difficult" or "complex" matters of customs administration and that US Customs, too, has encountered problems in grappling with these matters. But Article X:3(a) does not excuse non-uniform administration in difficult or complex cases. In fact, it is precisely the difficult or complex cases that highlight most prominently the lack of uniform administration in the EC.

4.857 In dealing with simple, commodity-type products, for example, the risk of non-uniform administration of classification rules would seem to be less than for more sophisticated products. But, when confronted with more sophisticated products or products embedding new technologies, the fact that classification decisions are being made by 25 different authorities increases the likelihood of divergent administration.

4.858 Moreover, far from supporting the EC's argument, its assertion that US Customs has encountered difficulty in grappling with certain issues actually underscores the difference between non-uniform administration of EC customs law and uniform administration of US customs law. Whatever challenges US Customs may have encountered in dealing with difficult-to-classify products, its decisions applied throughout the customs territory of the US

(d) Resolution of divergences among member States after months or years does not counter evidence of non-uniform administration.

4.859 Another EC line of argument is that illustrations of non-uniform administration identified by the US are inapposite, because the non-uniformities at issue were resolved. This argument does not rebut evidence of non-uniform administration, because in each instance non-uniform administration existed and, moreover, was allowed to persist for months or years.

4.860 It cannot be the case that a Member fulfills its obligation of uniform administration under Article X:3(a) as long as it reconciles instances of non-uniform administration eventually, even if it takes many months or years to do so. Such a construction would deprive Article X:3(a) of any meaning, as a Member could respond to any instance of non-uniform administration simply by asserting that it was in the process of resolving it.

3. Recent cases confirm that processes EC holds out as securing uniform administration fail to do so

4.861 The EC accuses the United States of basing its claims on "theoretical" scenarios. A poignant rebuttal of that critique is evident in the presentation made by a seasoned EC customs law practitioner, Mr. Philippe De Baere, at a recent forum sponsored by the American Bar Association (ABA). (Exhibit US-59).

4.862 The EC has referred to explanatory notes and conclusions of the Customs Code Committee as instruments to secure the uniform administration of EC customs law. In fact, what Mr. De Baere's presentation shows (p. 14) is just the opposite. In some member States, an explanatory note may be treated the same as a regulation and given prospective effect only. In others, an explanatory note may be treated as a clarification and given retrospective effect.

4.863 In particular, Mr. De Baere describes a recent case involving the classification of video camera recorders (i.e. camcorders) which demonstrates not only differences among member States in the treatment of EC explanatory notes, but also the problem of non-recognition of BTI from member State to member State, the problem of non-uniform administration of the EC law (CCC Article 221(3)) prescribing the period following importation during which a customs debt may be collected, and the problem of recourse to member State courts as a supposed tool of securing uniform administration. At issue in this case is the question whether certain camcorders should be classified under Tariff heading 8525.40.91 or 8525.40.99. A camcorder qualifies under the former heading if it is "[o]nly able to record sound and images taken by the television camera." (Exhibit US-60). "Other" camcorders qualify under heading 8525.40.99.

4.864 In July 2001, the Commission adopted an amendment to an explanatory note covering heading 8525.40.99. The amendment provided that this heading includes "'camcorders' in which the video input is obstructed by a plate, or in another way, or in which the video interface can be subsequently activated as video input by means of software." (Exhibit US-61). The amended note led to non-uniform administration of customs laws in at least three respects.

4.865 First, in view of the amended explanatory note, two member States (France and Spain) reached back to collect additional duty on certain camcorders imported prior to the amendment and classified under heading 8525.40.91. By contrast, other member States (in particular, the United Kingdom and Germany) have expressly declined to give retroactive effect to explanatory notes. (Exhibits US-63 and US-64).

4.866 Second, subsequent to issuance of the amended note, in June 2004, the Spanish customs authority issued BTI classifying 19 camcorder models produced by a particular company under heading 8525.40.91. (Exhibit US-65). In July 2004, the French affiliate of the Spanish importer informed the French customs authority of the existence of these BTI during the course of an audit by the French authority. Notwithstanding this information, in November 2005, the French authority informed the company that it intended to collect additional duty retroactively on certain camcorders, including cameras, that is, models covered by the Spanish BTI.

4.867 Third, in deciding to give retroactive effect to the July 2001 explanatory note, the French authority followed an interpretation of EC rules not followed by other member States on the period after importation during which a customs debt may be collected. Article 221(3) of the CCC (Exhibit US-5) sets that period as three years. The only exception to this rule is the lodging of an appeal, which suspends the three-year period. However, beginning with a 1998 judgment of the French Cour de Cassation (Exhibit US-66) concerning the predecessor to Article 221(3), the French customs authority has taken the position that any administrative proceeding (procès-verbal) investigating a possible customs infraction also has the effect of suspending the three-year period. In appeals from decisions following that position, litigants have consistently failed to persuade the French court to refer to the ECJ the question of whether this position is consistent with CCC Article 221(3) (Exhibits US-67 and US-68). And, indeed, as of December 2002, France's national interpretation of Article 221(3) has become entrenched through an amendment to France's customs law (Exhibit US-69). The refusal of even France's court of last instance to refer this question to the ECJ, even in the face of evidence that other member States interpret Article 221(3) differently, is further demonstration that the availability of appeals to member State courts is not the instrument of securing uniform administration that the EC claims.

4.868 A second illustration in the De Baere presentation reinforces the point that, contrary to the EC's argument, the opportunity to appeal customs administrative decisions to member State courts, with the possibility of eventual referral to the ECJ, does not secure uniform administration. The case involves classification of the Sony PlayStation2 (PS2). The UK customs authority had issued BTI for a good and then revoked it based on an EC Commission regulation adopting a different classification for the good. When that regulation was annulled by the EC Court of First Instance, rather than restore the BTI, the authority kept it revoked based on a re-evaluation of its original classification decision. It confirmed the BTI's continued revocation on new, national grounds only weeks after the ECJ's *Timmermans* decision. But for that action, the PS2 would have been subject to classification instruments with (in theory) uniform EC-wide effect continuously, beginning with issuance of the UK BTI, continuing with issuance of the Commission regulation, and continuing after the annulment of that regulation with restoration of the BTI. The *Timmermans* judgment permitted the UK to disrupt that presumably continuous uniformity by keeping the BTI revoked on grounds other than the Commission regulation that had led to its revocation in the first place. Compounding this disruption of uniform administration is the fact that the UK High Court of Justice declined to refer to the ECJ the question of whether the customs authority could do this.

4.869 A third recent case that calls into question the effectiveness of appeals to member State courts with the possibility of referral to the ECJ as a tool of uniform administration is the judgment of the ECJ in *Intermodal Transports* (Exhibit US-71). That case concerned the classification of certain tractors by the Dutch customs authority. Contrary to the importer's request, the authority had classified the tractors under heading 8701 rather than heading 8709. In its appeal, the importer called to the Dutch court's attention the fact that the Finnish customs authority had classified similar goods under heading 8709. Despite the apparent divergence, the court declined to refer the matter to the ECJ. When the appeal reached the Supreme Court of the Netherlands, that court referred to the ECJ the question of whether a member State court should make a preliminary reference to the ECJ when a party brings to its attention conflicting BTI for similar goods issued by another member State authority to a third party and the court believes that the BTI wrongly classified those goods.

4.870 The ECJ found that a national court is under no such obligation to refer. With respect to courts other than courts of last instance, the ECJ said that evidence of divergent BTI "cannot limit the freedom of assessment thus vested in [the national] court under Article 234 EC." (Exhibit US-71, paras. 32 and 45). Moreover, it said that even a court of last instance is under no obligation to refer if, for example, it finds correct classification of the goods in question to be "so obvious as to leave no scope for any reasonable doubt." (paras. 33 and 45). It went on to note that the national court has "sole responsibility" for determining whether the correct classification of goods is "so obvious as to leave no scope for any reasonable doubt." (para. 37).

4.871 Perhaps the EC's advisor, Mr. Vermulst, put it best in his article, "EC Customs Classification Rules: Does Ice-Cream Melt?" (Exhibit US-72, p. 21) when he said:

> The EC system with respect to judicial review in classification matters and, more in general, all customs issues is not only expensive and time-consuming for affected parties, it also may lead to inconsistent judgments by national courts, at least in first instance. This problem is exacerbated by the fact that courts of certain member States are much less likely to request preliminary rulings than those of other member States.

4. *It is appropriate for the Panel to exercise its authority under DSU Article 13*

4.872 With respect to the US suggestion that the Panel exercise its authority under Article 13.1 of the DSU, the United States was not asking the Panel to make its *prima facie* case. The United States has already done that with the evidence and arguments it has put before the Panel. Rather, the United States was suggesting that if an understanding of the statistical incidence of non-uniform administration of EC customs law would help the Panel to evaluate the evidence, it should exercise its authority under Article 13.1 to obtain certain information, which is exclusively in the hands of the EC or EC member States. As the panel in *US – Upland Cotton* recently explained, "Any suggestion that a panel 'makes the complainant's case', when it merely exercises its powers under the *DSU*, is entirely inaccurate." (para. 7.633).

5. *The EC fails to rebut evidence that classification rules are administered in a non-uniform manner*

(a) BTI does not secure uniform administration

4.873 With respect to US arguments showing that BTI does not secure uniform administration, the EC first denies that the ability of an importer to obtain BTI from any of 25 different member State customs authorities, without any centralized control, encourages "BTI shopping." In particular, it contends that its acknowledgment in the *EC – Chicken Cuts* dispute that "it is possible under EC law to withdraw an application for BTI where the outcome is considered unfavourable by the importer" (para. 7.261) does not indicate that BTI shopping occurs. But that contention is illogical. In a system in which the administration of customs law was uniform, there would be little point in an importer's withdrawing a request for a classification ruling upon learning the authority's proposed decision.

4.874 The EC also contends that the heavy skewing of BTI issuance in favour of certain member States does not indicate BTI shopping, but merely differences in various commercial factors from member State to member State. Such factors might be a logical explanation if the skewing were not as dramatic as it actually is. However, it seems remarkable that in a system which, according to the EC, does not encourage BTI shopping, a single member State (Germany), representing just over 19% of imports into the EC by value in 2004, issued about 37% of all BTI with a start date in 2004, while, for example, another member State (Italy), representing about 11% of imports, issued less than 1% of all BTI with a start date in 2004, and a member State representing almost 2% of imports into the EC (Greece), issued only a single BTI with a start date in 2004 (and only 10 with a start date in 2003 and 17 with a start date in 2002).

4.875 As the EC's advisor, Mr. Vermulst, has remarked (Exhibit US-74, pp. 1314-15):

> Unfortunately, the same disparity with respect to the origin of preliminary rulings is reflected in the requests for BTI, with several times more rulings issued by Germany than by any other country. Such a disparity of numbers of proceedings has several regrettable consequences. It implies that Germany has proportionally too much influence in this part of customs law. Moreover, the authority of a procedure is not enhanced if most member States barely apply it.

4.876 Moreover, it is not just the opportunity to shop for a favourable classification that makes BTI an inadequate instrument for securing uniform administration of customs classification rules. The lack of narrative explanation in BTI makes it difficult to see how a given member State authority came to its classification decision and thus for other authorities to determine whether they should follow that decision in classifying similar goods.

4.877 Further limiting the utility of BTI as a means of securing uniform administration is the very narrow sense in which BTI issued by one member State authority governs the actions of other member State authorities. BTI issued by one member State authority is binding on other member State authorities only to the extent that the person invoking the BTI is the person to whom it was issued (the "holder") and the goods at issue are identical to those described in the BTI. But for such cases, there is no obligation on the part of one member State authority to take account of BTI issued by other member State authorities for similar goods when such BTI is brought to its attention. This problem is evident in the EC's response to the US discussion of the *EC – Chicken Cuts* dispute. Despite the EC's acknowledgment there that different customs offices classified the identical goods differently, the EC now states that "[n]owhere in the Panel Report in *EC – Chicken Cuts* has the EC said that BTI was not recognized when presented by the holder."

4.878 The point is illustrated again by the EC's discussion of the blackout drapery lining case. In response to evidence that the EC customs office in Germany failed to explain why it was not following the classification decisions reflected in other offices' BTI, the EC simply states that "BTI is binding on the customs authorities only as against the holder of the BTI."

4.879 The EC attempts to draw a comparison to the practice of US Customs. However, the very regulation that the EC cites as evidence of US practice illustrates the difference between the US advance ruling system, which promotes uniformity, and the EC BTI system, which does not. Thus, section 177.9(a) of the regulation (Exhibit EC-129) states that where US Customs issues a ruling letter with respect to a particular transaction or issue, "the principle of the ruling set forth in the ruling letter ... may be cited as authority in the disposition of transactions involving the same circumstances." The EC BTI system contains no such provision.

(b) LCD monitors

4.880 With respect to evidence showing that the LCD monitors case is an important example of the lack of uniform administration of EC rules on customs classification, the EC first asserts that the duty suspension regulation concerning LCD monitors with DVI has resolved the lack of uniformity of administration with respect to this particular classification question and that the trading community is satisfied with the outcome. In fact, this assertion simply glosses over the fact that the suspension regulation applies only to monitors below a certain size threshold, that it does not actually resolve the underlying classification question, and that, for monitors above the size threshold, a state of non-uniformity with serious financial consequences remains. Moreover, the implication that the trading community is satisfied is belied by recent statements from the very industry concerned with this classification question (Exhibit US-75).

4.881 The EC next contests the US argument that an EC Customs Code Committee conclusion that conflicts with an applicable chapter note in the Combined Nomenclature detracts from rather than promotes uniform administration. The Committee's conclusion stated that a monitor should not be classified under Tariff heading 8471 unless an importer can show that it is "*only* to be used with an ADP machine," whereas the applicable chapter note states that a monitor is classifiable under heading 8471 if "it is of a kind solely *or principally* used in an automatic data-processing system." The Committee's conclusion has put member State authorities in the quandary of having to decide what weight to give the conclusion in view of an apparently conflicting chapter note.

4.882 For example, in a Tariff Notice issued in 2004, the UK authority, evidently following the Customs Code Committee's conclusion, stated that "from October 2004, LCD/TFT Monitors that incorporate a DVI connector are to be classified in Combined Nomenclature (CN) code 8528 21 90." (Exhibit US-76). The Netherlands, by contrast, has taken a very different approach. In a decree of July 2005, the Dutch customs authority explained that since April 2004 it had been classifying LCD monitors with DVI under Tariff heading 8528, in view of a Commission regulation concerning plasma monitors. It then went on to state (Exhibit US-77) that

> [n]ot all member States are following this policy. The result is a diverted flow of business, which is harmful to the competitiveness of Dutch industry in the logistics and services sector. For this reason, The Netherlands is making the policy as regards classification of certain LCDs in the Combined Nomenclature more precise.

Accordingly, the decree set forth criteria that the Netherlands follows as of 22 November 2004.

4.883 Moreover, despite the Customs Code Committee's conclusion, the German authority, too, appears to have continued classifying LCD monitors with DVI under heading 8471, even where they are principally though not solely for use with computers (Exhibit US-78).

4.884 Finally, the EC once again tries to divert the focus from its own practice to the practice of US Customs. However, unlike the EC, where US Customs found LCD monitors difficult to classify, its rulings still applied throughout the territory of the United States.

(c) Blackout drapery lining

4.885 Similarly, the EC fails to rebut evidence demonstrating that the blackout drapery lining case is yet another example of non-uniform administration of customs classification rules. The EC erroneously calls into question whether the lining produced by Rockland Industries at issue in the decision by the Main Customs Office in Bremen, which was classified under Tariff heading 3921, was materially identical to lining that other member States had classified under heading 5907. In particular, the EC asserts that the product before the Bremen Customs Office lacked a textile flocking, while the product at issue in other classification decisions contained flocking. In fact, however, as Rockland's President and Chief Executive Officer attests under oath (Exhibit US-79), "All coated products produced by Rockland incorporate textile flocking as part of the coating process. Rockland has never produced a coated product that does not incorporate textile flocking.... Textile flocking is required to prevent the fabric from sticking together."

4.886 Moreover, in context it appears that the Bremen Customs Office did not find an absence of flocking *per se* but, rather, that flocking did not constitute a distinct layer in the Rockland product at issue. What was relevant to the Bremen Customs Office was the existence of plastic in the coating, regardless of whether textile flocking or other elements were mixed into that coating. That the German customs authority takes this approach, contrary to the approach taken by other member State authorities, is confirmed by the letter from the Hamburg customs office concerning Rockland's lining product (Exhibit US-50).

4.887 Having ruled out classification of the lining under heading 5907, apparently based on its view that the existence of plastic in the coating precluded such classification, the German authority then looked to a German interpretive aid, which the EC states was derived by analogy to an EC regulation classifying ski trousers. Though the EC states that the interpretive aid was "without any legally binding character," the German authority relied on it in a way that turned out to be determinative. In any event, it is not consistent with uniform administration for the German authority to classify a textile product based on the selection of one prong from a three-prong test for the classification of an apparel item, where no other member State authority has done this.

4.888 Finally, the EC asserts without any basis that density of weave, the key criterion under Germany's interpretive aid, is relevant to determining whether textile fabric is present merely for reinforcing purposes. In fact, the notes pertaining to Chapter 39 of the Tariff make no reference to density of weave as a relevant criterion, and the notes to Chapter 59 expressly provide that classification under that chapter is to be determined *regardless* of weight per square meter. The EC asserts without basis that the reference to weight per square meter is different from density of weave. In fact, however, weight per square meter necessarily is a function of density of weave.

6. *The EC fails to rebut evidence that valuation rules are administered in a non-uniform manner*

4.889 Nor does the EC succeed in rebutting evidence that EC valuation rules are administered in a non-uniform manner. In addition to the EC's failure to explain away the findings of non-uniformity in the Court of Auditors report, two other points should be noted.

4.890 First, as previously noted, one of the ways in which member States administer the EC's customs valuation rules non-uniformly is through different auditing practices. In response, the EC states that "under Article 76(2) CCC, every Member State may proceed to all necessary verifications in order to satisfy themselves of the accuracy of the particulars contained in the declaration." But, the fact that member States "may" do this proves nothing. It does not change the fact that member States' audit practices in fact vary dramatically such that, as the EC Court of Auditors put it, "individual customs authorities are reluctant to accept each other's decisions." (Exhibit US-14, para. 37).

4.891 The EC also claims that the EC Customs Audit Guide "ensures a uniform practice across" the EC. However, given that the Guide was only "recently finalized," and, in any event, given that it is merely "intended as an aid to member States," rather than a binding obligation on them, there is no basis for this assertion.

4.892 Second, with respect to the Reebok case, the EC fails to rebut that this is a stark illustration of non-uniform administration of valuation rules. The EC states that RIL's appeals to Spanish courts show that there is indeed a forum to which this trader can go to seek uniform administration. But, the EC cannot seriously contend that, from the point of view of uniform administration, the right to appeal a dispute to a member State court is comparable to a right to take a matter directly to an institution with authority to give an answer that is definitive for the entire EC – a right which does not now exist. GATT Article X:3(a) does not concern a trader's right to appeal adverse customs decisions; it concerns a Member's requirement to administer specified laws uniformly, whether or not traders appeal administrative actions in particular cases.

4.893 Further, the EC mistakenly suggests that because RIL withdrew its complaint to the EC Ombudsman the problem with respect to non-uniform administration has been resolved. That simply is not so. RIL's decision to withdraw its complaint does not change the Commission's evident avoidance of the non-uniformity for over three years. Nor does it change the fact that there is a divergence between the Spanish authority's administration of EC valuation rules and other member States' administration of those rules.

7. *The EC fails to rebut evidence that customs procedures are administered in a non-uniform manner*

(a) Processing under customs control

4.894 With respect to processing under customs control, the United States has shown that certain member States approach the economic conditions assessment in very different ways. The United Kingdom, for example, makes a two-prong assessment, looking first at whether processing under customs control will enable processing activities to be created or maintained in the EC, and second at whether it will harm essential interests of Community producers of similar goods. In contrast, France applies only the first prong.

4.895 The EC's response to this evidence is that the United States mis-reads the customs bulletin explaining how France applies the economic conditions assessment. The EC asserts that the bulletin in fact makes reference to harm to Community producers. However, that reference is merely an introductory paraphrase of the CCC provision on processing under customs control. The operative text of the French bulletin sets forth a one-prong test, referring only to the creation or maintenance of processing activity in the EC.

4.896 The EC replies with a circular argument. It says that "the French guidance ...has to be interpreted in the context of the EC legislation". In other words, even though the text of the French guidance plainly says something different from the text of the UK guidance, the EC contends that in fact it should not be read as diverging from the UK guidance because that would be inconsistent with EC law. However, the EC fails to substantiate its assertion that inconsistency with the applicable EC regulation automatically causes non-uniformity in member State administration of that regulation to disappear.

4.897 The EC also faults the United States for not providing "evidence on the application of the guidance issued by the French authorities". However, there was no need for the United States to do so. This is not a case in which the United States is alleging that either the French guidance or the UK guidance is itself inconsistent with WTO obligations and therefore, according to the EC, "has the burden of proving that the measure in question has the alleged content or meaning". Rather, the inconsistency with WTO obligations that the United States is alleging is a lack of uniform administration on *the EC's* part and, in the case of processing under customs control, the lack of uniformity is evident on the face of divergent guidance from two different member States.

(b) Penalties

4.898 With respect to penalties, the EC first asserts that the GATT Article X:3(a) obligation of uniform administration does not apply to penalties because penalties "are not among the matters referred to in Article X:1 GATT". Contrary to the EC's claim, the United States does not concede this point. On the contrary, the terms of Article X:1 plainly encompass penalty provisions. For example, a law imposing a penalty for negligence in mis-declaring a good's classification or valuation certainly "pertain[s] to the classification or valuation of products for customs purposes". A penalty also may be considered an "other charge[] ...on imports". Or, considered as a consequence for failing to make a truthful declaration, for example, a penalty pertains to "requirements ...on imports".

4.899 A key flaw in the EC's argument is that it assumes that a law or regulation must either be the thing being administered or a tool of administration. But, according to the EC, it cannot have one aspect or the other, depending on one's perspective. That contention is groundless.

4.900 Further, although the EC appears to admit that penalties "ensur[e] compliance with EC law", which is another way of saying that they administer EC law by giving effect to that law, the EC goes on to avoid the US argument, which is that the diversity of member State penalty laws for giving effect to EC customs law is an important instance of non-uniform administration of EC customs law. Instead, the EC responds to an argument that the United States does not make. It contends that "Article X:3(a) GATT does not create an obligation to harmonize laws which may exist within a WTO Member at the sub-federal level". The US asserts no such generic requirement. It simply argues that Article X:3(a) requires that the EC's customs law be administered uniformly. Since different member States deploy different tools – that is, different penalty provisions – to give effect to EC customs law, the EC does not administer its customs law uniformly.

4.901 Additionally, the EC errs in arguing that penalties are outside the scope of Article X:3(a) because they apply to actions that violate customs laws. Article X:3(a) does not make the distinction between "illegitimate actions" and "legitimate trade" that the EC posits. In any event, contrary to the EC's assertion, penalty provisions *do* "establish the conditions for legal trade." In a system that relies heavily on the actions of traders at every step of the way, penalty provisions administer the customs laws – that is, they give effect to those laws – by setting consequences for the breach of those laws. The problem is that in the EC those consequences vary dramatically from member State to member State.

4.902 The EC argues in the alternative that while penalty provisions vary from member State to member State, this does not mean that there is a lack of uniform administration. Its basis for this statement is the proposition that to the extent member State penalty laws must meet the test of being "dissuasive and effective," pursuant to ECJ "guidelines," they administer EC customs law uniformly, regardless of differences among them. The EC's theory seems to be that as long as two different penalty provisions both secure compliance with EC customs laws, any differences between them simply are irrelevant.

4.903 But, the possibility that traders generally comply with the customs laws in two different member States, despite differences in penalties, is beside the point. It does not change the fact that a trader must take such difference into account, much the same way that it takes into account the likelihood that an authority will interpret classification or valuation rules in a favorable way.

8. *Member State courts, whose decisions govern only the customs authorities in their respective territories, do not fulfil the EC's obligation under Article X:3(b) of the GATT 1994*

4.904 The EC fails to meet its Article X:3(b) obligation, because the decisions of member State courts "govern the practice" of only a subset of the agencies entrusted with enforcement of EC customs laws, and because the fragmentation of review is inconsistent with the context of Article X:3(b), which includes the requirement of uniform administration of EC customs law.

4.905 The EC argues that "govern the practice" means nothing more than "implement in fair terms". However, Article X:3(b) already contains a separate requirement that agencies "implement[]" the decisions of review tribunals or procedures. The EC's construction of "govern the practice" would make it redundant with the separate "implement[]" requirement.

4.906 The decisions of an EC member State court govern the practice only of agencies within that member State. Even where a court is presented with a clear divergence between practice within its member State and practice in other member States – as was the case in *Intermodal Transport* and the French cases on CCC Article 221(3) – there is no obligation to make a reference to the ECJ. Moreover, as the EC has acknowledged, there is no mechanism in the EC for courts to be kept apprised of customs review decisions of other member State courts, much less a mechanism for customs authorities to be kept apprised of the decisions of courts other than those in their respective member States.

4.907 The EC also argues incorrectly that Article X:3(b) should not be read in the light of Article X:3(a) as context. In the EC's view, the absence of an "explicit link" or a "chapeau" means the latter is not context for the former, even though the two provisions are adjoining subparagraphs. This position is in stark contrast to the EC's invocation of Article XXIV:12 as context for the interpretation of Article X:3(a). And, while no rule of treaty interpretation requires an "explicit link" or a "chapeau" for one provision to constitute context for the interpretation of another, there is in fact an explicit link between the provisions at issue here.

4.908 Article X:3(a) requires a Member to administer its customs laws in a uniform manner. Article X:3(b) requires that the decisions of review tribunals or procedures "govern the practice" of the agencies entrusted with administrative enforcement. The "govern the practice" requirement means that review court decisions must control the way agencies administer the customs laws. In this sense, the two provisions are linked.

4.909 The EC rejects the proposition that review of customs decisions by member State courts whose decisions govern only certain customs agencies is inconsistent with the obligation of uniform administration. However, its argument in this respect is in conflict with its Article X:3(a) argument. It states that review by member State courts "is perfectly compatible with the obligation of uniform administration, *provided that the latter is ensured by other means that are appropriate to this aim*." Yet, in its Article X:3(a) argument the EC itself contends that review by member State courts is a key means to achieving the aim of uniform administration. Now it is arguing that that aim must be achieved by "other means" and that review by member State courts is merely "compatible" with that aim.

4.910 Additionally, the EC wrongly purports to draw from the US argument an implicit requirement for "the establishment of a central court of first instance with jurisdiction over the whole territory of any WTO Member". However, that is not the logical implication of the US argument. The logical implication of the US argument is that under Article X:3(b), every WTO Member must give effect throughout its territory to the decisions of its review tribunals. Where a Member has a single customs administration it may well be able to do this even though it provides for multiple regional customs courts. In the EC, perhaps uniquely, fragmented administration is coupled with fragmented review, and the result is inconsistent with Article X:3(b).

4.911 The EC also wrongly accuses the United States of "interpreting Article X:3(b) through the glass of its own legal system". Ironically, in the very next breath the EC urges an interpretation of Article X:3(b) through the glass of *its* own legal system. It asserts that establishing an EC customs court – assuming that this would be the only way for the EC to comply with its Article X:3(b) obligation – would "run[] contrary to one of [the EC's] fundamental constitutional principles" .

4.912 Finally, while the EC has consistently professed that creating an EC customs court would breach "fundamental constitutional principles", it should be noted that the Treaty of Nice (inserting Article 225a into the EC Treaty) in fact laid the groundwork for the establishment of new EC courts. Also, its amendment of EC Treaty Article 220 contemplates that "judicial panels may be attached to the Court of First Instance under the conditions laid down in Article 225a". In light of the authority to create special courts established by the Treaty of Nice, it seems that establishment of a court as one option that would bring the EC into compliance with its GATT Article X:3(b) obligation would not breach "fundamental constitutional principles".

9. *Closing statement*

4.913 The manner in which the EC has argued this dispute gives the impression that the issues are far more complicated than they actually are. At times, the EC has contended that the dispute is about larger philosophical questions, such as differences in the doctrines undergirding federalism in the United States and in the EC. At other times, the EC has contended that the dispute is about the minutiae of whether one or another EC customs authority decided a particular question correctly. It is easy to get lost in the back-and-forth between political theory and technical arcana. But when the arguments on questions that have no bearing on this dispute are cleared away, the case is in fact very simple.

4.914 With respect to Article X:3(a), the EC has an obligation to administer its customs laws in a uniform manner. In practice, it administers its laws through 25 different authorities in different parts of its territory. The decisions of any one authority do not bind any of the other authorities. If the EC authority in Spain issues binding tariff information classifying a good in a particular way, the EC authority in Germany is under no obligation to give any weight at all to that decision (other than in the very limited case in which the BTI is invoked by its holder). If a third party urges the EC authority in Germany to follow the classification decision of the EC authority in Spain, even if that third party is an affiliate of the holder, the EC authority in Germany is under no obligation to do so. In short, one part of the EC customs administration apparatus is under no obligation to act consistently with other parts of the EC customs administration apparatus.

4.915 The EC states that this is not so. It states that processes and institutions are in place to ensure that different parts of the EC customs administration apparatus act uniformly. But this assertion does not withstand scrutiny. With one exception (appeals to member State courts), the processes and institutions are general obligations, non-binding guidance, and discretionary mechanisms. This point was well illustrated in the EC's preliminary response to the Panel's question 164(a). When asked to comment on the observation that the EC refers to no measures making EC Treaty Article 10 – the general duty of member State cooperation – operational in the context of customs administration, the EC still referred to no specific measures. It stated simply that the duty of cooperation in Article 10 is a binding legal obligation, which can be enforced through infringement proceedings. Repeatedly, the EC states that matters *may* get referred to the Customs Code Committee, that infringement actions *may* be brought, that member States *may* give deference to the decisions of other member States. But, the constant theme is that all of these so-called tools are discretionary.

4.916 In the absence of any processes or institutions that *obligate* different parts of the EC customs administration apparatus to act uniformly, the design and structure of the EC customs administration system is such as to *necessarily* result in non-uniform administration. Even the one binding instrument to which the EC has alluded does not cure this problem. Even when confronted with direct evidence of a divergence in member State administration of customs law, a member State court is under no obligation to refer a question to the ECJ.

4.917 In its opening statement at this Panel meeting, in discussing a point pertaining to classification, the EC stated that "[a]t any given moment, there is only one correct classification for a particular product". The United States does not disagree. But, the question is: Who decides what that correct classification is? In the EC, each of the 25 different customs authorities decides, each only with respect to a particular territory, and none with the power to bind the others. The processes and institutions to which the EC refers do not change this. For this reason, the EC does not comply with its obligation under GATT Article X:3(a).

4.918 With respect to Article X:3(b), the EC has an obligation to provide tribunals or procedures for the prompt review and correction of administrative action relating to customs matters, and the decisions of such tribunals or procedures must be implemented by and govern the practice of the agencies entrusted with administrative enforcement. The tribunals that the EC points to as providing for the review and correction of administrative action relating to customs matters are the member State courts. The decisions of each member State court apply only within the territory of that member State. The EC customs authority in France is not required to follow the decisions of UK courts. Indeed, there is not even a mechanism to make member State courts aware of customs review decisions by other member State courts.

4.919 Under the foregoing structure, the decisions of the tribunals that the EC provides do not govern the practice of the EC's agencies entrusted with administrative enforcement. Each court's decisions govern the practice only of a discrete subset of such agencies. Not only is this inconsistent with the text of Article X:3(b), but it also is inconsistent with the context provided by Article X:3(a), which indicates that the obligation to provide review tribunals should be read in a manner consistent with the obligation to administer customs laws uniformly. The EC's only response is to argue that the phrase "govern the practice" really means "implement in fair terms". (Second Submission, para. 230). As this interpretation would render the separate "implement" requirement in Article X:3(b) superfluous, it should be rejected. Accordingly, the EC fails to meet its obligation to provide review tribunals consistent with Article X:3(b).

4.920 The second point the United States makes in closing is that the Panel should not be distracted by the EC's constant reference to dire consequences that supposedly would flow from making the findings the United States requests. Not only are the EC's predictions not relevant, but they are not accurate.

4.921 The first 19 paragraphs of the EC's Oral Statement at this meeting were devoted to recasting the US claims incorrectly as claims that GATT Article X:3(a) requires the EC "to set up a centralized customs agency and a customs court". (Second Oral Statement, para. 3). Having thus misstated the U.S. claims, the EC went on to accuse the United States of seeking to change "a fundamental characteristic of the EC" and to bring about "a radical shift in the federal balance within the EC".

4.922 Moreover, the cataclysmic scenario the EC predicts is not confined to its own system. It contends that the findings the United States seeks "would make the involvement of sub-federal entities in the execution of federal laws generally impossible in large areas of economic regulation". It claims that "[t]his is of considerable concern to the entire WTO membership".

4.923 These themes have been echoed throughout the EC's submissions and interventions. The EC is trying to dissuade the Panel from drawing the obvious conclusions that the facts and the law compel by resorting to scare tactics. In effect, the EC is saying that its obligations under Article X:3 should be interpreted in light of the consequences that any given interpretation would have. This was evident when the EC said at one and the same time that GATT Article XXIV:12 is not relevant to interpretation of GATT Article X:3(a), but that it would be relevant to interpretation of Article X:3(a) if it were found that Article X:3(a) requires the EC to create a centralized customs agency and customs court. (EC provisional response to Panel Provisional Question No. 155).

4.924 In the EC's view, an interpretation should be rejected if, for example, it would require a radical shift in the federal balance within the EC. But this is simply backwards. Relative difficulty of compliance is not a basis for adopting or rejecting a given interpretation of a treaty provision. Moreover, under customary international law, as reflected in Article 27 of the Vienna Convention on the Law of Treaties, "[a] party may not invoke the provisions of its internal law as justification for its failure to perform a treaty".

4.925 At paragraph 12 of the EC's Opening Statement at this Panel meeting, the EC reminded the Panel that "the EC is an original Member of the WTO", and that when the Contracting Parties agreed that the EC should become an original Member, they did so with knowledge of the EC's "system of customs administration and judicial review". The EC reasons that in light of this knowledge, it cannot be argued that the EC's system is inconsistent with GATT Article X:3. But, again, the EC has it exactly backwards. It is not the case that the other original Members of the WTO must be considered to have acquiesced in the EC's breach of a GATT obligation by having agreed that the EC should become an original Member. Rather, the EC had to have considered and accepted the consequences of Article X:3 when it decided to become a Member of the WTO in its own right. The EC is not now free to argue that it does not like those consequences and so should be relieved of the obligations it freely accepted.

4.926 In short, the picture that the EC portrays of the institutional changes that would have to be made in the EC if the Panel were to make the findings the United States requests is pure hyperbole, with no bearing at all on the issue at hand. The Panel should decline the EC's invitation to interpret Article X:3 in light of the EC's prediction of what it would take for the EC to come into compliance with its obligations. It also should give no credit to the proposition that the US claims will have dire consequences for other WTO Members. The US claims are directed at a problem unique to the EC, given its unique combination of geographically fragmented administration and geographically fragmented review.

V. ARGUMENTS OF THE THIRD PARTIES[701]

5.1 The arguments of those third parties who made written and/or oral statements to the Panel are summarized in this section. The summaries are based on the executive summaries submitted by those third parties. Where a third party has provided written responses to questions posed by the Panel, these responses are set out in Annex A. (See list of Annexes at page xvi).

A. *Third Party Written Submission of China*

5.2 China believes that it has substantial interests in the matter before this panel whether European Communities' ("EC") administration of customs law is in a uniform manner, as required by Article X:3(a) of the General Agreement on Tariffs and Trade 1994 ("the GATT 1994"), and the requirements of prompt review and correction of administrative actions relating to customs matters by Article X:3(b) of the GATT 1994 have been met by the EC .

1. *Issues relating to interpretation and application of Article X:3(a)*

(a) The scope of application of Article X:3(a) of the GATT 1994

5.3 Article X:3(a) of GATT 1994 concerns the administration of customs laws, not the customs laws themselves. The EC seems concerned with whether Article X:3(a) GATT applies to the administration of customs laws at the local level as well as at the central level.

5.4 Based on Article XXIV:12 of the GATT 1994 and the GATT Panel report in *Canada – Gold Coins*, the EC drew its conclusion that "Article X:3(a) GATT

[701] The texts of the footnotes in sections V:A – V:I are the original texts of the footnotes in the third parties' submissions.

does not require that customs laws be regulated at the central level of each WTO Member"[702].

5.5 Taking no position on this EC assertion, however, China does not think Article XXIV:12 of the GATT 1994 and the GATT Panel report in *Canada – Gold Coins* are proper in supporting EC's argument.

5.6 Article XXIV:12 requires that the provisions of GATT be observed by both the central government and the regional or local authorities of a Contracting Party, and that the central government take the responsibility for ensuring the observance of the provisions of GATT by its local authorities. So, if there are any difficulties, encountered by the federal government of a Contracting Party because of its particular administrative or legal structures, in ensuring the observance of the provisions of GATT by its local authorities, the federal government shall still seek such reasonable measures as are available to it to secure the observance of the provisions of GATT by its local authorities in accordance with Article XXIV:12 until the actions or measures inconsistent with any provisions of GATT by its local authorities are removed. The federal government of such a Contracting Party shall compensate, because of such actions or measures by its local authorities, for any nullified or impaired benefits accruing to other Contracting Parties under the provisions of the GATT.[703]

5.7 According to the GATT panel in *Canada – Gold Coins*, Article XXIV:12 applies to those measures taken by the local level authority of contracting parties with federal regimes when administering their laws or regulations of local level.[704] The present dispute does not concern a measure taken by the local authority when administering their laws or regulations of local level, but concerns whether the EC customs laws (i.e. laws of central level) can be administered by the EC member States (i.e. local level authority) and whether such administration is in a uniform manner.

5.8 The GATT panel in *Canada – Gold Coins* further stated that Article XXIV:12 does not change the scope of application of the provisions of the GATT.[705] China agrees with the EC that "Article X:3(a) GATT does not prescribe the specific way in which WTO Members should administer their customs laws"[706]. However, the obligation of uniform administration of customs laws should not be varied.

(b) The meaning of "uniform" as used in Article X:3(a) of the GATT 1994

5.9 The ordinary meaning of "uniform", as relevant here, is "of one unchanging form, character, or kind; that is or stays the same in different places or circumstances, or at different times"[707].

---

702 EC First Written Submission, para. 221.
703 GATT Panel Report, *Canada – Gold Coins*, para. 65.
704 GATT Panel Report, *Canada – Gold Coins*, para. 56.
705 GATT Panel Report, *Canada – Gold Coins*, para. 63.
706 EC First Written Submission, para. 222.
707 *The New Shorter Oxford English Dictionary*, Vol. II at 3488 (1993) (Exhibit US-4).

5.10 The panel in *Argentina – Hides and Leather* stated: "Customs laws should not vary, that every exporter and importer should be able to expect treatment of the same kind, in the same manner both over time and in different places and with respect to other persons. Uniform administration requires that Members ensure that their laws are applied consistently and predictably. This is a requirement of uniform administration of Customs laws and procedures between individual shippers and even with respect to the same person at different times and different places"[708].

5.11 China considers that the interpretation clarified by the panel in *Argentina – Hides and Leather* of the word "uniform" as used in Article X:3(a) is of the same substance with this ordinary meaning of "uniform".

5.12 China believes that when addressing the meaning of the word "uniform" reference should be made to the interpretation given by the panel in *Argentina – Hides and Leather.*

(c) The standard of uniformity required by Article X:3(a) of the GATT 1994

5.13 The EC argues that "Article X:3(a) GATT only lays down minimum standards"[709]. The EC referred to the Appellate Body report in *US – Shrimp* to support its argument. The paragraph referred to by the EC of the Appellate Body report in *US – Shrimp* reads:

> "It is also clear to us that Article X:3 of the GATT 1994 establishes certain minimum standards *for transparency and procedural fairness in the administration of trade regulations* which, in our view, are not met here. ……"[710] (emphasis added by China).

5.14 The minimum standards articulated by the Appellate Body are for transparency and procedural fairness in the administration of trade regulations, not for directly the uniformity requirement of the administration of customs law.

5.15 The EC also referred to the Panel report in *Argentina – Hides and Leather* to support its argument. However, the paragraphs referred to by the EC address the meaning of the word "uniform", and do not directly concern the standard of the uniformity.

2. *Conclusion*

5.16 China thanks the Panel to provide an opportunity to comment on the issues involved in this proceedings, and hopes that its comments will prove to be helpful.

---

708 Panel Report, *Argentina – Hides and Leather*, WT/DS155/R, para. 11.83.

709 EC First Written Submission, para. 231.

710 Appellate Body Report, *US – Shrimp*, para. 183.

B. Third Party Written Submission of Japan

1. Introduction

5.17 Japan participates in this dispute based on its systemic interests in the correct interpretation and application of Articles X:3(a) and (b) of the General Agreement on Tariffs and Trade 1994 ("the GATT 1994").

2. Consistency of the challenged measures with Article X:3(a) of the GATT

(a) The meaning of the term "uniform" administration in Article X:3(a) of the GATT 1994

5.18 As a premise, Japan agrees with the United States that the EC, as a Contracting Party, is responsible for ensuring a uniform administration of customs matters throughout its territory[711], and that the term "general application" in Article X:1 GATT would in EC's case mean the general application within the EC as a whole.

5.19 The United States claims that the "EC's customs laws are administered by 25 different authorities, among which divergences inevitably occur, and the EC does not provide for the systemic reconciliation of such divergences."[712] The United States elaborates that such divergences and the lack of systemic reconciliation of the divergences occur in customs classification, customs valuation and customs procedures of the EC member States.[713]

5.20 In determining the meaning of the term "uniform" required under Article X:3(a) GATT, it is useful to first recall the Panel's finding in US – Hot-Rolled Steel. The Panel held that, for a Member's measure to be inconsistent with GATT X:3(a) GATT, it would have to have a significant impact on the overall administration of that Member's law and not simply on an impact on the outcome in the single case in question. The Panel found:

> While it is not inconceivable that a Member's actions in a single instance might be evidence of lack of uniform, impartial, and reasonable administration of its laws, regulations, decisions and rulings, we consider that the actions in question would have to have a significant impact on the overall administration of the law, and not simply on the outcome in the single case in question. Moreover, we consider it unlikely that such a conclusion could be reached where actions in the single case in question were, themselves, consistent with more specific obligations under other WTO Agreements. 714

---

711 US First Written Submission, paras. 29 and 36.

712 US First Written Submission, para 19.

713 US First Written Submission paras. 24-26, 40ff.

714 Panel Report, *United States – Anti-Dumping Measures on Certain Hot-Rolled Steel Products from Japan*, WT/DS184/R, adopted 23 August 2001, para. 7.268.

5.21 The panel's finding in *Argentina – Hides and Leather* is also relevant. The Panel found that:

> We are of the view that this provision should not be read as a broad anti-discrimination provision. We do not think this provision should be interpreted to require all products be treated identically. That would be reading far too much into this paragraph which focuses on the day to day application of Customs laws, rules and regulations. There are many variations in products which might require differential treatment and we do not think this provisions should be read as a general invitation for a panel to make such distinctions.[715]

5.22 The GATT Panel in *EEC – Dessert Apples*, has also made a finding regarding Article X:3(a) of the GATT that minimal differences do not constitute a breach thereof, as follows:[716]

> The Panel further noted that the EEC Commission Regulations in question were directly applicable in all of the ten member States concerned in a substantially uniform manner, although there were some minor administrative variations, e.g., concerning the form in which licence applications could be made and the requirement of pro-forma invoices. The Panel found that these differences were minimal and did not in themselves establish a breach of Article X:3.

5.23 In light of the above findings as well as the complex nature and vast amount of imports that customs authorities handle, Japan shares the EC's view that "Article X:3(a) lays down minimum standards"[717] to ensure the impartial administration of trade related laws. The Panel should consider the nature of customs administration which often times involve a vast number of imports and numerous different products which are complicated to classify, reflecting realities such as the speed of technological advances and the resulting production of new products. Therefore, the fact that divergences between individual decisions of various customs authorities may exist in itself is not inconsistent with Article X:3(a) of the GATT, as both the United States and the EC confirm.[718] In this context, it is necessary to analyze whether the alleged divergences exist, as claimed by the United States, and if so, whether such divergences exist to a degree that would be considered to be inconsistent with Article X:3(a) GATT in light of the particular customs system as a whole.

(b) Article X:3(a) of the GATT does not prescribe the specific means a Member must employ in order to

---

[715] Panel Report, *Argentina – Measures Affecting the Export of Bovine Hides and Import of Finished Leather*, WT/DS155/R and Corr.1, adopted 16 February 2001, para. 11.84.

[716] GATT Panel Report, *EEC – Restrictions on Imports of Dessert Apples* (L/6491-36S/93), adopted on 22 June 1989, para.12.30.

[717] EC First Written Submission, para. 231.

[718] US First Written Submission para. 25; EC First Written Submission para. 238.

> ensure a uniform administration of customs laws; such uniformity should be determined in respect of the particular customs system as a whole

5.24 In respect of the United States' claim that the EC does not provide a systematic reconciliation of divergences, Article X:3(a) GATT "do[es] not concern the customs laws themselves, but only their administration"[719] and "does not prescribe the specific means a Member must employ in order to ensure a uniform administration of customs laws", as stated by the EC.[720] This is also in line with Japan's above-mentioned view that the issue is whether or not the results of applying a specific means of a Member ensure a uniform administration as a whole.

5.25 While Japan hopes that, where appropriate, Members further harmonize their customs administration within their respective territories in the future, Japan is of the view that the specific means to ensure a uniform administration of customs laws is one of the matters which should be addressed through the Doha Negotiations on Trade Facilitation which aims "to clarify and improve relevant aspects of Articles V, VIII and X of the GATT 1994…"

5.26 In respect of the BTI system or the function of the Customs Code Committee (CCC), it is useful to recall that the BTI and the CCC are each individual means that the EC provides to ensure a uniform administration of customs matters, and not each the only means. It is necessary to analyze other means such as classification regulations, the HS explanatory notes and opinions, and the EC explanatory notes to determine whether the EC's customs system as a whole ensures a uniform administration consistent with Article X:3(a) GATT.

3. *Consistency of the challenged measures with Article X:3(b) of the GATT*

(a) The measure in question

5.27 The United States claims that the EC does not provide tribunals or procedures for the prompt review and correction of administrative actions relating to customs matters, as required by Article X:3(b) GATT.[721] Japan agrees with the United States that as the EC is the responsible entity in administering regulation of customs matters, the EC should provide tribunals or procedures for the prompt review and correction.

5.28 The United States claims that the EC does not provide an opportunity to review and correct administration of customs matters because, for example, the "Community Customs Code says little on the question of appeal"[722] and "in fact, the time periods for first instance reviews conducted by Member State customs

[719] EC First Written Submission, para. 216.
[720] EC First Written Submission, para. 303.
[721] US First Written Submission, Section V, sub-section D.
[722] US First Written Submission, paras. 141-143.

authorities can vary widely...with the exception of courts of last resort, referral of questions by Member State courts [to the ECJ] is discretionary."[723]

(b) The consistency of the challenged measure with Article X:3(b) of the GATT

5.29 In respect of the United States' challenge that the EC does not provide an opportunity to review and correct administration of customs matters due to a lack of a common appeals procedure, Japan would like to point out that although a central court or procedure would likely ensure this result, again, this may not be the only means to realize an opportunity to review and to correct by the EC, especially in light of the principles of supremacy and of direct effect of Community law binding the national courts of the EC's member States.[724] As explained by the EC, the national courts could "assume the status of Community courts of general competence."[725]

5.30 Japan shares the view of the EC that Article X:3(b) of the GATT "does not require a central court or procedure to appeal administrative decisions in customs matters. There is no obligation under the GATT for WTO Members to establish a court similar to the United States Court of International Trade."[726]

5.31 As each Member is obliged to administer in a uniform manner all its customs matters pursuant to Article X:3(a) GATT, it is reasonable to deduce that the *results* of the tribunals or procedures of a prompt review pursuant to Article X:3(b) GATT shall ensure uniform administration of customs matters. However, this would be an issue of Article X:3(a) GATT.

5.32 In respect of the United States' challenge that "in fact, the time periods for first instance reviews conducted by member State customs authorities can vary widely"[727], the EC refers to the meaning of the word "prompt" as "without delay", while "delay" is "(a period of) time lost by inaction or inability to proceed."[728] Japan agrees that the GATT does not provide any specific standard for a "prompt" review and correction that should be taken, and refrains at this juncture from delving into factual issues. However, if one sees two different systems within the EC – whereas in one member State such review or correction can take up to one year, in another member State it is limited to 30 days – it seems to suggest that the former member State whose review or correction takes one year is not providing a "prompt review or correction" in a reasonably short term.

4. Conclusion

5.33 As set out at the beginning, based on its systemic interests in the correct interpretation and application of Articles X:3(a) and (b) of the GATT, Japan re-

---

723 US First Written Submission, paras. 146-149.
724 EC First Written Submission, Section III.A.3.
725 EC First Written Submission, para. 166.
726 EC First Written Submission, para. 465.
727 US First Written Submission, paras. 146-149.
728 EC First Written Submission, para. 459.

spectfully looks forward to the Panel's deliberation on issues concerning these provisions brought forward by the United States in this dispute.

C. *Third Party Written Submission of the Republic of Korea*

1. *Introduction*

5.34 Korea believes that certain aspects of the EC's customs system fails to be administered in an uniform manner, as required by the relevant provisions of GATT 1994. Rather than reiterating all the arguments, however, Korea will address in this submission certain critical issues.

2. *Legal arguments*

(a) The EC's non-uniform administration of laws and regulations concerning customs classification, valuation and other procedures violate Article X:3(a) of GATT 1994

5.35 The key issue in this dispute is whether, taken together, the EC's customs system provides uniformity in terms of administration of customs laws and regulations.

5.36 Korea does not dispute the fact that, by nature, customs laws and regulations involve discretion on the part of customs authorities of WTO Members.[729] Discretion, however, does not mean that the Customs authorities have the flexibility to administer customs laws and regulations in a non-uniform, partial or unreasonable manner. If such administration occurs, it is not an instance of exercising discretion; rather it is simply a deviation from the explicit obligation imposed by Article X:3(a) of GATT 1994.

5.37 In the area of customs control, the EC does have "uniform" laws and regulations. However, what Article X:3(a) requires and what the United States challenges here (and thus what causes Korea's concern as a third party participant) are not the laws and regulations themselves. Rather, the core of the challenge in this dispute is the fact that these EC laws and regulations are administered individually by 25 member States in a non-uniform manner. The 25 member States have their own customs authorities that administer customs laws and regulations in a way they see fit, in terms of classification, valuation and customs procedures.

5.38 Korea duly recognizes and respects the unique characteristics of the EC where all 25 member States individually exercise their authorities in the customs area. The unique characteristics, however, should not be referred to as a pretext to deviate from otherwise applicable WTO obligations, including GATT 1994. As a Member of the WTO in its own right, separate from its constituent member

---

[729] EC First Written Submission, dated 16 August 2005, at 60 ("A further important point is that Article X:3(a) [of] GATT does not prescribe the specific way in which WTO Members should administer customs laws in a uniform manner").

States, the EC has an obligation to make sure there are mechanisms in place which produce the effect of a uniform administration of its customs laws and regulations. Even if all its member States preserve individual customs authorities under the constituent legal document, the EC, at least, should have known that divergent customs regulations and practices among member States would be rampant, and thus established a mechanism through which such divergent regulations and practices are harmonized and reconciled.

5.39 From Korea's perspective, this problem caused by the EC's unique customs system will be aggravated as time passes by. Given the continued technological development and advent of new or hybrid products, customs control and regulation becomes increasingly complicated.

5.40 The EC's effort to downplay this widely known confusion and inconsistency simply falls apart when one looks at what is happening "in the field." Korea stresses that what is important in examining Article X:3(a) is the reality foreign exporters have to face at the border. The panel in *Argentina – Hides and Leather* pointed out that "Article X:3(a) requires an examination of the 'real effect' that a measure might have on traders operating in the commercial world."[730] Under the current system of disarray in the EC, it is simply impossible for "[e]very exporter and importer…to expect treatment of the same kind, in the same manner both over time and in different places…"[731]

5.41 Particularly with respect to the classification, the so-called Binding Tariff Information ("BTI") system of the EC simply further complicates the situation rather than alleviates the current problem because of its non-universal binding effect and the possibility of 'BTI shopping'.

5.42 Having 25 different manners as to how customs laws and regulations are administered is by no means "uniform" in the ordinary meaning of the term.[732] Korea believes that "uniformity" is only to be attained through an identical way of administration (or something comparable to such identical administration) of customs laws and regulation throughout the entire territory of a WTO member; in this case the territories of the 25 member States of the EC.[733] No matter how the EC attempts to justify it, the fact of the matter is the EC customs administration, as it currently stands, guarantees neither consistency nor predictability in classification, valuation or other customs procedures. This is exactly the situation the *Argentina – Hides and Leather* panel warned against.[734]

5.43 Korean exporters have had to deal with each customs agency of each member State on an *ad hoc* basis without any guarantee that other members of the EC would render the same or a similar conclusion for the same or similar issue.

---

[730] *Argentina – Measures Affecting the Export of Bovine Hides and the Import of Finished Leather*, WT/DS155/R, Report of the Panel, adopted 16 February 2001 ("*Argentina – Hides and Leather*"), at para. 11.77 (emphasis added).

[731] *Argentina – Hides and Leather*, at para. 11.83.

[732] Article 31(1) of the Vienna Convention on the Law of Treaties.

[733] *Argentina – Hides and Leather*, at para. 11.83.

[734] *Ibid.*

5.44 Taking all these into account, by failing to administer customs laws and regulations in a "uniform" manner, the EC violates its obligation under Article X:3(a) of GATT 1994.

(b) EC judicial system's failure to provide a viable mechanism to promptly review customs related administrative actions violate Article X:3(b) of GATT 1994

5.45 In addition, a WTO Member is also obligated to provide an aggrieved trader with "prompt" judicial review of an administrative decision rendered by its customs authorities. It should be noted that the obligation for a WTO Member is not simply to provide a review, but a "prompt" review. The EC's judicial system, however, is far from providing a "prompt" judicial review with respect to administrative decisions and actions by the customs authorities of its member States. In fact, traders are forced to deal with one more layer of complication due to the slow-moving, inconclusive judicial review in the EC.

5.46 The unique characteristics and structural organization of the EC should not be referred to as a pretext to violate otherwise applicable provisions of GATT 1994.

5.47 As noted above, each EC member State operates its own customs agency, which renders administrative decisions independent of each other. Needless to say, among EC member States there is frequent discrepancy in customs administrative decisions on the same issues. This discrepancy is further complicated by yet another layer of divergence: the administrative decision is then appealed to the courts of each member State, which has the authority to pronounce and apply the legal standard in the customs issue being appealed, yet again independent of national courts of another member. As such, each member State has wide discretion in conducting judicial review of customs administrative actions "in its own way." For example, there is no common rule for the timeframe of the review.[735] As a result, the judicial review by member States usually exacerbates the already laden confusion and inconsistency caused by non-uniform administration of customs laws and regulations, as explained in the Section 2(a) above, rather than provides reliable finality.

5.48 Only after going through the judicial review by national courts does a foreign trader have a chance to pursue judicial review by an EC court that has jurisdiction in the entire EC territory: the ECJ. In short, in the EC the traders have to go through one more process, and a lengthy one at that, before they get a viable judicial review by an EC court than they would have to do with other WTO members.

5.49 The EC argues that the ECJ fulfills its obligation under Article X:3(b) of GATT 1994.[736] But, given the fact that an aggrieved trader can reach the ECJ only upon the completion of judicial review at the member States, the ECJ is not

---

[735] US First Written Submission, at 106-107.

[736] EC First Written Submission, at 127-128.

a viable forum that provides "prompt" review of the challenged action. Furthermore, even if the ECJ renders its decision at long last, what basically follows from such a decision is yet another "back and forth" between the ECJ and national courts rather than an immediate finality of the dispute.[737] Under these circumstances, Korea does not believe that this is a "prompt" judicial review.

5.50 The EC's effort to justify the situation by repeating the unique structural aspects of the EC cannot be sustained either.[738] As a single economic entity, the EC, in its own right, assumes both rights and obligations under the WTO as a single package. It cannot simply claim the benefit as a single economic entity while disregarding obligations flowing from it, particularly so if such disregard creates unreasonable burden on its trading partners.

5.51 In the light of the foregoing reasons, Korea submits that the EC does not provide a judicial forum for a prompt review of customs related administrative actions, and thus violates its obligation under Article X:3(b) of GATT 1994.

3. *Conclusion*

5.52 For the reasons set forth above, the EC fails to fulfill its obligation under Articles X:3(a) and X:3(b) of GATT 1994. Korea respectfully submits that the Panel should hold that the EC's customs system as identified above is inconsistent with Articles X:3(a) and X:3(b) of GATT 1994.

D. *Third Party Written Submission of the Separate Customs Territory of Taiwan, Penghu, Kinmen and Matsu*

1. *Introduction*

5.53 The Separate Customs Territory of Taiwan, Penghu, Kinmen and Matsu welcomes the opportunity to present its views in this dispute given its substantial systemic and trade interest in the outcome of this case, and also given the fact that the European Communities (EC) is one of the major trading powers in the world. As such, it is imperative that the EC, as a WTO Member in its own right, adheres to the obligations of uniform administration of its customs laws and regulations as stated in Article X:3(a) and (b) of GATT 1994, without exception.

2. *Arguments*

5.54 The Separate Customs Territory of Taiwan, Penghu, Kinmen and Matsu finds much of the arguments by the EC to be either irrelevant or misleading, especially with regard to the characterization of the arguments made by the United States. At the outset, it is important to point out that the EC itself is a full Member of the WTO, and conducts its affairs as such, despite having 25 separate member States who are themselves Members of the WTO. Therefore, the EC,

---

[737] US First Written Submission, at 109-110.

[738] *See* generally, EC First Written Submission, at Section III.

like any other WTO Member, has the obligation to observe the rules set forth in Article X:3 of GATT 1994.

5.55 With regard to the interpretation of Article X:3(a), the Separate Customs Territory of Taiwan, Penghu, Kinmen and Matsu is puzzled by the deliberate effort of the EC to emphasize the reference to the *administration* of laws, regulations, decisions and rulings, as if that were not the challenge brought by the United States. We do not wish to dispute that Article X:3(a) applies to the administration of rather than the laws, regulations, decisions and rulings themselves, and that the Appellate Body in *EC – Bananas* has drawn precisely such a distinction.[739] However, this reading of Article X:3(a) does not negate the fact that the EC, as a WTO Member, does have the obligation to *administer* its laws and regulations in a *uniform* manner. This, in our view, is precisely what the United States claims that the EC violates. The EC has not presented any relevant arguments to the contrary.

5.56 The EC suggests that the way it has administered its customs laws, regulations, decisions and rulings is a result of its executive federalism, which is a fundamental and legitimate constitutional choice of government and should be afforded the same respect as those of the United States.[740] Neither the EC's constitutional choice nor that of the United States, in our view, seems to be relevant to this dispute. The United States, in our view, is not challenging the structure of the EC's government, nor is it seeking to interpret Article X:3(a) to require the formation of a single customs authority. It is true that the WTO does not dictate how a Member should organize its government, much like Article X:3(a) of GATT does not "prejudge the question of how the customs authorities in a WTO Member are structured and organized," as the EC states.[741] However, it is equally true that the structure and organization of a Member's government should not diminish in any way a Member's obligations under the WTO. After all, the same government agreed to the set of obligations under the WTO. Regardless of the constitutional choice by the EC, the issue in this case comes down to whether the EC has fulfilled its obligations.

5.57 The EC also speculates that political consideration to influence the Doha Round negotiations on trade facilitation played into the decision by the United States to bring this dispute.[742] This, again, is irrelevant, as speculation into the motivation behind a Member's decision to bring a challenge to the WTO by the Panel is neither constructive nor relevant to resolving the dispute. The Panel is tasked to decide whether the allegations of the United States are supported by the provisions of Article X:3(a) and (b) of the GATT and the relevant facts. Thus, a decision in favour of the United States does not mean that the Panel has yielded to political considerations, merely that the EC has not properly adhered to its obligations under the relevant provisions.

---

[739] *European Communities – Regime for the Importation, Sale and Distribution of Bananas*, Appellate Body Report, WT/DS27/AB/R, para. 200.

[740] EC First Written Submission, para. 204.

[741] *Ibid.*, para. 252.

[742] *Ibid.*, paras. 229, 230.

5.58 The EC cites the Panel in *Argentina – Hides and Leather* and GATT Panel in *EC – Dessert Apples* to support its argument that differential treatment and minor variations between EC member States in the administration of customs laws do not constitute a breach of Article X:3(a) of the GATT.[743] This is a mischaracterization of the precedents and the facts at issue. The quotation from *Argentina – Hides and Leather* cited in the EC First Written Submission speaks to the "many variations in products which might require differential treatment."[744] This is not the issue in the current dispute. The current dispute concerns the *same products* that are required to be treated in a "uniform...manner," in different ports of entry at different times. The quotation, therefore, does not support EC's argument.

5.59 Turning to *EC – Dessert Apples*, the "minor administrative variations" concerns the form in which licence applications could be made and the requirement of pro-forma invoices. In the present dispute, the differential treatments are the result of classification, valuation, and customs procedures. The divergences in the areas of classifications, valuation and customs procedures (regarding penalties and processing under customs control) go directly to the heart of the work of customs authorities, have enormous impact on trade, and cannot be compared to the minor variations in the form of licence applications and the requirement of pro-forma invoices mentioned in *EC – Dessert Apples*. Customs classifications, valuations and procedures at issue in this dispute cannot be characterized as minor administrative variations. If that were so, Article X:3(a) would be rendered completely meaningless.

5.60 On the sufficiency of evidence, the EC's argument that the United States has failed to discharge its burden of proof is again without merit. The United States cites "blackout drapery lining"[745] and DVI and LCD[746] as examples to support its complaint about non-uniform administration of EC customs classification law. On non-uniform administration of EC law on customs valuation, the US cites the discussion by the EC Court of Auditors on different member States having taken different positions on whether the costs of automobile repair that are covered by a seller's warranty should be deducted from customs value.[747] In one illustration, the United States notes that different member States of the EC have taken different positions on whether an importer is related to the non-EC companies that manufacture its products and on how those products should be valued.[748] And with regard to customs procedures, the United States cites a decision by the European Court of Justice that, as a matter of EC law, different member States are entitled to impose, and do impose, different sanctions.[749]

---

743 *Ibid.*, paras. 232, 233.

744 *Ibid.*, para. 232.

745 US First Written Submission, para. 67.

746 *Ibid.*, para. 74.

747 *See* Court of Auditors, Special Report No 23/2000 concerning valuation of imported goods for customs purposes (customs valuation), together with the Commission's replies, reprinted in the *Official Journal of the European Communities* C84, paras. 73-74 (14 March 2001) ("Court of Auditors Valuation Report") (Exhibit US-14); US First Written Submission, paras. 78-96.

748 US First Written Submission, para. 91.

749 *Ibid.*, para. 101.

Concerning the procedure known as "processing under customs control," the United States points out that different member States apply these tests differently, which can have a significant commercial impact.[750] As the United States demonstrates, the actual requirements that users of "local clearance procedures" must meet vary significantly from member State to member State, with the process being significantly more burdensome in some member States than others.[751] As illustrated above, the United States does not rely merely on an argument that the EC's customs laws being administered by 25 different authorities, among which divergences inevitably occur.[752] The Separate Customs Territory of Taiwan, Penghu, Kinmen and Matsu believes that the United States has sufficiently discharged its initial burden of proof. It is the EC who has so far failed to rebut the *prima facie* case presented by the United States.

5.61 Finally, with regard to Article X:3(b), the provision requires Members to "maintain…judicial, arbitral or administrative tribunals or procedures for the purpose…of the *prompt review and correction* of administrative action relating to customs matters." (emphasis added). The EC argues that it is possible to fulfill this requirement by maintaining several tribunals, each of them covering a part of the territory of the Member.[753] However, it is difficult to see how the stated purpose of prompt review and correction of administrative action can be met unless the Member establishes a procedure where the decisions and rulings of the tribunals ultimately have authority throughout the entire territory of the Member. It is unclear how the decisions and rulings of one tribunal on an administrative action relating to customs matters in an EC member State can be accepted and executed by the customs authority located within another EC member State. In addition, the length of time it takes to obtain a decision or ruling by the various tribunals may vary a great deal among different member States. It is also unclear how the EC can ensure the promptness of the review and correction by the various tribunals located in different member States.

3. *Conclusion*

5.62 The Separate Customs Territory of Taiwan, Penghu, Kinmen and Matsu respectfully requests that the Panel take the above views into careful consideration.

E. *Third Party Oral Statement of Argentina*

1. *Introduction*

5.63 Argentina's attention focuses on the fact that interpretation of Article X:3(b) establishes the obligation to institute or maintain functional tribunals or procedures for the object and purpose of Article X:3 of the GATT 1994; in

[750] *Ibid.*, paras. 106-108.
[751] *Ibid.*, paras. 110-118.
[752] *Ibid.*, para. 20.
[753] EC First Written Submission, para. 454.

other words, to ensure the "prompt" review and uniform correction of the trade regulations in the EC as a whole.

2. *The link between subparagraph (b) and subparagraph (a) of Article X:3 of the GATT 1994*

5.64 Argentina agrees with the United States that subparagraph (a) of Article X:3 is the immediate and relevant context for interpreting the meaning and scope of the obligation laid down in subparagraph (b) of Article X:3 of the GATT 1994 as it is precisely within the context of the obligation to apply trade regulations in a uniform manner that each WTO Member's obligation to institute or maintain tribunals or procedures for the purpose of reviewing or correcting trade regulations is situated.

5.65 Argentina considers that – irrespective of the different nature that the obligations laid down in subparagraphs (a) and (b) of Article X:3 of the GATT 1994 may have – there is a clear link between them, inasmuch as Article X:3 as a whole should be read and interpreted as a coherent ensemble without any internal contradictions so that compliance with one obligation does not alter or diminish compliance with another (the principle of effectiveness). It should also be borne in mind that, in addition, this link arises from the fact that the legislator placed these obligations in different subparagraphs of the same paragraph.

5.66 Consequently, according to subparagraph (a) of Article X:3, every WTO Member must apply its laws, regulations, judicial decisions and administrative provisions in a uniform impartial and reasonable manner. Moreover, according to subparagraph (b) of Article X:3, every WTO Member must institute judicial, arbitral or administrative procedures for reviewing or correcting administrative action if it is applied in a non-uniform, partial or unreasonable manner. The procedures referred to in subparagraph (b) of Article X:3 should, therefore, ensure, *inter alia*, the uniform application of trade regulations in accordance with subparagraph (a) of Article X:3 of the GATT 1994.

1. 5.67 For the foregoing reasons, Argentina does not question the *sui generis* nature of the EC nor the fact that the WTO's Members retain a certain degree of discretion when complying with obligations under Article X as a result of the specific wording of the Article. Nevertheless, Argentina considers that this should not constitute an obstacle and – being a WTO Member distinct from the member States belonging to it – the EC is subject to the obligations laid down in subparagraphs (a) and (b) of Article X:3 and, as such, should institute or maintain tribunals or procedures for review and correction that ensure uniform application of trade regulations throughout the EC.

3. *"Promptness" as an obligation in Article X:3(b)*

5.68 Argentina agrees with the parties to this dispute that the obligation laid down in subparagraph (b) of Article X:3 of the GATT 1994 is not confined solely to instituting or maintaining tribunals or procedures for reviewing or correcting administrative action but also means that these procedures must be instituted in such a way as to allow "*prompt*" review and correction of decisions by the customs authorities.

5.69 Argentina agrees with the EC regarding the meaning of the term "prompt" namely that the review or correction of the decision by the customs authority should occur within a "reasonably short period of time".

5.70 In order to determine when the period is "reasonably short", Article X:3 of the GATT 1994 is primarily addressed to importers and exporters. Its object and purpose is to preserve certain competitive situations, as pointed out by the Panel in the *Argentina – Hides and Leather* case.

5.71 Argentina therefore considers that Article X:3(b) is violated if the judicial, arbitral or administrative procedures do not allow review or correction of administrative action within a "reasonably short" period (promptly) so as to preserve the legitimate competitive prospects of exporters and importers.

5.72 Argentina wishes to emphasize that both paragraphs 1 and 3 of Article X of the GATT 1994 and WTO case law make exporters and importers the main beneficiaries of the obligations laid down in this Article.

5.73 Argentina therefore considers that the *sui generis* situation of the EC does not contradict the fact that – as a WTO Member independently of the States making up the EC – according to Article X:3(b), the European Communities should not only ensure that there are mechanisms for review and correction but also that such review and correction of decisions by the customs authorities of the EC member States as a whole should be "prompt".

5.74 In this regard, notwithstanding the degree of discretion given by the EC to its member States (as regards procedures for reviewing and correcting decisions by the customs authorities), the absence of any specific reference in Community legislation to the time-limits for such reviews and correction implies that the EC does not in any case guarantee to the other Members of the WTO that review and correction will be "prompt" throughout the Community, as required by subparagraph (b) of Article X:3.

F. Third Party Oral Statement of Australia

5.75 Australia joined this dispute as a third party in view of its systemic interests in the questions under consideration by the Panel. Australia therefore refrains at this stage from taking a position on the facts of this particular dispute.

5.76 The European Communities as a WTO Member in its own right has the obligation to comply with Article X:3(a) of the GATT 1994 by ensuring its customs system operates in a uniform, impartial and reasonable manner.

5.77 Australia agrees that Article X:3(a) is not prescriptive and is concerned with the administration of customs laws and not the laws themselves. It is clear that WTO Members retain discretion as to their administrative system provided it is uniform, impartial and reasonable.

5.78 Australia also acknowledges that, given the complex nature of customs systems, some divergences may occur from time to time, but these should not be so widespread or frequent as to render the customs administration inconsistent with Article X:3(a).

5.79 The question for the panel is whether the alleged divergences resulting from the European Communities' particular system (that is, reliance on the national systems of its member States) fall into this category.

5.80 As with Article X:3(a), the European Communities as a WTO Member in its own right has an obligation to comply with Article X:3(b) of the GATT 1994 by ensuring there exist tribunals or procedures for prompt review and correction of administrative action relating to customs matters.

5.81 Australia would argue that Article X:3(b) is not a prescriptive Article and includes no obligation to have a central court. However, Australia does support the view that the decisions and rulings of the review bodies should be applied consistently and be available equally throughout the territory of the WTO Member. The question for the Panel is whether the European Communities' system for review of customs matters achieves this result.

5.82 With regard to the requirement of prompt review, Australia would see it as desirable that the timeframe for review should be reasonably comparable from wherever review is sought within the territory of the member. This prevents, among other things, traders from seeking review in the forum they expect to produce the quickest outcome and contributes to a uniform approach (consistent with Article X:3(a)).

G. *Third Party Oral Statement of China*

1. *The scope of application of Article X:3(a) of the GATT 1994*

5.83 China considers that Article X:3(a) of GATT 1994 concerns the administration of customs laws, not the customs laws themselves. The EC seems concerned with whether Article X:3(a) GATT applies to the administration of customs laws at the local level as well as at the central level.

5.84 Based on Article XXIV:12 of the GATT 1994 and the GATT Panel report in *Canada – Gold Coins*, the EC drew its conclusion that "Article X:3(a) GATT does not require that customs laws be regulated at the central level of each WTO Member".

5.85 Taking no position on this EC assertion, however, China does not think Article XXIV:12 of the GATT 1994 and the GATT Panel report in *Canada – Gold Coins* are proper in supporting the EC's argument.

5.86 Article XXIV:12 requires that the provisions of GATT be observed by both the central government and the regional or local authorities of a Contracting Party, and that the central government take the responsibility for ensuring the observance of the provisions of GATT by its local authorities. So, if there are any difficulties, encountered by the federal government of a Contracting Party because of its particular administrative or legal structures, in ensuring the observance of the provisions of GATT by its local authorities, the federal government shall still seek such reasonable measures as are available to it to secure the observance of the provisions of GATT by its local authorities in accordance with Article XXIV:12 until the actions or measures inconsistent with any provisions of GATT by its local authorities are removed. The federal government of such a Contracting Party shall compensate, because of such actions or measures by its local authorities, for any nullified or impaired benefits accruing to other Contracting Parties under the provisions of the GATT.

5.87 According to the GATT panel in *Canada – Gold Coins*, Article XXIV:12 applies to those measures taken by the local authority of Contracting Parties with federal regimes when administering their laws or regulations of local level. The present dispute does not concern a measure taken by the local authority when administering their laws or regulations of local level, but concerns whether the EC customs laws (i.e. laws of central level) can be administered by only the EC member States (i.e. local level authority) and whether such administration is in a uniform manner.

5.88 The GATT panel in *Canada – Gold Coins* further stated that Article XXIV:12 does not change the scope of application of the provisions of the GATT. China agrees with the EC that "Article X:3(a) GATT does not prescribe the specific way in which WTO Members should administer their customs laws". However, the obligation of uniform administration of customs laws should not be varied.

2. *The meaning of "uniform" as used in Article X:3(a) of the GATT 1994*

5.89 The ordinary meaning of "uniform", as relevant here, is "of one unchanging form, character, or kind; that is or stays the same in different places or circumstances, or at different times."[754]

5.90 The panel in *Argentina – Hides and Leather* stated: "Customs laws should not vary, that every exporter and importer should be able to expect treatment of the same kind, in the same manner both over time and in different places and with respect to other persons. Uniform administration requires that Members ensure that their laws are applied consistently and predictably. This is a requirement of uniform administration of Customs laws and procedures between individual shippers and even with respect to the same person at different times and different places."

5.91 China considers that the interpretation clarified by the panel in *Argentina – Hides and Leather* of the word "uniform" as used in Article X:3(a) is of the same substance with this ordinary meaning of "uniform".

5.92 China believes that when addressing the meaning of the word "uniform" reference should be made to the interpretation given by the panel in *Argentina – Hides and Leather*.

---

[754] *The New Shorter Oxford English Dictionary*, Vol. II at 3488 (1993) (Exhibit US-4).

3. *The standard of uniformity required by Article X:3(a) of the GATT 1994*

5.93 The EC argues that "Article X:3(a) GATT only lays down minimum standards". The EC referred to the Appellate Body report in *US – Shrimp* to support its argument. The paragraph referred to by the EC of the Appellate Body report in *US – Shrimp* reads:

> "It is also clear to us that Article X:3 of the GATT 1994 establishes certain minimum standards *for transparency and procedural fairness in the administration of trade regulations* which, in our view, are not met here. ......" (emphasis added by China)

5.94 The minimum standards articulated by the Appellate Body are for transparency and procedural fairness in the administration of trade regulations, not for directly the uniformity requirement of the administration of customs law.

5.95 The EC also referred to the Panel report in *Argentina – Hides and Leather* to support its argument. However, the paragraphs referred to by the EC address the meaning of the word "uniform", and do not directly concern the standard of the uniformity.

H. *Third Party Oral Statement of Japan*

1. *Arguments relating to the consistency of the challenged measures with Article X:3(a) of the GATT*

5.96 Japan would like to add, as a basis for our argument that "Article X:3(a) lays down minimum standards"[755], the Appellate Body's finding in *US – Shrimp* that "[i]t is clear to us that Article X:3 of the GATT 1994 establishes certain minimum standards for transparency and procedural fairness in the administration of trade regulations"[756]. China has pointed out that this finding does not directly concern the requirement of uniformity. Article X:3(a) does not stipulate the "transparency and procedural fairness" of administration, but rather the "uniform, impartial and reasonable manner" in which trade regulations shall be implemented. The Appellate Body in *US – Shrimp*, however, characterized the requirements under Article X:3(a) as "transparency and procedural fairness." This is indeed apparent from the meanings of the terms "uniform", "transparent" and "fair." "Uniformity" in an administration would ensure an application which is of an unchanging form, character, or kind; that is or stays the same in different places or circumstances, or at different times."[757]. A "fair" administration would be implemented in a "just, unbiased, equitable, impartial..."[758] manner. As

---

[755] Japan, Third Party Submission, para. 8.

[756] Appellate Body Report, *United States – Import Prohibition of Certain Shrimp and Shrimp Products*, WT/DS58/AB/R, adopted 6 November 1998, para. 183.

[757] Panel Report, *Argentina – Measures Affecting the Export of Bovine Hides and Import of Finished Leather*, WT/DS155/R and Corr.1, adopted 16 February 2001, para. 11.80 (quoting *The New Shorter Oxford English Dictionary*, Vol. II at 3488 (1993)).

[758] *The New Shorter Oxford English Dictionary*, Vol. I at 907 (1993).

"transparency" is the "quality or condition of being transparent"[759], a "transparent" administration would be "easily discerned; evident; ...open" as well as "extrapolated from every occurrence of the phenomenon; to which there are no exceptions"[760], "not subject to ... more than one interpretation"[761]. An administration of regulations lacking "uniformity" would in general terms be unjust, biased, inequitable, partial and opaque – in other words, unfair and nontransparent. Therefore, uniformity is an element of a transparent and fair administration, or procedural fairness, and the above finding by the Appellate Body would be relevant in interpreting the uniformity required under Article X:3(a) of the GATT.

5.97 Japan agrees with the statement of the Separate Customs Territory of Taiwan, Penghu, Kinmen and Matsu which had correctly pointed out that while the Panel in *Argentina – Hides and Leather* determined that "many variations in products which might require differential treatment,[...] [t]he current dispute concerns the same products that are required to be treated in a 'uniform...manner'".[762] However, we view that this Panel's finding in *Argentina – Hides and Leather* is still relevant to the present case. It demonstrates that the scope and level of "uniformity" required by Article X:3(a) of the GATT, which had been determined by the Panel in *Argentina – Hides and Leather* to mean an administration applied in an unchanging form, character, or kind; that is or stays the same in different places or circumstances, or at different times"[763], is subject to interpretation. It also indicates that Article X:3(a) "focuses on the day to day application of Customs laws, rules and regulation"[764], providing a context in which this provision should be interpreted.

5.98 Japan agrees with the United States and other third parties that the EC, as a Contracting Party, is responsible for ensuring a uniform administration of customs matters throughout its territory, irrespective of the number of customs authorities within its territory. Japan also agrees that a central function within the government which has the primary responsibility to interpret trade regulations such as those relating to customs classification or customs valuation is desirable. However, Article X:3(a) of the GATT does not prescribe a specific means a Member must employ, and such specific means to ensure a uniform administration of customs laws is one of the matters which should be addressed through the Doha Negotiations on Trade Facilitation which aims "to clarify and improve relevant aspects of Articles V, VIII and X of the GATT 1994..." [765]. Japan would like to draw the Panel's attention to the fact that it is because such means are not specifically provided under the current GATT, that Japan has, together with Mongolia, Pakistan, Peru and the Separate Customs Territory of Taiwan, Pen-

---

[759] *Ibid.*, at 3373.
[760] *Ibid.*
[761] *Merriam-Webster Online Thesaurus*: http://www.m-w.com/cgi-bin/thesaurus?book=Thesaurus&va=transparent&x=13&y=16.
[762] Separate Customs Territory of Taiwan, Penghu, Kinmen and Matsu, Third Party Written Submission, para. 6.
[763] *Supra* footnote 757.
[764] *Supra* footnote 757, para. 11.84.
[765] WT/L/579, Annex D, para. 1.

ghu, Kinmen and Matsu, made a proposal on this matter.[766] Therefore, the issue before the Panel is whether the EC's administration of customs regulation as a whole ensures a uniform administration consistent with Article X:3(a) of the GATT, not whether the EC provides a specific means to achieve uniformity.

5.99 Furthermore, even if divergences exist in light of the particular customs system as a whole, the issue of whether the "degree" of such divergences is inconsistent with Article X:3(a) of the GATT would arise. In regard to this point, Japan recalls the Panel's finding in *US – Hot-Rolled Steel* which held that, for a Member's measure to be in consistent with Article X:3(a) of the GATT, "it would have to have a significant impact on the overall administration of that Member's law as opposed to a mere impact on the outcome in the individual case in question"[767]. In addition, the panel in *Argentina – Hides and Leather* pointed out that "Article X:3(a) requires an examination of the 'real effect' that a measure might have on traders operating in the commercial world" and that the examination of such real effect "can involve the examination of whether there is a possible impact on the competitive situation"[768]. Therefore, if the Panel considers the cases referred to by the United States as divergences, then further examination is necessary to determine whether the EC's administration lacks uniformity to the "degree" that would be inconsistent with Article X:3(a) of the GATT. Such a determination should be based on whether the cases mentioned by the United States are individual outcomes of the EC's customs administration, or evidences of the non-uniformity of the overall administration of the EC's customs regulation that may have a significant impact on the competitive situation.

I. Third Party Oral Statement of the Republic of Korea

5.100 Korea supports the arguments raised by the United States in its First Written Submission dated 12 July 2005. Korea believes that certain aspects of the EC's customs system in general and laws and regulations in particular are inconsistent with the relevant provisions of GATT 1994. With this in mind, Korea offers its position on the following issues.

1. The EC's non-uniform administration of laws and regulations concerning customs classification, valuation and other procedures violate Article X:3(a) of GATT 1994

5.101 As a Member of the WTO in its own right, the EC assumes the obligation to administer its customs laws and regulations in a "uniform, impartial and reasonable manner" in accordance with Article X:3(a) of GATT 1994. The EC, however, fails to abide by this important obligation. The EC laws and regulations

[766] TN/TF/W/8, page 5, TN/TF/W/8/Add.1.

[767] Panel Report, *United States – Anti-Dumping Measures on Certain Hot-Rolled Steel Products from Japan*, WT/DS184/R, adopted 23 August 2001, as modified by the Appellate Body Report, WT/DS184/AB/R, para. 7.268.

[768] *Supra* note 3, para. 11.77.

are administered individually and separately by the 25 member States in a non-uniform manner. In terms of classification, valuation and customs procedures, the 25 member States have their own customs authorities that administer customs laws and regulations in the way they see fit. Like other traders from outside the bloc, Korean exporters have had to deal with these 25 different customs authorities and their varying procedures for entry of the same or similar products into the EC.

5.102 Having 25 different manners of customs administration is by no means "uniform" in the ordinary meaning of the term. Korea believes that "uniformity" is only to be attained through identical administration (or something comparable to such identical administration) of customs laws and regulation throughout the entire territory of a WTO Member; in this case the territories of the 25 member States of the EC. No matter how the EC attempts to justify it, the fact of the matter is the EC customs administration, as it currently stands, guarantees neither consistency nor predictability in classification, valuation or other customs procedures. This is exactly the situation the *Argentina – Hides and Leather* panel warned against.

5.103 Korea duly recognizes and respects the unique characteristics of the EC where all 25 member States individually exercise their authorities in the customs area. The unique characteristics, however, should not become a pretext for deviating from otherwise applicable WTO obligations, including GATT 1994. Taking all these into account, by failing to administer customs laws and regulations in a "uniform" manner, the EC violates its obligation under Article X:3(a) of GATT 1994.

2. *The EC judicial system's failure to provide a viable mechanism to promptly review customs related administrative actions violates Article X:3(b) of GATT 1994*

5.104 Furthermore, each member State has wide discretion in conducting judicial reviews of customs administrative actions "in its own way." For example, there is no common rule for the timeframe of the review. As a result, the variety of approaches to judicial review by member States exacerbates the already widespread confusion and inconsistency caused by customs agencies' non-uniform administration of customs laws and regulations, as explained above.

5.105 Only after going through this lengthy, unpredictable and inconsistent judicial review by national courts does a foreign trader have a chance to pursue judicial review by an EC court that has jurisdiction in the entire EC territory: namely, the ECJ. The EC argues that the ECJ fulfills its obligation under Article X:3(b) of GATT 1994. Given the fact that an aggrieved trader can reach the ECJ only upon the completion of a judicial review at the level of the member States, the ECJ is not a viable forum for providing "prompt" review of the challenged action.

5.106 To provide a prompt review of customs decisions, the EC should have introduced and maintained a judicial forum that has jurisdiction throughout the territory of the EC. The EC, however, fails to provide a judicial forum for a prompt review of customs related administrative actions, and thus violates its obligation under Article X:3(b) of GATT 1994.

VI. INTERIM REVIEW

6.1 The Panel's Interim Report was issued to the parties on 10 February 2006. Pursuant to Article 15.2 of the DSU and paragraph 16 of the Panel's Working Procedures, the United States and the European Communities submitted written requests for review of the Interim Report on 24 February 2006. On 3 March 2006, the United States and the European Communities submitted further written comments on the comments that had been provided by the parties on 24 February 2006.

6.2 Pursuant to Article 15.3 of the DSU, this section of the Panel Report contains the Panel's response to the comments made by the parties in relation to the Interim Report, to the extent that an explanation is necessary. The Panel has modified aspects of its report in light of the parties' comments where it considered appropriate, as explained below. The Panel has also made certain revisions and editorial corrections for the purposes of clarity and accuracy. References to sections, paragraph numbers and footnotes in this Section VI relate to the Interim Report.

A. New Evidence Referred to in Comments During the Interim Review Stage

6.3 In its comments on the Interim Report, the **European Communities** referred to a number of exhibits that it had not relied upon previously in the Panel proceedings. In particular, the European Communities referred to: (a) Commission Regulation (EC) No. 2171/2005 concerning the tariff classification of certain LCD monitors (Exhibit EC-167); (b) Dutch Ministry of Finance, Telefaxbericht BCPP 2006/389 M (Exhibit EC-168); (c) an extract from the EBTI database concerning expired BTI DE M/2975/05-1 (Exhibit EC-169); (d) replies of customs authorities of member States concerning the alleged requirement of prior approval for valuation on a basis other than the last sale (Exhibit EC-170); (e) Greek Presidential decree No. 203 (Exhibit EC-171); and (f) Opinion 1/94 of the ECJ concerning accession to the WTO (Exhibit EC-172).

6.4 The **United States** objected to the European Communities' reference to and reliance upon Exhibits EC-167 – EC-172. More specifically, the United States submitted that the introduction of new evidence during the interim review stage of the Panel's proceedings is entirely impermissible and the Panel should give no consideration to that evidence. In support, the United States relied upon the Appellate Body's decision in *EC – Sardines*, which the United States argued stands for the proposition that, pursuant to Article 15 of the DSU, the interim review stage cannot include an assessment of new and unanswered evidence.

6.5 The **Panel** notes that Article 15.2 of the DSU, which governs the interim review stage of panel proceedings, provides in relevant part that:

> "Following the expiration of the set period of time for receipt of comments from the parties to the dispute, the panel shall issue an interim report to the parties, including both the descriptive sections and the panel's findings and conclusions. Within a period of time set by the panel, a party may submit a written request for the panel to review precise aspects of the interim report prior to circulation of the final report to the Members. ..."

6.6 In the Panel's view, Article 15.2 of the DSU clearly indicates that the purpose of the interim review stage of the Panel's proceedings is to review "precise aspects" of the Interim Report that was issued to parties on 10 February 2006. We consider that the terms of Article 15.2 preclude us from taking into consideration evidence which is not reflected in the Interim Report.[769] Therefore, the Panel declines to consider Exhibits EC-167 – EC-172.

B. Panel's Terms of Reference

1. Manner of administration

6.7 The **United States** requested the Panel to reconsider its finding in Section VII.B that the "measure at issue" for the purposes of a claim under Article X:3(a) of the GATT 1994 is the "manner of administration" of laws, regulations, decisions and rulings of the kind described in Article X:1 of the GATT 1994.

6.8 The **European Communities** submitted that it agreed with the Panel's analysis in Section VII.B in this regard and that, therefore, the United States' request should be rejected.

6.9 The **Panel** has taken careful note of the arguments advanced by the United States but has decided not to accept the United States' request. The Panel fully explained its reasoning for concluding that, for the purposes of a claim under Article X:3(a) of the GATT 1994, the measure at issue is the manner of administration that is allegedly non-uniform, partial and/or unreasonable in paragraphs 7.18 – 7.22. The United States has not convinced the Panel that its reasoning should be revised and, therefore, the Panel has retained these paragraphs in its Final Report.

2. Challenge of the EC system as a whole/overall

6.10 The **United States** questioned whether the Panel properly considered the United States' request for establishment of a panel as a whole in Section VII.B when it concluded that its terms of reference did not include the United States' challenge of the EC system of customs administration as a whole or overall. The United States further submitted that a claim that a Member is in breach of a WTO obligation in a request for establishment of a panel is sufficient to put that

---

[769] We find support for this view in the Appellate Body Report, *EC – Sardines*, para. 301.

Member on notice as to the obligation that has allegedly been violated and the measure at issue. According to the United States, it is not necessary to specifically identify whether the challenge is "overall" or "as a whole" or, rather, whether the challenge relates to specific instances of violation.

6.11 The **European Communities** submitted that the United States' request for reconsideration of the Panel's analysis in Section VII.B should be rejected. According to the European Communities, the Panel's approach is consistent with relevant Appellate Body jurisprudence, which merely requires that requests for establishment of a panel be read as a whole.

6.12 The **Panel** notes that, in paragraphs 7.24 – 7.32 and 7.42 – 7.46, the Panel referred to and discussed all relevant aspects of the United States' request for establishment of a panel. Further, in paragraph 7.40, we emphasised that a challenge of a system as a whole or overall must meet the important due process requirements contained in Article 6.2 of the DSU. We have modified paragraph 7.46 to make it clear that, when considered as a whole, the various elements of the United States' request for establishment of a panel preclude a challenge of the EC system of customs administration overall or as a whole.

3. Administration by "national customs authorities of EC member States" of "laws, regulations, handbooks, manuals and administrative practices"

6.13 The **United States** requested the Panel to delete the reference to administration by "national customs authorities of EC member States" in paragraphs 7.25, 7.33, 7.50 and 7.55. The United States submitted that, if this reference were to be retained, it would create the false impression that administration in the European Communities may be undertaken other than through the national customs authorities. The United States also requested modification of paragraph 7.25 to make it clear that it does not allege that the "laws, regulations, handbooks, manuals, and administrative practices" to which it refers in its request for establishment of a panel are themselves in violation of Article X:3(a) of the GATT 1994 but, rather, that they evidence such violation.

6.14 The **Panel** has decided to retain the reference to administration by "national customs authorities of EC member States" in paragraphs 7.25, 7.33, 7.50 and 7.55 given that, *inter alia*, this reference is drawn directly from the United States' own request for establishment of a panel. With respect to the reference to "laws, regulations, handbooks, manuals, and administrative practices", the Panel has modified paragraph 7.25 to clarify that the United States' request for establishment of a panel indicates that the specific forms of administration "challenged" by the United States under Article X:3(a) of the GATT 1994 include, *inter alia*, "laws, regulations, handbooks, manuals, and administrative practices".

4. *Temporal issues*

(a) Expired measures or measures not yet in existence at the time of panel establishment

6.15 The **United States** requested deletion of the statement in the last sentence of paragraph 7.28 that measures that amend, implement or are related to the Community Customs Code, the Implementing Regulation, the Common Customs Tariff or the TARIC are within the Panel's terms of reference, "to the extent that they do not change the essence of the measures being amended or implemented and/or do not change the essential nature of the United States' case under Article X.3(a) of the GATT 1994".

6.16 The **European Communities** submitted that it could accept the United States' request provided that the Panel agreed to the European Communities' request regarding paragraphs 7.90 – 7.92. More specifically, the European Communities requested that these paragraphs be moved to the section dealing with the Panel's terms of reference.

6.17 The **Panel** has decided to accede to the requests of both the United States and the European Communities. In particular, we deleted the statement in the last sentence of paragraph 7.28 to which the United States objected and we inserted paragraphs 7.90 – 7.92 in a new section entitled "Temporal matters concerning the Panel's terms of reference" following the section dealing with "The measure(s) at issue" in accordance with the European Communities' request.

6.18 The **European Communities** requested the Panel to reconsider its reasoning in paragraph 7.91 regarding expired measures and measures not yet in existence. The European Communities argued that the test formulated by the Panel in those paragraphs was excessively wide. In this regard, the European Communities noted that, pursuant to Article 3.7 of the DSU, the aim of dispute settlement is to secure a positive solution to a dispute. However, the European Communities argued that, with regard to measures no longer in existence at the time of establishment of a panel, the responding Member cannot bring them into conformity. Regarding measures that are not yet in existence at the time of establishment of a panel, the European Communities submitted that these could not be "covered" by a request for establishment.

6.19 The **United States** submitted that the European Communities' request should be rejected. The United States argued that evidence of instances of administration that pre-date or post-date establishment of a panel remain relevant to a panel's analysis inasmuch as they provide context for the examination of particular instances of alleged violations of Article X:3(a) of the GATT 1994. The United States further argued that circumstances that lead to a particular manner of administration in one instance may be the same circumstances affecting administration in other instances.

6.20 The **Panel** has carefully considered the parties' arguments regarding its reasoning in paragraph 7.91 (which, as noted in paragraph 6.17 above, is now contained in the section dealing with the Panel's terms of reference in the Final Report). At the outset, the Panel recalls its statement in paragraph 7.91 that, as a general principle, a panel is competent to make findings and recommendations on measures in existence at the time of establishment of a panel. In other words, from a temporal perspective, the time of establishment of a panel is of critical importance because it is at that time that the panel must focus its attention to determine whether or not a violation of the covered agreements exists. We disagree with the United States' argument that evidence of instances of administration that pre-date and post-date establishment of a panel remain relevant to a panel's analysis insofar as the United States suggests that anything that occurs before or after the establishment of panel, however remote in temporal terms from panel establishment, may have a bearing on a panel's analysis at the time of establishment. Rather, as the Panel clearly stated in paragraph 7.91, expired measures may properly be the subject of findings and recommendations by a panel *only to the extent that they affect the operation of a covered agreement at the time of establishment of a panel.* Further, a request for establishment of a panel may be drafted in such a way that anticipates measures not yet in existence at the time of panel establishment. As stated in paragraph 7.91, the Panel considers that, in such cases, the "future" measures which have come into existence since the establishment of a panel, may fall within the scope of a panel's terms of reference *only if they do not change the essential nature of the complaining Member's case as reflected in its request for establishment of a panel.* In light of the foregoing, the Panel does not consider it necessary to modify its reasoning in paragraph 7.91.

(b) The temporal scope of "administration"

6.21 The **European Communities** requested the Panel to reconsider its reasoning in paragraph 7.92. In particular, the European Communities argued that the statement by the Panel in that paragraph that the manner of administration may not have a clear starting point or ending point would make it impossible for a responding Member found in violation of Article X:3(a) of the GATT 1994 to prove that the violation had ended.

6.22 The **United States** submitted that, given the interlinked nature of "administration", findings about administration that pre-dates or post-dates the establishment of a panel could well shed light on administration that was indisputably in existence at the time of establishment. Additionally, the United States noted that it does not object to the Panel's reasoning in paragraph 7.92 but suggests that the Panel frame its reasoning not as a matter concerning the Panel's terms of reference but, rather, as context that will shed light on instances of administration that were indisputably in existence at the time of panel establishment. The United States also argued that the findings about past instances of non-uniform administration are evidence regarding the EC system of customs administration as a whole.

6.23 The **Panel** has taken note of the parties' comments regarding paragraph 7.92. In light of those comments, the Panel has decided to modify its reasoning in that paragraph (which, as noted in paragraph 6.17 above, is now contained in the section dealing with the Panel's terms of reference in the Final Report). The modifications make it clear that the Panel does not wish to suggest that administration that has occurred before or may occur after the establishment of a panel may be the subject of findings and recommendations of a panel in the context of a claim made under Article X:3(a) of the GATT 1994. Rather, the nature of administration is such that it may not be possible to clearly identify the point in time at which the administration exists. As we stated in paragraph 7.92, administration "may not have a clear starting point or end point. More particularly, administration may be part of an ongoing series of interlinked acts or measures, which could thereby, implicate acts or measures that no longer existed or did not exist at the time of establishment of the panel." The Panel has amended paragraph 7.92 to clarify that administration may comprise a continuum of steps and acts, some of which may pre-date or post-date the step or act that forms part of the administration that is considered by a panel at the time of establishment of that panel. The steps and acts pre-dating or post-dating the administration that is the subject of consideration may be relevant to determining whether or not a violation of Article X:3(a) of the GATT 1994 exists at the time of establishment of a panel.

6.24 By way of example, the Panel refers to paragraph 7.294 of its Interim Report. In respect of that paragraph, the **European Communities** argued that some of the evidence adduced by the United States to prove divergent classification of LCD monitors entails measures that post-date establishment of the Panel (namely, Exhibits US-76, 77 and 78) and that, therefore, they are outside the Panel's terms of reference.

6.25 The **United States** countered that the European Communities' objections should be rejected because they assume that the non-uniform administration evidenced by the exhibits in question only came into existence when those documents were issued and not before. According to the United States, the non-uniform administration reflected in those documents is simply a continuation of "an ongoing series of interlinked acts or measures" that existed at the time of establishment of the Panel.

6.26 The **Panel** considers that it is clear from its reasoning in paragraph 7.294, particularly when read in the light of paragraphs 7.91 – 7.92 and 7.295, that the Panel did not rely upon Exhibits US-76, 77 and 78 as proof of the existence of non-uniform administration at the time of the Panel's establishment. Rather, the Panel made reference to those exhibits because they contained evidence of the continuum of steps and acts comprising the administration of the Common Customs Tariff concerning the tariff classification of LCD monitors and illustrated that, at the time of establishment of the Panel, the European Communities was not administering the Common Customs Tariff in a uniform manner.

(c) "Currently"

6.27 The **European Communities** requested deletion of the word "currently" in paragraphs 7.207 and 7.448 and in the paragraphs containing conclusions drawn from the findings in those paragraphs. The European Communities reasoned that the inclusion of this word incorrectly suggests that a distinction should be drawn between cases where there never was a violation under Article X:3(a) of the GATT 1994 and cases where there once was a violation which has since been removed. The European Communities also argued that the use of the word "currently" suggests that there is a risk of recurrence of the violation in question.

6.28 The **United States** argued that the European Communities' requests should be rejected because circumstances that lead to a particular manner of administration in one instance may be the same circumstances affecting administration in other instances.

6.29 The **Panel** notes that, by using the term "currently" in those paragraphs, the Panel intends merely to highlight that, at one point in time, the act or measure in question amounted to non-uniform administration within the meaning of Article X:3(a) of the GATT 1994 but that, at the time of establishment of the Panel, such non-uniformity did not exist.

5. *Retroactive recovery of customs duties*

6.30 The **European Communities** requested deletion of paragraphs 7.375 – 7.385. According to the European Communities, those paragraphs concern the retroactive recovery of customs duties following adoption of an explanatory note, which is not within the Panel's terms of reference.

6.31 The **United States** submitted that the European Communities' request should be rejected. The United States noted that, if an EC customs authority views an explanatory note as a mere clarification of the Common Customs Tariff and, therefore, applies it retrospectively, it is administering the Common Customs Tariff differently from another EC customs authority that views the note as being more akin to an amendment and only applies it prospectively. The United States submitted that this cannot be understood as anything other than a divergence in administration of the tariff classification rules in the European Communities.

6.32 The **Panel** considers that paragraph 7.381 makes it clear that, in paragraphs 7.375 – 7.385, the Panel is dealing with alleged differences in the interpretation and application of explanatory notes by customs authorities in the member States (a matter which is clearly within the Panel's terms of reference) rather than the retroactive recovery of customs duties. Therefore, the Panel sees no need to delete paragraphs 7.375 – 7.385.

C. *Interpretation of Article x:3(a) of the GATT 1994*

1. *"Object and purpose"*

6.33 The **United States** requested deletion of paragraph 7.109. It argued that, with respect to the reference to "object and purpose" in Article 31(1) of the *Vienna Convention*, WTO jurisprudence does not indicate that an object and purpose of the WTO Agreement is to ensure security and predictability. Rather, the reference to security and predictability in such jurisprudence derives from Article 3.2 of the DSU, which concerns the aim of WTO dispute settlement.

6.34 The **Panel** considers that the architecture of the WTO system, which is a rules-based system, implies that security and predictability is an object and purpose of the WTO Agreement. In the Panel's view, this is implicit in Article 3.2 of the DSU which states, *inter alia*, that "[t]he dispute settlement system of the WTO is a central element in providing security and predictability to the multilateral trading system". In our view, this provision indicates that security and predictability is an object and purpose not only of the DSU but also of the entire multilateral trading system, of which the DSU is a part. Nevertheless, since the Panel's findings in paragraph 7.109 are not essential for its interpretation of the term "administer" in Article X:3(a) of the GATT 1994, the Panel has decided to delete paragraphs 7.108 – 7.109.

2. *"Supplementary means of interpretation"*

6.35 The **United States** requested the Panel to delete its reference to the "factual context" under Article 32 of the *Vienna Convention* as "supplementary means of interpretation" in paragraphs 7.131 – 7.136. The United States suggested that the Panel's discussion of the factual context should be substituted for a discussion of the relationship between Articles X:3(a) and X:3(b) of the GATT 1994.

6.36 The **European Communities** submitted that the United States' request should be rejected. In support, the European Communities referred to the Appellate Body's decision in the *EC – Chicken Cuts* case, which its says confirms the inclusive nature of Article 32 of the *Vienna Convention*.

6.37 The **Panel** notes that the United States does not appear to dispute the Panel's reference to the "factual context". Rather, its primary concern appears to be the legal basis upon which the Panel made such reference. In this regard, the Panel recalls its observation in footnote 262 of the Interim Report that, in the *EC – Chicken Cuts* case, the Appellate Body affirmed the panel's reliance upon the "factual context" when interpreting the ordinary meaning of a treaty term pursuant to Article 31 of the *Vienna Convention*. The Panel also stated in footnote 262 that the Appellate Body' approval of the use of "factual context" under Article 31 of the *Vienna Convention* indicates that it may alternatively/additionally be taken into consideration under Article 32 of the *Vienna Convention*. We find support for this view in *EC – Chicken Cuts*, where the Appellate Body stated that: "We stress, moreover, that Article 32 does not define exhaustively the supplementary means of interpretation to which an interpreter may have recourse. It states only that they *include* the preparatory work of the treaty and the circumstances of its conclusion. Thus, an interpreter has a certain flexibility in considering relevant supplementary means in a given case so as to assist in ascertaining the common intentions of the parties."[770] In the light of the foregoing, the Panel has decided not to delete reference to the "factual context" under Article 32 of the *Vienna*

[770] Appellate Body Report, *EC – Chicken Cuts*, para. 283.

Convention as "supplementary means of interpretation" in paragraphs 7.131 – 7.136 but has amended footnote 262 to reflect additional support for the Panel's approach.

6.38 Regarding the United States' suggestion that the Panel's discussion of the "factual context" should be replaced with a discussion of the relationship between Articles X:3(a) and X:3(b) of the GATT 1994, the Panel notes that the United States made no reference to such a relationship when demonstrating its claim under Article X:3(a) of the GATT 1994. In any case, the Panel considers that it is far from clear that the requirement to provide for prompt review and correction of administrative decisions by domestic tribunals and procedures under Article X:3(b) of the GATT 1994 supports the view that the obligation of uniformity in Article X:3(a) of the GATT 1994 should be interpreted flexibly, as has been suggested by the United States in its comments.

3. *"Minimum standards"*

6.39 The **United States** requested the Panel to delete its reference to "minimum standards of due process" in paragraph 7.135. The United States reasoned that such a reference could be misread as adding to the text of Article X:3(a) of the GATT 1994.

6.40 The **Panel** accepts that there is no explicit reference to "minimum standards of due process" in Article X:3(a) of the GATT 1994. Nevertheless, the Panel considers that such a notion is implicit in Article X:3(a) of the GATT 1994 in light of the immediate context of that provision, which was considered by the Panel in paragraphs 7.126 – 7.130. Furthermore, the Panel recalls its observation in footnote 264 that the Appellate Body stated in *US – Shrimp* that "[i]t is also clear to us that Article X:3 of the GATT 1994 establishes certain minimum standards for transparency and procedural fairness in the administration of trade regulations".[771] Therefore, the Panel declines to accept the United States' request with respect to paragraph 7.135.

4. *"Uniform"*

(a) Nature of the challenge

6.41 The **United States** submitted that the Panel's discussion of the term "uniform" in paragraph 7.136 implies that different standards apply depending upon the scope of the challenge that is being made under Article X:3(a) of the GATT 1994. The United States argued that this could be misread to imply that, for example, in the context of a narrow challenge, the same product would need to be classified under the same tariff heading by a Member, but that, in the context of a broader challenge, the same product could be classified under different tariff headings and the Member's tariff classification would be considered "uniform" for the purposes of Article X:3(a) of the GATT. The United States requested the Panel to clarify whether its finding is that the nature of the obligation of uniform

[771] Appellate Body Report, *US – Shrimp*, para. 183.

administration of measures would vary depending on how broadly a Member has framed its panel request.

6.42 The **Panel** considers that the response to the question in respect of which clarification is sought by the United States is already provided in paragraph 7.136. In particular, in that paragraph, the Panel stated that the form, nature and scale of the alleged non-uniform administration and the laws, regulations, judicial decisions and rulings that are allegedly being administered in a non-uniform manner should be taken into consideration when interpreting the term "uniform" in Article X:3(a) of the GATT 1994 in the context of a particular case. The Panel further stated that the narrower the challenge both in terms of the administration that is being challenged and the laws, regulations, decisions and rulings which are alleged to be administered in a non-uniform manner in a particular case, the more demanding the requirement of uniformity. The broader and more wide-ranging the challenge both in terms of the nature of administration that is being challenged and the specific laws, regulations, decisions and rulings or provisions thereof that are alleged to be administered in a non-uniform manner in a particular case, a less exacting standard of uniformity should be applied. Accordingly, the Panel sees no reason to further clarify paragraph 7.136.

(b) "Reasonable period of time"

6.43 The **United States** requested the Panel to amend paragraph 7.136 where the Panel states that, for the purposes of Article X:3(a) of the GATT 1994, uniformity must be attained within a reasonable period of time. The United States submitted that the obligation under Article X:3(a) of the GATT 1994 is to administer in a uniform manner currently. Further, the United States argued that the reference to a "reasonable period of time" could be confused with the reference to the same term in Article 21.3 of the DSU.

6.44 The **European Communities** argued that the United States' request should be rejected. According to the European Communities, the obligation of uniform administration under Article X:3(a) of the GATT 1994 applies at all times, not just currently, but compliance with Article X:3(a) of the GATT 1994 should be assessed at the time of the Panel's establishment. The European Communities also argued that the context of paragraph 7.136 makes it clear that the Panel is not referring to a "reasonable period of time" for the purposes of Article 21.3 of the DSU.

6.45 The **Panel** has taken note of the parties comments and has decided to clarify paragraph 7.133 upon which the summary in paragraph 7.136 is based. Specifically, in order to avoid a finding of non-uniform administration under Article X:3(a) of the GATT 1994, it must be clear at the time of establishment of the panel that any non-uniformity that may have existed was remedied within a period of time that is reasonable.

D. *Panel's Observations Regarding the EC System of Customs Administration*

6.46 The **European Communities** agreed that its system of customs administration is relevant context for the consideration of the United States' specific claims of violation of Article X:3(a) of the GATT 1994. Nevertheless, the European Communities requested that paragraphs 7.156 – 7.191, describing relevant aspects of the EC system of customs administration be deleted. The European Communities made similar but more specific comments regarding paragraphs 7.165, 7.168, 7.169, 7.272 and 7.534. The European Communities argued that those paragraphs overlap with the description of the EC system in the Descriptive Part of the Panel's report; they follow a different structure to that adopted in the Descriptive Part, which could lead to confusion; they contain errors; and/or concern matters outside the Panel's terms of reference.

6.47 The **United States** submitted that the Panel should reject the European Communities' request regarding paragraphs 7.156 – 7.191, 7.272 and 7.534. In this regard, the United States argued that the discussion of the EC system in the Descriptive Part is inadequate because it is merely factual and does not contain any analysis. Nevertheless, the United States submitted that all but the first sentence of paragraph 7.535 (which is linked to paragraphs 7.156 – 7.191 and 7.534) should be deleted given that the text in question concerns matters outside the Panel's terms of reference.

6.48 The **Panel** has taken careful note of the parties' comments regarding paragraphs 7.156 – 7.191, 7.272 and 7.534 – 7.535. The Panel has decided to retain those paragraphs because, as stated in paragraph 7.156, they explain the Panel's understanding of certain aspects of the manner in which the EC system of customs administration functions, which have been raised in the context of the particular instances of violations of Article X:3(a) of the GATT 1994 alleged by the United States. In the section of the Panel's report dealing with the particular instances of alleged violations, we have included cross-references to the general description of the EC system, which illustrates this point. The Panel does not consider that any overlap between the description of the EC system of customs administration in the Descriptive Part and in paragraphs 7.156 – 7.191 and 7.534 – 7.535 leads to any confusion. On the contrary, we consider that the elaboration provided in paragraphs 7.156 – 7.191, 7.272 and 7.534 – 7.535 ensures that the reader has a clear and complete picture of the way the EC system of customs administration works. In retaining paragraphs 7.156 – 7.191, 7.272 and 7.534 – 7.535, the Panel emphasizes that those paragraphs merely contain the Panel's observations about aspects of the EC system that arise in the context of the particular instances of violations of Article X:3(a) of the GATT 1994 alleged by the United States.

E. *Specific Instances of Alleged Violation of Article X:3(A) of the GATT 1994*

1. *Tariff classification of blackout drapery lining*

6.49 The **European Communities** requested deletion of paragraphs 7.265 – 7.276 because, according to the European Communities, those paragraphs reflect a logical inconsistency. In this regard, the European Communities implied that it is impossible to find that non-uniformity associated with an administrative process is in violation of Article X:3(a) of the GATT 1994 unless the result of the administrative process has also been found to be non-uniform in violation of that provision.

6.50 The **United States** submitted that the European Communities' request should be rejected. The United States noted in this regard that the Panel did not find that the tariff classification of blackout drapery lining was uniform in the European Communities. Rather, on the basis of the evidence presented to it, the Panel found that it could not conclude that the products before the various EC customs authorities were materially identical. The United States submitted that, accordingly, that finding does not preclude a finding of non-uniform administration with respect to the administrative process leading to the classification of blackout drapery lining.

6.51 The **Panel** has carefully considered the parties' comments and has decided not to delete paragraphs 7.265 – 7.276. The Panel recalls its finding in paragraph 7.264 that, on the basis of the limited evidence before it, it could only assume that the products in question were not identical. It was for that reason that the Panel was obliged to conclude that the tariff classification of the products before the German customs authorities, on the one hand, and those before customs authorities of the United Kingdom, Ireland, the Netherlands and Belgium, on the other, was not non-uniform for the purposes of Article X:3(a) of the GATT 1994. In any case, the Panel considers that non-uniform administrative processes may lead to a violation of Article X:3(a) of the GATT 1994 even though the results of those processes are uniform. Indeed, the Panel is of the view that, irrespective of the substantive outcome of an administrative process, non-uniformity in the process itself may have the effect of dissuading traders from importing into a particular part of Member. In particular, this could be the case where the administrative processes applied in one part of a Member are more burdensome or onerous as compared to the administrative processes applied in another part of that Member.

6.52 The **European Communities** also requested amendment of paragraph 7.274 to the extent that it indicates that the Main Customs Office of Bremen did not properly take into account classification decisions by other customs authorities. The European Communities argued that such a statement is not justified because the products that were the subject of classification by the Main Customs Office of Bremen were different from the products that were the subject of classification by the customs authorities of the United Kingdom, Ireland, the Netherlands and Belgium.

6.53 The **United States** submitted that the European Communities' request should be rejected because it was based on a misunderstanding of the facts.

6.54 The **Panel** has considered the parties' comments and has decided not to modify paragraph 7.274. In the Panel's view, even if the Main Customs Office of Bremen considered that the products in question were different, it should have had regard to the classification decisions of other customs authorities. It was incumbent upon the Main Customs Office of Bremen to do so in light of the numerous complaints made by the trader requesting reclassification and given that the Main Customs Office of Bremen was aware of the existence of classification decisions of other customs authorities for "comparable goods".

6.55 Additionally, the **European Communities** requested inclusion in paragraph 7.253 of a reference to the statement made by the Hamburg ZPLA in the case of the Ornata protest, asking the trader in question to provide "further information and receipts to show that identical merchandise was treated differently in other EU countries".

6.56 The **United States** submitted that the European Communities' request should be rejected because paragraph 7.253 merely contains a description of the products that were the subject of classification by the Hamburg ZPLA.

6.57 The **Panel** considers that it is not necessary to include a reference in paragraph 7.253 to the statement referred to by the European Communities because the statement in question is already fully excerpted in footnote 501.

6.58 The **European Communities** requested deletion from paragraph 7.275 of the statement that "the apparent failure on the part of the German customs authorities may have had an impact and may continue to have an impact in the future upon the tariff classification of blackout drapery lining in the European Communities". The European Communities questioned the "impact" that the alleged failure may have.

6.59 The **United States** submitted that the European Communities' request should be rejected. According to the United States, the potential impact is clear. In particular, the United States argued that, to the extent that traders can expect the German customs authorities to administer EC classification rules with respect to blackout drapery lining by using its own national interpretative aid and by not seriously considering the decisions of other customs authorities, the exports of that trader may be diverted.

6.60 In light of the parties' comments, the **Panel** has decided to clarify the nature of the impact that it had in mind in paragraph 7.275.

6.61 The **European Communities** requested deletion of the statement in paragraph 7.276 that the EC system does not require German customs authorities to make reference to the classification decisions of other customs authorities. The European Communities noted that implementation of this finding would require changes to the EC system of customs administration, which is a matter outside the Panel's terms of reference.

6.62 The **United States** submitted that the European Communities' request should be rejected. The United States reasoned that the Panel's findings should not be dictated by what the European Communities consider it will or will not have to do for implementation purposes.

6.63 The **Panel** has carefully considered the parties' comments and has modified paragraph 7.276 to make it clear that the acts of the German customs authorities regarding the administrative process leading to the tariff classification of blackout drapery lining, rather than the EC system itself, resulted in the Panel's finding of violation of Article X:3(a) of the GATT 1994.

2. *Tariff classification of liquid crystal display flat monitors with digital video interface*

6.64 The **European Communities** requested deletion of the statement in paragraph 7.294 that the European Communities does not appear to dispute that, in 2004, a divergence in the tariff classification of LCD monitors occurred. The European Communities submitted that, while it has recognised in its submissions that the classification of LCD monitors was a complex issue involving the classification of numerous products, it has not recognised that there was any lack of uniformity in its classification practice concerning LCD monitors at the time of the Panel's establishment.

6.65 The **Panel** acknowledges that the European Communities did not *explicitly* state in its submissions that it agreed that divergence in tariff classification of LCD monitors existed at the relevant point in time. Nevertheless, the Panel considers that the European Communities *implicitly* conceded the existence of such divergence in the various paragraphs of its submissions cited in footnote 540. We have expanded this footnote to further substantiate this point. Further, in the same footnote, we have elaborated on our discussion of the Press Release issued by Greenberg Traurig, 24 May 2005, contained in Exhibit US-29, which tends to confirm that, in 2004, divergent tariff classification of LCD monitors with DVI existed between, on the one hand, Dutch customs authorities and, on the other hand, customs authorities in the other member States.

3. *Revocation of BTI concerning candlesticks and preserved fruits and nuts in the context of the* Timmermans *case*

6.66 The **European Communities** requested that paragraphs 7.347 – 7.360 be deleted because the United States did not make a claim of non-uniformity regarding candlesticks and preserved fruits and nuts. Further, the European Communities submitted that these paragraphs should be deleted because they concern the United States' challenge of the EC system of customs administration "as such", a matter which is outside the Panel's terms of reference.

6.67 The **United States** submitted that it could accept the European Communities request provided that paragraphs 7.357 and 7.358 are retained in Section VII.D.6(a).

6.68 In light of the parties' comments, the **Panel** has decided to delete paragraphs 7.347 – 7.360, except for paragraphs 7.357 and 7.358 which have been retained in Section VII.D.6(a).

4. Penalties against infringements of EC customs legislation

6.69 The **European Communities** requested deletion of paragraph 7.490 on the ground that the United States did not allege a violation of Article X:3(a) of the GATT 1994 in the manner formulated by the Panel in that paragraph. Further, the European Communities argued that the Panel's statements in these paragraphs are inconsistent with its reasoning that substantive penalty laws cannot be regarded as acts of administration.

6.70 The **United States** submitted that the European Communities' request should be rejected. The United States acknowledged that it did not frame its claim with respect to penalties in the manner adopted by the Panel in paragraph 7.490. However, the United States argued that it is not the case that the United States did not allege a violation in this regard. Further, the United States submitted that there is no inconsistency between the Panel's reasoning in para. 7.490 and the Panel's other findings regarding penalties. According to the United States, the issue in para. 7.490 is not whether individual penalty laws can be regarded as acts of administration. Rather, the issue is whether the *Andrade* decision and the EC Council Regulation in question are EC customs laws susceptible to administration within the meaning of Article X:3(a) of the GATT 1994.

6.71 The **Panel** has decided not to modify paragraph 7.490. First, the Panel notes that there is nothing to prevent it from making observations, even if they are not based on allegations that were specifically made by the parties during the Panel proceedings. Further, as stated in the first sentence of paragraph 7.490, the Panel's observations in that paragraph relate to the *application* of the ECJ's judicial decision in *Jose Teodoro de Andrade* v. *Director da Alfândega de Leixões* and EC Council Resolution of 29 June 1995, on the effective uniform application of Community law and on the penalties applicable for breaches of Community law in the internal market. The Panel's observations do not concern substantive differences in laws, regulations or other measures.

F. EC and Member State Obligations

6.72 The **European Communities** requested amendment of paragraph 7.593 to make it clear that the European Communities and not the member States have exclusive competence for matters concerning the WTO Agreements regarding trade in goods.

6.73 The **United States** submitted that the European Communities' request should be rejected. In support, the United States argued that, through its request, the European Communities introduces an issue that was never discussed before in this dispute, attempts to support its argument with evidence that it adduced for the first time during the interim review stage and asks the Panel to make a statement about the relative competence of the European Communities and its member States that has implications that go well beyond this dispute and is wrong as a matter of law.

6.74 The **Panel** has taken careful note of the parties' comments and has decided not to accept the European Communities' request regarding paragraph 7.593. The Panel notes that the statement to which the European Communities objects concerns the obligations of the European Communities and its member States under the WTO agreements *as a matter of international law*. However, the arguments made by the European Communities in support of the proposed amendment of paragraph 7.593 relate to the relative competence of the European Communities and its member States *as a matter of domestic law*, which have no bearing on the statement in question.

G. *Other Requests for Review*

6.75 The United States and the European Communities requested certain changes to the representation of their respective arguments in the following paragraphs of the Interim Report: 7.73, 7.98, 7.99, 7.115, 7.116, 7.119, 7.254, 7.280, 7.526, 7.546 and 7.595. The Panel accepted those changes to the extent that they were consistent with what the parties stated in the various submissions they made to the Panel during the Panel proceedings.

6.76 The United States and the European Communities requested modification or clarification of the Panel's description of specific aspects associated with the EC system of customs administration in the following paragraphs: 2.26, 2.33, 2.57, 2.72, 7.160, 7.166, 7.168, 7.181, 7.187, 7.299, 7.319, 7.343 and footnotes 306, 650. The Panel acceded to those requests to the extent that they were consistent with the evidence that had been presented by the parties to the Panel during the Panel proceedings.

6.77 The European Communities requested changes to the English translations of certain exhibits filed by the United States, the original language of which was German (namely, Exhibits US-23, US-41 and US-50) in the following paragraphs: 7.251 and 7.253. The Panel accepted those changes to the extent that they were faithful to the German version of the exhibits in question.

6.78 In the case of the following paragraphs, suggestions were made by one party and were not objected to by the other party: 7.327, 7.329 – 7.346, 7.347 – 7.356, 7.360, 7.386 – 7.399, 7.402, 7.444, 8.1 (concerning the Panel's terms of reference), 8.1(a)(vii), (viii) and (xi), and 8.2. The Panel accepted all such suggested changes.

6.79 In addition, the United States and/or the European Communities requested clarification of certain factual matters in paragraphs 7.262 and 7.265. The Panel made the necessary clarifications to those paragraphs.

VII. FINDINGS

A. *Article x of the GATT 1994*

7.1 Article X of the GATT 1994, entitled "Publication and Administration of Trade Regulations" provides that:

> "1. Laws, regulations, judicial decisions and administrative rulings of general application, made effective by any contracting party, pertaining to the classification or the valuation of products for customs purposes, or to rates of duty, taxes or other charges, or to requirements, restrictions or prohibitions on imports or exports or on the transfer of payments therefor, or affecting their sale, distribution, transportation, insurance, warehousing inspection, exhibition, processing, mixing or other use, shall be published promptly in such a manner as to enable governments and traders to become acquainted with them. Agreements affecting international trade policy which are in force between the government or a governmental agency of any contracting party and the government or governmental agency of any other contracting party shall also be published. The provisions of this paragraph shall not require any contracting party to disclose confidential information which would impede law enforcement or otherwise be contrary to the public interest or would prejudice the legitimate commercial interests of particular enterprises, public or private.
>
> 2. No measure of general application taken by any contracting party effecting an advance in a rate of duty or other charge on imports under an established and uniform practice, or imposing a new or more burdensome requirement, restriction or prohibition on imports, or on the transfer of payments therefor, shall be enforced before such measure has been officially published.
>
> 3. (a) Each contracting party shall administer in a uniform, impartial and reasonable manner all its laws, regulations, decisions and rulings of the kind described in paragraph 1 of this Article.
>
> (b) Each contracting party shall maintain, or institute as soon as practicable, judicial, arbitral or administrative tribunals or procedures for the purpose, inter alia, of the prompt review and correction of administrative action relating to customs matters. Such tribunals or procedures shall be independent of the agencies entrusted with administrative enforcement and their decisions shall be implemented by, and shall govern the practice of, such agencies unless an appeal is lodged with a court or tribunal of superior jurisdiction within the time prescribed for appeals to be lodged by importers; Provided that the central administration of such agency may take steps to obtain a review of the matter in another proceeding if there is good cause to believe that the decision is inconsistent with established principles of law or the actual facts.

> (c) The provisions of subparagraph (b) of this paragraph shall not require the elimination or substitution of procedures in force in the territory of a contracting party on the date of this Agreement which in fact provide for an objective and impartial review of administrative action even though such procedures are not fully or formally independent of the agencies entrusted with administrative enforcement. Any contracting party employing such procedures shall, upon request, furnish the CONTRACTING PARTIES with full information thereon in order that they may determine whether such procedures conform to the requirements of this subparagraph."

7.2 In this dispute, the United States has made claims under Article X:3(a) and Article X:3(b) of the GATT 1994. The Panel will address each of these claims in turn, following consideration of a number of matters concerning the Panel's terms of references and procedural issues that have been raised.

B. The Panel's Terms of Reference

1. The measure(s) at issue

(a) Summary of the parties' arguments

7.3 The **United States** clarified in its first written submission that it is exclusively concerned with the requirement of "uniform" administration contained in Article X:3(a) of the GATT 1994.[772] The United States claims that the following measures are not being administered in a uniform way by the European Communities in violation of Article X:3(a) of the GATT 1994: the "Community Customs Code" contained in Council Regulation (EEC) No. 2913/92 of 12 October 1992; the "Implementing Regulation" implementing the Community Customs Code contained in Commission Regulation (EEC) No. 2454/93 of 2 July 1993; and the "Common Customs Tariff", which was originally promulgated in Council Regulation (EEC) No. 2658/87 but which is updated annually in the EC Official Journal.[773] The United States explains that, while it is principally challenging these three measures because they comprise the substance of EC customs laws, they are "supplemented" by miscellaneous Commission regulations and other measures.[774] The United States submits that these supplementary measures pertain to specific products or groups of products in ways that elaborate on provisions set forth in the three principal measures. According to the United States, because of their specificity and the diverse range of issues covered, it would be impossible to identify all such supplementary measures. Nevertheless, by way of example, the United States refers to Council Regulation (EC) No. 493/2005 regarding the suspension of duties on a subset of LCD monitors.[775] The United States also refers to an explanatory note to the Combined Nomenclature on the

772 United States' first written submission, footnote 15.

773 United States' first written submission, para. 3.

774 United States' replies to Panel question Nos. 3 and 128.

775 Exhibit US-28.

classification of certain camcorders.[776] The United States submits that the three principal measures and the supplementary measures are not administered in a uniform manner in violation of Article X:3(a) of the GATT 1994.[777]

7.4 The **European Communities** argues that the laws and regulations listed in the United States' request for establishment of a panel are not the "measures at issue" for the United States' claims under Article X:3(a) of the GATT 1994 within the meaning of Article 6.2 of the DSU. According to the European Communities, it is clear from that request that the United States' claim relates to the manner in which the European Communities administers the measures listed in the request, not to the measures themselves. The European Communities submits that the enumeration of laws and other measures in the request merely serves the purpose of identifying the laws which the European Communities allegedly fails to administer in a non-uniform manner.[778]

7.5 In response, the **United States** notes that it is not challenging the substance of the measures mentioned in its request for establishment of a panel.[779] Rather, it is challenging the manner in which EC customs law is administered. However, according to the United States, the manner in which the European Communities administers its customs law may not itself be a "measure". Therefore, the "specific measures at issue" for the purposes of Article 6.2 of the DSU are the laws, regulations, decisions and rulings that make up EC customs law, although in some cases these are being administered through laws and regulations which are themselves measures.[780]

7.6 The **European Communities** does not agree that the manner of administration of laws may not itself be a measure. In this regard, the European Communities submits that the Appellate Body has confirmed that any act or omission attributable to a WTO Member can be a measure of that Member for purposes of WTO dispute settlement. According to the European Communities, this statement also applies to the administration of laws referred to in Article X:3(a) of the GATT 1994. Whether a particular measure is challengeable in the WTO depends entirely on the substance of the WTO obligation in question.[781] The European Communities argues that the identification of the measure(s) at issue in the present dispute is particularly necessary given the specific features of Article X:3(a) of the GATT 1994.[782] The European Communities submits that the United States' suggestion that the "manner of administration" may not be a measure would lead to the absurd result that non-compliance with Article X:3(a) of the GATT 1994 could never be challenged under the DSU.[783] The European Communities also

---

[776] Explanatory Notes to the Combined Nomenclature of the European Communities, 13 July 2000, p. 316 (Exhibit US-62).
[777] United States' reply to Panel question No. 128.
[778] European Communities' second written submission, para. 7.
[779] United States' replies to Panel question Nos. 1, 4 and 128.
[780] United States' replies to Panel question Nos. 1 and 4.
[781] European Communities' second written submission, para. 8 referring to Appellate Body Report, *US – Corrosion-Resistant Steel Sunset Review*, para. 81.
[782] European Communities' second written submission, para. 9 referring to Appellate Body Report, *EC – Bananas III*, para. 200.
[783] European Communities' second written submission, para. 10.

notes in this regard that the Appellate Body has confirmed that Article X:3(a) of the GATT 1994 only relates to the administration of the laws and regulations referred to in Article X:1 of the GATT 1994, not to the substance of those laws and regulations.[784]

(b) Analysis by the Panel

7.7 In the context of the United States' claim that the European Communities has violated Article X:3(a) of the GATT 1994, the question has arisen as to what the "measure(s) at issue" is under Article 6.2 of the DSU for the purposes of a claim made pursuant to Article X:3(a) of the GATT 1994. In particular, the Panel has been called upon to determine whether the measures at issue in this dispute are the laws, regulations and other measures referred to in the United States' request for establishment of a panel as has been submitted by the United States or, rather, the manner of administration of the EC customs system as has been submitted by the European Communities.

(i) Interpretation of the term "measures at issue" under Article 6.2 of the DSU

7.8 By way of background for the Panel's consideration of the "measure(s) at issue" for the purposes of a claim under Article X:3(a) of the GATT 1994, the Panel will first examine more generally the meaning of the term "measures at issue", which appears in Article 6.2 of the DSU.

7.9 Article 6.2 of the DSU provides in relevant part that:

> "The request for the establishment of a panel shall … identify the specific *measures at issue* and provide a brief summary of the legal basis of the complaint sufficient to present the problem clearly." (emphasis added)

7.10 In summary, Article 6.2 of the DSU contains two distinct requirements that must be fulfilled in respect of a request for establishment of a panel: (1) the request must identify the specific measures at issue; and (2) it must contain a brief summary of the legal basis of the complaint.

7.11 The "measure at issue" identified in a request for establishment of a panel plays a pivotal role in a WTO dispute for a number of reasons.

7.12 *First*, the "measure at issue" together with the "legal basis of the complaint" comprise the "matter referred to the DSB", which forms the basis for a panel's terms of reference under Article 7.1 of the DSU.[785] In turn, a panel's terms of reference define the scope of a dispute and serve the due process objective of notifying the parties and third parties to a dispute of the nature of the complainant's case.[786]

---

[784] European Communities' second written submission, para. 9 referring to Appellate Body Report, *EC – Bananas III*, para. 200.

[785] Appellate Body Report, *US – Carbon Steel*, para. 125.

[786] Appellate Body Report, *US – Carbon Steel*, para. 126.

7.13 *Second*, it is the "measure at issue" identified in the request for establishment of a panel that must be brought into conformity in the event that that measure is found to be in violation of a WTO obligation. This is evident, *inter alia*, from Article 19.1 of the DSU, which provides in relevant part that:

> "Where a panel or the Appellate Body concludes that a *measure* is inconsistent with a covered agreement, it shall recommend that the Member concerned bring the *measure* into conformity with that agreement." (emphasis added)

7.14 The Panel understands that there is an inter-linkage between the reference to the term "measure" in Article 19.1 of the DSU and to the term "measures at issue" in Article 6.2 of the DSU. In particular, a panel and the Appellate Body may only make recommendations under Article 19.1 of the DSU with respect to a measure that has been specifically identified in the relevant request for establishment of a panel in accordance with Article 6.2 of the DSU and which has been found to be inconsistent with a WTO obligation.

7.15 Of relevance to the interpretation of the term "measure" in Article 6.2 of the DSU is the following statement by the Appellate Body:

> "In principle, any act or omission attributable to a WTO Member can be a measure of that Member for purposes of dispute settlement proceedings.[787] The acts or omissions that are so attributable are, in the usual case, the acts or omissions of the organs of the state, including those of the executive branch.[788]
>
> In addition, in GATT and WTO dispute settlement practice, panels have frequently examined measures consisting not only of particular acts applied only to a specific situation, but also of acts setting forth rules or norms that are intended to have general and prospective application.[789] In other words, instruments of a Member containing rules or norms could constitute a 'measure', irrespective of how or whether those rules or norms are applied in a particular instance. This is so because the disciplines of the GATT and the

[787] (*original footnote*) We need not consider, in this appeal, related issues such as the extent to which the acts or omissions of regional or local governments, or even the actions of private entities, could be attributed to a Member in particular circumstances.

[788] (*original footnote*) Both specific determinations made by a Member's executive agencies and regulations issued by its executive branch can constitute acts attributable to that Member. See, for example, the Panel Report in *US – DRAMS*, where the measures referred to the panel included a USDOC determination in an administrative review as well as a regulatory provision issued by USDOC.

[789] (*original footnote*) See, for example Panel Report, *US – Superfund*; Panel Report, *US – Malt Beverages*; Panel Report, *EEC – Parts and Components*; Panel Report, *Thailand – Cigarettes*; Panel Report, *US – Tobacco*; Panel Report, *Argentina – Textiles and Apparel*; Panel Report, *Canada – Aircraft*; Panel Report, *Turkey – Textiles*; Panel Report, *US – FSC*; Panel Report, *US – Section 301 Trade Act*; Panel Report, *US – 1916 Act (EC)*; Panel Report, *US – 1916 Act (Japan)*; Panel Report, *US – Hot-Rolled Steel*; Panel Report, *US – Export Restraints*; Panel Report, *US – FSC (21.5 – EC)*; and Panel Report, *Chile – Price Band System*. See also Appellate Body Report, *US – Carbon Steel*, paras. 156 and 157. See also Appellate Body Report, *US – 1916 Act*, footnotes 34 and 35 to paras. 60 and 61, respectively.

> WTO, as well as the dispute settlement system, are intended to protect not only existing trade but also the security and predictability needed to conduct future trade. This objective would be frustrated if instruments setting out rules or norms inconsistent with a Member's obligations could not be brought before a panel once they have been adopted and irrespective of any particular instance of application of such rules or norms.[790] It would also lead to a multiplicity of litigation if instruments embodying rules or norms could not be challenged as such, but only in the instances of their application. Thus, allowing claims against measures, as such, serves the purpose of preventing future disputes by allowing the root of WTO-inconsistent behaviour to be eliminated."[791]

7.16 Regarding the significance that should be attached, if any, to the term "at issue" in Article 6.2 of the DSU when referring to the specific measures that are required to be identified in a request for establishment of a panel, the Panel notes that the ordinary meaning of that term indicates that it refers to what is being challenged by the complainant.[792] Therefore, we understand that the term "measure at issue" in Article 6.2 of the DSU refers to the measure that is the subject of the challenge in a particular dispute.

7.17 In the Panel's view, the term "measure at issue" in Article 6.2 of the DSU should be interpreted in the light of the specific WTO obligation that is allegedly being violated by that measure in a particular dispute. The Panel considers that such an approach is necessary because the "measure at issue", which has been referred to in a request for establishment of a panel in accordance with Article 6.2 of the DSU, will be the subject of a recommendation to be brought into conformity pursuant to Article 19.1 of the DSU by a panel and/or the Appellate Body, if that measure is found to be in violation of a WTO obligation. The manner in which the measure is to be brought into conformity is clearly linked to the substance of the WTO obligation with which the measure in question has been found to be inconsistent. Therefore, the Panel considers that, at least in the context of some claims, the substance of the WTO obligation with which a measure may have been found to be inconsistent might have an impact upon the interpretation of the term "measures at issue" in Article 6.2 of the DSU. Having said this, the Panel does not wish to suggest that the distinct requirements in Article 6.2 of the DSU to identify the specific measures at issue and to provide a brief summary of the legal basis of the complaint should be merged and assessed as a single requirement. On the contrary, these requirements serve different purposes. On the one hand, the requirement to refer to the specific "measure at issue" in the request for establishment of a panel serves the purpose of identifying the act or omission of a WTO Member that is being challenged, whereas the requirement to provide a legal basis of the complaint indicates the legal benchmark or stan-

---

[790] (*original footnote*) Panel Report, *US – Superfund*, para. 5.2.2.

[791] Appellate Body Report, *US – Corrosion-Resistant Steel Sunset Review*, paras. 81-82.

[792] The New Shorter Oxford English Dictionary defines "at issue" as "the position of parties of which one affirms and the other denies a point": *The New Shorter Oxford English Dictionary*, 1993, p. 1428.

dard against which the act or omission is to be assessed to determine WTO-inconsistency or otherwise. While these are clearly distinct requirements that serve different purposes, they are, nevertheless, interrelated such that the interpretation of one in the context of a particular dispute may help to inform the interpretation of the other.

(ii) The "measure(s) at issue" for the purposes of a claim under Article X:3(a) of the GATT 1994

7.18 Bearing these general considerations in mind, the Panel now turns to the question of what are the "measure(s) at issue" for the purposes of a claim under Article X:3(a) of the GATT 1994? We commence with an analysis of the relevant aspects of Article X:3(a) of the GATT 1994 because, as noted in paragraph 7.17 above, the term "measure at issue" in Article 6.2 of the DSU should be interpreted in the light of the specific WTO obligation that is allegedly being violated by that measure.

7.19 Article X:3(a) of the GATT 1994 provides that:

> "Each contracting party shall administer in a uniform, impartial and reasonable manner all its laws, regulations, decisions and rulings of the kind described in paragraph 1 of this Article."

7.20 In the Panel's view, the essential aspect of the obligation contained in Article X:3(a) of the GATT 1994 that has a bearing upon the interpretation of the term "measures at issue" in Article 6.2 of the DSU for the purposes of a claim under Article X:3(a) of the GATT 1994 is the obligation to "administer in a uniform, impartial and reasonable manner". The Panel considers that, in the light of this essential aspect of the obligation contained in Article X:3(a) of the GATT 1994, when a violation of Article X:3(a) of the GATT 1994 is being claimed, the relevant request for establishment of a panel must identify the manner of administration that is allegedly non-uniform, partial and/or unreasonable.

7.21 In this regard, the Panel recalls that it is evident from Articles 6.2 and 19.1 of the DSU that it is the "measure at issue" in the request for establishment of a panel that must be brought into conformity in the event that that measure is found to be in violation of a WTO obligation. If a WTO Member were found to be in violation of Article X:3(a) of the GATT 1994, this would mean that the manner in which laws, regulations, decisions and/or rulings of the kind described in Article X:1 of the GATT 1994 are being administered by that Member is not uniform, impartial and/or reasonable. If, in the light of such a violation, a panel or the Appellate Body has recommended to the DSB that the Member bring the measure in question into conformity, the Member would need to alter the *manner* in which the relevant laws, regulations, decisions and/or rulings are being *administered* in order to abide by that recommendation.

7.22 While the "measure at issue" for the purposes of a claim under Article X:3(a) of the GATT 1994 is the manner of administration that is allegedly non-uniform, partial and/or unreasonable, this does not necessarily mean that the mere identification of the manner of administration in a request for establishment of a panel will meet the requirement in Article 6.2 of the DSU to identify the *specific* measure at issue. In the Panel's view, what is necessary to meet the requirement of specificity in Article 6.2 of the DSU will vary from case to case. In the following section of our report, we discuss, *inter alia*, the specificity requirement under Article 6.2 of the DSU for the purposes of the present dispute.

(iii) The "measure at issue" for the purposes of the United States' claim under Article X:3(a) of the GATT 1994 in this dispute

7.23 The Panel will now consider the United States' request for establishment of a panel as a whole, to determine the specific measure(s) at issue for the purposes of the United States' claim under Article X:3(a) of the GATT 1994 in this dispute. In its request for establishment of a panel, the United States makes reference to the essential aspect of the obligation contained in Article X:3(a) of the GATT 1994 set out in paragraph 7.20 above, namely, the manner of administration that allegedly results in non-uniformity.[793]

Manner of administration

7.24 In particular, the United States' request for establishment of a panel states in relevant part that:

> "The United States considers that the *manner* in which the European Communities ('EC') *administers* its laws, regulations, decisions and rulings of the kind described in Article X:1 of the *General Agreement on Tariffs and Trade 1994* ('GATT 1994') is not uniform, impartial and reasonable, and therefore is inconsistent with Article X:3(a) of the GATT 1994.
>
> ...
>
> Administration of [the measures set out in paragraph 7.26 below] in the European Communities is *carried out by the national customs authorities* of EC member States. Such administration takes numerous different forms. The United States understands that the *myriad forms of administration* of these measures include, but are not limited to, laws, regulations, handbooks, manuals, and administrative practices of customs authorities of member States of the European Communities."[794] (emphasis added)

7.25 The terms of the United States' request for establishment of a panel indicate that it challenges the manner of administration of certain aspects of EC cus-

[793] As noted previously, in footnote 15 of its first written submission, the United States clarified that, in the context of the present dispute, it only claims that the manner of administration of the EC system of customs administration is not "uniform" in violation of Article X:3(a) of the GATT 1994. The United States explicitly stated that it does not take a position on whether or not the manner of administration of the EC system is "impartial" or "unreasonable" within the meaning of Article X:3(a) of the GATT 1994.

[794] WT/DS315/8, which is contained in Annex D of the Panel's report.

toms law.[795] The request clarifies that the administration challenged by the United States is that undertaken by the "national customs authorities of EC member States". In addition, the request indicates that the specific forms of administration by national customs authorities challenged by the United States under Article X:3(a) of the GATT 1994 include, *inter alia*, laws, regulations, handbooks, manuals, and administrative practices.

"Laws, regulations, decisions and rulings of the kind described in Article X:1 of the GATT 1994"

7.26 Notably, the United States' request also refers to the "laws, regulations, decisions and rulings of the kind described in Article X:1 of the GATT 1994", which the United States alleges are not being administered in a uniform manner in violation of Article X:3(a) of the GATT 1994. In particular, the United States' request for establishment of a panel states in relevant part that:

> "For purposes of this request, the laws, regulations, decisions and rulings (collectively, 'measures') that the European Communities fails to administer in such a manner pertain to the classification and valuation of products for customs purposes and to requirements, restrictions or prohibitions on imports. The measures consist of:
>
> - Council Regulation (EEC) No 2913/92 of 12 October 1992 establishing the Community Customs Code, including all annexes thereto, as amended [the 'Community Customs Code'];
> - Commission Regulation (EEC) No 2454/93 of 2 July 1993 laying down provisions for the implementation of Council Regulation (EEC) No 2913/92 of 12 October 1992 establishing the Community Customs Code, including all annexes thereto, as amended [the 'Implementing Regulation'];
> - Council Regulation (EEC) No 2658/87 of 23 July 1987 on the tariff and statistical nomenclature and on the Common Customs Tariff, including all annexes thereto, as amended [the 'Common Customs Tariff'];
> - the Integrated Tariff of the European Communities established by virtue of Article 2 of Council Regulation (EEC) No 2658/87 of 23 July 1987 on the tariff and statistical nomenclature and on the Common Customs Tariff, including all annexes thereto, as amended [the 'TARIC']; and

[795] In its submissions to the Panel in these proceedings, the United States has confirmed that it is challenging the manner of administration of the measures mentioned in its request for establishment of a panel and not the substance of those measures: United States' replies to Panel question Nos. 1, 4 and 128.

- for each of the above laws and regulations, all amendments, implementing measures and other related measures."[796]

7.27 In the Panel's view, the specificity requirement in Article 6.2 of the DSU requires the inclusion of the "laws, regulations, decisions and rulings of the kind described in [Article X:1 of the GATT 1994]" alleged to be administered in a manner that is in violation of Article X:3(a) of the GATT 1994 in the United States' request for establishment of a panel. In this regard, the Panel recalls that the requirements in Article 6.2 of the DSU, including the obligation to *specifically* identify the "measure at issue", serve the important due process objective of notifying the parties and third parties to a dispute of the nature of the complainant's case. We consider that this due process objective would not be fully achieved if a responding Member were only informed about the manner of administration that allegedly results in non-uniformity, partiality and/or unreasonableness but not the laws, regulations, decisions or rulings that are allegedly being administered in a manner contrary to the requirements of Article X:3(a) of the GATT 1994.

7.28 The Panel also notes that the United States' request for establishment of a panel refers to all "amendments, implementing measures and other related measures" for the Community Customs Code, the Implementing Regulation, the Common Customs Tariff and the TARIC. This broad language used by the United States indicates that measures that amend, implement, or are related to the Community Customs Code, the Implementing Regulation, the Common Customs Tariff or the TARIC could be within our terms of reference.[797]

Areas of customs administration

7.29 An issue that has arisen in the context of this dispute is whether Article 6.2 of the DSU, when read in the light of Article X:3(a) of the GATT 1994, also requires identification of the specific areas of customs administration in respect of which it is being alleged that Article X:3(a) of the GATT 1994 has been violated.

7.30 The Panel notes that, in this case, the United States has challenged the administration of the Community Customs Code, the Implementing Regulation, the Common Customs Tariff, the TARIC and related measures. These measures cumulatively contain, literally, thousands of different provisions, they relate to a vast array of different customs areas, and may entail administration in a multitude of diverse ways.[798] Consequently, we consider that, in the context of this

[796] WT/DS315/8, which is contained in Annex D of the Panel's report.

[797] In this regard, see the Panel's analysis in paragraphs 7.36 – 7.37 below.

[798] The Community Customs Code (Exhibit US-5) comprises 253 articles and is divided into nine Titles, dealing with the following topics – Title I: General Provisions; Title II: Factors on the basis of which import duties or export duties and the other measures prescribed in respect of trade in goods are applied; Title III: Provisions applicable to goods brought into the customs territory of the Community until they are assigned a customs-approved treatment or use; Title IV: Customs-approved treatment or use; Title V: Goods leaving the customs territory of the Community; Title VI: Privileged operations; Title VII: Customs debt; Title VIII: Appeals; Title IX: Final provisions.

dispute, the specificity requirement in Article 6.2 of the DSU additionally requires the identification of the customs areas in the context of which the obligation contained in Article X:3(a) of the GATT 1994 is alleged by the United States to be violated. In our view, without such additional specificity regarding the customs areas at issue, the European Communities would not have been accorded its due process right to be informed of the nature of the United States' claim under Article X:3(a) of the GATT 1994.

7.31 In this regard, we note that, in *EC – Computer Equipment*, the Appellate Body addressed the question of whether the measures at issue and the products affected by those measures had been identified with sufficient specificity for the purposes of Article 6.2 of the DSU. The Appellate Body noted in that case that, even though "Article 6.2, does *not* explicitly require that the products to which the 'specific measures at issue' apply be identified ... with respect to certain WTO obligations, *in order to identify 'the specific measures at issue' it may also be necessary to identify the products subject to the measures in dispute*".[799] The Panel considers that, in the context of this case, identification of the areas of customs administration at issue is necessary to *specifically* identify the "measures at issue" in the same way suggested by the Appellate Body in *EC – Computer Equipment*. In other words, the areas of customs administration help to *specifically* identify the "measure at issue", namely, the manner of administration.

7.32 In this case, the United States' request for establishment of a panel specifically identifies the following areas of customs administration:

- classification and valuation of goods;
- procedures for the classification and valuation of goods, including the provision of binding classification and valuation information to importers;
- procedures for the entry and release of goods, including different certificate of origin requirements, different criteria among member States for the physical inspection of goods, different licensing requirements for importation of food

The Implementing Regulation (Exhibit US-6) comprises 915 articles covering the following topics – *PART I: General Implementing Provisions*: Title I: General; Title II: Binding Information; Title III: Favourable Tariff Treatment by reason of the nature of goods; Title IV: Origin of Goods; Title V: Customs Value; Title VI: Introduction of Goods into the Customs Territory; Title VII: Customs Declarations – Normal Procedure; Title VIII: Examination of the Goods, Findings of the Customs Office and other measures taken by the Customs Office; Title IX: Simplified Procedures. *PART II: Customs-approved Treatment of Use*: Title I: Release for free circulation; Title II: Customs Status of Goods and Transit; Title III: Customs Procedures with Economic Impact; Title IV: Implementing Provisions relating to Export; Title V: Other Customs-approved Treatments or Uses; Title VI: Goods Leaving the Customs Territory of the Community. *PART III: Privileged Operation*: Title I: Returned Goods. *PART IV: Customs Debt*: Title I: Security; Title II: Incurrence of the Debt; Title III: Recovery of the Amount of the Customs Debt; Title IV: Repayment or Remission of Import or Export Duties. *PART IVA: Controls on the Use and/or Destination of Goods*. *PART V: Final Provisions*.

The Common Customs Tariff consists of 21 sections, covering 99 chapters and includes more than 5000 tariff headings.

[799] Appellate Body Report, *EC – Computer Equipment*, para. 67.

products, and different procedures for processing express delivery shipments;

- procedures for auditing entry statements after goods are released into the stream of commerce in the European Communities;
- penalties and procedures regarding the imposition of penalties for violation of customs rules; and
- record-keeping requirements.[800]

(iv) Summary

7.33 In the Panel's view, when read as a whole, the United States' request for establishment of a panel indicates that the "specific measure at issue" in this dispute for the purposes of Article 6.2 of the DSU is the manner of administration by the national customs authorities of the member States of the Community Customs Code, the Implementing Regulation, the Common Customs Tariff, the TARIC and related measures in the areas of customs administration specifically identified in the United States' request for establishment of a panel – namely, the classification and valuation of goods, procedures for the classification and valuation of goods, procedures for the entry and release of goods, procedures for auditing entry statements after goods are released into free circulation, penalties and procedures regarding the imposition of penalties for violation of customs rules and record-keeping requirements. Therefore, pursuant to Article 7.1 of the DSU, under our terms of reference, we are only authorized to consider the manner of administration by the national customs authorities of the member States of the Community Customs Code, the Implementing Regulation, the Common Customs Tariff, the TARIC and related measures in the areas of customs administration specifically identified in the United States' request for establishment of a panel.

2. *Temporal matters concerning the Panel's terms of reference*

(a) Summary of the parties' arguments

7.34 The **European Communities** submits that the Panel's terms of reference only include measures that were in existence at the time the matter was referred to it by the DSB. Therefore, according to the European Communities, the Panel cannot make findings on measures which no longer existed at the time it was established nor on measures which were not yet in existence at the time the Panel was established.[801]

---

[800] WT/DS315/8, which is contained in Annex D of the Panel's report.

[801] European Communities' comments on the United States' reply to Panel question No. 124.

(b) Analysis by the Panel

7.35 The Panel notes that the European Communities has raised the issue of whether or not there are any temporal limitations on the measures upon which the Panel may make findings in addressing the United States' claim under Article X:3(a) of the GATT 1994. In particular, the European Communities argues that the Panel's terms of reference only include measures in existence at the time the matter was referred to it by the DSB. Therefore, according to the European Communities, the Panel cannot make findings on measures which no longer existed at the time it was established nor on measures which were not yet in existence at that time it was established.[802]

7.36 We understand that, as a general principle, a panel is competent to make findings and recommendations on measures in existence at the time of establishment of the panel, assuming that the request for establishment of a panel covers those measures. Nevertheless, a panel may also be competent to make findings and make recommendations on measures that have expired or are not yet in existence at the time of establishment, assuming again that the request covers those measures. More specifically, we understand that, to the extent that expired measures affect the operation of a covered agreement at the time of establishment of a panel, they may properly be the subject of findings and recommendations by a panel, particularly if such findings and recommendations are necessary to secure a positive solution to the dispute.[803] Further, measures that are not in existence at the time of establishment may be the subject of findings and recommendations by a panel when they come into existence provided that they do not change the essential nature of the complaining Member's case as reflected in its request for establishment of a panel.[804]

7.37 In the context of this dispute, the Panel recalls that the "specific measure at issue" in this dispute comprises the *manner of administration* of the Community Customs Code, the Implementing Regulation, the Common Customs Tariff, the TARIC and related measures. As will become evident when the Panel interprets and applies Article X:3(a) of the GATT 1994 in the context of the specific instances of violation alleged by the United States, the manner of administration in a particular case may not have a clear starting point or end point. More particularly, administration may be part of an ongoing series of interlinked acts or measures, which could, thereby, implicate acts or measures that no longer existed or did not exist at the time of establishment of the panel. In other words, administration may comprise a continuum of steps and acts, some of which may pre-date or post-date the step or act of administration that is considered by a panel at the time of establishment of that panel.[805] In our view, the steps and acts of administration that pre-date or post-date the establishment of a panel may be relevant to determining whether or not a violation of Article X:3(a) of the GATT

---

[802] *Ibid.*

[803] See, Appellate Body Report, *US – Upland Cotton*, para. 261; Appellate Body Report, *Chile – Price Band System*, paras. 126 – 144; Appellate Body Report, *EC – Chicken Cuts*, para. 156.

[804] See, Appellate Body Report, *Chile – Price Band System*, paras. 126 - 144.

[805] In this regard, the Panel recalls that, as a general rule, panels are required to consider measures in existence at the time of establishment of the panel.

1994 exists at the time of establishment. The relevance of these observations will become apparent when we address the particular instances of alleged violation of Article X:3(a) of the GATT 1994 by the European Communities later in our report.

3. *The scope of the United States' challenge of the EC system of customs administration under Article X:3(a) of the GATT 1994*

(a) Summary of the parties' arguments

7.38 The **United States** submits that, with respect to its claim under Article X:3(a) of the GATT 1994, it is challenging the absence of uniformity in the administration of EC customs law overall.[806] The United States submits that its request for establishment of a panel indicates that its challenge under Article X:3(a) of the GATT 1994 relates to the absence of uniformity of administration of EC customs law overall and demonstrates that a challenge based on the administration of EC customs law as a whole is within the Panel's terms of reference. More specifically, the United States explains that, first, the request identifies the Community Customs Code, the Implementing Regulation and the Community Customs Tariff. In the United States' view, these are the principal elements of EC customs law as a whole. The United States further submits that, later in its request for establishment of a panel, it makes clear that the lack of uniform administration that forms the basis for the United States' complaint is "manifest in differences among member States in a number of areas, including but not limited to" those that are enumerated. According to the United States, these aspects of its request for establishment of a panel demonstrate that a challenge based on the administration of EC customs law as a whole is within the Panel's terms of reference.[807] The United States further argues that, in its various submissions, it described the problem of non-uniform administration in the European Communities in systemic terms and then described how that problem manifests itself in the three areas of tariff classification, customs valuation and customs procedures.[808]

7.39 The **European Communities** argues that the United States has refused to identify the specific aspects of EC customs administration under challenge.[809] According to the European Communities, the measure at issue in the present dispute is the administration of EC customs law in the areas specifically referred to in the United States' request for establishment of a panel, as further refined in the United States' first written submission, notably tariff classification, customs valuation, processing under customs control, local clearance procedures and penalties. The European Communities submits that these more limited terms of reference are confirmed by the title of the present dispute – "*Selected* Customs Mat-

---

806 United States' reply to Panel question No. 1.

807 United States' reply to Panel question No. 124.

808 United States' reply to Panel question No. 3.

809 European Communities' second written submission, para. 12.

ters" (emphasis added). The European Communities concludes that the United States cannot seek to include all customs matters in the Panel's terms of reference by challenging the EC customs administration system as a whole.[810] The European Communities adds that such a wide interpretation of the United States' request for establishment of a panel is not in accordance with the requirements of Article 6.2 of the DSU, which requires a sufficient identification of the specific measures at issue.[811] The European Communities submits that it cannot be expected to defend itself against nebulous charges of non-uniform administration pursuant to Article X:3(a) of the GATT 1994 in areas that the United States has not identified in its request for establishment of a panel and its first written submission.[812]

(b) Analysis by the Panel

7.40 In the context of this dispute, the Panel has been called upon to determine whether the United States is entitled to challenge the EC system of customs administration overall or as a whole as has been submitted by the United States or, rather, whether the United States is limited to making arguments with respect to the specific customs areas that have been identified in its request for establishment of a panel, as has been submitted by the European Communities.

7.41 Before addressing that specific question, the Panel would like to make some general comments regarding its terms of reference that would appear to bear upon that question.

7.42 *First*, a panel's terms of reference do not change over time and are not affected by the way in which complaining Members advance their case.[813] As we have stated previously, a panel's terms of reference are defined by the request for establishment of a panel. If a request is drafted in broad terms, the panel's terms of reference will have corresponding breadth for the duration of the time for which the panel is seized of a dispute. A complaining Member that argues its case at any point during the panel proceedings in more limited terms than those provided for in its request for establishment of a panel is not obliged to confine itself to those more limited terms for the remainder of the proceedings before the Panel.

7.43 *Second*, the title of a case has no bearing upon the scope of a Panel's terms of reference. As mentioned previously, a Panel's terms of reference are defined by the measures and the claims that have been identified in the request for establishment of a panel. Neither Article 7 of the DSU, which defines the panel's terms of reference, nor the linked requirements of Article 6.2 of the DSU,

[810] European Communities' second written submission, para. 13.

[811] European Communities' comments on the United States' reply to Panel question No. 124.

[812] European Communities' second written submission, para. 14.

[813] That is not to say, however, that a panel would be obliged to make findings and/or rulings and recommendations with respect to all the measures and claims identified in a request for establishment of a panel. On the contrary, the panel is vested with a discretion to only rule on those matters necessary to secure a positive solution to a dispute: Appellate Body Report, *US – Wool Shirts and Blouses*, p. 19.

make any reference to the title of the case.[814] Ultimately, the breadth or narrowness of a particular challenge will be governed exclusively by the terms of the relevant request for establishment of a panel.

7.44 Turning now to the specific question we have been called upon to address identified in paragraph 7.40 above, there is nothing in the DSU nor in the other WTO Agreements that would prevent a complaining Member from challenging a responding Member's system as a whole or overall. Nevertheless, if a complaining Member wishes to make such a challenge, the request for establishment of a panel in which the responding Member's system is challenged as a whole or overall must meet the requirements of Article 6.2 of the DSU. Whether or not the requirements of Article 6.2 of the DSU have been fulfilled in an individual case will depend upon the particular request for establishment of a panel and the relevant facts surrounding that case.

7.45 The United States has submitted that its challenge of the EC system of customs administration as a whole or overall is evident from two aspects of its request for establishment of a panel. *First*, it submits that the request identifies the Community Customs Code, the Implementing Regulation and the Community Customs Tariff, which it argues are the principal elements of EC customs law as a whole. In other words, the United States submits that, since it has identified what it labels as the "principal elements" of the EC system of customs administration in its request, by implication, it challenges the EC system as a whole. *Second*, the United States submits that its request makes clear that the lack of uniform administration that forms the basis of its claim under Article X:3(a) of the GATT 1994 is "manifest in differences among member States in a number of areas, *including but not limited to*" the areas specifically enumerated in the request. The United States argues that the inclusive language in its request indicates that the whole EC system of customs administration is implicated by its claim under Article X:3(a) of the GATT 1994.

7.46 In the Panel's view, pursuant to the terms of the United States' request for establishment of a panel, the United States is precluded from challenging the EC system of customs administration as a whole or overall in this dispute. The Panel is of the view that, due to the wording and content of the United States' request, the Panel's terms of reference regarding the scope of the United States' claim under Article X:3(a) of the GATT 1994 are restricted to the specific areas of customs administration referred to in such request, which are set out in paragraph 7.32 above. Our reasoning is as follows.

7.47 *First*, the Panel considers that the references by the United States in its request for establishment of a panel to the Community Customs Code, the Implementing Regulation and the Community Customs Tariff cannot be considered in isolation from the reference in that request to a number of areas of customs administration.[815] When these aspects of the United States' request for establish-

---

[814] Further, the Panel notes that the title of a dispute usually originates from the WTO Secretariat.

[815] The Panel recalls its finding in paragraph 7.33 above that the "specific measure at issue" in this dispute for the purposes of Article 6.2 of the DSU is the manner of administration by the national customs authorities of the member States of the Community Customs Code, the Implementing Regu-

ment of a panel are read together, they indicate that the United States' claim under Article X:3(a) of the GATT 1994 extends to some, but not all, areas of customs administration covered by the Community Customs Code, the Implementing Regulation and the Community Customs Tariff.

7.48 *Second*, the Panel notes that the areas of customs administration listed in the United States' request for establishment of a panel do not cover the entire spectrum of areas that comprise the totality of the EC system of customs administration. The scope of the spectrum is evident from the contents of the various measures referred to by the United States in its request – namely, the Community Customs Code, the Implementing Regulation, the Common Customs Tariff, the TARIC and other "related measures". Areas that are part of the EC system of customs administration but which have not been referred to in the United States' request include transit procedures, customs debt, inward processing, outward processing, exportation and re-exportation.[816] In the Panel's understanding, these areas of the EC system of customs administration are not insignificant in terms of frequency of usage and volume of trade affected. Therefore, their absence from the United States' request for establishment of a panel is notable and supports the Panel's finding in paragraph 7.46 above that, on the basis of its request for establishment of a panel, the United States is precluded from challenging the EC system of customs administration overall or as a whole under Article X:3(a) of the GATT 1994 in this dispute.

7.49 *Finally*, the Panel notes that the list of the areas of customs administration contained in the United States' request for establishment of a panel is preceded by the following text: "Lack of uniform, impartial and reasonable administration of the above-identified measures is manifest in differences among member States in a number of areas, *including, but not limited to, the following...*". We do not consider that the phrase "including, but not limited to" on its own has the legal effect of incorporating into the Panel's terms of reference *all* areas of customs administration in the EC system and not just those specifically identified in the United States' request. In our view, if we were to interpret that phrase as having the legal effect of including areas not specifically identified in the request, such

---

lation, the Common Customs Tariff, the TARIC and related measures in the areas of customs administration specifically identified in the United States' request for establishment of a panel. The Panel also notes that, by referring to various elements of its request for establishment of a panel in support of its argument that the request relates to the EC system of customs administration as a whole, the United States itself appears to advocate the approach that the various aspects of the "measures at issue" for the purposes of a claim under Article X:3(a) of the GATT 1994 are to be considered together: United States' reply to Panel question No. 124.

816 "Transit procedures" are governed *inter alia* by Articles 54-55, 91-97 and 163-165 of the Community Customs Code and Articles 309-495, 616-623 and 712-716 of the Implementing Regulation. "Customs debt" is governed *inter alia* by Articles 189-242 of the Community Customs Code and Articles 857-912 of the Implementing Regulation. "Inward processing" is governed by Articles 114-129 of the Community Customs Code and Articles 275-276, 538-547, 549-649 and 829-839 of the Implementing Regulation. "Outward processing" is governed *inter alia* by Articles 145-160 of the Community Customs Code and Articles 277 and 748-787 of the Implementing Regulation. "Exportation" is governed *inter alia* by Articles 161-162 of the Community Customs Code and Articles 788-798 and 843-856 of the Implementing Regulation. "Re-exportation" is governed *inter alia* by Article 182 of the Community Customs Code and Articles 841-842 of the Implementing Regulation.

interpretation would undermine an important due process objective of the requirements of Article 6.2 of the DSU – namely, to provide sufficient notice and information to the responding party and third parties to a dispute of the nature of the complainant's case.[817]

7.50 In the light of the foregoing, after having considered the United States' request for establishment of a panel as a whole, the Panel concludes that its terms of reference regarding the United States' claim under Article X:3(a) of the GATT 1994 do not include a challenge to the EC system of customs administration overall or as a whole under Article X:3(a) of the GATT 1994. Rather, as stated in paragraph 7.33 above, our terms of reference are confined to the manner of administration by the national customs authorities of the member States of the Community Customs Code, the Implementing Regulation, the Common Customs Tariff, the TARIC and related measures in the areas of customs administration specifically identified in the United States' request for establishment of a panel.

4. *The nature of the United States' challenge of the EC system of customs administration under Article X:3(a) of the GATT 1994*

(a) Summary of the parties' arguments

7.51 The **United States** submits that it challenges the design and structure of the EC system of customs administration "as such". According to the United States, while it is true that Article X:3(a) of the GATT 1994 is concerned with administration, it is possible that a system of customs administration "as such" will be in violation of Article X:3(a) of the GATT 1994 if it necessarily results in non-uniform administration.[818] The United States submits that, in the case of the EC system of customs administration, it is the absence of a critical feature from the design and structure of the European Communities' system of customs administration that necessarily results in non-uniform administration in breach of Article X:3(a) of the GATT 1994 – namely, a procedure or institution that ensures that divergences of administration among the customs authorities of the 25 member States do not occur or that promptly reconciles such divergences as a matter of course when they do occur. In the United States' view, the procedures and institutions identified by the European Communities as instrumental in achieving uniform administration in the European Communities cannot and do not result in uniform administration of EC customs law by 25 independent, regionally limited customs authorities. Rather, according to the United States, such procedures and institutions constitute a loose network within which various responses to non-uniform administration may but need not necessarily occur. The United States argues that since the EC system of customs administration lacks any procedures or institutions to ensure that divergences do not occur or, when divergences come to light, they will be reconciled promptly and as a matter of course, that system necessarily results in non-uniform administration in breach of

---

[817] Appellate Body Report, *India – Patents (US)*, para. 90.
[818] United States' reply to Panel question No. 173.

Article X:3(a) of the GATT 1994.[819] The United States submits that this structural shortcoming in the EC system results in non-uniform administration with respect to all areas of customs administration. The United States argues that, in each of these areas, the only procedures or institutions that allegedly secure uniform administration are general, non-binding, discretionary procedures and institutions, with the exception of review by national courts. However, in the United States' view, review by national courts does not secure uniform administration given the discretion that courts have in deciding whether or not to refer matters to the ECJ, the lack of an obligation on the part of the customs authority in a given member State to follow the decisions of courts in other member States, and the lack of any mechanism to inform the customs authorities in the various member States of relevant customs decisions by courts in other member States.[820]

7.52 The **European Communities** submits that the United States' request for establishment of a panel only referred to the administration of EC customs law as the measure at issue. According to the European Communities, the United States did not challenge measures of general application which constitute the EC system of customs administration. The European Communities submits that, therefore, these general measures are not within the Panel's terms of reference.[821] The European Communities also submits that, in cases where a law or regulation "mandates" a form of administration that is not uniform, reasonable, or impartial, such law or regulation could be regarded *per se* as a violation of Article X:3(a) of the GATT 1994. According to the European Communities, a law or regulation will be "mandatory" if it does not leave the authorities any possibility to administer the laws or regulations in question in a uniform, impartial, or reasonable manner.[822] However, the European Communities submits that the specific design and structure of the European Communities' system could become relevant under Article X:3(a) of the GATT 1994 only if it necessarily led to a lack of uniformity.[823] In this regard, the European Communities recalls that whether or not the EC system of customs administration ensures uniform administration must be evaluated on the basis of the system as a whole and not on the basis of individual measures considered in isolation.[824] The European Communities further submits that, whether the EC system of customs administration "as such" leads to non-uniform administration is a question of fact regarding the interpretation and application of a large body of EC municipal law. The burden of proof to establish that such municipal law is in violation of WTO obligations rests with the United States as the complainant.[825] The European Communities concludes that the United States has failed to show that there are any features in the EC system of

[819] United States' reply to Panel question No. 126(a).
[820] United States' reply to Panel question No. 126(b).
[821] European Communities' reply to Panel question No. 173.
[822] European Communities' reply to Panel question No. 154.
[823] European Communities' oral statement at the second substantive meeting, para. 44; European Communities' reply to Panel question No. 173.
[824] European Communities' oral statement at the second substantive meeting, para. 45; European Communities' comments on the United States' reply to Panel question No. 127.
[825] European Communities' reply to Panel question No. 173.

customs administration which necessarily would lead to a lack of uniformity.[826] The European Communities explains that, in the European Communities, no law mandates non-uniform administration of EC customs law.[827] On the contrary, according to the European Communities, the EC system of customs administration contains numerous, interlocking mechanisms which, together, provide a high degree of assurance for a uniform interpretation and application of EC customs law.[828]

(b) Analysis by the Panel

7.53 Another question raised for the Panel's consideration in the context of this dispute is whether the United States is entitled to challenge "as such" the EC system of customs administration. In this regard, the Panel notes that the United States has clearly submitted that it challenges the design and structure of the EC system of customs administration "as such".[829] The European Communities argues that the United States' challenge of the EC system of customs administration "as such" is outside the Panel 's terms of reference.[830]

7.54 By way of preliminary comment, the Panel notes that the United States implicitly challenges "as such" the design and structure of the EC system of customs administration *as a whole or overall.* This is evident, *inter alia*, from the fact that the United States submits that alleged structural deficiencies in the EC system necessarily result in a violation of Article X:3(a) of the GATT in *all* areas of customs administration in the European Communities.[831] The Panel recalls its findings in paragraph 7.46 *et seq* above, that the United States is precluded from challenging the EC system of customs administration as a whole or overall under Article X:3(a) of the GATT 1994 because, as previously stated, such a challenge is outside our terms of reference. Nevertheless, we also found in paragraph 7.33 above that our terms of reference authorise us to consider the manner of administration by the national customs authorities of the member States of the Community Customs Code, the Implementing Regulation, the Common Customs Tariff, the TARIC and related measures in the areas of customs administration specifically identified in the United States' request for establishment of a panel. In the light of the fact that the United States has submitted that structural deficiencies in the EC system necessarily result in a violation of Article X:3(a) of the GATT in all areas of customs administration in the European Communities, we will consider whether or not the United States is entitled to make an "as such" challenge with respect to the design and structure of the EC system in the areas of customs administration that have been specifically identified in the United States' request for establishment of a panel.

---

[826] European Communities' oral statement at the second substantive meeting, para. 64.
[827] European Communities' reply to Panel question No. 154.
[828] European Communities' oral statement at the second substantive meeting, para. 64.
[829] United States' reply to Panel question No. 173.
[830] European Communities' first written submission, para. 14; European Communities' reply to Panel question No. 173.
[831] United States' reply to Panel question No. 126(b).

7.55 The Panel notes first that a Member's *legislation* can be challenged "as such" as being in violation of a WTO obligation.[832] There also appears to be support for the view that a *system* (and, presumably, components thereof) can be challenged "as such", provided that the system comprises rules or norms that are intended to have general and prospective application.[833]

7.56 The Panel again refers to the language of the United States' request for establishment of a panel to determine whether or not our terms of reference permit consideration of an "as such" challenge with respect to the design and structure of the EC system in the areas of customs administration that have been specifically identified in the United States' request. We note in this regard that, in *US – Oil Country Tubular Goods Sunset Reviews*, the Appellate Body stated that:

> "... In our view, 'as such' challenges against a Member's measures in WTO dispute settlement proceedings are serious challenges. By definition, an 'as such' claim challenges laws, regulations, or other instruments of a Member that have general and prospective application, asserting that a Member's conduct – not only in a particular instance that has occurred, but in future situations as well – will necessarily be inconsistent with that Member's WTO obligations. In essence, complaining parties bringing 'as such' challenges seek to prevent Members *ex ante* from engaging in certain conduct. The implications of such challenges are obviously more far-reaching than 'as applied' claims.
>
> We also expect that measures subject to 'as such' challenges would normally have undergone, under municipal law, thorough scrutiny through various deliberative processes to ensure consistency with the Member's international obligations, including those found in the covered agreements, and that the enactment of such a measure would implicitly reflect the conclusion of that Member that the measure is not inconsistent with those obligations. The presumption that WTO Members act in good faith in the implementation of their WTO commitments is particularly apt in the context of measures challenged 'as such'. We would therefore urge complaining parties to be *especially diligent* in setting out 'as such' claims in their panel requests as clearly as possible. In particular, we would expect that 'as such' claims state unambiguously the specific measures of municipal law challenged by the complaining party and the legal basis for the allegation that those measures are not consistent with particular provisions of the covered agreements. Through such straightforward presentations of 'as such' claims, panel requests should leave respondent parties in little doubt that, notwithstanding their own considered views on the WTO-consistency of

---

[832] Appellate Body Report, *US – 1916 Act*, para. 75.

[833] Appellate Body Report, *US – Corrosion-Resistant Steel Sunset Review*, paras. 81-82 set out above in para. 7.15.

their measures, another Member intends to challenge those measures, as such, in WTO dispute settlement proceedings."[834]

7.57 In the present case, the Panel considers that it is not clear from the United States' request for establishment of a panel that it intended to challenge the design and structure of aspects of the EC system of customs administration "as such".

7.58 *First*, in the Panel's view, there is nothing in the text of the United States' request for establishment of a panel that could be construed as clearly suggesting that the United States' challenge under Article X:3(a) of the GATT 1994 relates to the design and structure of the EC system of customs administration.

7.59 *Second*, the request for establishment of a panel suggests that the United States is concerned with the way in which administration is undertaken by member State customs authorities rather than with the design and structure of the customs administration system at the EC level "as such". In particular, the request starts by stating that "[t]he United States considers that the *manner* in which the European Communities ('EC') administers its laws, regulations, decisions and rulings of the kind described in Article X:1 of the General Agreement on Tariffs and Trade 1994 ('GATT 1994') is not uniform, impartial and reasonable, and therefore is inconsistent with Article X:3(a) of the GATT 1994" (emphasis added). We note that the term "manner" is defined as "the way in which something is done or happens; a method of action; a mode of procedure".[835] In our view, there is nothing in the ordinary meaning of the term "manner" to suggest that it relates to the design and structure of something. Rather, the ordinary meaning of that term suggests that it relates to application in practice.

7.60 In addition, when identifying the manner of administration that is allegedly in violation of Article X:3(a) of the GATT 1994, the request places emphasis on the actions of customs authorities of the member States whereas, in contrast, there is no mention of actions taken and/or procedures and institutions existing at the EC level, including the design and structure of the EC system of customs administration. In particular, the request states that:

> "Administration of these measures in the European Communities is *carried out by the national customs authorities of EC member States*. Such administration takes numerous different forms. The United States understands that the myriad forms of administration of these measures include, but are not limited to, laws, regulations, handbooks, manuals, and administrative practices of *customs authorities of member States of the European Communities*."[836] (emphasis added)

7.61 *Third*, we recall our finding in paragraph 7.20 above that the essential aspect of Article X:3(a) of the GATT 1994 is the obligation to "administer in a uniform, impartial and reasonable manner". By challenging the design and struc-

[834] Appellate Body Report, *US – Oil Country Tubular Goods Sunset Reviews*, paras. 172-173.

[835] *The New Shorter Oxford English Dictionary*, 1993, p. 1687.

[836] WT/DS315/8, which is contained in Annex D of the Panel's report.

ture of the EC system of customs administration "as such" under Article X:3(a) of the GATT 1994, the United States is effectively arguing that the design and structure *necessarily* results in administration that is not uniform.[837] In other words, the United States is arguing that it is not challenging specific instances of administration of laws, regulations, decisions or rulings, at least, not exclusively. Rather, it is challenging the system, which is the institutional framework and context within which specific acts of administration take place. In the Panel's view, the United States' purported challenge of the design and structure of the EC system "as such" is not obviously linked to the essence of the obligation contained in Article X:3(a) of the GATT 1994 – namely, the obligation to administer in a uniform manner. In the light of the lack of obvious connection between the United States' purported challenge of the EC system of customs administration "as such" and this essential aspect of the obligation contained in Article X:3(a) of the GATT 1994, it was all the more necessary for the United States to have been clear about the nature of its challenge in its request for establishment of a panel.

7.62 *Finally*, the Panel observes that the United States' request for establishment of a panel makes no explicit reference to the terms "as such" or *per se*. The Panel considers that, generally speaking, the absence of these terms from a request for establishment of a panel, the significance of which is well understood in WTO dispute settlement parlance, would not necessarily mean that a complaining Member would be precluded from making an "as such" challenge, provided that the responding Member is in no doubt that an "as such" challenge is intended.[838] However, for the reasons referred to above, the Panel considers that the United States' request for establishment of a panel did not make clear that an "as such" challenge of the EC system of customs administration was being alleged.[839]

7.63 In the light of the foregoing factors taken in totality, the Panel concludes that, on the basis of the language and content of its request for establishment of a panel, the United States is precluded from making an "as such" challenge with respect to the design and structure of the EC system of customs administration as a whole and also with respect to the design and structure of the EC system in the areas of customs administration that have been specifically identified in the United States' request. Nevertheless, pursuant to the terms of its request for establishment of a panel, the United States is still entitled to claim that the admini-

---

[837] Indeed, the United States explicitly argues as much in its reply to Panel question No. 126(a).

[838] We recall in this regard that the panel request serves the important due process objective of notifying the parties and third parties to a dispute of the nature of the complainant's case. See paragraph 7.12 above.

[839] Additionally, the Panel notes that the United States only clearly indicated its intention to make an "as such" challenge regarding the design and structure of the EC system of customs administration at a late stage in the Panel's proceedings, in response to a question posed by the Panel following the second substantive meeting (namely, United States' reply to Panel question No. 173. See also the United States' reply to Panel question No. 126). Prior to that stage of the Panel's proceedings, the United States made no explicit mention that its challenge under Article X:3(a) of the GATT 1994 was an "as such" challenge. This tends to support the view that, in its request for establishment of a panel, the United States did not intend to challenge the EC system of customs administration "as such".

stration of the Community Customs Code, the Implementing Regulation, the Common Customs Tariff and the TARIC and related measures in the areas of customs administration specifically identified in the United States' request in particular instances is in violation of Article X:3(a) of the GATT 1994. Indeed, the United States itself submits that its claims are not confined to an "as such" challenge of the design and structure of the EC system of customs administration. The United States explains that it has demonstrated in its submissions specific examples of non-uniform administration within the context of the EC system.[840]

5. *Overall conclusions regarding the Panel's terms of reference*

7.64 The Panel concludes that, for the reasons set forth above, its terms of reference authorise the Panel to consider the manner of administration by the national customs authorities of the member States of the Community Customs Code, the Implementing Regulation, the Common Customs Tariff, the TARIC and related measures in the areas of customs administration specifically identified in the United States' request for establishment of a panel. The Panel also concludes that, based on the language and content of the Panel's terms of reference, the Panel is precluded from considering "as such" challenges of the design and structure of the EC system of customs administration as a whole and also the design and structure of the EC system in the areas of customs administration that have been specifically identified in the United States' request for establishment of a panel. However, we are authorized to examine particular cases or instances of administration of the Community Customs Code, the Implementing Regulation, the Common Customs Tariff and the TARIC and related measures in those areas of customs administration specifically identified in the United States' request, where such cases or instances have been presented and relied upon by the United States in the context of this dispute. The Panel will examine each of those cases or instances later in its report after having first considered a number of procedural issues and general matters concerning the interpretation and application of Article X:3(a) of the GATT 1994.

C. *Procedural Issues*

1. *Admissibility of certain evidence*

(a) Evidence contained in section III of the United States' oral statement at the second substantive meeting

7.65 The issue of whether certain evidence relied upon by the United States in the context of its claim under Article X:3(a) of the GATT 1994 should be admitted by the Panel was raised by the European Communities during the Panel's second substantive meeting with the parties, which took place on 22 – 23 No-

[840] United States' reply to Panel question No. 126(b).

vember 2005. In particular, on 22 November 2005, following presentation by the United States of its oral statement at that substantive meeting, the European Communities argued that evidence contained in section III of the United States' oral statement[841] constituted "new" evidence, that it was submitted too late and that, therefore, it should be found to be inadmissible by the Panel. The United States defended its reliance upon such evidence on the basis that it constituted "evidence necessary for the purposes of rebuttals" within the meaning of paragraph 12 of the Working Procedures.[842] The United States argued that, as such, the evidence had not been adduced too late.

7.66 On 23 November 2005, the Panel issued a letter to the parties indicating that it had decided to admit the evidence in question. In particular, the Panel's letter stated the following:

> "The Panel refers to a procedural issue raised orally by the European Communities on 22 November 2005 during the Panel's second substantive meeting with the parties. In particular, the European Communities argued that evidence contained in exhibits to section III of the United States' oral statement for the second substantive meeting should be considered inadmissible by the Panel because paragraph 12 of the Panel's Working Procedures prohibits the submission of 'new' factual evidence after the first substantive meeting. The United States responds that the evidence in question is not 'new'. Rather, according to the United States, it constitutes 'evidence necessary for purposes of rebuttals' within the meaning of paragraph 12 of the Working Procedures.
>
> The Panel has carefully considered the parties' arguments in light of paragraph 12 of its Working Procedures and relevant provisions of the DSU. Without concluding whether or not the evidence in question can be construed either as 'new' factual evidence or as evidence that is 'necessary for purposes of rebuttals' within the meaning of paragraph 12 of the Working Procedures, the Panel has decided to admit the evidence referred to by the United States in section III of its oral statement for the second substantive meeting. The Panel considers that it is authorized to admit the evidence on the basis of the following. Paragraph 12 of the Working Procedures provides that '[p]arties shall submit all factual evidence to the Panel no later than during the first substantive meeting, except with respect to evidence necessary for purposes of rebuttals'. Article 12.1 of the DSU authorises a panel to decide to deviate from the Working Procedures following consultation with the parties. Further, Article 11 of the DSU requires the Panel to make an objective assessment of the facts. We do not consider that we would

841 Section III of the United States' oral statement is entitled "Recent Cases Confirm That Processes EC Holds Out As Securing Uniform Administration Fail To Do So" and relates to the United States' claim under Article X:3(a) of the GATT 1994.

842 The Panel's Working Procedures for this dispute are contained in Annex E of the Panel's report.

> be abiding by our duty in Article 11 of the DSU if we were to rule as inadmissible evidence that may have a bearing on the Panel's findings in this dispute.
>
> In order to avoid any prejudice to the European Communities regarding the reference by the United States to evidence in section III of its oral statement, the Panel has decided to provide the European Communities with the right to comment on the contents of section III of the United States' oral statement for the second substantive meeting. ... The Panel reserves its right to pose questions to the United States and the European Communities regarding the contents of section III, including the evidence referred to therein and any comments made by the European Communities thereon.
>
> ...
>
> The parties should note that the decision taken by the Panel in this communication only relates to the admissibility of evidence referred to by the United States in section III of its oral statement at the second substantive meeting. The decision has no bearing on the weight, if any, that the Panel may ultimately attribute to such evidence."

7.67 The Panel granted the European Communities a period of three weeks within which to provide its comments, commencing on the date the United States made its oral statement at the second substantive meeting in which it referred to the evidence in question.[843] Specifically, the European Communities was granted until 14 December 2005 to provide its comments. In its comments, the European Communities acknowledged that the working procedures contained in Appendix 3 of the DSU do not establish specific time limits for the presentation of evidence.[844] The European Communities also acknowledged that the Panel may, in consultation with the parties to the dispute, adopt more specific procedures than those contained in Appendix 3 of the DSU and/or may also amend the procedures in consultation with the parties.[845] The European Communities argued that, nevertheless, the submission by the United States of "new" factual evidence was not in accordance with the requirements of due process and procedural fairness, as reflected in paragraph 12 of the Panel's Working Procedures.[846] More specifically, the European Communities argued that the United States had not demonstrated any good cause for the late submission of the evidence, asserting that the United States had abstained from filing supporting evidence in its previous submissions and noting that the evidence referred to in section III of the United

[843] The Panel provided the European Communities with the opportunity to comment through a question posed by the Panel to the European Communities at the conclusion of the Panel's second substantive meeting with the parties. In particular, in Panel question No. 172, the Panel requested the European Communities to comment on section III of the United States' oral statement at the second substantive meeting, including any exhibits referred to in that section.

[844] European Communities' reply to Panel question No. 172, para. 6.

[845] *Ibid.*

[846] European Communities' reply to Panel question No. 172, para. 9.

States' oral statement dated back several years.[847] The European Communities further submitted that the Panel's decision to grant it additional time to comment on section III did not address its due process concerns because it was required to present a third submission containing comments on section III of the United States' oral statement at the second substantive meeting in parallel to replying to the Panel's questions following the second substantive meeting and providing comments on the United States' replies to those questions.[848]

7.68 On 15 December 2005, following receipt of the European Communities' comments, the Panel sent the parties a supplementary list of questions regarding section III of the United States' oral statement at the second substantive meeting and the European Communities' comments thereon. One of those questions requested the United States to explain why it had not referred to the evidence contained in section III prior to the Panel's second substantive meeting with the parties. In response, the United States submitted that it only became aware of that evidence through a presentation made on 27 October 2005[849] – that is, after the United States' second written submission had been filed. The United States submitted that, in any event, the illustrative cases referred to in that presentation, which were subsequently relied upon by the United States in section III of its oral statement at the second substantive meeting, rebutted the European Communities' contention during the first stage of the Panel's proceedings that the United States was basing its claims on theoretical scenarios. The United States further submitted that that evidence highlighted issues that had been developed during earlier stages of this dispute and it also involved relatively recent events. The United States submitted that, therefore, the evidence in question fell within the scope of paragraph 12 of the Panel's Working Procedures.[850]

7.69 As noted in paragraph 7.66 above, the Panel decided on 23 November 2005 to admit the evidence contained in section III of the United States' oral statement at the second substantive meeting. Given that the parties have made additional comments concerning the admissibility of such evidence since that decision was taken, the Panel considers it necessary to affirm the decision to admit that evidence. The Panel does not consider it necessary to decide whether the evidence in question amounts to "new" factual evidence as submitted by the European Communities or evidence that is "necessary for purposes of rebuttals" within the meaning of paragraph 12 of the Working Procedures as submitted by the United States. We hold this view because, as explained in our letter of 23 November 2005, regardless of the way in which that evidence is characterized, we have the authority to admit it pursuant to Article 12.1 of the DSU and paragraph 12 of the Working Procedures.

7.70 In any case, the Panel feels compelled to admit the evidence contained in section III of the United States' oral statement at the second substantive meeting

---

[847] European Communities' reply to Panel question No. 172, paras. 12-13.

[848] European Communities' reply to Panel question No. 172, para. 15.

[849] Philippe De Baere, "Coping with customs in the EU: The uniformity challenge: Judicial review of customs decisions and implementing legislation", PowerPoint Presentation at ABA International Law Section, 27 October 2005 (Exhibit US-59).

[850] United States' reply to Panel question No. 177.

in the light of Article 11 of the DSU. Under that Article, we are obliged to make an objective assessment of, *inter alia*, the facts of the case. As stated in our letter of 23 November 2005, we would not be abiding by our duty in Article 11 if we were to ignore evidence that may have a bearing on our findings in this dispute. Furthermore, even if the evidence in question could be construed as "new" evidence, the Panel provided the European Communities with a period of three weeks to comment on that evidence, commencing on the date the evidence in question was referred to by the United States. The period of three weeks was discussed and agreed upon by the Panel and the parties at the second substantive meeting.[851] At that time, the European Communities did not indicate to the Panel that that period would be insufficient to allow it to fully respond to the arguments made and evidence adduced in section III of the United States' oral statement.

(b) Evidence relied upon by the United States in sections of its oral statement at the second substantive meeting other than that contained in section III

7.71 In its comments on section III of the United States' oral statement at the second substantive meeting, which were filed on 14 December 2005, the European Communities referred to "additional" evidence relied upon by the United States in sections of its oral statement at the second substantive meeting other than that contained in section III.[852] With respect to such "additional" evidence, the European Communities stated that "it is not clear why this evidence has not been presented in earlier submissions"[853]. In its supplementary list of questions regarding section III of the United States' oral statement at the second substantive meeting sent to the parties on 15 December 2005, the Panel requested the European Communities to clearly identify the "additional" evidence it was referring to in the cited comment.[854] In response, the European Communities referred to the evidence contained in Exhibits US-73[855], US-74[856], US-75[857], US-76[858], US-77[859], US-78[860], US-79[861] and US-80.[862]

[851] In particular, this period was agreed upon during the closing phase of the Panel's second substantive meeting with the parties.

[852] European Communities' reply to Panel question No. 172, para. 15.

[853] European Communities' reply to Panel question No. 172, para. 11.

[854] Panel question No. 182.

[855] European Commission, *External and intra-European Union trade*, pp. 94-95, September 2005.

[856] Edwin A. Vermulst, *EC Customs Classification Rules: Should Ice Cream Melt?*, 15 Mich. J. Int'l L. 1241, pp. 1314-15, 1994.

[857] Letter from Mark MacGann, Director General, EICTA, to Manuel Arnal Monreal, Director International Affairs and Tariff Matters, European Commission, 2 September 2005.

[858] HM Customs & Excise, Tariff Notice 13/04.

[859] Douanerechten. Indeligen van bepaalde LCD monitoren in de gecombineerde nomenclatuur, No. CPP2005/1372M, 8 July 2005 (original and unofficial English translation).

[860] BTI DEM/2975/05-1 (start date of validity 19 July 2005).

[861] Affidavit of Mark R. Berman, President and Chief Executive Officer of Rockland Industries, Inc., 10 November 2005.

7.72 The Panel has decided to admit what the European Communities describes as "additional" evidence contained in sections of the United States' oral statement at the second substantive meeting other than section III. Our reasoning is as follows.

7.73 *First*, when the European Communities raised the issue of the admissibility of the "additional" evidence, it did not clearly and specifically request the Panel to reject such evidence on the ground that it constituted "new" evidence.[863] Rather, the European Communities merely noted that the Panel's decision of 23 November 2005 to admit certain evidence only related to section III, but not to "additional evidence referred to in other parts" of the United States' oral statement made at the second substantive meeting.[864] Further, the European Communities merely questioned why the evidence had not been submitted earlier without explicitly requesting its rejection.

7.74 *Second*, even if the European Communities' comments regarding the "additional" evidence could be construed as a request to the Panel to reject that evidence on the ground that it constitutes "new" evidence, the Panel considers that the European Communities did not raise its objections to such evidence early enough so as to allow the Panel to seek the United States' response, if the Panel were to have considered it necessary. In this regard, the Panel notes that, at the second substantive meeting, the European Communities did not raise any concerns regarding the admissibility of evidence contained in sections of the United States' oral statement other than section III. Nor did the European Communities raise any concerns immediately thereafter. The first mention of the European Communities' apparent concerns regarding the admissibility of such evidence was made in its comments on the evidence contained in section III of the United States' oral statement, three weeks after the point in time when the so-called "additional" evidence was referred to by the United States at the second substantive meeting. We consider that the European Communities should have raised its concerns regarding the evidence other than that contained in section III earlier, rather than at a stage when only one step remained before closure of the Panel's factual record.[865]

---

862 Treaty of Nice, Amending the Treaty on European Union, the Treaties Establishing the European Communities, and Certain Related Acts, reprinted in *Official Journal of the European Communities*, pp. C80/22 to C80/24 & C80/80, 10 March 2001.

863 In contrast, when referring to the evidence contained in section III of the United States' oral statement at the second substantive meeting, the European Communities clearly stated that such evidence constituted "new evidence". See, for example, European Communities' reply to Panel question No. 172, para. 10. Further, the European Communities alleged that there was no good cause for the late submission of evidence contained in section III of the United States' oral statement at the second substantive meeting but made no reference to evidence contained in other sections of the United States' oral statement in making this allegation: European Communities' reply to Panel question No. 172, para. 12.

864 European Communities' reply to Panel question No. 172, para. 15.

865 In light of the European Communities' objections to the evidence contained in section III of the United States' oral statement made at the second substantive meeting, the Panel and the parties agreed upon the steps that would occur to take account of those objections. The first step entailed the European Communities making comments on evidence contained in section III of the United States' oral statement, which comments were received on 14 December 2005. The final step entailed responding

7.75 *Finally*, the Panel recalls that, under Article 11 of the DSU, the Panel is obliged to make an objective assessment of, *inter alia*, the facts of the case. We consider that, pursuant to that Article, we are authorized to have regard to the evidence contained in Exhibits US-73, US-74, US-75, US-76, US-77, US-78, US-79 and US-80 because it may have a bearing on our findings in this dispute regarding the United States' claim under Article X:3(a) of the GATT 1994.

(c) Summary and conclusions

7.76 In summary, the Panel considers that, for the reasons set forth above, the evidence contained in the United States' oral statement at the second substantive meeting, including but not limited to that contained in section III of the statement, is admissible. The Panel considers that it is authorized to admit such evidence pursuant to Article 12.1 of the DSU and paragraph 12 of the Working Procedures. Furthermore, the Panel is of the view that the admission of such evidence is necessary in the light of the Panel's obligation under Article 11 of the DSU to make an objective assessment of, *inter alia*, the facts of the case. The Panel also considers that, with respect to the evidence contained in section III of the United States' oral statement at the second substantive meeting, it ensured the preservation of the due process rights of the European Communities by providing the European Communities with an opportunity to comment on the evidence in question within what the Panel considers to be a reasonable amount of time.[866]

2. *Requests by the United States that the Panel exercise its discretion under Article 13 of the DSU*

7.77 As previously noted, in this dispute the United States makes claims, *inter alia*, under Article X:3(a) of the GATT 1994. Specifically, the United States claims that the administration of EC customs law is not uniform and is, therefore, in violation of Article X:3(a) of the GATT 1994. Following the Panel's first substantive meeting with the parties, the Panel posed a number of questions to the United States requesting it to provide all relevant statistical evidence and/or other information to demonstrate the incidence of non-uniform administration with respect to tariff classification[867], customs valuation[868] and customs procedures[869] in the context of the overall administration of the EC customs regime. In response to the Panel's questions regarding tariff classification and customs valuation, the United States first argued that the information sought by the Panel was not needed to reach the conclusion that the European Communities is not in

---

to the Panel's questions on section III of the United States' oral statement at the second substantive meeting and the European Communities' comments thereon. The Panel's questions were sent to the parties on 15 December 2005 and the parties' replies were received on 22 December 2005.

[866] In addition, the Panel notes that it received a letter dated 21 December 2005, entitled "DS315 Amicus Curiae". By letter dated 9 January 2006, the Panel informed the parties to this dispute of its decision not to admit the letter as part of the Panel's record because, *inter alia*, it was filed too late and its admission would have unduly delayed the Panel's proceedings.

[867] Panel question No. 16.

[868] Panel question No. 24.

[869] Panel question No. 33.

compliance with its obligation of uniform administration under Article X:3(a) of the GATT 1994. In the alternative, the United States requested the Panel to exercise its discretion under Article 13 of the DSU because the European Communities, rather than the United States, was likely to have the information sought.

7.78 Article 13 of the DSU provides that:

> "1. Each panel shall have the right to seek information and technical advice from any individual or body which it deems appropriate. However, before a panel seeks such information or advice from any individual or body within the jurisdiction of a Member it shall inform the authorities of that Member. A Member should respond promptly and fully to any request by a panel for such information as the panel considers necessary and appropriate. Confidential information which is provided shall not be revealed without formal authorization from the individual, body, or authorities of the Member providing the information.
>
> 2. Panels may seek information from any relevant source and may consult experts to obtain their opinion on certain aspects of the matter. With respect to a factual issue concerning a scientific or other technical matter raised by a party to a dispute, a panel may request an advisory report in writing from an expert review group. Rules for the establishment of such a group and its procedures are set forth in Appendix 4."

7.79 In the area of *tariff classification*, the United States requested the Panel to seek from the European Communities a statistically significant sample of binding tariff information ("BTI") and other classification decisions from various member States in order to determine the frequency of divergent administration in that area pursuant to Article 13 of the DSU.[870] Additionally, the United States requested the Panel to seek a copy of a 2003 study to which reference had been made in the European Communities' draft Modernized Customs Code.[871] The United States submitted that it had requested a copy of that study during consultations with the European Communities for this dispute but that the European Communities refused to provide it. In making its request that the Panel exercise its discretion under Article 13 of the DSU regarding the study referred to in the draft Modernized Customs Code, the United States submitted that the Panel should draw an adverse inference should the European Communities refuse to provide it.[872]

[870] United States' reply to Panel question No. 16.

[871] United States' reply to Panel question No. 16. The draft Modernized Customs Code (European Commission, Directorate-General for Taxation and Customs Union, TAXUD/458/2004 – Rev 4, *Draft Modernized Customs Code*, 11 November 2004) is contained in Exhibit US-33. The study to which the United States refers is mentioned on page 4 of Exhibit US-33. In particular, the draft Modernized Customs Code refers to "[a]n external study in 2003 [which] has allowed the Commission to gain a clearer understanding of the current situation in the Member States and of the potential costs and benefits".

[872] United States' reply to Panel question No. 16.

7.80 In the *customs valuation* area, the United States requested the Panel to seek information from the European Communities of the type that enabled the EC Court of Auditors to make the findings contained in its report on customs valuation, Special Report No. 23/2000 pursuant to Article 13 of the DSU.[873] In this regard, the United States noted that, in evaluating the incidence of non-uniform administration with respect to valuation rules, the EC Court of Auditors had had access to "documents handled in the Customs Valuation Committee, customs authority valuation audit files, written valuation rulings, decisions of appeal tribunals and the actual customs declarations" for more than 200 companies and groups of companies.[874]

7.81 In response, the European Communities submitted that the United States' requests that the Panel exercise its discretion pursuant to Article 13 of the DSU should be rejected because they amounted to an attempt by the United States to rid itself of its burden to make a prima facie case and, therefore, went considerably beyond the functions of a panel under Article 13 of the DSU. The European Communities also submitted that it is not credible for the United States to claim, on the one hand, that there is widespread non-uniform administration of EC customs law in violation of Article X:3(a) of the GATT 1994, but that it does not have any evidence to support this claim, and that the European Communities should provide the information requested.[875] In response specifically to the United States' request concerning the EC Court of Auditors report, the European Communities submitted that it would not be practicable to comply if the Panel were to make such a request. According to the European Communities, the EC Court of Auditors' Special Report No. 23/2000 was based on audit visits that took place on the premises of the Commission and the customs administrations of 12 member States in 1999 – 2000.[876] The European Communities submitted that, whatever information the EC Court of Auditors may have collected at that time is in the possession of the EC Court of Auditors only. In addition, such information would reflect the situation in 1999 – 2000, but not the situation today.[877]

7.82 At the second substantive meeting with the parties, the Panel stated that, at that stage, it did not intend to exercise its discretion under Article 13 of the DSU. The Panel noted that, when the United States made its requests that the Panel exercise its discretion pursuant to Article 13 of the DSU, the United States submitted that it "does not believe that the [requested] information at issue is

[873] United States' reply to Panel question No. 24 referring to Court of Auditors, Special Report No. 23/2000 concerning valuation of imported goods for customs purposes (customs valuation), together with the Commission's replies, 14 March 2001 contained in Exhibit US-14.

[874] United States' reply to Panel question No. 24 referring to Court of Auditors, Special Report No. 23/2000 concerning valuation of imported goods for customs purposes (customs valuation), together with the Commission's replies, 14 March 2001, para. 10 (Exhibit US-14).

[875] European Communities' second written submission, paras. 48-50.

[876] Court of Auditors, Special Report No 23/2000 concerning valuation of imported goods for customs purposes (customs valuation), together with the Commission's replies, 14 March 2001, paras. 9-10 (Exhibit US-14).

[877] European Communities' second written submission, para. 155.

necessary for the Panel to find that the EC is not in compliance with its obligation of uniform administration".[878]

7.83 The Panel affirms the decision it took at the second substantive meeting not to exercise its discretion under Article 13 of the DSU because, since the Panel took that decision, the United States has not made any additional arguments to the effect that the requested information is necessary. In fact, the United States has repeatedly submitted to the Panel, both before the second substantive meeting and subsequently, that it has proved that the European Communities is in violation of Article X:3(a) of the GATT 1994[879], even in the absence of the evidence it requests pursuant to Article 13 of the DSU. Accordingly, since the United States – being the party that requested the Panel to exercise its discretion under Article 13 of the DSU – does not consider that the information it suggests should be sought from the European Communities is necessary for the Panel to find that the European Communities is not in compliance with its obligation under Article X:3(a) of the GATT 1994, the Panel does not see any compelling reason to exercise its discretion under Article 13 of the DSU to request that information. The Panel's decision not to exercise its discretion under Article 13 of the DSU dispenses with the need to address the United States' argument that adverse inferences should be drawn if the European Communities were to have refused to provide a copy of the study referred to in the draft Modernized Customs Code despite a request by the Panel for its production.[880]

D. Claims under Article x:3(a) of the GATT 1994

1. Article X:3(a) of the GATT 1994

7.84 Article X:3(a) of the GATT 1994 provides that:

> "Each contracting party shall administer in a uniform, impartial and reasonable manner all its laws, regulations, decisions and rulings of the kind described in paragraph 1 of this Article."

2. Findings requested by the United States under Article X:3(a) of the GATT 1994

(a) Summary of the parties' arguments

7.85 The **United States** submits that, with respect to its claim under Article X:3(a) of the GATT 1994, it is exclusively concerned with the requirement of "uniform" administration.[881] The United States notes that the principal finding it is asking the Panel to make is that the EC system of customs administration as a whole is inconsistent with the obligation of uniform administration under Arti-

---

[878] United States' replies to Panel question Nos. 16, 24 and 33.

[879] United States' reply to Panel question Nos. 16, 24, 33, 124, 126(b), 173 and 179; United States' oral statement at the second substantive meeting, paras. 4 and 6; United States' comments on the European Communities' reply to Panel question No. 173.

[880] United States' reply to Panel question No. 16.

[881] United States' first written submission, footnote 15.

cle X:3(a) of the GATT 1994. The United States considers that such a finding does not preclude findings of non-uniform administration regarding the specific areas of customs administration to which it has referred in its submissions to substantiate its claim of violation of Article X:3(a) of the GATT 1994 by the European Communities. According to the United States, while findings on specific areas of customs administration in the European Communities are not necessary to make the finding requested with respect to the EC system of customs administration as a whole, they would tend to support the finding requested by the United States that the EC system overall is in violation of Article X:3(a) of the GATT 1994.[882]

7.86 The United States submits that the evidence it has presented supports subsidiary findings that the European Communities fails to meet its obligation of uniform administration under Article X:3(a) of the GATT 1994 with respect to administration:

(a) in the area of tariff classification, of the Common Customs Tariff;

(b) in the area of customs valuation, of:

(i) Article 32(1)(c) of the Community Customs Code regarding the treatment of royalty payments for customs valuation purposes;

(ii) Article 147 of the Implementing Regulation regarding customs valuation on a basis other than the last sale that led to the introduction of a good into the customs territory of the European Communities;

(iii) Article 29 of the Community Customs Code and Article 143(1)(e) of the Implementing Regulation regarding circumstances under which parties are to be treated as "related" for customs valuation purposes;

(c) in the area of customs procedures, of:

(i) the valuation provisions contained in the Community Customs Code (Articles 28 – 36) and the Implementing Regulation (Articles 141 – 181a and Annexes 23 –29), to the extent that different member State authorities employ different audit procedures with respect to products following their release for free circulation[883];

(ii) all classification and valuation provisions in the Common Customs Tariff, the Community Customs Code and the Implementing Regulation, to the extent that different member State authorities have at their disposal different penalties to ensure compliance with those provisions;

---

882 United States' reply to Panel question No. 124.

883 The United States made it clear that its allegations concerning audit procedures related to products following their release for free circulation in United States' first written submission, para. 96 and the United States' reply to Panel question No. 28.

(iii) Article 133 of the Community Customs Code and Articles 502(3) and 552 of the Implementing Regulation regarding assessment of the economic conditions for allowing processing under customs control;

(iv) Articles 263-267 of the Implementing Regulation regarding local clearance procedures; and

(d) Article 221 of the Community Customs Code regarding the period following the incurrence of a customs debt during which liability for the debt may be communicated to the debtor and the suspension of that period during the pendency of an appeal.[884]

7.87 The United States notes that it is challenging non-uniformity in the administration of EC customs law under Article X:3(a) of the GATT 1994. According to the United States, that law is administered principally by authorities located in each of the European Communities' 25 member States. The United States notes that, therefore, it is the administration of EC customs law by the authorities located in each of the 25 member States that is the focus of the United States' claim under Article X:3(a) of the GATT 1994. However, the United States also notes that decisions and actions taken by the EC Commission and other EC institutions play a role in the administration of EC customs law. In particular, the United States submits that they are relevant to the United States' claim under Article X:3(a) of the GATT 1994 inasmuch as such institutions do not step in to ensure uniform administration among the customs authorities located throughout the territory of the European Communities.[885]

7.88 In response, regarding the United States' claim that it is challenging the administration of the EC system of customs administration as a whole, the **European Communities** submits that such a wide interpretation of the United States' request for establishment of a panel is not in accordance with the requirements of Article 6.2 of the DSU, which requires identification of the specific measures at issue. The European Communities also submits that the Panel's terms of reference regarding the United States' claim under Article X:3(a) of the GATT 1994 only cover the areas of customs administration specifically enumerated in the United States' request for establishment of a panel.

(b) Analysis by the Panel

7.89 During the course of the Panel's proceedings, the United States requested the Panel to make a finding that the EC system of customs administration as a whole is inconsistent with Article X:3(a) of the GATT 1994. The United States also requested the Panel to make "subsidiary" findings regarding the specific areas of customs administration to which the United States has referred in its submissions to substantiate its claim of violation of Article X:3(a) of the GATT 1994 by the European Communities. Finally, the United States requests findings regarding administration of EC customs law by customs authorities in the 25

[884] United States' replies to Panel question Nos. 124 and 179.

[885] United States' reply to Panel question No. 125.

member States of the European Communities but notes that decisions and actions taken by the EC Commission and other EC institutions may be relevant to the Panel's findings to the extent that those institutions do not intervene to ensure uniform administration among the 25 member States.[886]

7.90 The Panel recalls that its terms of reference in this dispute are governed by the United States' request for establishment of a panel. The Panel is only authorized to make findings, conclusions and recommendations with respect to matters within its terms of reference.

7.91 Regarding the United States' request for a finding that the EC system of customs administration as a whole is inconsistent with Article X:3(a) of the GATT 1994, the Panel refers to its finding in paragraph 7.50 above that the United States' challenge of the EC system of customs administration as a whole or overall is outside the Panel's terms of reference. Accordingly, the Panel is not authorized to make any findings, conclusions and recommendations regarding the EC system of customs administration as a whole.

7.92 With respect to the United States' request for "subsidiary" findings in respect of particular areas of customs administration, the Panel recalls its finding in paragraph 7.33 above that its terms of reference relate to the manner of administration of the Community Customs Code, the Implementing Regulation, the Common Customs Tariff, the TARIC and related measures in the areas of customs administration specifically identified in the United States' request for establishment of a panel – namely, the classification and valuation of goods, procedures for the classification and valuation of goods, procedures for the entry and release of goods, procedures for auditing entry statements after goods are released into free circulation, penalties and procedures regarding the imposition of penalties for violation of customs rules and record-keeping requirements. Therefore, the Panel is authorized to make findings with respect to the manner of administration of the Community Customs Code, the Implementing Regulation, the Common Customs Tariff, the TARIC and related measures with respect to the areas of customs administration specifically identified in the United States' request for establishment of a panel.

7.93 We recall our finding in paragraph 7.63 above that the United States is precluded from making an "as such" challenge with respect to the design and structure of the EC system in the areas of customs administration that have been specifically identified in the United States' request for establishment of a panel. Nevertheless, as previously stated, we are authorized to make findings with respect to particular instances of alleged violations of Article X:3(a) of the GATT 1994 regarding the administration of the Community Customs Code, the Implementing Regulation, the Common Customs Tariff and the TARIC and related measures in the areas of customs administration specifically identified in the United States' request. Accordingly, in the succeeding section of our report, we will address the particular instances of alleged violations of Article X:3(a) of the GATT 1994.

---

886 United States' replies to Panel question Nos. 124 and 125.

3. *Interpretation of Article X:3(a) of the GATT 1994*

7.94 Before considering the particular instances of violation of Article X:3(a) of the GATT 1994 alleged by the United States, the Panel will first explain its interpretation of the relevant terms of Article X:3(a) of the GATT 1994.

(a) Interpretation of "administer"

(i) Summary of the parties' arguments

Ordinary meaning

7.95 The **United States** submits that the ordinary meaning of "administer" that is relevant to the use of that term in Article X:3(a) of the GATT 1994 is to "carry on or execute (an office, affairs, etc.)".[887] The United States submits that a Member does not administer its law in a uniform manner if identical products or identical transactions receive different treatment in different geographical regions and the Member provides no mechanism for the systematic reconciliation of such differences.[888] The United States explains that, by its reference to "treatment" in this context, it means the application to a particular good or a particular transaction of laws, regulations, decisions and rulings of the kind described in Article X:1 of the GATT 1994. For example, according to the United States, when a customs authority applies a measure of general application – such as a classification rule of interpretation – to a particular good and thereby determines the good's classification and the corresponding duty owed, it accords "treatment" to that good.[889]

7.96 The **European Communities** submits that the term "administer" relates to the execution of something. In the case of Article X:3(a) of the GATT 1994, "administration" relates to the laws, regulations, decision and rulings of general application referred to in Article X:1 of the GATT 1994. In other words, in the context of Article X:3(a) of the GATT 1994, to "administer" means to execute general laws and regulations, i.e. to apply them in concrete cases. The European Communities submits that this interpretation is confirmed by the French and Spanish texts, which use the terms "appliquera" and "aplicará", both of which can be translated as "shall apply". Therefore, according to the European Communities, the French and Spanish texts confirm that Article X:3(a) of the GATT 1994 is concerned with the application of the general laws and regulations referred to in Article X:1 of the GATT 1994.[890] The European Communities further submits that Article X:3(a) of the GATT 1994 exists to provide certain minimum standards of predictability for traders. Accordingly, Article X:3(a) of the GATT 1994 is primarily concerned with the administrative outcomes affecting traders, and not with laws and procedures as such. The European Communities submits that, only to the extent that a particular procedure results necessarily

---

[887] United States' first written submission, para. 34 referring to *The New Shorter Oxford English Dictionary*, 1993, p. 28 (Exhibit US-3).

[888] United States' first written submission, para. 20.

[889] United States' reply to Panel question No. 7.

[890] European Communities' reply to Panel question No. 109.

and inevitably in a violation of Article X:3(a) of the GATT 1994, could such a procedure itself be said to be in violation of this provision.[891]

Substance versus administration

7.97 Referring to comments made by the Appellate Body in *EC – Bananas III*, the **European Communities** submits that the requirements of Article X:3(a) of the GATT 1994 do not concern the customs laws themselves, but only the administration of those laws.[892] According to the European Communities, this means that Article X:3(a) of the GATT 1994 does not require harmonization of laws within a Member where, for instance, different legal regimes are applicable within different parts of the territory of a WTO Member.[893]

7.98 In response, the **United States** submits that the line the European Communities draws between substance and administration would render Article X:3(a) of the GATT 1994 meaningless. The United States argues more specifically that, by characterizing all laws, regulations, and rules pertaining to customs matters as substantive measures, the European Communities would put all laws, regulations and rules that are instruments of customs administration beyond the reach of the disciplines Members have agreed to in Article X:3 of the GATT 1994.[894]

Forms of administration

7.99 The **United States** submits that Article X:3(a) of the GATT 1994 requires uniformity of administration and is indifferent to the various forms that administration may take.[895] The United States submits that Article X:3(a) of the GATT 1994 applies to administrative procedures applicable to traders, such as penalty and audit procedures, inasmuch as those procedures evidence non-uniform administration of laws, regulations, decisions, and rulings of the type described in Article X:1 of the GATT 1994.[896] According to the United States, Article X:3(a) of the GATT 1994 also applies to substantive decisions and the results of administrative processes that affect traders, such as particular decisions with respect to classification and valuation.[897] The United States submits that any decision by a member State customs authority that applies a measure of general application to a particular good or transaction may amount to "administration" within the meaning of Article X:3(a) of the GATT 1994. Where substantive decisions differ from one member State to another, this is evidence of a lack of uniform administration of the laws at issue.[898]

---

[891] European Communities' reply to Panel question No. 94.

[892] European Communities' first written submission, para. 216 referring to Appellate Body Report, *EC – Bananas III*, para. 200.

[893] European Communities' first written submission, para. 217.

[894] United States' oral statement at the first substantive meeting, para. 23.

[895] United States' replies to Panel question Nos. 93 and 94.

[896] United States' reply to Panel question No. 90.

[897] United States' reply to Panel question No. 94.

[898] United States' reply to Panel question No. 12.

7.100 The United States further submits that customs laws may be administered through instruments which are themselves laws.[899] In the United States' view, the laws, regulations, judicial decisions and administrative rulings of general application referred to in Article X:1 of the GATT 1994 are the objects of administration under Article X:3(a) of the GATT 1994. That is, they are the measures being administered. According to the United States, in principle, any of these measures is capable of being administered through tools that are themselves laws, regulations or other measures.[900] The United States submits that such tools which take the form of laws, regulations or other measures and which are administrative in nature are examined under Article X:3(a) of the GATT 1994 for their substance. In contrast, administration which takes the form of laws, regulations or other measures that are not administrative in nature is examined under Article X:3(a) of the GATT 1994 not for their substance but to see whether they are being administered in a uniform manner.[901] The United States explains that, where the substance of measures that administer customs laws differs from region to region, logically, administration of the customs laws is non-uniform in violation of Article X:3(a) of the GATT 1994.[902]

7.101 The **European Communities** recalls that the term to "administer" in Article X:3(a) of the GATT 1994 is defined as to "execute" or to "apply", which means that Article X:3(a) of the GATT 1994 applies to the execution in concrete cases of the laws, regulations, decisions and rulings of general application referred to in Article X:1 of the GATT 1994. According to the European Communities, a law is itself of general application, and itself needs to be executed or applied. Accordingly, it cannot be said that such a law "executes" or "applies" another law. The European Communities submits that arguing that a law can itself constitute "administration" of a law would undermine the clear distinction between the administration of laws and the laws themselves.[903] The European Communities adds that, since the laws, regulations, judicial decisions and administrative rulings referred to in Article X of the GATT 1994 all have in common that they must be "of general application", they cannot be said to be executed or applied by another law which is equally of general application.[904]

(ii) Analysis by the Panel

7.102 The United States' claim under Article X:3(a) of the GATT 1994 raises the question of the scope of the term "administer" in that Article. Some particular questions the Panel has been called upon to address in the context of this dispute are: Does the term "administer" relate to the application of laws, regulations, decisions and rulings in particular cases? If so, does it concern the manner in which administrative processes are conducted? Does it also extend to the substantive results of those processes? Does the term "administer" cover measures

899 United States' oral statement at the first substantive meeting, para. 21.
900 United States' reply to Panel question No. 93.
901 United States' reply to Panel question No. 90.
902 United States' reply to Panel question No. 133.
903 European Communities' reply to Panel question No. 93(a).
904 European Communities' reply to Panel question No. 93(b).

that are themselves in the form of laws and regulations? In interpreting Article X:3(a) of the GATT 1994 to address these questions, among others, the Panel will undertake its analysis pursuant to Articles 31 and 32 of the *Vienna Convention on the Law of Treaties (Vienna Convention)*.

Ordinary meaning

7.103 Article 31(1) of the *Vienna Convention* indicates that a treaty provision must be interpreted in accordance with its *ordinary meaning*. Regarding the ordinary meaning of the term "administer", the verb is defined as to "carry on or execute (an office, affairs etc.)" and to "execute or dispense (justice)"[905]. In turn, the term "execute" is defined as "carry out, put into effect (a plan, purpose, command, sentence, law, will)".[906] The noun "administration" is defined as "the action of administering something (a sacrament, justice, remedies, an oath etc.) to another" and "the management of public affairs; government"[907].

7.104 The definition of the term "administer" when read in conjunction with the definition of the term "execute" suggests that, in the context of Article X:3(a) of the GATT 1994, "administer" refers to any action that puts into practical effect the relevant laws, regulations, decisions and/or rulings of the kind described in Article X:1 of the GATT 1994. In the Panel's view, this indicates that the term covers the *application* of laws, regulations, decisions and rulings in particular cases because the application of a law etc. in a particular case necessarily involves giving practical effect to that law etc.

7.105 In the Panel's view, the application of a law in a particular case encompasses the *administrative process*[908] entailed in that application, because the administrative process represents the series of steps, actions or events that are taken or occur in pursuance of what is required by the law in question. In addition, we consider that the application of a law in a particular case encompasses the *results of administrative processes*. We hold this view because the results of administrative processes are the final manifestation of the application of a law in a particular case. Furthermore, the results of administrative processes are, by definition, the product of administrative processes which, as we have already said, would seem to fall within the scope of the ordinary meaning of the term "administer".

7.106 However, the Panel notes that there would appear to be nothing in the ordinary meaning of the term "administer" that would suggest that it covers *laws and regulations as such*. On the contrary, the relevant dictionary definitions indicate that the term "administer" refers to positive action or steps taken to put into effect measures such as laws and regulations, but not the laws and regulations

---

[905] *The New Shorter Oxford English Dictionary*, 1993, p. 28.

[906] *The New Shorter Oxford English Dictionary*, 1993, p. 877.

[907] *The New Shorter Oxford English Dictionary*, 1993, p. 28.

[908] In this regard, we note that the term "process" is defined, *inter alia*, as a continuous series of actions, events or changes; a course of action, a procedure; esp. a continuous and regular action or succession of actions occurring or performed in a definite manner: *The New Shorter Oxford English Dictionary*, 1993, p. 2364.

themselves, which merely exist without effect until they are actually applied in practice.

Context

7.107 Article 31(1) of the *Vienna Convention* indicates that a treaty provision must be interpreted in its *context.* As for the relevant context for the interpretation of Article X:3(a) of the GATT 1994, notably, it is contained in Article X of the GATT 1994, which is entitled "Publication and Administration of Trade Regulations". The title as well as the content of the various provisions of Article X of the GATT 1994 indicate that that Article, at least in part, is aimed at ensuring that due process is accorded to traders when they import or export. In this regard, we note that Article X:1 of the GATT 1994 requires that customs laws, regulations etc. should be published "in such a manner as to enable governments and traders to become acquainted with them". Article X:2 of the GATT 1994 prohibits the enforcement of a customs law "before such measure has been officially published". Article X:3(b) of the GATT 1994 requires the establishment of bodies or procedures for the "review and correction of administrative action relating to customs matters". This due process theme, which would appear to be reflected in each of sub-paragraphs of Article X of the GATT 1994, has been referred to by the Appellate Body when interpreting that Article.[909]

7.108 The due process theme underlying Article X of the GATT 1994 suggests that the aim of Article X:3(a) of the GATT 1994 is to ensure that traders are treated fairly and consistently when seeking to import from or export to a particular WTO Member.[910] This, in turn, suggests to us that the term "administer" in Article X:3(a) of the GATT 1994 relates to the *application* of laws in particular cases and, particularly, to *administrative processes and their results*, since the application of the obligation of uniformity (and, for that matter, the obligations of reasonableness and impartiality) to such processes and their results pursuant to Article X:3(a) of the GATT 1994, helps to ensure that traders are treated fairly and consistently. It is unclear whether the due process objective underlying Article X of the GATT 1994 also indicates that the term "administer" in Article X:3(a) of the GATT 1994 also relates to *laws and regulations as such.* Presumably, the publication of laws (which is required under Article X:1 of the GATT 1994) coupled with an obligation to ensure uniform, reasonable and impartial *application* of such laws and regulations would suffice to meet the due

---

909 In particular, the Appellate Body referred to the fundamental importance of the transparency standards contained in Article X of the GATT 1994 and stated that that Article has due process dimensions: Appellate Body Report, *US – Underwear,* pp 20-21. In addition, the Appellate Body has stated that "[i]t is clear to us that Article X:3 of the GATT 1994 establishes certain minimum standards of transparency and procedural fairness in the administration of trade regulations.": Appellate Body Report, *US - Shrimp*, para. 183. With respect to the latter case, the Panel notes that the meaning of the "minimum standards" referred to by the Appellate Body is discussed in paragraph 7.134 below.

910 This interpretation appears to be reflected in the statement made by the panel in *Argentina – Hides and Leather* that "[u]niform administration requires that Members ensure that their laws are applied *consistently and predictably.*" (emphasis added): Panel Report, *Argentina – Hides and Leather*, para. 11.83.

process objective underlying Article X of the GATT 1994. Therefore, it is not clear that it should be inferred from this objective that Article X:3(a) of the GATT 1994 requires *laws and regulations themselves* to also be uniform, reasonable and impartial.

Interpretation of Spanish and French versions of Article X:3(a) of the GATT 1994

7.109 The final clause of the WTO Agreement indicates that, for that Agreement, of which the GATT 1994 is a part, the English, French and Spanish texts are authentic.

7.110 Article X:3(a) of the French version of the GATT 1994 provides that:

> "Chaque partie contractante appliquera d'une manière uniforme, impartiale et raisonnable, tous les règlements, lois, décisions judiciaires et administratives visés au paragraphe premier du présent article."

7.111 Article X:3(a) of the Spanish version of the GATT 1994 provides that:

> "Cada parte contratante aplicará de manera uniforme, imparcial y razonable sus leyes, reglamentos, decisiones judiciales y disposiciones administrativas a que se refiere el párrafo 1 de este artículo."

7.112 The Panel understands that the terms "appliquera" and "aplicará" in the French and Spanish versions of Article X:3(a) of the GATT 1994 respectively are synonymous with the term "shall apply" in English.[911] Therefore, it is the Panel's view that the use of the terms "appliquera" and "aplicará" in the French and Spanish versions of Article X:3(a) of the GATT 1994 respectively tends to confirm that Article X:3(a) of the GATT relates to the application of laws, regulations, etc. but not to the laws and regulations as such.

Summary and conclusions

7.113 In summary, the interpretative material the Panel is entitled to rely upon under the *Vienna Convention* in interpreting the term "administer" in Article X:3(a) of the GATT 1994 indicates that that term relates to the application of laws and regulations, including administrative processes and their results, but not to laws and regulations as such. In this regard, we note that this view tends to be supported by statements made by panels and the Appellate Body in other cases, which have stressed that Article X:3(a) of the GATT is not concerned with the *substance* of laws, regulations, decisions and rulings themselves but, rather, with their *administration*.[912] In other words, these statements tend to support the view that Article X:3(a) of the GATT 1994 does not concern what a particular law

[911] "Aplicar" is defined, *inter alia,* as "to apply": *Collins Spanish Dictionary*, 1985, p.41. "Appliquer" is defined, *inter alia,* as "to apply": *Robert & Collins Senior*, 2002, p. 49. We note that, in turn, the term "apply" is defined as "to put use with a particular subject matter <apply the law to the facts>": *Black's Law Dictionary*, 1999, p. 96.

[912] See, for example, Appellate Body Report, *EC – Bananas III*, para. 200.

says (i.e. its substance) but, instead, concerns the way the law is applied in practice (i.e. the way in which it is administered).

7.114 The Panel recalls the United States' argument that laws or regulations that may be construed as "tools of administration" or "administrative in nature" may be examined under Article X:3(a) of the GATT 1994 for their substance to determine whether or not they evidence non-uniform administration of laws, regulations or other measures whereas other laws and regulations (that is, those that cannot be considered as "tools of administration" or "administrative in nature") are examined under Article X:3(a) of the GATT 1994 to determine whether they are being administered in a uniform fashion.[913] However, the Panel is not persuaded by this contention. Our reasons are as follows.

7.115 *First*, the Panel considers that the interpretation put forward by the United States would blur a distinction which the Panel considers is demanded by the text of Article X:3(a) of the GATT 1994. In particular, in our view, the text of Article X:3(a) of the GATT 1994 effectively requires a distinction to be drawn between, on the one hand, the instruments being administered (i.e. laws, regulations, decisions and rulings of the kind described in Article X:1 of the GATT 1994) and, on the other hand, the acts of administration of those laws, regulations, judicial decisions and administrative rulings. However, according to the United States, laws and regulations that are "tools of administration" or "administrative in nature" are evidence of non-uniform administration of laws, regulations, judicial decisions and administrative rulings of the kind described in Article X:1 of the GATT 1994 because they put into effect those laws, regulations, decisions and rulings, but they may also simultaneously be laws and regulations of the kind described in Article X:1 of the GATT 1994. In our view, the text of Article X:3(a) of the GATT 1994 does not contemplate the possibility that laws and regulations can *simultaneously* qualify as laws, regulations, judicial decisions and administrative rulings of the kind described in Article X:1 of the GATT 1994 and as acts of administration within the meaning of Article X:3(a) of the GATT 1994.

7.116 In this regard, the Panel recalls that the obligation of uniform administration under Article X:3(a) of the GATT 1994 relates to "laws, regulations, decisions and rulings of the kind described in [Article X:1 of the GATT 1994]". In turn, Article X:1 of the GATT 1994 refers to "[l]aws, regulations, judicial decisions and administrative rulings *of general application*" (emphasis added). The ordinary meaning of the term "general", which is of relevance in the context of Article X:1 of the GATT 1994, is: "Not specifically limited in application; related to a whole class of objects, cases, occasions, etc.; (of a rule, law etc.) true for all or nearly all cases coming under its terms."[914] The ordinary meaning of the term "application" of relevance for the purposes of Article X:1 of the GATT 1994 is: "The bringing of a general or figurative statement, a theory, principle,

[913] In this regard, the Panel notes that the United States relies upon comments made by the panel in *Argentina – Hides and Leather*, paras. 11.69-11.72.

[914] *The New Shorter Oxford English Dictionary*, p. 1073.

etc., to bear upon a matter."[915] The Panel understands that, therefore, the "[l]aws, regulations, judicial decisions and administrative rulings *of general application*" described in Article X:1 of the GATT 1994 are laws, regulations, judicial decisions and administrative rulings that apply to a range of situations or cases, rather than being limited in their scope of application. Accordingly, the "laws, regulations, decisions and rulings of the kind described in [Article X:1 of the GATT 1994]" to which Article X:3(a) of the GATT 1994 refers are laws, regulations, judicial decisions and administrative rulings that apply to a range of situations or cases, rather than being limited in their scope of application.

7.117 *Second*, the Panel notes that the United States' interpretation suggests that, when applied to what the United States describes as laws or regulations that are "tools of administration" or "administrative in nature", the obligation to administer in a uniform manner under Article X:3(a) of the GATT 1994 means that the *substance* of those laws or regulations may be considered. In other words, the United States submits that, pursuant to the obligation of uniform administration under Article X:3(a) of the GATT 1994, the substance of laws or regulations that are "tools of administration" or "administrative in nature" must be uniform (i.e. the same) throughout the territory of a WTO Member. In the Panel's view, the interpretation put forward by the United States would render redundant in Article X:3(a) of the GATT 1994 either the term "administer" or the reference to "laws, regulations, decisions and rulings of the kind described in [Article X:1 of the GATT 1994]", at least with respect to laws and regulations the United States labels as "tools of administration" or "administrative in nature". More specifically, such an interpretation would mean that, in essence, "laws, regulations, decisions and rulings of the kind described in [Article X:1 of the GATT 1994]" that are "tools of administration" or "administrative in nature" must be uniform or that "tools of administration" which are laws or regulations (regardless of whether or not they are laws, regulations, decisions and rulings of the kind described in Article X:1 of the GATT 1994) must be uniform. We note that, such an interpretation, which in the first alternative effectively reads out the term "administer" from Article X:3(a) of the GATT 1994 and in the second alternative effectively reads out the reference to "laws, regulations, decisions and rulings of the kind described in [Article X:1 of the GATT 1994]" (at least, with respect to laws, regulations, decisions or rulings that are "tools of administration" or "administrative in nature"), is precluded by the principle of effective treaty interpretation, which requires us to give meaning and effect to all the terms of Article X:3(a) of the GATT 1994.[916]

7.118 *Third*, according to the United States, all laws and regulations, whether "tools of administration" or "administrative in nature" or otherwise, are subject to the obligation of uniform administration under Article X:3(a) of the GATT 1994.

---

[915] *The New Shorter Oxford English Dictionary*, p. 100.

[916] The Appellate Body in *US – Gasoline* stated that one of the corollaries of the "general rule of interpretation" in Article 31 of the *Vienna Convention* is that "interpretation must give meaning and effect to all the terms of a treaty," and that an interpreter must not "adopt a reading that would result in reducing whole clauses or paragraphs of a treaty to redundancy or inutility.": Appellate Body Report, *US – Gasoline*, p. 23.

However, in the United States' view, those that qualify as "tools of administration" or "administrative in nature" are examined under Article X:3(a) of the GATT 1994 for their substance as evidence of non-uniform administration of the laws, regulations or other measures that they put into effect whereas those that do not so qualify are examined under Article X:3(a) of the GATT 1994 to determine whether or not they are being administered in a uniform fashion. In the Panel's view, there is no textual support in Article X:3(a) of the GATT 1994 for this two-track, differential approach.

7.119 Therefore, in the light of the foregoing, the Panel confirms its conclusion that the term "administer" in Article X:3(a) of the GATT 1994 relates to the application of laws and regulations, including administrative processes and their results but not to laws and regulations as such.

(b) Interpretation of "uniform"

(i) Summary of the parties' arguments

7.120 The **United States** submits that the ordinary meaning of the term "uniform" that is relevant to the use of that term in Article X:3(a) of the GATT 1994 is "of one unchanging form, character, or kind; that is or stays the same in different places or circumstances, or at different times."[917] The United States argues that the obligation of uniform administration under Article X:3(a) of the GATT 1994 requires uniform administration across the territory of a WTO Member. The United States submits that a Member does not administer its law in a uniform manner if identical products or identical transactions receive different treatment in different geographical regions of that Member and the Member provides no mechanism for the systematic reconciliation of such differences.[918]

7.121 The **European Communities** submits that it agrees with the definition of the term "uniform" as "of one unchanging form, character, or kind; that is or stays the same in different places or circumstances, or at different times". The European Communities further submits that identical standards must apply to the requirement of uniformity over time, across the territory, or as between individuals.[919]

(ii) Analysis by the Panel

7.122 The Panel has been called upon to determine the test that should be applied in determining whether or not the obligation of "uniform" administration in Article X:3(a) of the GATT 1994 has been violated. In determining what is meant by the term "uniform" in the context of Article X:3(a) of the GATT 1994, the Panel will undertake its analysis pursuant to Articles 31 and 32 of the *Vienna Convention*.

---

[917] United States' first written submission, paras. 34 and 35, referring to *The New Shorter Oxford English Dictionary*, 1993, p. 3488 (Exhibit US-4) and relying upon the panel report in *Argentina – Hides and Leather,* para. 11.80.

[918] United States' first written submission, para. 20.

[919] European Communities' reply to Panel question No. 151 referring to Panel Report, *Argentina – Hides and Leather*, para. 11.80.

Ordinary meaning

7.123 Regarding the *ordinary meaning* of the term "uniform", a WTO panel has noted that the dictionary defines the term "uniform" as "of one unchanging form, character, or kind; that is or stays the same in different places or circumstances, or at different times."[920] This definition, which has been relied upon by both the United States and the European Communities and was supported by a number of third parties to this dispute, indicates, that the term "uniform" requires, *inter alia*, geographic uniformity.[921] In other words, according to this definition, administration should be uniform in different places within a particular WTO Member pursuant to Article X:3(a) of the GATT 1994. The Panel sees no reason to disagree with this interpretation.

7.124 As for the standard that should be applied in determining whether or not administration is "uniform" in a particular case, the use of the term "the same" in the definition relied upon by the panel cited in the previous paragraph suggests that administration should be absolutely and instantaneously identical, when such administration concerns the same facts. However, the Panel notes that the term "uniform" has also been defined as "conforming to one standard, rule, or pattern; alike, similar".[922] This definition appears to imply a less exacting standard of uniformity than the former, requiring that the same rules be applied but not necessarily that the results of administration be identical. We now turn to the context for the interpretation of the term "uniformity" in Article X:3(a) of the GATT 1994 to determine which, if either, of these two interpretations of the standard of uniformity is more appropriate for the purposes of Article X:3(a) of the GATT 1994.

Context

7.125 The Panel will first consider the *immediate context* of the term "uniform", namely the other terms that appear in Article X:3(a) of the GATT 1994. The Panel recalls that Article X:3(a) of the GATT 1994 requires Members, *inter alia*, to "administer" in a uniform manner all their "laws, regulations, decisions and rulings of the kind described in Article X:1". It is clear from the terms of Article X:3(a) of the GATT 1994 that the uniformity obligation is intrinsically tied to the meaning of "administer" and to the "laws, regulations, decisions and rulings of the kind described in Article X:1 of the GATT 1994".

7.126 The Panel found in paragraph 7.113 above that the term "administer" in Article X:3(a) of the GATT 1994 relates to the application of laws and regulations, including administrative processes and their results but not to laws and regulations as such. The Panel understands that the specific form, nature and scale of administration that may be at issue in a dispute concerning the application of Article X:3(a) of the GATT 1994 may vary from case to case. In particu-

---

[920] Panel Report, *Argentina – Hides and Leather*, para. 11.83.

[921] The Panel notes that, in the context of this dispute, it has only been called upon to address issues of alleged geographical non-uniformity. Therefore, the Panel will restrict its interpretation of the term "uniformity" to this aspect of the term.

[922] *The New Shorter Oxford English Dictionary*, 1993, p. 3488.

lar, one case may involve administration concerning a specific, self-contained administrative process whereas another case may involve the administration of an entire system. The Panel considers that, therefore, in order to interpret the term "uniform" in a particular case involving an alleged violation of Article X:3(a) of the GATT 1994, it is necessary to first clarify the administration that is being challenged in a particular case.

7.127 Similarly, the Panel is of the view that, in order to interpret the term "uniform" in a particular case, it is necessary to clarify "laws, regulations, decisions and rulings of the kind described in [Article X:1 of the GATT 1994]", which are allegedly being administered in a non-uniform manner in violation of Article X:3(a) of the GATT 1994. At one end of the spectrum, it may be the case that a challenge under Article X:3(a) of the GATT 1994 relates to the administration of a single, specific legislative provision. At the other end of the spectrum, a challenge under Article X:3(a) of the GATT 1994 may relate to the administration of a vast body of legislative provisions. There are numerous possibilities between these two extremes of the spectrum.

7.128 It is evident from the foregoing that the form, nature and scale of administration[923] that may be at issue in a dispute concerning the application of Article X:3(a) of the GATT 1994, both in terms of the type of administration and the legislative framework within which the administration in question is occurring, may vary greatly from case to case. Given the range of possibilities in this regard, the Panel does not consider it possible to define a single concept of "uniformity" that would apply across the board. Indeed, in the Panel's view, the form, nature and scale of the alleged non-uniform administration and the laws, regulations, decisions and rulings that are allegedly being administered in a non-uniform manner should be taken into consideration when interpreting the term "uniform" in Article X:3(a) of the GATT 1994 in the context of a particular case.

7.129 The Panel considers that the narrower the challenge both in terms of the administration that is being challenged and the laws, regulations, decisions and rulings which are alleged to be administered in a non-uniform manner in a particular case, the more demanding the requirement of uniformity. On the other hand, the broader and more wide-ranging the challenge both in terms of the nature of administration that is being challenged and the specific laws, regulations, decisions and rulings or provisions thereof that are alleged to be administered in a non-uniform manner in a particular case, a less exacting standard of uniformity should be applied.

Supplementary means of interpretation

7.130 In the Panel's view, the approach set out in paragraph 7.129 above, which entails a notion of uniformity, the threshold for which differs depending upon the form, nature and scale of the challenge under Article X:3(a) of the GATT 1994

[923] When we refer to the "scale of administration" here and elsewhere in our report, we mean the scale of the particular act or acts of administration that are the subject of challenge under Article X:3(a) of the GATT 1994. We do *not* mean the scale of a system of administration that exists in a particular WTO Member.

in question, is warranted by reference to the factual context, which, in our view, may be taken into consideration pursuant to Article 32 of the *Vienna Convention* as *supplementary means of interpretation*.[924]

7.131 In particular, the Panel considers that, if we were to interpret Article X:3(a) of the GATT 1994 to impose a requirement of absolute uniformity – that is, uniformity in every case where the facts are identical, which is suggested by one interpretation of the ordinary meaning of the term "uniform" – this would lead to a result which is unreasonable. In this regard, the Panel notes that the practical reality of many systems of customs administration is that they involve millions of acts of administration every year. The Panel does not consider that it is practically viable to achieve absolute uniformity in each and every case involving identical facts, particularly in the context of large Members across whose borders many products are being imported and exported every day and where there are many customs officials involved.

7.132 The Panel considers that the factual context also indicates that the interpretation of the term "uniform" in Article X:3(a) of the GATT 1994 does not necessarily entail instantaneous uniformity, which could be inferred from one interpretation of the ordinary meaning of the term "uniform". In our view, interpreting Article X:3(a) of the GATT 1994 to impose an obligation of instantaneous uniformity would lead to an unreasonable result since achieving such instantaneous uniformity would not always be practically feasible in respect of many systems of customs administration. We consider that, rather, uniformity must be attained within a period of time that is reasonable. The Panel considers that, in order to avoid a finding of non-uniform administration under Article X:3(a) of the GATT 1994, it must be clear at the time of establishment of the panel that any non-uniformity that may have existed was remedied within a period of time that is reasonable. In our view, what is reasonable will depend upon the form,

---

[924] We note that the panel in *EC – Chicken Cuts* relied upon "factual context" when interpreting the ordinary meaning of the term "salted" in the European Communities' GATT Schedule: Panel Report, *EC – Chicken Cuts*, para. 7.105. On appeal, the European Communities challenged the panel's reliance upon the so-called "factual context". The Appellate Body upheld the panel's analysis stating that "... we would agree with the European Communities that there is no reference in the *Vienna Convention* to "factual context" as a separate analytical step under Article 31. Nevertheless, we do not believe that the Panel was incorrect to consider elements such as the 'products covered by the concession contained in heading 02.10', 'flavour, texture, [and] other physical properties' of the products falling under heading 02.10, and 'preservation' when interpreting the term 'salted' as it appears in heading 02.10. The Panel's consideration of these elements under 'ordinary meaning' of the term 'salted' complemented its analysis of the dictionary definitions of that term. In any event, even if we were to agree with the European Communities that these elements are not to be considered under 'ordinary meaning', they certainly could be considered under 'context'.": Appellate Body Report, *EC – Chicken Cuts*, para. 176. In the Panel's view, the Appellate Body' approval of the use of the "factual context" under Article 31 of the *Vienna Convention* indicates that it may alternatively/additionally be taken into consideration under Article 32 of the *Vienna Convention*. We find support for this view in *EC – Chicken Cuts*, where the Appellate Body stated that: "We stress, moreover, that Article 32 does not define exhaustively the supplementary means of interpretation to which an interpreter may have recourse. It states only that they *include* the preparatory work of the treaty and the circumstances of its conclusion. Thus, an interpreter has a certain flexibility in considering relevant supplementary means in a given case so as to assist in ascertaining the common intentions of the parties.": Appellate Body Report, *EC – Chicken Cuts*, para. 283.

nature and scale of the administration at issue. It will also depend upon the complexity of the factual and legal issues raised by the act of administration that is being challenged.

7.133 In our view, in no case can non-uniform administration persist for indefinite periods of time as this would effectively render redundant the term "uniform" in Article X:3(a) of the GATT 1994, which would be contrary to the principle of effective treaty interpretation.[925] Furthermore, such an interpretation would be inconsistent with our obligation under the *Vienna Convention* to interpret Article X:3(a) of the GATT 1994 in good faith.

7.134 In all cases, regardless of the form, nature and scale of administration at issue, the Panel considers that administration should not fall below certain minimum standards of due process, which encompass notions such as notice, transparency, fairness and equity.[926] In the Panel's view, such standards derive from the broader due process context of Article X:3(a) of the GATT 1994, which has been discussed above in paragraphs 7.107 – 7.108.

Summary and conclusions

7.135 In summary, the interpretative material upon which the Panel is entitled to rely under the *Vienna Convention* in interpreting the term "uniform" in Article X:3(a) of the GATT 1994 indicates that that term covers, *inter alia*, geographic uniformity. In other words, administration should be uniform in different places within a particular WTO Member. Further, the Panel considers that the form, nature and scale of the alleged non-uniform administration and the laws,

---

[925] In this regard, we recall that in *US – Gasoline*, the Appellate Body stated that one of the corollaries of the "general rule of interpretation" in Article 31 of the *Vienna Convention* is that "interpretation must give meaning and effect to all the terms of a treaty," and that an interpreter must not "adopt a reading that would result in reducing whole clauses or paragraphs of a treaty to redundancy or inutility.": Appellate Body Report, *US – Gasoline*, p. 23.

[926] We note in this regard that, in *US – Shrimp*, the Appellate Body stated that:

"It appears to us that, effectively, exporting Members applying for certification whose applications are rejected are denied basic fairness and due process, and are discriminated against, vis-à-vis those Members which are granted certification.

The provisions of Article X:3 of the GATT 1994 bear upon this matter. In our view, Section 609 falls within the 'laws, regulations, judicial decisions and administrative rulings of general application' described in Article X:1. Inasmuch as there are due process requirements generally for measures that are otherwise imposed in compliance with WTO obligations, it is only reasonable that rigorous compliance with the fundamental requirements of due process should be required in the application and administration of a measure which purports to be an exception to the treaty obligations of the Member imposing the measure and which effectively results in a suspension pro hac vice of the treaty rights of other Members.

It is also clear to us that *Article X:3 of the GATT 1994 establishes certain minimum standards for transparency and procedural fairness in the administration of trade regulations* which, in our view, are not met here. The non-transparent and ex parte nature of the internal governmental procedures applied by the competent officials in the Office of Marine Conservation, the Department of State, and the United States National Marine Fisheries Service throughout the certification processes under Section 609, as well as the fact that countries whose applications are denied do not receive formal notice of such denial, nor of the reasons for the denial, and the fact, too, that there is no formal legal procedure for review of, or appeal from, a denial of an application, are all contrary to the spirit, if not the letter, of Article X:3 of the GATT 1994." (emphasis added): Appellate Body Report, *US – Shrimp*, paras. 181 - 183.

regulations, judicial decisions and rulings that are allegedly being administered in a non-uniform manner should be taken into consideration when interpreting the term "uniform" in Article X:3(a) of the GATT 1994 in the context of a particular case. The Panel considers that the narrower the challenge both in terms of the administration that is being challenged and the laws, regulations, decisions and rulings which are alleged to be administered in a non-uniform manner in a particular case, the more demanding the requirement of uniformity. The broader and more wide-ranging the challenge both in terms of the nature of administration that is being challenged and the specific laws, regulations, decisions and rulings or provisions thereof that are alleged to be administered in a non-uniform manner in a particular case, a less exacting standard of uniformity should be applied. The Panel also considers that the interpretation of the term "uniform" in Article X:3(a) of the GATT 1994 does not necessarily entail instantaneous uniformity. Rather, uniformity must be attained within a period of time that is reasonable. What is reasonable will depend upon the form, nature and scale of the administration at issue as well as the complexity of the factual and legal issues raised by the act of administration that is being challenged. It is the Panel's view that, in all cases, regardless of the form, nature and scope of administration at issue, administration should not fall below certain minimum standards of due process, which encompass notions such as notice, transparency, fairness and equity.

4. *Relevance of Article XXIV:12 of the GATT 1994 for the interpretation of Article X:3(a) of the GATT 1994 in the context of this dispute*

(a) Summary of the parties' arguments

7.136 The **European Communities** submits that the reality of the United States' claim under Article X:3(a) of the GATT 1994 is that it is effectively seeking to require the European Communities to establish a central customs agency.[927] The European Communities argues that Article X:3(a) of the GATT 1994 does not prescribe the ways in which a WTO Member must implement its customs laws, including the question of through what authorities or administration customs laws are administered. According to the European Communities, Article X:3(a) of the GATT 1994 in no way excludes that, in a federal or quasi-federal state or entity, customs laws could be administered by authorities at the sub-federal level.[928] In support, the European Communities refers to Article XXIV:12 of the GATT 1994, which provides that "[e]ach contracting party shall take such reasonable measures as may be available to it to ensure observance of the provisions of this Agreement by the regional and local governments and authorities within its territories".[929] The European Communities notes that the GATT panel in *Canada – Gold Coins* found that Article XXIV:12 of the GATT 1994 has the "func-

---

927 European Communities' second written submission, para. 30.

928 European Communities' first written submission, para. 252.

929 European Communities' first written submission paras. 220-221.

tion of allowing federal States to accede to the General Agreement without having to change the federal distribution of competence". The European Communities submits that, accordingly, any interpretation of Article X:3(a) of the GATT 1994 that would affect the internal distribution of competence is incompatible with Article XXIV:12 of the GATT 1994.[930]

7.137 In response, the **United States** clarifies that the United States has never insisted that the European Communities must create an EC customs agency and an EC customs court and must harmonize member States' laws. The United States simply argues that the European Communities, like other WTO Members, must administer its customs laws in a manner consistent with Article X:3(a) of the GATT 1994.[931] The United States submits that Article XXIV:12 of the GATT 1994 concerns "the observance of the General Agreement by regional and local government authorities." According to the United States, in contrast, this dispute does not concern the observance of an obligation under the GATT 1994 by regional and local government authorities but, rather, by the European Communities itself. The United States argues that, therefore, this case is distinguishable from *Canada – Gold Coins*, which involved a provincial government of Canada adopting a measure for the raising of provincial revenue – a power that Canada's constitution vested exclusively in the provincial legislature – in a manner that put Canada in breach of its obligation under Article III of the GATT 1994.[932] Additionally, the United States notes that, if the European Communities has sought to invoke Article XXIV:12 of the GATT 1994 as a defence, this entails a burden to demonstrate that lapses in the uniform administration of EC customs law concern matters "which the central government cannot control under the constitutional distribution of powers".[933] According to the United States, if the European Communities is arguing that it is not able to control the administration of customs law by the customs authorities in the member States under its constitutional distribution of powers, this reinforces the point that the European Communities is not meeting its obligation to administer its customs law uniformly under Article X:3(a) of the GATT 1994.[934]

7.138 The **European Communities** responds that Article XXIV:12 of the GATT 1994 must have a useful meaning. In the context of Article XXIV:12 of the GATT 1994, it must be considered whether the WTO Member in question has regional or local governments and authorities within its territories which have responsibilities for implementing the provisions of the GATT. According to the European Communities, if it does, the Member in question must take "reasonable measures" to ensure compliance.[935] The European Communities argues that, in order to determine what is a "reasonable measure", the panel in *Canada –*

[930] European Communities' first written submission paras. 220-221, referring to GATT Panel Report, *Canada – Gold Coins*, para. 58.
[931] United States' comments on the European Communities' reply to Panel question No. 158.
[932] *Ibid.*
[933] GATT Panel Report, *United States – Measures Affecting Alcoholic and Malt Beverages*, BISD 39S/206, para. 5.79 (adopted 19 June 1992).
[934] United States' comments on the European Communities' reply to Panel question No. 158.
[935] European Communities' comments on the United States' reply to Panel question No. 176.

Gold Coins held that "the consequences of [...] non-observance [of the provisions of the GATT] by the local government for trade relations with other contracting parties are to be weighed against the domestic difficulties of securing observance".[936]

7.139 The **United States** submits that, even if Article XXIV:12 of the GATT 1994 were relevant to this dispute, it would not excuse the European Communities from its obligation under Article X:3(a) of the GATT 1994 or in any way affect its obligation under that Article. In this regard, the United States refers to paragraph 13 of the Understanding on the Interpretation of Article XXIV of the GATT 1994 which, according to the United States, makes clear that "[e]ach Member is fully responsible under GATT 1994 for the observance of all provisions of GATT 1994... ." That is, in the United States' view, Article XXIV:12 of the GATT 1994 imposes an obligation on Members with federal structures to take "reasonable measures" to "ensure observance" by local or regional governments of a Member's obligations but does not alter the content of any GATT 1994 obligation for such Members. Further, according to the United States, even where observance of WTO obligations by regional or local governments is at issue, paragraph 14 of the Understanding on Article XXIV and Article 22.9 of the DSU provide that "[t]he provisions of Articles XXII and XXIII of GATT 1994 as elaborated and applied by the [DSU]" and "[t]he provisions of the covered agreements and [the DSU]," respectively, "relating to compensation and suspension of concessions or other obligations apply in cases where it has not been possible to secure such observance." The United States submits that, therefore, even if, pursuant to Article XXIV:12 of the GATT 1994, the European Communities' only obligation under Article X:3(a) of the GATT 1994 was to take "reasonable measures" to secure uniform administration of EC customs law, its failure to actually administer its customs law in a uniform manner would not excuse it from relevant provisions on compensation and suspension of concessions.[937]

(b) Analysis by the Panel

7.140 The Panel notes that, in the context of this dispute, the United States argues that the European Communities has breached its obligation under Article X:3(a) of the GATT 1994 by virtue of its failure to administer EC customs law in a uniform manner.[938] The United States acknowledges that the administration of EC customs law is carried out by the customs authorities in the member States but submits that, to the extent that the European Communities does not control the administration by those customs authorities to ensure uniform administration, the European Communities is in violation of Article X:3(a) of the GATT 1994.[939]

---

936 GATT Panel Report, *Canada – Gold Coins*, para. 69.

937 United States' comments on the European Communities' reply to Panel question No. 158.

938 *Ibid.*

939 *Ibid.*

7.141 By way of preliminary comment, the Panel notes that the terms of Article X:3(a) of the GATT 1994 simply require Members to administer laws, regulations, decisions and rulings of the kind described in Article X:1 in a manner that is, *inter alia*, uniform. Article X:3(a) of the GATT 1994 does not prescribe how uniform administration must be achieved. Therefore, the Panel considers that Article X:3(a) of the GATT 1994 vests discretion in Members to determine how to achieve uniform administration, including the nature and level of entities that are charged with administration and the tools that are put in place to achieve uniform administration. Accordingly, the Panel considers that there is nothing in Article X:3(a) of the GATT 1994 to prevent the European Communities from administering its customs laws through, *inter alia*, customs authorities of its constituent member States.[940]

7.142 The question has arisen in this dispute as to whether or not Article XXIV:12 of the GATT 1994 has the effect of limiting the European Communities' obligations under Article X:3(a) of the GATT 1994 so that it is only required to take "reasonable measures" to ensure uniform administration by the customs authorities of the member States.[941] Article XXIV:12 of GATT 1994 provides that:

> "Each contracting party shall take such reasonable measures as may be available to it to ensure observance of the provisions of this Agreement by the regional and local governments and authorities within its territories."

7.143 The Understanding on the Interpretation of Article XXIV of GATT 1994 ("the Understanding"), which is part of the GATT 1994[942] and which was agreed upon during the Uruguay Round negotiations, provides the following with respect to Article XXIV:12 of the GATT 1994:

> "Each Member is fully responsible under GATT 1994 for the observance of all provisions of GATT 1994, and shall take such reasonable measures as may be available to it to ensure such observance by regional and local governments and authorities within its territory.
>
> The provisions of Articles XXII and XXIII of GATT 1994 as elaborated and applied by the Dispute Settlement Understanding may be invoked in respect of measures affecting its observance taken by regional or local governments or authorities within the territory of a Member. When the Dispute Settlement Body has ruled that a provision of GATT 1994 has not been observed, the responsible Member shall take such reasonable measures as may

---

[940] The Panel notes that, in the context of this dispute, the United States has not challenged as such the fact that the European Communities administers its customs laws through, *inter alia*, customs authorities of its constituent member States.

[941] See, for example, European Communities' comments on the United States' reply to Panel question No. 176 and United States' comments on the European Communities' reply to Panel question No. 158.

[942] See Article 1(c) of the GATT 1994.

> be available to it to ensure its observance. The provisions relating to compensation and suspension of concessions or other obligations apply in cases where it has not been possible to secure such observance.
>
> Each Member undertakes to accord sympathetic consideration to and afford adequate opportunity for consultation regarding any representations made by another Member concerning measures affecting the operation of GATT 1994 taken within the territory of the former."

7.144 The Panel notes that Article XXIV:12 of the GATT 1994 is drafted as a positive obligation rather than as a defence. More specifically, the use of the word "shall"[943] in Article XXIV:12 of the GATT 1994 indicates that that Article imposes an obligation on Members to take all reasonable measures to ensure that local authorities comply with WTO obligations. This would tend to indicate that Article XXIV:12 of the GATT 1994 cannot be relied upon to attenuate nor to derogate from the provisions of the GATT 1994 (including Article X:3(a) of the GATT 1994), to which Article XXIV:12 of the GATT 1994 refers. The Understanding supports the view that Article XXIV:12 of the GATT 1994 imposes a positive obligation rather than attenuating or derogating from the provisions of the GATT 1994. Specifically, it states that "[e]ach Member is fully responsible under GATT 1994 for the observance of all provisions of GATT 1994", suggesting that Article XXIV:12 of the GATT 1994 does not protect Members from being found in violation of their WTO obligations.[944] In addition, we note that the Understanding clearly states that, when the DSB has ruled that a provision of GATT 1994 has not been observed by regional or local governments or authorities of a WTO Member, "the provisions relating to compensation and suspension of concessions or other obligations apply in cases where it has not been possible to secure such observance".

7.145 In the light of the foregoing, it is the Panel's view that, irrespective of whether or not Article XXIV:12 of the GATT 1994 is applicable in the context of this dispute[945], that Article does not constitute an exception nor a derogation from the obligation of uniform administration in Article X:3(a) of the GATT

---

[943] Black's Law Dictionary defines the term "shall" as "has a duty to; more broadly, is required to.": *Black's Law Dictionary*, 1999, p. 1379.

[944] Further support for the view that Article XXIV:12 of the GATT 1994 does not attenuate nor derogate from the provisions of the GATT 1994, including Article X:3(a) of the GATT 1994 derives from Article XVI:4 of the WTO Agreement. Article XVI:4 of the WTO Agreement provides that: "Each Member shall ensure the conformity of its laws, regulations and administrative procedures with its obligations as provided in the annexed Agreements." We understand that Article XVI:4 of the WTO Agreement establishes a clear obligation for all WTO Members to ensure the conformity of its laws, regulations and administrative procedures with their obligations under the covered Agreements, including the GATT 1994. See Appellate Body Report, *EC – Sardines*, para. 213.

[945] In this regard, the Panel recalls that the United States has suggested that Article XXIV:12 is inapplicable in the context of this dispute: United States' comments on the European Communities' reply to Panel question No. 158. The Panel notes that it does not need to take a position on whether or not the member States of the European Communities qualify as "regional and local governments or authorities" within the meaning of Article XXIV:12 of the GATT 1994.

1994. Therefore, Article XXIV:12 of the GATT 1994 has no impact upon our examination of the United States' claims under Article X:3(a) of the GATT 1994.

5. *Burden of proof*

(a) Summary of parties' arguments

7.146 The **United States** submits that, under Article X:3(a) of the GATT 1994, it is necessary to examine the real effect that a measure might have on traders operating in the commercial world.[946]. According to the United States, this is evident from the context of Article X:3(a) of the GATT 1994, which includes in Article X:1 of the GATT 1994 an obligation to promptly publish certain customs measures and in Article X:3(b) of the GATT 1994 an obligation to provide fora for prompt review and correction of customs decisions, both of which plainly are oriented to facilitating the operations of traders.[947]

7.147 The **European Communities** agrees that the effect of administration on traders is a relevant consideration in the interpretation of Article X:3(a) of the GATT 1994. According to the European Communities, this means that the treatment which a trader can expect to receive from the customs authorities of a WTO Member should be reasonably predictable. This does not mean that individual instances of administrative error, which can be corrected through administrative and judicial mechanisms provided by a WTO Member's system, can be regarded as constituting a violation of Article X:3(a) of the GATT 1994. The European Communities submits that, rather, the effect on traders should be demonstrable through adequate evidence. The European Communities also submits that measures which entail no relevant difference in treatment between traders cannot be held to constitute a violation of Article X:3(a) of the GATT 1994.[948] The European Communities also considers that there is no requirement to show trade damage in order to prove a violation of Article X:3(a) of the GATT 1994. Rather, the question to be addressed is whether the complainant has suffered nullification and impairment within the meaning of Article XXIII of the GATT 1994. According to the European Communities, it follows from Article 3.8 of the DSU that, where there is an infringement of the obligations under the covered agreements, this is normally presumed to constitute a case of nullification and impairment. However, this presumption can be rebutted by the Member complained against.[949]

7.148 In response, the **United States** submits that an examination of the real effect that a measure might have on traders is not confined to an examination of whether traders in similar situations are required to pay different customs duties but includes consideration of the possible impact on the competitive situation. The United States submits that, therefore, in determining whether Article X:3(a)

---

[946] United States' first written submission, para. 117 referring to Panel Report, *Argentina – Hides and Leather*, para. 11.77.

[947] United States' first written submission, para. 117 referring to Panel Report, *Argentina – Hides and Leather*, para. 11.76.

[948] European Communities' reply to Panel question No. 174.

[949] European Communities' reply to Panel question No. 175.

of the GATT 1994 has been violated, a panel should ask not whether one WTO Member has been treated differently from other WTO Members. Rather, it should ask whether traders have been treated differently based, for example, on the part of the Member's territory through which they import their goods. If the manner in which a Member administers its customs law might encourage a trader to prefer importation through one region rather than another, this would be probative of non-uniform administration, in breach of Article X:3(a) of the GATT 1994.[950] The United States submits that benefits accruing to the United States are nullified or impaired if traders are effectively compelled to alter shipping patterns or incur additional costs as a result of non-uniform administration in violation of Article X:3(a) of the GATT 1994.[951]

7.149 The **European Communities** submits that a minimal threshold applies under Article X:3(a) of the GATT 1994, which implies that a variation in administrative practice must have a significant impact on the administration of customs laws in order to constitute a breach of Article X:3(a) of the GATT 1994.[952] According to the European Communities, this minimum threshold reflects the fact that Article X:3(a) of the GATT 1994 does not require uniformity for its own sake but, rather, intends to protect the interests of traders.[953] In support, the European Communities refers to the Appellate Body's comments in *EC – Poultry* which, according to the European Communities, indicate that individual instances of administration are not probative for a violation of Article X:3(a) of the GATT 1994.[954] Further, the European Communities submits that the panel's comments in *US – Hot Rolled Steel* indicate that a pattern of decision-making is needed for the purposes of Article X:3(a) of the GATT 1994.[955] The European Communities argues that such an interpretation of Article X:3(a) of the GATT 1994 is particularly necessary given that customs authorities have to operate in complex and rapidly changing circumstances, to which they constantly need to adapt. Moreover, according to the European Communities, customs administration is a complex system, whose outcomes are determined by many factors, not all of which are attributable to the Member in question.[956]

7.150 In response, the **United States** submits that the European Communities urges on the Panel a relative view of Article X:3(a) of the GATT 1994 which requires an assessment of the particularities of the system of customs administration in question.[957] The United States also argues that, while the text of Article X:3(a) of the GATT 1994 refers to administration in a "uniform manner", it

---

950 United States' replies to Panel question Nos. 174 and 175.

951 United States' comments on the European Communities' reply to Panel question No. 175.

952 European Communities' oral statement at the first substantive meeting, para. 25 referring to GATT Panel Report, *EEC – Dessert Apples*, para. 12.30.

953 European Communities' reply to Panel question No. 46.

954 European Communities' first written submission, para. 239 referring to Appellate Body Report, *EC – Poultry*, paras. 111 and 113.

955 European Communities' first written submission, para. 240 referring to Panel Report, *US – Hot Rolled Steel*, para. 7.268; European Communities' oral statement at the first substantive meeting, para. 26; European Communities' oral statement at the second substantive meeting, para. 28.

956 European Communities' oral statement at the first substantive meeting, para. 26.

957 United States' second written submission, para. 12.

does not refer to a "pattern of non-uniform" administration.[958] Further, the United States argues that the European Communities' contention that non-uniformity is impermissible only when it amounts to a pattern of non-uniformity is misplaced because it draws this proposition from two reports that are not on point. First, with respect to the Appellate Body's report in *EC – Poultry*, the United States submits that the relevant issue there was not the meaning of uniform administration under Article X:3(a) of the GATT 1994 but, rather, whether or not Article X of the GATT 1994 applies to a particular import licence issued with respect to a particular shipment.[959] The United States submits that, similarly, the European Communities relies upon a single sentence in the panel report in *US – Hot-Rolled Steel*.[960] According to the United States, the panel in that case was not referring to a pattern as a generic requirement for making out a claim under Article X:3(a) of the GATT 194, but a pattern that might have enabled the panel to determine whether the particular application of the anti-dumping law at issue in that case was uniform or not.[961] The United States contends that the claim at issue in the present dispute is very different from the claim Japan was making in *US – Hot-Rolled Steel*. The United States submits that it is not arguing that a particular application of EC customs law represents non-uniform administration. Rather, it is arguing that the EC system of customs administration as a whole does not result in the uniform administration that Article X:3(a) of the GATT 1994 requires.[962]

(b) Analysis by the Panel

7.151 The Panel considers that the burden of proof for the purposes of the United States' claim under Article X:3(a) of the GATT 1994 is closely linked to the Panel's interpretation of the terms of that Article. Of particular relevance to the burden proof in the context of this dispute is the Panel's finding in paragraph 7.135 above that a notion of uniformity applies in the context of Article X:3(a) of the GATT 1994, the threshold for which differs depending upon the nature of the challenge in question. Such a notion of the term "uniform" would appear to entail a different burden of proof corresponding to the form, nature and scale of the administration that is being challenged under Article X:3(a) of the GATT 1994 in a particular case. As the Panel stated in paragraph 7.135 above, the narrower the challenge, the higher the degree of uniformity required; the broader the challenge, the less exacting the standard of uniformity to be applied.

7.152 With respect to this dispute, the Panel recalls its finding in paragraph 7.64 above that its terms of reference authorise the Panel to consider the manner of administration by the national customs authorities of the member States of the Community Customs Code, the Implementing Regulation, the Common Customs Tariff, the TARIC and related measures in the areas of customs administration

[958] United States' second written submission, para. 28.
[959] United States' oral statement at the first substantive meeting, paras. 17-19.
[960] United States' second written submission, para. 33.
[961] United States' second written submission, para. 35.
[962] United States' second written submission, paras. 36-38.

specifically identified in the United States' request for establishment of a panel. Pursuant to the Panel's terms of reference, the Panel is precluded from considering "as such" challenges of the design and structure of the EC system of customs administration, including challenges of the design and structure of the EC system in the areas of customs administration specifically identified in the United States' request for establishment of a panel. However, we are authorized to consider particular instances of administration of the Community Customs Code, the Implementing Regulation, the Common Customs Tariff and the TARIC and related measures in the areas of customs administration specifically identified in the United States' request in particular instances which have been relied upon by the United States in the context of this dispute.

7.153 In the light of our terms of reference, for the purposes of resolving this dispute, the Panel considers that it is only necessary to determine the burden of proof applicable for particular instances of administration of the Community Customs Code, the Implementing Regulation, the Common Customs Tariff and the TARIC and related measures in the areas of customs administration specifically identified in the United States' request, which have been relied upon by the United States in the context of this dispute. In the Panel's view, as will be explained in further detail below, such instances constitute narrow challenges when considered in the context of the EC system of customs administration as a whole. Therefore, in the Panel's view, a high degree of uniformity should apply in the context of such instances.

7.154 We do not consider it necessary to determine precisely how demanding the requirement of uniformity should be in this regard. The Panel considers that this will depend upon the circumstances surrounding the particular instance of alleged non-uniform administration. In deciding whether or not the standard has been met in a particular instance, the Panel considers it necessary to bear in mind the minimum standards of due process that underlie Article X:3(a) of the GATT 1994.[963] It is also necessary to ensure that the threshold is not set so high that Article X:3(a) of the GATT 1994 could never be violated as this is clearly not what the drafters of Article X:3(a) of the GATT 1994 intended. In addition, it is the Panel's view that a violation of Article X:3(a) of the GATT 1994 will be demonstrated if the non-uniform administration in question results in an actual or possible future adverse impact on the trading environment.[964]

[963] See paragraph 7.134 above.

[964] We note in this regard that Article 3.8 of the DSU provides that: "In cases where there is an infringement of the obligations assumed under a covered agreement, the action is considered *prima facie* to constitute a case of nullification or impairment. This means that there is normally a presumption that a breach of the rule has an adverse impact on other Members parties [sic] to that covered agreement, and in such cases, it shall be up to the other Member against whom the complaint has been brought to rebut the charge".

6. *Specific alleged violations of Article X:3(a) of the GATT 1994*

7.155 In this section of the Panel's report, the Panel will address the particular instances of alleged violations of Article X:3(a) of the GATT 1994 regarding the administration of the Community Customs Code, the Implementing Regulation, the Common Customs Tariff, the TARIC and related measures in the areas of customs administration specifically identified in the United States' request for establishment of a panel. Before doing so, however, the Panel considers it necessary to explain its understanding of certain aspects of the manner in which the EC system of customs administration functions because this is important context for the examination of the particular instances of alleged violations of Article X:3(a) of the GATT 1994 in respect of which such aspects have been raised. To the extent necessary, the Panel will consider other aspects of the EC system of customs administration when examining the particular instances of alleged violations of Article X:3(a) of the GATT 1994.

(a) Relevant aspects of the EC system of customs administration

(i) Administration by customs authorities in the EC member States

7.156 The Panel has been informed by the European Communities that the administration of EC customs law is primarily the responsibility of the member States.[965] The Panel understands that EC customs law is directly applicable in the member States, which means that such law must be fully and uniformly applied in all the member States.[966] Moreover, the European Communities has informed the Panel that the customs authorities of the member State authorities must apply EC customs law in accordance with all available guidance regarding its proper meaning, including the EC Treaty and the case law of the ECJ.[967]

(ii) Institutions and mechanisms involved in the administration of the EC customs laws

Institutions and mechanisms applicable generally in all areas of customs administration[968]

Customs Code Committee

---

965 European Communities' reply to Panel question No. 146.

966 Case 106/77, *Simmenthal II*, [1978] ECR 629 (Exhibit EC-5).

967 European Communities' reply to Panel question No. 77.

968 The Panel notes that, in addition to the institutions and mechanisms dealt with below, the European Communities referred to budgetary and financial control mechanisms in place in the European Communities, which it argues helps to achieve uniform administration of EC customs law by the customs authorities of the member States: European Communities' first written submission, para. 158. These budgetary and financial control mechanisms are dealt with in paragraph 2.33 above.

7.157 The European Communities identifies the Customs Code Committee as an important institution that helps to ensure uniform administration of EC customs law among the customs authorities of the member States.[969] As noted in paragraph 2.51 above in the factual aspects of the Panel's report, the Customs Code Committee is established by Articles 247a(1) and 248a(1) of the Community Customs Code. The Customs Code Committee is composed of representatives from each member State and is chaired by a representative of the Commission. Article 249 of the Community Customs Code states that the Customs Code Committee has the authority to examine any question concerning customs legislation which is raised by its chairperson, either on his or her own initiative or at the request of a member State's representative. A similar provision is found in Article 8 of Regulation No. 2658/87 establishing the Common Customs Tariff, according to which the Committee may examine any matter referred to it by its chairperson, either on his or her own initiative or at the request of a representative of a member State, concerning the Combined Nomenclature or the TARIC. The European Communities notes that the total number of meetings of the Customs Code Committee was 77 in 2002 (with 113 ½ days of meetings), 47 in 2003 (with 77 ½ days of meetings) and 85 in 2004 (with 118 ½ days of meetings).[970]

7.158 The Panel understands that, in practice, the Customs Code Committee gives opinions on amendments to the Community Customs Code or implementing measures proposed by the Commission; examines questions concerning the interpretation of customs provisions or definitions of terms used in customs legislation; and exercises powers granted by virtue of specific customs legislation. More particularly, in the *tariff classification area*, the Panel has been informed by the European Communities that the Customs Code Committee is frequently asked to provide opinions on measures proposed by the Commission which will secure a uniform application of the Common Customs Tariff, such as classification regulations and EC explanatory notes. In addition, the Committee may adopt opinions on specific issues of tariff classification.[971] In the *customs valuation area*, the Panel has been informed by the European Communities that the Customs Code Committee will consider divergence in the application of EC customs law on customs valuation which is brought before it by the Commission or a member State.[972] After such consideration, the Customs Code Committee may issue opinions, which may take the form of conclusions or commentaries on the rules on customs valuation.[973] Additionally, the Commission will consult the Customs Code Committee on draft amendments to the valuation rules contained in the Implementing Regulation.[974]

---

[969] European Communities' first written submission, para. 85.

[970] European Communities' reply to Panel question No. 58(c). The European Communities also refers to Exhibit EC-103, which contains an overview of the number of meetings per section of the Customs Code Committee.

[971] European Communities' reply to Panel question No. 58(i)(iii).

[972] European Communities' reply to Panel question No. 58(j)(ii).

[973] These conclusions and commentaries are contained in Compendium of Customs Valuation Texts of eth Customs Code Committee, 2 December 2004 (Exhibit EC-37).

[974] European Communities' reply to Panel question No. 58(j)(iii).

7.159 It is apparent that not all matters entailing divergence in the administration of EC customs law between the customs authorities of the member States are brought before the Customs Code Committee for its consideration.[975] Moreover, the Committee may consider matters only if raised by the chairperson of the Committee or at the request of the member States' representatives.[976] The European Communities has stressed that the Customs Code Committee will not substitute itself for the individual customs authorities nor the competent courts of the member States in pending cases and, therefore, it will not usually examine individual cases.[977] Even in cases where matters are brought before the Customs Code Committee, the European Communities has acknowledged that, under the Rules of Procedure of the Customs Code Committee, there is no specific provision bestowing the Commission with the power to ask customs authorities of the member States to provide specific information.[978] Furthermore, in such cases, difficulties in coming to an agreement and delays may occur due, *inter alia* to the fact that the Committee is composed of representatives from each member State[979] and that decisions are determined by means of a qualified majority vote.[980]

7.160 In addition, it is notable that the opinions of the Customs Code Committee are not legally binding on the customs authorities of the member States.[981] As

---

[975] In the EC Court of Auditors Special Report No. 23/2000 concerning valuation of imported goods for customs purposes dated 14 March 2001, the EC Court of Auditors stated that "[m]any complex subject matters within the valuation area are not brought before the Valuation Committee.": EC Court of Auditors Special Report No 23/2000 concerning valuation of imported goods for customs purposes, 14 March 2001, para. 29 (Exhibit US-14).

[976] Article 249 of the Community Customs Code provides that: "The Committee may examine any question concerning customs legislation which is raised by its chairman, either on his own initiative or at the request of a Member State's representative." (Exhibit US-5).

[977] European Communities' replies to Panel question Nos. 58(j)(i) and 58(j)(v).

[978] European Communities' reply to Panel question No. 58(j)(v). The European Communities refers to Article 10 of the EC Treaty in this regard, which is dealt with below in paragraph 7.161 *et seq*.

[979] In the EC Court of Auditors Special Report No. 23/2000 concerning valuation of imported goods for customs purposes dated 14 March 2001, the EC Court of Auditors stated that: "Although the Valuation Committee offers a platform for the Member States to establish a common approach to similar individual cases, inevitably, with 15 different customs authorities, progress towards achieving consensus is slow. The Valuation Committee frequently becomes entrenched in details and disagreements between the representatives of the Member States"": EC Court of Auditors Special Report No 23/2000 concerning valuation of imported goods for customs purposes, 14 March 2001, para. 26 (Exhibit US-14). In addition, the EC Court of Auditors notes that "the Valuation Committee is too cumbersome a vehicle to achieve the Commission objectives": EC Court of Auditors Special Report No 23/2000 concerning valuation of imported goods for customs purposes, 14 March 2001, para. 29 (Exhibit US-14). Further, in a statement made by the Head of Customs Legislation Unit, European Commission in June 2004, Michael Lux noted that "organising a majority decision [of the Customs Code Committee] will be more difficult, since one will have to negotiate with 25 – instead of 15 – Member States. With so many members, the chairing of meetings will have to be firm to obtain any results at all.": *EU enlargement and customs law: What will change?*, Taxud/463/2004, Rev. 1, 14 June 2004, p. 4 (Exhibit US-15). In addition, in the context of this dispute, the European Communities has acknowledged that there are no specific time limits for how long a matter can remain on the agenda of the Customs Code Committee: European Communities' reply to Panel question No. 159(a).

[980] Article 6 of the Rules of Procedures of the Customs Code Committee, 5 December 2001 (Exhibit US-9).

[981] Joined Cases 69 and 70/76, *Dittmeyer*, [1977] ECR 231 (Exhibit EC-31).

stated by the European Communities itself, the Customs Code Committee does not have the authority to take decisions with respect to customs matters. Rather, the Customs Code Committee merely assists the competent EC institutions in the context of the management or regulatory procedures foreseen under the Customs Code Committee.[982] However, even in this capacity, it is unclear whether the opinions and recommendations made by the Customs Code Committee to the EC institutions can be enforced.[983] Therefore, in the light of the foregoing, it would appear that the Customs Code Committee has limited power to impose uniform administration of EC customs law on customs authorities of the member States.[984]

Article 10 of the EC Treaty

7.161 The European Communities submits that the "duty of cooperation" contained in Article 10 of the EC Treaty makes an important contribution to the uniform administration of EC customs law by the customs authorities of the member States.[985]

7.162 Article 10 of the EC Treaty provides that:

> "Member States shall take all appropriate measures, whether general or particular, to ensure fulfilment of the obligations arising out of this Treaty or resulting from action taken by the institutions of the Community. They shall facilitate the achievement of the Community's tasks.
>
> They shall abstain from any measure which could jeopardise the attainment of the objectives of this Treaty."

7.163 According to the European Communities, the "duty of cooperation" in Article 10 of the EC Treaty is legally binding and directly applicable in all member States. The European Communities submits that, therefore, the obligation contained in Article 10 of the EC Treaty must be respected by member States' authorities in the administration of EC customs law. The European Communities

---

[982] European Communities' first written submission, para. 266. See paragraphs 2.20 – 2.21 above, where the regulatory and management procedures are described.

[983] In the EC Court of Auditors Special Report No. 23/2000 concerning valuation of imported goods for customs purposes dated 14 March 2001, the EC Court of Auditors stated that "the Commission has not the authority to enforce the results of the Valuation Committee's work": EC Court of Auditors Special Report No 23/2000 concerning valuation of imported goods for customs purposes, 14 March 2001, para. 29 (Exhibit US-14).

[984] In the EC Court of Auditors Special Report No. 23/2000 concerning valuation of imported goods for customs purposes dated 14 March 2001, the EC Court of Auditors stated that: "The Commission uses the [Valuation section of the Customs Code Committee] to try to achieve its objective of ensuring that the valuation rules are applied correctly and in a uniform manner but has no powers to direct Member States to adopt a particular interpretation of the customs valuation legislation. The Commission views its mission as to encourage any form of convergence of practice between the administrations represented in the Valuation Committee, and has to rely on discussion, persuasion and encouragement as the means of achieving common treatment of identical problems in Member States.": EC Court of Auditors Special Report No 23/2000 concerning valuation of imported goods for customs purposes, 14 March 2001, para. 26 (Exhibit US-14).

[985] European Communities' reply to Panel question No. 58(l).

also submits that, where a member State infringes the duty of cooperation, this constitutes an infringement of the EC Treaty, against which the European Commission can bring infringement proceedings pursuant to Article 226 of the EC Treaty.[986]

7.164 Notably, Article 10 of the EC Treaty does not prescribe the "appropriate measures" which the member States (including customs authorities of the member States) must take to ensure fulfilment of their obligations under EC law, including EC customs law. Further, the European Communities has only referred to a handful of cases in which Article 10 of the EC Treaty was invoked as a basis for ensuring uniform administration of EC customs law among the customs authorities of the member States.[987] Therefore, the Panel observes that the extent to which Article 10 of the EC Treaty contributes to the uniform administration of EC customs law is unclear.

Preliminary reference system

7.165 According to Article 234 of the EC Treaty, national courts of the member States may refer any question regarding the interpretation of EC law to the ECJ. The European Communities has informed the Panel that national courts or tribunals against whose decisions there is a judicial remedy under national law, are entitled, but in principle not required, to refer a question to the ECJ for a preliminary ruling. Subject to certain exceptions, member States' courts against whose decisions there is no judicial remedy under national law are obliged to refer such questions to the ECJ.[988]

7.166 The European Communities submits that the main objective of the ECJ preliminary reference system provided for under Article 234 of the EC Treaty is to guarantee the uniform interpretation and application of EC law, including EC customs law, throughout the member States. The European Communities further submits that it is through preliminary rulings issued by the ECJ, which are binding on all courts of the member States, that divergences within and between the member States can be avoided and the effective application of Community law be assured.[989]

---

[986] European Communities' reply to Panel question No. 147. Infringement proceedings under, *inter alia*, Article 226 of the EC Treaty are discussed in paragraphs 7.169 – 7.170 below.

[987] In particular, in the *tariff classification area*, the European Communities refers to Case C-206/03, *Commissioners of Customs & Excise v. SmithKline Beecham*, Order of the Court of 19 January 2005 (not yet reported) (Exhibit EC-142) and to Case C-453/00, *Kühne & Heitz v. Productschap voor Pluimvee en Eieren* [2004] ECR I-837 (Exhibit EC-61). In the *area of customs procedures* (and, specifically, with respect to the imposition of penalties in the context of violations of EC customs law), the European Communities refers to Case C-213/99 *José Teodoro de Andrade v. Director da Alfândega de Leixoes, de Andrade* [2000] ECR I-11083 (Exhibit US-31), Case C-91/02 *Hannle + Hofstetter Internationale Spedition v. Fianzlandesdirektion für Wien, Niederosterreich* Judgment of 16 October 2003 (not yet reported) (Exhibit EC-143), Case C-36/94 *Siesse v. Director da Alfândega de Alcântara, Siesse* [1995] ECR I-3573 (Exhibit EC-40), Case 68/88 *Commission v. Greece* 1989 [ECR] 2965 (Exhibit EC-38).

[988] European Communities' first written submission, para. 95.

[989] European Communities' first written submission, para. 185.

7.167 The Panel notes that the preliminary reference system only becomes operational when two cumulative conditions have been satisfied. The first condition is that a trader disgruntled by the decision of a customs authority in a member State must appeal to a national court of the member State in question. Given the cost and time implicated by such an appeal, it is unclear whether traders will resort to such an option in all cases in which non-uniform application of EC customs law among the customs authorities of the member States becomes apparent. Notably, a trader is not authorized under EC law to proceed directly to the ECJ for a preliminary ruling. The second condition is that the national court to whom the trader has appealed must be obliged to or must decide to refer the matter to the ECJ for a preliminary ruling. Even in cases where a national court is technically obliged to refer a matter to the ECJ for a preliminary ruling[990], there are exceptions to this obligation. In particular, a national court is not obliged to refer a matter to the ECJ for a preliminary ruling when: the question raised is irrelevant; the provision of EC law in question has already been interpreted by the ECJ; or the correct application of EC law is so obvious as to leave no scope for any reasonable doubt.[991]

7.168 The European Communities provided the Panel with statistics concerning the use of the preliminary reference system in the context of the administration of EC customs law, including in the specific areas of custom administration listed in the United States' request for establishment of a panel. The European Communities explains that the total number of preliminary rulings requested by member State courts during the period 1995 – 2005 was 2,314, of which 249 concerned customs administration. The European Communities notes that, of the 249 requests for preliminary ruling in the area of customs administration, 55 related to tariff classification, 9 related to customs valuation and 162 concerned customs procedures.[992] The Panel notes that the use of the preliminary reference system to secure uniform administration by the customs authorities of the member States in the area of customs administration during the period of 1995 – 2005 appears low, especially in the light of the European Communities assertion that literally millions of customs decisions are taken by customs authorities in the member States each year in the European Communities.[993]

Infringement proceedings

7.169 "Infringement proceedings" may be instituted before the ECJ against member States for failure to fulfil an obligation under EC law pursuant to Articles 226-228 of the EC Treaty. The European Communities submits that infringement proceedings against authorities of the member States play an impor-

---

[990] That is, because there is no judicial remedy under national law from the national court or where a national court considers that an act of a Community institution is invalid.

[991] Case C-495/03 *Intermodal Transports BV v. Staatssecretaris van Financiën*, 15 September 2005, para. 33 (Exhibit US-71) and Case 283/81, *Cilfit*, [1982], ECR 3415, paras. 10-16 (Exhibit EC-160).

[992] European Communities' reply to Panel question No. 162.

[993] European Communities' closing statement at the second substantive meeting, para. 20.

tant role in ensuring uniform administration among customs authorities of the member States of EC customs law.[994]

7.170 The European Communities notes that, since 1995, 83 infringement proceedings have been commenced by the EC Commission against the member States concerning the administration of customs law.[995] Of those 83 cases, 2 cases related to tariff classification, 1 case related to customs valuation and 44 cases related to customs procedures.[996] The Panel notes that the use of infringement proceedings to secure uniform administration by the customs authorities of the member States in the area of customs administration during the period of 1995 – 2000 appears low, especially in the light of the European Communities assertion that literally millions of customs decisions are taken each year in the European Communities.[997]

The European Ombudsman

7.171 The European Communities submits that the European Ombudsman is a mechanism that contributes to the uniform administration of EC customs law by the customs authorities of the member States.[998]

7.172 The Panel considers that the extent to which the European Ombudsman is effective in ensuring uniform administration among the customs authorities of the member States of EC customs law is unclear in the light of the following facts. *First*, it is apparent that the European Ombudsman's jurisdiction is limited to consideration of complaints of maladministration on the part of the institutions and bodies of the European Union.[999] Therefore, it would appear that the European Ombudsman cannot investigate complaints against customs authorities in the member States for the non-uniform application of EC customs law. *Second*, since 1999, the European Ombudsman has issued only four decisions on matters of customs administration. In one case, the European Ombudsman made a critical remark. In two cases, the European Ombudsman found no maladministration. In a further case, the complaint was withdrawn, so that the European Ombudsman did not take a decision on the substance of the complaint.[1000] The Panel notes that the use of the European Ombudsman to secure uniform administration by the customs authorities of the member States in the area of customs administration since 1999 appears low, especially in the light of the European Commu-

[994] European Communities' first written submission, para. 46; European Communities' second written submission, para. 172; European Communities' oral statement at the second substantive meeting, para. 49.

[995] European Communities' reply to United States' question No. 1.

[996] European Communities' reply to Panel question No. 164.

[997] European Communities' closing statement at the second substantive meeting, para. 20.

[998] European Communities' first written submission, para. 50; European Communities' second written submission, para. 167.

[999] The European Ombudsman at a Glance, p. 2 (Exhibit US-82).

[1000] European Communities' reply to Panel question No. 165 referring to the Reebok case (Exhibit US-52).

nities assertion that literally millions of customs decisions are taken each year in the European Communities.[1001]

Complaints to the EC Commission

7.173 The European Communities submits that any individual with a concern regarding the administration of customs matters can bring the issue to the attention of the EC Commission, which will consider the matter and respond in accordance with the Commission's Code of Conduct.[1002]

7.174 The European Communities has informed the Panel that, during the period of 1996 – 2004, over 17,000 letters were received by the EC Commission from private bodies and operators on customs matters. The European Communities noted that it was not possible to determine the number of letters that concerned the areas of tariff classification, customs valuation and customs procedures, but was willing to provide the Panel with a representative table for the period of 2002 – 2005.[1003] Further, the European Communities informed the Panel that it was not feasible to explain the reaction and/or action taken by the Commission in each of the cases and the time taken by the Commission to respond.[1004]

Restrictions on the adoption of national measures by customs authorities of the member States

7.175 The European Communities submits that national measures implemented by customs authorities of the member States (including national practices and provisions) must strictly respect EC law and may otherwise be set aside by the courts.[1005] Nevertheless, the European Communities itself submits that a member State may act to supplement provisions contained in EC law if it is explicitly authorized to do so[1006], or if a specific issue is not covered by EC law.[1007] Moreover, the European Communities submits that member States' authorities are not prevented from issuing administrative guidelines or other non-binding documents for administrative purposes, although the ECJ has indicated that such measures cannot derogate in any way from the application of EC law by the cus-

[1001] European Communities' closing statement at the second substantive meeting, para. 20.

[1002] European Communities' first written submission, para. 275 referring to Commission communication to the European Parliament and the European Ombudsman on relations with the complainant in respect of infringements of Community law, 10 October 2002 (Exhibit EC-11) and to Rules of Procedure of the Commission, 8 December 2000 (Exhibit EC-12).

[1003] European Communities' reply to Panel question No. 166 referring to Tables of correspondence 2002 – 2005, DG TAXUD (Exhibit EC-149).

[1004] European Communities' reply to Panel question No. 166.

[1005] European Communities' reply to Panel question No. 78 referring to Case 230/78, Eridania-Zuccherifici [1979] ECR 2749, para. 34 (Exhibit EC-114).

[1006] The European Communities clarifies that the authorisation does not necessarily have to be "explicit"; it is sufficient if it follows from the text of the Community legislation.

[1007] European Communities' reply to Panel question No. 78; European Communities' reply to Panel question No. 157.

toms authorities and the courts.[1008] More specifically, the ECJ has stated that national authorities cannot issue binding guidelines for the interpretation of EC law. Accordingly, the interpretation of EC law by national administrations and courts must be guided exclusively by the text of EC law, and all contrary provisions or guidelines of national origin must be set aside.[1009]

7.176 The European Communities notes that, in areas that are not regulated by EC law, member States are free to legislate and to administer their own laws. The European Communities acknowledges that there are no mechanisms in place at the EC level to ensure a uniform interpretation and application of the laws of member States in such areas. However, the European Communities submits that, in such areas, the member States may still be required to respect certain principles of EC law, including Article 10 of the EC Treaty discussed in paragraph 7.161 *et seq* above and ECJ jurisprudence.[1010]

Consultations and mutual assistance between member State customs authorities

7.177 The European Communities has acknowledged that there is no general obligation contained in EC customs law requiring the customs authorities of the member States to consult other customs authorities of other member States before making customs decisions, although obligations of mutual consultation may arise in specific situations, for instance in the context of the issuance of BTI, which is discussed in more detail in paragraph 7.181 below.[1011] Further, Council Regulation (EC) No. 515/97 on mutual assistance between the administrative authorities of the member States and cooperation between the latter and the Commission seeks to ensure the correct application of, *inter alia*, EC customs law.[1012] The European Communities explains that, under Regulation No. 515/97, member States have the general right to request relevant information from other member States, on either persons or transactions involving imports of goods, from other administrations. Member States also have the obligation to provide assistance (including communication of all information in their possession) where they consider it useful for ensuring compliance with customs legislation, or where breaches (actual or potential) of customs legislation arise.[1013]

Best practice guidelines

1008 European Communities' reply to Panel question No. 157.

1009 European Communities' reply to Panel question No. 78.

1010 European Communities' reply to Panel question No. 85.

1011 The European Communities submits that examples would include the following provisions: single authorisation for end-use (Article 292 [2] of the Implementing Regulation); customs procedures with economic impact (Article 500 of the Implementing Regulation); regular shipping service (Articles 313a-313b of the Implementing Regulation); proof of Community status by authorized consignor (Article 324e of the Implementing Regulation); simplified transit procedure for air transport - level 2 (Article 445 of the Implementing Regulation); simplified transit procedure for sea transport - level 2 (Article 448 of the Implementing Regulation): European Communities' reply to Panel question No. 79.

1012 Exhibit EC-42.

1013 European Communities' reply to Panel question No. 149.

7.178 Article 4 of Decision No. 253/2003/EC of the European Parliament and the Council of 11 February 2003 adopting an action programme for customs in the Community refers to the need, *inter alia* to identify, develop and apply best working practices, especially in the areas of post-clearance audit control, risk analysis and simplified procedures; to improve the standardization and simplification of customs procedures, systems and controls; to improve the coordination of and co-operation between laboratories carrying out analysis for customs purposes in order to ensure, in particular, a uniform and unambiguous tariff classification throughout the European Union; and to develop common training measures and the organisational framework for customs training that would respond to the needs arising from programme actions. The European Communities refers to a list of programme actions which fall into the above-mentioned categories.[1014] The European Communities also submits that the Community and its member States have undertaken a series of actions to improve working practices.[1015] In the area of *tariff classification*, the European Communities refers to the EBTI guidelines as a form of best working practice guidelines.[1016] Regarding the best practice guidelines that exist in the area of *customs valuation*, the European Communities refers to the Compendium of Customs Valuation texts[1017], which is regularly updated, and into which all relevant conclusion and commentaries are integrated.[1018] Regarding best working practice guidelines in the *customs procedure area* (audit following release for circulation, penalties for infringements of EC customs legislation, processing under customs control and local clearance procedures), the European Communities refers to a Risk Analysis Guide issued to Member States in 1998[1019]; a Standard Risk Management Framework issued in 2002[1020]; the Customs Audit Guide[1021]; and Council Resolution of 29 June 1995 on the effective and uniform application of Community law and on the penalties applicable for breaches of Community law in the internal market.[1022]

Institutions and mechanisms applicable in specific areas of customs administration referred to in the United States' request for establishment of a panel

Tariff classification

7.179 The European Communities notes that the administration of EC rules in the area of tariff classification is, in principle, the responsibility of the customs

---

1014 Exhibit EC-117.
1015 European Communities' reply to Panel question No. 83.
1016 European Communities' reply to Panel question No. 167 referring to Exhibit EC-32. These guidelines are discussed in more detail in paragraph 7.181 below.
1017 This Compendium, which is contained in Exhibit EC-37, is discussed in more detail in paragraph 7.186 *et seq* below.
1018 European Communities' reply to Panel question No. 167.
1019 Exhibit EC-150.
1020 Exhibit EC-151.
1021 Exhibit EC-90.
1022 European Communities' reply to Panel question No. 167 referring to Exhibit EC-41.

authorities of the member States. However, according to the European Communities, there are a number of tools to ensure uniform administration by the customs authorities of the member States, including classification regulations, explanatory notes to the Common Customs Tariff, opinions of the Customs Code Committee and BTI. These tools are explained in the factual aspects of the Panel's report in paragraphs 2.37 – 2.48 above.

7.180 The European Communities submits that, when there is disagreement among customs authorities of the member States regarding tariff classification, the customs authorities concerned *should* consult with one another. Nevertheless, the European Communities acknowledges that the customs authorities of the member States are *not obliged* to consult with one another.[1023] The European Communities also submits that, if the disagreement persists, the matter *must* be raised with the Customs Code Committee. However, as noted above in paragraph 7.159, the Customs Code Committee may consider matters only if raised by the chairperson of the Committee or a member State representative.[1024] Furthermore, as submitted by the European Communities itself, the Customs Code Committee will not usually examine individual cases of divergent application of EC customs law, including in the area of tariff classification.[1025] Moreover, the Panel recalls that the opinions of the Customs Code Committee are not legally binding.[1026] Additionally, the Panel notes that EC customs law does not appear to make provision for the situation where a customs authority of a member State refuses to consult with a customs authority of another member State regarding disagreements concerning the tariff classification of a particular good.

7.181 With respect to the issuance of BTI by the customs authorities of the member States, Article 8(1) of the Implementing Regulation provides that a copy of the application for BTI and a copy of BTI notified to the applicant must be transmitted to the EC Commission, which are then stored in a central database run by the EC Commission – namely, the EBTI database. According to the administrative guidelines issued by the Commission on the EBTI system, the EBTI database should be consulted by customs authorities prior to the issuance of BTI in cases where there is a doubt regarding the correct classification, or where different headings merit consideration.[1027] Notably, however, the European Communities acknowledges that the administrative guidelines on the EBTI system are not legally binding and, therefore, there is no obligation on the part of customs authorities of the member States to consult the EBTI database when they classify a good.[1028] The European Communities submits that, nevertheless, in the administration of EC customs law, all member States are bound by the duty of cooperation contained in Article 10 of the EC Treaty according to which member States must use all tools available to ensure the proper and uniform administra-

[1023] European Communities' reply to Panel question No. 56.
[1024] Article 249 of the Community Customs Code.
[1025] European Communities' replies to Panel question Nos. 58(j)(i) and 58(j)(v).
[1026] Joined Cases 69 and 70/76, *Dittmeyer*, [1977] ECR 231 (Exhibit EC-31).
[1027] Administrative Guidelines on the European Binding Tariff Information (EBTI) System and its Operation, 28 October 2004, p. 7 (Exhibit EC-32).
[1028] European Communities' reply to US question No. 3 following the first substantive meeting.

tion of EC customs law, including the EBTI system.[1029] Moreover, the European Communities explains that customs authorities of the member States are not obliged to consult the EBTI database because, in the majority of cases, the classification of goods is unproblematic. Therefore, according to the European Communities, it would be disproportionate and result in a considerable slowing-down of customs procedures, to require consultation of the EBTI database in each and every case involving a classification of goods by customs authorities of the member States.[1030] The European Communities further explains that the purpose of BTI is primarily to provide holders with a measure of legal certainty as regards the tariff classification of goods throughout the European Communities, rather than to ensure uniform administration of EC rules in the area of tariff classification.[1031]

7.182 Concerning the revocation of BTI, the Panel understands that, in the context of the EC system of customs administration, such revocation is not imposed on other customs authorities operating within the context of the same system and there is no obligation to inform other customs authorities of the decision to revoke BTI.[1032] For example, cases may arise where a customs authority of a member State considers that its interpretation of a particular tariff heading is erroneous and decides to revoke BTI that was issued in accordance with its former interpretation. The Panel observes that, if the system of customs administration does not provide for uniform application of the revocation and/or does not oblige the revoking customs authority to consult and/or to notify other customs authorities of the decision to revoke, the customs authorities in other member States may continue classifying under the heading formerly used by the revoking customs authority.[1033]

[1029] European Communities' reply to Panel question No. 55. Article 10 of the EC Treaty is discussed above in paragraph 7.161 *et seq*.

[1030] European Communities' reply to US question No. 3 following the first substantive meeting.

[1031] According to the European Communities, this objective can be deduced from numerous provisions of Community law concerning the granting and effect of binding tariff information, in particular Article 12 of the Community Customs Code and Articles 5, 10, and 11 of the Implementing Regulation: European Communities' reply to Panel question No. 50.

[1032] The Panel understands that, under EC customs law, there is no provision that provides that the revocation of BTI is immediately binding on the customs authorities of all member States. Furthermore, we understand that there is no specific provision in EC customs law requiring the transmission of the revocation of BTI by customs authorities of the member States to the Commission.

[1033] Indeed, the Advocate General in the decision in *Timmermans Transport & Logistics BV v. Inspecteur der Belastingdienst Douanedistrict Roosendaal and Hoogenboom Production Ltd v. Inspecteur der Belastingdienst Douanedistrict Rotterdam* pointed out the risks of non-uniform administration in such a scenario, stating that:

> "[T]he view may be taken that BTI must be revoked where the customs authorities have actually made an error (i.e. one established as such rather than one which they merely claim to have committed) in the interpretation of the customs nomenclature and, therefore, in the tariff classification of the goods covered by the BTI in question. ...
>
> However, I do not share the opinion ... that customs authorities are entitled to revoke BTI in cases where they take the view at their own discretion (i.e. on the basis of their assessment alone) that they have made an error in the interpretation of the customs nomenclature and in the corresponding tariff classification. After all, such revocation is not necessarily justified because the error in question has not necessarily been established as such. Furthermore, the possibility of revoking BTI in this way

Customs valuation

7.183 The European Communities submits that the administration of EC rules in the area of customs valuation is primarily the responsibility of the customs authorities of the member States.[1034] However, according to the European Communities, there are a number of tools to ensure uniform administration by the customs authorities of the member States, including amendments to EC rules regarding customs valuation, opinions of the Customs Code Committee and the Compendium of Customs Valuation texts. These tools are explained in the factual aspects of the Panel's report in paragraphs 2.49 – 2.56 above.

7.184 The European Communities submits that, where a need for further detailed rules on valuation exists, the EC Commission may, in accordance with the procedure of Article 247 of the Community Customs Code, amend the valuation rules contained in the Implementing Regulation, which amendments will be legally binding in all member States.[1035]

7.185 With respect to the utility of opinions of the Customs Code Committee to achieve uniform administration by the customs authorities of the member States in the customs valuation area, the European Communities notes that the Customs Code Committee may adopt guidelines and conclusions on questions of customs valuation wherever necessary.[1036] In this regard, the Panel recalls that the opinions of the Customs Code Committee are not legally binding on the customs authorities of the member States.[1037]

---

is not readily compatible either with the objective of the uniform application of the customs nomenclature or with the objective of legal certainty pursued by the introduction of BTI.

As regards the objective of the uniform application of the customs nomenclature, I consider that, while a Commission decision ordering the revocation of BTI is necessarily aimed at, and has the effect of ensuring the correct and uniform application of the customs nomenclature, the same cannot be said of the practice whereby the customs authorities decide at their own discretion to revoke BTI which they have issued following a change in their own interpretation of the relevant nomenclature, even though, in so doing, the authorities in question may be motivated by the desire to align their interpretation with that given by other customs authorities.

After all, it should be borne in mind that, unlike the Commission, the customs authorities issuing BTI do not necessarily have an overview of all the BTI notices issued by all the other customs authorities within the Community in respect of identical or similar goods.

In my opinion, where customs authorities consider that they have made an error in the interpretation of the customs nomenclature when issuing BTI, they should notify the Commission to that effect in order to ensure that it is indeed an error such as to justify revocation of the BTI in question. Only a mechanism such as this would be capable of ensuring that the customs nomenclature is applied correctly, or at least uniformly. In my view, the need for customs authorities to notify the Commission in this way follows both from the objectives of legal certainty and the uniform application of the customs nomenclature pursued through the introduction of BTI, and from the obligation incumbent on Member States, under Article 10 EC, to cooperate dutifully with the Community institutions.": *Timmermans Transport & Logistics BV v. Inspecteur der Belastingdienst - Douanedistrict Roosendaal and Hoogenboom Production Ltd v. Inspecteur der Belastingdienst - Douanedistrict Rotterdam*, Opinion of the Advocate General, Cases C-133/02 and C-134/02, 2004 ECR I-01125, 11 September 2003, paras. 58-62 (Exhibit US-21).

[1034] European Communities' reply to Panel question No. 146.

[1035] European Communities' first written submission, para. 128.

[1036] European Communities' reply to Panel question No. 146.

[1037] Joined Cases 69 and 70/76, *Dittmeyer*, [1977] ECR 231 (Exhibit EC-31).

7.186 The European Communities also notes that the Commission has issued a Compendium of Customs Valuation texts. This Compendium contains commentaries prepared and conclusions reached by the Customs Code Committee on specific issues of customs valuation. In addition, it contains excerpts from relevant judgments of the ECJ on valuation issues, as well as indices of other relevant texts.[1038] However, the Panel understands that the commentaries contained in the Compendium of Customs Valuation texts have no legal status and, therefore, do not have binding effect.[1039] Furthermore, as far as the Panel is aware, EC customs law does not oblige customs authorities of the member States to make reference to the Compendium when making decisions on customs valuation matters.

7.187 The Panel also understands that, in the area of customs valuation, there is no obligation under EC law to consult when there is disagreement among customs authorities of the member States regarding customs valuation in a particular situation. The European Communities refers to what it labels as a "best practice guide", dealing with the exchange of information between member States in relation, *inter alia*, to valuation decisions.[1040] The Panel notes that the document to which the European Communities refers is a report of the Customs 2002 Project Group "to examine possible working tools to assist information exchange in customs valuation matters", which was set up in response to the EC Court of Auditors Special Report No. 23/2000 concerning valuation of imported goods for customs purposes.[1041] The report of the Customs 2002 Project Group notes that current informal bilateral contacts among customs authorities of the member States work well regarding the exchange of customs valuation information but states that this situation could be usefully complemented by a more formalized system available to all administrations.[1042] As far as the Panel is aware, such a system has not yet been implemented in the European Communities.

Customs procedures

7.188 Concerning customs procedures, the European Communities submits that the conduct of processing under customs control, local clearance procedure, customs audits and the administration of penalty provisions are the responsibility of the customs authorities of the member States authorities.[1043]

[1038] European Communities' first written submission, para. 130 referring to the Compendium of Customs Valuation texts of the Customs Code Committee, 2 December 2004 (Exhibit EC-37).

[1039] Indeed, the version of the Compendium available on the Internet states that: "[T]he present compendium has no legal status. It has been prepared primarily for Member States administrations but can be circulated to all interested parties": http://ec.europa.eu/comm/taxation_customs/resources/documents/ ccut.en.pdf referred to by the European Communities in paragraph 130 of its first written submission.

[1040] European Communities' reply to Panel question No. 149 referring to Final report, Customs 2002 Project Group to examine possible working tools to assist information exchange in customs valuation matters, 21 November 2002 (Exhibit EC-144).

[1041] Exhibit US-14.

[1042] Final report, Customs 2002 Project Group to examine possible working tools to assist information exchange in customs valuation matters, 21 November 2002, p. 7 (Exhibit EC-144).

[1043] European Communities' reply to Panel question No. 146.

7.189 The Panel notes that Article 250 of the Community Customs Code provides that, where a customs procedure is used in several member States, the decisions, measures and documents issued by one member State shall have the same legal effects in other member States as such decisions, measures taken and documents issued by each of those member States.

7.190 The Panel understands that, in the area of customs procedures, there is no obligation under EC law to consult when there is disagreement among customs authorities of the member States regarding customs procedures in a particular situation. The European Communities submits, and the United States has not contested, that, with respect to local clearance procedure and processing under customs control, where such a procedure involves more than one member State, exchange of information is practised among customs authorities of the member States.[1044]

General observations regarding the institutions and mechanisms involved in the administration of the EC customs laws

7.191 The European Communities submits that whether or not a lack of uniformity exists in a particular system of customs administration can only be determined on the basis of all relevant facts, which necessarily includes a consideration of all the features of the customs system in question.[1045] The European Communities contends that, in the context of its system of customs administration, it is not appropriate to consider a small number of instruments in isolation, ignoring the wider range of instruments that contribute to the uniform interpretation and application of EC customs law.[1046] In this regard, the Panel notes that, in its consideration of the EC system of customs administration as a whole, the Panel found the system complicated and, at times, opaque and confusing. We can imagine that the difficulties we encountered in our efforts to understand the EC system of customs administration would be multiplied manifold for traders in general and small traders in particular who are trying to import into the European Communities.

7.192 The Panel will now consider the particular instances of alleged violations of Article X:3(a) of the GATT 1994 regarding the administration of the Community Customs Code, the Implementing Regulation, the Common Customs Tariff, the TARIC and related measures. More particularly, the Panel will consider the United States' allegations of: non-uniform administration of the Common Customs Tariff in the area of tariff classification; non-uniform administration of the Community Customs Code and the Implementing Regulation in the area of customs valuation; non-uniform administration of the Community Customs Code and the Implementing Regulation in the area of customs procedures; and non-uniform administration regarding Article 221(3) of the Community Customs Code.

[1044] European Communities' reply to Panel question No. 149.

[1045] European Communities' oral statement at the second substantive meeting, para. 10.

[1046] European Communities' first written submission, para. 260.

(b) Allegations of non-uniform administration of the Common Customs Tariff in the area of tariff classification

(i) Tariff classification of network cards for personal computers

Summary of the parties' arguments

7.193 The **United States** submits that the case of *Peacock AG* v. *Hauptzollamt Paderborn* describes divergence in classification of network cards for personal computers between Denmark, Netherlands, and the United Kingdom, on the one hand, and Germany, on the other.[1047] The United States notes that, in the context of that case, the Advocate General observed that "customs authorities of various Community Member States issued conflicting BTIs classifying items of LAN equipment variously under headings 8471, 8473 and 8517 [of the Common Customs Tariff]".[1048]

7.194 In response, the **European Communities** notes that the *Peacock* case relates to importations of network cards for personal computers before 1995. In 1995, the European Communities adopted Regulation No. 1165/95 foreseeing the classification of the network cards in question under heading 8517 (electrical apparatus for line telegraphy).[1049] However, Regulation No. 1165/95 did not apply to importations that took place before its entry into force.[1050] Further, the European Communities submits that the classification of network cards for personal computers by the German customs authorities which came to light in the *Peacock* case was appealed in a competent court in Germany, which referred the question to the ECJ for a preliminary ruling. By judgment of 19 October 2000, the ECJ decided that the classification by the German authorities had been erroneous, and that the products in question had to be classified under heading 8471 (automatic data-processing machines and parts thereof).[1051] The European Communities submits that, in a further ruling, the ECJ confirmed this interpretation and decided that Regulation No. 1165/95 was invalid.[1052]

7.195 The **United States** notes in response that, even though the divergence in classification of network cards for personal computers may have been resolved through litigation that ultimately led to an ECJ decision, this does not rebut evidence of non-uniform administration because non-uniform administration existed

[1047] United States' first written submission, footnote 33 referring to Case C-339/98, *Peacock AG* v. *Hauptzollamt Paderborn*, Opinion of the Advocate General, 2000 ECR I-08947, 28 October 1999, paras. 7-8 (Exhibit US-17).

[1048] United States' comments on the European Communities' reply to Panel question No. 161 referring to Case C-339/98, *Peacock AG* v. *Hauptzollamt Paderborn*, Opinion of the Advocate General, 2000 ECR I-08947, 28 October 1999, para. 15 (Exhibit US-17).

[1049] Commission Regulation No. 1165/95 of 23 May 1995 concerning the classification of certain goods in the Combined Nomenclature (Exhibit EC-135).

[1050] European Communities' second written submission, para. 134.

[1051] Case C-339/98, *Peacock*, [2000] ECR I-8497, 19 October 2000 (Exhibit EC-87).

[1052] European Communities' second written submission, para. 135 referring to Case C-463/98, *Cabletron System Ltd* v *The Revenue Commissioners* [2001] ECR I-3495, 10 May 2001 (Exhibit EC-136).

and, moreover, was allowed to persist for years. The United States notes in this regard that the divergence in network cards for personal computers occurred in 1995 but was not resolved until five years later, when the ECJ rendered a decision in 2000.[1053]

7.196 The **European Communities** argues that BTI is only binding against the holder of the BTI and is not binding against other persons.[1054] Further, the European Communities submits that what is significant is not that a divergence may occur but, rather, that it is addressed and removed once it occurs. According to the European Communities, this is precisely what happened in the context of the *Peacock* case.[1055] In addition, the European Communities submits that the correct classification of network equipment is a complex technical question with which many customs authorities have had to come to terms.[1056] In this regard, the European Communities notes that the classification of network equipment has also led to a WTO dispute between the European Communities and the United States concerning the correct classification of LAN equipment (including network cards).[1057]

Analysis by the Panel

7.197 The Panel notes that the United States challenges an alleged divergence in the tariff classification of network cards for personal computers among customs authorities of the member States of the European Communities.[1058]

7.198 In the Panel's view, the tariff classification of a product, such as network cards for personal computers, constitutes an act of administration within the meaning of Article X:3(a) of the GATT 1994. This act of administration is a matter within the Panel's terms of reference since it amounts to an instance of administration of the Common Customs Tariff in the tariff classification area.[1059]

7.199 With respect to the question of whether or not the tariff classification of network cards for personal computers is "uniform" within the meaning of Article X:3(a) of the GATT 1994, the Panel recalls its finding in paragraph 7.135 above that geographic uniformity is required under Article X:3(a) of the GATT 1994. That is, administration should be uniform in different places within a particular WTO Member. The Panel also recalls its finding in paragraph 7.135

[1053] United States' reply to Panel question No. 20; United States' oral statement at the second substantive meeting, para. 21.

[1054] European Communities' reply to Panel question No. 161 referring to Case C-495/03, *Intermodal Transports BV v. Staastsecretaris van Financiën*, 15 September 2005, not yet reported, para. 27 (Exhibit US-71).

[1055] European Communities' second written submission, para. 136.

[1056] Case C-339/98, *Peacock AG* v. *Hauptzollamt Paderborn*, Opinion of the Advocate General, 2000 ECR I-08947, 28 October 1999, para. 11 *et seq.* (Exhibit US-17).

[1057] European Communities' second written submission, para. 137 referring to Appellate Body Report and Panel Reports, *EC – Computer Equipment*.

[1058] United States' first written submission, footnote 33 referring to Case C-339/98, *Peacock AG* v. *Hauptzollamt Paderborn*, Opinion of the Advocate General, 2000 ECR I-08947, 28 October 1999, paras. 7-8 (Exhibit US-17).

[1059] For information on EC institutions and mechanisms applicable in the tariff classification area, see paragraphs 7.179 – 7.182 above.

above that the form, nature and scale of the alleged non-uniform administration and the laws, regulations, judicial decisions and rulings that are allegedly being administered in a non-uniform manner should be taken into consideration when interpreting the term "uniform" in Article X:3(a) of the GATT 1994. The Panel considers that the United States' challenge with respect to the tariff classification of network cards for personal computers is narrow in nature. It involves the interpretation of only a few tariff headings in the Common Customs Tariff to determine the classification of a single product – namely, network cards for personal computers. Therefore, given the narrowness of this challenge, the Panel considers that a high degree of uniformity is required for the purposes of Article X:3(a) of the GATT 1994. We now turn to the facts to determine whether or not this high degree of uniformity has been achieved with respect to the tariff classification of network cards for personal computers.

7.200 The Panel notes that, in support of the United States' allegation of the existence of divergent tariff classification of network cards for personal computers among the member States of the European Communities, it relies upon the following explanation of the factual background of the main proceedings of the case before the ECJ in *Peacock AG* v. *Hauptzollamt Paderborn*, which is contained in the Advocate General's opinion:

> "According to the order for references, Peacock AG (the applicant), a German company, imported large quantities of network cards from the United States of America and other non-member countries between July 1990 and May 1995, having them cleared through customs under CN subheading 8473 3000 as electronic circuits, for use solely as parts for computers falling under heading 8471 (cards). In 1993, the applicant and two of its subsidiaries received binding customs tariff information (BTIs) from the Danish, Netherlands and United Kingdom customs authorities, to the effect that such network cards were to be classified under heading 8473 of the CN.
>
> The Hauptzollamt (Principal Customs Office) Paderborn (the defendant), however, subsequently issued amendment notices and claimed the extra customs duty which should have been paid had the goods been classified under what it considered to be the correct CN heading, namely 8517. The applicant challenged both those notices and the group customs declarations which it had made in compliance with them. By decision of 11 September 1995 the defendant rejected the objections as unfounded, holding that network cards were to be classified under heading 8517."[1060]

7.201 The facts as contained in the Advocate General's opinion do indicate the existence at one point in time of differences in tariff classification between, on the one hand, the German customs authorities (who classified the product in question under heading 8517) and, on the other hand, Danish, Dutch and UK

[1060] Case C-339/98, *Peacock AG* v. *Hauptzollamt Paderborn*, Opinion of the Advocate General, 2000 ECR I-08947, 28 October 1999, paras. 7 - 8 (Exhibit US-17).

customs authorities (who classified it under heading 8473). The Panel notes that the European Communities has not contested the existence of such differences.[1061] In the light of the foregoing, the Panel considers that, sometime during the period 1990 – 1995, the European Communities was not administering the Common Customs Tariff concerning the tariff classification of network cards for personal computers in a uniform manner in violation of Article X:3(a) of the GATT 1994.

7.202 Nevertheless, the Panel is of the view that the efforts taken by EC institutions to reconcile such differences need to be taken into consideration for the purposes of this dispute. In the year 2000, following the reference by the German national court to the ECJ for a preliminary ruling in the *Peacock* case, the ECJ concluded that the products in question were to be classified under heading 8471 – that is, under a heading that had not been the basis for classification neither by the German customs authorities nor by the Danish, Dutch and UK customs authorities.[1062]

7.203 Notably, the importations that gave rise to the ECJ's preliminary ruling in the *Peacock* case occurred between 1990 and 1995.[1063] They took place before adoption of Commission Regulation (EC) No. 1165/95 of 23 May 1995, according to which certain products were classified under sub-heading 8517 82 90.[1064] The products classified under heading 8517 pursuant to Regulation No. 1165/95 were apparently identical to the products at issue in the *Peacock* case.[1065]

7.204 Given that the importations at issue in the *Peacock* case pre-dated the adoption of Regulation No. 1165/95, Regulation No. 1165/95 was not at issue in that case.[1066] Nevertheless, in the light of the apparent inconsistency between, on the one hand, the classification of network cards for personal computers under heading 8471 by the ECJ in its 2000 preliminary ruling in the *Peacock* case and, on the other hand, in Regulation No. 1165/95, which classified the products under heading 8517, the ECJ ruled the latter Regulation legally invalid in a preliminary ruling in the case of *Cabletron Systems Ltd v The Revenue Commis-*

[1061] European Communities' second written submission, paras. 134-137.

[1062] Case C-339/98, *Peacock*, [2000] ECR I-8497, 19 October 2000 (Exhibit EC-87).

[1063] At paragraph 3, the Advocate General states that the goods with which the main proceedings are concerned were imported between 1990 and 1995: Case C-339/98, *Peacock AG* v. *Hauptzollamt Paderborn*, Opinion of the Advocate General, 2000 ECR I-08947, 28 October 1999 (Exhibit US-17).

[1064] In particular, Regulation No. 1165/95 classified the following products under sub-heading 8517 82 90: "An adapter card for incorporation in cable linked digital automatic data-processing (ADP) machines enabling the exchange of data over a local area network (LAN) without using a modem)". (Exhibit EC-135).

[1065] This is evident from paragraph 6 of Case C-339/98, *Peacock AG* v. *Hauptzollamt Paderborn*, Opinion of the Advocate General, 2000 ECR I-08947, 28 October 1999 (Exhibit US-17).

[1066] Indeed, as noted by the Advocate General in his opinion, "[t]he national court has not sought a ruling on the validity of Regulation No. 1165/95, which came into force after the importations with which the main proceedings are concerned, but has expressed the view that a ruling that the network cards were to be classified under heading 8473 would indirectly entail its invalidity in so far as it classified them elsewhere": Case C-339/98, Opinion of the Advocate General, 2000 ECR I-08947, para. 9 (28 October 1999) (Exhibit US-17).

sioners.[1067] In the *Cabletron* case, the ECJ specifically took note of its ruling in the *Peacock* case[1068] and stated that "[t]he Commission [in drafting Regulation No. 1165/95] ought to have realised, in the light of the wording of headings No 8471 and No 8517, read in conjunction with the explanatory notes, as worded when those regulations were adopted, that it was wrong to classify those types of network equipment under heading No 8517. ... [they] must be classified under heading No. 8471 of the Combined Nomenclature".[1069]

7.205 In summary, on the basis of the evidence that has been submitted to the Panel in the context of this dispute, divergence in tariff classification of network cards for personal computers existed between 1990 and 1995. Such divergence came to the attention of an EC institution – namely, the ECJ – through a request for preliminary ruling in the *Peacock* case in the year 2000. In its preliminary ruling in the *Peacock* case as well as in a preliminary ruling issued in the year 2001 in the *Cabletron* case, the ECJ clarified the correct classification of the network cards for personal computers. The Panel understands that a preliminary ruling issued by the ECJ is binding on the national court hearing the case in which the ruling is given.[1070] Further, we understand from the European Communities that a preliminary ruling issued by the ECJ, including those issued in the context of the *Peacock* and *Cabletron* cases, are binding on all courts of the member States.[1071] The Panel has not been provided with any evidence to indicate that divergence in tariff classification of network cards for personal computers among member States persisted following the issuance of the ECJ's preliminary rulings in the *Peacock* and *Cabletron* cases.

7.206 In the light of the foregoing, the Panel concludes that differences in administration did appear to exist in the tariff classification of the products in question between, on the one hand, the German customs authorities and, on the other hand, Danish, Dutch and UK customs authorities between 1990 and 1995. The Panel considers that, during that period, the European Communities was not administering the Common Customs Tariff concerning the tariff classification of network cards for personal computers in a uniform manner in violation of Article X:3(a) of the GATT 1994. However, the non-uniform administration in question occurred more than 10 years ago. Therefore, we do not consider that the differences in question demonstrate that the European Communities currently administers the Common Customs Tariff non-uniformly with respect to the tariff classification of network cards for personal computers. In this regard, we recall our finding in paragraph 7.36 above that, as a general principle, a panel is competent to consider measures in existence at the time of establishment of the panel but a panel may also be competent to consider measures that had expired at the

---

[1067] Case C-463/98, *Cabletron System Ltd v The Revenue Commissioners*, [2001] ECR I-3495, 10 May 2001 (Exhibit EC-136).

[1068] Case C-463/98, *Cabletron System Ltd v The Revenue Commissioners*, [2001] ECR I-3495, 10 May 2001, para. 16 *et seq*. (Exhibit EC-136).

[1069] Case C-463/98, *Cabletron System Ltd v The Revenue Commissioners* [2001] ECR I-3495, 10 May 2001, paras. 1 and 2 (Exhibit EC-136).

[1070] Case 29/68, *Milchkontor v Hauptzollamt Saarbrücken*, [1969] ECR 165 (Exhibit EC-59).

[1071] European Communities' reply to Panel question No. 163.

time of establishment to the extent that such expired measures affect the operation of a covered agreement at that time. In this case, the Panel has no evidence before it to indicate that the differences in tariff classification of network cards for personal computers that existed between 1990 and 1995 persist and/or continue to have effect today. On the contrary, the Panel understands that, once the differences in question were brought to the attention of EC institutions through the *Peacock* and *Cabletron* cases, such differences were resolved.

7.207 The Panel concludes that the tariff classification of network cards for personal computers does not currently amount to non-uniform administration within the meaning of Article X:3(a) of the GATT 1994. Therefore, the Panel finds no violation of Article X:3(a) of the GATT 1994 with respect to the tariff classification of network cards for personal computers.

(ii) Tariff classification of drip irrigation products

Summary of the parties' arguments

7.208 The **United States** refers to a case in which customs authorities in France and Spain differed over whether a drip irrigation product should be classified as an irrigation system or as a pipe.[1072] The United States explains that French customs authorities issued BTI for the product in question in 1999, classifying it as an irrigation system under tariff heading 8424 of the Common Customs Tariff, which carried an *ad valorem* duty rate of 1.7%. In December 2000, when an importer of the same product attempted to import the product through Spain, the Spanish customs authorities disregarded the French BTI and classified the product as a pipe, under tariff heading 3717 of the Common Customs Tariff, which carried an *ad valorem* duty rate of 6.4%.[1073]

7.209 In response, the **European Communities** clarifies that BTI was issued by French customs authorities on 6 July 1999 for a Roberts Irrigation Product (Ro-Drip) under CN code 8424 81 10, which covers water appliances. On 9 February 2001, Spanish customs authorities issued BTI in which it classified the same product under CN code 3917 32 99. According to the European Communities, the issue of divergent BTI was discussed by the Tariff and Statistical Nomenclature Section of the Customs Code Committee. The issue was resolved by adoption of Commission Regulation (EC) No. 763/2002 of 3 May 2002, which classified the product under heading 3917 32 99.[1074] Consequently, France revoked and replaced the previously issued BTI.[1075]

7.210 The **United States** responds that, even though the divergence in classification of drip irrigation products may have been resolved through the adoption of a regulation, this does not rebut evidence of non-uniform administration, be-

[1072] United States' first written submission, footnote 33.

[1073] United States' reply to Panel question No. 15.

[1074] Commission Regulation (EC) No. 763/2002 of 3 May 2002 concerning the classification of certain goods in the Combined Nomenclature (Exhibit EC-88).

[1075] European Communities' second written submission, para. 142.

cause non-uniform administration existed and, moreover, was allowed to persist for a year and a half.[1076] Specifically, the United States submits that the divergence in classification of the drip irrigation product occurred in February 2001 and was not resolved until 15 months later, in May 2002. During that time, the divergence effectively compelled the exporter to modify its shipping practices, sending its product to France rather than Spain.[1077]

7.211 The **European Communities** responds that BTI is binding only against the holder of the BTI and is not binding against other persons.[1078] According to the European Communities, the BTI issued by France and Spain were not issued for the same holders. Further, the European Communities submits that what is significant is not that a divergence in tariff classification may occur but, rather, that it is addressed and removed once it occurs.[1079] According to the European Communities, this is precisely what happened in the case of drip irrigation products. Once the divergent BTI had been detected, the case was promptly addressed and resolved within a period of time that is reasonable. The European Communities submits that a period of less than 15 months between the issuance of the divergent BTI to the adoption of the classification regulation does not constitute an excessively long period for definitively resolving a complex classification issue.[1080]

Analysis by the Panel

7.212 The Panel notes that the United States challenges divergence in the tariff classification of drip irrigation products among customs authorities of the member States of the European Communities.[1081]

7.213 In the Panel's view, the tariff classification of a product, including drip irrigations products, constitutes an act of administration within the meaning of Article X:3(a) of the GATT 1994. This act of administration is a matter within the Panel's terms of reference since it amounts to an instance of administration of the Common Customs Tariff in the tariff classification area.[1082]

7.214 With respect to the question of whether or not the tariff classification of drip irrigation products is "uniform" within the meaning of Article X:3(a) of the GATT 1994, the Panel recalls its finding in paragraph 7.135 above that geographic uniformity is required under Article X:3(a) of the GATT 1994. That is, administration should be uniform in different places within a particular WTO Member. The Panel also recalls its finding in paragraph 7.135 above that the form, nature and scale of the alleged non-uniform administration and the laws,

---

[1076] United States' replies to Panel question Nos. 15 and 20.

[1077] United States' oral statement at the second substantive meeting, para. 21.

[1078] European Communities' reply to Panel question No. 161 referring to Case C-495/03, *Intermodal Transports BV v. Staatssecretaris van Financiën*, 15 September 2005, not yet reported, para. 27 (Exhibit US-71).

[1079] European Communities' second written submission, para. 143.

[1080] *Ibid.*

[1081] United States' first written submission, footnote 33.

[1082] For information on EC institutions and mechanisms applicable in the tariff classification area, see paragraphs 7.179 – 7.182 above.

regulations, judicial decisions and rulings that are allegedly being administered in a non-uniform manner should be taken into consideration when interpreting the term "uniform" in Article X:3(a) of the GATT 1994. The Panel considers that the United States' challenge with respect to the tariff classification of drip irrigation products is narrow in nature. It involves the interpretation of only a few tariff headings in the Common Customs Tariff to determine the classification of a single product – namely, drip irrigation products. Therefore, given the narrowness of this challenge, the Panel considers that a high degree of uniformity is required for the purposes of Article X:3(a) of the GATT 1994. We now turn to the facts to determine whether or not this high degree of uniformity has been achieved with respect to the tariff classification of drip irrigation products.

7.215 The Panel notes that the United States has not provided any evidence to support its allegation of divergence in the tariff classification of drip irrigation products. Rather, it merely asserts the existence of a difference between French and Spanish BTI for drip irrigation products in its submissions.[1083] Nevertheless, the Panel is willing to accept this assertion in light of the fact that the European Communities does not dispute the existence of divergence in this regard.[1084]

7.216 On the basis of the European Communities' explanation of the facts[1085], the divergence in tariff classification of drip irrigation products occurred between 1999 and 2001. In particular, the French customs authorities classified drip irrigation products under sub-heading 8424 81 10 of the Common Customs Tariff in BTI that was issued in July 1999 whereas the Spanish customs authorities classified the products under sub-heading 3917 32 99 of the Common Customs Tariff in BTI that was issued in February 2001. In Commission Regulation (EC) No. 763/2002 of 3 May 2002, drip irrigation products were classified under subheading 3917 32 99.[1086] The Panel has not been provided with any evidence indicating that the divergence in tariff classification of drip irrigation products among member States persisted following the adoption of Regulation No. 763/2002.

7.217 In the light of the foregoing facts, the Panel concludes that the tariff classification of drip irrigation products does not amount to non-uniform administration in violation of Article X:3(a) of the GATT 1994. On the basis of the parties' description of the facts, it would appear that differences existed in classification of the products in question between, on the one hand, the French customs authorities and, on the other hand, Spanish customs authorities. However, the evidence submitted to the Panel in this dispute indicates that those differences existed during a relatively short period of time, namely between early 2001 and mid-2002. Further, the differences in question occurred some time ago. There-

[1083] United States' first written submission, footnote 33; United States' reply to Panel question No. 15.

[1084] European Communities' second written submission, paras. 142-143.

[1085] This explanation largely corresponds to the United States' description of the facts. In any case, the Panel notes that neither party provided the Panel with evidence to enable it to verify which version of the facts was correct.

[1086] Commission Regulation (EC) No 763/2002 of 3 May 2002 concerning the classification of certain goods in the Combined Nomenclature (Exhibit EC-88).

fore, even if such differences qualify as instances of geographical non-uniformity within the meaning of Article X:3(a) of the GATT 1994, we do not consider that such differences demonstrate that the European Communities currently administers the Common Customs Tariff non-uniformly with respect to the tariff classification of drip irrigation products. In this regard, we recall our finding in paragraph 7.36 above that, as a general principle, a panel is competent to consider measures in existence at the time of establishment of the panel but a panel may also be competent to consider measures that had expired at the time of establishment to the extent that such expired measures affect the operation of a covered agreement at that time. Moreover, we have not been provided with any evidence to suggest that the differences in administration regarding the tariff classification of drip irrigation products that existed between 2001 and 2002 persist and/or continue to have effect today. On the contrary, the Panel understands that the differences have been resolved through adoption of Regulation No. 763/2002 of 3 May 2002.

7.218 The Panel concludes that the tariff classification of drip irrigation products does not amount to non-uniform administration within the meaning of Article X:3(a) of the GATT 1994. Therefore, the Panel finds no violation of Article X:3(a) of the GATT 1994 with respect to the tariff classification of drip irrigation products.

(iii) Tariff classification of unisex articles or shorts

Summary of the parties' arguments

7.219 The **United States** argues that, in response to a recent survey among the membership of a trade association consisting of importers of products into the European Communities, respondents observed that "[u]nisex-articles or shorts have different classifications in Italy and Spain to those in Germany". According to the United States, because of this divergence in classification among the member States, these articles have to be imported via Germany, which causes additional costs.[1087]

7.220 In response, the **European Communities** submits that the so-called "survey" relied upon by the United States is based on a comment from a single, unidentified company in the context of a trade association questionnaire of March 2005 and is not supported by any additional evidence. The European Communities submits that, therefore, it is impossible to ascertain the precise nature of the products concerned, nor to identify the tariff classification issues that might be involved. Accordingly, the European Communities considers that the statement cited by the United States does not provide any evidence of a lack of uniformity

[1087] United States' first written submission, para. 76 referring to Foreign Trade Association, Questionnaire on the topic "Trade Facilitation": Facilitation of Trade in WTO States, March 2005, response to question 1.4, (Exhibit US-30).

in classification practice in the European Communities with respect to unisex articles or shorts.[1088]

Analysis by the Panel

7.221 The Panel notes that the United States challenges divergence in the tariff classification of unisex articles or shorts among customs authorities of the member States of the European Communities.[1089]

7.222 In the Panel's view, the tariff classification of a product, including unisex articles or shorts, constitutes an act of administration within the meaning of Article X:3(a) of the GATT 1994. This act of administration is a matter within the Panel's terms of reference since it amounts to an instance of administration of the Common Customs Tariff in the tariff classification area.[1090]

7.223 With respect to the question of whether or not the tariff classification of unisex articles or shorts is "uniform" within the meaning of Article X:3(a) of the GATT 1994, the Panel recalls its finding in paragraph 7.135 above that geographic uniformity is required under Article X:3(a) of the GATT 1994. That is, administration should be uniform in different places within a particular WTO Member. The Panel also recalls its finding in paragraph 7.135 above that the form, nature and scale of the alleged non-uniform administration and the laws, regulations, judicial decisions and rulings that are allegedly being administered in a non-uniform manner should be taken into consideration when interpreting the term "uniform" in Article X:3(a) of the GATT 1994. The Panel considers that the United States' challenge with respect to the tariff classification of unisex articles or shorts is narrow in nature. It involves the interpretation of only a few tariff headings in the Common Customs Tariff to determine the classification of a single product – namely, unisex articles or shorts. Therefore, given the narrowness of this challenge, the Panel considers that a high degree of uniformity is required for the purposes of Article X:3(a) of the GATT 1994. We now turn to the facts to determine whether or not this high degree of uniformity has been achieved with respect to the tariff classification of unisex articles or shorts.

7.224 The Panel does not consider that the evidence relied upon by the United States demonstrates the existence of non-uniform administration within the meaning of Article X:3(a) of the GATT 1994 for the following reasons.

7.225 *First*, the *only* evidence relied upon by the United States is the March 2005 report of the Foreign Trade Association regarding a questionnaire on the topic of "Trade Facilitation": Facilitation of Trade in WTO States.[1091] We do not consider that this report, on its own, constitutes probative evidence for the pur-

---

[1088] European Communities' second written submission, para. 133.

[1089] United States' first written submission, para. 76 referring to Foreign Trade Association, Questionnaire on the topic "Trade Facilitation": Facilitation of Trade in WTO States, March 2005, response to question 1.4, (Exhibit US-30).

[1090] For information on EC institutions and mechanisms applicable in the tariff classification area, see paragraphs 7.179 – 7.182 above.

[1091] Foreign Trade Association, Questionnaire on the topic "Trade Facilitation": Facilitation of Trade in WTO States, March 2005 (Exhibit US-30).

poses of a claim under Article X:3(a) of the GATT 1994 given that it merely contains a sample of comments made by individual traders in response to questions posed in the questionnaire. The extent to which those comments are representative of concerns held by all traders seeking to import products into the European Communities is unclear. Indeed, the opening paragraph of the Foreign Trade Association's report itself states that "[t]he Trade Facilitation Questionnaire was sent to 70 FTA member companies. 20 answers reached the FTA ... The following represents quotations from the answers. Although the [quotations] do not always fully comply with the political consensus among all members, they highlight the practical problems European traders, especially importers, face at borders".

7.226 *Second*, the Panel is not convinced that the paragraph of the Foreign Trade Association's report cited by the United States in support of its allegations proves that a lack of uniform administration on the part of the European Communities in violation of Article X:3(a) of the GATT 1994 has occurred with respect to unisex articles or shorts. In our view, if anything, the cited paragraph suggests that the alleged differences in the tariff classification of unisex articles or shorts are linked to a lack of clarity in the relevant tariff heading(s) of the Harmonized System.[1092] In this regard, we note that the comment upon which the United States relies reads as follows:

> "The classification of garments causes in general many problems. For example: Unisex-articles or shorts have different classifications in Italy and Spain to those in Germany. These articles have to be imported via Germany which causes additional costs. *The HS-Code should be simplified (one category for all clothes above waist and one for all clothes below waist).*"[1093] (emphasis added)

7.227 *Finally*, even if the Foreign Trade Association's report could be read as indicating differences regarding the classification of unisex articles or shorts among the customs authorities of the member States, without any additional supporting evidence, it is impossible for the Panel to know whether or not such differences exist despite identity in the products being classified or, rather, because the products are not the same.

7.228 The Panel concludes that the United States has not proved that the tariff classification of unisex articles or shorts amounts to non-uniform administration within the meaning of Article X:3(a) of the GATT 1994.

[1092] The European Communities is a signatory to the HS Convention. Therefore, pursuant to Article 3.1 of the HS Convention, the European Communities is obliged to use the HS headings and subheadings at the 6-digit level. The European Communities does, however, have flexibility to add headings and subheadings beyond the 6-digit level.

[1093] Foreign Trade Association, Questionnaire on the topic "Trade Facilitation": Facilitation of Trade in WTO States, March 2005, para. 1.4 (Exhibit US-30).

(iv) Tariff classification of blackout drapery lining

Summary of the parties' arguments

Evidence of divergence in classification

7.229 The **United States** submits that the blackout drapery lining case is a glaring example of non-uniform administration of the Common Customs Tariff in the context of which no EC institution has stepped in to cure the non-uniformity.[1094] Specifically, the United States notes that, in BTI issued from 1999 to 2002, customs authorities in the United Kingdom, Ireland, and the Netherlands and, subsequently, in Belgium, classified similar drapery linings under tariff heading 5907 of the Common Customs Tariff ("Textile fabrics otherwise impregnated, coated or covered; painted canvas being theatrical scenery, studio back-cloths or the like"). However, during this same period, customs authorities in Germany classified the product under tariff heading 3921 of the Common Customs Tariff ("Other plates, sheets, film, foil and strip, of plastics"). The United States submits that, after almost five years of various requests by importers for review by different branches of the German customs authority, the Main Customs Office of Bremen issued a decision in September 2004, finding that imports of the product in question in October and November 1999 were properly classified under heading 3921.[1095] According to the United States, the German customs authority acknowledged the existence of BTI for comparable goods but made no effort to explain why it was declining to follow the classification decisions reflected in that BTI.[1096] Nor did it attempt to reconcile its classification decision with the classification decisions reflected in BTI issued by other member States' customs authorities. Moreover, according to the United States, the German customs authority relied on a rationale that is not compelled by the Common Customs Tariff.[1097]

7.230 The **European Communities** argues that the present case does not concern the question of the heading under which a particular product should properly have been classified but, rather, the question of uniformity of administration of EC classification rules.[1098]

Goods in question the same?

7.231 The **European Communities** submits that the products described in the decision of the Main Customs Office Bremen were not identical to the products described in the BTI issued by customs authorities in the United Kingdom, Ireland, and the Netherlands, since the former were not flocked with textile flock,

---

[1094] United States' reply to Panel question No. 4.

[1095] United States' first written submission, para. 66.

[1096] Hauptzollamt Bremen, Letter Decision to Bautex-Stoffe GmbH regarding classification of blackout drapery lining, 22 September 2004 (original and English translation) (Exhibit US-23).

[1097] United States' reply to Panel question No. 4.

[1098] European Communities' second written submission, para. 116.

while the products in the BTI are described as having been flocked. On the basis of these product descriptions, the products had to be classified differently.[1099] According to the European Communities, the presence of a layer of textile flock is an important criterion for determining whether, under Chapter Note 2(a)(5) to Chapter 59 of the Common Customs Tariff, the textile fabric is used for reinforcement purposes only which, in turn, could affect classification.[1100] Therefore, according to the European Communities, the difference in tariff classification referred to by the United States is not a lack of uniformity but, rather, the result of a correct application of the Common Customs Tariff.[1101] The European Communities also submits that, even if a mistake had occurred in the factual appraisal of the products, this does not mean that there is a lack of uniformity in the application of EC customs law in violation of Article X:3(a) of the GATT 1994. In particular, if the importer felt that the German customs authorities had erred in their appraisal of the good in question, he could have appealed the decision of the Main Customs Office of Bremen before the Bremen Tax Court. According to the European Communities, if the importer has chosen not to appeal, then this cannot be used to claim a lack of uniformity in the EC system of customs classification. The European Communities adds that neither the importer nor the producer have ever brought the issue of classification of blackout drapery lining to the attention of the European Commission.[1102]

7.232 The **United States** responds that it is not correct that the product before the German authorities was not flocked. According to the United States, as a matter of fact, the determination of the Main Customs Office of Hamburg upon which the Main Customs Office of Bremen relied found the product to contain "flocking with individual fibers."[1103] The United States submits that the Main Customs Office of Bremen did not find an absence of flocking *per se* but, rather, that flocking did not constitute a distinct layer in the product at issue. What was relevant to the Main Customs Office of Bremen was the existence of plastic in the coating, regardless of whether textile flocking or other elements were mixed into that coating. The United States argues that the fact that the German customs authority took this approach, contrary to the approach taken by other member State authorities, is confirmed by the letter from the Main Customs Office of Hamburg.[1104]

7.233 In response, the **European Communities** submits that the letter of the Main Customs Office Hamburg relied upon by the United States relates to an administrative appeal introduced by a company called Ornata GmbH. According to the European Communities, it does not appear that that appeal is in any way

[1099] European Communities' second written submission, para. 117.

[1100] European Communities' first written submission, para. 337.

[1101] European Communities' second written submission, para. 117.

[1102] European Communities' first written submission, para. 340.

[1103] United States' reply to Panel question No. 17(a) referring to Letter from Main Customs Office Hamburg-Waltershof to ORNATA GmbH, 29 July 1998 (original and English translation), p. 1 (Exhibit US-50).

[1104] United States' oral statement at the second substantive meeting, para. 62 referring to Letter from Main Customs Office Hamburg-Waltershof to ORNATA GmbH, 29 July 1998 (original and English translation) (Exhibit US-50).

related to the administrative appeal introduced by Bautex-Stoffe GmbH, which was the subject of the decision of the Main Customs Office Bremen. Nor does it indicate that the Main Customs Office of Bremen relied on the letter of the Main Customs Office of Hamburg.[1105]

7.234 The **United States** responds that the letter from the Main Customs Office of Bremen and the letter from the Main Customs Office of Hamburg both concern blackout drapery lining produced by Rockland Industries. The Main Customs Office of Bremen decided to exclude Rockland Industries' product from classification under tariff heading 5907 on a ground evidently not applied by other EC customs authorities – that is, on the ground that the product had plastic in its coating, regardless of whether textile flocking or other elements were mixed into that coating.[1106] The United States further submits that the European Communities erroneously calls into question whether the lining produced by Rockland Industries at issue in the decision by the Main Customs Office of Bremen, which was classified under tariff heading 3921, was materially identical to lining that other member States had classified under heading 5907. In support, the United States submits that Rockland Industries' President and Chief Executive Officer attests under oath that: "All coated products produced by Rockland incorporate textile flocking as part of the coating process. Rockland has never produced a coated product that does not incorporate textile flocking. ... Textile flocking is required to prevent the fabric from sticking together."[1107]

7.235 In response, the **European Communities** submits that an affidavit by the Chairman of Rockland Industries, the producer of blackout drapery lining, is a statement by a person with a clear interest in the classification of blackout drapery lining and, therefore, has no probative value. Moreover, the affidavit does not concern the question of whether the products before the EC authorities were in fact identical.[1108] More specifically, while the affidavit indicates that the product which was the subject of the decision by the Main Customs Office of Bremen was produced by Rockland Industries, it provides no answer as to whether the products for which the BTI were issued by the Dutch, Irish and UK authorities were also products of Rockland Industries.[1109] Rather, it merely contains an assurance that Rockland Industries has never produced any product that is not flocked.[1110] The European Communities adds that, in order to determine the correct classification of the product, the question is not whether the product incorporates textile flocking as part of the coating process but, rather, whether there is a layer of textile flocking visible to the naked eye. According to the European

[1105] European Communities' second written submission, para. 108.

[1106] United States' reply to Panel question No. 137(a).

[1107] United States' oral statement at the second substantive meeting, para. 61 referring to Affidavit of Mark R. Berman, President and Chief Executive Officer of Rockland Industries, Inc., 10 November 2005 (Exhibit US-79).

[1108] European Communities' closing statement at the second substantive meeting, para. 16.

[1109] European Communities' comments on the United States' reply to Panel question No. 137(a).

[1110] European Communities' closing statement at the second substantive meeting, para. 16.

Communities, this is not a question that can be answered through an affidavit sworn by the President of the producer of the good.[1111]

Explanatory Note to sub-heading 5907 of the Harmonized System

7.236 The **United States** refers to the explanatory note accompanying heading 5907 of the Harmonized System, which provides, *inter alia*, that "[t]he fabrics covered [under subheading 5907] include ... [f]abric, the surface of which is coated with glue (rubber glue or other), *plastics*, rubber or other materials and sprinkled with a fine layer of other material such as ... textile flock or dust to produce imitation suedes. ...".[1112] The United States submits that, in the light of that explanatory note, for classification purposes, the relative density of the flocking is not a material point of distinction. According to the United States, customs authorities of member States other than Germany have classified black-out drapery lining under heading 5907 in cases where the flocking on the products surface was found to be "sparsely applied".[1113] The United States submits that, in contrast, the Main Customs Office of Bremen stated that "[a]ssignment of the goods to class 5907 could only be considered if, in accordance with the label of that class: 'other webs,' the goods were not plastic-coated as per class 3921."[1114]

7.237 The **European Communities** responds that it is wrong to say that the decision of the Main Customs Office of Bremen is incompatible with the explanatory note to heading 5907 of the Harmonized System. According to the European Communities, explanatory note (G)(1) to heading 5907 provides that the fabrics covered include "fabric, the surface of which is coated with glue (rubber glue or other), plastics, rubber or other materials and sprinkled with a fine layer of other materials such as (1) textile flock or dust to produce imitation suèdes".[1115] The European Communities submits that, therefore, the presence of textile flock or dust was a relevant criterion for the classification under heading 5907. The decision of the Main Customs Office of Bremen took account of this factor by noting the absence of a layer of textile flock. Since the product was not flocked, it could not be classified under heading 5907.[1116]

German interpretative aid

[1111] European Communities' comments on the United States' reply to Panel question No. 137(a).

[1112] United States' reply to Panel question No. 17(a) referring to Harmonized System Explanatory Note, subheading 5907 (Exhibit US-48).

[1113] United States' reply to Panel question No. 17(a) referring to BTI UK103424227 (Exhibit US-51).

[1114] United States' reply to Panel question No. 17(a) referring to Hauptzollamt Bremen, Letter Decision to Bautex-Stoffe GmbH, 22 September 2004 (original and English translation) (Exhibit US-23). The Panel notes that the English translation of the decision of Main Customs Office of Bremen submitted by the United States refers to heading 3921 whereas the German version of the decision refers to heading 5903.

[1115] Harmonized System Explanatory Note, subheading 5907 (Exhibit US-48; Exhibit EC-127).

[1116] European Communities' second written submission, para. 111.

7.238 The **United States** submits that the Hamburg Customs Office relied upon an interpretive aid particular to Germany and not uniformly used by member State customs authorities in applying the Common Customs Tariff to coated textile fabrics, such as blackout drapery lining. The United States submits that the aid in question directed the customs authority to consider the density of the product's fibre. According to the United States, the Main Customs Office of Bremen plainly relied on the findings of the Hamburg Customs Office and, moreover, expressly referred to the fact that "[t]he web is not fine", an apparent allusion to the finding of the Main Customs Office of Hamburg based on the interpretive aid.[1117]

7.239 In response, the **European Communities** submits that the aid in question was referred to only by the Main Customs Office of Hamburg, not by the Main Customs Office of Bremen, which decided the appeal.[1118] Further, according to the European Communities, the text contains nothing which is contrary to EC law. In particular, the criterion that the web is not fine was developed in analogy to another EC classification regulation and is a relevant factor to determine whether the textile fabric is present merely for reinforcing purposes.[1119] The European Communities also submits that the text in question is purely an interpretative aid prepared for administrative purposes which does not have the force of law and does not derogate from EC law. In this regard, the European Communities argues that the ECJ has clarified that handbooks, guidance or other compilations prepared by member States have no legally binding character in EC law.[1120]

7.240 The **United States** submits in response that the EC classification regulation with respect to which the European Communities argues the German interpretative aid was developed by way of analogy is a regulation pertaining to the classification of ski trousers, which are classifiable under Chapter 62 of the Common Customs Tariff.[1121] The United States submits that the interpretative rules referred to in that regulation are relevant to classification of an apparel item, but make no sense when applied for a product such as blackout drapery lining. The particular aspect of the ski trousers rule on which the German authority relied in this case was the tightness of the weave of the fabric. However, according to the United States, Note 2(a) to Chapter 59 of the Common Customs Tariff expressly makes that criterion irrelevant to the classification of coated fabrics. In particular, it states that heading 5903 applies to "textile fabrics, impregnated, coated, covered or laminated with plastics, *whatever the weight per*

1117 United States' reply to Panel question No. 17(a) referring to Hauptzollamt Bremen, Letter Decision to Bautex-Stoffe GmbH, 22 September 2004 (original and English translation) (Exhibit US-23).

1118 European Communities' first written submission, para. 342.

1119 European Communities' first written submission, para. 343 referring to Commission Regulation (EC) No. 1458/97 concerning the classification of certain goods in the Combined Nomenclature (Exhibit EC-78).

1120 European Communities' first written submission, para. 344 referring to Case C-161/88, *Friedrich Binder*, [1989] ECR 2415, 12 July 1989, para. 19 (Exhibit EC-79).

1121 Commission Regulation (EC) No. 1458/97 concerning the classification of certain goods in the Combined Nomenclature (Exhibit EC-78).

square meter and whatever the nature of the plastic material. ..."[1122] The United States explains that, having ruled out classification of the blackout drapery lining in question under heading 5907, apparently based on its view that the existence of plastic in the coating precluded such classification, the German customs authority then looked to a German interpretive aid. The United States submits that the German customs authority relied on it in a way that turned out to be determinative.[1123]

7.241 The **European Communities** submits that the United States' criticism of the reference to a classification regulation concerning a type of ski trousers is unwarranted. Commission Regulation (EC) No. 1458/97 concerned the classification of garments under heading 6210, which covers "garments made up of fabrics of heading 5602, 5603, 5903, 5906 or 5907".[1124] The European Communities submits that, implicitly, the classification regulation in question concerned the classification of the fabric out of which garments are made. That regulation implicitly required application of Note 2(a)(5) to Chapter 59 of the Common Customs Tariff to determine whether the fabric serves merely reinforcing purposes. The European Communities submits that it was in this context that the Main Customs Office of Hamburg took into account the "tight weave" of the fabric.[1125] The European Communities submits that the weight referred to in the chapeau of Note 2(a) to Chapter 59 is the weight of the entire product – that is, the fabric as impregnated, coated, covered or laminated. The Main Customs Office of Bremen did not consider the weight of the product, but rather the density of the web of the polyester fabric, which is only a part of the product.[1126] The European Communities submits that, according to Note (2)(a)(5) to Chapter 59 of the Common Customs Tariff, heading 5903 does not apply to plates, sheets, or strips of cellular plastics, combined with textile fabric, where the textile fabric is present merely for reinforcing purposes. For the application of heading 5903, it is, therefore, necessary to determine whether the textile fabric is present merely for reinforcing purposes and, consequently, the question whether the web was fine is a relevant criterion for establishing whether it is present for reinforcement purposes or not.[1127]

7.242 In response, the **United States** submits that the notes pertaining to Chapter 39 of the Common Customs Tariff make no reference to density of weave as a relevant criterion, and the notes to Chapter 59 expressly provide that classification under that chapter is to be determined *regardless* of weight per square meter. The European Communities asserts without basis that the reference to weight per square meter is different from density of weave. In fact, however, weight per square meter necessarily is a function of density of weave.[1128]

1122 United States' reply to Panel question No. 17(a).
1123 United States' oral statement at the second substantive meeting, para. 63.
1124 Excerpt of heading 6210 of the Common Customs Tariff (Exhibit EC-132).
1125 European Communities' second written submission, para. 113.
1126 European Communities' second written submission, para. 115.
1127 European Communities' second written submission, para. 112.
1128 United States' oral statement at the second substantive meeting, para. 64.

Compatibility with WCO opinion

7.243 The **United States** submits that, in October 2004, the Secretariat of the World Customs Organization (WCO) issued an opinion agreeing that the product in question should be classified under heading 5907 of the Harmonized System.[1129] According to the United States, shortly thereafter, Belgian customs authorities issued a decision classifying blackout drapery lining under heading 5907. However, the German decision remains unchanged.[1130]

7.244 In response, the **European Communities** submits that the WCO opinion is irrelevant. The European Communities notes that the opinion states that "the visible outer layer consists of cotton flocking which completely covers the acrylic cellular plastic". According to the European Communities, this does not correspond to the description of the product before the German customs authorities. The European Communities also notes that the opinion is purely the opinion of an official of the WCO, which does not have any legally binding status under the Harmonized System Convention. Moreover, if the United States believed there was a dispute concerning the application of the Harmonized System Convention, it could submit this dispute to the Harmonised System Committee in accordance with Article 10 of the HS Convention but has not done so as yet.[1131]

Analysis by the Panel

General

7.245 The Panel notes that the United States challenges divergence in the tariff classification of blackout drapery lining among customs authorities of the member States of the European Communities.[1132]

7.246 In the Panel's view, the tariff classification of a product, including blackout drapery lining, constitutes an act of administration within the meaning of Article X:3(a) of the GATT 1994. This act of administration is a matter within the Panel's terms of reference since it amounts to an instance of administration of the Common Customs Tariff in the tariff classification area.[1133]

7.247 With respect to the question of whether or not the tariff classification of blackout drapery lining is "uniform" within the meaning of Article X:3(a) of the GATT 1994, the Panel recalls its finding in paragraph 7.135 above that geographic uniformity is required under Article X:3(a) of the GATT 1994. That is, administration should be uniform in different places within a particular WTO Member. The Panel also recalls its finding in paragraph 7.125 above that the form, nature and scale of the alleged non-uniform administration and the laws,

---

[1129] Letter from Mr. Chriticles Mwansa, Director, World Customs Organization, Tariff and Trade Affairs Directorate, to Mr. Myles B. Harmon, Director, Office of Regulations and Rulings, U.S. Customs and Border Protection, 26 October 2004 (Exhibit US-24).

[1130] United States' first written submission, para. 68.

[1131] European Communities' first written submission, para. 341.

[1132] United States' first written submission, para. 66.

[1133] For information on EC institutions and mechanisms applicable in the tariff classification area, see paragraphs 7.179 – 7.182 above.

regulations, judicial decisions and rulings that are allegedly being administered in a non-uniform manner should be taken into consideration when interpreting the term "uniform" in Article X:3(a) of the GATT 1994. The Panel considers that the United States' challenge with respect to the tariff classification of blackout drapery lining is narrow in nature. It involves the interpretation of only a few tariff headings in the Common Customs Tariff to determine the classification of a single product – namely, blackout drapery lining. Therefore, given the narrowness of this challenge, the Panel considers that a high degree of uniformity is required for the purposes of Article X:3(a) of the GATT 1994. We now turn to the facts to determine whether or not this high degree of uniformity has been achieved with respect to the tariff classification of blackout drapery lining.

Evidence relied upon by the United States to prove the existence of divergence in the tariff classification of blackout drapery lining

7.248 The United States alleges the existence of divergence in tariff classification of blackout drapery lining from 1999 to 2002 between, on the one hand, customs authorities in the United Kingdom, Ireland, and the Netherlands and, subsequently, in Belgium, who classified the product in question under tariff heading 5907 of the Common Customs Tariff (which covers "Textile fabrics otherwise impregnated, coated or covered; painted canvas being theatrical scenery, studio back-cloths or the like") and, on the other hand, customs authorities in Germany, who classified the product in question under heading 3921 of the Common Customs Tariff (which covers "Other plates, sheets, film, foil and strip, of plastics").

7.249 To support its allegation the United States refers to a number of BTI notices issued for blackout drapery lining by customs authorities in the United Kingdom (dated 17 March 1999, 12 June 1999 and 22 December 1999), in Ireland (dated 1 April 1999) and in the Netherlands (dated 13 February 2002).[1134] Each BTI relied upon by the United States classifies the product under heading 5907. The descriptions of the products in each of those BTI are set out immediately below:

> *BTI issued by UK customs authority dated 17 March 1999*
>
> "Thermal curtain lining; also known as blackout material. Consisting of a plain weave fabric of 50% polyester and 50% cotton fibres. Visibly coated on one side only with a layer of acrylic foam. Textile flock then appears to have been sparesly [sic] applied to the top of this coating giving it a slightly raised or brushed effect. Used in such places as hotels etc to darken and block out sunlight in rooms where the sun is a problem. The fabric may also be applied to the back of existing transparent/translucent curtains; as lin-

[1134] BTI issued from 1999 through 2002 by customs authorities in the United Kingdom, Ireland, and the Netherlands (Exhibit US-22).

ing material; giving the same net result. Similar in appearance to the fabric used in photographic studios etc."

BTI issued by UK customs authority dated 12 June 1999

"Plain weave fabric 70% Polyester 30% Cotton. Visibly coated on one side only. Textile flock has been applied giving the fabric a slightly raised or brushed effect. Used as a blackout material"

BTI issued by UK customs authority dated 22 December 1999

"Textile fabric constructed of textile flock with a layer of cellular plastic and a knitted textile backing. 71.3% foam (PU/PVC); 16.6% polyester; 12.1% viscose"

BTI issued by Irish customs authority dated 1 April 1999

"Thermal curtain lining (blackout curtain lining), plain weave fabric of 50% polyester and 50% cotton, visibly coated on one side with a layer of acrylic foam. Textile flock has then been applied on top of this coating."

BTI issued by Dutch customs authority dated 13 February 2002

"Fabric of 100% cottons covertly with low acrylic resin polymers, on which a layer has been textielvezeltjes introduced (flock). The fabric is provided on roles [sic] of approximately 50 meters length, packs in plastic and by 4 roles [sic] in a hamper box."

7.250 In addition, with respect to the tariff classification of blackout drapery lining in Belgium, it is evident from a decision issued by the Hamburg ZPLA[1135], aspects of which are excerpted in paragraph 7.252 below, that certain products imported into Belgium by Rockland Industries were classified by the Belgian customs authorities under heading 5907.[1136] An affidavit of Mr Mark Berman, Chief Executive Officer of Rockland Industries, states in relevant part that:

"6. All coated products produced by Rockland incorporate textile flocking as part of the coating process. Rockland has never produced a coated product that does not incorporate textile flocking.

[1135] The Panel understands that the acronym ZPLA can be translated in English as "Testing and Training Establishment for Technical Customs Matters". The body referred to by the Panel in its findings as the "Hamburg ZPLA" is referred to by the parties variously as the "Hamburg Customs Office", the "Main Customs Office of Hamburg" and the "Hamburg ZPLA".

[1136] Letter from Oberfinanzdirektion Hamburg to HZA Bremen regarding Protest of Bautex-Stoffe GmbH, 3 February 2003 (original and English translation) (Exhibit US-41). Further, in a letter from Marc De Schutter, Federal Government Services, Financial Section, Administration of Border Police and Import Taxes, Western Board to Inspector of Border Police and Import Taxes in Antwerp - C.T.D.A.I., 26 November 2004, (original and English translation) (Exhibit US-25), it is evident that "tissue" with "a covering surface of non-cellular synthetic material which contains filler materials (titanium dioxide and silicates), which are covered at its surface with body hair" were classified by Belgian customs authorities under tariff heading 5907.

7. Textile flocking is required to prevent the fabric from sticking together."[1137]

7.251 The United States contrasts the tariff classification of blackout drapery lining by the customs authorities in the United Kingdom, Ireland, the Netherlands and Belgium with certain decisions and opinions issued by German customs authorities. In particular, the United States refers to an expert opinion issued by the Main Customs Office of Bremen to Bautex-Stoffe GmbH ("Bautex") dated 29 September 2004.[1138] In that expert opinion, the Main Customs Office of Bremen found that certain products that had been imported into Germany by Bautex in October and November 1999 had been properly classified under heading 3921.[1139] The Main Customs Office of Bremen's expert opinion states in relevant part that:[1140]

> "According to the classification opinion of the Hamburg ZPLA as well as three supplementary opinions on the matter, the goods in question consist of rolls of a white fabric made of polyester, coated on one side with acrylate. The fabric is not dense and not further treated. The plastic coating consists of cellular plastic. The fabric and the coating are of approximately the same thickness. The fabric is to be considered as no more than an underlay. The imported goods are covered by heading 3921.
>
> According to the classification opinion, a hardened oil-based coating is not present. The surface is not covered with a thin layer of textile flock. The fabric is not dense, and is uniform in color. The fabric serves only as a reinforcement.
>
> Classification of the goods under heading 5907 could only be considered if, in accordance with the wording of that heading, "other textile fabrics ... ", the goods were not plastic-coated as required by heading 5903. The fact that the plastic coating has been treated with flame retardant and the like does not change the fact that the plastic coating exists. Therefore, classification under heading 5907

[1137] Affidavit of Mark R. Berman, President and Chief Executive Officer of Rockland Industries, Inc., 10 November 2005, paras. 6 - 7 (Exhibit US-79). The Panel notes the European Communities' objections to this affidavit on the ground that it constitutes a statement by a person with a clear interest in the classification of blackout drapery lining and, therefore, has no probative value: European Communities' closing statement at the second substantive meeting, para. 16. Nevertheless, the Panel considers that the affidavit contains evidence that contributes constructively to our duty under Article 11 of the DSU to conduct an objective assessment of the matter before us.

[1138] The Panel notes that the European Communities characterises this expert opinion of the Main Customs Office of Bremen as a "decision": European Communities' first written submission, para. 333.

[1139] Hauptzollamt Bremen, Letter Decision to Bautex-Stoffe GmbH regarding classification of blackout drapery lining, 29 September 2004 (Exhibit US-23).

[1140] The Panel notes that it found the United States' translation into English of various exhibits that were originally in German difficult to understand and, at times, incorrect. Therefore, in its findings, the Panel relies upon its own unofficial translations of Exhibits US-23, 41 and 50. Nevertheless, the Panel considers that differences between, on the one hand, the United States' translations of Exhibits US-23, 41 and 50 and, on the other hand, the Panel's translations of those exhibits do not affect the substance of the Panel's findings regarding the tariff classification of blackout drapery lining.

is excluded. Given that the plastic coating has a cellular structure, it is excluded from classification under heading 5903 and should be classified under heading 3921.

As cellular plastic sheets made of other plastics, the imported goods are to be assigned code number 3921 1900 990. The legal grounds for this classification are to be found in Note 2(a)(5) to Chapter 59 of the Customs Tariff.

The Main Customs Office of Bremen is convinced of the correctness of the Hamburg ZPLA's findings regarding the material composition of the goods.

Numerous other binding customs decisions [BTI] have been handed down for comparable goods (darkening material)."

7.252 In reaching its conclusion that the products in question should be classified under heading 3921, the Main Customs Office of Bremen relied, *inter alia*, on a decision issued by the Hamburg ZPLA dated 3 February 2003 regarding a "protest" filed by Bautex.[1141] The decision of the Hamburg ZPLA (the "Bautex decision issued by the Hamburg ZPLA") states in relevant part that:

"According to the expert opinion, the coating does not consist of hardened oil; the IR-spectrum, however, indicates traces of oil and polyallylesters are present in the extract. The main ingredient of the coating, however, is likely to be acrylate, according to the IR-spectrum. ...

There is a series of vZTA[1142] regarding various darkening materials ... in which the cellular plastic was coated with a synthetic layer, which shows a little flocking and which corresponds to the merchandise in question. Among these, vZTA 55/03 provides a good basis for comparison because the applicant submitted the same documents as Bautex-Stoffe GmbH in its protest filing. I am referring to the letters of the Belgian Customs Office according to which a product of the company Rockland Industries was classified under sub-heading 5907 000 90. This use of the same documents for classification in all cases strengthens the suspicion that the documents do not necessarily match the merchandise...

An important difference lies in the fact that, in the case of vZTA 55/03, the fabric is dense whereas the fabric is not dense in the merchandise under consideration. ...

[1141] Letter from Oberfinanzdirektion Hamburg to HZA Bremen regarding Protest of Bautex-Stoffe GmbH, 3 February 2003 (original and English translation) (Exhibit US-41). It is apparent from the decision of the Main Customs Office of Bremen that the opinion of the Hamburg ZPLA was relied upon by the Main Customs Office of Bremen, in addition to "three supplementary opinions on the same matter": Hauptzollamt Bremen, Letter Decision to Bautex-Stoffe GmbH regarding classification of blackout drapery lining, 29 September 2004 (Exhibit US-23).

[1142] The Panel understands that the German acronym "vZTA" corresponds to the English acronym "BTI".

> Because the product in question consists of a cellular plastic, I adhere to my suggested opinion that [sub-heading] 3921 19 is appropriate."

7.253 The affidavit of Mr Mark Berman, Chief Executive Officer of Rockland Industries, referred to in paragraph 7.250 above, stated that the products that were the subject of the classification in the expert opinion of the Main Customs Office of Bremen and in the Bautex decision issued by Hamburg ZPLA were identical in all material respects to those that were the subject of a 1998 classification letter by the Hamburg ZPLA concerning a "protest" filed by Ornata GmbH (the "Ornata letter issued by the Hamburg ZPLA").[1143] In the Ornata letter issued by the Hamburg ZPLA,[1144] the products in question were described in the following terms:

> "According to ZPLA's findings, the tested merchandise shows under magnification on the surface *isolated* fibres; a cohesive layer is not present. A coating of the fabric with a thin layer of flock is not present. Because the surface treatment (flocking with individual fibres) is not visible to the naked eye, classification of the merchandise under heading 5907 is out of the question according to Chapter 59, Note 5 (a) and (c).
>
> ...
>
> In this particular case, ZPLA determined the following composition of the merchandise: a *white* fabric made out of polyester/cotton, which is on *one side* covered with cellular plastic (and flock fibres) with the layer built up – white fabric (0.20 mm thickness) – white/black/white cellular plastic layers made from polyacrylate with additives (0.20 mm thickness) – flock. The spun fabric is not dense and is not further processed. According to the above-mentioned definition, the white fabric is merely a base for reinforcement purposes. The merchandise is therefore excluded from heading 5903, according to Note 2(a)(5) to Chapter 59 and should be classified under Chapter 39.
>
> ...
>
> According to your opinion, as expressed in your letter ..., a coating of the merchandise with flock dust is visible with the naked eye, whereas ZPLA determined that flock dust fibers were *only visible under magnification.*
>
> The expression "visible with the naked eye" means, according to established jurisprudence that the impregnation, coating or covering of the fabric has to be directly visible in a simple visual examination ...

1143 Affidavit of Mark R. Berman, President and Chief Executive Officer of Rockland Industries, Inc., 10 November 2005 (Exhibit US-79).

1144 Letter from Main Customs Office Hamburg-Waltershof to ORNATA GmbH in response to protest regarding classification, 29 July 1998 (Exhibit US-50).

> Because a magnifier (aid) is necessary for the determination of flock dust fibres, therefore, the covering of the fabric with flock dust *is not visible to the naked eye.* According to the objective features and characteristics, as specified by the wording of the tariff headings in the Common Customs Tariff and the sections or chapter notes, classification under heading 5907 is therefore not possible ..." (emphasis in original)

7.254 The European Communities argues that the products classified, on the one hand, by customs authorities in the United Kingdom, Ireland, the Netherlands and Belgium and, on the other hand, by customs authorities in Germany, were not identical in relevant respects and, therefore, had to be classified differently.[1145] In addressing this argument, the Panel notes that its task here is not to determine the correct classification under the Common Customs Tariff of the products being considered by, on the one hand, customs authorities in the United Kingdom, Ireland, the Netherlands and Belgium and, on the other hand, customs authorities in Germany. Rather, our task is to determine whether the divergence in tariff classification with respect to those products demonstrates non-uniform administration within the meaning of Article X:3(a) of the GATT 1994. In undertaking this task, we will focus on determining whether or not there was any objectively justifiable basis upon which the German customs authorities considered that the products, the subject of classification by the customs authorities in United Kingdom, Ireland, the Netherlands and Belgium, were different from the products that were the subject of classification by the German customs authorities. If not, this would tend to indicate the existence of non-uniform administration in violation of Article X:3(a) of the GATT 1994.

Physical characteristics of the products that were the subject of classification by on the one hand, customs authorities in the United Kingdom, Ireland, the Netherlands and Belgium and, on the other hand, customs authorities in Germany

7.255 Regarding the products that were the subject of classification by the customs authorities in United Kingdom, Ireland, the Netherlands and Belgium, the Panel notes that the BTI submitted by the United States indicates that the products classified by the customs authorities in the United Kingdom, Ireland and the Netherlands are all textile products covered with a layer of flocking.[1146] Further, when read in conjunction with the affidavit of Mr Mark Berman, Chief Executive Officer of Rockland Industries, the relevant decision of the Hamburg ZPLA

[1145] See, for example, European Communities' second written submission, para. 117 and European Communities' closing statement at the second substantive meeting, para. 16.
[1146] See paragraph 7.249 above.

indicates that the products classified by the customs authorities in Belgium were all textile products incorporating textile flocking.[1147]

7.256 With respect to the products classified by the German customs authority, the Panel notes that the only evidence provided that casts light on the physical characteristics of those products are the expert opinion of the Main Customs Office of Bremen[1148], the Bautex decision issued by the Hamburg ZPLA[1149], the Ornata letter issued by the Hamburg ZPLA[1150] and the affidavit of Mr Mark Berman, Chief Executive Officer of Rockland Industries, concerning products manufactured by Rockland Industries.[1151]

7.257 It is evident from the excerpts of the expert opinion of the Main Customs Office of Bremen set out in paragraph 7.251 above, that, unlike the customs authorities in the United Kingdom, Ireland, the Netherlands and Belgium, the Main Customs Office of Bremen did not characterize the products as textile products. Rather, the products were described as "cellular plastic sheets". The Main Customs Office of Bremen explained that the products also possessed a fabric component but that such component "is to be considered as no more than underlay" and "serves only as a reinforcement".

7.258 Like the expert opinion of the Main Customs Office of Bremen, the Bautex decision issued by the Hamburg ZPLA also appeared to characterize the products in question as a plastic. In particular, in its decision set out in paragraph 7.252 above, the Hamburg ZPLA described the product as being predominantly an "acrylate"[1152] and consisting of a "cellular plastic". The Hamburg ZPLA appeared to acknowledge the presence of textile elements. For example, the Hamburg ZPLA referred to "traces of ... polyallylesters" and "a little flocking". However, the Hamburg ZPLA considered that the fabric in question was not "dense" enough to warrant classification of the product under heading 5907 (i.e. as a textile product).

7.259 According to the Ornata letter issued by the Hamburg ZPLA set out in paragraph 7.253 above, the products that were the subject of classification were considered flocked, thus sharing an important feature in common with the products the subject of classification by the customs authorities in the United King-

---

1147 See paragraph 7.250 above. In the Harmonized System (heading 5603) "textile flock" is defined as consisting of textile fibres not exceeding 5 mm in length (silk, wool, cotton, man-made fibres, etc.). It is obtained as waste during various finishing operations and, in particular, from the shearing of velvets. It is also produced by cutting textile tow or fibres. Textile dust is obtained as waste, or by grinding textile fibres to a powder. Textile flock and dust fall in this heading even if bleached or dyed or if the fibres have been artificially curled.

1148 Hauptzollamt Bremen, Letter Decision to Bautex-Stoffe GmbH regarding classification of black-out drapery lining, 29 September 2004 (Exhibit US-23).

1149 Letter from Oberfinanzdirektion Hamburg to HZA Bremen regarding Protest of Bautex-Stoffe GmbH, 3 February 2003 (original and English translation) (Exhibit US-41).

1150 Letter from Main Customs Office Hamburg-Waltershof to ORNATA GmbH in response to protest regarding classification. 29 July 1998 (Exhibit US-50).

1151 Affidavit of Mark R. Berman, President and Chief Executive Officer of Rockland Industries, Inc., 10 November 2005, paras. 6 – 7 (Exhibit US-79).

1152 The term "acrylate" is defined as "a salt or ester of acrylic acid": *The New Shorter Oxford English Dictionary*, 1993, p. 21.

dom, Ireland, the Netherlands and Belgium. However, unlike the customs authorities in the United Kingdom, Ireland, the Netherlands and Belgium, the Hamburg ZPLA considered that such flocking was not sufficient so as to warrant classification under heading 5907 because the "flock dust fibres" were not "visible to the naked eye". The Hamburg ZPLA further stated that the fabric component of the product in question was "merely a base for reinforcement purposes".

7.260 It is apparent that the products that were the subject of classification in the expert opinion by the Main Customs Office of Bremen and in the Bautex decision issued by the Hamburg ZPLA were produced by Rockland Industries and were identical.[1153] It is less clear whether the products that were the subject of classification by the Main Customs Office of Bremen and in the Bautex decision issued by the Hamburg ZPLA were identical with the products that were the subject of classification in the Ornata letter issued by the Hamburg ZPLA. In this regard, we recall that, in his affidavit, Mr Mark Berman states that the product that was the subject of classification in the Ornata letter issued by the Hamburg ZPLA was "identical in all material respects to the product sold to [Bautex] by Rockland".[1154] The United States has not submitted any evidence to support Mr Berman's assertion that the products that were the subject of classification in the Ornata letter issued by the Hamburg ZPLA were "identical in all material respects" with those that were the subject of classification by the Main Customs Office of Bremen and in the Bautex decision issued by the Hamburg ZPLA. In this regard, the Panel notes that Mr Berman's appraisal of what is material may be different from the matters that are relevant for the purposes of determining whether or not the tariff classification of blackout drapery lining in the European Communities amounts to non-uniform administration in violation of Article X:3(a) of the GATT 1994.

7.261 In any event, the Panel notes that the three decisions by the German customs authorities did not consider that the textile/fabric/flocking components of the products that were the subject of classification were significant and/or visible to the naked eye. This would appear to contrast with the physical characteristics of the products that were the subject of classification by the customs authorities in the United Kingdom, Ireland, the Netherlands and Belgium. In this regard, the Panel recalls that the United States has referred to an affidavit of Mr Mark Berman, Chief Executive Officer of the company whose products were the subject of classification by the Main Customs Office of Bremen and the Hamburg ZPLA in respect of the Bautex decision.[1155] The Panel acknowledges that that affidavit indicates that the products that were the subject of classification by those two

---

[1153] The decision issued by the Main Customs Office of Bremen specifically notes that the products the subject of classification were manufactured by Rockland Industries: Hauptzollamt Bremen, Letter Decision to Bautex-Stoffe GmbH regarding classification of blackout drapery lining, 29 September 2004 (Exhibit US-23). As noted in paragraph 7.252 above, in reaching its decision that the products in question should be classified under heading 3921, the Main Customs Office of Bremen relied, *inter alia*, on the Bautex decision issued by the Hamburg ZPLA.

[1154] Affidavit of Mark R. Berman, President and Chief Executive Officer of Rockland Industries, Inc., 10 November 2005, para. 8 (Exhibit US-79).

[1155] Affidavit of Mark R. Berman, President and Chief Executive Officer of Rockland Industries, Inc., 10 November 2005 (Exhibit US-79).

German customs authorities were "coated products" incorporating "textile flocking". However, as was submitted by the European Communities during the Panel's proceedings[1156], the affidavit does not address the question of whether the products before the customs authorities in the United Kingdom, Ireland, the Netherlands and Belgium were, in fact, identical to the products that were the subject of classification by the German customs authorities. Indeed, the Panel has not been provided with any evidence that proves that the products in question were, in fact, identical.

7.262 With regard to the opinion of the WCO Secretariat referred to by the United States in which the WCO Secretariat suggested that the products that were the subject of classification there were classifiable under heading 5907 (i.e. different from the heading relied upon by the German customs authorities),[1157] the Panel notes that there is no compelling evidence in that opinion to indicate that the products the subject of the WCO Secretariat's opinion had the same key physical characteristics as those possessed by the products that were the subject of classification by the German customs authorities. In particular, the WCO Secretariat described the products in question as follows:

> "[T]he product at issue would appear to be woven fabric made from 70% polyester and 30% cotton, which is coated on one side, in a three-pass operation, with a three-layer foam mixture of clay, titanium dioxide, carbon black, flame retardant, acrylic and textile flock. The layer closest to the woven fabric is an acrylic cellular plastic. The middle layer is composed mainly of titanium dioxide with carbon black. The outer layer is composed of an acrylic cellular plastic with cotton flocking fibers. The woven fabric, which is used to make blackout drapery lining, accounts for 24.7% of the weight of the blackout lining, and the coating for 75.3%.
>
> ...
>
> [I]t could be argued that the product at issue, consisting of a textile fabric which is neither figured nor worked, and which is uniformly dyed and coated with cellular plastic, should be classified in heading 39.21 by virtue of Note 2(a)(5) to Chapter 59.
>
> However, judging by the information submitted and the sample supplied, this product is not merely a textile fabric laminated with cellular plastic. It also incorporates a middle layer composed mainly of titanium dioxide and carbon black, and in addition the *visible* outer layer consists of cotton flocking which completely covers the acrylic cellular plastic.
>
> ...

[1156] European Communities' closing statement at the second substantive meeting, para. 16.

[1157] Letter from M. Chriticles Mwansa, Director, World Customs Organization, Tariff and Trade Affairs Directorate, to M. Myles B. Harmon, Director, Office of Regulations and Rulings, U.S. Customs and Border Protection regarding classification of blackout drapery lining (26 October 2004) (Exhibit US-24).

> [I]t is the titanium dioxide and the carbon black which confer on this product its blackout properties, while the cotton flocking covers the external surface of the fabric, preventing the layer of acrylic plastic from sticking and giving the fabric a hand similar to that of a suede fabric.
>
> The Secretariat shares your Administration's view that the significance of these additional layers cannot be ignored, given the use which will be made of this textile product (manufacture of linings for blackout curtains).
>
> The Secretariat can also agree with you that the product at issue can be likened to a coated fabric of the kind described on page 1036 of the Explanatory Notes under item (g)(1), and as a result the Secretariat would tend to classify it in heading 59.07 by application of Interpretative Rule 1."

7.263 It would appear that the products under consideration by the WCO Secretariat comprised textile fabric laminated with cellular plastic. Further, the product in question included a visible outer layer consisting of cotton flocking, which completely covered the acrylic cellular plastic. As noted previously, the products that were the subject of classification by the Main Customs Office of Bremen and in the Bautex decision issued by Hamburg ZPLA were characterised as predominantly plastic rather than textile, which arguably, distinguish them from the products under consideration by the WCO Secretariat. Further, the products that were the subject of classification in the Ornata letter issued by the Hamburg ZPLA were characterised as possessing "flock dust fibres" which were not "visible to the naked eye". Again, the absence of a visible layer of textile flocking arguably distinguish them from the products under consideration by the WCO Secretariat. Indeed, while not binding, the WCO Secretariat opinion appears to suggest that, in the absence of a visible outer layer of cotton flocking completely covering the acrylic cellular plastic (which apparently characterised the products the subject of the WCO Secretariat's classification opinion), the products would have been classifiable under heading 3921.

7.264 On the basis of the limited evidence before the Panel, the Panel can only assume that the products that were the subject of classification by the Main Customs Office of Bremen, in the Bautex decision issued by the Hamburg ZPLA and in the Ornata letter issued by Hamburg ZPLA, were not identical to those that were the subject of classification by the customs authorities in the United Kingdom, Ireland, the Netherlands and Belgium. This indicates to the Panel that there was an objectively justifiable basis upon which the German customs authorities considered that the products that were the subject of classification by the customs authorities in the United Kingdom, Ireland, the Netherlands and Belgium were different from the products that were the subject of classification by the German customs authorities.

7.265 Therefore, the Panel does not consider that the divergent *decisions* regarding the tariff classification by, on the one hand, the German customs authorities and, on the other hand, the customs authorities in the United Kingdom, Ireland, the Netherlands and Belgium amounts to non-uniform administration in violation of Article X:3(a) of the GATT 1994. As stated previously, we consider that, on the basis of the limited evidence before the Panel, there was an objective factual basis that justifies the decision by the German customs authorities to classify the product in question in a manner differently from the customs authorities in the United Kingdom, Ireland, the Netherlands and Belgium. Nevertheless, the Panel notes that the United States has also implicitly challenged the *administrative process* that led to divergent classification decisions regarding blackout drapery lining.[1158] We consider that process immediately below.

Administrative process leading to tariff classification decisions for the product in question by German customs authorities

7.266 The Panel recalls its finding that the term "administer" in Article X:3(a) of the GATT 1994 relates to the application of laws and regulations, including administrative processes. In the Panel's view, the administrative process leading to a tariff classification decision, such as the tariff classification of blackout drapery lining, constitutes an act of administration within the meaning of Article X:3(a) of the GATT 1994. Further, it amounts to an instance of administration of the Common Customs Tariff in the tariff classification area, a matter that is within the Panel's terms of reference.

German interpretative aid

7.267 In the Panel's view, a system of customs administration which allows or, at least, does not prevent customs authorities from unilaterally relying upon interpretative aids in carrying out their functions, which are not provided for in the binding rules applicable to all customs authorities, such as in the European Communities, could lead to non-uniform administration in violation of Article X:3(a) of the GATT 1994 in certain circumstances.

7.268 The Bautex decision issued by the Hamburg ZPLA makes explicit reference to an interpretative aid that was particular to Germany.[1159] In particular, that decision refers to a note to Chapter 59 of the Tariff entitled "Erl. Zu Kap. 59 NEH Rz. 02.0 ff".[1160] Notably, the interpretative aid sets out criteria, which are aimed at determining whether or not the textile component of a product is present merely for reinforcing purposes in accordance with Note 2(a)(5) to Chapter 59 of the Common Customs Tariff. The interpretative aid states, *inter alia*, that, in determining whether or not the textile component of a product is present merely for reinforcing purposes, it is necessary to consider whether the fabric in

[1158] United States' first written submission, paras. 71 – 72.

[1159] The European Communities does not dispute that the Bautex decision issued by the Hamburg ZPLA was based, at least in part, on an interpretative aid that was particular to Germany: European Communities' first written submission, para. 343.

[1160] This note is contained in "National Decisions and Indications accompanying Chapter 59 of the German Tariff Schedule" (original and English translation) (Exhibit US-43).

question is "tightly woven". This criterion appears to have been relied upon by the German customs authorities in each of the three decisions with which we have been provided.

7.269 In particular, as previously noted, the Bautex decision issued by the Hamburg ZPLA makes explicit reference to an interpretative aid that was particular to Germany and then proceeds to state that "the fabric is not dense in the merchandise under consideration".[1161] In other words, the Hamburg ZPLA appeared to correlate the criterion of "tightly woven" in the German interpretative aid with the criterion of density of the fabric. This criterion of density was also relied upon by the Main Customs Office of Bremen[1162] and by the Hamburg ZPLA in respect of the opinion concerning Ornata[1163].

7.270 Notably, the interpretative aid relied upon by the German customs authorities in each of these cases is not contained in the relevant chapters of the Common Customs Tariff, namely Chapters 39 and 59.[1164] The European Communities submits that the fabric density criterion was developed pursuant to Commission Regulation (EC) No. 1458/97.[1165] As the European Communities itself explains, that regulation concerned the classification of garments. The Panel considers it difficult to reconcile the fact that a product that was considered as predominantly plastic by two of the German customs authorities in question (i.e. the Main Customs Office of Bremen and the Hamburg ZPLA in respect of the Bautex decision) would be classified by those customs authorities based on an interpretative aid developed in analogy to a regulation concerning textile products. Moreover, even if the fabric density criterion amounted to what the European Communities describes as a "purely interpretative aid prepared for administrative purposes which does not in any way have force of law, and does not derogate from Community law"[1166], the Panel notes that the criterion appears to have played a critical role for the German customs authorities in deciding how to classify the products in question.[1167]

7.271 The Panel has not been provided with any evidence to indicate that any other member States are relying upon an aid akin to that used by the German customs authorities with respect to the tariff classification of blackout drapery lining. Further, the interpretative aid relied upon by the German customs authori-

[1161] See paragraph 7.252 above.

[1162] In particular, the Main Customs Office of Bremen states that "[t]he fabric is not dense". See paragraph 7.251 above.

[1163] The Ornata decision issued by the Hamburg ZPLA states that: "[t[he spun fabric is not dense": See paragraph 7.253 above.

[1164] In this regard, see paragraphs 7.175 – 7.176 above.

[1165] Commission Regulation (EC) No. 1458/97 concerning the classification of certain goods in the Combined Nomenclature (Exhibit EC-78).

[1166] European Communities' first written submission, para. 344 referring to Exhibit EC-79, para. 19.

[1167] In this respect, the Panel notes that the European Communities submits that member States' customs authorities are not prevented from issuing administrative guidelines or other non-binding documents for administrative purposes. However, the ECJ has confirmed that such measures cannot derogate in any way from the application of EC law: European Communities' reply to Panel question No. 157.

ties is not contained in the relevant chapters of the Common Customs Tariff.[1168] Additionally, the German interpretative aid apparently has in the past and may continue in the future to have an impact upon the tariff classification of blackout drapery lining in the European Communities. These factors demonstrate that the German customs authorities' reliance upon the interpretative aid in question amounts to non-uniform administration in violation of Article X:3(a) of the GATT 1994.

Tariff classification decisions in other member States

7.272 By way of observation, a customs administration system which does not *require* reference by customs authorities to decisions taken by other customs authorities operating within the same system and/or cooperation between customs authorities before customs decisions are taken, such as in the European Communities, could lead to non-uniform administration in violation of Article X:3(a) of the GATT 1994 in certain circumstances.[1169]

7.273 In the present case, the Panel also notes that, while the Main Customs Office of Bremen acknowledged the existence of "numerous binding customs tariff decisions ... handed down regarding comparable goods"[1170], without any explanation, it went on to state that it "sees no reason to vacate the contested Notice of Change to Tax". Similarly in the Bautex decision issued by the Hamburg ZPLA, the German customs authority referred to a classification decision by Belgian customs authority but distinguished it on the basis that "[t]he use of the same documents for classification in all cases strengthens the suspicion that the documents do not necessarily match the merchandise."[1171]

7.274 The Panel is of the view that the failure on the part of the Main Customs Office of Bremen to take into account "numerous binding customs tariff decisions ... handed down regarding comparable goods" or, at a minimum, to explain why they were deemed irrelevant to the classification at hand is not consistent with the obligation of uniform administration in Article X:3(a) of the GATT 1994. The Panel considers that it was all the more incumbent upon the Main Customs Office of Bremen to provide such explanations in the light of the fact that Bautex-Stoffe GmbH – the company requesting review of the classification of products before the Main Customs Office of Bremen – objected on numerous occasions to the classification of the products under heading 3921 on the ground

---

[1168] In this regard, the Panel notes that the European Communities submits that member States can only act to supplement provisions contained in EC law if they have been specifically authorized to do so or if a specific issue is not covered by EC law: European Communities' reply to Panel question No. 157. In the case of the tariff classification of blackout drapery lining, the Panel notes that this appears to be covered by the Common Customs Tariff. Further, the Panel has not been provided with any evidence to indicate that member States have been specifically authorized to supplement the Common Customs Tariff with respect to the tariff classification of blackout drapery lining.

[1169] In this regard, see paragraph 7.177 above,

[1170] Hauptzollamt Bremen, Letter Decision to Bautex-Stoffe GmbH, Sep. 22, 2004 (original and English translation) ("Bautex-Stoffe Decision") (Exhibit US-23).

[1171] Letter from Oberfinanzdirektion Hamburg to HZA Bremen regarding Protest of Bautex-Stoffe GmbH, 3 February 2003 (original and English translation) (Exhibit US-41).

that the goods consisted of a fabric comprising polyester and wool, coated with acrylic and flocked with cotton fibers[1172] and because the Main Customs Office of Bremen was clearly aware of the existence of classification decisions by other customs authorities for "comparable goods". For the same reasons, the Panel considers that it was not appropriate for the German customs authority in the Bautex decision issued by the Hamburg ZPLA to have dismissed the tariff classification by Belgian customs authorities on the basis of a mere "suspicion" that the documents filed for classification of those products by the Belgian customs authorities did not correspond to the products themselves.[1173]

7.275 Indeed, it is possible that, had the German customs authorities' consideration of classification decisions for blackout drapery lining issued by customs authorities in other member States gone beyond the merely superficial reference that their respective decisions evidence, the classification of the products before the German customs authorities might not have been different from the classification of the products before the customs authorities in United Kingdom, Ireland, the Netherlands and Belgium. In the Panel's view, the apparent failure on the part of German customs authorities to seriously consider classification decisions for blackout drapery lining of other customs authorities may have had an impact and may continue to have an impact in the future upon trade in blackout drapery lining in the European Communities.[1174] These factors demonstrate that the treatment by the German customs authorities of classification decisions for blackout drapery lining issued by other customs authorities amounts to non-uniform administration in violation of Article X:3(a) of the GATT 1994.

Conclusion

7.276 In conclusion, the Panel considers that the administrative process leading to the tariff classification of blackout drapery lining amounts to non-uniform administration within the meaning of Article X:3(a) of the GATT 1994. The Panel considers that the acts of non-uniform administration which occurred between 1999 and 2002 with respect to the tariff classification of blackout drapery lining continue to have potential effect. In particular, German customs authori-

---

[1172] This is evident from page 2 of Hauptzollamt Bremen, Letter Decision to Bautex-Stoffe GmbH, 22 September 2004 (original and English translation) ("Bautex-Stoffe Decision") (Exhibit US-23) which refers to letters dated 2 May 2001, 25 August 2001, 22 August 2002 and 14 May 2003.

[1173] With respect to its letter concerning Ornata, the Hamburg ZPLA states that: "In your protest letter of 18/12/1997 you mention that a number of fundamental decisions were taken by the EU finance authorities in Brussels with reference to merchandise under code 5907 0090 900. May I request you to inform me of the document numbers and dates of the decisions, if they are known to you. If you have further information and receipts to show that identical merchandise was treated differently in other EU countries (i.e. a classification other than heading 3921), please send me the documents, in order to clarify this situation.": Letter from Main Customs Office Hamburg-Waltershof to ORNATA GmbH in response to protest regarding classification (29 July 1998), p. 2 (Exhibit US-50). The Panel has not been provided with any evidence to suggest that the documentation for identical merchandise requested by the Hamburg ZPLA was not provided and/or that such documentation was not taken into account by the Hamburg ZPLA.

[1174] For example, the impact might be trade diversion to member States other than Germany because of the administrative processes applied by at least some customs authorities in Germany with respect to the tariff classification of blackout drapery lining.

ties may rely upon an interpretative aid particular to Germany in deciding how to classify blackout drapery lining whereas, apparently, customs authorities in other member States do not rely upon the same aid. Furthermore, German customs authorities are not obliged to make reference to the decisions of other customs authorities when classifying blackout drapery lining, even in cases where there is a possibility that the products the subject of those decisions are the same or similar. Therefore, the Panel finds a violation of Article X:3(a) of the GATT 1994 with respect to the tariff classification of blackout drapery lining.

(v) Tariff classification of liquid crystal display flat monitors with digital video interface

Summary of the parties' arguments

Evidence of divergence in classification

7.277 The **United States** refers to a case involving BTI for the classification of liquid crystal display (LCD) flat monitors with digital video interface (DVI). The United States notes that, until 2004, member State customs authorities had consistently classified LCD flat monitors with DVI as "computer monitors" under heading 8471 of the Common Customs Tariff ("Automatic data processing machines and units thereof ..."). The United States submits that, however, in 2004, customs authorities in the Netherlands began classifying the goods as "video monitors" under heading 8528 of the Common Customs Tariff ("Reception apparatus for television, whether or not incorporating radio-broadcast receivers or sound or video recording or reproducing apparatus; video monitors and video projectors"). The United States submits that this matter was brought to the attention of the Customs Code Committee. According to the United States, the Customs Code Committee did not definitively resolve the classification question. Instead, in March 2005, the Council of the European Union issued a regulation temporarily resolving the matter for some of the monitors at issue (i.e. monitors with a diagonal measurement of 19 inches or less and an aspect ratio of 4:3 or 5:4). However, the United States submits that that regulation merely suspends duties on this subset of monitors until 31 December 2006 and, meanwhile, leaves unresolved the classification of monitors with a diagonal measurement greater than 19 inches, which at least one member State (i.e. the Netherlands) continues to classify as video monitors.[1175] According to the United States, products above the size threshold defined in the Council regulation remain subject to duties depending on the classification assigned by customs authorities in different member States.[1176]

7.278 The **European Communities** responds that the correct classification of the monitors at issue is a relatively recent question, which has arisen due to the

[1175] United States' first written submission, para. 74 referring to Council Regulation (EC) No. 493/2005 of 16 March 2005 (Exhibit US-28).
[1176] United States' reply to Panel question No. 4.

increasing convergence of information technology and consumer electronics. Many LCD monitors, by virtue of their design and technical characteristics, can serve both as a computer monitor and as a video monitor. The European Communities submits that it is, therefore, difficult for customs authorities to establish on an objective basis the precise purpose for which a particular monitor is intended.[1177] The European Communities also notes that there are a large number of different types of LCD monitors on the market that differ in various aspects, including size, the interfaces they possess, the signals they can process, and general design. According to the European Communities, to the extent that such features may have an impact on their use, differences between different types of monitors may also need to be taken into account.[1178] The European Communities submits that the evidence referred to by the United States in support of its claims does not show that there is a problem of non-uniform administration contrary to Article X:3(a) of the GATT 1994, but rather that there is an issue in the process of resolution. In this regard, the European Communities submits that the classification of the relevant monitors is an issue which is currently under review, and relevant measures will be submitted to the Customs Code Committee in the near future.[1179]

Measures taken by the European Communities to resolve the divergence in classification

7.279 The **European Communities** notes that Council Regulation (EC) No. 493/2005 of 16 March 2005 temporarily suspends, until 31 December 2006, the duties for video monitors with a diagonal screen measurement of 48.5 cm or less and with an aspect ratio of 4:3 or 5:4.[1180] The European Communities explains that the purpose of this measure is to provide certainty about tariff treatment to the concerned importers for a transitional period of time. This suspension was limited to those monitors which, on account of their size, are more likely to serve as computer monitors than larger monitors. The adoption of a temporary duty suspension was preferred to a classification regulation because, according to the European Communities, it allows further observation of the technological and commercial developments in this segment of the market.[1181] The European Communities explains that, from a practical perspective, the suspension of the duties fulfils exactly the same purpose as that of a classification regulation. It assures traders that, regardless of whether the goods fall under headings 8471 or 8528, their goods will receive the same tariff treatment. The European Communities notes that the relevant industry association has characterised Regulation No. 493/2005 as "a very important suspension request which, when adopted as pro-

[1177] European Communities' first written submission, para. 349.
[1178] European Communities' first written submission, para. 350.
[1179] European Communities' closing statement at the second substantive meeting, para. 15.
[1180] European Communities' first written submission, para. 356 referring to Council Regulation (EC) No 493/2005 of 16 March 2005 (Exhibit US-28).
[1181] European Communities' first written submission, para. 357.

posed, will benefit all importers of such products".[1182] The European Communities submits that, before the expiration of the suspensive measure, EC institutions will review the situation and adopt any necessary measures.[1183]

7.280 The **United States** submits that faced with the problem of divergent classification, the European Communities merely adopted a regulation that temporarily suspends duties on certain LCD monitors with DVI regardless of their classification. The United States notes that the temporary duty suspension only applies to monitors below a specified size threshold. Monitors above that threshold continue to be subject to divergent classification from member State to member State.[1184] The United States also questions whether adoption of a Council regulation to deal temporarily with a subset of LCD monitors rather than a classification regulation, approved by the Customs Code Committee amounts to uniform administration within the meaning of Article X:3(a) of the GATT 1994. According to the United States, a duty suspension regulation is very different from a classification regulation. One is a temporary policy solution, while the other is a definitive determination of a technical issue. In the United States' view, the ability of the Council to adopt a duty suspension regulation does not demonstrate the system's ability to achieve uniformity when it comes to the administration of classification rules. Indeed, the very fact that the question of classification remains unresolved shows an inability of the system to achieve uniformity in this area.[1185] The United States submits that, therefore, since the suspension regulation applies only to monitors below a certain size threshold, that it does not actually resolve the underlying classification question, for monitors above the size threshold, a state of non-uniformity with serious financial consequences remains.[1186] According to the United States, traders organize their business affairs with a long-term view, and in making their shipping decisions, they are likely to take account of which customs authorities will accord the more favourable tariff treatment after the temporary regulation expires.[1187]

7.281 The **European Communities** submits that the United States seems to insinuate that the European Communities chose Regulation No. 493/2005 in order to somehow circumvent the Customs Code Committee. The European Communities disputes this, arguing that the adoption of Regulation No. 493/2005 required a qualified majority of the member States in the Council, just as a favourable opinion of the Committee in management or regulatory procedure does. Rather, the instrument of a Council Regulation was chosen because this seemed better adapted to the specific circumstances of the case.[1188] The European Communities adds that it has adopted another relevant measure, namely Regulation No. 634/2005, which classifies LCD monitors of a particular type under heading 8528. Currently, the Commission keeps monitoring the situation, and

---

[1182] European Communities' first written submission, para. 358 referring to Exhibit EC-84.
[1183] European Communities' first written submission, para. 357.
[1184] United States' reply to Panel question No. 17(b).
[1185] United States' reply to Panel question No. 4.
[1186] United States' oral statement at the second substantive meeting, para. 53.
[1187] United States' reply to Panel question No. 137(b).
[1188] European Communities' first written submission, para. 360.

may adopt further classification regulations for LCD monitors or other appropriate measures as and when the need arises.[1189]

7.282 The European Communities also submits that the reference to the long-term planning on the part of traders is irrelevant for the purposes of Article X:3(a) of the GATT 1994. The European Communities submits that Article X:3(a) of the GATT 1994 requires uniform administration; it does not prohibit legislative changes nor does it protect expectations of traders regarding the continuation of certain measures. Accordingly, the question of what measures the European Communities will adopt after the expiration of Regulation No. 493/2005 in order to ensure uniform administration is not prejudged by Article X:3(a) of the GATT 1994.[1190] The European Communities also argues that the fact that Regulation No. 493/2005 is only valid until 31 December 2006 does not reduce its value for ensuring uniform tariff treatment throughout the European Communities presently. Moreover, before the expiration of the measure, the European Communities will examine the situation and will adopt the measures which are necessary. The European Communities submits that the United States cannot build an allegation of non-uniform administration on the mere speculation that the European Communities might fail to take certain measures in the future.[1191] Therefore, according to the European Communities, it is irrelevant whether any provision compels the European Communities to take the necessary measures after the expiration of Regulation No. 493/2005.[1192]

7.283 The European Communities also argues that the United States is wrong to claim that Regulation No. 493/2005 fails to ensure uniform administration because the measure concerns the suspension of a duty rate, rather than the classification of a product. In this regard, the European Communities notes that Article X:3(a) of the GATT 1994 does not require uniform administration for its own sake, but rather in order to ensure uniform conditions of treatment for traders. Accordingly, Article X:3(a) of the GATT 1994 can be held to be violated only where a variation of practice in fact has a significant impact on traders. In the case of LCD monitors, due to Regulation No. 493/2005, for the monitors covered by the regulation, there is no difference in tariff duties between monitors classified under heading 8471 and those classified under heading 8528, since the tariff rate for both will be 0%. Nor are there any other relevant differences in treatment. Accordingly, even if there were differences in tariff classification for the monitors at issue, this would have no impact on traders. The European Communities explains that this is why the trading community was in fact strongly supportive of the measure.[1193] In addition, the European Communities considers that, even if the Panel were to hold that there was an incompatibility with Arti-

[1189] European Communities' first written submission, para. 361 referring to Exhibit EC-85.

[1190] European Communities' comments on the United States' reply to Panel question No. 137(b).

[1191] European Communities' second written submission, para. 122; European Communities' comments on the United States' reply to Panel question No. 137(b).

[1192] European Communities' comments on the United States' reply to Panel question No. 137(b)

[1193] European Communities' second written submission, para. 123 referring to letter containing industry response to Regulation No. 493/2005 concerning LCD Video Monitors, 16 November 2004 (Exhibit EC-84).

cle X:3(a) of the GATT 1994, this incompatibility could not be held to constitute nullification or impairment of any benefit accruing to the United States under Article X:3(a) of the GATT 1994. In the case of LCD monitors, the tariff treatment for the monitors covered by Regulation No. 493/2005 is uniform and the duty rate is 0%. Therefore, the presumption of nullification and impairment established by Article 3.8 of the DSU would have to be considered as rebutted in the present case.[1194]

7.284 In response, the **United States** submits that the implication that the trading community is satisfied by the measures taken by the European Communities so far regarding the tariff classification of LCD monitors is belied by recent statements from the industry concerned with this classification question. Specifically, in a September 2005 letter to the Commission's Director for International Affairs and Tariff Matters, the industry association that has focused on this matter ("EICTA") stated that: "[w]ithout such clarification [of the classification of monitors above the size threshold set forth in the duty suspension regulation], the industry is faced with an unacceptable situation were [sic] various Member States are applying classification rules in an inconsistent manner, causing competitive disadvantage for some importers and making the consequences of sourcing and routing decisions almost impossible to predict".[1195] Further, as recently as 6 December 2005, EICTA advised the Commission of its profound concerns regarding this matter. According to the United States, EICTA noted not only its substantive disagreement with the Commission's proposed regulation, but also its dismay at the Commission's lack of consultation with the trade association, including its lack of response to the association's 2 September 2005 letter on this matter.[1196]

7.285 In response, the **European Communities** submits that, in its letter, EICTA specifically calls on the Commission to postpone the discussion of the classification regulation. The European Communities question how postponement of a measure that will contribute to uniform administration, supports the United States' submission that the European Communities is not doing enough to ensure uniform administration. With reference to EICTA's letter, the European Communities submits that this, together with a number of other measures[1197], are outside the Panel's terms of reference. Finally, the European Communities submits that, on the basis of ongoing consultations with the customs authorities of the member States as well as with concerned industry, the EC Commission has prepared a draft classification regulation regarding LCD monitors. This measure

[1194] European Communities' second written submission, para. 124.

[1195] United States' oral statement at the second substantive meeting, para. 53 referring to Letter from Mark MacGann, Director General, EICTA, to Manuel Arnal Monreal, Director International Affairs and Tariff Matters, European Commission, 2 September 2005, p. 1 (Exhibit US-75).

[1196] United States' reply to Panel question No. 137(b) referring to *See* Letter from Mark MacGann, Director General, EICTA, to Manuel Arnal Monreal, Director International Affairs and Tariff Matters, European Commission, 6 December 2005 (Exhibit US-81).

[1197] Specifically, the European Communities refers to Exhibits US 75-78.

will be submitted for the opinion of the Customs Code Committee at its meeting of 16 December 2005.[1198]

Opinion of the Customs Code Committee

7.286 The **European Communities** submits that the Customs Code Committee was seized of the issue of the classification of LCD monitors for the first time in April 2004 and has reviewed the situation at regular intervals ever since. Since the classification issue requires technical input from industry, the Committee has, in accordance with Article 9 of its Rules of Procedure, heard representatives of the industry.[1199] The European Communities notes that, at its 346th meeting of 30 June – 2 July 2004, the Customs Code Committee concluded that "unless an importer can demonstrate that a monitor is only to be used with an ADP machine (heading 8471) or to be used as an indicator panel (heading 8531), it has to be classified under heading 8528".[1200] On the basis of the foregoing, the European Communities submits that the United States' allegations that the Netherlands wrongly classifies LCD monitors as video monitors is misplaced since, in principle, such a classification is in line with the Common Customs Tariff, as confirmed by the Customs Code Committee.[1201]

7.287 In response, the **United States** submits that by characterizing the Dutch classification as "in line" with the Common Customs Tariff, the European Communities suggests that more than one classification may be "in line". According to the United States, where more than one classification is "in line" with the Common Customs Tariff, the European Communities does not provide a mechanism for systematically reconciling different classifications adopted by different member State authorities. The United States adds that the Customs Code Committee conclusion with which the Dutch classification supposedly is "in line" is not itself in line with the relevant Chapter Note from the Common Customs Tariff. Specifically, the Committee's conclusion would prohibit a monitor from being classified as a computer monitor under tariff heading 8471 unless an importer can demonstrate that it is "*only* to be used with an ADP machine"[1202] – a computer machine. However, according to the United States, under the relevant chapter notes, a monitor may be classified as a computer monitor if "it is of a kind *solely or principally* used in an automatic data-processing system".[1203]

[1198] European Communities' comments on the United States' reply to Panel question No. 137(b) referring to proposed new regulation on LCD monitors, 29 November 2005,(Exhibit EC-163) and Agenda for Customs Code Committee, 21 November 2005 (Exhibit EC-164).

[1199] European Communities' first written submission, para. 352.

[1200] European Communities' first written submission, para. 353.

[1201] European Communities' first written submission, para. 354.

[1202] European Communities' first written submission, para. 353.

[1203] United States' oral statement at the first substantive meeting, para. 28; United States' reply to Panel question No. 4 referring to Commission Regulation No. 1810/2004 of 7 September 2004 amending Annex I to Council Regulation (EEC) No 2658/87 on the tariff and statistical nomenclature and on the Common Customs Tariff, 30 October 2004 at 504 (Chapter 84, note 5(B)(a)) (emphasis added). (Exhibit US-46).

7.288 The United States also notes that Regulation No. 634/2005 classifying monitors of a particular type under heading 8528, states that "[c]lassification under subheading 8471 60 is excluded, as the monitor is not of a kind solely or principally used in an automated data processing system. ...".[1204] The United States observes that the regulation applied the sole or principal use test, as indicated in Note 5 to Chapter 84 of the Common Customs Tariff. By contrast, the conclusion of the Customs Code Committee is that an importer must demonstrate that "a monitor is *only* to be used with an ADP machine" in order to have it classified under heading 8471. According to the United States, the Customs Code Committee's conclusion, which abandons the sole or principal use test set out in the Common Customs Tariff in favour of a sole use test, detracts from rather than promotes uniformity. In the view of the United States, member State authorities are now confronted with two conflicting tests for classifying LCD monitors with DVI for ADP machines – the sole or principal use test in the Common Customs Tariff chapter notes or the sole use test in the Customs Code Committee's conclusion.[1205]

7.289 The **European Communities** responds that the Customs Code Committee reached its conclusion on the basis of several presentations by the industry concerned. On this basis, the Committee concluded that industry had not succeeded in presenting any criteria on which principal use could be established.[1206] The European Communities adds that it does not understand what purpose conclusions of the Customs Code Committee could have if it should be limited to restating the language of the Combined Nomenclature. According to the European Communities, in order to provide for a uniform application of the Common Customs Tariff, it must be possible for the Committee to reach, on the basis of the facts available, and acting in conformity with the Common Customs Tariff, specific conclusions concerning the classification of particular goods. It is in this way that the Committee can and does contribute to the uniform classification of goods throughout the European Communities.[1207]

7.290 In counter-response, the **United States** submits that the Customs Code Committee's conclusions have put member State authorities in the quandary of having to decide what weight to give the conclusions in view of an apparently conflicting chapter note, namely Note 5 to Chapter 84 of the Common Customs Tariff.[1208] The United States submits that this quandary is evidenced by different approaches taken by member State authorities. For example, in a tariff notice issued in 2004, the UK customs authority, evidently following the Customs Code Committee's conclusion, stated that "from October 2004, LCD/TFT Monitors that incorporate a DVI connector are to be classified in Combined Nomenclature (CN) code 8528 21 90".[1209] Thus, according to the United States, the United

---

[1204] Commission Regulation (EC) No. 634/2005 of 26 April 2005 concerning the classification of certain goods in the Combined Nomenclature (Exhibit EC-85).

[1205] United States' reply to Panel question No. 17(b).

[1206] European Communities' second written submission, para. 127.

[1207] European Communities' second written submission, para. 128.

[1208] United States' oral statement at the second substantive meeting, para. 54.

[1209] HM Customs & Excise, Tariff Notice 13/04 (Exhibit US-76).

Kingdom appears to be following the opinion of the Customs Code Committee and classifying all such monitors under heading 8528, regardless of sole or principal use. In the case of the Netherlands, the United States submits that it has abandoned the guidance of the Customs Code Committee for fear of adverse commercial impact and is now applying its own set of criteria for deciding whether to classify monitors under heading 8528 and 8471. Specifically, in a decree of July 2005, the Dutch customs authority explained that, since April 2004, it had been classifying LCD monitors with DVI under tariff heading 8528, in view of a Commission regulation concerning plasma monitors. It then went on to state that: "[n]ot all member states are following this policy. The result is a diverted flow of business, which is harmful to the competitiveness of Dutch industry in the logistics and services sector. For this reason, the Netherlands is making the policy as regards classification of certain LCDs in the Combined Nomenclature more precise".[1210] Accordingly, the decree set forth criteria that the Netherlands follows as of 22 November 2004 for determining whether LCD monitors with DVI should be classified under heading 8471 or heading 8528. These criteria, which cover a number of factors, including how a good is presented in brochures, are evidently unique to the Netherlands, appearing in no EC regulation or even in EC guidance. Moreover, despite the Customs Code Committee's conclusion, the German authority appears to have continued classifying LCD monitors with DVI under heading 8471, even where they are principally though not solely for use with computers.[1211]

Analysis by the Panel

7.291 The Panel notes that the United States challenges divergence in the tariff classification of LCD monitors with DVI among customs authorities of the member States of the European Communities.[1212]

7.292 In the Panel's view, the tariff classification of a product, including of LCD monitors with DVI, constitutes an act of administration within the meaning of Article X:3(a) of the GATT 1994. This act of administration is a matter within the Panel's terms of reference since it amounts to an instance of administration of the Common Customs Tariff in the tariff classification area.[1213]

7.293 With respect to the question of whether or not the tariff classification of LCD monitors with DVI is "uniform" within the meaning of Article X:3(a) of the GATT 1994, the Panel recalls its finding in paragraph 7.135 above that geographic uniformity is required under Article X:3(a) of the GATT 1994. That is, administration should be uniform in different places within a particular WTO Member. The Panel also recalls its finding in paragraph 7.135 above that the

---

[1210] Douanerechten. Indeling van bepaalde LCD monitoren in de gecombineerde nomenclatuur, No. CPP2005/1372M, 8 July 2005, (original and unofficial English translation) (Exhibit US-77).

[1211] United States' reply to Panel question No. 137(b) referring to BTI DEM/2975/05-1 (start date of validity 19 July 2005) (Exhibit US-78).

[1212] United States' first written submission, para. 74 referring to Council Regulation (EC) No. 493/2005 of 16 March 2005 (Exhibit US-28).

[1213] For information on EC institutions and mechanisms applicable in the tariff classification area, see paragraphs 7.179 – 7.182 above.

form, nature and scale of the alleged non-uniform administration and the laws, regulations, judicial decisions and rulings that are allegedly being administered in a non-uniform manner should be taken into consideration when interpreting the term "uniform" in Article X:3(a) of the GATT 1994. The Panel considers that the United States' challenge with respect to the tariff classification of LCD monitors with DVI is narrow in nature. It involves the interpretation of only a few tariff headings in the Common Customs Tariff to determine the classification of a single product – namely, of LCD monitors with DVI. Therefore, given the narrowness of this challenge, the Panel considers that a high degree of uniformity is required for the purposes of Article X:3(a) of the GATT 1994. We now turn to the facts to determine whether or not this high degree of uniformity has been achieved with respect to the tariff classification of LCD monitors with DVI.

7.294 The Panel notes that the European Communities does not appear to dispute that, in 2004, a divergence in the tariff classification of LCD monitors with DVI among customs authorities of the member States occurred, namely that customs authorities in the Netherlands classified LCD flat monitors with DVI "video monitors" under heading 8528 ("Reception apparatus for television, whether or not incorporating radio-broadcast receivers or sound or video recording or reproducing apparatus; video monitors and video projectors") whereas customs authorities in other member States classified such LCD monitors as "computer monitors" under heading 8471 ("Automatic data processing machines and units thereof ...").[1214] Further, the European Communities itself has noted that many LCD monitors, by virtue of their design and technical characteristics, can serve both as a computer monitor and as a video monitor.[1215] In these proceedings, the European Communities has not submitted that the divergence in tariff classification is limited to a subset of LCD monitors that can serve both as a computer monitor and as a video monitor.

7.295 The European Communities does submit, however, that the divergence in the tariff classification of LCD monitors with DVI among customs authorities of the member States has been the subject of past and ongoing action on the part of

[1214] European Communities' first written submission, para. 349; European Communities closing statement at the second substantive meeting, para. 15; European Communities' comments on the United States' reply to Panel question No. 137(b). For example, in its closing statement at the second substantive meeting, the European Communities stated that "these recent developments do not show that there is a problem of non-uniform application contrary to Article X:3(a) GATT, but rather that there is an issue which is currently under review...": European Communities closing statement at the second substantive meeting, para. 15. Divergent tariff classification of LCD monitors with DVI between, on the one hand, Dutch customs authorities and, on the other hand, customs authorities in the other member States, tends to be supported by a press release entitled "Additional tax assessments again reveal the Netherlands to be the odd one out in the EU", which states that "[t]he Dutch Customs authorities have completely unexpectedly introduced importation criteria – newly published in November 2004 – and levies on LCD monitors with retrospective effect on all such products which were imported through the Netherlands by importers and logistical service providers in the period from 2002 – 2004. ... This situation is in marked contrast to the other EU countries, which have not issued additional assessments.": Press Release issued by Greenberg Traurig, 24 May 2005 (Exhibit US-29).

[1215] European Communities' first written submission, para. 349.

the European Communities to resolve the divergence.[1216] After appraising all the relevant evidence before us, we are of the view that the action taken by the European Communities since 2004 when the existence of non-uniform administration became apparent has not had the effect of rectifying the divergence in the tariff classification of LCD monitors with DVI among customs authorities of the member States.[1217] Our reasoning is as follows.

7.296 *First*, by the European Communities' own admission, Council Regulation (EC) No. 493/2005 of 16 March 2005, which was enacted in response to the divergence in tariff classification of LCD monitors with DVI, only applies to video monitors with a diagonal screen measurement of 48.5 cm or less and with an aspect ratio of 4:3 or 5:4.[1218] The Regulation explains the rationale for the limited scope of its application in the preamble as follows: "Trade data indicate that currently monitors using liquid crystal display technology, with a diagonal measurement of the screen of 48,5 cm or less and a screen aspect ratio of 4:3 or 5:4, are mainly used as output units of automatic data-processing machines. However, such monitors are frequently also capable of reproducing video images from a source other than an automatic data-processing machine and therefore do not meet the condition of being solely or principally for use with such machines".[1219] In other words, the Regulation limits its scope of application to monitors with a diagonal screen measurement of 48.5 cm or less and with an aspect ratio of 4:3 or 5:4 because, according to the Regulation, monitors with those features are mainly used as output units of automatic data-processing machines and are also capable of reproducing video images from a source other than an automatic data-processing machine. The Panel has not been provided with evidence to suggest that monitors falling outside the scope of the Regulation (because they do not have a diagonal screen measurement of 48.5 cm or less and do not have an aspect ratio of 4:3 or 5:4) would not also be used as outputs of automatic data-processing machines as well as reproducing video images from a source other than an automatic data-processing machine. In fact, to the contrary, the European Communities itself has submitted that many LCD monitors, by virtue of their design and technical characteristics, can serve both as a computer monitor and as a video monitor.[1220] Moreover, the preamble to Regulation No. 493/2005 states that:

[1216] European Communities' first written submission, para. 361 referring to Commission Regulation No. 634/2005 (Exhibit EC-85); European Communities' closing statement at the second substantive meeting, para. 15; European Communities' comments on the United States' reply to Panel question No. 137(b) referring to proposed new regulation on LCD monitors, 29 November 2005,(Exhibit EC-163) and Agenda for Customs Code Committee, 21 November 2005 (Exhibit EC-164).

[1217] The Panel notes that the action taken by the European Communities to address the divergence in the tariff classification of LCD monitors with DVI is not part of the "measure at issue" for the purposes of the United States' claim under Article X:3(a) of the GATT 1994. Rather, such action is relevant evidence to determine whether or not the divergence in the tariff classification of LCD monitors with DVI among customs authorities of the member States, which has not been disputed by the European Communities, has been resolved.

[1218] Council Regulation (EC) No. 493/2005 of 16 March 2005 (Exhibit US-28).

[1219] Council Regulation (EC) No. 493/2005 of 16 March 2005, 3rd preamble (Exhibit US-28).

[1220] European Communities' first written submission, para. 349.

> "[T]he convergence of information technology, consumer electronics industries and new technologies has created a situation where it is becoming impossible, when classifying monitors, to determine, by reference to simple technical characteristics, the main purpose of a particular monitor. It follows from the case law of the Court of Justice of the European Communities that classification cannot be based on actual use. The correct classification of individual products is to be based on objective and quantifiable data. It is currently not feasible to establish unambiguous criteria meeting this requirement."[1221]

Therefore, while Regulation No. 493/2005 may have remedied the divergence in tariff classification with respect to those monitors falling within the scope of the Regulation, it would not have the same effect with respect to monitors that fall outside the scope of the Regulation.[1222]

7.297 *Second*, Regulation No. 493/2005 indicates that the duty suspension applies to LCD monitors with DVI which are "classifiable under CN code 8528 21 90".[1223] In other words, Regulation No. 493/2005 only applies to products that qualify under heading 8528. Accordingly, this Regulation would not be applicable and, therefore, would not be helpful in resolving the divergence in tariff classification in cases where it is unclear whether an LCD monitor should be classified under heading 8528 or, rather, under heading 8471. Such cases would appear to be at the core of the United States' allegation that tariff classification of LCD monitors with DVI diverges among customs authorities of the member States.

7.298 *Third*, the Panel notes the European Communities' statement that it has adopted another relevant measure – namely, Commission Regulation (EC) No. 634/2005 of 26 April 2005 – which classifies LCD monitors of a particular type under heading 8528.[1224] This Regulation would appear to assist in resolving the ambiguity regarding whether a product should be classified under heading 8528 or, rather, under heading 8471. In particular, Regulation No. 634/2005 indicates that the classification of LCD monitors under heading 8528 is limited to "a colour monitor of the liquid crystal device (LCD) type with a diagonal measurement of the screen of 38,1 cm (15") and overall dimensions of 30,5 (W) x 22.9 (H) x 8.9 (D) cm". The Regulation also stipulates that "the product must display signals received from various sources, such as an automatic data-processing machine, a closed circuit television system, a DVD player or a camcorder" in order for the monitor to be classifiable under heading 8528. The Regulation further clarifies that: "Classification under subheading 8471 60 is excluded, as the moni-

---

[1221] Council Regulation (EC) No. 493/2005 of 16 March 2005, 2nd preamble (Exhibit US-28).

[1222] The Panel notes that, here, it is not addressing the administration of Council Regulation (EC) No. 493/2005 of 16 March 2005 for the purposes of the United States' claim under Article X:3(a) of the GATT 1994. Rather, we are considering that Regulation to determine whether or not it indicates that the divergence in tariff classification of LCD monitors with DVI, which became apparent in 2004, has been resolved.

[1223] Council Regulation (EC) No. 493/2005 of 16 March 2005, 4th preamble (Exhibit US-28).

[1224] Exhibit EC-85.

tor is not of a kind solely or principally used in an automatic data-processing system (see Note 5 to Chapter 84) in view of its capabilities to display signals from various sources".[1225]

7.299 The Panel considers that the steps that Regulation No. 634/2005 may have made towards resolving the divergent classification of LCD monitors could be undermined when read in light of the opinion of the Customs Code Committee taken at its 346th meeting of 30 June – 2 July 2004, especially in light of the fact that, as a matter of practice, representatives of member State customs authorities participate in the Customs Code Committee decision-making process and the same customs authorities apply Regulation No. 634/2005.[1226] In particular, the Customs Code Committee opined that "unless an importer can demonstrate that a monitor is only to be used with an ADP machine (heading 8471) or to be used as an indicator panel (heading 8531), it has to be classified under heading 8528".[1227] In other words, the Customs Code Committee's opinion requires that a monitor must *only* be used with an ADP machine in order for it to be classifiable under heading 8471. This statement contrasts with the formulation used in Regulation No. 634/2005 which implicitly states that heading 8471 60 only applies to monitors of a kind *solely or principally used* (not *only* used) in an automatic data-processing system.[1228] This difference in formulation used in Regulation No. 634/2005 on the one hand and by the Customs Code Committee on the other could well have significant practical effects. We note in this regard the European Communities' submission that opinions of the Customs Code Committee play an important role in the uniform administration of the Common Customs Tariff and that member State customs authorities attach some importance to those opinions.[1229]

[1225] Commission Regulation No. 634/2005 of 26 April 2005, Annex, para. 4 (Exhibit EC-85). The Panel notes that, here, it is not addressing the administration of Commission Regulation No. 634/2005 for the purposes of the United States' claim under Article X:3(a) of the GATT 1994. Rather, we are considering that Regulation to determine whether or not it indicates that the divergence in tariff classification of LCD monitors with DVI, which became apparent in 2004, has been resolved.

[1226] In this regard, see paragraphs 7.157 – 7.160 above.

[1227] The relevant excerpt of the minutes of the Customs Code Committee's 346th meeting of 30 June-2 July 2004 meeting is set out in paragraph 353 of the European Communities' first written submission.

[1228] The formulation used in Regulation No. 634/2005 is based on Note 5 to Chapter 84 of the Common Customs Tariff.

[1229] For example, the European Communities notes that opinions of the Customs Code Committee are not legally binding but further notes that, as stated by the ECJ in Joined Cases 69 and 70/76, *Dittmeyer v Hauptzollamt Hamburg - Waltershof* (Exhibit EC-31), they constitute an important means of ensuring the uniform application of the common customs tariff and, as such, may be considered as a valid aid to the interpretation of the tariff. The European Communities further notes that member States' customs authorities are not legally bound by the opinions of the Customs Code Committee. However, they are bound by the duty of cooperation contained in Article 10 of the EC Treaty, which includes an obligation to contribute to the uniform application of Community law. For this reason, member States are bound to give due weight to interpretations of EC customs law set out in opinions of the Customs Code Committee. The European Communities adds that, from a practical point of view, opinions of the Committee typically reflect a common approach agreed by all member States: European Communities' reply to Panel question No. 58(l).

7.300 *Fourth*, the Panel has evidence that customs authorities of the member States do not appear to have a clear idea of the practical effect of the various measures existing at the Community level regarding the tariff classification of LCD monitors with DVI. For example, in Tariff Notice 13/04, which, apparently, was issued following issuance of the opinion of the Customs Code Committee, the UK customs authority, stated that "from October 2004, LCD/TFT Monitors that incorporate a DVI connector are to be classified in Combined Nomenclature (CN) code 8528 21 90".[1230] This tends to suggest that the UK customs authorities considered that monitors that did not incorporate DVI would not be classifiable under heading 8528 and, presumably, would, therefore, be classifiable under heading 8471. In other words, the UK authorities appear to have adopted the approach indicated by the Customs Code Committee.

7.301 More recently and subsequent to the coming into force of Regulation No. 634/2005, in a decree of 8 July 2005 concerning the classification of certain LCD monitors, the Dutch customs authorities stated that:

> "In accordance with Regulation (EC) number 754/2004 of 23 April 2004 (published in OJL 118), the European Commission has classified plasma-monitors with a screen diameter of 42 inches accompanied by a DVI connection, within heading 8528.
>
> The Customs committee, tariff and statistical nomenclature section, work instruments sector (329th meeting of 15 December 2003), by qualified majority agreed on advice to be given on the above-mentioned Regulation. Since then, The Netherlands, supported by the European Commission, has put forth the policy that LCD monitors which meet the requirements of the Regulation, are to be classified in heading 8528. Not all member states are following this policy. The result is a diverted flow of business, which is harmful to the competitiveness of Dutch industry in the logistics and services sector. For this reason, The Netherlands is making the policy as regards classification of certain LCDs in the Combined Nomenclature more precise."[1231]

The decree goes on to list criteria for the classification of LCD monitors, a number of which do not appear in any of the instruments existing at the Community level.[1232]

[1230] HM Customs & Excise, Tariff Notice 13/04 (Exhibit US-76).

[1231] Douanerechten. Indeling van bepaalde LCD monitoren in de gecombineerde nomenclatuur, No. CPP2005/1372M (8 July 2005) (original and unofficial English translation) para. 1 (Exhibit US-77).

[1232] The Dutch decree refers to the following criteria:

"- no other connection other than a VGA and/or DVI connection (the presence of an audio connection is allowed);

- a screen diameter not greater than 20 inches (51centimeters) with screen measurements (height/width) of approximately 3:4 (thus no "widescreen");

- the absence of a remote control/absence of an infra-red sensor on the monitor;

- the absence of an instrument which allows choice of channels or points to the use of the monitor as a television;

7.302 Further, in BTI dated 19 July 2005, the German customs authority appears to have continued classifying LCD monitors with DVI under heading 8471, even where they are principally though not solely for use with computers.[1233]

7.303 Moreover, there appears to be some confusion among participants in the industry regarding the tariff classification of LCD monitors with DVI. In particular, in a letter dated 2 September 2005 to the Commission's Director for International Affairs and Tariff Matters, the industry association dealing with LCD monitors ("EICTA") stated that "[w]ithout ... clarification [of the classification of LCD monitors], the industry is faced with an unacceptable situation were [sic] various Member States are applying classification rules in an inconsistent manner, causing competitive disadvantage for some importers and making the consequences of sourcing and routing decisions almost impossible to predict".[1234] Further, by letter dated 6 December 2005, EICTA advised the EC Commission of its concerns regarding the enactment of a Regulation concerning the classification of goods under headings 8471 and 8528, which had not been enacted at the time the letter was sent to the EC Commission.[1235]

7.304 On the basis of the evidence submitted to it, it is the Panel's view that the action taken by the European Communities has not had the effect of rectifying the divergence in the tariff classification of LCD monitors with DVI among customs authorities of the member States, the existence of which divergence since 2004 has not been disputed by the European Communities. In this regard, the evidence indicates that the ongoing existence of divergent tariff classification has had and is likely to continue to have an adverse impact on the trading environment[1236], until the divergence is resolved. The Panel considers that the precise manner in which such divergence is resolved is not a matter for its consideration. Nor is it a matter that is dictated by Article X:3(a) of the GATT 1994. However, the tools and mechanisms should be effective in removing the divergent tariff classification, which in our view, did not occur despite the various steps taken by

---

- no provision (covered by a metal plate or by other norms – ("slot-in type") allowing the monitor to be used as a video-monitor ("tariff engineering");

- the opportunity to place the screen in varying positions (adjust height, tilt forwards/backwards, turn in 90 degree angle (portrait/landscape)."

[1233] United States' reply to Panel question No. 137(b) referring to BTI DEM/2975/05-1 (start date of validity 19 July 2005) (Exhibit US-78). The BTI indicates that the product that was classified by the German customs authorities was an LCD monitor with a 20,1" display screen with a network cable for connection with ADP machines, of a kind mainly used for ADP processing.

[1234] United States' oral statement at the second substantive meeting, para. 53 referring to letter from Mark MacGann, Director General, EICTA, to Manuel Arnal Monreal, Director International Affairs and Tariff Matters, European Commission, p. 1, 2 September 2005 (Exhibit US-75).

[1235] United States' reply to Panel question No. 137(b) referring to letter from Mark MacGann, Director General, EICTA, to Manuel Arnal Monreal, Director International Affairs and Tariff Matters, European Commission, 6 December 2005 (Exhibit US-81).

[1236] The impact on the trading environment is evident, *inter alia*, from the evidence referred to by the Panel in paragraphs 7.300 – 7.303. The Panel considers that the fact that traders may be subject to the same duty (or, for that matter, no duty) whether the LCD monitors they are importing into the European Communities are classified under heading 8471 or 8528 does not detract from our conclusion that the trading environment has been affected as a result of the divergent tariff classification.

the European Communities to resolve the divergence in tariff classification of LCD monitors with DVI.

7.305 In conclusion, the Panel considers that the tariff classification of LCD monitors with DVI amounts to non-uniform administration within the meaning of Article X:3(a) of the GATT 1994. The Panel considers that measures adopted by the European Communities so far have not had the effect of removing divergence in tariff classification of such monitors which became evident in 2004.[1237] Therefore, the Panel finds a violation of Article X:3(a) of the GATT 1994 with respect to the tariff classification of LCD monitors with DVI.

(vi) Treatment of BTI in member States other than the issuing member State

Summary of the parties' arguments

7.306 The **United States** notes that the Community Customs Code provides for the issuance by member State customs authorities of advance rulings in the form of BTI, which informs traders of the classification that will be assigned to particular goods on importation.[1238] The United States further notes that Article 11 of the Implementing Regulation states that BTI issued by the authorities of one member State is "binding on the competent authorities of all the member States under the same conditions"[1239] but submits that, in reality, member States do not always treat BTI issued by other member States as binding.[1240] More particularly, the United States argues that BTI from one member State does not bind another member State to classify similar or identical goods imported by a person other than the holder of the BTI in the same way, with the result that the same product can be classified under different tariff classifications, and be subject to different tariff treatment, from one member State to another.[1241] In support, the United States submits that, in a recent survey among the membership of a trade association consisting of importers of products into the European Communities, companies observed that "[b]inding tariff information from German authorities is still not accepted by other EU countries, especially Greece and Portugal."[1242]

7.307 In response, the **European Communities** contests the existence of any problem regarding the recognition of BTI from Germany in other member States. The European Communities argues that the so-called "survey" relied upon by the

[1237] The Panel notes the existence of a draft Regulation concerning the classification of LCD monitors contained in Exhibit EC-163. However, at the time the Panel issued its Interim Report to the parties, the Panel had not been provided with evidence to indicate that that draft regulation had the effect of removing divergence in tariff classification of such monitors which became evident in 2004.

[1238] United States' first written submission, para. 22.

[1239] Commission Regulation (EEC) No. 2454/93 of 2 July 1993 laying down provisions for the implementation of Council Regulation (EEC) No. 2913/92 of 12 October 1992 establishing the Community Customs Code, Article 11 (Exhibit US-6).

[1240] United States' first written submission, para. 47.

[1241] United States' first written submission, para. 22.

[1242] United States' first written submission, para. 76 referring to Foreign Trade Association, Questionnaire on the topic "Trade Facilitation": Facilitation of Trade in WTO States, March 2005, response to question 1.4 (Exhibit US-30).

United States is based on a comment from a single unidentified company in the context of a trade association questionnaire of March 2005 and is not supported by any additional evidence. Accordingly, it is impossible to verify the accuracy of the statement. The European Communities further submits that, even if an importer claims that BTI was not accepted, this might reflect a range of problems of an entirely different kind, for instance a lack of identity of the products imported with those described in the BTI. Moreover, if a customs authority fails to recognize BTI issued by another member State, the importer can obtain judicial review or inform the EC Commission. However, the European Communities submits that it is not aware of this having occurred.[1243]

7.308 The **United States** submits that the case of *Peacock AG* v. *Hauptzollamt Paderborn* describes divergence in classification of network cards for personal computers between Denmark, Netherlands, and United Kingdom, on the one hand, and Germany, on the other.[1244] According to the United States, the *Peacock* case illustrates that one or more member States did not treat BTI issued by other member States as binding[1245]

7.309 The **European Communities** argues that BTI is only binding against the holder of the BTI and is not binding against other persons.[1246] Further, the European Communities submits that what is significant is not that a divergence may occur but, rather, that it is addressed and removed once it occurs. According to the European Communities, this is precisely what happened in the context of the *Peacock* case.[1247]

7.310 The **United States** refers to divergence in classification of drip irrigation products. The United States explains that French customs authorities issued BTI for the product in question in 1999, classifying it as an irrigation system under tariff heading 8424 of the Common Customs Tariff, which carried an *ad valorem* duty rate of 1.7%. In December 2000, when an importer of the same product attempted to import the product through Spain, the Spanish customs authorities disregarded the French BTI and classified the product as a pipe, under tariff heading 3717 of the Common Customs Tariff, which carried an *ad valorem* duty rate of 6.4%.[1248] According to the United States, this case illustrates that one or more member States did not treat as binding BTI issued by other member States.[1249]

[1243] European Communities' second written submission, para. 95.

[1244] United States' first written submission, footnote 33 referring to Case C-339/98, *Peacock AG* v. *Hauptzollamt Paderborn*, Opinion of the Advocate General, 2000 ECR I-08947, 28 October 1999, paras. 7-8 (Exhibit US-17).

[1245] United States' reply to Panel question No. 20; United States' oral statement at the second substantive meeting, para. 21.

[1246] European Communities' reply to Panel question No. 161 referring to Case C-495/03, *Intermodal Transports BV v. Staastsecretaris van Financiën*, 15 September 2005, not yet reported, para. 27 (Exhibit US-71).

[1247] European Communities' second written submission, para. 136.

[1248] United States' reply to Panel question No. 14.

[1249] United States' reply to Panel question No. 20.

7.311 The **European Communities** responds that BTI is binding only against the holder of the BTI and is not binding against other persons.[1250] According to the European Communities, the BTI issued by customs authorities in France and Spain for the drip irrigation products were not issued for the same holders. Further, the European Communities submits that what is significant is not that a divergence in tariff classification may occur but, rather, that it is addressed and removed once it occurs.[1251]

7.312 The **United States** refers to the *Camcorders* case and submits that, following amendment of an explanatory note regarding camcorders in June 2004, the Spanish customs authority issued BTI classifying 19 camcorder models produced by a particular company under sub-heading 8525 40 91.[1252] The French affiliate of the holder of the BTI informed the customs authority in France of the BTI's existence during the course of an audit by that office. Nevertheless, according to the United States, the French customs authority informed the company that it intended not to follow the classification set forth in the BTI, but instead, to collect duty based on its own determination of the correct classification of the camcorder models at issue.[1253] The United States submits that while the context in which this matter emerged involved the post-clearance recovery of duties, nevertheless, determining the amount of duties to be recovered first requires a determination of classification.[1254]

7.313 In response, the **European Communities** submits that the BTI issued by the Spanish authorities for camcorders are in full accordance with EC classification rules. According to the European Communities, the United States has not provided any evidence of any other member States having classified camcorders contrary to EC classification rules. Moreover, according to the European Communities, the United States does not provide any evidence on when the importation into France took place and whether indeed they related to products corresponding to those described in the BTI issued by the Spanish authorities. Further, the European Communities submits that it appears that the question addressed by the French authorities was one of post-clearance recovery of customs duties, and not one of tariff classification. Since the question is, therefore, not one regarding the uniform administration of tariff classification rules, but rather of the post-clearance recovery of customs debts, the European Communities considers that the issue is outside the Panel's terms of reference.[1255]

7.314 The **United States** refers to the report of the panel in the dispute *EC – Chicken Cuts*. The United States notes that at issue there was whether a certain

---

[1250] European Communities' reply to Panel question No. 161 referring to Case C-495/03, *Intermodal Transports BV v. Staatssecretaris van Financiën*, 15 September 2005, not yet reported, para. 27 (Exhibit US-71).

[1251] European Communities' second written submission, para. 143 referring to United States' reply to Panel question No. 2, para 4.

[1252] BTI issued by Spanish customs authority classifying camcorders under sub-heading 8525 40 91, with start date of validity in June 2004 (Exhibit US-65).

[1253] United States' oral statement at the second substantive meeting, para. 30.

[1254] United States' reply to Panel question No. 180.

[1255] European Communities' reply to Panel question No. 172, para. 37.

product should be classified under tariff heading 0210 or 0207 of the Common Customs Tariff. The complaining parties relied on issuance of BTI by several member States consistently classifying the product under heading 0210. In response, the European Communities asserted that "this interpretation was not followed in other EC customs offices".[1256]

7.315 The **European Communities** submits that there was no difference of interpretation nor application of EC classification rules in the context of the *EC – Chicken Cuts* case. Further, the European Communities' statement related only to "interpretation". Nowhere in the panel's report in *EC – Chicken Cuts* was the European Communities reported as having said that BTI was not recognized when presented by the holder. Accordingly, in the European Communities' view, the statement quoted by the United States is not pertinent.[1257]

Analysis by the Panel

7.316 The Panel notes that the essence of the United States challenge under Article X:3(a) of the GATT 1994 here is that customs authorities of the member States do not always treat BTI issued by customs authorities of other member States as binding.[1258]

7.317 In the Panel's view, the treatment of BTI issued by customs authorities constitutes an act of administration within the meaning of Article X:3(a) of the GATT 1994. This act of administration is a matter within the Panel's terms of reference since it amounts to an instance of administration of the Common Customs Tariff in the tariff classification area.[1259]

7.318 The context for the United States' challenge is Article 12(2) of the Community Customs Code, which provides that:

> Binding tariff information ... shall be binding on the customs authorities as against the holder of the information only in respect of the tariff classification ... of goods.

7.319 Article 11 of the Implementing Regulation is also relevant. It provides that:

> "Binding tariff information supplied by the customs authorities of a Member State since 1 January 1991 shall become binding on the competent authorities of all the Member States under the same conditions."[1260]

7.320 As a starting point, the Panel notes that its task in this dispute is to determine whether or not Article X:3(a) of the GATT 1994 has been violated by the European Communities, not to determine the consistency or otherwise of EC acts

---

[1256] Panel Report, *EC – Chicken Cuts*, para. 7.260.

[1257] European Communities' second written submission, para. 96.

[1258] United States' first written submission, para. 47.

[1259] For information on EC institutions and mechanisms applicable in the tariff classification area, see paragraphs 7.179 – 7.182 above.

[1260] Commission Regulation (EEC) No. 2454/93 of 2 July 1993 laying down provisions for the implementation of Council Regulation (EEC) No. 2913/92 of 12 October 1992 establishing the Community Customs Code, Article 11 (Exhibit US-6).

with EC customs law. Having said that, the Panel can see that the failure on the part of customs authorities of member States to accept BTI issued by customs authorities in other member States when that BTI is presented by the holder in contravention of Article 12(2) of the Community Customs Code and Article 11 of the Implementing Regulation could simultaneously lead to non-uniform administration in violation of Article X:3(a) of the GATT 1994. In particular, if a customs authority of a member State refuses to acknowledge and treat as binding BTI issued by a customs authority of another member State for a product that is identical in all material respects to that which is the subject of the BTI when such BTI is invoked by the holder and, instead, classifies the product differently, this will necessarily result in non-uniform administration of the Common Customs Tariff in violation of Article X:3(a) of the GATT 1994. Nevertheless, the Panel notes that it has not been provided with sufficient evidence to prove that non-uniform administration in violation of Article X:3(a) of the GATT 1994 has occurred regarding the treatment of BTI in member States other than the issuing member State in the specific instances relied upon by the United States.

7.321 In particular, in support of its allegation that customs authorities of the member States do not always treat BTI issued by customs authorities of other member States as binding in violation of Article X:3(a) of the GATT 1994, the United States relies first upon the March 2005 report of the Foreign Trade Association regarding a questionnaire on the topic of "Trade Facilitation": Facilitation of Trade in WTO States.[1261] More specifically, the United States relies upon the following statement made by one trader, which is contained in the report: "Binding tariff information from German authorities is still not accepted by other EU countries, especially Greece and Portugal."[1262] The Panel does not consider that this statement on its own constitutes probative evidence to support the United States' allegation given that it is simply a single, anecdotal comment made by one trader in response to questions posed in the questionnaire and is not supported by any factual evidence. The opening paragraph of the Foreign Trade Association's report itself states that "[t]he Trade Facilitation Questionnaire was sent to 70 FTA member companies. 20 answers reached the FTA ... The following represents quotations from the answers. Although the [quotations] do not always fully comply with the political consensus among all members, they highlight the practical problems European traders, especially importers, face at borders". Further, with respect to the specific statement relied upon by the United States, the Panel notes that it is very broad and general. It does not identify the products covered by the German BTI that is allegedly not being accepted elsewhere, particularly in Greece and Portugal. Nor does the statement indicate the period during which the German BTI was not accepted by customs authorities in other member States. Finally, the statement does not indicate whether or not BTI issued by German customs authorities that was not accepted by customs authorities in Greece and Portugal was invoked by the holder of the German BTI.

[1261] Foreign Trade Association, Questionnaire on the topic "Trade Facilitation": Facilitation of Trade in WTO States, March 2005 (Exhibit US-30).

[1262] Foreign Trade Association, Questionnaire on the topic "Trade Facilitation": Facilitation of Trade in WTO States, March 2005, para. 1.4 (Exhibit US-30).

7.322 By way of additional support for its allegation that customs authorities of the member States do not always treat BTI issued by customs authorities of other member States as binding in violation of Article X:3(a) of the GATT 1994, the United States relies upon an alleged failure by German customs authorities to treat as binding BTI issued by customs authorities in Denmark, Netherlands, and United Kingdom for network cards for personal computers.[1263] The United States makes additional allegations regarding tariff classification for this product, which are dealt with in detail in paragraph 7.193 *et seq* above. We note in that discussion that the facts indicate the existence of differences in tariff classification for network cards for personal computers between, on the one hand, the German customs authorities (who classified the product in question under heading 8517 of the Common Customs Tariff) and, on the other hand, Danish, Dutch and UK customs authorities (who classified it under heading 8473 of the Common Customs Tariff) at one point in time, the existence of which differences has not been contested by the European Communities.[1264] Nevertheless, the Panel notes that it has not been presented with any evidence to indicate that German customs authorities refused to accept the classification by Danish, Dutch and UK customs authorities. Therefore, the Panel considers that there is no reason to deviate from our conclusion in paragraph 7.207 above that the tariff classification of network cards for personal computers does not currently amount to non-uniform administration within the meaning of Article X:3(a) of the GATT 1994.

7.323 The United States also relies upon an alleged failure by Spanish customs authorities to treat as binding BTI issued by French customs authorities for drip irrigation products. The United States makes additional allegations regarding tariff classification for this product, which are dealt with in detail in paragraph 7.208 *et seq* above. We note in that discussion that the United States has not provided any evidence to support its allegation of differences in the tariff classification of drip irrigation products between customs authorities of the member States but that we are willing to accept its assertion in this regard in light of the fact that the European Communities does not dispute the existence of differences in this regard. Nevertheless, the Panel notes that it has not been presented with any evidence to indicate that Spanish customs authorities refused to accept the classification by French customs authorities. Therefore, the Panel considers that there is no reason to deviate from our conclusion in paragraph 7.218 above that the tariff classification of drip irrigation products does not amount to non-uniform administration within the meaning of Article X:3(a) of the GATT 1994.

7.324 The United States also relies upon the circumstances surrounding the *Camcorders* case, in which an explanatory note relating to camcorders was amended.[1265] The United States submits that BTI issued by Spanish customs authorities following the amendment was not accepted by French customs authorities even though the application for BTI before the French authorities was made

---

[1263] In particular, the United States refers to Case C-339/98, *Peacock AG* v. *Hauptzollamt Paderborn*, Opinion of the Advocate General, 2000 ECR I-08947, 28 October 1999, paras. 7 - 8 (Exhibit US-17).

[1264] See paragraph 7.201 above.

[1265] This case is discussed by the Panel again in paragraph 7.348 *et seq* below.

by the French affiliate of the company that had secured BTI from the Spanish authorities and despite the fact that the Spanish BTI had been brought to the attention of the French authorities. The Panel notes that, in support of its allegation that French authorities refused to accept BTI issued by Spanish authorities in the context of the *Camcorders* case, the United States has provided copies of the BTI issued by the Spanish customs authorities.[1266] However, it has provided no evidence of BTI and/or classification decisions issued by the French customs authorities. Nor has the United States submitted any evidence to prove that the French customs authorities were made aware of the Spanish BTI before classifying the products in question. Therefore, the Panel considers that the United States has not proved that the *Camcorders* case supports the United States' allegation that customs authorities of member States do not always treat BTI issued by customs authorities of other member States as binding.

7.325 The United States also refers to a statement made by the European Communities during the panel proceedings in the *EC – Chicken Cuts* case. In particular, the United States submits that, in those proceedings, the European Communities asserted that the interpretation contained in BTI issued by customs authorities in several member States concerning the classification of certain chicken products consistently classifying the product under heading 0210 of the Combined Nomenclature was not followed by other EC customs offices.[1267]

7.326 *First*, the Panel notes that, on the basis of the panel's report in that case, the European Communities did not assert that BTI issued by customs authorities in certain member States had not been accepted in other member States. Rather, the European Communities submitted that the interpretation that the product in question should be classified under heading 0210 of the Common Customs Tariff had not been followed by certain customs offices in the European Communities.[1268]

7.327 *Second*, despite the statements made by the European Communities in that case suggesting the existence of divergent tariff classification regarding the product in question, the panel noted that the European Communities had not produced BTI of instances where the products at issue had been classified under a heading other than heading 0210.[1269] In other words, the panel did not find any evidence of divergent tariff classification regarding the product in question. Moreover, on the basis of the contents of the panel's report in that case, there would appear to have been no evidence before the panel to indicate that BTI is-

---

[1266] Exhibit US-65.

[1267] Specifically, the United States relies upon the panel's summary of the European Communities' in that case contained in Panel Report, *EC – Chicken Cuts*, para. 7.260.

[1268] According to the Panel Report in *EC – Chicken Cuts*, the European Communities accepted that a number of BTIs were issued by EC member State customs authorities (principally Hamburg in Germany, Rotterdam in the Netherlands and various offices in the United Kingdom), which classified the products at issue under subheading 0210.90. The European Communities further accepted that, given the commercial importance of some of the customs offices – namely, Hamburg and Rotterdam – substantial trade entered the European Communities under this incorrect interpretation. However, the European Communities submitted that this interpretation was not followed in other EC customs offices: Panel Report, *EC – Chicken Cuts*, para. 7.260.

[1269] Panel Report, *EC – Chicken Cuts*, para. 7.270.

sued by customs authorities in certain member States had not been accepted in other member States.

7.328 The Panel notes that, in the context of the United States' allegation that the tariff classification of blackout drapery lining is non-uniform in violation of Article X:3(a) of the GATT 1994, the United States alleged that the German customs authorities acknowledged the existence of BTI for comparable goods but made no effort to explain why it was declining to follow the classification decisions reflected in that BTI.[1270] The Panel recalls its finding in paragraph 7.265 above that there would appear to have been an objective factual basis justifying the decision by the German customs authorities to classify the products in question differently from those being classified by other customs authorities in the European Communities. In turn, this would explain why the German customs authorities did not treat as binding BTI issued in other member States.[1271] In addition, there is no indication that any BTI which was brought to the attention of the German customs authorities was invoked by the *holder*.

7.329 In the light of the foregoing, the Panel concludes that the United States has not proved that customs authorities in the member States have failed to treat as binding BTI issued by customs authorities in other member States and that such failure amounts to non-uniform administration within the meaning of Article X:3(a) of the GATT 1994.

(vii) Refusal to withdraw revocation of BTI concerning Sony PlayStations2 in the context of the Sony PlayStation2 case

Summary of the parties' arguments

7.330 The **United States** refers to a case involving the tariff classification of the Sony PlayStation2 (PS2). The United States submits that the UK customs authority issued BTI for that good and then revoked it based on an EC Commission regulation adopting a different classification for the good. When that regulation was annulled by the EC Court of First Instance, rather than restore the BTI, the authority maintained the revocation based on new, national grounds only weeks after the ECJ's decision in the *Timmermans* case.[1272] The United States submits that, prior to the ECJ's judgment in the *Timmermans* case which was issued in January 2004, the customs authority in the United Kingdom evidently believed

---

[1270] Hauptzollamt Bremen, Letter Decision to Bautex-Stoffe GmbH regarding classification of blackout drapery lining, 22 September 2004 (original and English translation), p. 1 (Exhibit US-23).

[1271] Nevertheless, the Panel recalls its findings in paragraphs 7.272 – 7.275 above that the failure on the part of the German customs authorities to have regard to classification decisions of customs authorities in other member States or at a minimum, to explain why they were deemed irrelevant to the classification at hand is not consistent with the obligation of uniform administration in Article X:3(a) of the GATT 1994. The Panel also considered that the dismissal by another German customs authority of the tariff classification by Belgian customs authorities on the basis of a mere "suspicion" that the documents filed for classification of those products by the Belgian customs authorities did not correspond to the products themselves was not consistent with Article X:3(a) of the GATT 1994.

[1272] United States' oral statement at the second substantive meeting, para. 33.

that it was required to restore the BTI following the annulment of the regulation in question and that, in view of the Advocate General's opinion in the *Timmermans* case issued in September 2003, it could not amend the BTI based on its own, independent reinterpretation of the applicable classification rules. However, following the judgement by the ECJ in the *Timmermans* case, the UK customs authority was free to maintain the revocation of the BTI, not on the basis of the EC regulation that had been annulled, but on the basis of its own reinterpretation of the applicable classification rules. According to the United States, whether or not the BTI correctly classified the PS2, the *Sony PlayStation2* case stands for the broader proposition that, in accordance with the ECJ's judgement in the *Timmermans* case, each of the European Communities' 25 independent, geographically limited customs offices has the power to depart from a path of uniform administration of the classification rules based on its own reconsideration of those rules.[1273]

7.331 In response, the **European Communities** submits the United States' allegation that the UK High Court of Justice revoked the BTI based on its own re-evaluation of the classification rules in the *PS2* case is misleading. The revocation took place because of the entry into force of an EC classification regulation. Accordingly, rather than following its own interpretation of classification rules, the UK High Court of Justice in fact duly applied Community law. According to the European Communities, the UK High Court of Justice upheld the validity of the revocation with explicit reliance on the ECJ's judgement in the *Timmermans* case and on the basis of clear evidence supporting the reasoning behind that revocation.[1274]

Analysis by the Panel

7.332 The Panel notes that the essence of the United States' challenge with respect to the *Sony PlayStation2* case (*PS2* case) is that customs authorities of the member States are able to refuse to withdraw revocation of BTI even though such a refusal deviates from uniform administration.[1275]

7.333 The Panel recalls its finding in paragraph 7.64 above that, on the basis of its request for establishment of a panel, the United States is precluded from making an "as such" challenge with respect to the design and structure of the EC system of customs administration as a whole and also with respect to the design and structure of the EC system in the areas of customs administration that have been specifically identified in the United States' request. In the context of the specific allegation made by the United States that customs authorities of the member States are able to refuse to withdraw revocation of BTI even though such a refusal deviates from uniform administration, the Panel considers that this is a matter outside our terms of reference because it concerns the structural aspects asso-

[1273] United States' reply to Panel question No. 184.

[1274] European Communities' reply to Panel question No. 172, para. 54 referring to *Sony Computer Entertainment Europe Ltd. v. Commissioners of Customs and Excise*, Judgment of the High Court of Justice, Chancery Division, EWHC 1644 (Ch), para. 118 (Exhibit US-70).

[1275] United States' reply to Panel question No. 184.

ciated with the EC system of customs administration. Nevertheless, the Panel considers that, on the basis of the United States' request for establishment of a panel, the United States is able to claim and the Panel is authorized to consider whether or not there is evidence to indicate that the refusal to withdraw revocation of BTI regarding PS2 in the context of the *PS2* case by the UK customs authorities resulted in non-uniform administration in violation of Article X:3(a) of the GATT 1994. In this regard, the Panel notes that the refusal to withdraw revocation of BTI constitutes an act of administration within the meaning of Article X:3(a) of the GATT 1994. This act of administration is a matter within the Panel's terms of reference since it amounts to an instance of administration of the Common Customs Tariff in the tariff classification area.[1276]

7.334 The relevant facts are set out in the judgement of the UK High Court of Justice, Chancery Division in the case of *Sony Computer Entertainment Europe Limited v the Commissioners of Customs and Excise.*[1277] Specifically, on 28 August 2000, Sony applied to the UK customs authority for BTI for certain PS2 models under tariff heading 8471 of the Common Customs Tariff. On 19 October 2000, the UK customs authority issued BTI classifying the PS2 under heading 9504 of the Common Customs Tariff rather than under heading 8471 of the Common Customs Tariff. The UK customs authority explained that the basis for the decision was that the product was not considered to be freely programmable and, therefore, did not meet the criteria of Note 5(A)(a)(2) to Chapter 84 of the Common Customs Tariff. Accordingly, the product could not be classified under heading 8471. The UK customs authority noted that the classification under heading 9504 was justified *inter alia* on the basis of Commission Regulation (EC) No. 1508/2000 for a set of electronic devices consisting of a video game console.

7.335 On 22 November 2000, Sony requested a formal departmental review of the decision of 19 October 2000 by the UK customs authority to classify the PS2 under heading 9504 rather than under 8471. By letter dated 5 January 2001, the decision to classify the PS2 under heading 9504 was upheld following the departmental review. The decision was also confirmed by the Tariff and Nomenclature Section of the Customs Code Committee during its meeting of 26 – 27 February 2001. By letter dated 29 March 2001, Sony was informed of the Committee's decision and was notified that a draft regulation classifying the products in question under heading 9504 was being prepared. The justification in the draft regulation for the classification of PS2 under heading 9504 was as follows: "Of the various functions (including playing video games, playback of CD audio, DVD video, automatic data processing etc.) playing video games gives the apparatus its essential character and determines classification under heading 9504 as a game console".[1278]

[1276] For information on EC institutions and mechanisms applicable in the tariff classification area, see paragraphs 7.179 – 7.182 above.

[1277] *Sony Computer Entertainment Europe Ltd. v. Commissioners of Customs and Excise*, Judgment of the High Court of Justice, Chancery Division, EWHC 1644 (Ch), (Exhibit US-70).

[1278] The draft regulation was subsequently adopted as Commission Regulation (EC) No. 1400/2001 of 10 July 2001 (Exhibit EC-157).

7.336 Prior to adoption of the draft regulation, Sony appealed to the UK VAT and Duties Tribunal against the decision issued following the departmental review, contained in the letter of 5 January 2001. This appeal was allowed. In allowing the appeal, the Tribunal noted that the UK customs authority's decision had been based on the fact that the PS2 was not "freely programmable" and, therefore, that it did not meet the criteria for coverage under heading 8471 in accordance with Note 5(A)(a)(2) to Chapter 84. The departmental review had upheld this rationale. The Tribunal to which Sony appealed found that the basis for the decision of the UK customs authority (and for the subsequent departmental review) was invalid in light of the fact that the draft regulation classified PS2 under heading 9504 for different reasons. The Tribunal concluded that, therefore, the UK customs authority's decision could not stand.

7.337 Following the Tribunal's decision allowing Sony's appeal, Sony requested the UK customs authority to issue new BTI classifying PS2 under tariff heading 8471. By letter dated 12 June 2001, Sony's request was granted but was made subject to the qualification that, following publication of the draft regulation which would classify PS2 under heading 9504, the BTI issued classifying PS2 under heading 8471 would be revoked.

7.338 On 10 July 2001, the draft regulation was adopted as Commission Regulation (EC) No. 1400/2001.[1279] Pursuant to Article 1 of that Regulation, when read in conjunction with the Annex to that Regulation, PS2 was classified under heading 9504. Accordingly, on 25 July 2001, the UK customs authority wrote to Sony revoking the BTI which had classified PS2 under heading 8471. On 6 September 2001, Sony requested departmental review of the decision to revoke the BTI on the ground that the Regulation which provoked the revocation (i.e. Regulation No. 1400/2001) was illegal. Further, on 3 October 2001, Sony lodged an application with the ECJ to annul the Regulation No. 1400/2001 under Article 230 of the EC Treaty. On 30 September 2003, the Court of First Instance annulled the Regulation finding that, although PS2 could be classified under heading 9504, the explanation of the legal basis for classification of PS2 under heading 9504 pursuant to the Regulation was wrong.[1280]

7.339 Following the annulment of Regulation No. 1400/2001, the UK customs authority sought advice from the Directorate-General, Taxation and Customs Union regarding the status of the BTI that had classified PS2 under heading 8471. The Directorate-General's response, contained in a letter dated 8 January 2004 and circulated to the customs authorities of all current and future member States, stated that in the light of the CFI's findings that the PS2 could not be classified under heading 8471 and that it could be classified in heading 9504, the EC Commission's view was that the PS2 was still correctly classifiable under heading 9504. On or about 1 May 2004, the WCO adopted a classification opinion which classified the PS2 under heading 9504.

[1279] Commission Regulation (EC) No. 1400/2001 of 10 July 2001 (Exhibit EC-157).

[1280] CFI Judgement: Sony Computer Entertainment Europe Ltd. v. Commission of the European Communities, Case T-243/01, 30 September 2003, paras. 120-128 (Exhibit US-12).

7.340 The Panel can see that the circumstances surrounding the *PS2* case could have resulted in non-uniform administration in violation of Article X:3(a) of the GATT 1994. Specifically, in the context of that case, the UK customs authority refused to withdraw the revocation of BTI classifying PS2 under heading 8471 even though Regulation No. 1400/2001, which had triggered the revocation, had been annulled. The UK customs authority refused to do so on the ground that Regulation No. 1400/2001 had been found invalid not because the classification of PS2 under heading 9504 had been incorrect in the Regulation but because the explanation of the legal basis for the classification under the Regulation was wrong. It is conceivable that other customs authorities in the European Communities could have adopted an approach other than that adopted by the UK customs authorities. In particular, they could have decided to honour BTI classifying the PS2 under heading 8471 given that the Regulation classifying the product under heading 9504 had been annulled. Alternatively, they could have decided to withdraw revocations of BTI that had classified PS2 under heading 8471. Had either of these possibilities eventuated, the Panel considers that a situation of non-uniform administration in violation of Article X:3(a) of the GATT 1994 would have resulted. In particular, while the UK authority classified the product under heading 9504, the other customs authorities would have classified the product under heading 8471. This scenario is possible in the context of the EC system of customs administration because it does not provide for uniform withdrawal of revocations of BTI. Nor does the system impose an obligation on member State customs authorities to consult with and/or notify other customs authorities of decisions to withdraw revocations of BTI.[1281]

7.341 Nevertheless, the Panel notes that it has not been provided with any evidence to indicate that divergent tariff classification among member States occurred following the refusal by the UK customs authority to withdraw its revocation of BTI classifying PS2 under heading 8471. Indeed, the only evidence submitted by the United States regarding classification of PS2 are the judgements of the UK High Court of Justice[1282] and the CFI[1283] concerning the *PS2* case. The Panel considers that these judgements on their own do not prove that divergent tariff classification among member States occurred following the refusal by the UK customs authority to withdraw its revocation of BTI classifying PS2 under heading 8471.

7.342 The Panel also considers that the circumstances surrounding the *PS2* case could have resulted in non-uniform administration in violation of Article X:3(a) of the GATT 1994 in another respect. In particular, by letter dated 12 June 2001,

[1281] The Panel understands that, under EC customs law, there is no provision that provides that the withdrawal of revocation of BTI is immediately binding on the customs authorities of all member States. Furthermore, we understand that there is no specific provision in EC customs law requiring the transmission of the withdrawal of revocation of BTI by customs authorities of the member States to the Commission.

[1282] *Sony Computer Entertainment Europe Ltd. v. Commissioners of Customs and Excise*, Judgment of the High Court of Justice, Chancery Division, [2005] EWHC 1644 (Ch), 27 July 2005 (Exhibit US-70).

[1283] CFI Judgement: Sony Computer Entertainment Europe Ltd. v. Commission of the European Communities, Case T-243/01, 30 September 2003 (Exhibit US-12).

the UK customs authorities decided to grant Sony BTI classifying PS2 under heading 8471 even though the UK authorities knew that the adoption of Regulation No. 1400/2001 was imminent and that that Regulation would have the effect of classifying the PS2 under heading 9504.[1284] When the UK customs authorities issued BTI classifying PS2 under heading 8471 to Sony, it made it clear that the BTI would be revoked once Regulation No. 1400/2001 had been adopted. However, in the meantime, it is quite possible that other customs authorities classified PS2 under heading 9504 knowing that, eventually, Regulation No. 1400/2001 would apply to PS2 and would require classification under heading 9504. Nevertheless, as previously noted, the Panel has not been provided with any evidence to indicate that divergent classification among member States occurred following the issuance by the UK customs authority of BTI classifying PS2 under heading 8471.

7.343 The Panel concludes that the United States has not proved that the failure to withdraw the revocation of BTI by the UK customs authorities with respect to the tariff classification of PS2 in the context of the *PS2* case amounts to non-uniform administration within the meaning of Article X:3(a) of the GATT 1994.

(viii) Interpretation and application of an amendment to an explanatory note concerning camcorders in the Camcorders case

Summary of the parties' arguments

7.344 The **United States** submits that a presentation made by Mr De Baere, an EC customs law practitioner, points out that the consequences of an explanatory note may vary from member State to member State. In some member States, an explanatory note may be treated the same as a regulation and given prospective effect only. In other member States, an explanatory note may be treated as a clarification of the state of the law and given retrospective effect.[1285] By way of example, the United States refers to a case involving the classification of video camera recorders ("camcorders"). The United States explains that at issue in that case was whether certain camcorders should be classified under tariff heading 8525 40 91 of the Common Customs Tariff (attracting a 4.9% tariff) or under tariff heading 8525 40 99 of the Common Customs Tariff (attracting a 14% tariff).[1286]

[1284] We note in this regard that, even the European Communities stated in its submissions to the Panel that "even though the BTI in question should not have been issued, this was a unique case due to the very specific circumstances of the case.": European Communities' reply to Panel question No. 184.

[1285] United States' oral statement at the second substantive meeting, para. 26 referring to Exhibit US-59.

[1286] United States' oral statement at the second substantive meeting, para. 27 referring to Commission Regulation No. 1810/2004 of 7 September 2004 amending Annex I to Council Regulation (EEC) No. 2658/87 on the tariff and statistical nomenclature and the Common Customs Tariff, 30 October 2004, p. 573 (Exhibit US-60).

7.345 The United States notes that a camcorder qualifies under heading 8525 40 91 if it is "[o]nly able to record sound and images taken by the television camera" whereas "other" camcorders qualify under heading 8525 40 99. The United States submits that, in July 2001, the Commission adopted an amendment to an earlier explanatory note covering heading 8525 40 99. The amendment provided that heading 8525 40 99 includes "'camcorders' in which the video input is obstructed by a plate, or in another way, or in which the video interface can be subsequently activated as video input by means of software."[1287] The United States submits that, pursuant to the amended explanatory note, if a camcorder was susceptible to certain modifications, it should be classified under heading 8525 40 99, even if at the time of importation it appeared to be classifiable under heading 8525 40 91.[1288]

7.346 The United States argues that, in view of the amended explanatory note, two member States (namely, France and Spain) reached back to collect additional duty on certain camcorders imported prior to the amendment that had been classified under heading 8525 40 91. That is, in view of the explanatory note, customs authorities in those member States revised the classification of merchandise that had already been imported and collected additional customs duties accordingly. By contrast, customs authorities in other member States refrained from giving retrospective effect to the explanatory note because, in their view, the note effectively established a new substantive rule – that is, it made susceptibility of camcorders to modification of use following importation a criterion for their classification. The United States submits that this was evidenced, for example, by the announcement of the explanatory note by the customs authority in the United Kingdom, in which it indicated that the note "does involve a change in practice for [the] United Kingdom".[1289] Thus, according to the United States, different EC customs offices applied the amended explanatory note to the same situation differently, demonstrating that the European Communities fails to administer its customs law uniformly in violation of Article X:3(a) of the GATT 1994.[1290]

7.347 In response, the **European Communities** submits that the United States has presented its reference to the *Camcorders* case as a rebuttal to the European Communities' argument that EC explanatory notes are a tool for securing uniform administration of EC classification rules.[1291] However, according to the

---

[1287] Uniform Application of the Combined Nomenclature (CN), Official Journal of the European Communities, 6 July 2001, p. C 190/10 (Exhibit US-61). Explanatory Notes to the Combined Nomenclature of the European Communities, Official Journal of the European Communities, 13 July 2000, p. 316 (Exhibit US-62).

[1288] United States' oral statement at the second substantive meeting, para. 28.

[1289] HM Customs & Excise, Tariff Notice 19/01, July 2001 (Exhibit US-63). Vorschriftensammlung Bundesfinanzverwaltung, VSF-Nachrichten N 46 2003, sec. I(3) 5 August 2003, (German customs notice on application of the EC provisions on reimbursement/remission and recovery of import duties, together with unofficial English translation) (Exhibit US-64).

[1290] United States' oral statement at the second substantive meeting, para. 29.

[1291] In particular, the European Communities submitted that, in considering the EC system of customs administration in the tariff classification area, it was necessary to consider all relevant features of the EC system, including EC explanatory notes: European Communities' first written submission,

European Communities, the United States discusses that case to address the question of whether member States, subsequent to the adoption of an EC explanatory note, may reach back to collect additional duty on importations made prior to the issuance of the explanatory note. According to European Communities, this issue has nothing to do with the value of explanatory notes as tools for securing the uniform administration of tariff classification rules. Further, according to the European Communities, the United States has not shown that there has been any lack of uniformity as regards tariff classification in the European Communities following the issuance of the explanatory note in question.[1292]

Analysis by the Panel

7.348 The Panel notes that the essence of the United States' challenge in the context of the *Camcorders* case appears to be that the way in which an amendment to an explanatory note to the Common Customs Tariff concerning camcorders was interpreted and applied varied from member State to member State. Specifically, in the context of the *Camcorders* case, the United States submits that, in some member States – namely, the United Kingdom and Germany – the explanatory note was treated as equivalent to a regulation and given prospective effect only. In other member States – namely, France and Spain, the explanatory note was treated as merely a clarification of the law and given retrospective effect.[1293]

7.349 In the Panel's view, the interpretation and application of amendments to explanatory notes to the Common Customs Tariff by the customs authorities of the member States constitutes an act of administration within the meaning of Article X:3(a) of the GATT 1994. This act of administration is a matter within the Panel's terms of reference since it amounts to an instance of administration of the Common Customs Tariff in the tariff classification area.[1294]

7.350 The Panel can see that differences in the interpretation and application of amendments to explanatory notes to the Common Customs Tariff among the member States could result in non-uniform administration in violation of Article X:3(a) of the GATT 1994. In particular, such differences could result in the imposition of duty treatment to importers of identical products that is not the same in different member States. For example, if one member State decides to treat an amendment to an explanatory notes as a mere clarification of the law and, therefore, retrospectively applies the amendment, this could mean that importers who had imported products into that member State prior to the amendment of the explanatory note would be liable for duty that is retrospectively being claimed. If, on the other hand, another member State decides to treat the amendment as akin to a substantive classification regulation and, therefore, ap-

paras. 262, 291 and 292; European Communities' oral statement at the first substantive meeting, paras. 38-39.

[1292] European Communities' reply to Panel question No. 172, paras. 38-39.

[1293] United States' oral statement at the second substantive meeting, paras. 26-27.

[1294] At a minimum, the Panel considers that amendments to explanatory notes to the Common Customs Tariff are "related measures" to the Common Customs Tariff. In this regard, see paragraph 7.28 above. See also paragraphs 7.175 – 7.176 above.

plies it only prospectively, this would mean that importers who had imported products into that member State prior to the amendment of the explanatory note would not be retrospectively liable for duty. In the Panel's view, in the context of the EC system of customs administration, the absence of an obligation imposed upon the member States to treat the explanatory note in the same way, could amount to an instance of non-uniform administration in violation of Article X:3(a) of the GATT 1994.[1295] Nevertheless, the Panel notes that it has not been provided with evidence to prove that non-uniform administration regarding the interpretation and application of the amended explanatory notes concerning camcorders actually occurred in the context of the *Camcorders* case.

7.351 In particular, the United States relies primarily upon a PowerPoint presentation made by Mr De Baere, an EC customs law practitioner.[1296] According to the United States, that presentation points out that the consequences of an explanatory note may vary from member State to member State.[1297] However, the only comment in the presentation that appears relevant to divergent interpretation and application of explanatory notes (and, presumably, amendments thereto) is that, with respect to camcorders, "Member States interpret the retrospective effect of the Explanatory Note differently (France and Spain)".[1298] The Panel notes that the bullet point in Mr De Baere's presentation containing this statement makes no reference to any supporting factual material.

7.352 Relying upon the statement in Mr De Baere's presentation, the United States seeks to contrast the interpretation and application of the amendment to the explanatory note concerning camcorders in, on the one hand, France and Spain with, on the other hand, the interpretation and application of the same amendment in the United Kingdom and Germany. The United States does so by referring to a UK tariff notice[1299] and to a German notice.[1300] However, notably, the Panel has not been provided with any evidence regarding the treatment of the

---

[1295] We note in this regard that, according to Article 9(1)(a) of Regulation No. 2658/87, the Commission may issue explanatory notes to the Combined Nomenclature. Explanatory notes to the CN are not legally binding, and cannot amend the CN. However, the ECJ has repeatedly acknowledged that explanatory notes are an important aid in the interpretation of the CN: Case C-396/02, *DFDS*, judgment of 16 September 2004 (not yet published), para. 28 (Exhibit EC-25); Case C-259/97, *Clees*, [1998] ECR I-8127, para. 12 (Exhibit EC-29).

[1296] Philippe De Baere, "Coping with customs in the EU: The uniformity challenge: Judicial review of customs decisions and implementing legislation", Presentation at ABA International Law Section, 27 October 2005 (Exhibit US-59).

[1297] United States' oral statement at the second substantive meeting, para. 26 referring to Philippe De Baere, *Coping with customs in the EU: The uniformity challenge: Judicial review of customs decisions and implementing legislation*, Presentation at ABA International Law Section, 27 October 2005 (Exhibit US-59).

[1298] Philippe De Baere, "Coping with customs in the EU: The uniformity challenge: Judicial review of customs decisions and implementing legislation", Presentation at ABA International Law Section, 27 October 2005, page 14 (Exhibit US-59).

[1299] HM Customs & Excise, Tariff Notice 19/01, July 2001 (Exhibit US-63).

[1300] Vorschriftensammlung Bundesfinanzverwaltung, VSF Nachrichten N 46 2003, sec. I(3), 5 August 2003, (German customs notice on application of the EC provisions on reimbursement/remission and recovery of import duties, together with unofficial English translation) (Exhibit US-64).

relevant amended explanatory note in France and Spain.[1301] In the absence of such evidence, the Panel considers that it is impossible to draw any conclusions regarding the existence of non-uniform administration of the amended explanatory notes as between customs authorities in France and Spain on the one hand and those in United Kingdom and Germany on the other.

7.353 Moreover, in the Panel's view, the evidence submitted regarding the interpretation and application of the amended explanatory note in the United Kingdom and Germany does not clearly prove that those two member States treat the explanatory note as akin to a substantive classification regulation and, therefore, prospectively apply the amendment, as has been submitted by the United States. Specifically, the UK tariff notice merely states that the amended explanatory note "does involve a change in practice for the United Kingdom". However, it does not contain any evidence as to whether or not the amendment will be given prospective or retrospective effect. The German notice constitutes an instruction from the federal finance administration. It appears to contain general statements regarding the recovery of import duties in cases where, *inter alia*, explanatory notes are amended. In this regard, the German notice states that: "To the extent that changes to the Explanatory Notes do not constitute changes of the content they may be applied retroactively, i.e. also to imports prior to their entry into force. In other cases where, for instance, the changes to the HS Explanatory Notes constitute a compromise in substance or a fundamental position without a conclusive character, they only apply for the future regarding the classification in the Combined Nomenclature."[1302] In other words, the German notice tends to indicate that amendments to explanatory notes may be given either retroactive or prospective effect, depending upon the nature of the change. It does not, however, indicate that the amendment to the explanatory note at issue in the *Camcorders* case should be treated prospectively, as has been contended by the United States. In fact, the German notice contains no mention whatsoever of how the explanatory note at issue in the *Camcorders* case should be treated.

7.354 Following consideration of the evidence submitted by the United States as a whole, the Panel concludes that the United States has not proved that the interpretation and application of the amended explanatory note to the Common Customs Tariff concerning camcorders in the context of the *Camcorders* case was divergent among the member States in violation of Article X:3(a) of the GATT 1994.

[1301] The explanatory note in question was amended by notice dated 6 July 2001 (Uniform Application of the Combined Nomenclature, 6 July 2001, p. C 190/10 (Exhibit US-61). That explanatory note concerned the interpretation of sub-heading 8525 40 99. The Panel notes that it has been provided with copies of BTI classifying products under tariff heading 8525 40 91, issued by Spanish customs authorities in 2004 (Exhibit US-65). However, we have not been provided with any evidence to indicate that French and Spanish customs authorities applied the amended explanatory note to retrospectively classify products under sub-heading 8525 40 99 imported before July 2001.

[1302] Vorschriftensammlung Bundesfinanzverwaltung, VSF Nachrichten N 46 2003, sec. I(3), 5 August 2003, (German customs notice on application of the EC provisions on reimbursement/remission and recovery of import duties, together with unofficial English translation), p. 2 (Exhibit US-64).

(ix) Summary and conclusions

7.355 In summary, the Panel finds that, with respect to the United States' allegations of non-uniform administration of the Common Customs Tariff in the area of tariff classification:

(a) During 1990 – 1995, the European Communities was not administering the Common Customs Tariff regarding the tariff classification of network cards for personal computers in a uniform manner in violation of Article X:3(a) of the GATT 1994. However, the tariff classification of network cards for personal computers does not currently amount to non-uniform administration within the meaning of Article X:3(a) of the GATT 1994. Therefore, the Panel finds no violation of Article X:3(a) of the GATT 1994 with respect to the tariff classification of network cards for personal computers.

(b) The tariff classification of drip irrigation products does not amount to non-uniform administration within the meaning of Article X:3(a) of the GATT 1994. Therefore, the Panel finds no violation of Article X:3(a) of the GATT 1994 with respect to the tariff classification of drip irrigation products.

(c) The United States has not proved that the tariff classification of unisex articles or shorts amounts to non-uniform administration within the meaning of Article X:3(a) of the GATT 1994.

(d) The administrative process leading to the tariff classification of blackout drapery lining amounts to non-uniform administration within the meaning of Article X:3(a) of the GATT 1994. Therefore, the Panel finds a violation of Article X:3(a) of the GATT 1994 with respect to the tariff classification of blackout drapery lining.

(e) The tariff classification of liquid crystal display monitors with digital video interface amounts to non-uniform administration within the meaning of Article X:3(a) of the GATT 1994. Therefore, the Panel finds a violation of Article X:3(a) of the GATT 1994 with respect to the tariff classification of liquid crystal display monitors with digital video interface.

(f) The United States has not proved that customs authorities in the member States have failed to treat as binding BTI issued by customs authorities in other member States and that such failure amounts to non-uniform administration within the meaning of Article X:3(a) of the GATT 1994.

(g) The United States has not proved that the refusal to withdraw the revocation of BTI by the UK customs authorities with respect to the tariff classification of the Sony PlayStation2 in the context of the *Sony PlayStation2* case amounts to non-uniform administration within the meaning of Article X:3(a) of the GATT 1994.

(h) The United States has not proved that the interpretation and application of the amended explanatory notes to the Common Customs Tariff concerning camcorders in the context of the *Camcorders* case amounts to non-uniform administration in violation of Article X:3(a) of the GATT 1994.

(c) Allegations of non-uniform administration of the Community Customs Code and the Implementing Regulation in the area of customs valuation

(i) Royalty payments

Summary of the parties' arguments

7.356 The **United States** notes that the EC Court of Auditors found in its report that, in a number of cases, different member States apportioned royalties differently to the customs value of identical goods imported by the same company. The United States submits that the Court found that, in the cases identified, the member States involved either did not bring the disparate treatment to the attention of the Customs Code Committee, or that the matter was not examined by the Committee.[1303]

7.357 In response, the **European Communities** notes that the treatment of royalties is regulated by Article 32(1)(c) of the Community Customs Code. The European Communities submits that it is not correct to state that different member States apportioned royalties differently to the customs value of identical goods imported by the same company since the examples referred to by the Court of Auditors mostly involved different subsidiaries established in various member States.[1304] The European Communities adds that, following the report of the EC Court of Auditors, the Commission together with the Customs Code Committee worked through the cases examined by the Court of Auditors in order to clarify the issues and establish whether there had been a lack of uniformity. According to the European Communities, in most cases, it was confirmed that the questions involved were purely factual issues concerning the establishment of the conditions of Article 32(1)(c) of the Community Customs Code. The European Communities argues that, since no systematic lack of uniformity was found, it was concluded that no amendment to the Community Customs Code nor the Implementing Regulation was required.[1305]

7.358 The **United States** submits that, even if the European Communities' assertions were correct, they still would not rebut the broader findings of the Court of Auditors report. For example, the Court of Auditors found "weaknesses" in the European Communities' administration of customs valuation rules to include, among others, "the absence of common control standards and working prac-

---

[1303] United States' first written submission, para. 86 referring to Court of Auditors Valuation Report, paras. 58-61 (Exhibit US-14).

[1304] European Communities' first written submission, para. 392.

[1305] European Communities' first written submission, para. 393.

tices"; "the absence of common treatment of traders with operations in several member States"; and "the absence of Community law provisions allowing the establishment of Community-wide valuation decisions."[1306]

Analysis by the Panel

7.359 The Panel notes that, in essence, the United States alleges differences between customs authorities in the member States regarding the manner in which royalties are apportioned to the customs value of identical goods imported by the same company.[1307] In its submissions, the United States indicated that it specifically challenges the administration in the European Communities of Article 32(1)(c) of the Community Customs Code regarding the treatment of royalty payments for customs valuation purposes.[1308]

7.360 In the Panel's view, the manner in which royalties are apportioned to the customs value of identical goods imported by the same company constitutes an act of administration within the meaning of Article X:3(a) of the GATT 1994. This act of administration is a matter within the Panel's terms of reference since it amounts to an instance of administration of Article 32(1)(c) of the Community Customs Code in the customs valuation area.[1309]

7.361 With respect to the question of whether or not the manner in which royalties are apportioned to the customs value of identical goods imported by customs authorities in the member States is "uniform" within the meaning of Article X:3(a) of the GATT 1994, the Panel recalls its finding in paragraph 7.135 above that geographic uniformity is required under Article X:3(a) of the GATT 1994. That is, administration should be uniform in different places within a particular WTO Member. The Panel also recalls its finding in paragraph 7.135 above that the form, nature and scale of the alleged non-uniform administration and the laws, regulations, judicial decisions and rulings that are allegedly being administered in a non-uniform manner should be taken into consideration when interpreting the term "uniform" in Article X:3(a) of the GATT 1994. The Panel considers that the United States' challenge with respect to manner in which royalties are apportioned to the customs value of identical goods imported by the same company is narrow in nature. It involves the application of a single provision of the Community Customs Code – namely, Article 32(1)(c). Therefore, given the narrowness of this challenge, the Panel considers that a high degree of uniformity is required for the purposes of Article X:3(a) of the GATT 1994. We now turn to the facts to determine whether or not this high degree of uniformity has been achieved with respect to the manner in which royalties are apportioned to the customs value.

7.362 Article 32(1)(c) of the Community Customs Code provides that:

[1306] United States' reply to Panel question No. 137(c) referring to Court of Auditors Valuation Report, para. 86 (Exhibit US-14).

[1307] United States' first written submission, para. 86 referring to Court of Auditors Valuation Report, paras. 58-61 (Exhibit US-14).

[1308] United States' reply to Panel question No. 124.

[1309] In this regard, see paragraphs 7.183 – 7.187 above.

> "In determining the customs value under Article 29 [of the Community Customs Code], there shall be added to the price actually paid or payable for the imported goods:
>
> ...
>
> (c) Royalties and licence fees related to the goods being valued that the buyer must pay, either directly or indirectly, as a condition of sale of the goods being valued, to the extent that such royalties and fees are not included in the price actually paid or payable."

7.363 The only evidence upon which the United States relies in support of its claim that Article 32(1)(c) of the Community Customs Code is not being administered in a uniform manner in violation of Article X:3(a) of the GATT 1994 is contained in the EC Court of Auditors Special Report No. 23/2000 concerning valuation of imported goods for customs purposes dated 14 March 2001.[1310] We consider each of the relevant aspects of the report in turn.

7.364 *First*, the EC Court of Auditor's report makes general comments regarding the administration of the royalty provisions in EC customs law:

> "Royalties and licence fees may be included in the invoice price of imported goods or shown separately on the invoice as an addition to the basic price. They may also be calculated yearly as a percentage of the total value of sales of imported goods. ...
>
> ...
>
> The Commission has invested considerable effort to ensure uniform application of the rules. Even so the Court found several cases of apparently different treatment between the Member States. Given the present diversity of control methods within the customs union this is not surprising."[1311]

7.365 In the Panel's view, while the excerpt of the EC Court of Auditor's report set out in the preceding paragraph indicates the existence of "different treatment" in the context of EC customs rules regarding royalties, it does not provide any detail of the nature of the different treatment. Therefore, in the Panel's view, these statements on their own are an insufficient basis upon which to infer that

---

[1310] By way of background, the Panel notes that EC Court of Auditors' report states that:

"The audit conducted by the EC Court of Auditors took place at the Commission and in all member States except the three that joined the Union on 1 January 1995 (Austria, Finland and Sweden). Visits were also made to the World Trade Organisation and the World Customs Organisation.

The audit included an examination of documents handled in the Commission Valuation Committee, customs authority valuation audit files, written valuation rulings, decisions of appeal tribunals and the actual customs declarations. Files and documentation concerning customs valuation procedures for more than 200 companies and groups of companies were examined.

In order to select its sample the Court used a predetermined list of the 50 most important trading companies worldwide, combined with lists, obtained in each Member State visited, of the 50 most important companies in terms of customs duties established.": EC Court of Auditors Special Report No 23/2000 concerning valuation of imported goods for customs purposes, 14 March 2001, paras. 9-11 (Exhibit US-14).

[1311] EC Court of Auditors Special Report No 23/2000 concerning valuation of imported goods for customs purposes, 14 March 2001, paras. 55-57 (Exhibit US-14).

the "different treatment" in question corresponds to non-uniform administration within the meaning of Article X:3(a) of the GATT 1994.

7.366 *Second*, the EC Court of Auditor's report refers to the payment by a particular company of customs duties on royalties in some member States but, apparently, not in others. Specifically, the report states:

> "In one case, the customs authority of the Member State where the headquarters of the company was based considered that three different transaction situations might apply for customs valuation purposes. All of them were legal and in some cases royalties and other payments would be included in the customs valuation. If the analysis of this customs authority is correct it is quite likely that the customs valuation of the imports by the company in six of the seven Member States examined by the Court are incorrect. In 1997 the company concerned paid more than 43 million euro in customs duties in these seven Member States. Uplifts for royalties applied by the different national customs ranged from 0% to 10% of the value of the imported goods."[1312]

7.367 The Panel notes that the EC Court of Auditor's statement excerpted in the preceding paragraph refers to "three different transactions" engaged in by the company in question, some of which apparently entailed the payment of customs duties on royalties. The excerpt refers to the existence of errors in appraising these transactions on the part of a number of member States but there is insufficient information in the report for us to conclude that such errors resulted in non-uniform administration in violation of Article X:3(a) of the GATT 1994. The last sentence of the excerpt states that uplifts for royalties "applied by the different national customs" payable by the company in question "ranged from 0% to 10%". The Panel considers that, when read in context, this statement does not necessarily indicate non-uniform administration within the meaning of Article X:3(a) of the GATT 1994 given that it is unclear whether or not the different amounts of uplifts for royalties corresponded to the fact that materially different transactions were implicated, which could be inferred from the first sentence of the excerpt.

7.368 *Third*, the EC Court of Auditor's report refers to another instance in which a particular company paid customs duties on royalties in some member States but, apparently, not in others. Specifically, the report states:

> "In another case the majority of a company's Community imports passed through a distribution centre in one Member State. The customs authority in that Member State decided that none of the royalty payments made by the company formed part of the customs value. The Court found that in five of the Member States to which the importer had previously imported, the customs authorities had

[1312] EC Court of Auditors Special Report No 23/2000 concerning valuation of imported goods for customs purposes, 14 March 2001, para. 58 (Exhibit US-14).

> charged duty on at least part of the royalty and other additional payments by the importer.
>
> In this case some Member States had exchanged information. However, even taking into account the different solutions and the extended timescale involved, the Member States authorities clearly had difficulties in accepting that the principal valuation questions were the same. The company paid over 33 million euro in customs duty in 1998. Notwithstanding its declared objective of maintaining equivalent conditions for operators in the Member States ... the Commission did not examine the valuation treatment of this company."[1313]

7.369 The Panel notes that the excerpt of the EC Court of Auditor's report set out in the preceding paragraph does tend to indicate the existence of differences in treatment of royalty payments for the purposes of customs valuation as between the member States. In particular, the report refers to the fact that the customs authority in one member State decided that royalty payments made by a particular importer did not form part of the customs value whereas the customs authorities in five other member States to which the importer had previously imported, did include royalty payments as part of the customs value. However, the question arises as to whether or not the transactions in question were, in fact, identical.

7.370 Regarding the question of whether or not the transactions in question were, in fact, identical, the report notes that customs authorities of one member State decided that royalty payments made by a particular company *did not* form part of the customs value but it was clear that, in the case of that member State, the imports were passed through a distribution centre. The report does not indicate that the imports into other member States, where customs authorities decided that royalty payments made by a particular company *did* form part of the customs value, were also passed through a distribution centre. Therefore, it is impossible to know whether or not the transactions in question were, in fact, identical. In summary, the Panel considers that the EC Court of Auditor's report does not contain sufficient information to know whether or not the "different treatment" in the context of EC customs rules regarding royalties constituted non-uniform administration in violation of Article X:3(a) of the GATT 1994.[1314]

[1313] EC Court of Auditors Special Report No 23/2000 concerning valuation of imported goods for customs purposes, 14 March 2001, para. 60 (Exhibit US-14).

[1314] The Panel notes in this regard that the purpose of the EC Court of Auditor's report was not to ascertain the existence or otherwise of non-uniform administration within the meaning of Article X:3(a) of the GATT 1994. Rather, paragraph 12 of the report notes that: "The general objective of the audit was to examine the accuracy and consistency of the valuation for customs purposes of goods imported into the European union. The audit sought to establish: (a) how international rules on customs valuation have been incorporated into Community legislation; (b) what steps the Commission or Member States take to ensure proper application of Community rules on customs valuation and what control procedures the customs authorities of the Member States have put in place to comply with the requirements of Community legislation; (c) to what extent the Community legislation is applied consistently to imports, in particular to imports by companies with operations in more than

7.371 The Panel concludes that the United States has not proved that differences between member States regarding the manner in which royalties are apportioned to the customs value of identical goods imported by the same company exist that amount to non-uniform administration of Article 32(1)(c) of the Community Customs Code within the meaning of Article X:3(a) of the GATT 1994.

(ii) Valuation on a basis other than the transaction of the last sale (or "successive sale")

Summary of the parties' arguments

7.372 According to the **United States**, the EC Court of Auditors found in its report that, with respect to the application of the rule that allows imported goods, in certain cases, to be valued on a basis other than the transaction of the last sale which led to the introduction of the goods into the customs territory of the European Communities, authorities in some member States required importers to obtain prior approval for valuation on a basis other than the transaction value of the last sale, whereas authorities in other member States imposed no such requirement.[1315] The United States also submits that it is significant not only that some EC customs authorities administer Article 147(1) of the Implementing Regulation by imposing a form of prior approval, while others do not, but also that the prior approval obtained from an EC customs authority in one region has no binding force in other parts of the territory of the European Communities.[1316]

7.373 In response, the **European Communities** submits that the conditions under which a sale other than the last sale may be used as the basis for establishing the transaction value are set out in Article 147 of the Implementing Regulation.[1317] The European Communities submits that, whereas the United States claims that the EC Court of Auditors "found that authorities in some member States required importers to obtain prior approval for valuation on a basis other than the transaction value of the last sale", the Court of Auditors merely stated that "*in practice*, some customs authorities do impose *a form of prior approval*". The European Communities submits that, contrary to the impression created by the United States, there is no form of legal requirement of prior approval in order to be able to rely on an earlier sale.[1318] Moreover, given the potential complexity of the issue involved, it is not unreasonable for a customs authority to encourage traders who want to rely on the possibility of establishing the transaction value on the basis of an earlier sale to have this issue settled in advance. The European Communities submits that, in any event, it considers that such a practice consti-

one Member State." : EC Court of Auditors Special Report No 23/2000 concerning valuation of imported goods for customs purposes, 14 March 2001 (Exhibit US-14).

1315 United States' first written submission, para. 87 referring to Court of Auditors Valuation Report, para. 64 (Exhibit US-14).

1316 United States' reply to Panel question No. 137(d).

1317 European Communities' first written submission, para. 394.

1318 European Communities' first written submission, para. 395.

tutes a minor variation in administrative practice, which does not amount to a lack of uniformity incompatible with Article X:3(a) of the GATT 1994.[1319]

7.374 The **United States** submits that there is no distinction between legally requiring importers to obtain prior approval and in practice imposing a form of prior approval.[1320] Further, the United States disputes that the differences in questions regarding the administration of Article 147(1) of the Implementing Regulation represent a "minor variation." The United States submits that, from the trader's point of view, if it must obtain prior approval in order to base customs value on a sale other than the last sale, this would be relevant in deciding where to enter its goods into the European Communities. In this regard, the United States submits that there is no basis for the proposition that Article X:3(a) of the GATT 1994 is breached only by non-uniform administration that affects the ultimate customs debt owed by the trader but not by non-uniform administration that affects the burden borne or risk faced by the trader.[1321]

7.375 The **European Communities** submits that, on the basis of a survey of the practices of the customs authorities of all member States, it can confirm that no member State, neither in law nor in practice, imposes a requirement of prior approval with respect to the conditions under which a sale other than the last sale may be used as the basis for establishing the transaction value for customs valuation purposes. According to the European Communities, the United States has not provided any evidence to the contrary.[1322]

Analysis by the Panel

7.376 The Panel notes that the United States challenges the administration of Article 147(1) of the Implementing Regulation. Specifically, the United States alleges that, in some member States, importers are practically required to obtain prior approval for valuation on a basis other than the transaction value of the last sale (also known as "successive sale"), whereas authorities in other member States impose no such requirement.[1323] In addition, according to the United States, the prior approval obtained from a customs authority in one member State has no binding force elsewhere in the European Communities.[1324]

7.377 In the Panel's view, the imposition of requirements regarding approval for valuation on a basis other than the transaction value of the last sale constitutes an act of administration within the meaning of Article X:3(a) of the GATT 1994. This act of administration is a matter within the Panel's terms of reference since it amounts to an instance of administration of the Article 147(1) of the Implementing Regulation in the customs valuation area.[1325]

[1319] European Communities' first written submission, para. 396.

[1320] United States' reply to Panel question No. 137(d) referring to European Communities' first written submission, paras. 394-396.

[1321] United States' reply to Panel question No. 137(d) referring to Panel Report, *Argentina – Hides and Leather*, paras. 11.91-11.93.

[1322] European Communities' comments on the United States' reply to Panel question No. 137(d).

[1323] United States' first written submission, para. 87.

[1324] United States' reply to Panel question No. 137(d).

[1325] In this regard, see paragraphs 7.183 – 7187 above.

7.378 With respect to the question of whether or not the imposition of requirements regarding approval for valuation on a basis other than the transaction value of the last sale in the member States is "uniform" within the meaning of Article X:3(a) of the GATT 1994, the Panel recalls its finding in paragraph 7.135 above that geographic uniformity is required under Article X:3(a) of the GATT 1994. That is, administration should be uniform in different places within a particular WTO Member. The Panel also recalls its finding in paragraph 7.135 above that the form, nature and scale of the alleged non-uniform administration and the laws, regulations, judicial decisions and rulings that are allegedly being administered in a non-uniform manner should be taken into consideration when interpreting the term "uniform" in Article X:3(a) of the GATT 1994. The Panel considers that the United States' challenge with respect to the imposition of requirements regarding approval for valuation on a basis other than the transaction value of the last sale is narrow in nature. It involves the application of a single provision of the Implementing Regulation – namely, Article 147(1) of the Implementing Regulation. Therefore, given the narrowness of this challenge, the Panel considers that a high degree of uniformity is required for the purposes of Article X:3(a) of the GATT 1994. We now turn to the facts to determine whether or not this high degree of uniformity has been achieved with respect to the administration of Article 147(1) of the Implementing Regulation regarding the imposition of requirements regarding approval for valuation on a basis other than the transaction value of the last sale.

7.379 Article 147(1) of the Implementing Regulation provides in relevant part that:

> "1. For the purposes of Article 29 of the Code, the fact that the goods which are the subject of a sale are declared for free circulation shall be regarded as adequate indication that they were sold for export to the customs territory of the Community. In the case of successive sales before valuation, only the last sale, which led to the introduction of the goods into the customs territory of the Community, or a sale taking place in the customs territory of the Community before entry for free circulation of the goods shall constitute such indication.
>
> Where a price is declared which relates to a sale taking place before the last sale on the basis of which the goods were introduced into the customs territory of the Community, it must be demonstrated to the satisfaction of the customs authorities that this sale of goods took place for export to the customs territory in question."

7.380 The only evidence upon which the United States relies in support of its claim that Article 147(1) of the Implementing Regulation is not being administered in a uniform manner in violation of Article X:3(a) of the GATT 1994 is contained in the EC Court of Auditors Special Report No. 23/2000 concerning valuation of imported goods for customs purposes dated 14 March 2001.

7.381 The relevant section of the Court's report states that:

> "The Court was unable to identify the full extent to which importers use or seek to use the successive sales provision. One reason for this is that, in order to apply to successive sales provision, unlike some other customs provisions, there is no legal requirement for an importer to obtain prior permission or authorisation. However, the Court found that, in practice, some customs authorities do impose a form of prior approval even though this has no basis in Community law. As in other aspects of customs valuation the Court found variations in the extent to which customs authorities allow the use of the provision or consult with each other. The Court has established that certain importers use the successive sales provision in one or more Member States but not in others and has drawn some significant examples of inconsistency to the attention of the Commission."[1326]

7.382 The Panel notes that, in the section of the EC Court of Auditor's report excerpted in the preceding paragraph, the Court noted the existence of a "practice" on the part of customs authorities to impose a form of prior approval with respect to the successive sales provision of EC customs law, namely Article 147(1) of the Implementing Regulation. The Court specifically noted that such a practice has no basis in Community law and is not being followed in other member States. During the course of the Panel's proceedings, the European Communities submitted that, on the basis of a survey of the practices of the customs authorities of all member States, no member State, neither in law nor in practice, imposes a requirement of prior approval with respect to the conditions under which a sale other than the last sale may be used as the basis for establishing the transaction value for customs valuation purposes.[1327] However, at the time the Panel issued its Interim Report to the parties, the European Communities had not submitted any evidence to substantiate its assertion in this regard.[1328] Further, at that time, the Panel had not been provided with any evidence that would suggest that the practice engaged in by some customs authorities of imposing a form of prior approval that had been identified by the EC Court of Auditors in its report had since been remedied in the European Communities. The Panel considers that evidence clearly indicating the imposition of a requirement by member States, whether in practice and/or as a matter of law, that is not justified by the terms of EC law and which is not being applied in other member States, such as that contained in the EC Court of Auditors' report regarding the successive sales provision, necessarily falls foul of the obligation of uniform administration in Article X:3(a) of the GATT 1994.

7.383 Therefore, the Panel concludes that the administration of Article 147(1) of the Implementing Regulation in the European Communities is non-uniform in

[1326] EC Court of Auditors Special Report No 23/2000 concerning valuation of imported goods for customs purposes, 14 March 2001, para. 64 (Exhibit US-14).

[1327] European Communities' comments on the United States' reply to Panel question No. 137(d).

[1328] The Panel considers that it was incumbent upon the European Communities to submit such evidence in the light of aspects of the EC Court of Auditor's report referred to in paragraph 7.383 above, which tend to call the European Communities assertion in this regard into question.

violation of Article X:3(a) of the GATT 1994 to the extent that customs authorities in some member States impose a form of prior approval with respect to the successive sales provision, which is inconsistent with EC customs laws, whereas customs authorities in other member States do not. The Panel notes in this regard that the practice of imposing a form of prior approval with respect to the successive sales provision results in an actual or possible adverse impact on the trading environment in that it might affect the member State into which a trader decides to import.

7.384 With regard to the United States' allegation that the European Communities has also violated Article X:3(a) of the GATT 1994 because the prior approval obtained from a customs authority in one member State has no binding force elsewhere in the European Communities, the Panel notes that the United States has provided no evidence to substantiate this allegation. Therefore, we consider that the United States has not met its burden to make a prima facie case that the administration of Article 147(1) of the Implementing Regulation is non-uniform in violation of Article X:3(a) of the GATT 1994 because the prior approval obtained from a customs authority in one member State has no binding force elsewhere in the European Communities.

7.385 In the light of the foregoing, the Panel finds that, the imposition by customs authorities in some member States of a form of prior approval with respect to the successive sales provision, which is inconsistent with EC customs laws and which is not imposed by customs authorities in other member States means that the European Communities does not administer its customs law concerning successive sales – in particular, Article 147(1) of the Implementing Regulation – in a uniform manner in violation of Article X:3(a) of the GATT 1994.

(iii) Vehicle repair costs covered under warranty

Summary of the parties' arguments

7.386 The **United States** submits that the EC Court of Auditors notes in its report that different member States have taken different positions on whether the costs of automobile repair covered by a seller's warranty should be deducted from the customs value.[1329] According to the United States, in at least one member State – namely, Germany – the Court found that customs authorities reduced the customs value of imported vehicles by the value of repairs undertaken in the territory of the European Communities and reimbursed by the foreign seller. Other member States – in particular, Italy, the Netherlands, and the United Kingdom – declined requests for similar customs value reductions. The United States submits that the Court observed that the Commission had been aware of differen-

[1329] United States' first written submission, para. 25 referring to Court of Auditors, Special Report No. 23/2000 concerning valuation of imported goods for customs purposes (customs valuation), together with the Commission's replies, paras. 73-74, 14 March 2001 (Exhibit US-14).

tial treatment among member States for at least ten years and had not taken any steps to reconcile the difference.[1330]

7.387 In response, as a preliminary matter, the **European Communities** notes that the EC Court of Auditors' report confirms that the Commission had not been aware of differential treatment among member States for 10 years. The Court merely referred to the German valuation practice, which it – contrary to the Commission – considered unjustified, as having been known for ten years.[1331] The European Communities submits that when, through the report of the Court of Auditors, it became apparent that differences existed between member States in the treatment of repair cost covered by a warranty, the Commission, after careful examination of the issue and due consultation of the Customs Code Committee, adopted Commission Regulation (EC) No. 444/2002 of 11 March 2002, which introduced an amended version of Article 145 into the Implementing Regulation and specifically addresses the issue raised in the Court of Auditor's report.[1332] According to the European Communities, with this amendment, the issue of warranties has been sufficiently clarified, and the uniform application of EC valuation law is secured. In the view of the European Communities, the example shows that the European Communities is perfectly capable of detecting and correcting non-uniform practices, if they arise.[1333] Further, the European Communities notes that, on a complex issue of customs valuation, the European Communities itself detected the problem, and took the necessary measures to correct it. Accordingly, rather than showing any failure in the European Communities' system, the example of repair costs under warranty shows that the EC system of customs administration functions properly.[1334]

7.388 In response, the **United States** submits that, as the EC Court of Auditors report explains, the Commission was first made aware of inconsistent member State practice in this area in a 1990 report. The fact that an instance of non-uniform administration first called to the Commission's attention in 1990 was resolved by a regulation adopted in 2002 hardly demonstrates that the system works in a manner consistent with the obligation of uniform administration in Article X:3(a) of the GATT 1994.[1335] Further, the United States submits that, while the regulation cited by the European Communities does appear to address the issue of treatment of repair costs covered by warranty, what is remarkable is that it took the European Communities 12 years to resolve this matter.[1336] According to the United States, a system that leads to resolution of non-uniformity of administration 12 years after it is brought to the attention of the relevant au-

[1330] United States' first written submission, para. 88 referring to Court of Auditors Valuation Report, paras. 73-74 (Exhibit US-14).

[1331] European Communities' first written submission, footnote 194.

[1332] European Communities' first written submission, para. 397 referring to Exhibit EC-89 and Exhibit EC-37, pp. 14-19.

[1333] European Communities' first written submission, para. 398.

[1334] European Communities' second written submission, para. 156.

[1335] United States' reply to Panel question No. 4.

[1336] Court of Auditors Valuation Report, paras. 73-74 (Exhibit US-14).

thority hardly satisfies the requirement of uniform administration in Article X:3(a) of the GATT 1994.[1337]

Analysis by the Panel

7.389 The Panel notes that, when the United States listed the "subsidiary findings" requested regarding the specific areas of customs administration it alleges are being administered by the European Communities in a non-uniform manner in violation of Article X:3(a) of the GATT 1994, the United States did not make mention of the European Communities' administration of valuation rules in cases involving vehicle repair costs covered under warranty.[1338] Nevertheless, elsewhere in its submissions, the United States did allege differences among member States regarding whether or not the costs of automobile repair covered by a seller's warranty should be deducted from the customs value.[1339] In light of these allegations, the Panel considers it necessary to address them.

7.390 The Panel notes that the United States challenges alleged differences in approaches taken by customs authorities in the member States regarding whether or not the costs of automobile repair covered by a seller's warranty should be deducted from the customs value.[1340] The Panel understands that, in alleging differences among member States as to whether or not the costs of vehicle repair covered by a seller's warranty should be deducted from the customs value, the United States is implicitly challenging the administration of Article 29(3)(a) of the Community Customs Code.

7.391 In the Panel's view, the deduction (or not) of the costs of vehicle repair covered by a seller's warranty constitutes an act of administration within the meaning of Article X:3(a) of the GATT 1994. This act of administration is a matter within the Panel's terms of reference since it amounts to an instance of administration of the Article 29(3)(a) of the Community Customs Code in the customs valuation area.[1341]

7.392 With respect to the question of whether or not the deduction (or not) of the costs of vehicle repair covered by a seller's warranty in the member States is "uniform" within the meaning of Article X:3(a) of the GATT 1994, the Panel recalls its finding in paragraph 7.135 above that geographic uniformity is required under Article X:3(a) of the GATT 1994. That is, administration should be uniform in different places within a particular WTO Member. The Panel also recalls its finding in paragraph 7.135 above that the form, nature and scale of the alleged non-uniform administration and the laws, regulations, judicial decisions and rulings that are allegedly being administered in a non-uniform manner should be taken into consideration when interpreting the term "uniform" in Arti-

---

[1337] United States' reply to Panel question No. 25.

[1338] United States' reply to Panel question No. 124.

[1339] See, for example, United States' first written submission, paras. 88 - 89.

[1340] United States' first written submission, para. 25 referring to Court of Auditors, Special Report No. 23/2000 concerning valuation of imported goods for customs purposes (customs valuation), together with the Commission's replies, paras. 73-74, 14 March 2001 (Exhibit US-14).

[1341] In this regard, see paragraphs 7.183 – 7.187 above.

cle X:3(a) of the GATT 1994. The Panel considers that the United States' challenge with respect to the deduction (or not) of the costs of vehicle repair covered by a seller's warranty is narrow in nature. It involves the application of a single provision of the Community Customs Code – namely, Article 29(3)(a) of the Community Customs Code. Therefore, given the narrowness of this challenge, the Panel considers that a high degree of uniformity is required for the purposes of Article X:3(a) of the GATT 1994. We now turn to the facts to determine whether or not this high degree of uniformity has been achieved with respect to the administration of Article 29(3)(a) of the Community Customs Code concerning the deduction (or not) of the costs of vehicle repair covered by a seller's warranty in the member States.

7.393 Article 29(3)(a) of the Community Customs Code provides that:

> "The price actually paid or payable is the total payment made or to be made by the buyer to or for the benefit of the seller for the imported goods and includes all payments made or to be made as a condition of sale of the imported goods by the buyer to the seller or by the buyer to a third party to satisfy an obligation of the seller. The payment need not necessarily take the form of a transfer of money. Payment may be made by way of letters of credit or negotiable instrument and may be made directly or indirectly."

7.394 The only evidence upon which the United States relies in support of its claim that Article 29(3)(a) of the Community Customs Code is not being administered in a uniform manner in violation of Article X:3(a) of the GATT 1994 is contained in the EC Court of Auditors Special Report No. 23/2000 concerning valuation of imported goods for customs purposes dated 14 March 2001. We consider each of the relevant aspects of that report in turn.

7.395 *First*, the EC Court of Auditor's report makes general comments regarding the administration of EC customs law with respect to the costs of vehicle repair covered by a seller's warranty:

> "Manufacturers often give a guarantee or warranty with their products. Such guarantees mean that if the goods are later shown not to be in accordance with the sale specification the buyer will be compensated. ...
>
> The treatment of manufacturer's guarantees for imported cars is a prime example of an area where the individual customs authorities of the Member States apply different interpretations of Community legislation."[1342]

7.396 In the Panel's view, while the excerpt of the EC Court of Auditor's report set out in the preceding paragraph indicates the existence of "different interpretations" in the context of EC customs rules regarding the costs of vehicle repair covered by a seller's warranty, it does not provide any detail of the nature of the different interpretations nor of the practical consequences of such different inter-

[1342] EC Court of Auditors Special Report No 23/2000 concerning valuation of imported goods for customs purposes, 14 March 2001, paras. 71-72 (Exhibit US-14).

pretations. Therefore, in the Panel's view, these statements on their own are an insufficient basis upon which to infer that the "different interpretations" in question correspond to non-uniform administration within the meaning of Article X:3(a) of the GATT 1994 regarding the treatment of the costs of vehicle repair covered by a seller's warranty for the purposes of customs valuation.

7.397 *Second*, the EC Court of Auditor's report refers specifically to differences among member States regarding whether or not they grant customs value reductions for the costs of vehicle repair covered by a seller's warranty. In particular, the report states:

> "In its annual report on the financial year 1990, the Court drew the Commission's attention to the practice of the German customs authority of granting value reductions on imports of motor vehicles against repair costs covered under warranty arrangements. The Court considered that these reductions were outside the provisions of Community law in force at that time. Ten years later, similar value reductions are still being applied by the German customs authority. The Court continues to consider this procedure as not conforming to the provisions of Community law.
>
> Similar situations are treated differently in other Member States. The customs authorities of three Member States (Italy, the Netherlands, the United Kingdom) have refused similar claims from importers of motor vehicles. The different approaches of Member States' customs administrations to this question may be one of the elements leading to trade diversion inside the Community.
>
> This is a clear indication of the lack of cohesion within the customs union, and one which may have resulted in losses of own resources. Regardless of any ultimate revision of the regulations, the fact remains that for over 10 years a practice of rebates, unchallenged by the Commission, has existed."[1343]

7.398 The Panel notes that, in the sections of the EC Court of Auditor's report excerpted in the preceding paragraph, the Court noted the existence of "different" treatment among the member States regarding "similar situations" in relation to the treatment of costs of vehicle repair covered by a seller's warranty. Specifically, the Court notes that, whereas German customs authorities had granted reductions in imports of vehicles subject to repair costs covered under warranty, customs authorities in Italy, the Netherlands and the United Kingdom had failed to do so in similar situations. In the Panel's view, these findings of the EC Court of Auditors tend to indicate the existence of non-uniform administration within the meaning of Article X:3(a) of the GATT 1994 regarding the treatment of costs of vehicle repair covered by a seller's warranty. Indeed, in the context of this

---

[1343] EC Court of Auditors Special Report No 23/2000 concerning valuation of imported goods for customs purposes, 14 March 2001, paras. 73-75 (Exhibit US-14).

dispute, the European Communities does not dispute that the different treatment in question amounted to non-uniform administration.[1344]

7.399 In the light of the foregoing, the Panel considers that, at the time the EC Court of Auditors prepared its report – namely, in 2001 – the European Communities was not administering its customs law concerning vehicle repair costs covered under warranty in a uniform manner in violation of Article X:3(a) of the GATT 1994. The Panel is of the view that this instance of non-uniform administration is all the more noteworthy in light of the fact that the Court of Auditors had already prepared a report noting the same instance of non-uniform administration more than ten years earlier in 1990.[1345] The Panel understands that, as in the case of the 2001 report, the EC Commission received a copy of the EC Court of Auditor's 1990 report and was provided with the opportunity to make comments thereon.[1346]

7.400 The Panel notes that it was only after receiving critical comments in two consecutive reports by the EC Court of Auditors, which were separated by a period of ten years, that the Commission finally took action to remedy non-uniform administration regarding the treatment of the costs of vehicle repair covered by a seller's warranty. Specifically, in 2002, the EC Commission adopted Commission Regulation (EC) No. 444/2002 of 11 March 2002.[1347] That Regulation had the effect, *inter alia*, of amending Article 145 of the Implementing Regulation. Following the amendment, Article 145(2) of the Implementing Regulation provided that and continues to provide that:

> "After release of the goods for free circulation, an adjustment made by the seller, to the benefit of the buyer, of the price actually paid or payable for the goods may be taken into consideration for the determination of the customs value in accordance with Article 29 of the Code, if it is demonstrated to the satisfaction of the customs authorities that:
>
> (a) the goods were defective at the moment referred to by Article 67 of the Code;
>
> (b) the seller made the adjustment in performance of a warranty obligation provided for in the contract of sale, concluded before release for free circulation of the goods;
>
> (c) the defective nature of the goods has not already been taken into account in the relevant sales contract."

[1344] European Communities' first written submission, para. 398; European Communities' second written submission, para. 156.

[1345] The Court of Auditors' Annual Report concerning the financial year 1990, Chapter 2, para. 2.52(a) (OJ C 324, 13.12.1991) referred to in EC Court of Auditors Special Report No 23/2000 concerning valuation of imported goods for customs purposes, 14 March 2001, paras. 73-75 (Exhibit US-14).

[1346] The Panel notes that the EC Court of Auditors Special Report No 23/2000 contains a section containing "The Commission's Replies" pp. 13 - 18 (Exhibit US-14).

[1347] Commission Regulation No. 444/2002 of 11 March 2002 (Exhibit EC-89).

7.401 The United States acknowledges that Regulation No. 44/2002 had the effect of resolving the non-uniform administration regarding the treatment of the costs of vehicle repair covered by a seller's warranty for the purposes of customs valuation.[1348] Indeed, the Panel understands that the non-uniform administration concerning such costs that had existed at least between 1990 and 2001, was finally removed in 2002. There is no evidence before the Panel that would suggest that the non-uniform administration has re-emerged since then.

7.402 In the light of the foregoing, the Panel concludes that, in 2001, the European Communities was not administering Article 29(3)(a) of the Community Customs Code regarding the costs of vehicle repair covered by a seller's warranty in a uniform manner in violation of Article X:3(a) of the GATT 1994. However, this violation was remedied in 2002 through the enactment of Regulation No. 44/2002.

7.403 The Panel concludes that the European Communities is not currently administering Article 29(3)(a) of the Community Customs Code concerning vehicle repair costs covered under warranty in a manner that is non-uniform within the meaning of Article X:3(a) of the GATT 1994. Therefore, the Panel finds no violation of Article X:3(a) of the GATT 1994 with respect to the administration of Article 29(3)(a) of the Community Customs Code concerning vehicle repair costs covered under warranty.

(iv) Relationship between EC importer and non-EC manufacturers

Summary of the parties' arguments

7.404 The **United States** argues that different member States have taken different positions on whether an importer is related to non-EC companies that manufacture its products and, accordingly, on how those products should be valued.[1349] By way of example, the United States refers to a case involving Reebok International Limited ("RIL"), which contracts with various suppliers outside the European Communities to manufacture shoes that are then imported and sold to customers in the European Communities.[1350] As for whether RIL's contracts with non-EC manufacturers establish a control relationship affecting the price at which the shoes are sold for export to the European Communities that should be taken into account in customs valuation, the United States notes that the Spanish customs authorities found that RIL's contracts with non-EC manufacturers established a control relationship vis-à- vis those suppliers. The relevant aspects of the contracts considered significant by the Spanish customs authorities related to quality approval, pricing conditions, and restrictions on delivery conditions. However, the contracts did not allow RIL to direct or restrain the management or activities of its suppliers. The United States submits that other member State customs authorities did not consider the contracts to have established a control

[1348] United States' reply to Panel question No. 4.

[1349] United States' first written submission, para. 25.

[1350] United States' first written submission, para. 90.

relationship between RIL and its non-EC manufacturers.[1351] According to the United States, RIL is in the process of appealing the valuation decisions of the Spanish customs authorities – a process that has already taken years and is expected to take even longer. The United States submits that coping with these inconsistencies has added costs to RIL's operations that would not be necessary if EC customs law were administered uniformly.[1352]

7.405 The United States explains that its claims with respect to this issue are based on a narrative account by the importer at issue. The United States notes that, due to concerns relating to the pendency of litigation over the matter at issue and the commercial sensitivity of the information that supporting documentation would contain, the importer declined to provide documentation at this time. However, according to the United States, its claims are substantiated in a decision of the European Ombudsman.[1353] The United States argues that that decision reveals how the Commission dealt with the company's complaint when it was brought to the Commission's attention in September 2000. According to the United States, rather than refer the matter to the Customs Code Committee, the Commission replied three months later "that the interpretation issues raised by the complainant were a matter for the national customs authorities, and that [the Commission] has no responsibility to undertake a detailed examination of very specific individual cases, this being the task of national administrations."[1354] When the company expressly requested referral to the Committee a year later, the Commission "rejected the idea."[1355] The company renewed its request in January 2002 and, over two years later, still had not received a reply from the Commission. The United States notes that the Ombudsman's decision indicates that, following a meeting between agents for the company and officials of the Commission's Directorate for Taxation and Customs Union in May 2004, the complainant stated that "he no longer wished to pursue the complaint".[1356] However, according to the United States, it does *not* indicate that the underlying lack of uniformity was resolved. The fact that the company is continuing to pursue its appeal through the Spanish courts indicates that, in fact, it has not been resolved.[1357]

7.406 In response, the **European Communities** submits that the United States cannot justify its failure to discharge its burden of proof on the basis of the refusal of the importer in question to provide the necessary evidence.[1358] Further, with respect to the decision by the European Ombudsman on a complaint by an individual importer, the European Communities confirms that the complaint was made on behalf of Reebok, which claimed that the European Commission was

---

1351 United States' first written submission, para. 91.

1352 United States' first written submission, para. 92.

1353 Exhibit US-52.

1354 Decision of the European Ombudsman on complaint 128/2004/OV against the European Commission, p. 2, 2 June 2004 (Exhibit US-52).

1355 *Ibid.*

1356 Decision of the European Ombudsman on complaint 128/2004/OV against the European Commission, p. 4, 2 June 2004 (Exhibit US-52).

1357 United States' reply to Panel question No. 26.

1358 European Communities' second written submission, para. 162.

not properly discharging its responsibilities in respect of the administration of customs valuation law.[1359] The European Communities notes that, however, the Ombudsman did not take a decision on the substance of the complaint. Rather, the complainant withdrew the complaint indicating that he "was satisfied with the position the Commission had adopted on the matter and with its proposal to look into pending problematic issues".[1360]

7.407 The European Communities also submits that the facts as set out in the Ombudsman's decision are not presented entirely correctly. Notably, the United States refers to a quotation from a letter of the European Commission of 20 December 2000, in which the Commission is supposed to have stated "that the interpretation issues raised by the complainant were a matter for the national customs authorities". According to the European Communities, this quotation is not correct. In its letter of 20 December 2000, the Commission stated the following (emphasis added): "The *application* of this criterion [of Article 143(1)(e) Implementing Regulation] in individual cases is of course a matter for national administrations and the Commission Services could only express an opinion if a detailed file on all aspects of the case was to be forwarded by the customs services in question. However, our services do not, in general, have a responsibility to undertake a detailed examination of very specific cases, this being the task of the national administrations."[1361] The European Communities considers that this statement correctly reflects the division of competences between the European Commission and the customs authorities of the member States, the latter of which are competent for the application of customs law in individual cases. According to the European Communities, it is neither possible nor appropriate for the Commission to substitute itself for the competent authority simply because, in an individual case of application, a trader is not satisfied with an approach taken by the customs authority.[1362] The European Communities notes that, nevertheless, the Commission is responsible for monitoring and ensuring the correct and uniform interpretation and application of EC customs law. This was explicitly acknowledged in the following paragraph of the letter: "On the other hand, cases involving the proven divergence of valuation treatment of a company at EC level, or a clear mis-application or mis-interpretation of EC law, can be notified and consideration can then be given to appropriate action by the Commission Services".[1363] According to the European Communities, in the case in question, at the time in question, Reebok had not submitted to the European Commission any evidence that showed an incorrect application of EC law or a divergence in the application of EC law. Accordingly, the Commission did not see any need to intervene in the specific pending case.[1364]

7.408 The European Communities also argues that the valuation dispute between Reebok and the Spanish customs authorities is a complex valuation dis-

---

[1359] European Communities' second written submission, para. 165.

[1360] European Communities' second written submission, para. 166 referring to Exhibit US-52, p. 4.

[1361] Exhibit EC-138.

[1362] European Communities' second written submission, paras. 168-169.

[1363] European Communities' second written submission, para. 170.

[1364] European Communities' second written submission, para. 171.

pute concerning the assessment of whether RIL controls certain of its suppliers. According to the European Communities, the Commission has kept this case, which is currently pending before the Spanish tribunals, under close review, and has also discussed it in the Customs Code Committee. However, neither the European Commission nor the Customs Code Committee are a substitute for the normal appeals mechanisms before the national courts. In addition, RIL has not, in fact, submitted a formal complaint to the European Commission in this matter.[1365] The European Communities explains that the Valuation Section of the Customs Code Committee examined the issue of the application of Article 143(1)(e) of the Implementing Regulation (dealing with related parties) by Spanish customs authorities but did not establish any incompatibility with EC law or lack of uniformity.[1366] The European Communities further explains that, during the meetings of the Customs Code Committee on 1 October and 20 December 2004, the delegates' view was that the facts tended to show that the parties were related, as was previously concluded by the Spanish authorities. The European Communities adds that, since similar cases had been raised by two other member States, it was considered that, in 2005, further work was desirable in this context. It was also recalled that, since similar cases had come in for attention, and these relate to manufacturing and processing operations which have become significant in trade and economy terms, the Commission decided to carry further the work on the basis of a working group of the Committee. In August 2005, Reebok submitted, at the Commission's request, material indicating that there could be a divergent approach among member States. The European Communities notes that this material will now be looked at and the working group will begin to meet and work shortly. The European Communities submits that it is intended that the working group will produce concrete outputs which will address both the general interpretation and application of Article 143(1)(e) of the Implementing Regulation, and the specific elements which have been the subject of disagreement between the customs authorities in Spain and the firm in question.[1367] The European Communities submits that, overall, it does not see that the Reebok case provides any support for the allegation that the European Communities fails to administer is customs valuation rules in a uniform manner.[1368]

Analysis by the Panel

7.409 The Panel notes that the United States challenges the administration of Article 29 of the Community Customs Code and Article 143(1)(e) of the Implementing Regulation, which concern the circumstances in which parties are to be treated as "related" for customs valuation purposes. In particular, the United States argues that different member States have taken different positions on

[1365] European Communities' oral statement at the first substantive meeting, para. 46.

[1366] European Communities' first written submission, para. 407.

[1367] European Communities' first written submission, para. 407; European Communities' reply to Panel question No. 62.

[1368] European Communities' first written submission, para. 410.

whether an importer is related to non-EC companies that manufacture its products and, accordingly, on how those products should be valued.[1369]

7.410 In the Panel's view, the treatment (or not) of parties as "related" for the purposes of customs valuation constitutes an act of administration within the meaning of Article X:3(a) of the GATT 1994. This act of administration is a matter within the Panel's terms of reference since it amounts to an instance of administration of Article 29 of the Community Customs Code and Article 143(1)(e) of the Implementing Regulation in the customs valuation area.[1370]

7.411 With respect to the question of whether the treatment (or not) of parties as "related" in the member States is "uniform" within the meaning of Article X:3(a) of the GATT 1994, the Panel recalls its finding in paragraph 7.135 above that geographic uniformity is required under Article X:3(a) of the GATT 1994. That is, administration should be uniform in different places within a particular WTO Member. The Panel also recalls its finding in paragraph 7.135 above that the form, nature and scale of the alleged non-uniform administration and the laws, regulations, judicial decisions and rulings that are allegedly being administered in a non-uniform manner should be taken into consideration when interpreting the term "uniform" in Article X:3(a) of the GATT 1994. The Panel considers that the United States' challenge with respect to the treatment (or not) of parties as "related" for customs valuation purposes is narrow in nature. It involves the application of a single provision of the Community Customs Code and a single provision of the Implementing Regulation – namely, Article 29 of the Community Customs Code and Article 143(1)(e) of the Implementing Regulation. Therefore, given the narrowness of this challenge, the Panel considers that a high degree of uniformity is required for the purposes of Article X:3(a) of the GATT 1994. We now turn to the facts to determine whether or not this high degree of uniformity has been achieved with respect to the treatment (or not) of parties as "related".

7.412 Article 29 of the Community Customs Code provides in relevant part that:

> "1. The customs value of imported goods shall be the transaction value, that is, the price actually paid or payable for the goods when sold for export to the customs territory of the Community, adjusted, where necessary, in accordance with Articles 32 and 33, provided:
>
> ...
>
> (d) that the buyer and seller are not related, or, where the buyer and seller are related, that the transaction value is acceptable for customs purposes under paragraph 2.
>
> 2.(a) In determining whether the transaction value is acceptable for the purposes of paragraph 1, the fact that the buyer and the seller are related shall not in itself be sufficient grounds for regarding the transaction value as unacceptable. Where

[1369] United States' first written submission, para. 25.

[1370] In this regard, see paragraphs 7.183 – 7.187 above.

necessary, the circumstances surrounding the sale shall be examined and the transaction value shall be accepted provided that the relationship did not influence the price. If, in the light of information provided by the declarant or otherwise, the customs authorities have grounds for considering that the relationship influenced the price, they shall communicate their grounds to the declarant and he shall be given a reasonable opportunity to respond. If the declarant so requests, the communication of the grounds shall be in writing.

(b) In a sale between related persons, the transaction value shall be accepted and the goods valued in accordance with paragraph 1 wherever the declarant demonstrates that such value closely approximates to one of the following occurring at or about the same time:

(i) the transaction value in sales, between buyers and sellers who are not related in any particular case, of identical or similar goods for export to the Community;

(ii) the customs value of identical or similar goods, as determined under Article 30 (2) (c);

(iii) the customs value of identical or similar goods, as determined under Article 30 (2) (d).

In applying the foregoing tests, due account shall be taken of demonstrated differences in commercial levels, quantity levels, the elements enumerated in Article 32 and costs incurred by the seller in sales in which he and the buyer are not related and where such costs are not incurred by the seller in sales in which he and the buyer are related."

7.413 Article 143(1)(e) of the Implementing Regulation provides that persons shall be deemed to be related only if one of them directly or indirectly controls the other.

7.414 To support its allegation that Article 29 of the Community Customs Code and Article 143(1)(e) of the Implementing Regulation are being administered in a non-uniform manner in violation of Article X:3(a) of the GATT 1994, the United States refers to a case involving Reebok International Limited ("RIL"). According to the United States, Spanish customs authorities found that RIL's contracts with non-EC manufacturers established a control relationship *vis-à-vis* those suppliers whereas other member State authorities did not consider the contracts to have established a control relationship between RIL and its non-EC manufacturers.

7.415 The United States explains that its claims with respect to the administration of Article 29 of the Community Customs Code and Article 143(1)(e) of the Implementing Regulation issue are based on a narrative account by RIL because, due to concerns relating to the pendency of litigation over the matter at issue in this dispute and the commercial sensitivity of the information that supporting documentation would contain, RIL declined to provide documentation. Apart from its narrative account of RIL's experiences, the United States also relies upon a decision of the European Ombudsman concerning a complaint by RIL.[1371] The United States argues that the decision reveals how the Commission dealt with the RIL's complaint when it was brought to the Commission's attention in September 2000. According to the United States, the European Ombudsman's decision does not indicate that the underlying lack of uniformity was resolved.

7.416 The Panel's appraisal of the Ombudsman's letter is that it does not, on its own, prove the existence of non-uniform administration of Article 29 of the Community Customs Code and Article 143(1)(e) of the Implementing Regulation in violation of Article X:3(a) of the GATT 1994.[1372] The Ombudsman's letter notes RIL's complaint that "Community legislation is not interpreted in the same way in different Member States, such as the Netherlands and Spain". However, apart from making this observation on RIL's complaint, the Ombudsman did not make any factual findings regarding the uniformity or lack thereof among member States with respect to the question of whether or not parties are related for the purposes of Article 29 of the Community Customs Code and Article 143(1)(e) of the Implementing Regulation. In fact, the Panel has no objective evidence before it to prove the existence or otherwise of non-uniform administration in this regard. Moreover, in light of the fact that the European Communities has contested the existence of non-uniform administration in this respect,[1373] the Panel does not consider it appropriate to make any inferences solely on the basis of the United States' narrative account.

7.417 With respect to the United States' more general comments regarding the manner in which the European Communities' handled RIL's complaint of alleged non-uniform administration, the Panel considers that these comments might be relevant for a claim of unreasonable or partial administration of EC customs law under Article X:3(a) of the GATT 1994, which claim the United States has not made in the context of this dispute.[1374] However, the Panel considers that such comments are not relevant for a claim of non-uniform administration under Article X:3(a) of the GATT 1994.

7.418 Accordingly, the Panel concludes that the United States has not proved that the manner of administration of Article 29 of the Community Customs Code and Article 143(1)(e) of the Implementing Regulation concerning the circumstances in which parties are to be treated as "related" for customs valuation purposes is non-uniform among the member States within the meaning of Article X:3(a) of the GATT 1994.

[1371] Exhibit US-52.

[1372] With regard to the European Ombudsman, see paragraphs 7.171 – 7.172 above.

[1373] European Communities' second written submission, para. 163.

[1374] The Panel recalls that the United States clarified in its first submission that it is exclusively concerned with the requirement of uniform administration under Article X:3(a) of the GATT 1994: United States' first written submission, footnote 15.

(v) Summary and conclusions

7.419 In summary, the Panel finds that, with respect to the United States' allegations of non-uniform administration of the Community Customs Code and the Implementing Regulation in the area of customs valuation:

(a) The United States has not proved that differences between member States regarding the manner in which royalties are apportioned to the customs value of identical goods imported by the same company exist that amount to non-uniform administration of Article 32(1)(c) of the Community Customs Code within the meaning of Article X:3(a) of the GATT 1994.

(b) The imposition by customs authorities in some member States of a form of prior approval with respect to the successive sales provision, which is inconsistent with EC customs laws and which is not imposed by customs authorities in other member States means that the European Communities does not administer its customs law concerning successive sales – in particular, Article 147(1) of the Implementing Regulation – in a uniform manner in violation of Article X:3(a) of the GATT 1994.

(c) In 2001, the European Communities was not administering Article 29(3)(a) of the Community Customs Code regarding the costs of vehicle repair covered by a seller's warranty in a uniform manner in violation of Article X:3(a) of the GATT 1994. However, the European Communities is not currently administering Article 29(3)(a) of the Community Customs Code concerning vehicle repair costs covered under warranty in a manner that is non-uniform within the meaning of Article X:3(a) of the GATT 1994. Therefore, the Panel finds no violation of Article X:3(a) of the GATT 1994 with respect to the administration of Article 29(3)(a) of the Community Customs Code concerning vehicle repair costs covered under warranty.

(d) The United States has not proved that the manner of administration of Article 29 of the Community Customs Code and Article 143(1)(e) of the Implementing Regulation concerning the circumstances in which parties are to be treated as "related" for customs valuation purposes is non-uniform among the member States within the meaning of Article X:3(a) of the GATT 1994.

(d) Allegations of non-uniform administration of the Community Customs Code and the Implementing Regulation in the area of customs procedures

(i) Audit following release for free circulation

Summary of the parties' arguments

7.420 The **United States** notes that audit procedures are procedures for verifying importers' statements with respect to classification, valuation and origin of goods.[1375] The United States submits that the EC Court of Auditors found in its report that different member State authorities take different approaches to valuation audits following the release of products into free circulation, with important consequences for importers.[1376] According to the United States, in the case of at least one member State, the Court found that the customs authorities lack the right to perform post-importation audits at all, except in cases of fraud. The United States asserts that, even among States in which authorities are permitted to perform post-importation audits, the Court found differences among working procedures with the consequence that "individual customs authorities are reluctant to accept each other's decisions".[1377] The United States also notes that, in its report, the EC Court of Auditors observed that authorities in Belgium and the Netherlands routinely provide the importer with a written valuation decision at the conclusion of each audit, which are binding for five years, thus providing the importer with a degree of legal certainty similar to BTI.[1378] According to the United States, by contrast, the Court found that "[c]ertain member States only issue such decisions when there are specific adjustments that have to be made (France, Ireland, Portugal, the United Kingdom). Others rarely make such written decisions (Denmark, Spain, Italy, Luxembourg). In Germany, the valuation decision does not exist as a separate written document. However, the detailed report that is given to the importer after an audit will normally contain the substance of a valuation decision".[1379]

7.421 In response, the **European Communities** submits that questions of auditing are not part of customs procedures and, therefore, do not concern the administration of customs laws as such.[1380] The European Communities submits that, in any event, under Article 78(2) of the Community Customs Code, every member State may proceed to all necessary verifications in order to satisfy themselves of the accuracy of the particulars contained in the customs declaration. According to the European Communities, this includes all questions regarding the value of the goods.[1381] The European Communities also argues that it does not believe that Article X:3(a) of the GATT 1994 can require complete certainty for traders concerning questions of auditing. On the contrary, a certain degree of uncertainty

---

[1375] United States' reply to Panel question No. 4.

[1376] United States' first written submission, para. 96.

[1377] United States' first written submission, para. 97 referring to EC Court of Auditors Valuation Report, paras. 33 and 37 (Exhibit US-14).

[1378] United States' first written submission, para. 98.

[1379] United States' first written submission, para. 99 referring to EC Court of Auditors Valuation Report, para. 46 (Exhibit US-14).

[1380] In this regard, the European Communities notes that Article 4(16) of the Community Customs Code defines a "customs procedure" as any of the following: release for free circulation; transit; customs warehousing; inward processing; processing under customs control; temporary admission; outward processing; and exportation: European Communities' reply to Panel question No. 64(a). The European Communities further submits that post-release audits are not considered as "customs procedures" because they are not one of the procedures referred to in Article 4(16) of the Community Customs Code.

[1381] European Communities' second written submission, para. 157.

as to when and under which conditions an audit will be carried out is in the interests of sound control and must be accepted by traders as part of a customs compliance policy. In addition, the European Communities submits that any administrative differences that might still exist are minor in nature, and do not amount to a violation of Article X:3(a) of the GATT 1994.[1382] The European Communities further notes that the member State referred to by the Court of Auditors in which the customs authorities lack the right to perform post-importation audits except in cases of fraud was Greece. In 2000, Greece established a service with powers to conduct post-clearance audits. Finally, the European Communities submits that the Commission in conjunction with the member States has recently finalized a Community Customs Audit Guide.[1383] According to the European Communities, this Guide ensures uniform audit practice across the European Communities.[1384]

7.422 The **United States** disputes the European Communities' argument that audits are not part of customs procedures. According to the United States, the specific sense in which the European Communities uses the term "customs procedure" for the purposes of the Community Customs Code has no bearing on whether audits are customs procedures (in the ordinary sense of that term) for administering the Code.[1385] The United States argues that, in any event, whether or not auditing is characterized as a customs procedure, audits are plainly tools for administering EC customs laws. According to the United States, to the extent that different member States use different audit procedures, they administer the underlying law differently.[1386] The United States argues that, flowing from the ordinary meaning of "administer", audit procedures put EC customs laws into effect by verifying and enforcing compliance with those laws. It is through the tools of audit procedures, among others, that member State authorities "execute" or "carry out" EC customs laws.[1387] The United States argues that the administration of EC customs laws depends in large part on the actions of traders themselves. Given the millions of declarations submitted to member State customs authorities each year, it would be impossible for the authorities to thoroughly inspect every shipment or verify the contents of every declaration before clearance. It is for this reason that tools for verifying and enforcing compliance with the customs laws are critical to "carrying out" or "putting into effect" those laws. Compliance with those laws is secured through traders' knowledge that the representations they make to the customs authorities ultimately are subject to verification and enforcement through audits and penalties.[1388] The United States also submits that, given that the Community Customs Audit Guide was only recently finalized and, in any event, given that it is merely intended as an aid to member States, rather than a binding obligation on them, there is no basis for the asser-

[1382] European Communities' first written submission, para. 400.
[1383] Community Customs Audit Guide (Exhibit EC-90).
[1384] European Communities' second written submission, para. 158.
[1385] United States' second written submission, para. 83.
[1386] United States' reply to Panel question No. 28.
[1387] United States' second written submission, paras. 79-80.
[1388] United States' second written submission, para. 81.

tion that it ensures a uniform practice across the European Communities.[1389] Finally, regarding the European Communities' dismissal of differences among member States in this area as "minor in nature", the United States submits that, whereas some member States provide traders with legal certainty as to how specified transactions will be treated going forward, others do not.[1390]

7.423 The **European Communities** submits that it does not believe that Article X:3(a) of the GATT 1994 requires harmonization of the relevant rules of general administrative law of the member States which govern audit procedures.[1391] In addition, the European Communities submits that Article 78(2) of the Community Customs Code gives customs authorities the power to conduct post-clearance inspections and audits. All member States have the necessary audit capacities, and are guided by the Community Customs Audit Guide. The European Communities submits that it does not believe that audit provisions as such are among the laws enumerated in Article X:1 of the GATT 1994 since Article X:1 only covers those laws and regulations which pertain to the matters referred to in this provision.[1392] In any event, the basic provisions exist at the EC level, not at the member State level, and a uniform audit practice is ensured throughout the European Communities.[1393]

7.424 The **United States** responds that tools of administration need not necessarily qualify as laws of general application within the meaning of Article X:1 of the GATT 1994. For the purposes of Article X:3(a) of the GATT 1994, it is the object of administration – the thing being administered – as opposed to the provision doing the administering, that must be a law of general application within the meaning of Article X:1. This is evident from the grammatical structure of Article X:3(a) of the GATT 1994, in which the phrase "laws, regulations, decisions and rulings of the kind described in paragraph 1 of this Article" is the object of the phrase "shall administer in a uniform, impartial and reasonable manner."[1394]

Analysis by the Panel

7.425 The Panel notes that, in essence, the United States challenges the fact that different member States take different approaches to audits following the release of products into free circulation.[1395] In support, the United States relies upon the EC Court of Auditors report, which it asserts, referred to differences among member States regarding the existence of the right of customs authorities to conduct post-importation audits and also regarding the working procedures adopted

---

1389 United States' oral statement at the second substantive meeting, para. 68.

1390 United States' oral statement at the first substantive meeting, para. 55.

1391 European Communities' first written submission, para. 401.

1392 European Communities' comments on the United States' reply to Panel question No. 138.

1393 European Communities' reply to Panel question No. 168(c).

1394 United States' reply to Panel question No. 129.

1395 United States' first written submission, para. 96.

among the customs authorities that do have the right to conduct post-importation audits.[1396]

7.426 With respect to its allegations concerning divergence in audit procedures among the member States, the United States does not specifically identify the provisions of EC customs laws it claims are being administered in a non-uniform fashion. Rather, the United States submits that it challenges the manner of administration of "the valuation provisions contained in the Community Customs Code (Articles 28 – 36) and the Implementing Regulation (Articles 141 – 181a and Annexes 23 –29), to the extent that different member State authorities employ different audit procedures"[1397]. Nevertheless, in the Panel's understanding, the only provision of the various instruments identified in the United States' request for establishment of a panel which it alleges are being administered in a non-uniform manner and which concerns audit procedures following release for free circulation is Article 78(2) of the Community Customs Code.

7.427 In the Panel's view, the conduct (or not) of post-importation audits and the working procedures adopted among the customs authorities regarding post-importation audits constitute acts of administration within the meaning of Article X:3(a) of the GATT 1994. These acts of administration are matters within the Panel's terms of reference since they amount to instances of administration of Article 78(2) of the Community Customs Code with respect to procedures for the entry and release of goods.

7.428 Article 78(2) of the Community Customs Code provides that:

> "The customs authorities may, after releasing the goods and in order to satisfy themselves as to the accuracy of the particulars contained in the declaration, inspect the commercial documents and data relating to the import or export operations in respect of the goods concerned or to subsequent commercial operations involving those goods. Such inspections may be carried out at the premises of the declarant, of any other person directly or indirectly involved in the said operations in a business capacity or of any other person in possession of the said document and data for business purposes. Those authorities may also examine the goods where it is still possible for them to be produced."

7.429 By way of general observation, the Panel notes that Article 78(2) of the Community Customs Code is discretionary rather than prescriptive in nature. More specifically, Article 78(2) of the Community Customs Code empowers customs authorities to conduct audits following the release of goods for free circulation but does not oblige them to do so. Further, Article 78(2) of the Community Customs Code does not impose any conditions on the manner in which audits are to be conducted other than to provide that the purpose of audits is to satisfy customs authorities of the accuracy of the particulars contained in the cus-

---

[1396] United States' first written submission, paras. 97 – 99 referring to EC Court of Auditors Valuation Report, paras. 33, 37 and 46 (Exhibit US-14).

[1397] United States' replies to Panel question Nos. 124 and 179.

toms declaration. In satisfying itself of the accuracy of the particulars contained in the customs declaration, the customs authority is authorized under Article 78(2) of the Community Customs Code to "inspect the commercial documents and data relating to the import or export operations in respect of the goods concerned or to subsequent commercial operations involving those goods". The Panel considers that the discretionary nature of Article 78(2) of the Community Customs Code is notable because it reflects a policy decision on the part of the legislator to provide administrators with a certain degree of freedom in the application of that provision.

7.430 The Panel notes that the ordinary meaning of the terms of Article X:3(a) of the GATT 1994 does not indicate that Article X:3(a) of the GATT 1994 requires laws to be prescriptive rather than discretionary. As the Panel has noted in paragraph 7.20 above, the essential aspect Article X:3(a) of the GATT is the obligation to "administer in a uniform, impartial and reasonable manner". The Panel recalls its findings in paragraph 7.113 above that Article X:3(a) of the GATT 1994 does not concern what a particular law says (i.e. its substance) but, instead, concerns the way the law is applied in practice (i.e. the way in which it is administered). Therefore, the Panel considers that Article X:3(a) of the GATT 1994 does not dictate whether or not a provision regulating a particular matter of customs administration should be drafted in prescriptive rather than discretionary terms.[1398]

[1398] In this regard, the Panel notes that the context of Article X:3(a) of the GATT 1994 could arguably be interpreted as suggesting that Article X:3(a) of the GATT 1994 is not aimed at harmonising WTO Members' customs laws by, *inter alia*, requiring prescriptive provisions to regulate customs matters. In fact, while the provisions of Article VIII of the GATT 1994 could be viewed as being aimed at, *inter alia*, harmonization of certain internal customs matters, notably, the relevant language used in Article VIII of the GATT 1994 is quite distinct from that used in Article X:3(a) of the GATT 1994. In particular, Article VIII of the GATT 1994, which, in general terms, covers certain import and export-related fees and formalities, provides in relevant part that:

"1. (a) All fees and charges of whatever character (other than import and export duties and other than taxes within the purview of Article III) imposed by contracting parties on or in connection with importation or exportation shall be limited in amount to the approximate cost of services rendered and shall not represent an indirect protection to domestic products or a taxation of imports or exports for fiscal purposes.

(b) The contracting parties recognize the need for reducing the number and diversity of fees and charges referred to in subparagraph (a).

(c) The contracting parties also recognize the need for minimizing the incidence and complexity of import and export formalities and for decreasing and simplifying import and export documentation requirements.*

2. A contracting party shall, upon request by another contracting party or by the CONTRACTING PARTIES, review the operation of its laws and regulations in the light of the provisions of this Article.

3. No contracting party shall impose substantial penalties for minor breaches of customs regulations or procedural requirements. In particular, no penalty in respect of any omission or mistake in customs documentation which is easily rectifiable and obviously made without fraudulent intent or gross negligence shall be greater than necessary to serve merely as a warning.

4. The provisions of this Article shall extend to fees, charges, formalities and requirements imposed by governmental authorities in connection with importation and exportation, including those relating to:

(a) consular transactions, such as consular invoices and certificates;

(b) quantitative restrictions;

7.431 The Panel notes that, by definition, discretionary provisions may be applied in different ways, which may or may not produce different substantive results. The Panel considers that, if such differences in application were to be interpreted as amounting to instances of non-uniform administration in violation of Article X:3(a) of the GATT 1994, this would mean that the application of many discretionary provisions would be in violation of Article X:3(a) of the GATT 1994. The Panel is of the view that the drafters of Article X:3(a) of the GATT 1994 could not have intended this result because there may be a justifiable rationale for the existence of discretion in such cases. Nevertheless, while the Panel considers that divergences resulting from the exercise of discretion in the law being administered do not necessarily fall foul of Article X:3(a) of the GATT 1994, the Panel does consider that there are certain limits implicit in Article X:3(a) of the GATT 1994 that circumscribe the types of provisions that may be couched in discretionary terms and that may have an impact upon the way in which discretion is exercised in particular cases. In particular, the Panel recalls its findings in paragraphs 7.107 and 7.108 above that the due process theme underlying Article X of the GATT 1994 suggests that the aim of Article X:3(a) of the GATT is to ensure that traders are treated fairly and consistently when seeking to import from or export to a particular WTO Member. The Panel also considers that an object and purpose of the WTO Agreement is to ensure security and predictability in the trading environment.[1399] In the Panel's view, the exis-

(c) licensing;
(d) exchange control;
(e) statistical services;
(f) documents, documentation and certification;
(g) analysis and inspection; and
(h) quarantine, sanitation and fumigation."

[1399] The preamble of the WTO Agreement specifies that one of the purposes of the Agreement is to "expand[] ... trade in goods and services." It also states that Members should contribute to such expansion "by entering into reciprocal and mutually advantageous arrangements directed to the substantial reduction of tariffs and other barriers to trade." In *EC – Computer Equipment*, the Appellate Body stated that: "[T]he security and predictability of 'the reciprocal and mutually advantageous arrangements directed to the substantial reduction of tariffs and other barriers to trade' is an object and purpose of the WTO Agreement, generally, as well as of the GATT 1994.": Appellate Body Report, *EC – Computer Equipment,* para. 82. This view was recently affirmed by the Appellate Body in Appellate Body Report, *EC – Chicken Cuts*, para. 243. The objective of security and predictability was also referred to by the Appellate Body in the context of Article III of the GATT 1994 (dealing with national treatment). In particular, in *Japan – Alcoholic Beverages II*, the Appellate Body stated that: "Our interpretation of Article III is faithful to the 'customary rules of interpretation of public international law'. WTO rules are reliable, comprehensible and enforceable. WTO rules are not so rigid or so inflexible as not to leave room for reasoned judgements in confronting the endless and ever-changing ebb and flow of real facts in real cases in the real world. They will serve the multilateral trading system best if they are interpreted with that in mind. In that way, we will achieve the 'security and predictability' sought for the multilateral trading system by the Members of the WTO through the establishment of the dispute settlement system.": Appellate Body Report, *Japan – Alcoholic Beverages II*, pp. 29-31. Finally, the objective of security and predictability has been referred to in the context of the DSU. In particular, in *US – Section 301 Trade Act*, the panel examined the European Communities' argument that Section 301 was inconsistent with Article 23 of the DSU ("Strengthening of the Multilateral System") as well as various articles of GATT 1994. In its examination, the panel discussed the importance of the concept of "security and predictability" and stated: "Providing security and predictability to the multilateral trading system is another central object and

tence and exercise of discretion should not unduly compromise the underlying due process objective of Article X:3(a) of the GATT 1994. Nor should they render the trading environment insecure and unpredictable without just cause.

7.432 The Panel takes note of the European Communities' argument that a certain degree of uncertainty as to when and under which conditions an audit will be carried out is in the interest of sound control and must be accepted by traders as part of a customs compliance policy.[1400] The Panel notes that the United States has not disputed the suggested rationale for the existence of discretion under Article 78(2) of the Community Customs Code put forward by the European Communities. The Panel has no reason to question this suggested rationale.[1401] Further, the Panel notes that the Community Customs Audit Guide[1402], which sets out a framework for post clearance and audit based controls, helps to ensure that the due process rights of traders are not unduly compromised.[1403]

7.433 In support of its allegation of non-uniform administration with respect to audit procedures, the United States points to a statement made in the EC Court of Auditors Special Report No. 23/2000 concerning valuation of imported goods for customs purposes dated 14 March 2001 that customs authorities in at least one member State (apparently, Greece) lacked the right to perform post-importation audits whereas, implicitly, customs authorities in other member States possessed that right. The Panel understands that both the approach adopted by Greece at the time the EC Court of Auditors' report was prepared on the one hand and that adopted in the other member States would be consistent with Article 78(2) of the Community Customs Code given that, as noted previously, Article 78(2) authorises member State customs authorities to conduct audits but does not oblige them to do so. The United States also relies upon statements by the EC Court of Auditors in its report to the effect that some member States (Belgium and the Netherlands) routinely provide the importer with a written binding valuation decisions at the conclusion of each audit, others only issue such decisions when there are specific adjustments that have to be made (France, Ireland, Portugal, the United Kingdom), yet others rarely make such written decisions (Denmark, Spain, Italy, Luxembourg) and, finally, in Germany, the valuation decision does not exist as a separate written document. Again, the Panel would merely note that Article 78(2) of the Community Customs Code contains no requirements concerning the action to be taken by customs authorities following conclusion of an audit. In

purpose of the system which could be instrumental to achieving the broad objectives of the Preamble. Of all WTO disciplines, the DSU is one of the most important instruments to protect the security and predictability of the multilateral trading system and through it that of the market-place and its different operators. DSU provisions must, thus, be interpreted in the light of this object and purpose and in a manner which would most effectively enhance it. In this respect we are referring not only to preambular language but also to positive law provisions in the DSU itself.": Panel Report, *US – Section 301 Trade Act*, para. 7.75.

[1400] European Communities' first written submission, para. 400.

[1401] Indeed, the Panel does not consider that it is in a position to second-guess policy choices made by legislators in the European Communities.

[1402] The Community Customs Audit Guide is contained in Exhibit EC-90. In this regard, see paragraph 7.178 above.

[1403] European Communities' first written submission, para. 400 referring to Exhibit EC-90.

particular, Article 78(2) of the Community Customs Code does not impose an obligation to prepare written decisions following an audit. Nor does Article 78(2) of the Community Customs Code preclude the issuance of such decisions. Therefore, it would appear that the various approaches taken by the member States regarding the issuance of written decisions are all consistent with the terms of Article 78(2) of the Community Customs Code.

7.434 By way of summary, the Panel recalls that Article X:3(a) of the GATT 1994 does not dictate whether or not a provision regulating a particular matter of customs administration should be drafted in prescriptive rather than discretionary terms. The Panel further recalls that divergences resulting from the exercise of discretion in the law being administered do not necessarily fall foul of Article X:3(a) of the GATT 1994 provided that the existence and exercise of discretion do not unduly compromise the underlying due process objective of Article X:3(a) of the GATT 1994 and do not render the trading environment insecure and unpredictable without just cause. In light of these findings and given that the Panel has no reason to question the rationale indicated by the European Communities for the existence of discretion in Article 78(2) of the Community Customs Code, the Panel finds no violation of Article X:3(a) of the GATT 1994 with respect to the manner of administration of the audit procedure requirements in the European Communities by the member States applicable to goods following their release for free circulation, in particular Article 78(2) of the Community Customs Code.[1404]

(ii) Penalties against infringements of EC customs legislation

Summary of the parties' arguments

7.435 The **United States** submits that, in the area of penalties for EC customs law violations, it is well recognized that, as a matter of EC law, different member States are entitled to impose, and do impose, different sanctions. The United States notes that the EC Commission itself has acknowledged that "[s]pecific offences may be considered in one Member State as a serious criminal act possibly leading to imprisonment, whilst in another Member State the same act may only lead to a small – or even no – fine".[1405] Further, the United States submits that this area of divergence is one that has been noted by the ECJ on a number of occasions. By way of example, the United States refers to the ECJ's decision in *Jose Teodoro de Andrade* v. *Director da Alfândega de Leixões*, where the Court stated that "[a]s regards customs offences, the Court has pointed out that in the absence of harmonization of the Community legislation in that field, the member

[1404] In light of this conclusion, the Panel does not consider it necessary to determine whether or not audits following the release of goods for free circulation are properly categorised as "customs procedures".

[1405] United States' second written submission, para. 72 referring to European Commission, Director-ate-General for Taxation and Customs Union, TAXUD/447/2004 Rev 2, *An Explanatory Introduction to the modernized Customs Code*, p. 13, 24 February 2005 (Exhibit US-32).

States are empowered to choose the penalties which seem appropriate to them".[1406]

7.436 The **European Communities** submits that the United States' claim regarding penalties for violations of customs laws must be rejected because penalty provisions are not covered by Article X:3(a) of the GATT 1994, because Article X:3(a) does not require the harmonization of member States' penalty provisions and because EC law ensures a sufficient degree of uniformity of member States' penalty provisions.[1407] Further, the European Communities submits that penalty provisions, which provide for a sanction in the case of a violation of a provision of customs laws, are not themselves customs laws[1408] and that, therefore, they are not covered by Article X:3(a) of the GATT 1994.[1409] More specifically, the European Communities submits that penalties for violations of customs laws are not among the matters referred to in Article X:1 of the GATT 1994. The European Communities further submits that it cannot be considered that penalties for violations of customs laws necessarily "pertain to" the classification or the valuation of products, or to rates of duties.[1410]

7.437 The European Communities also submits that member States' laws which contain penalty provisions are themselves laws of general application. Accordingly, even if these laws fell under Article X:1 of the GATT 1994, it would be the administration of those laws to which Article X:3(a) of the GATT 1994 applies. The European Communities submits that alleged differences between member States' penalty provisions to which the United States has referred are not differences in administration but, rather, differences between different legislative measures applicable in different territories. That a particular topic may be regulated differently in different parts of the territory of a WTO Member has nothing to do with non-uniform administration.[1411] The European Communities submits that, since Article X:3(a) of the GATT 1994 only concerns the *administration* of customs laws and not the *substance* of the customs laws themselves, Article X:3(a) of the GATT 1994 does not require the harmonization of member States' penalty provisions. The European Communities argues that, therefore, Article X:3(a) of the GATT 1994 does not create an obligation to harmonise laws which may exist within a WTO Member at the sub-federal level. It merely requires that such laws be administered uniformly within the territory in which they apply.[1412] The European Communities further submits that the penalties applicable for violations of EC customs laws are set out in the national laws of

[1406] United States' first written submission, para. 100 referring to *Jose Teodoro de Andrade* v. *Director da Alfândega de Leixões*, Case C-213/99, ECR I-11083 7 December 2000, paras. 4, 18-20. (Exhibit US-31).

[1407] European Communities' second written submission, para. 189.

[1408] European Communities' first written submission, para. 431.

[1409] European Communities' first written submission, para. 429; European Communities' oral statement at the first substantive meeting, para. 52.

[1410] European Communities' reply to Panel question No. 119; European Communities' oral statement at the second substantive meeting, para. 67.

[1411] European Communities' oral statement at the second substantive meeting, para. 69.

[1412] European Communities' first written submission, para. 434; European Communities' oral statement at the first substantive meeting, para. 53.

the member States, which must respect the principles set out by Community law. Accordingly, it is not the administration of penalty provisions which varies within the European Communities; it is the laws themselves which are different, albeit within the limits set by Community law.[1413] The European Communities concludes that the United States has not shown that the administration of those penalty provisions varies within the member States that have adopted them. Rather, according to the European Communities, the United States is effectively requiring a harmonization of penalty provisions within the European Communities but Article X:3(a) of the GATT 1994 provides no legal basis for such a claim.[1414]

7.438 The **United States** submits that the European Communities' argument ignores the distinction between the laws that a member State administers and the tools for administering those laws. It assumes, without foundation, that because penalty provisions take the form of laws they can only themselves be administered, and not also serve as tools of administration of other laws. However, according to the United States, to the extent that penal laws are tools of administration of customs laws and cause the administration of customs laws to be uniform or non-uniform, Article X:3(a) of the GATT 1994 applies to such laws.[1415] The United States argues that, flowing from the ordinary meaning of "administer", member States' penalty provisions put EC customs laws into effect by verifying and enforcing compliance with those laws. It is through the tools of penalty provisions, among others, that member State authorities "execute" or "carry out" EC customs laws.[1416] The United States notes that its arguments are directed at laws and regulations at the sub-federal level that are used to verify and enforce compliance with laws and regulations prescribed at the federal level; they are not directed at the vast body of laws and regulations at the sub-federal level that have nothing to do with verification and enforcement of compliance with other laws and regulations or that concern only verification and enforcement of compliance with other sub-federal laws and regulations.[1417] The United States also submits that the European Communities' argument that differences in penalty laws are differences of substance rather than differences of administration mistakenly assumes that a law (or other measure) cannot be administrative in nature. In the United States' view, penalty laws are administrative in nature, inasmuch as they presume the existence of other laws and prescribe consequences for the violation of those laws.[1418]

7.439 The **European Communities** responds that it does not agree that a penalty provision puts into effect or carries out the substantive rule the violation of which it is intended to sanction. For instance, a provision which provides for the imposition of a sanction for the failure to declare a good does not "carry out" or

[1413] European Communities' first written submission, para. 435; European Communities' oral statement at the first substantive meeting, para. 53.
[1414] European Communities' first written submission, para. 436.
[1415] United States' reply to Panel question No. 32.
[1416] United States' second written submission, paras. 79-80.
[1417] United States' second written submission, para. 7.
[1418] United States' replies to Panel question Nos. 4 and 32.

"put into effect" the provision which imposes the obligation to declare the good. The penalty provision itself needs to be carried out through an administrative or judicial act imposing the sanction. It is this latter act which can be regarded as executing the prohibition, and thus constitutes "administration". In contrast, the penalty provision complements the substantive provision, but does not itself put it into effect.[1419] According to the European Communities, penalty provisions and substantive provisions are both measures of general application which complement one another. That the former exists at the member States level and the latter at the EC level does not mean that the former administers the latter.[1420] The European Communities also notes that it does not contest that penalty provisions are relevant tools for ensuring uniform administration of customs law. However, the fact that penalty provisions are tools for the uniform administration of customs laws does not mean that they are themselves laws or regulations pertaining to the matters enumerated in Article X:1 of the GATT 1994, in particular tariff classification, customs valuation, or rates of duty.[1421] The European Communities submits that Article X:3(a) of the GATT 1994 requires the uniform administration only of the laws and regulations referred to in Article X:1 of the GATT 1994. If penalty provisions are merely "tools" to ensure a uniform administration of those laws, then penalty provisions as such do not fall within the scope of Article X:3(a) of the GATT 1994.[1422] Further, according to the European Communities, the United States has not shown that the fact that penalty provisions are contained in laws of the Member States leads in any way to a non-uniformity in the administration of the laws covered by Article X:1 of the GATT 1994, in particular laws regarding tariff classification, customs valuation, and rates of duty. In addition, the European Communities submits that it is not correct to assume that differences in penalties would necessarily lead to a lack of uniformity in the application of the provisions the violation of which is sanctioned. Such a consequence would result only if sanctions were not dissuasive or effective. If, on the contrary, sanctions are dissuasive and effective, then it must be assumed that the related substantive provisions will be respected, regardless of differences in the level of sanctions applicable.[1423]

7.440 The European Communities further submits that, even if Article X:3(a) of the GATT 1994 were considered to apply to the question of harmonization of penalty provisions, EC law provides for a sufficient level of harmonization in this respect.[1424] In this regard, the European Communities submits that the ECJ has developed clear guidelines for penalty provisions for violations of EC customs law, which must, in particular, be effective, proportionate, and dissuasive, and that these principles have also been confirmed by the Council of the European Union.[1425] The European Communities considers that these general re-

---

1419 European Communities' oral statement at the second substantive meeting, para. 71.

1420 European Communities' oral statement at the second substantive meeting, para. 72.

1421 European Communities' second written submission, para. 192.

1422 European Communities' second written submission, para. 193.

1423 European Communities' second written submission, para. 209.

1424 European Communities first written submission, paras. 429 and 437; European Communities' oral statement at the first substantive meeting, para. 54.

1425 European Communities' first written submission, para. 438.

quirements are sufficient for securing a uniform application of EC customs laws, in accordance with Article X:3(a) of the GATT 1994. According to the European Communities, the United States has not provided any evidence demonstrating that the absence of a full harmonization of penalty provisions in the EC leads to any lack of uniformity in the application of EC laws in areas referred to by Article X:1 of the GATT 1994.[1426] In addition, the European Communities submits that the ECJ in *Jose Teodoro de Andrade* v. *Director da Alfândega de Leixões* emphasised that member States cannot act freely when laying down penalty provisions, but must ensure that the penalty is effective, proportionate and dissuasive. The European Communities explains that, in other words, member States are limited in two directions. They cannot lay down penalties that are excessively severe and, therefore, violate the principle of proportionality. On the other hand, they cannot lay down penalties which are so lenient that they have no dissuasive effect and, therefore, do not ensure the effective application of Community law. The European Communities adds that these fundamental principles are sufficient to ensure uniformity in the application of customs laws, confirmed by Article VIII:3 of the GATT 1994, which specifically addresses the issue of sanctions for violations of customs regulations and which merely provides for certain minimum standards of proportionality.[1427]

7.441 In response, the **United States** submits that the fundamental principles to which the European Communities refers are very general principles, which permit a wide range of member State practices. The United States notes that the European Communities itself acknowledges that specific offences may be considered in one member State as a serious criminal act possibly leading to imprisonment, whilst in another member State the same act may only lead to a small – or even no – fine. According to the United States, the European Communities cannot suggest that it discharges its obligation of uniform administration where the applicable legal doctrines permit such dramatic divergences in administration. According to the United States, accepting that argument would effectively render Article X:3(a) of the GATT 1994 meaningless.[1428]

Analysis by the Panel

7.442 The Panel notes that the essence of the United States' challenge is that, in the area of penalties for EC customs law violations, different member States are entitled to impose, and do impose, different sanctions.[1429] The United States submits that penal laws are tools of administration of EC customs laws and, to the extent that they are different among member States, they result in non-uniform

[1426] European Communities' oral statement at the second substantive meeting, para. 79.
[1427] European Communities' first written submission, paras. 441-442.
[1428] United States' oral statement at the first substantive meeting, para. 52 referring to European Commission, Directorate-General for Taxation and Customs Union, TAXUD/447/2004 Rev 2, *An Explanatory Introduction to the Modernized Customs Code*, p. 13, 24 February 2005). (Exhibit US-32).
[1429] United States' first written submission, para. 26.

administration of customs laws in violation of Article X:3(a) of the GATT 1994.[1430]

7.443 There are no provisions in the Community Customs Code nor in the Implementing Regulation that define offences at the EC level and identify the consequences of such offences (e.g. in the form of penalties).[1431] As a result, the nature and level of such penalties are determined by the national laws of the member States. This fact was noted in the customs administration area by the ECJ in *Jose Teodoro de Andrade* v. *Director da Alfândega de Leixões*. In that case, the ECJ stated that "[a]s regards customs offences, the Court has pointed out that in the absence of harmonization of the Community legislation in that field, the member States are empowered to choose the penalties which seem appropriate to them."[1432]

7.444 In the light of the foregoing, the question for the Panel's consideration is whether penalty laws can be viewed as "tools" that administer EC customs law and, if so, whether substantive differences in such tools among the member States – the existence of which is not disputed between the parties – mean that administration of EC customs laws is non-uniform within the meaning of Article X:3(a) of the GATT 1994. In this regard, the Panel recalls its finding in paragraph 7.114 *et seq* that the term "administer" refers to the application of laws and regulations, including administrative processes and their results but not to laws and regulations as such. Accordingly, it is the Panel's view that, for the purposes of Article X:3(a) of the GATT 1994, the substantive content of penalty laws of the member States used to enforce EC customs law cannot be viewed as acts of administration with respect to laws, regulations, decisions and rulings covered by Article X:1 of the GATT. Therefore, substantive differences in penalty laws between member States cannot be considered to be in violation of Article X:3(a) of the GATT 1994. Therefore, the Panel finds no violation of Article X:3(a) of the GATT 1994 with respect to the substantive differences in penalty laws between member States.[1433]

7.445 The Panel does wish to note, however, that while the Panel is of the view that substantive differences in penalty laws between member States cannot be considered to be in violation of Article X:3(a) of the GATT 1994, nevertheless, differences in the way member States have applied the judicial decision issued by the ECJ in *Jose Teodoro de Andrade* v. *Director da Alfândega de Leixões*, which requires that infringements of EC law are penalized through measures that make the penalty effective, proportionate and dissuasive, could, in theory, be considered to be in violation of Article X:3(a) of the GATT 1994. In this regard, the Panel notes that judicial decisions of the kind issued by the ECJ in the

[1430] United States' oral statement at the first substantive meeting, para. 50;. United States' reply to Panel question No. 32.

[1431] In this regard, see paragraphs 7.175 – 7.176.

[1432] *Jose Teodoro de Andrade* v. *Director da Alfândega de Leixões*, Case C-213/99, ECR I-11083 7 December 2000, para. 20 (Exhibit US-31).

[1433] In light of this conclusion, the Panel does not consider it necessary to determine whether or not penalty laws are properly categorised as "customs procedures", which was questioned by the European Communities in footnote 127 of its first written submission.

Andrade case fall within the scope of "laws, regulations, decisions and rulings of the kind described in [Article X:1 of the GATT 1994]". Further, the ECJ's decision in the *Andrade* case was confirmed in EC Council Resolution of 29 June 1995 on the effective uniform application of Community law and on the penalties applicable for breaches of Community law in the internal market.[1434] In the Panel's view, this Council Resolution also falls within the scope of "laws, regulations, decisions and rulings of the kind described in [Article X:1 of the GATT 1994]". The Panel considers that the acknowledgement by the European Communities in the context of this dispute of substantive differences in penalty laws among member States could indicate that the judicial decision issued by the ECJ in *Jose Teodoro de Andrade* v. *Director da Alfândega de Leixões* and EC Council Resolution of 29 June 1995 on the effective uniform application of Community law and on the penalties applicable for breaches of Community law in the internal market are not being administered in a uniform manner by the member States in violation of Article X:3(a) of the GATT 1994. However, the Panel will not seek to determine whether or not the manner of administration by the member States of the judicial decision issued by the ECJ in *Jose Teodoro de Andrade* v. *Director da Alfândega de Leixões* and EC Council Resolution of 29 June 1995 on the effective uniform application of Community law and on the penalties applicable for breaches of Community law in the internal market is actually in violation of Article X:3(a) of the GATT 1994 given that the United States did not allege a violation of Article X:3(a) of the GATT 1994 in this regard.

(iii) Processing under customs control

Summary of the parties' arguments

7.446 The **United States** notes that "processing under customs control" allows duty to be assessed on a product that is imported into the European Communities once it has been further processed in the European Communities following importation rather than imposing duties on the imported product itself. According to the United States, in the European Communities, eligibility to use this procedure is determined according to an "economic conditions" assessment set out in EC law.[1435] The United States submits that, under Annex 76 of the Implementing Regulation, the "economic conditions" are deemed to be fulfilled for certain goods and operations but for all other goods and operations, an assessment of the economic conditions must be made on a case-by-case basis by the customs authorities of the member State in which an application is made.[1436]

7.447 The United States argues that, although the assessment of whether or not the "economic conditions" have been fulfilled in a given case entails an EC-wide

---

[1434] Exhibit EC-41. In particular, the Council Resolution requests the member States to "take action to ensure that, when Community acts are transposed into national legislation, Community law is duly applied with the same effectiveness and thoroughness as national law and that, in any event, the penalty provisions adopted are effective, proportionate and dissuasive".

[1435] United States' first written submission, paras. 27 and 103.

[1436] United States' first written submission, para. 104 referring to Article 552(1) of the Implementing Regulation (Exhibit US-6).

assessment, EC customs law makes no provision for uniform application of that assessment throughout the European Communities. The United States argues that different member States apply the tests differently, which can have a significant commercial impact.[1437] In this regard, the United States notes that Article 502(3) of the Implementing Regulation states that "the examination shall establish whether the use of non-Community sources enables processing activities to be created or maintained in the Community". The United States submits that at least one member State's authorities appear to apply tests that go beyond this basic guideline.[1438] The United States argues in particular that, in the United Kingdom, authorities require an importer to show not only that "the use of non-Community sources enables processing activities to be created or maintained in the Community" as provided by Article 502(3), but also that the proposed processing will not "harm[ ] the essential interests of Community producers of similar goods."[1439] The United States submits that, in contrast, the substance of French law implementing relevant provisions of EC customs law identifies a one-prong economic effects test for deciding whether to permit processing under customs control.[1440] The United States submits that, in essence, French regulations simply require an importer to satisfy the condition set out in Article 502(3) of the Implementing Regulation and, therefore, do not impose the additional test of demonstrating the absence of harm to competitors in the European Communities that is contained in UK law.[1441] Therefore, applicants to the French customs authority are not told that the information they provide must also show that the proposed processing activity will not adversely affect the essential interests of Community producers of similar goods. Nor are they told the types of evidence applicants should provide to satisfy the second prong to the economic test.[1442]

7.448 According to the United States, a straightforward comparison between the French guidance and the UK guidance demonstrates that France and the United Kingdom are administering Article 133 of the Community Customs Code and Articles 502(3) and 552 of the Implementing Regulation non-uniformly. The United States clarifies that it has not made any arguments with respect to the application of the French law. According to the United States, this is not necessary because French law and the UK law – both tools for the administration of the EC law – are facially divergent.[1443] According to the United States, the fact that different member States explicitly apply different tests, with at least one member State requiring affirmative evidence of the absence of harm to competitors in the European Communities and others simply requiring evidence of the creation or maintenance of processing within the European Communities, is stark

1437 United States' first written submission, para. 27.

1438 United States' first written submission, para. 105.

1439 United States' first written submission, para. 106 referring to HM Customs & Excise, Notice 237, "Processing Under Customs Control (PCC)", June 2003 (Exhibit US-34).

1440 Bulletin officiel des douanes no. 6527, 31 August 2001, para. 83 (as modified by BOD no. 6609, 4 November 2004) (Exhibit US-35).

1441 United States' first written submission, para. 107.

1442 United States' reply to Panel question No. 140.

1443 United States' reply to Panel question No. 139.

evidence of a lack of uniformity in administration.[1444] The United States submits that, therefore, the application of each of those laws will *necessarily* diverge from each other.[1445]

7.449 In response, the **European Communities** argues that the French and UK documents referred to in the United States' arguments do not constitute "law". Their nature is simply that of guidance, which must always be interpreted in line with EC law. The European Communities submits that, therefore, the United States challenges what it considers to be a divergence between the French and the UK guidance concerning processing under customs control.[1446]

7.450 The **United States** submits in response that, under the Community Customs Code and the Implementing Regulation, customs authorities must make an "economic conditions" assessment to determine whether certain applications for processing under customs control should be granted. The manner in which different member State authorities administer that measure of general application is sometimes set forth in manuals or bulletins or other member State-specific documents. These documents explain how member States administer the EC regulations on processing under customs control and, therefore, serve an administrative function. That is, they prescribe how other laws – certain articles of the Community Customs Code and the Implementing Regulation – will be carried out. The United States submits that, to the extent that different member States' manuals or bulletins prescribe different means of carrying out the relevant EC rules, they evidence non-uniformity in the administration of those rules. According to the United States, non-uniformity in the application of the economic conditions test by different member State authorities is evident in the substance of manuals and bulletins that prescribe how the test is to be carried out in different member States.[1447]

7.451 The **European Communities** argues that Article 133(e) of the Community Customs Code restricts authorisation for processing under control to cases "where the necessary conditions for the procedure to help create or maintain a processing activity in the Community without adversely affecting the essential interests of Community producers of similar goods (economic conditions) are fulfilled". According to the European Communities, Article 502(3) of the Implementing Regulation repeats the first part of the sentence, which must be considered as an abbreviated reference to the requirements laid down in Article 133(e) of the Community Customs Code. The European Communities submits that the situation could not be otherwise considering that the Implementing Regulation, which has been adopted by the Commission, is implementing legislation and cannot modify the requirements laid down by the Community Customs Code.[1448] The European Communities submits that, furthermore, the French "Bulletin officiel des douanes" also refers to the test relating to the absence of

1444 United States' first written submission, para. 107.
1445 United States' reply to Panel question No. 139.
1446 European Communities' comments on the United States' reply to Panel question No. 139.
1447 United States' reply to Panel question No. 27.
1448 European Communities' first written submission, para. 413.

harm to competitors in the European Communities.[1449] The European Communities submits that the second subparagraph in paragraphs 78 and 79 of the French guidance underline the obligation upon the requesting party to provide information on the lack of adverse effects on the essential interests of Community producers of similar goods.[1450]

7.452 The European Communities concludes that there is no divergence between the French and UK documents and that, therefore, it is for the United States to prove the existence of divergent application of the conditions for processing under customs control. According to the European Communities, the United States has submitted no such proof.[1451] The European Communities submits that, in the absence of any evidence demonstrating that the French authorities follow a constant practice deviating from Article 133(e) of the Community Customs Code, the United States has failed to prove the existence of a pattern of non-uniform administration in relation to the processing under customs control procedure.[1452]

7.453 The **United States** responds that the mention of absence of harm to competitors in the French customs bulletin is simply an introductory paraphrase of certain provisions from the Community Customs Code. After the introduction, the bulletin specifies that the economic conditions test will be carried out according to the modalities set forth thereafter ("il s'effectue selon les modalités définies ci-après"). The relevant modality makes no reference to harm to Community producers.[1453]

7.454 The **European Communities** argues in response that the United States' criticism is based on an isolated and incorrect interpretation of the French guidance, which has to be interpreted in the context of the EC legislation. The guidance refers to the economic conditions required to obtain an authorisation to process under customs control in the same way as Article 502(3) of the Implementing Regulation – namely, by using an abbreviation of the requirements laid down in Article 133(e) of the Community Custom Code. The French authorities require the same kind of information as the United Kingdom: the information needed to assess whether "the necessary conditions for the procedure to help create or maintain a processing activity in the Community without adversely affecting the essential interests of Community producers of similar goods (economic conditions) are fulfilled".[1454] The European Communities submits that this interpretation is supported by paragraph 78 of the French guidance, which, within Chapter III "Examination of economic conditions", plays the role of a chapeau to Section I, where paragraph 83 is located. Paragraph 78 provides that: "Articles 117-c, 133-e, and 148-c of the Community Customs Code stipulate that

[1449] European Communities' first written submission, para. 415 referring to Bulletin officiel des douanes no. 6527 at para. 78, 31 August 2001, p. 17 (as modified by BOD no. 6609, 4 November 2004) (Exhibit US-35).

[1450] European Communities' comments on the United States' reply to Panel question No. 140.

[1451] European Communities' comments on the United States' reply to Panel question No. 139.

[1452] European Communities' second written submission, para. 183.

[1453] United States' reply to Panel question No. 4.

[1454] European Communities' second written submission, para. 178.

the granting of an authorization for inward processing, outward processing, or processing under customs control must not adversely affect the essential interests of Community producers of goods comparable to those used."[1455] The European Communities submits that paragraph 78 is more than simply an introductory paraphrase of certain provisions from the Community Customs Code. This paragraph reminds, for Section I as a whole, that the absence of adverse effects on the essential interests of Community producers is a general economic condition that is common to the three customs procedures therein covered (inward processing, outward processing and processing under customs control), as it is clearly laid down in Articles 117 (c), 148(c) and 133(e) of the Community Customs Code, respectively.[1456]

Analysis by the Panel

7.455 The Panel notes that the United States challenges substantive divergence in guidance between France and the United Kingdom regarding the administration of provisions of EC customs law concerning processing under customs control.[1457] The United States explains that such *substantive* divergences in such guidance necessarily result in divergent *application* of EC customs law in this area by French and UK customs authorities.[1458]

7.456 The law concerning processing under customs control which the United States alleges is being administered in a non-uniform fashion exists at the EC level. In particular, the United States challenges the manner of administration of Article 133 of the Community Customs Code and Articles 502(3) and 552 of the Implementing Regulation regarding assessment of the economic conditions for allowing processing under customs control.[1459]

7.457 In the Panel's view, the application of EC law regarding processing under customs control constitutes an act of administration within the meaning of Article X:3(a) of the GATT 1994. This act of administration is a matter within the Panel's terms of reference since it amounts to an instance of administration of the Article 133 of the Community Customs Code and Articles 502(3) and 552 of the Implementing Regulation with respect to procedures for the entry and release of goods.[1460]

7.458 With respect to the question of whether or not the application of EC law regarding processing under customs control in the member States is "uniform" within the meaning of Article X:3(a) of the GATT 1994, the Panel recalls its finding in paragraph 7.135 above that geographic uniformity is required under Article X:3(a) of the GATT 1994. That is, administration should be uniform in different places within a particular WTO Member. The Panel also recalls its finding in paragraph 7.135 above that the form, nature and scale of the alleged non-

[1455] European Communities' second written submission, para. 179 referring to Exhibit US-35.
[1456] European Communities' second written submission, para. 180.
[1457] United States' oral statement at the second substantive meeting, para. 75.
[1458] United States' reply to Panel question No. 139.
[1459] United States' replies to Panel question Nos. 124 and 139.
[1460] In this regard, see paragraphs 7.188 – 7.190 above.

uniform administration and the laws, regulations, judicial decisions and rulings that are allegedly being administered in a non-uniform manner should be taken into consideration when interpreting the term "uniform" in Article X:3(a) of the GATT 1994. The Panel considers that the United States' challenge with respect to the application of EC law regarding processing under customs control is narrow in nature. It involves the application of a few provisions of the Community Customs Code and the Implementing Regulation – namely, Article 133 of the Community Customs Code and Articles 502(3) and 552 of the Implementing Regulation. Therefore, given the narrowness of this challenge, the Panel considers that a high degree of uniformity is required for the purposes of Article X:3(a) of the GATT 1994. We now turn to the facts to determine whether or not this high degree of uniformity has been achieved with respect to the application of EC law regarding processing under customs control.

7.459 In summary, Article 133(e) of the Community Customs Code provides that, before granting authorization for processing under customs control pursuant to Article 85 of the Community Customs Code, customs authorities must examine the economic consequences of the use of the processing under customs control procedures to determine whether or not the procedure helps to create or maintain a processing activity in the European Communities without adversely affecting the essential interests of EC producers of similar goods. Article 502(3) of the Implementing Regulation provides that, in respect of processing under customs control arrangements, the examination shall establish whether the use of non-Community sources enables processing activities to be created or maintained in the Community. Article 552 and Part A of Annex 76 of the Implementing Regulation set out the cases in which the economic conditions are deemed to be fulfilled so that, in those cases, an examination of the economic conditions is not necessary. For the types of goods and operations mentioned in Part B of Annex 76 of the Implementing Regulation and those not covered by Part A of that Annex, the examination of the economic conditions must take place at Community level, through the relevant Committee procedure. For the types of goods and operations not mentioned in Annex 76 of the Implementing Regulation, pursuant to Articles 502(1) and 552(1) of the Implementing Regulation, the examination of the economic conditions shall take place at national level. When examinations take place at the national level, member States must communicate to the Commission relevant information in accordance with Article 522 of the Implementing Regulation. Furthermore, pursuant to Articles 503 and 504 of the Implementing Regulation, if a member State objects to an authorization issued or if the customs authorities concerned wish to consult before or after issuing an authorization, an examination of the economic condition may take place at Community level.

7.460 In the context of the United States' allegations of non-uniform administration of EC law regarding processing under customs control, the Panel understands that the act(s) of administration which the United States challenges is the manner in which the French and UK customs authorities apply EC customs law. In support of its challenge, the United States relies upon guidance issued by the French and UK customs authorities respectively concerning the administration of EC law on processing under customs control. According to the United States, the divergence in the contents of the French and UK guidance necessarily means that the manner in which the French and UK customs authorities implement or put into effect EC customs law will be non-uniform in violation of Article X:3(a) of the GATT 1994.

7.461 To demonstrate the manner of administration by the UK customs authorities, the United States refers to HM Customs & Excise Notice 237, entitled "Processing under Customs Control (PCC)" dated June 2003. The introduction states that the purpose of the Notice is to explain the procedure pertaining to processing under customs control.[1461] The Notice explains that the law on processing under customs control and other customs procedures is contained in the Community Customs Code and the Implementing Regulation.[1462] Additionally, the Notice states in capitals and bold that "Nothing In This Notice Overrides The Law" and subsequently that "this notice is not the law".[1463] The Notice also states that:

> "The DTI/DEFRA will use the evidence provided to establish whether the use of non-Community goods enables processing activities to be created or maintained in the Community without harming the essential interests of Community producers of similar goods. There are therefore two aspects to the economic test and you must provide evidence to show both the impact upon your business and the impact upon any other community producers of the imported goods. ..."[1464]

7.462 Regarding the manner of administration by the French customs authorities, the United States refers to Bulletin officiel des douanes no. 6527 dated 31 August 2001. The cover page of the Bulletin notes certain documentary references – namely, the Community Customs Code and the Implementing Regulation.[1465] The first paragraph of the chapter of Bulletin dealing with the "economic conditions" test (namely, Chapter III) also makes specific reference to relevant provisions of EC law, including Article 133(e) of the Community Customs Code, which concerns processing under customs control.[1466] Regarding the requirements applicable under the economic conditions test for all customs procedures to which the test applies, the first paragraph of Chapter III provides that: "Articles 117-c, 133-e, and 148-c of the Community Customs Code stipulate that the granting of an authorization for inward processing, outward processing, or processing under customs control must not adversely affect the essential interests of

---

[1461] HM Customs & Excise, Notice 237, "Processing Under Customs Control (PCC)", June 2003, para. 1.1 (Exhibit US-34).

[1462] HM Customs & Excise, Notice 237, "Processing Under Customs Control (PCC)", June 2003, para. 1.4 (Exhibit US-34).

[1463] *Ibid.*

[1464] HM Customs & Excise, Notice 237, "Processing Under Customs Control (PCC)", June 2003, para. 15 (Exhibit US-34). See also para. 3.4.

[1465] Bulletin officiel des douanes no. 6527, 31 August 2001, p. 1 (as modified by BOD no. 6609, 4 November 2004) (Exhibit US-35).

[1466] Bulletin officiel des douanes no. 6527, 31 August 2001, para. 78, p. 17 (as modified by BOD no. 6609, 4 November 2004) (Exhibit US-35).

Community producers of goods comparable to those used."[1467] A latter paragraph in Chapter III, which exclusively concerns processing under customs control, provides that: ""With regard to processing under customs control, block 10 of the model request must be completed with information showing that use of this customs regime will create or maintain a processing activity in the Community (goods and operations not mentioned in of Annex 76, Part A of the IPC)."[1468]

7.463 In the Panel's view, when read as a whole, the UK and French documents providing guidance regarding processing under customs control contain the same two substantive requirements that are mentioned in Article 133(e) of the Community Customs Code – namely, a requirement to determine whether or not the processing under customs control procedure helps to create or maintain a processing activity in the European Communities and a requirement to determine whether or not the essential interests of EC producers of similar goods are being affected. In particular, this is evident from the excerpt of the UK guidance set out in paragraph 7.461 above, which explicitly refers to the fact that the customs authority to whom an application for processing under customs control has been made will establish whether the use of non-Community goods enables processing activities to be created or maintained in the Community without harming the essential interests of Community producers of similar goods. Similarly, in the case of the French guidance, one paragraph of the Bulletin, which applies globally to all procedures to which an "economic conditions" test applies (of which processing under customs control is one), specifically refers to the need to determine whether or not the essential interests of EC producers of similar goods are being affected. Subsequently, in a paragraph that deals exclusively with processing under customs control, a reference is made to the requirement that the procedure must help to create or maintain a processing activity in the European Communities. Furthermore, as is evident from paragraphs 7.461 – 7.462 above, both the UK and French documents providing guidance make reference to the governing EC law. The Panel considers that anyone reading and/or applying the UK and French guidance documents would understand that those documents should be read in the light of the relevant aspects of EC law upon which they are based, including Article 133(e) of the Community Customs Code, to which the French guidance makes explicit reference.

7.464 In the light of the foregoing, the Panel considers that the United States has not proved the existence of a substantive divergence in French and UK guidance regarding the administration of provisions of EC customs law governing processing under customs control. Furthermore, the United States has provided no evidence that the manner in which the French and UK customs authorities actually apply such guidance results in practice is non-uniform within the meaning of Article X:3(a) of the GATT 1994.

[1467] *Ibid.*

[1468] Bulletin officiel des douanes no. 6527, 31 August 2001, para. 83, p. 19 (as modified by BOD no. 6609, 4 November 2004) (Exhibit US-35).

7.465 Accordingly, the Panel concludes that the United States has not proved that the manner of administration of Article 133 of the Community Customs Code and Articles 502(3) and 552 of the Implementing Regulation regarding processing under customs control is non-uniform among the member States in violation of Article X:3(a) of the GATT 1994.

(iv) Local clearance procedures

Summary of the parties' arguments

7.466 The **United States** notes that "local clearance procedures" include procedures whereby importers may cause goods to enter into free circulation in the European Communities at their place of business, rather than presenting goods for inspection by the customs authorities. According to the United States, the actual requirements that users of this procedure must meet vary significantly from member State to member State, with the process being significantly more burdensome in some member States than others.[1469] The United States argues that serious differences do, in fact, exist and their very existence illustrates lack of uniformity in the administration of EC customs law.[1470] The United States submits that different member States administer the local clearance procedures differently, including with respect to involvement of customs authorities prior to release of goods, post-release requirements, and document retention requirements.[1471]

7.467 The United States refers to the following table to illustrate the differences:[1472]

Member State	Requirements prior to release	Customs involvement prior to release	Requirements after release	Document retention requirements
United Kingdom	Manifest data provided to customs electronically without modification.	None.	Supplementary data on classification, valuation, origin transmitted to customs electronically.	Importer must retain supporting documents for 4 years.

[1469] United States' first written submission, paras. 28 and 110.
[1470] United States' first written submission, para. 117.
[1471] United States' reply to Panel question No. 30.
[1472] This table is contained in paragraph 116 of the United States' first written submission.

Member State	Requirements prior to release	Customs involvement prior to release	Requirements after release	Document retention requirements
France	Manifest data supplemented with classification, valuation and other data and registered in importer's inventory system; importer informs customs of initial declaration.	May inspect within specified time period prior to release.	Supplementary data, including supporting documents – DV1 valuation form, invoices, certificates – provided to customs in hard copy.	
Germany	Manifest data transmitted to customs, including translation of goods' description into German; initial declaration, including classification, valuation and origin information, made to customs.	May inspect within specified time period prior to release.	Supplementary data, including supporting documents – DV1 valuation form, invoices, certifications – provided to customs.	Importer must retain supporting documents for 6 years.
Italy	Manifest data transmitted to customs.	May inspect within 1 hour.	Supplementary declaration transmitted electronically; no DV1 valuation form required.	Importer must retain supporting documents for 5 years.
Netherlands	Initial declaration made through entry into importer's inventory system; contents of initial declaration negotiated locally.	May inspect within specified time prior to release.	DV1 valuation form transmitted electronically. Certain documents (e.g., licenses and certificates showing entitlement to preferential tariff treatment) required with supplementary declaration, but not invoices or airwaybills.	Importer must retain supporting documents for 10 years.

7.468 The **European Communities** submits that the United States does not provide a single exhibit to illustrate and support its claim, which renders it impossible for the European Communities to defend itself and does not allow the Panel to verify whether or not the United States' claim is substantiated. Further, it is clear that the United States has misunderstood the different steps in the process followed when goods are imported through this procedure. In addition, the United States' description of the procedure and of the documents retention requirements contains fundamental errors.[1473] Therefore, according to the European Communities, the claim of non-uniform administration under Article X:3(a) of the GATT with respect to local clearance procedures is not sustained.[1474]

7.469 In relation to customs involvement prior to release, the European Communities submits that the fact that, at the frontier, anti-smuggling and admissibility checks are made electronically does not mean that there is no involvement of customs. Moreover, if the goods do not fulfil these checks, there will be a customs action, such as a physical check and seizure. The European Communities submits that it is, therefore, wrong to state that there is no customs involvement prior to release in the United Kingdom.[1475] Taking the United Kingdom and France as representative examples in relation to inspection of goods by the customs authorities prior to release, according to the European Communities, there is no contradiction between the practices in these two member States. In both cases, customs officials may or may not inspect goods prior to release.[1476]

7.470 Concerning the requirements prior to release in the framework of the local clearance procedures, the European Communities submits that it is not the shipping manifest data itself which is provided but a simplified declaration containing certain data, where the trader has to insert a reference number.[1477] The European Communities adds that the use of both electronic clearance systems and paper-based systems is possible. The European Communities submits that, as far as local clearance procedures are concerned, detailed Community rules for paper-based clearance can be found in Articles 263 to 267 of the Implementing Regulation. Where the clearance system used is electronic, additional rules are applicable and can be found in Articles 4(a) – (c) and Articles 222-224 of the same Regulation.[1478] As regards supporting document requirements, the European Communities submits that all member States apply identical rules and that the issue raised by the United States concerning the valuation form "DV1" again stems from a confusion: all member States allow operators having regular trade flows with the same suppliers to submit only once the relevant DV1 together with the initial application to benefit from local clearance procedures.[1479]

7.471 In relation to the document retention requirements, the European Communities submits that the information provided by the United States regarding the Netherlands is wrong: the retention period is 7 years since 1 July 1998, under Article 8 (3) of the Douanewet (Customs Act). The European Communities submits that, besides, Article 16(1) of the Community Customs Code provides that the requisite documents shall be retained for a minimum period of three years, but leaves member States the possibility to stipulate longer periods taking

---

1473 European Communities' oral statement at the first substantive meeting, para. 49.
1474 *Ibid.*
1475 European Communities' first written submission, para. 423.
1476 European Communities' second written submission, para. 186.
1477 European Communities' first written submission, para. 422.
1478 European Communities' first written submission, para. 424.
1479 European Communities' first written submission, para. 425.

into account their general administrative and fiscal needs and practices. The European Communities argues that the resulting time-frame differences between the four member States for which the United States submits evidence (from 4 to 7 years) are not fundamental. In this regard, the European Communities reiterates that Article X:3(a) of the GATT 1994 concerns the administration of customs laws, not the customs laws themselves and this provision does not impose an obligation to harmonise legislation within a WTO member. The existing time-frame differences for document retention between some EC member States pertain to the content of customs law, not to their administration. Therefore, according to the European Communities, these differences do not come within the scope of Article X:3(a) of the GATT 1994.[1480] In addition, the European Communities argues that, in light of the GATT panel in *EEC – Dessert Apples*, any such differences are not substantial in nature and do not entail a lack of uniformity in the application of customs laws contrary to Article X:3(a) of the GATT 1994. The European Communities considers, therefore, that the United States' claim under Article X:3(a) of the GATT 1994 is not founded in relation to local clearance procedures.[1481]

7.472 The **United States** submits that the European Communities' statements regarding local clearance procedures identify the outer parameters in which different customs authorities in the European Communities must operate. The United States submits that, while it does not dispute the European Communities' characterization of what those outer parameters are, it does contend that different customs authorities in the European Communities administer the local clearance procedures differently within those parameters.[1482]

Analysis by the Panel

7.473 The Panel notes that the essence of the United States' challenge with respect to local clearance procedures is that the actual requirements users of this procedure must meet vary significantly from member State to member State, with the process being significantly more burdensome in some member States than in others.[1483] The United States submits that such differences regarding the requirements imposed by customs authorities of the European Communities in the context of local clearance procedures amount to non-uniform administration of Articles 263 – 267 of the Implementing Regulation.

7.474 In the Panel's view, the imposition of requirements regarding local clearance procedures constitutes an act of administration within the meaning of Article X:3(a) of the GATT 1994. This act of administration is a matter within the Panel's terms of reference since it amounts to an instance of administration of Articles 263 – 267 of the Implementing Regulation with respect to procedures for the entry and release of goods.[1484]

[1480] European Communities' first written submission, para. 426.

[1481] European Communities' first written submission, paras. 427 – 428.

[1482] United States' reply to Panel question No. 137(c).

[1483] United States' first written submission, paras. 28 and 110.

[1484] In this regard, see paragraphs 7.188 – 7.190 above.

7.475 Regarding the question of whether or not the imposition of requirements for local clearance procedures is "uniform" within the meaning of Article X:3(a) of the GATT 1994, the Panel recalls its finding in paragraph 7.135 above that geographic uniformity is required under Article X:3(a) of the GATT 1994. That is, administration should be uniform in different places within a particular WTO Member. The Panel also recalls its finding in paragraph 7.135 above that the form, nature and scale of the alleged non-uniform administration and the laws, regulations, judicial decisions and rulings that are allegedly being administered in a non-uniform manner should be taken into consideration when interpreting the term "uniform" in Article X:3(a) of the GATT 1994. The Panel considers that the United States' challenge with respect to the imposition of requirements regarding local clearance procedures is narrow in nature. It involves the application of a few provisions of the Implementing Regulation – namely, Articles 263 – 267 of the Implementing Regulation. Therefore, given the narrowness of this challenge, the Panel considers that a high degree of uniformity is required for the purposes of Article X:3(a) of the GATT 1994. We now turn to the facts to determine whether or not this high degree of uniformity has been achieved with respect to the imposition of requirements regarding local clearance procedures.

7.476 In support of its allegations of non-uniformity in violation of Article X:3(a) of the GATT 1994, the United States relies on a table which, it submits, proves the existence of differences among the member States in the context of local clearance procedures regarding requirements imposed prior to release, customs involvement prior to release, requirements imposed after release and document retention requirements. The Panel notes that the United States has not submitted any factual material to support what are, in essence, nothing more than assertions contained in the table of alleged differences upon which the United States relies.

7.477 Therefore, the Panel concludes that the United States has not proved that differences between member States exist regarding the actual requirements users of the local clearance procedures must meet between the member States. Consequently, the United States has not proved that Articles 263 – 267 of the Implementing Regulation are administered in a non-uniform manner in violation of Article X:3(a) of the GATT 1994.

(v) Summary and conclusions

7.478 In summary, the Panel finds that, with respect to the United States' allegations of non-uniform administration of the Community Customs Code and the Implementing Regulation in the area of customs procedures:

(a) The Panel finds no violation of Article X:3(a) of the GATT 1994 with respect to the manner of administration of Article 78(2) of the Community Customs Code regarding the requirements imposed for audit procedures[1485] following the release of products for free circulation in the European Communities.

(b) The Panel finds no violation of Article X:3(a) of the GATT 1994 with respect to the substantive differences in penalty laws[1486] between the member States.

(c) The United States has not proved that the manner of administration of Article 133 of the Community Customs Code and Articles 502(3) and 552 of the Implementing Regulation regarding processing under customs control is non-uniform in violation of Article X:3(a) of the GATT 1994.

(d) The United States has not proved that the administration of Articles 263 – 267 of the Implementing Regulation regarding local clearance procedures is non-uniform in violation of Article X:3(a) of the GATT 1994.

(e) Allegations of non-uniform administration regarding Article 221(3) of the Community Customs Code

(i) Summary of the parties' arguments

7.479 The **United States** submits that Article 221(3) of the Community Customs Code prescribes a three-year period following the incurrence of a customs debt during which liability for the debt may be communicated to the debtor. It also provides for suspension of the three-year period during the pendency of an appeal. The United States argues that Article 221(3) of the Community Customs Code does not provide any other circumstance under which the three-year period may be suspended.[1487] According to the United States, the customs offices of the 25 member States are each responsible for administering those rules but they administer those rules differently. The United States submits that the French customs authorities have taken the position that the three-year period may be suspended by the institution of any administrative proceeding (procès-verbal) investigating a possible customs infraction, even if that proceeding does not result in the imposition of any penalty against the debtor. According to the United States, despite divergence with other customs authorities in other parts of the European Communities, France's highest court (the Cour de Cassation) has declined to refer to the ECJ the question of this rule's consistency with EC law.[1488] The United States submits that the *Camcorders* case illustrates the non-uniform ad-

[1485] The Panel recalls its conclusion in footnote 747 above that the Panel does not consider it necessary to determine whether or not audits following the release of goods for free circulation are properly categorised as "customs procedures".

[1486] The Panel recalls its conclusion in footnote 776 above that the Panel does not consider it necessary to determine whether or not penalty laws are properly categorised as "customs procedures".

[1487] United States' reply to Panel question No. 179.

[1488] United States' comments on European Communities' reply to Panel question No. 146 referring Judgment of the Cour de Cassation, Case No. 143, 13 June 2001, pp. 439-40 (Exhibit US-67); Judgment of the Cour de Cassation, Case No. 144, 13 June 2001, p. 448 (Exhibit US-68).

ministration of Article 221(3) of the Community Customs Code. Specifically, in the context of that case, the French customs authorities take the view that the amended explanatory note to the Common Customs Tariff can be applied to imports pre-dating the note but, additionally, unlike customs offices in other parts of the European Communities, French customs authorities take the view that the note can be applied to imports even if the customs debt attributable to those imports arose more than three years in the past. Thus, according to the United States, the camcorders importer in France remains vulnerable for additional duty collections on imports made in 1999, even though customs offices in other parts of the European Communities would consider such additional collection to be time-barred. The United States argues that, therefore, in the context of the *Camcorders* case, France's unique interpretation of Article 221(3) of the Community Customs Code leaves the importer vulnerable to additional duty collections on imports that occurred six years ago, even though other member States would consider such additional collection to be barred.[1489]

7.480 The **European Communities** submits that the application of Article 221(3) of the Community Customs Code, which, according to the European Communities, concerns the period during which a customs debt may be communicated to the debtor, is not within the Panel's terms of reference because it does not fall within the scope of customs areas listed in the United States' request for establishment of a panel. The European Communities adds that the United States did not raise the alleged non-uniform application of Article 221(3) of the Community Customs Code until the Panel's second substantive meeting with the parties. Further, in a reply to a question from the Panel[1490], the United States lists a number of provisions in respect of which it claims to have established a lack of uniform administration but does not include Article 221 of the Community Customs Code. According to the European Communities, this implies that the United States either does not believe it has established its case regarding the non-uniform administration of Article 221 of the Community Customs Code or it concedes that this claim does not fall within the Panel's terms of reference.[1491]

7.481 In response, the **United States** accepts that Article 221(3) of the Community Customs Code concerns the period during which a customs debt may be communicated. However, the United States disagrees with the implication that this has nothing to do with collection of the customs debt. According to the United States, the period during which the customs debt may be communicated to the debtor is obviously essential to collection of the debt. The United States clarifies that, if the period for such communication has expired, then so has the possibility of collecting any debt not previously communicated.[1492] The United States also submits that the European Communities' assertion that Article 221(3) of the Community Customs Code does not concern any of the areas of customs administration referred to in the United States' request for establishment of a

[1489] United States' oral statement at the second substantive meeting, para. 31.

[1490] Panel question No. 124.

[1491] European Communities' reply to Panel question No. 172; European Communities' comments on the United States' reply to Panel question No. 124.

[1492] United States' reply to Panel question No. 180, footnote 31.

panel appears to confuse the claims made by the United States with arguments advanced by it in support of those claims. According to the United States, its claims under Article X:3(a) of the GATT are set out clearly and with specificity in the first paragraph of its panel request. There, the United States claims that "the manner in which the European Communities ('EC') administers its laws, regulations, decisions and rulings of the kind described in Article X:1 of the General Agreement on Tariffs and Trade 1994 ('GATT 1994') is not uniform, impartial and reasonable, and therefore is inconsistent with Article X:3(a) of the GATT 1994." The request then goes on to identify precisely the laws, regulation, decisions, and rulings of the kind described in Article X:1 the United States alleges the European Communities to have failed to administer in the manner required by Article X:3(a), including the Community Customs Code. The United States submits that Article 221(3) of the Community Customs Code forms a part of the Community Customs Code. Further, the subject-matter of Article 221(3) of the Community Customs Code falls within the illustrative, non-exhaustive list of customs areas contained in the United States' request. The United States adds that it discussed Article 221(3) of the Community Customs Code in its oral statement at the Panel's second substantive meeting.[1493]

7.482 The **European Communities** also submits that Article 221(3) of the Community Customs Code only addresses the period during which a customs debt may be communicated to the debtor. In contrast, the question of the substantive conditions under which the customs debt may be retroactively recovered is addressed in Article 220 of the Community Customs Code. Moreover, the European Communities submits that it is incorrect to state that the only permitted exception to Article 221(3) of the Community Customs Code is the lodging of an appeal, which suspends the three-year period for communicating the customs debt. Another relevant exception is Article 221(4) of the Community Customs Code, according to which, where the customs debt is the result of an act which, at the time it was committed, was liable to give rise to criminal court proceedings, the amount may, under the conditions set out in the provisions in force, be communicated to the debtor after the expiry of the three-year period. The European Communities notes that the ECJ has clarified that the question as to whether an act may give raise to criminal proceedings is a question of member States' law, not of Community law.[1494]

(ii) Analysis by the Panel

7.483 A preliminary question for the Panel's consideration is whether or not Article 221(3) of the Community Customs Code falls within the Panel's terms of reference. According to the European Communities, Article 221(3) of the Community Customs Code, which concerns the period during which a customs debt may be communicated to the debtor, is not within the Panel's terms of reference because it does not fall within the scope of customs areas listed in he United

[1493] United States' reply to Panel question No. 178.

[1494] European Communities' reply to Panel question No. 172, para. 42 referring to Case C-273/90, *Meico-Fell*, [1991] ECR I-5569, para 13 (Exhibit EC-155).

States' request for establishment of a panel. The United States accepts that Article 221(3) of the Community Customs Code concerns the period during which a customs debt may be collected but submits that it is within the Panel's terms of reference since it forms a part of the Community Customs Code, which is listed in the United States' request for establishment of a panel and the subject-matter of Article 221(3) of the Community Customs Code falls within the illustrative, non-exhaustive list of customs areas contained in the United States' request.

7.484 The Panel recalls its finding in paragraph 7.33 above that, under our terms of reference, we are only authorized to consider the manner of administration by the national customs authorities of the member States of the Community Customs Code, the Implementing Regulation, the Common Customs Tariff, the TARIC and related measures in the areas of customs administration specifically identified in the United States' request for establishment of a panel – namely, the classification and valuation of goods, procedures for the classification and valuation of goods, procedures for the entry and release of goods, procedures for auditing entry statements after goods are released into free circulation, penalties and procedures regarding the imposition of penalties for violation of customs rules and record-keeping requirements. While it is clear that Article 221(3) is contained in one of the measures identified in the United States' request that are allegedly not being administered in a uniform manner in violation of Article X:3(a) of the GATT 1994 – namely, the Community Customs Code – it is also necessary to determine whether or not the subject-matter of Article 221(3) of the Community Customs Code is covered by the areas of customs administration specifically identified in that request. We turn, therefore, to the terms of Article 221 of the Community Customs Code.

7.485 Article 221 of the Community Customs Code is found in Chapter 3 of the Community Customs Code, which is entitled "Recovery of the amount of the Customs Debt". More particularly, Article 221 is found in Section 1 of Chapter 3, which is entitled "Entry in the accounts and communication of the amount of duty to the debtor." Article 221 provides that:

> "1. As soon as it has been entered in the accounts, the amount of duty shall be communicated to the debtor in accordance with appropriate procedures.
>
> 2. Where the amount of duty payable has been entered, for guidance, in the customs declaration, the customs authorities may specify that it shall not be communicated in accordance with paragraph 1 unless the amount of duty indicated does not correspond to the amount determined by the authorities.
>
> Without prejudice to the application of the second paragraph of Article 218(1), where use is made of the possibility provided for in the preceding subparagraph, release of the goods by the customs authorities shall be equivalent to communication to the debtor of the amount of duty entered in the accounts.
>
> 3. Communication to the debtor shall not take place after the expiry of a period of three years from the date on which the cus-

> toms debt was incurred. This period shall be suspended from the time an appeal within the meaning of Article 243 is lodged, for the duration of the appeal proceedings.
>
> 4. Where the customs debt is the result of an act which, at the time it was committed, was liable to give rise to criminal court proceedings, the amount may, under the conditions set out in the provisions in force, be communicated to the debtor after the expiry of the three-year period referred to in paragraph 3."

7.486 In the Panel's view, Article 221 of the Community Customs Code, including Article 221(3), relates to the recovery of and communication of customs debt. This is evident from the ordinary meaning of the terms of Article 221 as well as the context in which that Article is found such as the title of the Chapter and Section in which it is contained.

7.487 The Panel considers that Article 221 of the Community Customs Code, including Article 221(3), is not covered by any of the areas of customs administration specifically identified in the United States' request for establishment of a panel. In particular, the ordinary meaning of those areas does not appear to encompass the recovery and communication of customs debts.[1495] Therefore, we conclude that Article 221(3) of the Community Customs Code is outside our terms of reference with regard to the United States' claim that the administration of that provision violates Article X:3(a) of the GATT 1994. More specifically, the United States is precluded from arguing in this dispute that the manner of administration of Article 221(3) of the Community Customs Code is in violation of Article X:3(a) of the GATT 1994. However, this does not mean that the United States is prevented from relying upon the manner of administration of Article 221(3) of the Community Customs Code to the extent that it is relevant to the United States' claim that measures in the areas of customs administration that have been specifically identified in its request for establishment of a panel (such as, tariff classification) are being administered in a manner that is in violation of Article X:3(a) of the GATT 1994.[1496]

[1495] In this regard we note that the *Dictionary of International Trade*, 2000, defines the areas of customs administration specifically identified in the United States' request for establishment of a panel as follows: "Classification" is defined as "the categorization of merchandise" (page 40). "Valuation" is defined as "the appraisal of the worth of imported goods by customs officials for the purpose of determining the amount of duty payable in the importing country" (page 201). "Entry" is defined as "the process of, and documentation required for securing the release of imported merchandise" (page 72). "Audit" is defined as "a formal examination of records or documents" (page 20). "Penalties" is defined as the "charges assessed or action taken by customs in response to a violation of a customs-enforced regulation or law" (page 154). The meaning of the term "record-keeping" is self-explanatory. In addition, the World Customs Organization Glossary of International Customs Terms defines "release" as "action by the Customs to permit goods undergoing clearance to be placed at the disposal of the persons concerned".

[1496] The Panel notes in this regard that the United States relied upon Article 221(3) of the Community Customs Code with respect to its allegation that the way in which an amendment to an explanatory note to the Common Customs Tariff concerning camcorders was interpreted and applied varied from member State to member State: See paragraph 7.344 *et seq* above.

(f) Overall observations regarding the United States' allegations of non-uniform administration under Article X:3(a) of the GATT 1994

7.488 The Panel recalls the United States' argument that, the absence of a procedure or institution in the European Communities to ensure that divergences of administration among the customs authorities of the 25 member States do not occur or that promptly reconcile such divergences as a matter of course when they occur, necessarily results in non-uniform administration in breach of Article X:3(a) of the GATT 1994.[1497] The Panel further recalls that the United States argued that these structural shortcoming result in non-uniform administration with respect to all areas of the EC system of customs administration.[1498]

7.489 In paragraphs 7.156 – 7.192 above, the Panel explained its understanding of the manner in which the EC system of customs administration functions. The Panel recalls that it provided that explanation because it considers that such understanding provides important context for the examination of the particular instances of alleged violations of Article X:3(a) of the GATT 1994, which the Panel has been called upon to examine in the context of this dispute. In that explanation, the Panel considered each of the institutions and mechanisms referred to by the European Communities as playing an instrumental role in achieving uniform administration of EC customs law by the customs authorities of the member States. In its explanation, the Panel observed that certain features associated with a number of those institutions and mechanisms would not necessarily enhance uniform administration of EC customs law by the customs authorities of the member States and, at worst, might even cause non-uniform administration.

7.490 Nevertheless, the Panel is not authorized to make any findings on those institutions and mechanisms given that, as stated above in paragraph 7.64, the Panel's terms of reference preclude it from considering "as such" challenges of the design and structure of the EC system of customs administration, including components thereof. However, even if the Panel were authorized to make such findings, the Panel notes that the United States did not demonstrate that the design and structure of the EC system of customs administration, including components thereof necessarily result in a violation of Article X:3(a) of the GATT 1994. Rather, the United States referred to a number of apparently random instances of alleged violation of Article X:3(a) of the GATT 1994, without demonstrating to us that those examples are symptomatic and representative of underlying structural deficiencies in the EC system of customs administration. Moreover, the Panel recalls that the United States only proved to the Panel that Article X:3(a) of the GATT 1994 had actually been violated in three of the various instances of alleged violation of Article X:3(a) of the GATT 1994 to which it had referred in support of its claims.

[1497] United States' reply to Panel question No. 126(a).
[1498] United States' reply to Panel question No. 126(b).

E. *Claims Under Article X:3(b) of the GATT 1994*

1. *Article X:3(b) of the GATT 1994*

7.491 Article X:3(b) of the GATT 1994 provides that:

> "Each contracting party shall maintain, or institute as soon as practicable, judicial, arbitral or administrative tribunals or procedures for the purpose, *inter alia*, of the prompt review and correction of administrative action relating to customs matters. Such tribunals or procedures shall be independent of the agencies entrusted with administrative enforcement and their decisions shall be implemented by, and shall govern the practice of, such agencies unless an appeal is lodged with a court or tribunal of superior jurisdiction within the time prescribed for appeals to be lodged by importers; *Provided* that the central administration of such agency may take steps to obtain a review of the matter in another proceeding if there is good cause to believe that the decision is inconsistent with established principles of law or the actual facts."

2. *Findings requested by the United States under Article X:3(b) of the GATT 1994*

(a) Summary of the parties' arguments

7.492 The **United States** submits that Article X:3(b) of the GATT 1994 requires the European Communities as a WTO Member to have in place certain "judicial, arbitral or administrative tribunals or procedures." It then defines certain qualities that these tribunals or procedures must have. The United States clarifies that, in the present dispute, its claim relates to the requirement under Article X:3(b) of the GATT 1994 that the decisions of the tribunals or procedures required by that Article "govern the practice of" the agencies entrusted with administrative enforcement "unless an appeal is lodged with a court or tribunal of superior jurisdiction within the time prescribed for appeals to be lodged by importers."[1499] In particular, the United States submits that the European Communities does not fulfil its obligation under Article X:3(b) of the GATT 1994 because each of the multiple review tribunals it provides renders decisions that govern the practice only of a subset of agencies entrusted with administrative enforcement within a particular region in the European Communities but does not "govern the practice" of the European Communities' agencies in other member States.[1500]

7.493 The **European Communities** notes that it understands that the United States' claims under Article X:3(b) of the GATT 1994 do not concern the material scope of the control exercised by review tribunals or procedures under Article X:3(b) of the GATT 1994 nor the purpose of such review. The European Communities submits that, in its understanding, the United States' claim under

[1499] United States' second written submission, paras. 102-109; United States' reply to Panel question No. 141.

[1500] United States' second written submission, para. 102.

Article X:3(b) of the GATT 1994 focuses on the nature of the review to be conducted under that Article.[1501] More specifically, the European Communities submits that the United States' claims under Article X:3(b) of the GATT 1994 exclusively relate to the requirement that tribunals or procedures must govern the practice of the agencies entrusted with administrative enforcement.[1502]

(b) Analysis by the Panel

7.494 The Panel notes that, in its request for establishment of a panel, the United States made its claim under Article X:3(b) of the GATT 1994 in the following terms:

> "... the European Communities has failed to maintain, or institute as soon as practicable, judicial, arbitral or administrative tribunals or procedures for the purpose, *inter alia*, of the prompt review and correction of administrative action relating to customs matters. The above-identified measures, including in particular Articles 243 through 246 of the Code, expressly provide that EC member States are responsible for the implementation of procedures for appeals from decisions by member State customs authorities. Accordingly, the ability to obtain review of a customs decision by a tribunal of the European Communities does not arise until after an importer or other interested party has pursued review through national administrative and/or judicial tribunals. For this reason, the European Communities is in breach of Article X:3(b) of the GATT 1994."[1503]

7.495 In a reply to a question posed by the Panel, the United States made it clear that its claim under Article X:3(b) of the GATT 1994 was confined to the allegation that the decisions of the tribunals or procedures in the European Communities do not "govern the practice of" all the "agencies entrusted with administrative enforcement" in the European Communities in violation of Article X:3(b) of the GATT 1994. More specifically, the United States alleges in the context of this dispute that the tribunals or procedures provided by individual member States for the review and correction of administrative action do not satisfy the European Communities' obligation under Article X:3(b) of the GATT 1994 because the decisions of such tribunals or procedures have effect only within the respective member States and not on EC agencies throughout the territory of the European Communities.[1504]

7.496 In light of the United States' clarification of its claim under Article X:3(b) of the GATT 1994 in its reply to a question posed by the Panel, the Panel will confine its analysis to the question of whether or not Article X:3(b) of the GATT 1994 requires that the decisions of the tribunals or procedures for the review and correction of administrative action relating to customs matters govern the prac-

---

[1501] European Communities' second written submission, para. 215.

[1502] European Communities' comment on the United States' reply to Panel question No. 141.

[1503] WT/DS315/8, which is contained in Annex D of the Panel's report.

[1504] United States' reply to Panel question No. 35.

tice of *all* the agencies entrusted with administrative enforcement *throughout the territory* of a particular Member, as has been asserted by the United States. For the purposes of resolving this dispute, the Panel will also consider whether or not the tribunals and procedures provided in the European Communities for the review and correction of administrative action fulfil the European Communities' obligation under Article X:3(b) of the GATT 1994 in this regard.[1505]

3. *Interpretation of Article X:3(b) of the GATT 1994*

(a) Summary of the parties' arguments

(i) Relevant features of review bodies

7.497 The **United States** submits that it is "administrative" action that must be eligible for prompt review and correction under Article X:3(b) of the GATT 1994. The United States submits that this suggests that the obligation of prompt review and correction under Article X:3(b) of the GATT 1994 applies to the first tribunal or procedure that a Member provides for the purpose of review and correction. The United States submits that this interpretation is supported by the reference in Article X:3(b) of the GATT 1994 to appeals to a "court or tribunal of superior jurisdiction within the time prescribed for appeals to be lodged by importers."[1506]

7.498 Similarly, the **European Communities** submits that the review established by Article X:3(b) of the GATT 1994 only pertains to first instance review.[1507] The European Communities reasons that, therefore, to require uniformity at the first instance would necessarily imply the establishment of a central court of first instance with jurisdiction over the whole territory of any WTO Member. According to the European Communities, this conclusion finds no support in the wording of Article X:3(b) of the GATT 1994.[1508]

7.499 The European Communities also notes that Article X:3(b) of the GATT 1994 provides that tribunals or procedures ensuring the prompt review and correction of administrative action on customs matters must be independent of the agencies entrusted with administrative enforcement. According to the European Communities, provided that first instance administrative review fulfils the requirement of independence, such review may be considered consistent with the obligation to ensure prompt review and correction of administrative action contained in Article X:3(b) of the GATT 1994.[1509] The European Communities submits that the requirement of independence in Article X:3(b) of the GATT 1994

[1505] The Panel notes that it does not consider it necessary to determine whether or not the review provided in the European Communities in fulfilment of Article X:3(b) of the GATT 1994 is "prompt" within the meaning of that Article in order to resolve this dispute: United States' replies to Panel question Nos. 40, 142 and 144.

[1506] United States' reply to Panel question No. 121.

[1507] European Communities' second written submission, para. 225.

[1508] *Ibid.*

[1509] European Communities' reply to Panel question No. 121.

imposes an external separation between the tribunals or procedures and the agencies.[1510]

(ii) Geographical coverage and substantive effect of decisions of review bodies

General

7.500 The **United States** submits that the relevant context for the interpretation of Article X:3(b) of the GATT 1994 includes the immediately preceding sub-paragraph, namely Article X:3(a) of the GATT 1994. The United States notes that that sub-paragraph calls for the "uniform, impartial, and reasonable" administration of customs laws. The United States submits that, therefore, when read in the light of Article X:3(a) of the GATT 1994, Article X:3(b) of the GATT 1994 means that the decisions of the tribunals or procedures must provide for the review and correction of customs matters for the European Communities as a whole, not just within limited geographical regions within the European Communities.[1511] More particularly, the United States submits that it is inconsistent with Article X:3(b) of the GATT 1994 to require a trader who had received adverse customs decisions in different member States, each at odds with the prevailing interpretation of EC customs law in other member States, to pursue separate appeals in each of those States.[1512]

Significance of the term "shall govern the practice of"

7.501 The **United States** argues that the second sentence of Article X:3(b) of the GATT 1994 provides that the tribunals or procedures provided by a Member "shall be independent of the agencies entrusted with administrative enforcement and their decisions shall be implemented by, *and shall govern the practice of, such agencies. ...*" According to the United States, the phrase "shall govern the practice of such agencies" requires that all enforcement agencies of a Member follow the reviewing tribunal's decisions.[1513] The United States adds that the "govern the practice" requirement in Article X:3(b) of the GATT 1994 means that decisions by review bodies must control the way agencies administer customs laws.[1514] In support, the United States submits that the ordinary meaning of the term "govern" in the context of Article X:3(b) of the GATT 1994 is "[c]ontrol, influence, regulate, or determine" or "[c]onstitute a law, rule, standard, or principle for."[1515] The United States submits that, accordingly, the distinct "govern the practice" requirement in Article X:3(b) of the GATT 1994 looks beyond the simple implementation of a decision in the case at hand and

[1510] European Communities' second written submission, para. 218.
[1511] United States' first written submission, para. 138.
[1512] United States' first written submission, paras. 134 and 139.
[1513] United States' reply to Panel question No.35.
[1514] United States' oral statement at the second substantive meeting, para. 88.
[1515] *The New Shorter Oxford English Dictionary*, 1993, pp. 1122-1123.

requires that the decision "control, influence, regulate or determine" the practice of or "constitute a law, rule, standard, or principle for" "the agencies entrusted with administrative enforcement" of the customs laws going forward.[1516] The United States further argues that, if Article X:3(b) of the GATT 1994, unlike Article X:3(a) of the GATT 1994, is not concerned with questions of uniformity, there would be no need for Article X:3(b) of the GATT to specify that the decisions of review tribunals must "govern the practice of" the agencies entrusted with administrative enforcement. It would suffice simply to require the provision of tribunals or procedures whose decisions are "implemented by" the agencies entrusted with administrative enforcement.[1517]

7.502 In response, the **European Communities** submits that it considers that the reference to the term "govern" in Article X:3(b) of the GATT 1994 indicates that it is aimed at securing a fair implementation of tribunal decisions in administrative law matters.[1518] According to the European Communities, if the term "govern" were to be interpreted to mean "control, regulate, determine, constitute a law, rule, standard or principle for", the decisions of first instance tribunals would be considered as having binding effect, contrary to a common element that is shared by most of the civil law and common law legal systems – namely, that only high level or last instance tribunals take decisions that are considered as binding and, therefore, a general source of law.[1519] The European Communities submits that the United States' interpretation imposes very far-reaching obligations for all WTO Members, which do not correspond to the legal traditions of most WTO Members of both civil law or roman-germanic law and the common law families.[1520] According to the European Communities, the decisions of a first instance tribunal are only binding for the specific cases decided by the same tribunal and, therefore, they are not an instrument ensuring uniform administration. The European Communities submits that a decision of a first instance review body plays the role of guidance to other first instance review bodies. Thus, the ordinary meaning of "govern" would be "influence".[1521]

Significance of the reference to "the agencies"

7.503 The **United States** argues that it is "*the* agencies entrusted with administrative enforcement" whose practice is required to be governed by the decisions of review tribunals or procedures under Article X:3(b) of the GATT 1994. According to the United States, that requirement is not fulfilled where the decisions of review tribunals or procedures govern the practice of only some of the agencies entrusted with administrative enforcement. Rather, for the practice of "the agencies" to be governed by the decisions of review tribunals, those decisions

[1516] United States' second written submission, para. 104.

[1517] United States' second written submission, para. 103.

[1518] European Communities' oral statement at the second substantive meeting, para. 93 and European Communities' second written submission, para 230.

[1519] European Communities' oral statement at the second substantive meeting, para. 94.

[1520] European Communities' closing statement at the second substantive meeting, para. 30.

[1521] European Communities' oral statement at the second substantive meeting, para. 95.

must govern "the agencies" throughout the Member's territory.[1522] The United States submits that this understanding is reinforced by the context provided by Article X:3(a) of the GATT 1994. In particular, where the decisions of review tribunals govern the practice of the agencies entrusted with administrative enforcement, they become part of the agencies' administration of the Member's customs laws in future cases. Since the Member's customs laws must be administered in a uniform manner, the decisions of review tribunals must govern the practice of "the agencies" throughout its territory. If they govern the practice of only some of the agencies then, by definition, the administration of the Member's laws will not be uniform; different interpretations of the Member's laws will govern the practice of different agencies within the Member's territory.[1523]

7.504 The **European Communities** responds that the use of the term "the agencies" in Article X:3(b) of the GATT 1994 does not mean that those agencies are all the agencies throughout the WTO Member's territory. According to the European Communities, "the agencies" must be read in context with the term to which it relates – that is, "tribunals", which are tribunals of first instance. The European Communities submits that, therefore, "the agencies" must be understood as "the agencies" whose decisions are reviewed by these tribunals of first instance. The European Communities adds that "the agencies" are those established in each of its member States, not the agencies established in the other member States.[1524]

Significance of the reference to the right to seek review by "the central administration of such agency"

7.505 The **United States** submits that further evidence for the proposition that the review and correction provided for pursuant to Article X:3(b) of the GATT 1994 must result in decisions that govern the administration of a Member's customs laws throughout its territory is the proviso in the second sentence of that Article, which states that "*the central administration of such agency* may take steps to obtain a review of the matter in another proceeding if there is good cause to believe that the decision is inconsistent with established principles of law or the actual facts." According to the United States, the proviso contemplates "the central administration" challenging a tribunal's decision collaterally – that is, "in another proceeding" – when the central administration determines that "the decision is inconsistent with established principles of law or the actual facts." In the United States' view, that possibility only makes sense if the decision in the original proceeding has effect outside that proceeding. If the decision's effects were confined to the proceeding in which it was rendered, there would be no need or basis for a collateral challenge.[1525] The United States submits that, where a Member has no "central administration" (as is the case in the European Communities),

[1522] United States' second written submission, para. 106.

[1523] United States' second written submission, para. 107.

[1524] European Communities' oral statement at the second substantive meeting, para. 97.

[1525] United States' second written submission, para. 113.

the possibility set out in the proviso would appear not to exist. However, according to the United States, that simply means that, in the unusual situation of a Member without a central administration, the various regional customs authorities would have to take other steps to ensure that the decisions of review tribunals "govern the practice of" "the agencies entrusted with administrative enforcement" *and* that the Member continues to administer its customs laws in a uniform manner.[1526]

7.506 In response, the **European Communities** submits that the possibility for the central administration of a customs agency to request review is not established to rectify the effects of the original decision in the practice of the agencies but to provide a remedy, based on limited grounds, against a decision that is no more challengeable through ordinary means because it is time-barred.[1527] According to the European Communities, this is clear from the structure of Article X:3(b) of the GATT 1994. Specifically, the proviso refers to the time limits for appeals contained in the previous phrase in sub-paragraph (b), not to the "govern the practice" requirement, which is placed in the second phrase of the second sentence of that sub-paragraph.[1528] In addition, the European Communities contends that the fact that the proviso is not intended to rectify the effects of the original decision in the practice of the agencies also derives from the nature of this type of exceptional review. When the review is based on a lack of consistency with established principles of law, its purpose is to protect the cornerstones of a legal system, with a view to eliminating conflicts with the case-law of the highest courts, which are responsible for refining those principles of law. When the review is based on a lack of consistency with the actual facts, its purpose is to annul a judicial decision on discovery of facts that were unknown to the court and to the party claiming the revision when the decision was given. According to the European Communities, neither of these two grounds of review is linked to the eventual effects of a first instance judicial decision on the practice of the customs agencies.[1529]

Legal relationship between Articles X:3(a) and X:3(b) of the GATT 1994

7.507 The **United States** argues that Article X:3(b) of the GATT 1994 must be read in light of the obligation of uniform administration in Article X:3(a) of the GATT 1994. The United States submits that, accordingly, where review leads to decisions whose effect is limited to particular regions within a Member's territory, such review is inconsistent with Article X:3(b) of the GATT 1994.[1530]

7.508 The **European Communities** submits that sub-paragraphs (a) and (b) of Article X:3 of the GATT 1994 lay down different obligations: one of uniform administration, the other on remedies. According to the European Communities,

[1526] United States' second written submission, para. 115.
[1527] European Communities' oral statement at the second substantive meeting, para. 106.
[1528] European Communities' oral statement at the second substantive meeting, para. 107.
[1529] European Communities' oral statement at the second substantive meeting, para. 108.
[1530] United States' second written submission, para. 99.

from a legal point of view, Article X:3 of the GATT 1994 does not make any link between sub-paragraphs (a) and (b), which should, therefore, be considered as separate obligations.[1531] First, sub-paragraph (b) does not make any reference to sub-paragraph (a), unlike sub-paragraph (c), which contains an explicit link to sub-paragraph (b). Further, Article X:3 GATT 1994 is not introduced by a chapeau to indicate that the two sub-paragraphs are linked so that one has to be interpreted in light of the other.[1532] The European Communities adds that the fact that sub-paragraphs (a) and (b) are both contained in Article X:3 of the GATT 1994 does not mean that they should be interpreted in such as way as to blur the distinction between the obligations which they contain. Obviously, the two provisions must be interpreted in a harmonious way, taking into account their respective object and purpose. However, this does not mean that obligations from one provision can simply be imported into the other. The European Communities submits that, in particular, Article X:3(a) of the GATT 1994 does not concern the administration of laws concerning the judicial procedure and judicial organisation, since such laws are not among those referred to in Article X:1 of the GATT 1994.[1533]

7.509 In response, the **United States** contends that the European Communities is wrong to assert that Article X:3 of the GATT 1994 does not make any link between sub-paragraphs (a) and (b). The United States submits that the second sentence of sub-paragraph (b) expressly states that the decisions of the tribunals or procedures maintained or instituted in accordance with that sub-paragraph "shall govern the practice of" "the agencies entrusted with administrative enforcement". According to the United States, the link derives from the fact that administrative enforcement, in turn, is the subject of sub-paragraph (a).[1534]

7.510 The **European Communities** responds that it considers that the term "administrative enforcement" in Article X:3(b) of the GATT 1994 does not establish a link between sub-paragraphs (a) and (b). In the European Communities' view, Article X:3(b) of the GATT 1994 refers to "agencies entrusted with administrative enforcement" to identify the agencies that are subject to prompt review, and from which the tribunals or procedures must be independent.[1535]

7.511 The **United States** submits that the European Communities itself argues that review of administrative actions by courts and uniform administration are inherently intertwined, such that the former, in its view, is a key tool for achieving the latter.[1536] More specifically, the United States submits that a theme repeated throughout the European Communities' submissions is that appeals of customs decisions to national courts, coupled with the possibility of national courts making preliminary references to the ECJ, constitutes a critical instrument of ensuring uniform administration of customs law. The United States submits

[1531] European Communities' first written submission, para. 461.

[1532] European Communities' second written submission, para. 223.

[1533] European Communities reply to Panel question No. 87.

[1534] United States' oral statement at the first substantive meeting, para. 59.

[1535] European Communities' Reply to Panel question No. 87

[1536] United States' oral statement at the first substantive meeting, para 58, referring to the European Communities' first written submission, para. 185.

that that position supports interpreting the obligation to provide reviews of customs decisions under Article X:3(b) of the GATT 1994 in light of the obligation to administer customs laws uniformly under Article X:3(a) of the GATT 1994.[1537]

7.512 In response, the **European Communities** argues that the fact that the European Communities has conceded that Articles X:3(a) and X:3(b) of the GATT 1994 must be interpreted in an harmonious way does not mean that the European Communities agrees to an interpretation that transforms Article X:3 of the GATT 1994 into a "totum revolutum" provision, where the various obligations in that Article are merged, with the unwarranted consequence that the obligation to grant independent review and correction of customs administrative decisions at first instance level is absorbed by the obligation to ensure uniform administration of the legislation.[1538] The European Communities submits that the relevant context for the interpretation of Article X:3(a) of the GATT 1994 is not Article X:3(b) of the GATT 1994, but Article X:1 of the GATT 1994, to which Article X:3(a) of the GATT 1994 makes a specific reference. The European Communities notes that Article X:1 of the GATT 1994 includes "judicial decisions of general application" among the instruments to be administered uniformly in accordance with Article X:3(a) of the GATT 1994. According to the European Communities, this evidences that Article X of the GATT 1994 covers two types of judicial decisions: those of general application, whose uniform administration is required under Article X:3(a) of the GATT 1994 and those adopted by first instance review courts, where uniform administration through all the WTO Member is not required. According to the European Communities, this contextual interpretation explains why there is no link between sub-paragraphs (a) and (b) in Article X:3 of the GATT 1994.[1539]

Significance of the reference to "tribunals" and "procedures" in the plural

7.513 The **European Communities** submits that Article X:3(b) of the GATT 1994 merely requires WTO Members to ensure that administrative decisions in customs matters are reviewed promptly by an independent tribunal or through an independent procedure.[1540] According to the European Communities, this is supported by the literal and multi-linguistic interpretation of Article X:3(b) of the GATT 1994.[1541] More specifically, the European Communities submits that, under Article X:3(b) of the GATT 1994, WTO members are obliged to have "tribunals or procedures" not "a tribunal" or "a procedure". According to the European Communities, the French and Spanish versions of the provision also use the equivalent terms in plural. This clearly allows the WTO Members to have several tribunals, each of them covering a part of its geography and being competent

[1537] United States' oral statement at the first substantive meeting, para. 58.

[1538] European Communities' oral statement at the second substantive meeting, para. 100.

[1539] European Communities' comments on the United States' reply to Panel question No. 142.

[1540] European Communities' oral statement at the first substantive meeting, para. 57.

[1541] European Communities' first written submission, para. 452.

for the review of the administrative decisions taken by their respective customs offices.[1542]

7.514 In response, the **United States** submits that the use of the plural form in Article X:3(b) of the GATT 1994 could indicate the permissibility of multiple fora for review of customs decisions for different types of review and/or by different types of review bodies, but it does not follow logically that separate and independent fora may be provided for each of several different regions within a Member's territory.[1543] The United States submits that it is not inconceivable that a WTO Member could provide several review tribunals or procedures, each covering a different part of its geography, in a manner consistent with Article X:3(b) of the GATT 1994. In the United States' view, what is important is that the decisions of these tribunals be given effect for the Member's agencies as a whole, so as to govern the practice of the Member's agencies entrusted with administrative enforcement of customs laws and not engender non-uniform enforcement. The United States submits that this might be accomplished where a Member has a single, centralized customs agency, required to give effect throughout the Member's territory to the decisions of any tribunals reviewing its actions. However, according to the United States, where review tribunals cover particular agencies and there is no other mechanism to give effect to the decisions of individual tribunals for the remaining agencies, the geographical fragmentation of review is inconsistent with Article X:3(b) of the GATT 1994.[1544]

7.515 The **European Communities** submits that the United States' interpretation of the use of the plural in Article X:3(b) of the GATT 1994 can perfectly live together with the one proffered by the European Communities. According to the European Communities, the use of the plural form may indicate that a WTO Member is entitled to maintain geographically limited tribunals and it may also indicate that a WTO Member is allowed to maintain multiple fora for review of customs decisions.[1545]

Decisions

7.516 The **United States** submits that the terms of Article X:3(b) of the GATT 1994 plainly provide that the decisions rendered by review tribunals or procedures must meet two independent requirements. Specifically, they must be implemented by the agencies entrusted with administrative enforcement, and they must govern the practice of those agencies. For decisions to govern the practice of the agencies entrusted with administrative enforcement, they must be given effect beyond simple implementation of the order in the case at hand.[1546] The United States submits that whether "decisions" in Article X:3(b) of the GATT 1994 is understood to have a narrower meaning according to which they are lim-

---

1542 European Communities' first written submission, para. 454.

1543 United States' oral statement at the first substantive meeting, para. 60; United States' reply to Panel question No. 38.

1544 United States' reply to Panel question No. 38.

1545 European Communities' second written submission, para. 232.

1546 United States' second written submission, paras. 104-106.

ited to the final mandate or order or a broader meaning that encompasses the review body's reasoning, that does not affect the "govern the practice" requirement. That is, even in a legal system in which a decision is understood as pertaining only to the court's mandate or order and not to its reasons, Article X:3(b) of the GATT 1994 still requires that the decision both be implemented by *and* govern the practice of the agencies entrusted with administrative enforcement. In the view of the United States, it does not make a difference whether a given Member's legal system treats a "decision" as consisting of only the court's order or mandate, or including the court's reasons.[1547]

7.517 The **European Communities** submits that the United States fails to give a proper meaning to the term "decision" in Article X:3(b) of the GATT 1994. The "decision" of a tribunal in a particular case must be distinguished from the reasoning which led it to this decision. For instance, if a tribunal decides on an action for the annulment of a decision of the customs authorities, then the decision will be to annul the decision or not. If the decision is to annul, then this decision will govern the practice of the agency. In contrast, there is no basis in Article X:3(a) of the GATT 1994 for assuming that all questions of interpretation which the tribunal may have considered in the course of its reasoning equally become binding on the agency. According to the European Communities, this would give a role to judicial precedent that would go far beyond the practice of numerous WTO Members which do not have a legal system based on case law.[1548] The European Communities clarifies that this does not imply that the decisions of a tribunal of first instance, including the reasoning contained in the tribunal's judgement, do not produce any effects in the EC system. According to the European Communities, such reasoning will constitute relevant judicial practice, which will be taken into account by the customs agencies. Moreover, if a customs agency or a court in a member State does not share the interpretation of the EC legislation given by a court of another member State, it will take the initiatives that are appropriate given its respective position in the system: the customs agency shall consult and discuss the issue with the Commission and the other member States, the court in another member State will or shall refer to the ECJ.[1549]

(b) Analysis by the Panel

7.518 The Panel recalls that, in order to resolve this dispute, the Panel needs only to address the question of whether or not Article X:3(b) of the GATT 1994 requires the decisions of the judicial, arbitral or administrative tribunals or procedures for the review and correction of administrative action relating to customs matters to govern the practice of *all* the agencies entrusted with administrative enforcement *throughout the territory* of a particular Member, as has been asserted by the United States. The Panel will interpret the various terms contained in Article X:3(b) of the GATT 1994 that would appear to have a bearing on this

---

[1547] United States' reply to Panel question No. 142.

[1548] European Communities' oral statement at the second substantive meeting, para. 98.

[1549] European Communities' oral statement at the second substantive meeting, para. 99.

question. In so doing, the Panel will use as its legal framework Articles 31 and 32 of the *Vienna Convention*.

Ordinary meaning

"Independent"

7.519 The Panel recalls that the first sentence of Article X:3(b) of the GATT 1994 requires WTO Members to maintain or institute judicial, arbitral or administrative tribunals or procedures for the purpose of the prompt review and correction of administrative action relating to customs matters. The second sentence of Article X:3(b) of the GATT 1994 goes on to provide that such tribunals or procedures must "be *independent* of the agencies entrusted with administrative enforcement". In the Panel's understanding, when read in the light of the qualification contained in the second sentence of Article X:3(b) of the GATT 1994, it is clear that the tribunals or procedures for the prompt review and correction of administrative action required by the first sentence of that Article must be "independent" of the agencies whose administrative action is the subject of review.

7.520 The Panel notes that the term "independent" is defined as "not subject to the control or influence of another; not associated with another (often larger) entity".[1550] On the basis of the ordinary meaning of the term "independent", the Panel understands that the judicial, arbitral or administrative tribunals or procedures for the review and correction of administrative action relating to customs matters under Article X:3(b) of the GATT 1994 must be free of control or influence from the administrative agencies whose decisions are the subject of review. More specifically, we understand that such tribunals and procedures must have the ability to conduct the review provided for under Article X:3(b) of the GATT 1994 with freedom in institutional and practical terms from interference by the agencies whose decisions are being reviewed.[1551]

Level of review

7.521 Regarding the level of review of administrative action to be provided under Article X:3(b) of the GATT 1994, the Panel notes that the terms of Article X:3(b) of the GATT 1994 indicate that the review required under Article X:3(b) of the GATT 1994 need not necessarily be the *last* instance review to which an administrative decision is subject because the decisions of tribunals and procedures that undertake the review demanded by Article X:3(b) of the GATT 1994 may be the subject of a further appeal. In this regard, the Panel notes that

---

[1550] *Black's Law Dictionary*, 1999, p. 774.

[1551] The Panel understands that, in some WTO Members, administrative action relating to customs matters may be reviewed by the same administrative authority that originally took the action. For example, two of the third parties to this dispute – namely, Japan and Chinese Tapei – indicated that administrative action may first be reviewed by the same administrative authority that took the action originally: Japan's reply to Panel question No. 105 and Chinese Taipei's reply to Panel question No. 105. Such review would not qualify under Article X:3(b) of the GATT 1994 because, in such cases, the reviewing body is not independent of the administrative authority whose decision is the subject of review.

Article X:3(b) of the GATT 1994 requires that the decisions of judicial, arbitral or administrative tribunals and procedures for the prompt review and correction of administrative action must "govern the practice of [administrative] agencies *unless an appeal is lodged with a court or tribunal of superior jurisdiction*" (emphasis added). In our view, this indicates that Article X:3(b) of the GATT 1994 contemplates the possibility that there may be appeals to bodies of "superior jurisdiction" from the decisions of the tribunals and procedures that provide the review required under Article X:3(b) of the GATT 1994. Moreover, the Panel notes that Article X:3(b) of the GATT 1994 refers to the possibility that the "central administration of such agency may take steps to obtain a review of the matter in another proceeding if there is good cause to believe that the decision is inconsistent with established principles of law or the actual facts". In the Panel's view, the possibility that the central administration of an agency whose administrative action is the subject of review may seek further review of that action in another proceeding confirms the view that the review anticipated by Article X:3(b) of the GATT 1994 is not necessarily the last instance review to which the administrative action in question may be subject.

7.522 The Panel also notes that both parties to this dispute are of the view that that provision relates to *first* instance review.[1552] Article X:3(b) of the GATT 1994 applies to review by the tribunals or procedures that are "independent" of the agencies whose administrative action is the subject of review. This indicates that Article X:3(b) of the GATT 1994 applies to first instance review by tribunals and procedures that are independent from the administering authority that took the administrative action that is the subject of review.

"Tribunals or procedures"

7.523 The parties have raised the question in this dispute of the significance that should be attached, if any, to the fact that Article X:3(b) of the GATT 1994 refers to judicial, arbitral or administrative "tribunals" and "procedures" in the plural in all three authentic versions of the GATT 1994.

7.524 The Panel notes that the obligation to maintain or institute "tribunals or procedures" in the plural is imposed upon the "contracting party" in the singular. This suggests to the Panel that Article X:3(b) of the GATT 1994 does not oblige a Member to set up a single tribunal or procedure for the review of all administrative action. Further, in the Panel's view, this indicates that Article X:3(b) of the GATT 1994 expressly contemplates the possibility that there may be multiple tribunals or procedures in place in a single WTO Member for the review of administrative action.

7.525 The existence of the possibility under Article X:3(b) of the GATT 1994 that there may be multiple review tribunals or procedures in place in a single

[1552] United States' reply to Panel question No. 121; European Communities' second written submission, para. 225. The Panel understands first instance review to mean review by the first body or procedure to consider a decision after that decision has been taken. By definition, we understand that first instance review may be the subject of subsequent review by higher level review bodies or procedures.

WTO Member for the review of administrative action may be explained in a number of different ways. One possible explanation could be that the various review tribunals or procedures maintained or instituted in a WTO Member have different areas of substantive competence. Other possible explanations could be that the various tribunals or procedures have responsibility for different geographical areas and/or for administrative action emanating from different administrative bodies.[1553] In the Panel's view, the use of the plural when referring to the tribunals and procedures to which Article X:3(b) of the GATT 1994 relates does not clearly indicate which, if any, of these possible explanations is the appropriate interpretation of Article X:3(b) of the GATT 1994.

"Such agencies"

7.526 Article X:3(b) of the GATT 1994 provides that the decisions of judicial, arbitral or administrative tribunals and procedures should "govern the practice, of *such agencies*" (emphasis added). The question has arisen in the context of this dispute as to the significance, if any, that should be ascribed to the reference to "such agencies" in the plural in Article X:3(b) of the GATT 1994.

7.527 One possible interpretation is that the use of the plural when referring to "agencies" in Article X:3(b) of the GATT 1994 merely flows from the fact that the review tribunals and procedures required under Article X:3(b) of the GATT 1994 are also referred to in the plural. To recall, the second sentence of Article X:3(b) of the GATT 1994 provides that: "Such tribunals or procedures ... shall govern the practice of, such agencies". Further, the Panel notes that the use of the plural to refer to administrative agencies in the second sentence of Article X:3(b) of the GATT 1994 contrasts with the reference to agencies in the singular in the proviso at the end of that Article. In particular, the proviso in Article X:3(b) of the GATT 1994 states that: "*Provided* that the central administration of *such agency* may take steps to obtain review of the matter in another proceeding ..." (emphasis added).

7.528 The Panel considers that it is difficult to know what significance should be attached, if any, to the reference to agencies in the plural in the second sentence of Article X:3(b) of the GATT 1994, especially in light of the reference to the same term in the singular in the proviso to that Article. Nevertheless, the Panel is of the view that it is clear from the terms of Article X:3(b) of the GATT 1994 that the decisions of judicial, arbitral or administrative tribunals and procedures for the prompt review and correction of administrative action must govern the practice of the agency whose action was the subject of review by a tribunal or procedure in a particular case.

"Govern the practice of"

7.529 Article X:3(b) of the GATT 1994 requires that "tribunals or procedures [for the review and correction of administrative action relating to customs mat-

[1553] In fact, the United States itself submits that a WTO Member could provide several review tribunals or procedures, each covering a different part of its geography, in a manner consistent with Article X:3(b) of the GATT 1994: United States' reply to Panel question No. 38.

ters] shall be independent of the agencies entrusted with administrative enforcement and their decisions shall be implemented by, and shall *govern* the practice of, such agencies" (emphasis added). Regarding the ordinary meaning of the term "govern", the Panel notes that it is defined as "control, influence, regulate, or determine (a person, another's action, the course or issue of events)".[1554] When considered in the light of this definition, it would appear that the term "govern" in Article X:3(b) of the GATT 1994 means that the decisions of judicial, arbitral or administrative tribunals and procedures, established for the review of administrative action relating to customs matters, must have binding effect.

7.530 The Panel recalls its conclusion in paragraph 7.528 that, under Article X:3(b) of the GATT 1994, the decisions of judicial, arbitral or administrative tribunals and procedures for the prompt review and correction of administrative action must govern the practice of the agency whose action was the subject of review by a tribunal or procedure in a particular case. Accordingly, when considered in the light of the ordinary meaning of the term "govern", the Panel understands that the decisions of tribunals or procedures for the review and correction of administrative action relating to customs matters must bind the administrative agency whose action is the subject of review pursuant to Article X:3(b) of the GATT 1994.

7.531 Moreover, it is the Panel's view that the ordinary meaning of the term "govern" when read in conjunction with the term "practice"[1555] in Article X:3(b) of the GATT 1994 implies a prospective notion. More specifically, the Panel understands that the binding effect of a decision of a tribunal or procedure for the review and correction of administrative action means that the administrative agency whose action was the subject of review by a tribunal or procedure pursuant to Article X:3(b) of the GATT 1994 is bound by that decision with respect to the specific factual situation that was the subject of the review but also with respect to identical factual situations that may arise in the future concerning identical legal issues.[1556]

[1554] *The New Shorter Oxford English Dictionary*, 1993, p. 1122.

[1555] The Panel notes that the Appellate Body's interpretation of the term "practice" in the context of the reference to "subsequent practice" under Article 31.3(c) of the *Vienna Convention* in *Japan – Alcoholic Beverages II* would appear to be relevant in this regard. In particular, the Appellate Body stated that "practice" entails the following features: "a 'concordant, common and consistent' sequence of acts or pronouncements which is sufficient to establish a discernible pattern...": Appellate Body Report, *Japan – Alcoholic Beverages II*, p. 13.

[1556] The Panel notes that Article X:3(b) of the GATT 1994 also provides that the decisions of tribunals and procedures for the review and correction of administrative action "shall be implemented by" administrative agencies. In the Panel's view, this means that, in addition to being bound to follow a decision of a tribunal or procedure for the review and correction of administrative action (which flows from the term "govern" in Article X:3(b) of the GATT 1994), the administrative agency is also obliged to *apply* the decision in practice, in accordance with the requirement to "implement" such decisions in Article X:3(b) of the GATT 1994.

Context

Legal relationship between Articles X:3(a) and X:3(b) of the GATT 1994

7.532 The Panel has been called upon to determine the relationship, if any, between Articles X:3(b) and X:3(a) of the GATT 1994, for the purposes of the interpretation of Article X:3(b) of the GATT 1994.

7.533 The Panel notes that Article X:3(b) of the GATT 1994 itself does not contain an express textual link between that Article and the obligation of uniform administration in Article X:3(a) of the GATT 1994. In this regard, Article X:3(b) of the GATT 1994 contrasts with Article X:3(c) of the GATT 1994, which, like Article X:3(b) of the GATT, is contained in Article X of the GATT, but which explicitly cross-refers to Article X:3(b).[1557]

7.534 In considering whether or not a link between Articles X:3(a) and X:3(b) of the GATT 1994 can be inferred, the Panel notes that in *India – Patents*, the Appellate Body stated that the principles of treaty interpretation in the *Vienna Convention* "neither require nor condone the imputation into a treaty of words that are not there or the importation into a treaty of concepts that were not intended."[1558] Given the absence of an express reference to Article X:3(a) of the GATT 1994 in Article X:3(b) of the GATT 1994, which contrasts with the explicit cross-reference between Articles X:3(b) and X:3(c) of the GATT 1994, the Panel considers that it is not possible to infer that the drafters of the GATT intended that the obligation to provide tribunals or procedures for the purpose of the prompt review and correction of administrative action relating to customs matters under Article X:3(b) of the GATT 1994 is to be read as simultaneously requiring uniform administration in accordance with Article X:3(a) of the GATT 1994. Indeed, such an interpretation would amount to merging different requirements that are currently contained in separate sub-paragraphs of Article X of the GATT 1994.

7.535 Nevertheless, the Panel does not wish to suggest that Articles X:3(a) and X:3(b) of the GATT 1994 are completely unrelated. In fact, we consider that they are related in the same way that each and every provision of the WTO Agreements is related. More specifically, we consider each provision of the WTO Agreements must be interpreted and applied in a manner that is harmoni-

---

[1557] Article X:3(c) of the GATT 1994 provides that: "The provisions of subparagraph (b) of this paragraph shall not require the elimination or substitution of procedures in force in the territory of a contracting party on the date of this Agreement which in fact provide for an objective and impartial review of administrative action even though such procedures are not fully or formally independent of the agencies entrusted with administrative enforcement. Any contracting party employing such procedures shall, upon request, furnish the CONTRACTING PARTIES with full information thereon in order that they may determine whether such procedures conform to the requirements of this subparagraph."

[1558] Appellate Body Report, *India – Patents (US)*, para. 45. Similarly, in interpreting the relationship between various provisions of the SCM Agreement, the Appellate Body stated that "we attach significance to the absence of any textual link between Article 21.3 reviews and the *de minimis* standard set forth in Article 11.9.": Appellate Body Report, *US – Carbon Steel*, para. 69.

ous with the interpretation and application of other provisions of the WTO Agreements. The Panel considers that, in practical terms, this means that the various provisions of the WTO Agreements should not be interpreted and applied in a manner that would undermine and/or circumvent any other provision of the WTO Agreements.[1559]

Article X of the GATT 1994

7.536 In addition, the Panel recalls its observation in the context of its interpretation of Article X:3(a) of the GATT 1994 in paragraphs 7.107 and 7.108 above that a due process theme underlies Article X of the GATT 1994. In the Panel's view, this theme suggests that an aim of the review provided for under Article X:3(b) of the GATT 1994 is to ensure that a trader who has been adversely affected by a decision of an administrative agency has the ability to have that adverse decision reviewed by a tribunal or procedure that is independent from the agency that originally took the adverse decision.

Overall summary and conclusions

7.537 In the Panel's view, neither the ordinary meaning of the various terms of Article X:3(b) of the GATT 1994 nor the legal context for the interpretation of Article X:3(b) of the GATT 1994 provide a clear answer to the specific question the Panel has been called upon to address – namely, whether Article X:3(b) of the GATT 1994 requires the decisions of the judicial, arbitral or administrative tribunals or procedures for the review and correction of administrative action relating to customs matters to govern the practice of *all* the agencies entrusted with administrative enforcement *throughout the territory* of a particular Member.

7.538 Having said that, the Panel considers that the interpretation of the relevant terms of Article X:3(b) of the GATT 1994 does clearly indicate that the decisions of the review tribunals and procedures required under Article X:3(b) of the GATT 1994 may be the subject of an appeal. Further, the Panel recalls the parties' understanding that Article X:3(b) of the GATT 1994 relates to first instance review.[1560] In this regard, the Panel does not consider that it would be reasonable to infer that first instance independent review tribunals and bodies, whose jurisdiction in most legal systems is normally limited in substantive and geographical terms, should have the authority to bind all agencies entrusted with administrative enforcement throughout the territory of a Member. Further, the Panel recalls that the due process theme that underlies Article X of the GATT 1994, in which Article X:3(b) of the GATT 1994 is contained, indicates that Article X:3(b) of the GATT 1994 exists to ensure that a trader who has been adversely affected by

---

[1559] In this regard, the Panel notes that, in *Argentina – Footwear (EC)*, the Appellate Body stated that the provisions of the WTO Agreements "are all provisions of one treaty, the WTO Agreement. They entered into force as part of that treaty at the same time. They apply equally and are equally binding on all WTO Members.... a treaty interpreter must read all applicable provisions of a treaty in a way that gives meaning to all of them, harmoniously.": Appellate Body Report, *Argentina – Footwear (EC)*, para 81.

[1560] United States' reply to Panel question No. 121; European Communities' second written submission, para. 225.

a decision of an administrative agency has the ability to have that adverse decision reviewed. In the Panel's view, to require decisions issued by judicial, arbitral or administrative tribunals or procedures pursuant to Article X:3(b) of the GATT 1994 to apply and have effect throughout the territory of a Member would go beyond what is demanded by this due process objective.

7.539 The factors set out in the preceding paragraph, taken in conjunction, incline us to conclude that Article X:3(b) of the GATT 1994 does not necessarily mean that the decisions of the judicial, arbitral or administrative tribunals or procedures for the review and correction of administrative action relating to customs matters must govern the practice of *all* the agencies entrusted with administrative enforcement *throughout the territory* of a particular Member.

4. *Specific alleged violations of Article X:3(b) of the GATT 1994*

(a) Summary of the parties' arguments

7.540 The **United States** submits that, under Article X:3(b) of the GATT 1994, it is the WTO Member (as opposed to regional subdivisions of the Member) that has an obligation to provide tribunals or procedures for the prompt review and correction of administrative action relating to customs matters. The United States further submits that the decisions of such tribunals or procedures must govern the practice of that Member's agencies – that is, in the context of this case, the European Communities' agencies, as a whole, not just individual member States' agencies – and that the Member's agencies must implement those decisions.[1561]

7.541 The United States also submits that the provision of tribunals or procedures by individual member States within the European Communities does not satisfy the European Communities' obligation under Article X:3(b) of the GATT 1994, as the decisions of these tribunals or procedures have effect only within the respective member States and not on EC agencies generally.[1562] More specifically, the United States submits that the European Communities does not fulfil its obligation under Article X:3(b) of the GATT 1994 because each of the multiple review tribunals it provides renders decisions that govern the practice only of a subset of agencies entrusted with administrative enforcement within a particular region in the European Communities but does not "govern the practice" of the European Communities' agencies in another member State.[1563] The United States submits that, given that the ECJ is not set up to be an EC customs court, what is left is a patchwork of member State customs authorities whose work is reviewed by member State courts, with no EC tribunal nor procedure providing prompt review and correction of customs decisions in a way that would bring about uniformity in the administration of EC customs law.[1564]

[1561] United States' reply to Panel question No. 35.
[1562] *Ibid.*
[1563] United States' second written submission, para. 102.
[1564] United States' first written submission, para. 153.

7.542 The **European Communities** argues that the United States has focused entirely on the absence of an EC customs court.[1565] According to the European Communities, Article X:3(b) of the GATT 1994 is neutral as to the means which WTO Members employ for ensuring prompt review. In other words, that provision does not prescribe the specific bodies or instruments, structure and time periods which WTO Members should use to ensure prompt review of customs decisions.[1566] The European Communities submits that the Appellate Body's interpretation of Article X of the GATT 1994 in *EC – Poultry* and *EC – Bananas III* further supports the view that that Article does not impose any specific structure for the review system.[1567] The European Communities argues that, moreover, the panel in *EC – Trademarks and Geographical Indications (US)* confirmed that the European Communities may comply with its obligation under Article X:3(b) of the GATT 1994 through the courts of its member States.[1568] According to the European Communities, where the tribunals of the member States provide judicial review of decisions taken by the member States' customs authorities, they act as organs of the European Communities, through which the European Communities discharges its obligations under Article X:3(b) of the GATT 1994.[1569]

7.543 In response, the **United States** contends that the European Communities appears to reason that, if the individual member States are complying with their obligations under Article X:3(b) of the GATT 1994, then the European Communities is necessarily complying with its obligation under Article X:3(b) of the GATT 1994. However, the fact that the same tribunal may be considered, as a matter of internal EC law, as both a member State tribunal and an EC tribunal does not mean that it meets the requirements of Article X:3(b) of the GATT 1994 with respect to both the European Communities and the member States' obligations. The United States concludes that, as a matter of EC law, a tribunal may serve a dual function as both a member State tribunal and an EC tribunal. However, this does not mean that it also satisfies both the member State's obligation under Article X:3(b) of the GATT 1994 and the European Communities' obligation under Article X:3(b) of the GATT 1994.[1570] The United States clarifies that its complaint in this dispute is not about the review bodies provided by each of the member States. The United States has not argued, for example, that review at the member State level breaches member States' obligations under Article X:3(b) of the GATT 1994. Rather, the thrust of the United States' claim is that existing review at the member State level alone lacks features that would enable it to satisfy the European Communities' obligations under Article X:3(b) of the GATT 1994.[1571] In particular, the United States submits that the appellate mechanism in each member State is different, and the decisions of each member

---

[1565] European Communities' oral statement at the second substantive meeting, para. 5.

[1566] European Communities' oral statement at the first substantive meeting, para. 62.

[1567] European Communities' first written submission, para. 455.

[1568] European Communities' first written submission, para. 456.

[1569] European Communities' oral statement at the first substantive meeting, para. 70 referring to Panel Report, *EC – Geographical Indications and Trademarks (US)*, para. 7.725.

[1570] United States' comments on the European Communities' reply to Panel question No. 169.

[1571] United States' reply to Panel question No. 142.

State's courts apply only in the territory of that member State.[1572] The United States submits that this arrangement does not meet the European Communities' obligation under Article X:3(b) of the GATT 1994.[1573]

7.544 In response, the **European Communities** notes that decisions of the member States' customs authorities, which are based on EC law, are reviewed by the national courts and tribunals acting as the ordinary judges for EC law. Customs decisions adopted by the EC institutions are reviewed by the ECJ (and, in some cases, by the Court of First Instance) through direct actions or preliminary rulings on validity. The European Communities submits that there is, therefore, a complete system of judicial protection in place.[1574] The European Communities submits that, further, in the European Communities, the review of customs decisions currently takes place as part of the general system for review of administrative decisions in the field of administrative law or tax law.[1575] According to the European Communities, Article X:3(b) of the GATT 1994 does not require a central court or procedure to appeal administrative decisions in customs matters.[1576] The European Communities also notes that, with respect to direct appeals to the Court of First Instance and to the ECJ, there is no prior administrative review of administrative decision adopted by the EC institutions on customs matters. Pursuant to Article 230(5) of the EC treaty, an action for annulment must be brought directly to the relevant Court within two months from the notification or the publication of the challenged decision.[1577] With respect to the Court of First Instance and the ECJ, the European Communities submits that, pursuant to the second paragraph of Article 230 of the EC Treaty, the grounds of illegality which parties may plead in an action for annulment are lack of competence, infringement of an essential procedural requirement, infringement of the Treaty or of any rule of law relating to its application or misuse of powers.[1578]

7.545 With respect to review by the ECJ pursuant to Article 230 of the EC Treaty, the **United States** submits that Article 230 of the EC Treaty pertains to review by the ECJ of the legality of acts adopted by EC institutions, including the Commission and Council. The United States notes that, in the context of the present dispute, the United States has not raised any issue with respect to ECJ review pursuant to Article 230 of the EC Treaty.[1579]

(b) Analysis by the Panel

7.546 The main question for the Panel's consideration here is whether or not the European Communities is fulfilling its obligations under Article X:3(b) of the GATT 1994. In this regard, the Panel recalls that the United States alleges that decisions of the tribunals or procedures in the European Communities do not

---

[1572] United States' first written submission, para. 133.

[1573] United States' oral statement at the first substantive meeting, paras. 62 - 64.

[1574] European Communities' first written submission, para. 465.

[1575] European Communities' oral statement at the first substantive meeting, para. 61.

[1576] European Communities' first written submission, para. 465.

[1577] European Communities' reply to Panel question No. 70(a).

[1578] European Communities' reply to Panel question No. 71(a) and (b).

[1579] United States' reply to Panel question No. 143.

"govern the practice of" all the "agencies entrusted with administrative enforcement" in the European Communities in violation of Article X:3(b) of the GATT 1994.[1580] The Panel also notes that the United States exclusively argues that the European Communities is in violation of Article X:3(b) of the GATT 1994; it does not claim that the individual member States of the European Communities are also in violation of Article X:3(b) of the GATT 1994. In addition, the United States does not challenge the review of acts jointly adopted by the European Parliament and the Council, the European Commission and the European Central Bank, or by the Council itself or the Parliament where the act is intended to produce legal effects *vis-à-vis* third parties pursuant to Article 230 of the EC Treaty.[1581]

(i) Discharge of the European Communities' obligation under Article X:3(b) of the GATT 1994

7.547 A preliminary issue that has arisen with respect to the United States' claim that the European Communities is in violation of Article X:3(b) of the GATT 1994 is whether the European Communities is able to discharge its obligations under that provision through the member States. In particular, the United States argues that the provision of judicial, arbitral or administrative tribunals or procedures for the review and correction of administrative action by individual member States within the European Communities does not satisfy the European Communities' obligation under Article X:3(b) of the GATT 1994.

7.548 The Panel notes that the European Communities is a Member of the WTO.[1582] In addition, all the constituent member States of the European Communities are Members of the WTO. The member States were either founding Members of the GATT[1583]; they acceded to the GATT[1584]; or they have since acceded to the WTO[1585]. Therefore, it would appear that the European Communities as well as its constituent member States concurrently bear the obligations contained in the WTO Agreements, including those contained in Article X:3(b)

[1580] United States' reply to Panel question No. 35.

[1581] United States' oral statement at the second substantive meeting, para. 85; United States' closing statement at the second substantive meeting, paras. 8-9.

[1582] Articles IX, XI and XIV of the WTO Agreement recognise the European Communities as a WTO member. Article IX:1 of the WTO Agreement provides *inter alia* that: "Where the European Communities exercise their right to vote, they shall have a number of votes equal to the number of their member States". Article XI:1 of the WTO Agreement provides that: "The contracting parties to GATT 1947 as of the date of entry into force of this agreement, and the European Communities, which accept this Agreement and the Multilateral Trade agreements and for which Schedules of Concessions and Commitments are annexed to GATT 1994 and for which Schedules of Specific Commitments are annexed to GATS shall become original Members of the WTO." Article XIV:1 of the WTO Agreement provides that: "This Agreement shall be open for acceptance, by signature or otherwise, by contracting parties to GATT 1947, and the European Communities, which are eligible to become original Members of the WTO in accordance with Article XI of this Agreement."

[1583] Belgium, France, Luxembourg, the Netherlands and the United Kingdom.

[1584] Austria, Cyprus, Czech Republic, Denmark, Finland, Germany, Greece, Hungary, Ireland, Italy, Malta, Poland, Portugal, Slovak Republic, Spain and Sweden.

[1585] Estonia, Latvia, Lithuania, Slovenia.

of the GATT 1994. However, the Panel recalls that the United States exclusively argues that the European Communities is in violation of Article X:3(b) of the GATT 1994; it does not claim that the member States of the European Communities are also in violation of Article X:3(b) of the GATT 1994. Therefore, the Panel will confine its attention to the question of whether or not the European Communities is in violation of Article X:3(b) of the GATT 1994.

7.549 In this regard, the Panel recalls that the EC Treaty establishes a common commercial policy which, according to Article 133(1) of the EC Treaty, is based on uniform principles, particularly with regard to changes in tariff rates, the conclusion of tariff and trade agreements, the achievement of uniformity in measures of liberalization, export policy, and measures to protect trade such as those to be taken in the event of dumping or subsidies. The ECJ has confirmed that the customs union and the common commercial policy, which includes administration of customs matters, fall within the exclusive competence of the European Communities.[1586] One of the main instruments comprising the legislative framework for customs administration in the European Communities is the Community Customs Code, which covers, *inter alia*, review of decisions on customs matters.

7.550 The European Communities has informed the Panel that, where the tribunals of the member States provide review of decisions taken by the member States' customs authorities, they act as organs of the European Communities[1587] and that the consideration of the member State courts as bodies entrusted with the ordinary application of EC law is based on the existence of the preliminary reference procedure to the ECJ and on the basic principles of primacy of EC law and direct effect.[1588] We find support for this view in Article 243 of the Community Customs Code, which provides in relevant part that:

> 1. Any person shall have the right to appeal against decisions taken by the customs authorities which relate to the application of customs legislation, and which concern him directly and individually.
>
> ...
>
> The appeal must be lodged in the Member State where the decision has been taken or applied for.
>
> 2. The right of appeal may be exercised:
>
> (a) initially before the customs authorities designated for that purpose by the Member States;
>
> (b) subsequently, before an independent body, which may be a judicial authority or an equivalent specialized body, according to the provisions in force in the Member States.

7.551 The Panel understands that Article 243 of the Community Customs Code requires review of customs decisions to be undertaken, initially, by the customs

[1586] Opinion 1/75, *Local Cost Standard*, [1975] ECR 1355 (Exhibit EC-13).

[1587] European Communities' oral statement at the first substantive meeting, para. 70.

[1588] European Communities' reply to Panel question No. 169.

authorities designated for that purpose by the member States and subsequently, before an independent body, which may be a judicial authority or an equivalent specialized body, according to the provisions in force in the member States.

7.552 It is the Panel's view that the European Communities may comply with its obligations under Article X:3(b) of the GATT 1994 through organs in its member States. We consider that this follows from the fact that Article X:3(b) of the GATT 1994 does not contain any requirements regarding the institutional structure of the review mechanism required by that Article other than the requirement that the review be undertaken by judicial, arbitral or administrative tribunals.[1589]

7.553 In the light of the foregoing, the Panel concludes that the authorities in the member States – including customs authorities designated for that purpose by the member States and independent bodies, such as a judicial authority or an equivalent specialized body – act as organs of the European Communities when they review and correct administrative action taken pursuant to EC customs law.

(ii) Review of administrative action relating to customs matters by authorities in the member States

7.554 The United States challenges review by member State authorities under Article X:3(b) of the GATT 1994 on the ground that the decisions of such authorities only have effect within the respective member States. Indeed, there appears to be no dispute between the parties that this is a fact.[1590] However, the Panel recalls that, in paragraph 7.539 above, it found that the decisions of tribunals or procedures established or maintained pursuant to Article X:3(b) of the GATT 1994 need not necessarily govern the practice of *all* the agencies entrusted with administrative enforcement *throughout the territory* of a particular Member, as has been asserted by the United States. Therefore, in the context of this dispute, the Panel considers that the European Communities does not violate Article X:3(b) of the GATT 1994 merely because the decisions regarding review of administration action relating to customs matters, which are taken by authorities in the member States acting as organs of the European Communities, do not apply and have effect throughout the territory of the European Communities.

7.555 On the basis of the explanations provided by the European Communities, which have not been disputed by the United States, we understand that, pursuant to Article 243(2)(b) of the Community Customs Code, member States have in

[1589] The Panel considers that this also follows from Article 4 of the Draft Articles on Responsibility of States for Internationally Wrongful Acts, which provides that:

"1. The conduct of any State organ shall be considered as an act of that State under international law, whether the organ exercises legislative, executive, judicial or any other functions, whatever position it holds in the organization of the State, and whatever its character as an organ of the central government or of a territorial unit of the State.

2. An organ includes any person or entity which has that status in accordance with the internal law of the State."

[1590] Indeed, the European Communities appears to acknowledge as much in European Communities' first written submission, para. 454; European Communities' second written submission, para 99; European Communities' second written submission, para. 224.

place independent, administrative bodies and/or judicial bodies that perform the function of reviewing and correcting administrative action relating to customs matters. Specifically, the European Communities has indicated that, in the case of Spain, Italy, Ireland and Denmark, administrative review is carried out by a body that is independent of the agencies entrusted with administrative enforcement.[1591] The European Communities has also submitted that the courts of all member States review and correct the legality of the administrative decisions relating to customs matters.[1592]

(iii) Summary and conclusions

7.556 In summary, the Panel considers that, for the purposes of its obligations under Article X:3(b) of the GATT 1994, the authorities in the member States – namely, independent administrative and judicial bodies – act as organs of the European Communities when they review and correct administrative action taken pursuant to EC customs law. As a matter of fact, decisions of such member State authorities only have effect within the respective member States. However, the Panel considers that the European Communities does not violate Article X:3(b) of the GATT 1994 merely because the decisions regarding review of administration action relating to customs matters, which are taken by authorities in the member States acting as organs of the European Communities, do not apply to all agencies in the European Communities and do not have effect throughout the territory of the European Communities. The Panel recalls that the United States does not allege inconsistency with any other aspect of Article X:3(b) of the GATT 1994. Therefore, the Panel concludes that the European Communities is not in violation of Article X:3(b) of the GATT 1994.

VIII. CONCLUSIONS AND RECOMMENDATIONS

8.1 The Panel *concludes* that:

(a) With respect to the Panel's terms of reference in the context of the United States' claim under Article X:3(a) of the GATT 1994:

(i) The Panel's terms of reference authorise the Panel to consider the manner of administration by the national customs authorities of the member States of the Community Customs Code, the Implementing Regulation, the Common Customs Tariff, the TARIC and related measures in the areas of customs administration specifically identified in the United States' request for establishment of a panel.

(ii) Article 221 of the Community Customs Code, including Article 221(3), is not covered by any of the areas of customs administration specifically identified in the United States' request for establishment of a panel. Therefore, Arti-

[1591] European Communities' reply to Panel question No. 69(b).

[1592] European Communities' reply to Panel question No. 69(a).

cle 221(3) of the Community Customs Code is outside the Panel's terms of reference.

(iii) Under its terms of reference, the Panel is precluded from considering "as such" challenges of the design and structure of the EC system of customs administration as a whole and also the design and structure of the EC system in the areas of customs administration that have been specifically identified in the United States' request for establishment of a panel.

(b) With respect to the United States' claim of non-uniform administration of the Common Customs Tariff in the area of tariff classification in violation of Article X:3(a) of the GATT 1994:

(i) The European Communities is not currently administering the Common Customs Tariff regarding the tariff classification of network cards for personal computers in a manner that is non-uniform in violation of Article X:3(a) of the GATT 1994. Therefore, the Panel finds no violation of Article X:3(a) of the GATT 1994 with respect to the tariff classification of network cards for personal computers.

(ii) The tariff classification of drip irrigation products does not amount to non-uniform administration within the meaning of Article X:3(a) of the GATT 1994. Therefore, the Panel finds no violation of Article X:3(a) of the GATT 1994 with respect to the tariff classification of drip irrigation products.

(iii) The United States has not proved that the tariff classification of unisex articles or shorts amounts to non-uniform administration within the meaning of Article X:3(a) of the GATT 1994.

(iv) The administrative process leading to the tariff classification of blackout drapery lining amounts to non-uniform administration within the meaning of Article X:3(a) of the GATT 1994. Therefore, the Panel finds a violation of Article X:3(a) of the GATT 1994 with respect to the tariff classification of blackout drapery lining.

(v) The tariff classification of liquid crystal display monitors with digital video interface amounts to non-uniform administration within the meaning of Article X:3(a) of the GATT 1994. Therefore, the Panel finds a violation of Article X:3(a) of the GATT 1994 with respect to the tariff classification of liquid crystal display monitors with digital video interface.

(vi) The United States has not proved that customs authorities in the member States have failed to treat as binding BTI issued by customs authorities in other member States and that such failure amounts to non-uniform administration within the meaning of Article X:3(a) of the GATT 1994.

(vii) The United States has not proved that the refusal to withdraw the revocation of BTI by the UK customs authorities with respect to the tariff classification of Sony PlayStation2 in the context of the *Sony PlayStation2* case amounts to non-uniform administration within the meaning of Article X:3(a) of the GATT 1994.

(viii) The United States has not proved that the interpretation and application of the amended explanatory notes to the Common Custom Tariff concerning camcorders in the context of the *Camcorders* case amounts to non-uniform administration in violation of Article X:3(a) of the GATT 1994.

(c) With respect to the United States' allegations of non-uniform administration of the Community Customs Code and the Implementing Regulation in the area of customs valuation in violation of Article X:3(a) of the GATT 1994:

(i) The United States has not proved that differences between member States regarding the manner in which royalties are apportioned to the customs value of identical goods imported by the same company exist that amount to non-uniform administration of Article 32(1)(c) of the Community Customs Code within the meaning of Article X:3(a) of the GATT 1994.

(ii) The imposition by customs authorities in some member States of a form of prior approval with respect to the successive sales provision, which is inconsistent with EC customs laws and which is not imposed by customs authorities in other member States means that the European Communities does not administer its customs law concerning successive sales – in particular, Article 147(1) of the Implementing Regulation – in a uniform manner in violation of Article X:3(a) of the GATT 1994.

(iii) The European Communities is not currently administering Article 29(3)(a) of the Community Customs Code concerning vehicle repair costs covered under warranty in a manner that violates the uniformity obligation in Article X:3(a) of the GATT 1994. Therefore, the Panel finds no violation of Article X:3(a) of the GATT 1994 with respect to the administration of Article 29(3)(a) of the Community Customs Code concerning vehicle repair costs covered under warranty.

(iv) The United States has not proved that the manner of administration of Article 29 of the Community Customs Code and Article 143(1)(e) of the Implementing Regulation concerning the circumstances in which parties are to be treated as "related" for customs valuation purposes is non-uniform among the member States within the meaning of Article X:3(a) of the GATT 1994.

(d) With respect to the United States' allegations of non-uniform administration of the Community Customs Code and the Implementing Regulation in the area of customs procedures in violation of Article X:3(a) of the GATT 1994:

(i) The Panel finds no violation of Article X:3(a) of the GATT 1994 with respect to the manner of administration of Article 78(2) of the Community Customs Code regarding the requirements imposed for audit procedures following the release of products for free circulation in the European Communities.

(ii) The Panel finds no violation of Article X:3(a) of the GATT 1994 with respect to the substantive differences in penalty laws between member States.

(iii) The United States has not proved that the manner of administration of Article 133 of the Community Customs Code and Articles 502(3) and 552 of the Implementing Regulation regarding processing under customs control is non-uniform in violation of Article X:3(a) of the GATT 1994.

(iv) The United States has not proved that the administration of Articles 263 – 267 of the Implementing Regulation regarding local clearance procedures is non-uniform in violation of Article X:3(a) of the GATT 1994.

(e) With respect to the United States' claim of violation of the obligation to provide prompt review and correction of administrative action relating to customs matter in Article X:3(b) of the GATT 1994, the Panel finds no violation.

8.2 Therefore, the Panel *concludes* that the European Communities has acted inconsistently with the requirements of Articles X:3(a) of the GATT 1994 and, thus, nullified or impaired benefits accruing to the United States. Accordingly, the Panel *recommends* that the Dispute Settlement Body request the European Communities to bring itself into conformity with respect to:

(a) the administration of the Common Custom Tariff regarding the administrative process leading to the tariff classification of blackout drapery lining;

(b) the administration of the Common Customs Tariff regarding the tariff classification of liquid crystal display monitors with digital video interface;

(c) the administration of Article 147(1) of the Implementing Regulation regarding the imposition by customs authorities in some member States of a form of prior approval with respect to the successive sales provision in the context of customs valuation.

Cumulative List of Published Disputes

Argentina - Definitive Anti-Dumping Duties on Poultry from Brazil

Complaint by Brazil (WT/DS241)

Report of the Panel — DSR 2003:V, 1727

Argentina - Definitive Anti-Dumping Measures on Imports of Ceramic Floor Tiles from Italy

Complaint by the European Communities (WT/DS189)

Report of the Panel — DSR 2001:XII, 6241

Argentina - Definitive Safeguard Measure on Imports of Preserved Peaches

Complaint by Chile (WT/DS238)

Report of the Panel — DSR 2003:III, 1037

Argentina - Measures Affecting Imports of Footwear, Textiles, Apparel and Other Items

Complaint by the United States (WT/DS56)

Report of the Appellate Body — DSR 1998:III, 1003

Report of the Panel — DSR 1998:III, 1033

Argentina - Measures Affecting the Export of Bovine Hides and the Import of Finished Leather

Complaint by the European Communities (WT/DS155)

Report of the Panel — DSR 2001:V, 1779

Award of the Arbitrator under Article 21.3(c) of the DSU — DSR 2001:XII, 6013

Argentina - Safeguard Measures on Imports of Footwear

Complaint by the European Communities (WT/DS121)

Report of the Appellate Body — DSR 2000:I, 515

Report of the Panel — DSR 2000:II, 575

Australia - Measures Affecting Importation of Salmon

Complaint by Canada (WT/DS18)

Report of the Appellate Body — DSR 1998:VIII, 3327

Report of the Panel — DSR 1998:VIII, 3407

Award of the Arbitrator under Article 21.3(c) of the DSU — DSR 1999:I, 267

Report of the Panel - Recourse to Article 21.5 of the DSU — DSR 2000:IV, 2031

Australia - Subsidies Provided to Producers and Exporters of Automotive Leather

Complaint by the United States (WT/DS126)

Report of the Panel DSR 1999:III, 951

Report of the Panel - Recourse to Article 21.5 of the DSU DSR 2000:III, 1189

Brazil - Measures Affecting Desiccated Coconut

Complaint by the Philippines (WT/DS22)

Report of the Appellate Body DSR 1997:I, 167

Report of the Panel DSR 1997:I, 189

Brazil - Export Financing Programme for Aircraft

Complaint by Canada (WT/DS46)

Report of the Appellate Body DSR 1999:III, 1161

Report of the Panel DSR 1999:III, 1221

Report of the Appellate Body - Recourse to Article 21.5 of the DSU DSR 2000:VIII, 4067

Report of the Panel - Recourse to Article 21.5 of the DSU DSR 2000:IX, 4093

Report of the Panel - Second Recourse to Article 21.5 of the DSU DSR 2001:XI, 5481

Decision by the Arbitrators - Recourse to Arbitration by Brazil under Article 22.6 of the DSU and Article 4.11 of the *SCM Agreement* DSR 2002:I, 19

Canada - Certain Measures Affecting the Automotive Industry

Complaint by the European Communities (WT/DS142); Complaint by Japan (WT/DS139)

Report of the Appellate Body DSR 2000:VI, 2985

Report of the Panel DSR 2000:VII, 3043

Award of the Arbitrator under Article 21.3(c) of the DSU DSR 2000:X, 5079

Canada - Certain Measures Concerning Periodicals

Complaint by the United States (WT/DS31)

Report of the Appellate Body DSR 1997:I, 449

Report of the Panel DSR 1997:I, 481

Canada - Export Credits and Loan Guarantees for Regional Aircraft

Complaint by Brazil (WT/DS222)

Report of the Panel DSR 2002:III, 849

Decision by the Arbitrator under Article 22.6 of the DSU and Article 4.11 of the SCM Agreement DSR 2003:III, 1187

Canada - Measures Affecting the Importation of Milk and the Exportation of Dairy Products
Complaint by New Zealand (WT/DS113);
Complaint by the United States (WT/DS103)
Report of the Appellate Body DSR 1999:V, 2057
Report of the Panel DSR 1999:VI, 2097
Report of the Appellate Body - Recourse to Article 21.5 of the DSU DSR 2001:XIII, 6829
Report of the Panel - Recourse to Article 21.5 of the DSU DSR 2001:XIII, 6865
Report of the Appellate Body - Second Recourse to Article 21.5 of the DSU DSR 2003:I, 213
Report of the Panel - Second Recourse to Article 21.5 of the DSU DSR 2003:I, 255

Canada - Measures Affecting the Export of Civilian Aircraft
Complaint by Brazil (WT/DS70)
Report of the Appellate Body DSR 1999:III, 1377
Report of the Panel DSR 1999:IV, 1443
Report of the Appellate Body - Recourse to Article 21.5 of the DSU DSR 2000:IX, 4299
Report of the Panel - Recourse to Article 21.5 of the DSU DSR 2000:IX, 4315

Canada – Measures Relating to Exports of Wheat and Treatment of Imported Grain
Complaint by United States (WT/DS276)
Report of the Appellate Body DSR 2004:VI, 2807
Report of the Panel DSR 2004:VI, 2887

Canada - Patent Protection of Pharmaceutical Products
Complaint by the European Communities (WT/DS114)
Report of the Panel DSR 2000:V, 2289
Award of the Arbitrator under Article 21.3(c) of the DSU DSR 2002:I, 3

Canada - Term of Patent Protection
Complaint by the United States (WT/DS170)
Report of the Appellate Body DSR 2000:X, 5093
Report of the Panel DSR 2000:XI, 5121
Award of the Arbitrator under Article 21.3(c) of the DSU DSR 2000:IX, 4537

Chile - Price Band System and Safeguard Measures Relating to Certain Agricultural Products
Complaint by Argentina (WT/DS207)

Report of the Appellate Body — DSR 2002:VIII, 3045

Report of the Panel — DSR 2002:VIII, 30127

Award of the Arbitrator under Article 21.3(c) of the DSU — DSR 2003:III, 1237

Chile - Taxes on Alcoholic Beverages

Complaint by the European Communities (WT/DS87), (WT/DS110)

Report of the Appellate Body — DSR 2000:I, 281

Report of the Panel — DSR 2000:I, 303

Award of the Arbitrator under Article 21.3(c) of the DSU — DSR 2000:V, 2583

Dominican Republic - Measures Affecting the Importation and Internal Sale of Cigarettes

Complaint by Honduras (WT/DS302)

Report of the Appellate Body — DSR 2005:XV, 7367

Report of the Panel — DSR 2005:XV, 7425

Arbitration under Article 21.3(c) of the DSU (WT/DS302/17)

Report of the Arbitrator — DSR 2005:XXIII, 11663

Egypt - Definitive Anti-Dumping Measures on Steel Rebar from Turkey

Complaint by Turkey (WT/DS211)

Report of the Panel — DSR 2002:VII, 2667

European Communities - Anti-Dumping Duties on Imports of Cotton-Type Bed Linen from India

Complaint by India (WT/DS141)

Report of the Appellate Body — DSR 2001:V, 2049

Report of the Appellate Body (Recourse to Article 21.5 of the DSU by India) — DSR 2003:III, 965

Report of the Panel — DSR 2001:VI, 2077

Report of the Panel - Recourse to Article 21.5 of the DSU — DSR 2003:IV, 1269

European Communities - Anti-Dumping Duties on Malleable Cast Iron Tube or Pipe Fittings from Brazil

Complaint by Brazil (WT/DS219)

Report of the Appellate Body — DSR 2003:VI, 2613

Report of the Panel — DSR 2003:VII, 2701

European Communities – Conditions for the Granting of Tariff Preferences to Developing Countries

Complaint by India (WT/DS246)

Report of the Appellate Body — DSR 2004:III, 951

Report of the Panel DSR 2004:III, 1037

Award of the Arbitrator under Article 21.3 (c) of the DSU DSR 2004:IX, 4313

European Communities – Countervailing Measures on Dynamic Random Access Memory Chips from Korea

Complaint by Korea (WT/DS299)

Report of the Panel DSR 2005:XVIII, 8671

European Communities - Customs Classification of Certain Computer Equipment

Complaint by the United States (WT/DS62, WT/DS67, WT/DS68)

Complaint by the United States - Ireland

Complaint by the United States - United Kingdom

Report of the Appellate Body DSR 1998:V, 1851

Report of the Panel DSR 1998:V, 1891

European Communities - Customs Classification of Frozen Boneless Chicken Cuts

Complaint by Brazil and Thailand (WT/DS269, WT/DS286)

Report of the Appellate Body DSR 2005:XIX, 9157

Complaint by Brazil (WT/DS269)

Report of the Panel DSR 2005:XIX, 9295

Complaint by Thailand (WT/DS286)

Report of the Panel DSR 2005:XX, 9721

European Communities - Export Subsidies on Sugar

Complaint by Australia, Brazil, Thailand (WT/DS265, WT/DS266, WT/DS283)

Report of the Appellate Body DSR 2005:XIII, 6365

Complaint by Australia (WT/DS265)

Report of the Panel DSR 2005:XIII, 6499

Complaint by Brazil (WT/DS266) DSR 2005:XIV, 6793

Report of the Panel

Complaint by Thailand (WT/DS283)

Report of the Panel DSR 2005:XIV, 7071

Arbitration under Article 21.3(c) of the Understanding on Rules and Procedures Governing the Settlement of Disputes (WT/DS265/33, WT/DS266/33, WT/DS283/14)

Award of the Arbitrator DSR 2005:XXIII, 11579

European Communities - Measures Affecting Asbestos and Asbestos-Containing Products

Complaint by Canada (WT/DS135)

Report of the Appellate Body DSR 2001:VII, 3243

Report of the Panel DSR 2001:VIII, 3305

European Communities - Measures Affecting the Approval and Marketing of Biotech Products

Complaint by United States, Canada, Argentina (WT/DS291, WT/DS292, WT/DS293)

Report of the Panel DSR 2006:III, 847

European Communities - Measures Affecting the Importation of Certain Poultry Products

Complaint by Brazil (WT/DS69)

Report of the Appellate Body DSR 1998:V, 2031

Report of the Panel DSR 1998:V, 2089

European Communities – Measures Affecting Trade in Commercial Vessels

Complaint by Korea (WT/DS301)

Report of the Panel DSR 2005:XV, 7733

European Communities - Measures Concerning Meat and Meat Products (Hormones)

Complaint by Canada (WT/DS48);
Complaint by the United States (WT/DS26)

Report of the Appellate Body DSR 1998:I, 135

Report of the Panel (Canada) DSR 1998:II, 235

Report of the Panel (United States) DSR 1998:III, 699

Award of the Arbitrator under Article 21.3(c) of the DSU DSR 1998:V, 1833

Decision by the Arbitrators under Article 22.6 of the DSU (Canada) DSR 1999:III, 1135

Decision by the Arbitrators under Article 22.6 of the DSU (United States) DSR 1999:III, 1105

European Communities – Protection of Trademarks and Geographical Indications for Agricultural Products and Foodstuffs

Complaint by the United States (WT/DS174)

Report of the Panel DSR 2005:VIII-IX, 3499,4083

Complaint by Australia (WT/DS290)

Report of the Panel DSR 2005:X-XI, 4603,5121

European Communities - Regime for the Importation, Sale and Distribution of Bananas

Complaint by Ecuador; Guatemala; Honduras; Mexico; and the United States (WT/DS27)

Report of the Appellate Body DSR 1997:II, 589
Report of the Panel (Ecuador) DSR 1997:III, 3
Report of the Panel (Guatemala, Honduras) DSR 1997:II, 695
Report of the Panel (Mexico) DSR 1997:II, 803
Report of the Panel (United States) DSR 1997:II, 943
Award of the Arbitrator under Article 21.3(c) of the DSU DSR 1998:I, 3
Decision by the Arbitrators under Article 22.6 of the DSU (US) DSR 1999:II, 725
Report of the Panel - Recourse to Article 21.5 of the DSU (European Communities) DSR 1999:II, 783
Report of the Panel - Recourse to Article 21.5 of the DSU (Ecuador) DSR 1999:II, 803
Decision by the Arbitrators under Article 22.6 of the DSU (Ecuador) DSR 2000:V, 2237

European Communities - The ACP-EC Partnership Agreement - Recourse to Arbitration Pursuant to the Decision of 14 November 2001 (WT/L/616)

Award of the Arbitrator DSR 2005:XXIII, 11667

European Communities - The ACP-EC Partnership Agreement - Second Recourse to Arbitration Pursuant to the Decision of 14 November 2001 (WT/L/625)

Award of the Arbitrator DSR 2005:XXIII, 11701

European Communities - Trade Description of Sardines

Complaint by Peru (WT/DS231/R)

Report of the Appellate Body DSR 2002:VIII, 3359
Report of the Panel DSR 2002:VIII, 3451

European Communities - Trade Description of Scallops

Complaint by Canada (WT/DS7);
Complaint by Chile (WT/DS14);
Complaint by Peru (WT/DS12)

Report of the Panel (Canada) DSR 1996:I, 89
Report of the Panel (Chile, Peru) DSR 1996:I, 93

Guatemala - Anti-Dumping Investigation Regarding Portland Cement From Mexico

Complaint by Mexico (WT/DS60)

Report of the Appellate Body DSR 1998:IX, 3767
Report of the Panel DSR 1998:IX, 3797

Guatemala - Definitive Anti-Dumping Measures on Grey Portland Cement from Mexico

Complaint by Mexico (WT/DS156)

Report of the Panel DSR 2000:XI, 5295

India - Measures Affecting the Automotive Sector

Complaint by European Communities (WT/DS146)
Complaint by the United States (WT/DS175)

Report of the Appellate Body DSR 2002:V, 1821

Report of the Panel DSR 2002:V, 1827

India - Patent Protection for Pharmaceutical and Agricultural Chemical Products

Complaint by European Communities (WT/DS79);
Complaint by the United States (WT/DS50)

Report of the Appellate Body (United States) DSR 1998:I, 9

Report of the Panel (European Communities) DSR 1998:VI, 2661

Report of the Panel (United States) DSR 1998:I, 41

India - Quantitative Restrictions on Imports of Agricultural, - Textile and Industrial Products

Complaint by the United States (WT/DS90)

Report of the Appellate Body DSR 1999:IV, 1763

Report of the Panel DSR 1999:V, 1799

Indonesia - Certain Measures Affecting the Automobile Industry

Complaint by European Communities (WT/DS54);
Complaint by Japan (WT/DS55, WT/DS64);
Complaint by the United States (WT/DS59)

Report of the Panel DSR 1998:VI, 2201

Award of the Arbitrator under Article 21.3(c) of the DSU DSR 1998:IX, 4029

Japan - Measures Affecting Agricultural Products

Complaint by the United States (WT/DS76)

Report of the Appellate Body DSR 1999:I, 277

Report of the Panel DSR 1999:I, 315

Japan - Measures Affecting Consumer Photographic Film and Paper

Complaint by the United States (WT/DS44)

Report of the Panel DSR 1998:IV, 1179

Japan - Measures Affecting the Importation of Apples

Complaint by the United States (WT/DS245)

Report of the Appellate Body DSR 2003:IX, 4391

Report of the Panel DSR 2003:IX, 4481

Report of the Panel - Recourse to Article 21.5 of the DSU DSR 2005:XVI, 7911

Japan - Taxes on Alcoholic Beverages

Complaint by Canada (WT/DS10);
Complaint by the European Communities (WT/DS8);
Complaint by the United States (WT/DS11)

Report of the Appellate Body DSR 1996:I, 97

Report of the Panel DSR 1996:I, 125

Award of the Arbitrator under Article 21.3(c) of the DSU DSR 1997:I, 3

Korea - Anti-Dumping Duties on Imports of Certain Paper from Indonesia

Complaint by Indonesia (WT/DS312)

Report of the Panel DSR 2005:XXII, 10637

Korea - Definitive Safeguard Measure on Imports of Certain Dairy Products

Complaint by the European Communities (WT/DS98)

Report of the Appellate Body DSR 2000:I, 3

Report of the Panel DSR 2000:I, 49

Korea - Measures Affecting Imports of Fresh, Chilled and Frozen Beef

Complaint by Australia (WT/DS169);
Complaint by the United States (WT/DS161)

Report of the Appellate Body DSR 2001:I, 5

Report of the Panel DSR 2001:I, 59

Korea - Measures Affecting Government Procurement

Complaint by the United States (WT/DS163)

Report of the Panel DSR 2000:VIII, 3541

Korea - Measures Affecting Trade in Commercial Vessels

Complaint by the European Communities (WT/DS273)

Report of the Panel DSR 2005:VII, 2747

Korea - Taxes on Alcoholic Beverages

Complaint by the European Communities (WT/DS75);
Complaint by the United States (WT/DS84)

Report of the Appellate Body DSR 1999:I, 3

Report of the Panel DSR 1999:I, 44

Award of the Arbitrator under Article 21.3(c) of the DSU DSR 1999:II, 937

Mexico - Anti-Dumping Investigation of High Fructose Corn Syrup (HFCS) from the United States

Complaint by the United States (WT/DS132)

Report of the Panel — DSR 2000:III, 1345

Report of the Appellate Body - Recourse to Article 21.5 of the DSU — DSR 2001:XIII, 6675

Report of the Panel - Recourse to Article 21.5 of the DSU — DSR 2001:XIII, 6717

Mexico - Definitive Anti-Dumping Measures on Beef and Rice - Complaint with Respect to Rice

Complaint by the United States (WT/DS295)

Report of the Appellate Body — DSR 2005:XXII, 10853

Report of the Panel — DSR 2005 XXIII, 11005

Mexico – Measures Affecting Telecommunications Services

Complaint by the United States (WT/DS204)

Report of the Panel — DSR 2004:IV, 1579

Mexico – Tax Measures on Soft Drinks and Other Beverages

Complaint by the United States (WT/DS308)

Report of the Appellate Body — DSR 2006:I, 3

Report of the Panel — DSR 2006 I, 43

Thailand - Anti-Dumping Duties on Angles, Shapes and Sections of Iron or Non-Alloy Steel and H-Beams from Poland

Complaint by Poland (WT/DS122)

Report of the Appellate Body — DSR 2001:VII, 2701

Report of the Panel — DSR 2001:VII, 2741

Turkey - Restrictions on Imports of Textile and Clothing Products

Complaint by India (WT/DS34)

Report of the Appellate Body — DSR 1999:VI, 2345

Report of the Panel — DSR 1999:VI, 2363

United States - Anti-Dumping Act of 1916

Complaint by the European Communities (WT/DS136)

Decision by the Arbitrators under Article 22.6 of the DSU — DSR 2004:IX, 4269

Complaint by Japan (WT/DS162)

Report of the Appellate Body — DSR 2000:X, 4793

Report of the Panel (European Communities) — DSR 2000:X, 4593

Report of the Panel (Japan) — DSR 2000:X, 4831

Award of the Arbitrator under Article 21.3(c) of the DSU — DSR 2001:V, 2017

United States-Anti-Dumping and Countervailing Measures on Steel Plate from India

Complaint by India (WT/DS206)

Report of the Panel DSR 2002:VI, 2073

United States - Anti-Dumping Duty on Dynamic Random Access Memory Semiconductors (DRAMS) of One Megabit or Above from Korea

Complaint by Korea (WT/DS99)

Report of the Panel DSR 1999:II, 521

United States - Anti-Dumping Measures on Certain Hot-Rolled Steel Products from Japan

Complaint by Japan (WT/DS184)

Report of the Appellate Body DSR 2001:X, 4697

Report of the Panel DSR 2001:X, 4769

Award of the Arbitrator under Article 21.3(c) of the DSU DSR 2002:IV, 1389

United States - Anti-Dumping Measures on Oil Country Tubular Goods (OCTG) from Mexico

Complaint by Mexico and United States (WT/DS282)

Report of the Appellate Body DSR 2005:XX, 10129

Report of the Panel DSR 2005:XXI, 10225

United States - Anti-Dumping Measures on Stainless Steel Plate in Coils and Stainless Steel Sheet and Strip from Korea

Complaint by Korea (WT/DS179)

Report of the Panel DSR 2001:IV, 1295

United States - Continued Dumping and Subsidy Offset Act of 2000

Complaint by Australia, Brazil, Canada, Chile, the European Communities, India, Indonesia, Japan, Korea, Mexico and Thailand (WT/DS217)

Report of the Appellate Body DSR 2003:I, 375

Report of the Panel DSR 2003:II, 489

Award of the Arbitrator under Article 21.3(c) of the DSU DSR 2003:III, 1163

Complaint by Brazil

Decision by the Arbitrator under Article 22.6 of the DSU DSR 2004:IX, 4341

Complaint by Canada (WT/DS234)

Decision by the Arbitrator under Article 22.6 of the DSU DSR 2004:IX, 4425

Complaint by Chile (WT/DS217)

Decision by the Arbitrator under Article 22.6 of the DSU — DSR 2004:IX, 4511

Complaint by European Communities (WT/DS217)

Decision by the Arbitrator under Article 22.6 of the DSU — DSR 2004:IX, 4591

Original Complaint by India - Recourse to Arbitration by the United States under Article 22.6 of the DSU (WT/DS217)

Decision by the Arbitrator — DSR 2004:X, 4691

Original Complaint by Japan - Recourse to Arbitration by the United States under Article 22.6 of the DSU (WT/DS217)

Decision by the Arbitrator — DSR 2004:X, 4771

Original Complaint by Korea - Recourse to Arbitration by the United States under Article 22.6 of the DSU ((WT/DS217)

Decision by the Arbitrator — DSR 2004:X, 4851

Original Complaint by Mexico - Recourse to Arbitration by the United States under Article 22.6 of the DSU (WT/DS234)

Decision by the Arbitrator — DSR 2004:X, 4931

United States - Countervailing Duties on Certain Corrosion-Resistant Carbon Steel Flat Products from Germany

Complaint by European Communities (WT/DS213)

Report of the Appellate Body — DSR 2002:IX, 3781

Report of the Panel — DSR 2002:IX, 3835

United States - Countervailing Duty Investigation on Dynamic Random Access Memory Semiconductors (DRAMS) from Korea

Complaint by Korea (WT/DS296)

Report of the Appellate Body — DSR 2005:XVI, 8131

Report of the Panel — DSR 2005:XVII, 8243

United States - Countervailing Measures Concerning Certain Products from the European Communities

Complaint by European Communities (WT/DS212)

Report of the Appellate Body — DSR 2003:I, 5

Report of the Panel — DSR 2003:I, 73

Recourse to Article 21.5 of the DSU by the European Communities

Report of the Panel — DSR 2005:XVIII, 8950

United States - Definitive Safeguard Measures on Imports of Certain Steel Products

Complaint by Brazil (WT/DS259);
Complaint by China (WT/DS252);
Complaint by European Communities (WT/DS248);
Complaint by Japan (WT/DS249);
Complaint by Korea (WT/DS251);
Complaint by New Zealand (WT/DS258);
Complaint by Norway (WT/DS254);
Complaint by Switzerland (WT/DS253)

Report of the Appellate Body DSR 2003:VII, 3117
Report of the Panel DSR 2003:VIII, 3273

United States - Definitive Safeguard Measures on Imports of Circular Welded Carbon Quality Line Pipe from Korea

Complaint by Korea (WT/DS202)

Report of the Appellate Body DSR 2002:IV, 1403
Report of the Panel DSR 2002:IV, 1473
Award of the Arbitrator under Article 21.3(c) of the DSU DSR 2002:V, 2061

United States - Definitive Safeguard Measures on Imports of Wheat Gluten from the European Communities

Complaint by the European Communities (WT/DS166)

Report of the Appellate Body DSR 2001:II, 717
Report of the Panel DSR 2001:III, 779

United States - Final Countervailing Duty Determination with Respect to Certain Softwood Lumber from Canada

Complaint by Canada (WT/DS257)

Report of the Appellate Body DSR 2004:II, 587
Report of the Panel DSR 2004:II, 659

Recourse by Canada to Article 21.5 of the DSU

Report of the Appellate Body DSR 2005:XXIII, 11355
Report of the Panel DSR 2005:XXIII, 11399

United States - Final Dumping Determination on Softwood Lumber from Canada

Complaint by Canada (WT/DS264)

Report of the Appellate Body DSR 2004:V, 1917
Report of the Panel DSR 2004:V, 1981

Arbitration under Article 21.3(c) of the DSU (WT/DS264)

Report of the Arbitrator DSR 2004:X, 5011

United States - Import Measures on Certain Products from the European Communities

Complaint by the European Communities (WT/DS165)

Report of the Appellate Body DSR 2001:I, 373

Report of the Panel DSR 2001:II, 413

United States - Imposition of Countervailing Duties on Certain Hot-Rolled Lead and Bismuth Carbon Steel Products Originating in the United Kingdom

Complaint by the European Communities (WT/DS138)

Report of the Appellate Body DSR 2000:V, 2595

Report of the Panel DSR 2000:VI, 2623

United States - Import Prohibition of Certain Shrimp and Shrimp Products

Complaint by India (WT/DS58);
Complaint by Malaysia (WT/DS58);
Complaint by Pakistan (WT/DS58);
Complaint by Thailand (WT/DS58)

Report of the Appellate Body DSR 1998:VII, 2755

Report of the Panel DSR 1998:VII, 2821

Report of the Appellate Body - Recourse to Article 21.5 of the DSU (Malaysia) DSR 2001:XIII, 6481

Report of the Panel - Recourse to Article 21.5 of the DSU (Malaysia) DSR 2001:XIII, 6529

United States – Investigation of the International Trade Commission in Softwood Lumber from Canada

Complaint by Canada (WT/DS277)

Report of the Panel DSR 2004:VI, 2543

United States - Laws, Regulations and Methodology for Calculating Dumping Margins ("Zeroing")

Complaint by European Communities and the United States (WT/DS294)

Report of the Appellate Body DSR 2006:II, 417

Report of the Panel DSR 2006:II, 521

United States - Measure Affecting Imports of Woven Wool Shirts and Blouses from India

Complaint by India (WT/DS33)

Report of the Appellate Body DSR 1997:I, 323

Report of the Panel DSR 1997:I, 343

United States - Measures Affecting the Cross-Border Supply of Gambling and Betting Services
Complaint by Antigua (WT/DS285)
Report of the Appellate Body DSR 2005:XII, 5663
Report of the Panel DSR 2005:XII, 5797
Arbitration under Article 21.3(c) of the DSU (WT/DS285/13)
Award of the Arbitrator DSR 2005:XXIII, 11637

United States - Measures Treating Export Restraints as Subsidies
Complaint by Canada (WT/DS194)
Report of the Panel DSR 2001:XI, 5767

United States - Preliminary Determinations with Respect to Certain Softwood Lumber from Canada
Complaint by Canada (WT/DS236)
Report of the Panel DSR 2002:IX, 3597

United States - Restrictions on Imports of Cotton and Man-made Fibre Underwear
Complaint by Costa Rica (WT/DS24)
Report of the Appellate Body DSR 1997:I, 11
Report of the Panel DSR 1997:I, 31

United States - Rules of Origin for Textiles and Apparel Products
Complaint by India (WT/DS243)
Report of the Panel DSR 2003:VI, 2309

United States - Safeguard Measures on Imports of Fresh, Chilled or Frozen Lamb Meat from New Zealand and Australia
Complaint by Australia (WT/DS178);
Complaint by new Zealand (WT/DS177)
Report of the Appellate Body DSR 2001:IX, 4051
Report of the Panel DSR 2001:IX, 4107

United States - Section 110(5) of the US Copyright Act
Complaint by the European Communities (WT/DS160)
Report of the Panel DSR 2000:VIII, 3769
Award of the Arbitrator under Article 21.3(c) of the DSU DSR 2001:II, 657
Award of the Arbitrator under Article 25 of the DSU DSR 2001:II, 667

United States - Sections 301-310 of the Trade Act of 1974
Complaint by the European Communities (WT/DS152)
Report of the Panel DSR 2000:II, 815

United States - Section 211 Omnibus Appropriations Act of 1998
Complaint by the European Communities (WT/DS176)
Report of the Appellate Body DSR 2002:II, 589
Report of the Panel DSR 2002:II, 683

United States- Section 129(c)(1) of the Uruguay Round Agreements Act
Complaint by Canada (WT/DS221)
Report of the Panel DSR 2002:VII, 2581

United States - Standards for Reformulated and Conventional Gasoline
Complaint by Brazil (WT/DS4);
Complaint by Venezuela (WT/DS2)
Report of the Appellate Body DSR 1996:I, 3
Report of the Panel DSR 1996:I, 29

United States – Subsidies on Upland Cotton
Complaint by Brazil (WT/DS267)
Report of the Appellate Body DSR 2005:I, 3
Report of the Panell DSR 2005:II- III- IV- V- VI, 297

United States - Sunset Review of Anti-Dumping Duties on Corrosion-Resistant Carbon Steel Flat Products from Japan
Complaint by Japan (WT/DS244)
Report of the Appellate Body DSR 2004:I, 3
Report of the Panel DSR 2004:I, 87

United States – Sunset Reviews of Anti-Dumping Measures on Oil Country Tubular Goods from Argentina
Complaint by Argentina (WT/DS268)
Report of the Appellate Body DSR 2004:VII, 3341
Report of the Panel DSR:2004:VIII, 3421
Arbitration under Article 21.3(c) of the DSU (WT/DS268/12)
Award of the Arbitrator DSR:2005:XXIII, 11617

United States - Tax Treatment for "Foreign Sales Corporations"
Complaint by the European Communities (WT/DS108)
Report of the Appellate Body DSR 2000:III, 1619
Report of the Panel DSR 2000:IV, 1675

Report of the Appellate Body - Recourse to Article 21.5 of the DSU DSR 2002:I, 55
Report of the Panel - Recourse to Article 21.5 of the DSU DSR 2002:I, 119
Decision by the Arbitrator under Article 22.6 of the DSU and Article 4.11 of the SCM Agreement DSR 2002:VI, 2517

United States - Transitional Safeguard Measure on Combed Cotton Yarn from Pakistan

Complaint by Pakistan (WT/DS192)
Report of the Appellate Body DSR 2001:XII, 6027
Report of the Panel DSR 2001:XII, 6067